Classic Readings in Urban Planning

Second Edition

Edited by
JAY M. STEIN, FAICP

PLANNERS PRESS
AMERICAN PLANNING ASSOCIATION
Chicago, Illinois   Washington, D.C.

ISBN (paperback edition) 1-884829-90-2
ISBN (hardbound edition) 1-884829-91-0
Library of Congress Control Number 2003115360
Printed in the Untied States of America

The first edition of this book, *Classic Readings in Urban
Planning: An Introduction* was published by the McGraw-Hill
Companies in 1995. The copyright to that edition was
assigned to Jay M. Stein in 2001.

To Rhonda and our children: a full house

PREFACE

It has been almost a decade since the publication of my original *Classic Readings in Urban Planning: An Introduction* (New York: McGraw-Hill, Inc., 1995). In that time, several friends, students, and professional colleagues have offered many comments on how to improve the book, on the quality and usefulness of the selections, and suggestions to include writings in areas of planning not covered in the original edition, such as gender issues, sustainability, and strategic planning. Thus, *Classic Readings in Urban Planning, Second Edition* is a product of all this informal and valuable input. But, as with the first book, I decided it was important to go beyond anecdotal information and use a more formal process to select the readings. Indeed, I believe that the methodical process followed to select the readings for both editions gives a unique distinction and level of quality to these anthologies.

In September 2002 I mailed a questionnaire to 40 experts in different fields of planning selected from the Association of Collegiate Schools of Planning (ACSP) *Guide to Undergraduate and Graduate Education in Urban and Regional Planning, 11th Edition*, Appendix B, Faculty by Specialization (Washington, D.C.: American Planning Association, 2000). The experts were not selected in a "scientific" manner, but rather were chosen based on my own knowledge of their work and an interest in having diverse representation. Nineteen forms were returned, and those contributors are listed in the Acknowledgements.

The questionnaire had two parts. In Part I, respondents were asked to evaluate each of the readings in the first edition of the book on the following basis: strongly retain, retain, no opinion, reject, strongly reject. In Part II, respondents were asked the following:

"Please list below the three (3) articles or books that you consider to be **essential** reading *in the above field* (in their identified area of expertise on the form) for an introductory survey course in urban planning:"

"Also please list three books or articles, **regardless of field**, that you think are **absolutely essential**–that a student **must** read–in an introductory survey/survey course in urban planning."

Based on the results of the survey of our "panel of experts," approximately half of the selections from the original book were retained and half replaced with new selections. Also, the book was reorganized by reducing the number of parts from 13 in the original edition to seven in the second edition. The reorganization into a smaller number of parts allows for more depth of coverage and range of perspectives in each subject area.

As in the first edition, *Classic Readings in Urban Planning, Second Edition* is intended as a main or supplementary textbook for advanced undergraduate or beginning graduate level introductory courses in urban and regional planning. Planning commissioners, professional planners, lawyers, architects, and governmental officials should also find the book useful as a general overview of the field of urban planning.

Each reading is introduced with an abstract, and each part includes a list of recommended supplementary readings. This list contains current works in the sub-field, as well as "classic" readings that could not be included as a main selection. Both the instructor and students should find these lists useful for more extensive study of an area. The complete collection of readings contained in this book should serve as a comprehensive introduction to urban planning.

I have assumed that it is far more interesting and exciting to *directly* experience ideas and read – even struggle – with original writings than it is to review someone else's synopsis *about* those ideas. I have never read a summary or description of the work of Jane Jacobs, Lewis Mumford, Kevin Lynch, or Paul Davidoff, that adequately captures the eloquence of their writings and the passion of their convictions. I believe there is no better way to excite students about planning than to have them read the "classics" written by some of the leading authorities in our field.

THE "CLASSIC" CONCEPT

Webster's (1979:334) defines "classic" as "of the highest class; most representative of the excellence of its kind; having recognized worth." Classic readings are of superior quality, represent outstanding scholarship, and may have significantly influenced or changed the field. Nevertheless, in a field as broad as planning, selecting a small group of "classics" from a rich literature is a formidable task. As Johnson and Silver (Winter 1990: 101-102) noted in a *Journal of the American Planning Association* commentary, a consensus simply does not exist on what are "the" books in urban planning. Nevertheless, I have attempted to use a systematic approach for identifying the "classics" included in this book.

Despite using a very thorough process for screening the "classics," the selections included in *Classic Readings in Urban Planning, Second Edition* cannot be viewed as representing "the" works in urban planning. Several compromises with the concept of "classics" have been necessary in preparing this text. These compromises include consideration of the level and complexity of writings that students can comprehend in an advanced undergraduate or introductory graduate course; an attempt to represent several different voices and perspectives on issues; a need to address some of the contemporary issues of the day; and, finally, an unfortunate but real constraint has been the occasional prohibitive cost involved in obtaining reprint permissions from publishers.

Given the diversity, long history, and intellectual traditions of the planning field, the size of this text could easily be increased threefold and still not cover all the significant, major writings that truly deserve to be called "classic." Such an increase in size, would be impractical for one volume and make the price unaffordable to students. Yet the issues I faced in organizing this book are similar to those experienced by every instructor when preparing a course. Every instructor must select materials from a large universe of possibilities. There is never enough time or space to cover all that the student needs to learn. Choices must be made. The question in designing a course or a textbook is the same: In the very limited time or space available, what *must* absolutely be covered, what is *essential*, what *must* a student be exposed to, what *must* they read?

In addition to the survey of experts and the anecdotal feedback described previously, I also used two other sources of information—similar to the process followed in the first edition—to select the readings included in *Classic Readings in Urban Planning, Second Edition*: identification of award-winning writing, and a review of planning literature.

The identification of award winning writings and authors was an important input to the article selection process. Award designations included: the Association of Collegiate Schools of Planning's Distinguished Planning Educator Award, the Paul Davidoff Award, and the Chester Rapkin Award for the best article published in *The Journal of Planning Education and Research*; Society of American City and Regional Planning History Awards - Lewis Mumford Prize for Best Book and Catherine Bauer Wurster Prize for Best Article; and outstanding journal articles selected by the appointed annual committees of the *Journal of the American Planning Association*. Finally, I conducted my own review of the planning literature. This involved extensive study of *Urban Affairs Abstracts* and a careful reading of the book review sections and articles in the *Journal of the American Planning Association*, *Journal of Planning Education and Research*, and the *Journal of Planning Literature*.

CONCLUSION

Although the "classics" selected for this text have been chosen by a thorough, systematic process, the book is not intended to be a compilation of "the" writings in planning. Instead, the selections included in *Classic Readings in Urban Planning, Second Edition* are an attempt to balance the complex needs of an introductory textbook with the goal of creating a high quality anthology of classic readings in planning. The book is a treasure chest of outstanding writing by some of the most important contributors to the planning field. I hope the reader will enjoy the adventure of studying these selections, capture the excitement and commitment of the authors, and be encouraged to pursue additional work in urban planning.

Jay M. Stein, FAICP
Gainesville, Florida
October 2003

REFERENCES

Association of Collegiate Schools of Planning. *Guide to Undergraduate and Graduate Education in Urban and Regional Planning*, Eleventh Edition. 2000. Washington, D.C.: American Planning Association.

Gary T. Johnson and Christopher Silver. 1990. "From the Book Review Editors." *Journal of the American Planning Association* 56, 1:101-102.

Webster's New Twentieth Century Dictionary of the English Language Unabridged 2nd Edition. 1979. New York: Simon and Schuster.

Acknowledgments

I gratefully acknowledge the ideas and support of my colleagues and students in the College of Design, Construction and Planning at the University of Florida. Holly Maudlin, my research assistant, was simply terrific in her dedication, perseverance and attention to detail while always maintaining a cheerful disposition. I also wish to thank my friends and colleagues in the member schools of the Association of Collegiate Schools of Planning who served as a "panel of experts" in helping to select the classics that are this book. I am also most grateful to Sylvia Lewis, editor and publisher at the American Planning Association's Planners Press, for believing in this project and for being a good friend and colleague over many years.

I am most indebted, however, to my wife, Rhonda Phillips, a fellow planner and spiritual traveler, for all her support and encouragement; and to our children, a continuing source of both challenge and inspiration to make the world a better place - Jessie, Ariel, Melissa, Danielle, and Brannon.

ACSP PANEL OF EXPERTS

Alan Black, FAICP
Roy Bahl
Scott A. Bollens, AICP
John Bryson
Marcia Marker Feld
Sharon L. Gaber, AICP
David R. Godschalk, FAICP
Harvey M. Jacobs
Edward J. Kaiser, FAICP
Eric D. Kelly, FAICP
Norman Krumholz, FAICP
Barry Nocks, AICP
Mark B. Lapping
Mickey Lauria
Emil Malizia, AICP
Riad G. Mahayni, FAICP
James Nicholas
Gary Pivo

CONTENTS

I
Planning History and Theory

The Crystallization of the City: The First Urban Transformation

Lewis Mumford

In the introduction to *The City in History*, Lewis Mumford observes that the book begins "with a city that was, symbolically, a world; it closes with a world that has become, in many practical aspects, a city" (p.xi). Although it took many decades to realize this transformation, it is nevertheless a remarkable one. The selection included here, "The First Urban Transformation," is the opening section of the chapter, "The Crystallization of the City." Here, Mumford describes the "implosion" that led to the first great expansion of civilization: the creation of cities. Under the leadership of the new "institution of Kingship," the diverse and scattered elements of a civilization were compressed into the boundaries of cities. This contrasts to the explosion of our own era, as boundaries disappear and we become more of a global community. Mumford argues that to understand this process—and to understand the city in our own age—we must study its origins, form, functions, and historical development.

In view of its satisfying rituals but limited capabilities, no mere increase in numbers would, in all probability, suffice to turn a village into a city. This change needed an outer challenge to pull the community sharply away from the central concerns of nutrition and reproduction: a purpose beyond mere survival. The larger part of the world's population never in fact responded to this challenge: until the present period of urbanization, cities contained only a small fraction of mankind.

The city came as a definite emergent in the paleo-neolithic community: an emergent in the definite sense that Lloyd Morgan and William Morton Wheeler used that concept. In emergent evolution, the introduction of a new factor does not just add to the existing mass, but produces an over-all change, a new configuration, which alters its properties. Potentialities that could not be recognized in the pre-emergent stage, like the possibility of organic life developing from relatively stable and unorganized "dead" matter, then for the first time become visible. So with the leap from village culture. On the new plane, the old components of the village were carried along and incorporated in the new urban unit; but through the action of new factors, they were recomposed in a more complex an unstable pattern than that of the village—yet in a fashion that promoted further transformations and developments. The human composition of the new unit likewise became more complex: in addition to the hunter, the peasant, and the shepherd, other primitive types entered the city and made their contribution to its existence: the miner, the woodman, the fisherman, each bringing with him the tools and skills and habits of life formed under other pressures. The engineer, the boatman, the sailor arise from this more generalized primitive background, at one point or another in the valley section: from all these original types still other occupation groups develop, the soldier, the banker, the merchant, the priest. Out of this complexity the city created a higher unity.

This new urban mixture resulted in an enormous expansion of human capabilities in every direction. The city effected a mobilization of manpower, a command over long distance transportation, an intensification of communication over long distances in space and time, an outburst of invention along with a large scale development of civil engineering, and, not least, it promoted a tremendous further rise in agricultural productivity.

That urban transformation was accompanied, perhaps preceded, by similar outpourings from the collective unconscious. At some moment, it would seem, the local familiar gods, close to the hearth fire, were overpowered and partly replaced certainly outranked, by the distant sky gods or earth gods, identified with the sun, the moon, the waters of life, the thunderstorm, the desert. The local chieftain turned into the towering king, and became likewise the chief priestly guardian of the shrine now endowed with divine or almost divine attributes. The village neighbors would now be kept at a distance: no longer familiars and equals, they were reduced to subjects, whose lives were supervised and directed by military and civil officers, governors, viziers, tax-gatherers, soldiers, directly accountable to the king.

Even the ancient village habits and customs might be altered in obedience to divine command. No longer was it sufficient for the village farmer to produce enough to feed his family or his village: he must now work harder and practice self-denial to support a royal and priestly officialdom with a large surplus. For the new rulers were greedy feeders, and openly measured their power not only in arms, but in loaves of bread and jugs of beer. In the new urban society, the wisdom of the aged no longer carried authority: it was the young men of Uruk, who, against the advice of the Elders, supported Gilgamesh when he proposed to attack Kish instead of surrendering to the demands of the ruler of Kish. Though family connections still counted in urban society, vocational ability and youthful audacity counted even more, if it gained the support of the King.

When all this happened, the archaic village culture yielded to urban "civilization," that peculiar combination of creativity and control, of expression and repression, of tension and release, whose outward manifestation has been the historic city. From its origins onward, indeed, the city may be described as a structure specially equipped to store and transmit the goods of civilization, sufficiently condensed to afford the maximum amount of facilities in a minimum space, but also capable of structural enlargement to enable it to find a place for the changing needs and the more complex forms of a growing society and its cumulative social heritage. The invention of such forms as the written record, the library, the archive, the school, and the university is one of the earliest and most characteristic achievements of the city.

The transformation I now seek to describe was first called by Childe the Urban Revolution. This term does justice to the active and critically important role of the city; but it does not accurately indicate the process; for a revolution implies a turning things upside down, and a progressive movement away from outworn institutions that have been left behind. Seen from the vantage point of our own age, it seems to indicate something like the same general shift that occurred with our own industrial revolution, with the same sort of emphasis on economic activities. This obscures rather than clarifies what actually occurred. The rise of the city, so far from wiping out earlier elements in the culture, actually brought them together and increased their efficacy and scope. Even the fostering of non-agricultural occupations heightened the demand for food and probably caused villages to multiply, and still more land to be brought under cultivation. Within the city, very little of the old order was at first excluded: agriculture itself in Summer, for example, continued to be practiced on a large scale by those who lived permanently within the new walled towns.

What happened rather with the rise of cities, was that many functions that had heretofore been scattered and unorganized were brought together within a limited area, and the components of the community were kept in a state of dynamic tension and interaction. In this union, made almost compulsory by the strict enclosure of the city wall, the already well-established parts of the proto-city—shrine, spring, village, market, stronghold—participated in the general enlargement and concentration of numbers, and underwent a structural differentiation that gave them forms recognizable in every subsequent phase of urban culture. The city proved not merely a means of expressing in concrete terms the magnification of sacred and secular power, but in a manner that went far beyond any conscious intention it also enlarged all the dimensions of life. Beginning as a representation of the cosmos, a means of bringing heaven down to earth, the city became a symbol of the possible. Utopia was an integral part of its original constitution, and precisely because it first took form as an ideal projection, it brought into existence realities that might have remained latent for an indefinite time in more soberly governed small communities, pitched to lower expectations and unwilling to make exertions that transcended both their workaday habits and their mundane hopes.

In this emergence of the city, the dynamic element came, as we have seen, from outside the village. Here one must give the new rulers their due, for their hunting practices had accustomed them to a wider horizon than village culture habitually viewed. Archaeologists have pointed out that there is even the possibility that the earliest grain-gatherers, in the uplands of the Near East, may have been hunters who gathered the seeds in their pouch, for current rations, long before they knew how to plant them. The hunter's exploratory mobility, his willingness to gamble and take risks, his need to make prompt decisions, his readiness to undergo bitter deprivation and intense fatigue in pursuit of his game, his willingness to face death in coming to grips with fierce animals—either to kill or be killed—all gave him special qualifications for confident leadership. These traits were the foundations of aristocratic dominance. Faced with the complexities of large-scale community life, individualistic audacity was more viable than the slow communal responses that the agricultural village fostered.

In a society confronting numerous social changes brought on by its own mechanical and agricultural improvements, which provoked serious crises that called for prompt action, under unified command, the hoarded folk wisdom born solely of past experience in long-familiar situation was impotent. Only the self confident and adventurous could in some degree control these new forces and have sufficient imagination to use them for hitherto unimaginable purposes. Neolithic "togetherness" was not enough. Many a village, baffled and beset by flooded fields or ruined crops, must have turned away from its slow-moving, overcautious council of elders to a single figure who spoke with authority and promptly gave commands as if he expected instantly to be obeyed.

Doubtless the hunter's imagination, no less than his prowess, was there from the beginning, long before either flowed into political channel: for surely there is a more commanding esthetic sense in the Paleolithic hunter's cave than there is

in any early Neolithic pottery or sculpture. Nothing like the same superb esthetic flair as we find in the Aurignacian caves came back till the stone-and-copper age. But now heroic exertions, once confined mainly to the hunt, were applied to the entire physical environment. Nothing the mind projected seemed impossible. What one singularly self-assured man dared to dream of, under favor of the gods, a whole city obedient to his will might do. No longer would wild animals alone be subdued: rivers, mountains, swamps, masses of men, would be attacked collectively at the King's command and reduced to order. Backbreaking exertions that no little community would impose on itself, so long as nature met its customary needs, were now undertaken: the hunter-hero, from Gilgamesh to Herakles, set the example in his superhuman acts of strength. In conquering hard physical tasks every man became a bit of a hero, surpassing his own natural limits—if only to escape the overseer's lash.

The expansion of human energies, the enlargements of the human ego, perhaps for the first time detached from its immediate communal envelope the differentiation of common human activities into specialized vocations, and the expression of this expansion and differentiation at many points in the structure of t he city, were all aspects of a single transformation: the rise of civilization. We cannot follow this change at the moment it occurred, for, as Teilhard de Chardin notes of other evolutionary changes, it is the unstable and fluid emerging forms that leave no record behind. But later crystallizations clearly point to the nature of the earlier evolution.

To interpret what happened in the city, one must deal equally with technics, politics, and religion, above all with the religious side of the transformation. If at the beginning all these aspects of life were inseparably mingled, it was religion that took precedence and claimed primacy, probably because unconscious imagery and subjective projections dominated every aspect of reality, allowing nature to become visible only in so far as it could be worked into the tissue of desire and dream. Surviving monuments and records show that this general magnification of power was accompanied by equally exorbitant images, issuing from the unconscious, transposed into the "eternal" forms of art.

As we have seen, the formative stages of this process possibly took many thousands of years: even the last steps in the transition from the Neolithic country town, little more than an overgrown village, to the full-blown city, the home of new institutional forms, may have taken centuries, even millennia; so long that many institutions that we have definite historic record of in other parts of the world—such as ceremonial human sacrifice—may have had time both to flourish and to be largely cut down in Egypt or Mesopotamia.

The enormous time gap between the earliest foundation in the Valley of the Jordan, if their latest datings are correct, and those of the Sumerian cities allows of many profound if unrecorded changes. But the final outbreak of inventions that attended the birth of the city probably happened within a few centuries, or even, as Frankford suggested of kingship, within a few generations. Pretty surely it took place within a span of years no greater than the seven centuries between the invention of the mechanical clock and the unlocking of atomic power.

As far as the present record stands, grain cultivation, the plow, the potter's wheel, the sailboat, the draw loom, copper metallurgy, abstract mathematics, exact astronomical observation, the calendar, writing and other modes of intelligible discourse in permanent form, all came into existence at roughly the same time, around 3000 B.C. give or take a few centuries. The most ancient urban remains now knows, except Jericho, date from this period. This constituted a singular technological expansion of human power whose only parallel is the change that has taken place in our own time. In both cases men, suddenly exalted, behaved like gods: but with little sense of their latent human limitations and infirmities, or of the neurotic and criminal natures often freely projected upon the deities.

There is nevertheless one outstanding difference between the first urban epoch and our own. Ours is an age of multitude of socially undirected technical advances, divorced from any other ends than the advancement of science and technology. We live in fact in an exploding universe of mechanical and electronic invention, whose parts are moving at a rapid pace ever further and further away from their human center, and from any rational, autonomous human purposes. This tech-

nological explosion has produced a similar explosion of the city itself: the city has burst open and scattered its complex organs and organizations over the entire landscape. The walled urban container indeed has not merely been broken open: it has also been largely demagnetized, with the result that we are witnessing a sort of devolution of urban power into a state of randomness and unpredictability. In short, our civilization is running out of control, overwhelmed by its own resources and opportunities, as well as its superabundant fecundity. The totalitarian states that see ruthlessly to impose control are much the victim of their clumsy brakes as the seemingly freer economies coasting downhill are at the mercy of their runaway vehicles.

Just the opposite happened with the first great expansion of civilization: instead of an explosion of power, there was rather an *implosion.* The many diverse elements of the community hitherto scattered over a great valley system and occasionally into regions far beyond, were mobilized and packed together under pressure, behind the massive walls of the city. Even the gigantic forces of nature were brought under conscious human direction: tens of thousands of men moved into action as one machine under centralized command, building irrigation ditches, canals, urban mounds, ziggurats, temples, palaces, pyramids, on a scale hitherto inconceivable. As an immediate outcome of the new power mythology, the machine itself had been invented: long invisible to archaeologists because the substance of which it was composed—human bodies—had been dismantled and decomposed. The city was the container that brought about this implosion, and through its very form held together the new forces, intensified their internal reactions, and raised the whole level of achievement.

This implosion happened at the very moment that the area of intercourse was greatly enlarged, through raidings and tradings, through seizures and commandeerings, through migrations and enslavements, through tax-gatherings and the wholesale conscription of labor. Under pressure of one master institution, that of kingship, a multitude of diverse social particles, long separate and self-centered, if not mutually antagonistic, were brought together in a concentrated urban area. As with a gas, the very pressure of the molecules within that limited space produced more social collisions and interactions within a generation than would have occurred in many centuries if still isolated in their native habitats, without boundaries. Or to put it in more organic terms, little communal village cells, undifferentiated and uncomplicated, every part of performing equally every function, turned into complex structures organized on an axiate principle, with differentiated tissues and specialized organs, and with one part, the central nervous system, thinking for and directing the whole.

What made this concentration and mobilization of power possible? What gave it the special form it took in the city, with a central religious and political nucleus, the citadel, dominating the entire social structure and giving centralized direction to activities that had one been dispersed and undirected, or at least locally self governed? What I am going to suggest as the key development here had already been presaged, at a much earlier stage, by the apparent evolution of the protective hunter into the tribute-gathering chief: a figure repeatedly attested in similar developments in many later cycles of civilization. Suddenly this figure assumed superhuman proportions: all his powers and prerogatives became immensely magnified, while those of his subjects, who no longer had a will of their own or could claim any life apart from that of the ruler, were correspondingly diminished.

Now I would hardly be bold enough to advance this explanation if one of the most brilliant of modern archaeologists, the late Henri Frankfort, had not provided most of the necessary data, and unconsciously foreshadowed if not foreseen this conclusion. What I would suggest is that the most important agent in effecting the change from a decentralized village economy to a highly organized urban economy, was the king, or rather, the institution of Kingship. The industrialization and commercialization we now associate with urban growth was for centuries a subordinate phenomenon, probably even emerging later in time: the very word merchant does not appear in Mesopotamian writing till the second millennium, "when it designates the official of a temple privileged to trade abroad." Going beyond Frankfort, I suggest that one of the attributes of the ancient Egyptian god, Ptah, as revealed in a document derived from the third millennium B.C.—*that he founded cities*—is the special and all but universal function of kings. In the urban implosion, the king stands at the center: he is the polar magnet that draws to the heart of the city and brings under the control of the palace and temple all the new forces of civilization. Sometimes the king founded new cities; sometimes he transformed old country towns that had long been a-building, placing them under the authority of his governors: in either case his rule made a decisive change in their form and contents.

Towns, Time and Tradition: The Legacy of Planning in Frontier America

John Reps

Town Planning in Frontier America is a shortened version of John Reps's longer and more detailed book, *The Making of Urban America* (1965). In these books, Reps covers city plans from the first European settlement at St. Augustine in 1565 to the frontier planning experiences of the middle of the nineteenth century. In this section, Reps examines nineteenth-century frontier planning and discusses the obstacles involved in transferring planning knowledge from England to her former colony. Finally, he summarizes the planning failures and achievements of the era. He focuses on the lessons that can be learned from our frontier development-planning experiences and applied to the challenges of modern urbanization.

By the middle of the 19th century the basic pattern of urban settlement east of the Mississippi had been established. Virtually all of what were to become the major cities of an increasingly urban nation had begun as planned communities: Boston, New York, Philadelphia, Baltimore, Washington, Pittsburgh, Buffalo, Cleveland, Detroit, Chicago, Cincinnati, Indianapolis, St. Louis, and New Orleans. Not all had been planned with skill, and in every case the explosive growth of these urban centers was soon to outrun the bounds of their original borders. In each of these, as well as in dozens of planned cities of smaller size, something of the heritage of its planned beginnings remains. In many, indeed most, the character and quality of t he first settlement forms prescribed by their founders exceeds in merit the accretions of the later 19th century and of our own era.

We are now entering a period of American urbanization. By the year 2000 current projections indicate that we will develop as much additional land for urban purposes as we did in the first 400 years of city building from 1565 to 1965. In addition, we are setting about the complex task of reconstructing the blighted and congested centers of our existing cities. Increasingly the effort to create a better life will focus on the issues of city growth and control of the urban environment, along with attempts to grapple with the nagging social problems of poverty and racial segregation.

The American philosopher George Santayana once observed that those who are ignorant of history are condemned to re-live it. What are the lessons to be learned from our planning experience during the first period of frontier development as we approach the new frontier of making our cities habitable for ourselves and succeeding generations? Let us try to sum up our failures and our achievements during that remarkable era of our history when we laid the foundation for an urban civilization.

We must not let national pride warp our perspective. The North Atlantic proved a major barrier to the transplanting of town planning techniques and concepts which were highly developed in Europe at the beginning of colonization and which continued to advance and change in the centuries to follow. The resources of colonial settlers pitted against the difficulties of a harsh and often hostile environment permitted little more than the minimum requirements of town life let alone the amenities or embellishments which were commonplace in 17th- and 18th- century Europe.

Compare, for example, the Quebec of Champlain with the Charleville of its founder, Duke Charles III. Both date from 1608. Quebec consisted of Champlain's crude "Habitation" and a tiny grid of streets hugging the banks of the St. Lawrence River. Charleville embodied all the theories of Renaissance formal planning, with its elaborate hierarchy of streets and open squares on which fronted carefully scaled buildings all making up a sophisticated composition in civic design. Not until 1791, with L'Enfant's Baroque plan for Washington, did American urban planners produce a large-scale example of what had long been established as a standard plan form in Europe.

Or, contrast the development pattern of the West End of London in the mid-18th century with the plan of Savannah and its multiple squares. While the plan forms are essentially similar, the differences between them in the third dimension were striking. Fronting the London squares stood elegant and restrained terrace houses of urbane dignity and harmonious proportions. Lining the squares of frontier Savannah were the simplest of huts and cabins. Not for nearly a century did Savannah attain something of the character of even the least imposing of Georgian London's squares. The lag between city planning practice in Europe and what occurred in the colonial empires of North America was thus substantial.

The reasons for these differences between colony and mother country are readily understandable. The strangeness of the environment, the slowness of communications, the absence of traditions, the lack of institutional patterns, and the necessity to create anew even the most elementary of urban services and facilities—all contributed to prevent the speedy and complete transfer to the New World of what had been learned about city planning in the old. Today these inhibiting factors have vanished, yet one can argue that in comparison with such remarkably well-ordered European cities as Stockholm and Amsterdam we still lag far behind European practice in urban planning. No longer do we have the excuse of limited physical resources; indeed, their very abundance may contribute to our urban physical disarray. Yet in a sense we still act like primitive colonials, helpless to put into practice the latest lessons of how to arrange cities in patterns which are both functional and beautiful.

Our failure to achieve an urban order fitting for the time and within our capabilities may well stem from attitudes toward the city developed in our swaddling years. America was peopled by Europeans who were hungry for land. In a seemingly limitless continent the most insatiable appetites could be satisfied. For a time fear of Indian attack combined with old habits of settlement to promote the development of compact agricultural villages. But when the natives were overcome and when the boundless extent of the land became apparent, the old associations of village and town life gave way to a quite different agricultural settlement pattern of isolated farmsteads. As early as 1623 in Plymouth Governor Bradford regretfully described these events:

"For now as their stocks increased…there was no longer any holding them together, but now they must of necessitie goe to their great lots; they could not other wise keep their katle; and having oxen growne, they must have land for plowing and tillage. And no man now thought he could live, except he had catle and a great deale of ground to keep them; all striving to increase their stocks. By which means they were scatered all over the bay, quickly, and the town in which they lived compactly till now, was left very thine, and in a short time allmost desolate. …And this, I fear, will be the ruine of NewEngland."[1]

For a good many Americans it was rural life which represented the ideal. The town was something from which to escape. The Jeffersonian notion of an agrarian democracy represents an old and deep feeling in American culture which has its manifestation today in the attempt to find in endless suburbia the freedoms which our ancestors sought on the western frontier of settlement. It is perhaps a permissible exaggeration to state that today's urban sprawl began in the 17th-century Plymouth.

One feature of American planning in the frontier era is the almost total absence of three-dimensional design. This is not to say that effective bits of townscape were unknown—countless New England villages testify to the care taken by early settlers in the siting of individual buildings. For the most part, however, towns were c conceived of in only two dimensions. The example of Williamsburg is virtually unique. Here was a town in which the plan of streets and building sites was developed as part of a larger vision of the future which included the location, size, and elevational treatment of its major structures. This approach to total urban design is the great lesson which Williamsburg has to teach—not the plan itself, the architectural style of its buildings, or the layout of its gardens. These belong to another era, and mere imitation of their dimensions and appearance is an insult to the integrity of colonial designers. Many of the shortcomings of the nation's cities today have resulted from earlier failures to realize that the third dimension of architecture is a vital ingredient of urban planning.

Another characteristic of American town planning was the widespread use of the gridiron or checkerboard pattern. As in virtually all other periods of wholesale colonization in world history, early colonial and later frontier towns were planned mainly on a geometric pattern of rectangular blocks, straight streets, and right-angle intersections. As the plan form most economical to survey, quickest to build, and easiest to understand, it is not surprising that the orthogonal system prevailed. For European visitors this feature of the American scene was novel and, at first impression, desirable. Thus, Francis Baily, noting the "perfect regularity" of Philadelphia and Baltimore was moved to comment, "This is a plan of which the Americans are very fond, and I think with reason, as it is by far the best way of laying out a city. All the modern-built towns in America are on this principle." However, what may have at first seemed like a vision of a new world urban rationality all too quickly blurred into an impression of sterile dullness. By the time Baily reached Cincinnati his infatuation with the grid had given way to disenchantment:

"I have taken occasion to express my approbation of the American mode of laying out their new towns, in a general way, in straight lines; but I think that oftentimes it is a sacrifice of beauty to prejudice, particularly when they persevere in making all their streets cross each other at a right angles, *without any regard to the situation of the ground,* or the face of the surrounding country: whereas, these ought certainly to be taken into consideration, in order that a town may unite both utility and beauty; and, with a little attention to this, a town might still preserve the straight line, and yet avoid that disgusting appearance which many of the new towns in America make."[2]

The seeds of senseless mechanized and unimaginative town planning which was to characterize much of the 19th century were sown in colonial soil. Yet not all gridiron plans of the frontier era of American urban development were of this quality. One thinks of New Haven, with a generous one-ninth of the original town left as an open green; or of Savannah, with its multiple squares breaking the monotony of the grid; or of Jeffersonville, with its alternating pattern of open squares and building blocks. Even Philadelphia's original plan contained the five squared laid out by Penn, the largest intended as a town center and the four smaller as recreation grounds. And Williamsburg demonstrates that the orthogonal plan is not incompatible with an atmosphere of formality and dignity.

It was less the first gridiron plans, which, in most cases were too modest in size to be offensively dull, than the later extensions of cities that violated good sense in community planning. Without regard to topography or, more importantly, failing to include in the additions to the city some of the open spaces of the original design, these new areas mechanically repeated almost endlessly the grid street system without any relieving features. Savannah stands almost alone as an exception to this dreary tradition.

The reasons are not difficult to identify. Planning of towns and development of land, in the beginning a community enterprise, fell into the hands of individuals and corporations whose almost sole aim was private profit. Even if the proper skills and sensibilities had been present, there was little incentive to plan well when mediocre planning, or worse, yielded generous financial returns. Moreover, as most communities abandoned responsibility for town planning to individuals they failed to create adequate legal and administrative institutions for the public control of private land development.

Our present urban land policy has scarcely departed from this position. Most important decisions about the timing of development, its location, and its design remain in private hands, tempered only mildly by regulations supposedly intended to protect the public interest. Because memories are short and historical perspective lacking, our generation regards this as the American tradition. So it is, but it is not the only tradition of our town planning history, nor has it proved the most effective.

The examples of Annapolis, Williamsburg, Savannah, Washington, and many of the 19th-century planned state capital cities remind us that public initiative and investment for the planning of cities once served to create an urban environment superior in quality to that of the present when measured against available financial and intellectual resources. The history of modern American city planning since the turn of the century can be read as an attempt, faltering and so far largely ineffective, to recapture that earlier tradition which placed the planning of towns as a responsibility of the community at large.

If the American urban history has anything to contribute to the modern world aside from mere antiquarian enjoyment it is that good cities—beautiful, as well as safe and efficient—will arise only when it is the city itself that assumes the obligation for its own destiny.

NOTES

1. William Bradford, *History of Plymouth Plantation*, W. T. David, ed., New York, 1908, pp. 293-94.

2. Francis Baily, *Journal of a Tour in Unsettled Parts of North America in 1796 & 1797*, London, 1856, pp. 105, 226-27.

If Planning is Everything, Maybe It's Nothing

Aaron Wildavsky

In this selection Wildavsky addresses the growing importance and increasing exclusivity of the planning profession at the national level. He explores the concepts and motives behind various models of planning and speaks to the constant scrutiny that planners face as a result of the growing dimensions of their responsibilities. Wildavsky then concludes by examining the costs and benefits of formal planning, and the reasoning and purpose that keeps the profession in continuing practice.

INTRODUCTION

The planner has become the victim of planning; his own creation has overwhelmed him. Planning has become so large that the planner cannot encompass its dimensions. Planning has become so complex planners cannot keep up with it. Planning protrudes in so many directions, the planner can no longer discern its shape. He may be economist, political scientist, sociologist, architect or scientist. Yet the essence of his calling—planning—escapes him. He finds it everywhere in general and nowhere in particular. Why is planning so elusive?

The concept of planning stands between actors and their societies. It conditions the way they perceive social problems and it guides their choice of solutions. Their understanding of planning helps them to choose the questions they ask and the answers they find. It leads them to evaluate their experience, including their attempt to plan, in certain ways rather than others. The difficulties they experience in society are related to their understanding of the mechanism—planning—they believe will help them solve its problems.

Men think through language. They can hardly conceive of phenomena their words cannot express. The ways in which men think about planning affect how they act just as their attempts to plan affect how they think about it. The problems they have with the word mirror their problems with the world.

Planners begin by attempting to transform their environment and end by being absorbed into it. This pattern of failure is most evident in the poor countries of the world where glittering promise has been replaced b y discouraging performance.[1] Nor, despite the high economic growth, are the results different in rich countries; brief examination of two critical cases—France and Japan—will show they also do not follow their plans or make good on them when they do. Planning fails everywhere it has been tried.

How can this be? The reasonable man plans ahead. He seeks to avoid future evils by anticipating them. He tries to obtain a more desirable future by working toward it in the present. Nothing seems more reasonable than planning. And that is where the problem begins; for if planning is reason, then reasonable people must be for it. A reasonable author addressing a reasonable reader cannot be opposed to reason. Is it irrational to dissent from this position?

One good question deserves another: can it be rational to fail? Now anyone can do the best he can and still not succeed. Suppose, however, that the failures of planning are not peripheral or accidental but integral to its very nature. Suppose planning as presently constituted cannot work in the environment in which it is supposed to function. Is it irrational to entertain this hypothesis? If it is irrational to pursue any hypothesis that does not confirm the rational nature of planning, then you are about to read an irrational essay.

PLANNING AS FUTURE CONTROL

Practitioners and students of planning have given the word countless interpretations. Every writer, it seems, feels compelled to redefine the concept. And I am no exception. For the confusion resulting from this semantic Tower of Babel impinges on the practice of planning. How does one evaluate a phenomenon when there is little agreement about what it is? How can one say that planning is good or bad or in between when there are no accepted criteria for determining degrees of success or failure? Judgment of the performance of planning rests upon the nature of the expectations it arouses; and these expectations naturally vary with the definition one adopts. If planning is designed to make goals consistent on paper, one would judge it quite differently than if its purpose is actually to achieve social goals in the future.

Planning is the attempt to control the consequences of our actions. The more consequences we control, the more we have succeeded in planning. To use somewhat different language, planning is the ability to control the future by current acts. Instead of discovering his fate in the future, man plans to make it in his own image. But the present may be reluctant to give birth to the future. Man can attempt to plan and he can fail. As St. Paul put it in his letter to the Romans, "I do not understand my own actions. For I do not do what I want, but I do the very thing I hate...I can will what is right, but I cannot do it. For I do not do the good I want, but the evil I do not want is what I do." While man has helped cause these unanticipated events, he has not consciously intended (that is, planned) to bring them about. We must distinguish, therefore, between attempts to plan and actual success in planning.

Attempts to plan are no more planning than the desire to be wise may be called wisdom or the wish to be rich entitles a man to be called wealthy. Promise must be dignified by performance. The determination of whether planning has taken place must rest on an assessment of whether and to what degree future control has been achieved.

Planning must not be confused with the existence of a formal plan, people called planners, or an institution (henceforth called the planning commission) with the word planning in its official title. Formal plans are only one possible manifestation of planning, since planning may take place outside of formal planning organizations. The distinction here is between a written and an unwritten plan. No one today would claim that the British do not have a constitution (rules specifying the procedures for exercising political power) merely because theirs is found in legislation and custom rather than in a single document like that of the United States. Perhaps the existence of a formal plan suggests a greater commitment to the objectives and the subordinate goals in the plan than one would expect in the absence of such a visible public document. This question should be resolved by observation rather than by definition. Certainly the absence of a Bill of Rights in the "unwritten" British constitution does not reveal a lesser commitment to due process or democratic procedure than America's formal statement in its Constitution. In like manner, it would be wrong to say that a government t hat consciously improved the conditions of its people and increased their ability to live productive lives was not planning because it lacked the formal apparatus, while another government whose people suffered in these respects was planning because it had a plan and planners.

It is tempting to identify planning with government ownership of industry. Then the government is directly making decisions for the entire economy, and that would appear to eliminate the difficulties of plan implementation caused by a recalcitrant private sector. The decisions that are made, however, may turn out to run counter to the plan. Planned decisions often have unplanned consequences. It would be more accurate to say that these governments attempt to plan but do not necessarily succeed, if success means controlling the future direction of their society through a predetermined series of actions. Achievements and not the plan must be the final arbiter of planning. Otherwise, planning exists because there is a plan, no matter what fate has in store for it.

We want a definition of planning that will enable us to compare the efficacy of different ways of achieving control over the future. We want to b e able to say that one process or strategy or social structure is better or worse in enabling society to move in the direction it chooses in the most expeditious manner. Central direction of the economy, reliance on a price mechanism, devotion to traditional culture, emphasis on agriculture and small industry, any and all bases for action may be judged by their consequences so long as none are identified as planning itself.

A definition based on attempts to plan—planning as a goal-directed behavior—leaves open the question of whether the actions involved have resulted in the kind of future control envisaged. By defining planning according to its inputs (different modes of trying to control the future) rather than its outputs (extent of future control) the element of direction is removed from planning. Such a definition might be appropriate for those interested in different styles of decision for their own sake but not for people concerned with appraising purposeful social action.

For if a definition covers all attempts to plan, whether they succeed or not, planning encompasses whatever men intend to do in the world. Since practically all actions with future consequences are planned actions, planning is everything, and nonplanning can hardly be said to exist. Nonplanning only exists when people have no objectives, when their actions are random and not goal-directed. If everybody plans (well, almost) it is not possible to distinguish planned from unplanned actions.

A definition of planning based on formal position—planning is whatever planners do—is useful if one wishes to examine the activities of people who occupy these places. But a formal definition rules out on *a priori* grounds the likelihood that ability to control the consequences of current actions may be more widely diffused in society. The question becomes not "who in society succeeds in planning?" but "how successful are formal planners in planning?" The planners are the active element, their society the passive beneficiary of their efforts.

Planning is often used (though this definition is rarely made explicit) as if it were equivalent to rationality. Once norms associated with rational action are identified—efficiency, consistency, coordination—any process of decision may be appraised according to the degree to which it conforms to them. The assumption is that following these norms leads to better decisions. Defining planning as applied rationality focuses attention on adherence to universal norms rather than on the consequences of acting one way instead of another. Attention is directed to the internal qualities of the decisions and not to their external effects.

The confusions surrounding the meaning of planning may have a social explanation. Unable to control the future, planners have resisted any other definition that would brand them as failures. After all, no one else is forced to make public predictions that rarely turn out right. Planners want credit for their aspirations, for a noble effort, so they grope toward a definition that stresses the activities in which they engage or the processes through which they work. Exhibition displaces power. The focus of meaning can shift from events in the world to their own exemplary behavior.

These definitions are not merely different ways of looking at the same thing. They are not just words. They imply different standards for planning and they direct our attention to different phenomena. To define planning as future control, for instance, does away with distinction between drawing up plans and implementing them, setting goals and achieving them. The objective and its fulfillment are part of the same series of actions.[2] Separating goals from achievements, as most definitions do by emphasizing intention over accomplishment, blurs the distinction between planning and other purposeful behavior. Hence planning becomes a self-protecting hypothesis; so long as planners try to plan, it cannot be falsified.

In order to understand the implications of these rival definitions, let us consider what is involved in the statements about planning made by practitioner and theorist alike. Virtually everyone would agree that planning requires: (1) A specification of future objectives and (2) a series of related actions over time designed to achieve them. We can now try to discover in general terms what is entailed by national planning

PLANNING AS CAUSE

We can say (beginning with implementing actions) that the first requisite of national planning is causal knowledge: the existence of theory with at least some evidence to support it specifying causal relationships. If X and Y are done, then Z will result. If the consequences of contemplated actions cannot accurately be appraised, specified objectives will be achieved only by accident. The necessity for causal knowledge is made more stringent in long-range planning because the consequences of each action become the basis for the succeeding steps. Each error in prediction is magnified because of its impact on future decisions.

It will help if we specify the kinds of casual knowledge planning requires: knowledge of the relationships in each of dozens of areas of policy from fisheries to foreign exchange. These relationships may be further subdivided: (1) interaction among the elements of the policy itself, (2) incentives for the people involved to carry out the policy or mechanisms for insuring compliance, (3) sufficient resources at the time required. In agriculture, for example, knowledge of the elements of the policy itself—the technology of production, the mechanisms of distribution, the availability of markets—must be right if the policy is to work. If the farmers will not plant the crops called for or if the prices do not bring them sufficient remuneration, the will sabotage the policy, either overtly or through passive resistance. If there is insufficient money for seeds or fertilizer or if the farmer lacks the education or the motivation to employ the necessary techniques, the policy will fail.

Even if good theory exists somewhere in the world, people in a particular society must be able to apply it in the specific context of their own country. Yet knowledge of how to apply theory is often as weak as the theory itself. Social circumstances may make a mockery of general principles. There may be few men who are capable of utilizing existing theory for practical purposes. Where causal theory is absent or imperfect, where applications are poor or nonexistent, where personnel to carry out policies is lacking or badly trained, the preconditions of formal planning cannot be met.

Yet we have not begun to exhaust the requirements of casual knowledge. Not only is it required in each important area of policy (actually it is also necessary to know which areas are important), but among areas of policy as well. Energy policy, for example, cannot be pursued apart from transportation, industrial and agricultural policy. The major consequences of each set of policy decisions for other areas of policy must be known; if they are not, some objectives will be achieved at the expense of others or none of the objectives will be achieved. Scarce as causal theory is within specific areas of policy, it is superabundant compared to the lack of knowledge of interaction effects. There are no useful models of economies as a whole; either they contain so few variables as to be too general, or they contain so many that one cannot understand what goes on inside them, let alone in the world to which they are supposed to refer. If economic theory is weak, theories of society involving human motivation and incentive are barely alive. The provision of information itself is dependent on cultural norms, political support and administrative practices that usually work in the opposite direction. Thus the lack of theory means that one often does not what kind of information to collect, and, in any event, it would probably not be available.

Causal knowledge is also necessary to relate the policies of the nation over time to changes in the international economy and political systems. Low income countries are especially vulnerable to fluctuations in the price of imports and exports and in the willingness of previous donor nations to supply aid. Should the plan require a certain amount of foreign currency, it can easily disintegrate if commodity prices drop, imports rise, and foreign aid disappears. There are no good predictive models of international prices or of willingness to supply aid.

National planning provides a hard test of causal knowledge. Men, resources and institutions must be mobilized and related to one another at successive stages in time in order to obtain predicted results that lead to the achievement of objectives. Nothing less than control of the future is involved.

Any regime, whether it professes to love planning and enshrines *the plan* in its hall of fame, or whether it rejects formal planning entirely, plans to the extent that it can control its future. Planning takes place when people in a society are able to cause consequences they desire to occur. Planning is, therefore, a form of social causation. It requires causal knowledge and the ability to wield that knowledge effectively in society. Power and planning are different ways of looking at the same events.

PLANNING AS POWER

Power is the probability of changing the behavior of others against opposition.[3] As soon as the prevalence of disagreement over social goals or policies is admitted into discussion, it becomes clear that there can be no planning without the ability to cause other people to act differently than they otherwise would. Planning assumes power.

Planning is politics.

Power is a reciprocal relationship. It depends not only on what one actor can do but on how the other relevant actors respond in turn. A group may decide not to attempt to realize its intentions because doing so would use up resources that might be better employed elsewhere. Or its efforts may fail because others lack the ability to carry out their instructions. The wielders of power are restricted not only by the limits on their resources but also by the capacities of the respondents. Power must be viewed in its social context.[4]

Planning requires the power to maintain the preeminence of future objectives in the present. The nation's rulers must be able to commit its existing resources to the accomplishments of future objectives. If new rulers arise who make drastic changes in objectives, the original plan is finished. The continuity of the regime, of course, is one of the more problematical features of the poor country. Its unity may crumble, its devotion to original objectives may be undermined from within, and its ability to command the nation's resources may be dissipated through disagreement. Either the rulers must stay in power long enough to accomplish their original purposes or their successors must be people who share the same commitments.

If planning is to be more than an academic exercise, it must actually guide the making of governmental decision. Governmental actions (and the private activities they seek to influence) must in large measure conform to the plan if it is to have practical effect. Planning, then, at any point in time, involves governmental decisions on resource allocation. A theory of how planning should be done, therefore, would be a theory of governmental resource allocation over time. Planning theory becomes a theory of successive government budgets. If we substitute the words "what the government ought to do" for the words "ought to be in the plan," it becomes clear that a normative theory of planning would have to include a political theory detailing what the government's activities ought to be at a particular time.

To plan, therefore, is to govern. Planning thus becomes the process through which society makes its decisions. If one takes a narrow view of politics, only acts by official government bodies are planning acts. A broader view of politics would include all acts, whether ostensibly private or public, that have substantial future impact on society. To plan is to make decisions that affect others. Planners are presidents, ministers, bureaucrats, party leaders, scientists, entrepreneurs—anybody whose acts have large future consequences.

But the act of governing need not necessarily involve planning; intentions in actions may be unrealized. Political leaders, like planners, may find that they cannot control the future. All may try but none may succeed. Planners and politicians may compete for the right to attempt to plan but there may be no victor to claim the spoils.

Formal planners may be viewed as rivals for control of policy with other government agencies and private groups. Can planners dominate these competitors? They can be nothing if no one listens to them. They may be used by others but have no independent force of their own. Planners may also be everything. They may become the government and exert most of the public force in their nation. Although planning theory sometimes suggests that this is the position planners would need in order to carry out their purposes, and though planners in moments of frustration may wish they had this power, it would be fair to say they do not envisage total control. The vision they have of themselves is of a small but dedicated band that somehow enables the nation to meet goals by bringing it to its senses when necessary. They have in mind a regulator role of the type found in cybernetic systems: amidst a vast complex of machinery there is a small but sensitive device that returns the system to its true path whenever it strays. By pushing in the right direction at critical times the sum of the corrections adds up to achievement of the original goals. France and Germany might well adopt this thermostatic view of planning. But poor countries require far more than occasional correction; they need large inputs of energy in order to build important components of their systems. Thus planners vacillate between the thermostatic view, which is more in accordance with their potential, and the assumption of total power, which is beyond their grasp, when the small changes they can cause are overwhelmed by the large ones over which they have little control.

The experience of formal planners has a universal tinge. Life is full of small corrections. Rarely is it possible to pursue objectives on a once-

and-for-all basis. Relative success in meeting goals depends on new actions in response to changing circumstances. Learning, adjustment, adaptation are the keys to accomplishment. What happens to the original objectives when behavior changes in the light of new conditions?

PLANNING AS ADAPTATION

Until now I have taken for granted the existence of future objectives, each one neatly labeled as if they came out of a great national sausage machine in the sky. They have been assumed to exist somehow "out there". The time has come to inquire into the setting of objectives.

One way to determine future objectives is to extrapolate present trends. The goal in the future is to go where the society was headed in any event. The very idea of planning, however, suggests that one is not letting things go any which way, but intervenes to make them move in a different direction or faster or slower in the same direction. You do not need a plan to get you where you were going to be. How, then are new objectives created?

It turns out that there are no rules for determining objectives. The rules we do have for resource allocation—efficiency, productivity—assume that objectives are given. These rules specify: achieve a given objective at lowest costs or achieve as much of a given objective as possible from a fixed amount of resources. They posit relationships between inputs and outputs; they do not say what the outputs should be, other than getting the most out of the inputs related to them.

Suppose that governmental leaders simply pick any set that appeals to them. What validity should be accorded these objectives? The obvious answer is that they are authoritative if set out by leaders who will attempt to achieve them. This amounts to saying that they are valid because the government says so. Yet the idea of planning, with its connotations of reason and intelligence, resists the thought that objectives are just stuck out there. Presumably the planners must relate these objectives in some way to the capabilities of the nation as well as to the desires of its leaders.

An objective may be desirable but unobtainable. The result of seeking it may be a waste of resources. Fidel Castro publicly accepts blame for

setting a quota of sugar cane so high that cutting went far past the time and use of resources that were economically justified.[5] But no one knows what the right level would be. If sights are set too low, less may be done than desirable. If too high, unnecessary effort may be devoted to the task. Like Goldilocks, the leaders would like to come out just right. But that is too complex a task. So they simplify by allowing experience to modify the goals they set.

The Soviet Union's response to this dilemma has been instructive. The goals stated in their plans are meant to be targets. If a particular sector of the economy achieves its production goal, the standard is raised next time. Should the goal remain unfulfilled, the people involved are driven harder. If they still cannot make it, the target is lowered through negotiation.[6] There may be an implicit Pavlovian theory of human behavior in this process, but there is nothing scientific about the setting of objectives. Essentially, an arbitrary objective goal is set and then is modified with experience or sometimes just abandoned.

Another approach is to think of objectives as distant rather than near targets. Leaders spell out their objectives and hope to achieve them sometime, even if not in the period specified in the plan. Some might call this utopian, but others would say it represents a society going in a predetermined direction, though the pace of that effort is subject to change. Although this approach may be reasonable, it subverts the basic element of control which is supposed to differentiate planning from just mucking about.

What is the point of saying that the seven-year plan has been achieved in 22 months or that a certain industry has exceeded its quota or that it will take 9¼ years to achieve some part of the five-year plan? Presumably the idea of planning is that you get where you are going when you say you will and in the manner specified. Can it mean that you get some other place faster or the same place slower and in a way you did not anticipate? This is not a quibble. It goes to the heart of the idea of planning.

What has happened is that the objectives and the means for obtaining them are no longer fixed but have become subject to modification. The original set of objectives and the plan that embodies them are considered merely starting points.

They are altered on the basis of experience and necessity. A new regime, a change in commodity prices, discovery of a new theory, accumulation of changes in national cultural mores, may all signify the desirability of changing objectives and the policies to implement them. Adaptation to changing circumstances is certainly a virtue of the intelligent man. But is smacks of *ad hoc* decisionmaking.

When planning is placed in the context of continuous adjustment it becomes hard to distinguish from any other process of decision. By making planning reasonable it becomes inseparable from the processes of decision it was designed to supplant. One plans the way one governs; one does the best one can at the time and hopes that future information will enable one to do better as circumstances change. Some call this adaptive planning; others call it muddling through. Under the criteria of adaptation, almost any process for making decisions in a social context can be considered to be planning.

PLANNING AS PROCESS

One cannot, for instance, discuss democracy for long without using the terms—goals, alternatives, appraisals, objectives—which are the heart of almost any contemporary definition of planning. This suggests that electoral democracy may be considered a mode of planning.

The United States does not seek to achieve goals stated in a national plan. Yet that does not mean that the United States has no goals its decisionmakers try to achieve. There are institutions—the Federal Reserve Board, the Council of Economic Advisers, the Office of Management and Budget, Congressional committees, and more—whose task is to find goals and policies that embody them. There are specific pieces of legislation that are dedicated to full employment, ending or mitigating the effects of pollution, building highways, expanding recreational opportunities, improving agricultural productivity, and on and on. When these goals conflict, new decisions must be made concerning how much of each to try to achieve. Even a single goal like full employment may not be capable of achievements because there is not enough knowledge to do it or because it entails other costs, such as inflation, that prohibit

it. Moreover, these goals are related to ultimate objectives. The Preamble to the Constitution states national goals and the remainder presents an institutional plan for achieving them. The government of the United States seeks to achieve domestic prosperity and to protect its interests overseas. While these broad objectives remain constant the intermediate goals change in response to forces in society.

When he was a student in the City Planning Department of the University of California at Berkeley, Owen McShane wrote a paper making explicit the similarities between planning (as found in the model developed by West Churchman, in his book, *The Systems Approach*) and electoral democracy as a process of making decisions. Churchman postulates that planning is concerned with multi-stage decisionmaking and "hence it must study (1) a decisionmaker who (2) chooses among alternative courses of action in order to reach (3) certain first-stage goals, which lead to (4) other-stage objectives."[7] It is easy to parallel this model in terms of electoral democracy as the operation of (1) the electorate which (2) chooses from a group of candidates in order to reach (3) certain first-stage goals, which lead to (4) the implicit goals of the society at large.

Placing the steps in each system side by side, McShane found that the electoral process fitted Churchman's model with remarkable nicety. Every step has an operational equivalent in any electoral democracy.

Similar comparisons could b e made between the process of planning and the process of legislation and administration. Consider, for instance, a recent description of how public policy is made: "Generically, one can identify at least six different steps in the process of making government policy—publicizing a problem, initiating a search for a solution, evaluating alternative solutions, choosing a solution or a combination of solutions, implementing the measures decided upon, and finally evaluating consequences of a measure."[8] At this level of description there appears to be no significant difference between the United States (and almost any other government, for that matter) and societies that engage in planning.

When planning is conceived of as goal-directed behavior, almost any decisionmaking process will be found to contain similar elements. How

Table I.1

THE PLANNING SYSTEM	THE ELECTORAL DEMOCRATIC SYSTEM
Program 1: Legitimacy	**Program 1: Legitimacy**
Relationship between the planning system (P.S.) and the decisionmakers.	Relationship between the constitution, etc., and the electorate.
(a) Justification (why the P.S. should exist and its role).	(a) Justification (why democracy should exist and its role).
(b) Staffing the P.S. and establishing responsibility and authority.	(b) Designing the institutions of democracy and establishing responsibility and authority.
(c) The communication Subsystem	(c) The Communication Subsystem
(i) Persuasion (selling the P.S.)	(i) Persuasion (e.g. the Federalist, etc.)
(ii) Mutual education.	(ii) Public schools and media.
(iii) Politics identifying and changing the power structure of the organization.	(iii) Politics (constitutional amendments, judiciary).
(d) Implementation (installing the plan).	(d) Implementation (setting up the institutions and operating them).
Program 2: Analysis	**Program 2: Analysis**
Measurement (Identification, classification, prediction, etc.)	Measurement (Identification, classification, prediction, etc.)
(a) Identifying the decisionmakers, and customers of the larger system	(a) Identifying interest groups, setting the franchise, etc.
(b) Discovering and inventing the alternatives.	(b) Selecting candidates for office.
(c) Identifying the first stage goals.	(c) Identifying and lobbying for first stage goals and policies.
(d) Identifying the ultimate objectives.	(d) Identifying the ultimate aims of society (e.g., Goal for Americans, Bill of Rights, etc.)
(e) Measuring the effectiveness of each alternative for each stage goal.	(e) Assessing the candidate and his policy platform.
(f) Measuring the effectiveness of each first stage goal for the ultimate objectives.	(f) Assessing the effectiveness of policies for ultimate objectives (e.g. the Vietnam war as protecting democracy).
(g) Estimating the optimal alternative.	(g) Voting for the candidates of one's choice.
Program 3: Testing *(Verifying the Plan)*	**Program 3: Testing** *(Does the democracy work?)*
(a) Simulation and parallel testing.	(a) Comparison with other nations, self-appraisal by the citizenry.
(b) Controlling the plan once implemented.	(b) Checks and balances, news media, public debate, the opposition.

then can we evaluate planning? Asking what has been caused by goal-directed behavior is like requesting an explanation for all that has happened. If the process of planning cannot usefully be separated from other modes of choice, the observer will be unable to attribute consequences to planning that do not also belong to other ways of making decisions; its merits cannot be challenged by future events because they all have their origin in someone's efforts to secure his aims.

If planning is to be judged by its consequences, by what it accomplishes, we must return to the problem of causality. What has planning caused? What has happened differently because of the presence of plans, planners and planning commissions than would have happened without them? What, in the economist's language, is the value added by planning?

Evaluation of planning is not possible so long as it refers to mere effort. The only sportsmanlike response to a runner who has given his all, is "good try," especially if he has fallen at the first turn. Only if planning is defined to mean completed action, achieving a set goal, can its relative degree of success be appraised.

If we are willing to equate national planning with a formal plan, it is possible to ask whether the interventions specified in it have been carried out, and whether they have come close to achieving the desired ends. Evaluation of formal planning depends on forging a valid link between intentions expressed in the plan and future performance of the nation.

PLANNING AS INTENTION

I have grossly simplified the problem of deciding whether intentions have been carried out by placing them solely in the hands of planners and assuming that their intentions are manifested in the national plan. Judging plans and planners by their intentions nevertheless has strong attractions. The plan itself has the inestimable advantage of existing in time and space and being separable from other phenomena. The plan speaks of accomplishing certain things in specified ways and one can ask whether these future states of affairs have indeed come about. If the plan predicts a rate of economic growth, supported by the development of certain sectors of the economy,

propelled by various key projects, one can ascertain whether that rate has been achieved, whether the sectors singled out for special attention have grown in the way specified and whether the projects have been built and are bringing in the returns that were claimed for them. To the extent that the planners are not impossibly vague about what they intend, and relevant information is available and accurate, the plan may be judged by the degree to which its intentions have been carried out.

Yet the criterion of intention may easily prove superficial. Let us suppose that a plan has failed the test of accomplishing the goals set down in it. How might one explain that failure? If the plan is viewed as a series of predictions, it is evident that they have not come true. Yet calling a bad prediction a failure in an uncertain world seems harsh. More to the point would be a statement that the planners were unable to move the nation in the directions they intended. The claim can still be made, however, that much progress occurred, even if it fell short of the initial aims. Imagine a situation in which under Plan I a 4% growth rate was postulated and only 3% achieved, while in Plan II a 10% rate was set out and one of 6% achieved. Plan I was more successful in the sense that the growth rate came closer to the target, but Plan II was more successful in that the overall rate of growth was greater. Assume for the moment that both levels of growth are attributable to the plan. Why should one set of planners be criticized because of their higher level of aspirations if their actual accomplishments are greater? When the intentions in plans are not realized it is difficult to know whether this failure is due to poor performance or unreasonable expectations. Did the nation try to do too little or too much? Were its planners over ambitious or underachievers?

Planners are vulnerable. Unless they take the precaution of making their goals too vague to be tested, their failure is evident for all to see. They must spend their time not in explaining how they have succeeded but in arguing away their evident failures. A great deal can be learned about fulfilling intentions by noting what happens when early optimism is replaced by later rationalization.

When a venture runs into trouble there are a number of classic ways of justifying it without showing that its performance is actually better.

The usual tactic is to claim that the venture has not been tried hard enough, that doing more of the same would bring the results originally envisaged. If the bombing of North Vietnam does not waken the will of that government to resist, the answer is evidently not to stop but to do more of it. When the poverty programs in the United States lead to disappointing results, then the answer must be that not enough money has been poured into them. It is always difficult to know whether the theory behind the policy is mistaken, so input of resources would reach the critical mass presumed necessary to make it successful. The same argument is made in regard to formal planning: if only there were more effort, more dedication, more commitment, things would be better. This argument however, presumes on behalf of formal planning precisely what it is supposed to prove. If things were as they were supposed to be, planning would not be necessary to correct them. The argument is reminiscent of a practitioner's comment about planning around the world: in Russia it is imperative, in France it is indicative, and in poor countries it is subjunctive.

The usual way of justifying formal planning in the absence of (or contrary to the evidence about) accomplishment is to shift the focus of discussion from goals to process. The critic of planning, it is said, has evidently mistaken the nature of the enterprise: by focusing in his simple-minded way on the intentions of the planners he has missed the beneficial effects of the processes through which the plan is made. A similar argument is heard about the United States space program: it is not merely reaching the moon but all the wonderful things learned on the way up and down (cf. technological fallout) that justify the cost of the effort. Planning is good, therefore, not so much for what it does but for how it goes about not doing it.

The process of planning presumably inculcates habits of mind leading to more rational choice. Officials are sensitized to the doctrine of opportunity costs, to what must be given up in order to pursue certain alternatives, and to the notion of enterprise as a productive force in the nation's economy. Time horizons are expanded because the future is made part of present decisions. Because of the existence of the plans and the planners, data may have been collected that otherwise would not have been; men with eco-nomic skills have been introduced into government. Those who come in contact with these new men are said to benefit from their new ways of looking at the world. To ask how these spinoff benefits are made tangible would be to retreat to the fallacy—comparing the intentions of planners with their accomplishments—that the process argument was designed to subvert.

There is another way of getting around the problem of intention and its realization; instead of merely saying that the intentions specified in the plan are not the real ones, one can argue that the planners are not the people whose intentions count. An interest-group leader or a politician may have hidden agenda the plan is supposed to achieve. The plan thus becomes an instrument for the purposes of others; its provisions are to be judged by the degree to which it serves their needs. To determine whether planning was successful or not would, therefore require specific knowledge of the real purposes for which it was used and no *a priori* judgments from afar would be appropriate.

Plans and planners in this context are simply one element in a repertoire of responses in the political arena that are available to those powerful and clever enough to use them. Plans may be weapons wielded by one political faction against another. The forces of logic, reason and rationali-ty may be used by a president against a recalci-trant ministry or by one ministry or region versus another. The possibilities are endless. If national leaders wish to be though modern, for instance, they have a document with which to dazzle their visitors. Charts, tables, graphs, regressions, are trotted out, but no one who matters attends to them. The plan need not be a means of surmount-ing the nation's difficulties, but rather may become a mode of covering them up.

By taking the argument one step further, the idea of plans as intentions can be dissolved entire-ly. One no longer asks whether the intentions in the plan are carried out, but which of many com-peting intentions is validated, if, indeed, any are. In this view there is no single set of intentions, any more than there is a general will that can be embodied in a single plan. There are different wills and various interests that compete for shares in planning. Some of these "wills" get adopted as government plans for a time and then are altered or revised. The great questions then become: whose intentions are realized? Are anyone's plans made good by the unfolding of events?

One conflict over goals is admitted, intention evaporates as a useful criterion for judging the success of planning. The planners lose their hold over intention; it is no longer immutable but problematical, a subject for bargaining, a counter in the flux of events. The stage shifts from the intentions specified in the plan to a multitude of actors whose intentions are alleged to b e the real ones. The success of planning depends entirely on whose plans one has in mind.

My discussion of intention may be rejected, not necessarily because it's misleading (though that may be the case), but because it's seen as irrelevant. Sophisticated people, critics might say, have long since abandoned both the idea of national planning and of national intentions. They may go along with it for its symbolic value but they know it does not work. "So why bother to spend all this time discussing it," one can hear them say. Planners have a much more modest conception—to reduce the scope of efforts by concentrating on individual sectors of the economy and move in the direction of dealing with relatively small and circumscribed problems. They seek to discover an actual opportunity for decision, to elaborate a few alternatives and to discuss their probably consequences in a limited way. They cut their costs of calculations by vastly reducing the magnitude of the tasks they set for themselves.

This approach is basically conservative. It takes for granted the existing distribution of wealth and power. It works with whatever price mechanism exists. It seeks not to influence many decisions at once but only a few. Now the ordinary men who would otherwise have made these decisions in the absence of planners also concentrate on a very narrow area of specialization: they also consider a few different ways of doing things; they also estimate the probably consequences in a limited way, and they also choose the alternative that seems best under the circumstances. By making planning manageable it appears we have made it indistinguishable from ordinary processes of decision. Planning has been rescued by diminishing, if not entirely, obliterating, the difference between it and everyday decisionmaking. Of what, then, do the advantages of planning consist?

Maybe we have been looking at planning in the wrong way. The place to look for the virtues of planning, perhaps, is not in the world but in the word. Planning is good, it seems, because it is good to plan.

Planning is not really defended for what it does but for what is symbolizes. Planning, identified with reason, is conceived to be the way in which intelligence is applied to social problems. The efforts of planners are presumably better than other people's social problems. The efforts of planners are presumably better than other people's because they result in policy proposals that are systematic, efficient, coordinated, consistent, and rational. It is words like these that convey the superiority of planning. The virtue of planning is that it embodies universal norms of rational choice.

PLANNING AS RATIONALITY

Certain key terms appear over and over again: planning is good because it is *systematic* rather than random, *efficient* rather than wasteful, *coordinated* rather than helter-skelter, *consistent* rather than contradictory, and above all, *rational* rather than unreasonable. In the interest of achieving a deeper understanding of why planning is preferred, it will be helpful to consider these norms as instructions to decisionmakers. What would they do if they followed them?

Be systematic! What does it mean to say that decisions should be made in a systematic manner? A word like "careful" will not do because planners cannot be presumed to be more careful than other people. Perhaps "orderly" is better; it implies a checklist of items to be taken into account, but anyone can make a list. Being systematic implies further that one knows the right variables in the correct order to put into the list, and can specify the relationship among them. The essential meaning of systematic, therefore, is having qualities of a system, that is a series of variables whose interactions are known and whose outputs can be predicted from knowledge of their inputs. System, therefore, is another word for theory or model explaining and predicting events in the real world in a parsimonious way that permits manipulation.[9] To say that one is being systematic, consequently implies that one has causal knowledge.

Here we have part of the answer we have been seeking. Planning is good because inherent in the concept of the possession of knowledge that can be used to control the world. Knowledge is hard to obtain; the mind of man is small and simple while the world is large and complex. Hence the temptation to imply by a cover word possession of the very thing, causal knowledge, that is missing.

Be efficient! There is in modern man a deeply-rooted belief that objectives should be obtained at the least cost. Who can quarrel with that? But technical efficiency should never be considered by itself. It does not tell you where to go but only that you should arrive there (or part way) by the least effort.

The great questions are: efficiency for whom and for what? There are some goals (destroying other nations in nuclear war, decreasing the living standards of the poverty-stricken in order to bene-fit the wealthy) that one does not wish achieved at all, let alone efficiently. Efficiency, therefore, rais-es once more the prior question of objectives.

One of the most notable characteristics of national objectives is that they tend to be vague, multiple and contradictory. Increasing national income is rarely the only social objective. It has to be traded off against more immediate consump-tion objectives, such as raising the living standards of rural people. Cultural objectives such as encouraging the spread of native languages and crafts, may have to be undertaken at a sacrifice of income. Political objectives, such as the desire to improve racial harmony or assert national inde-pendence, may lead to distribution of investment funds to economically unprofitable regions and to rejection of certain kinds of foreign aid. A great deal depends on which objectives enter into national priorities first, because there is seldom room for emphasis one more than a few.

Stress on efficiency assumes that objectives are agreed upon. Conflict is banished. The very national unity to which the plan is supposed to contribute turns out to be one of its major assump-tions.

Coordinate! Coordination is one of the golden words of our time. I cannot offhand think of any way in which the word is used that implies disap-proval. Policies should be coordinated; they should not run every which-way. No one wishes their children to be described as uncoordinated.

Many of the world's ills are attributed to lack of coordination of government. Yet, so far as we know, there has never been a serious effort to ana-lyze the term. It requires and deserves full discus-sion. All that can be done here, however, is barely to open up the subject.

Policies should be mutually supportive rather than contradictory. People should not work at cross purposes. The participants in any particular activity should contribute to a common purpose at the right time and in the right amount to achieve coordination. A should facilitate B in order to achieve C. From this intuitive sense of coordina-tion four important (and possible contradictory) meanings can be derived.

If there is a common objective, then efficiency requires that it be achieved with the least input of resources. When these resources are supplied by a number of different actors, hence the need for coordination, they must all contribute their proper share at the correct time. If their actions are effi-cient, that means they contributed just what they should and no more or less.

Coordination, then, equals efficiency, which is highly prized because achieving it means avoid-ing bad things: duplication, overlapping and redundancy. These are bad because they result in unnecessary effort, thereby expending resources that might be used more effectively for other pur-poses. But now we shall complicate matters by introducing another criterion that is (for good rea-son) much less heard in discussion of planning. I refer to reliability, the probability that a particular function will be performed. Heretofore we have assumed that reliability was taken care of in the definition of efficiency. It has been discussed as if the policy in mind had only to work once. Yet we all know that major problems of designing policies can center on the need to have them work at a cer-tain level of reliability. For this reason, as Martin Landau has so brilliantly demonstrated, redun-dancy is built-in to most human enterprises.[10] We ensure against failure by having adequate reserves and by creating several mechanisms to perform a single task in case on should fail.

Coordination of complex activities requires redundancy. Telling us to avoid duplication gives us no useful instruction at all; it is just a recipe for failure. What we need to know is how much and what kind of redundancy to build-in to our programs. The larger the number of participants in an enterprise, the more difficult the problem of coordination, the greater the need for redundancy.

Participants in a common enterprise may act in a contradictory fashion because of ignorance; when informed of their place in the scheme of things, they may obediently be expected to behave properly. If we relax the assumption that a common purpose is involved, however, and admit the possibility (indeed the likelihood) of conflict over goals, then coordination becomes another term for coercion. Since actors A and B disagree with goal C, they can only be coordinated by being told what to do and doing it. The German word, *Gleichschaltung*, used by the Nazis in the sense of enforcing a rigid conformity, can give us some insight into this particular usage of coordination. To coordinate one must be able to get others to do things they do not want to do. Coordination thus becomes a form of coercive power.

When one bureaucrat tells another to coordinate a policy, he means that it should be cleared with other official participants who have some stake in the matter. This is a way of sharing the blame in case things go wrong (each initial on the documents being another hostage against retribution). Since they cannot be coerced, their consent must be obtained. Bargaining must take place to reconcile the differences with the result that the policy may be modified, even at the cost of compromising its original purposes. Coordination in this sense is another word for consent.

Coordination means achieving efficiency and reliability, consent and coercion. Telling another person to achieve coordination, therefore, does not tell him what to do. He does not know whether to coerce or bargain or what mixture of efficiency and reliability to attempt. Here we have another example of an apparently desirable trait of planning that covers up the central problems—conflict versus cooperation, coercion versus consent—that its invocation is supposed to resolve. Planning suffers from the same disability that Herbert Simon illustrated for proverbial wisdom in administration:[11] each apparently desirable trait may be countered by its opposite—look before you leap, but he who hesitates is lost. An apt illustration is the use of "consistency".

Be consistent! Do not run in all directions at once. Consistency may be conceived as horizontal (at a moment in time) or vertical (over a series of time periods extending into the future). Vertical consistency requires that the same policy be pursued, horizontal consistency that it mesh with others existing at the same time. The former requires continuity of a powerful regime able to enforce its preferences, the latter tremendous knowledge of how policies affect one another. These are demanding prerequisites. One requires extraordinary rigidity to ensure continuity, the other unusual flexibility to achieve accommodation with other policies. Be firm, be pliant, are hard directions to follow at one and the same time.

The divergent directions implied in the term suggest that the virtues of consistency should not be taken for granted. It may well be desirable to pursue a single tack with energy and devotion but it may also prove valuable to hedge one's bets. Consistency secures a higher payoff for success but also imposes a steeper penalty for failure. If several divergent policies are being pursued in the same area they may interfere with each other but there also may be a greater chance that one will succeed. The admonition "Be consistent" may be opposed by the proverb, "Don't put all your eggs in the same basket."

Consistency is not wholly compatible with adaptation. While it may be desirable to pursue a steady course it is also commonsensical to adapt to changing circumstances. There is a model of the unchanging objective pursued by numerous detours and tactical retreats but never abandoned and ultimately achieved. There is also the model of learning in which experience leads men to alter their objectives as well as the means of obtaining them. They may come to believe the cost is too high or they may learn they prefer different objectives. If both means and ends, policies and objectives, are changing simultaneously, consistency may turn out to be a will o' the wisp that eludes one's grasp whenever one tries to capture it.[12] The resulting inconsistency may not matter so much, however, as long as alternative courses of action are thoroughly examined at each point of decision.

Consider alternatives! Which ones? How many? Answers to these questions depend on the inventiveness of the planners; the acknowledged constraints; (such as limited funds, social values), and the cost in terms of time, talent, and money, that can be spent on each. While it used to be popular to say that all alternatives should be systematically compared, it has become evident that this won't work; knowledge is lacking and the cost is too high. The number of alternatives considered could easily be infinite if the dimensions of the problem (such as time, money, skill and size) are continuous.

Let us suppose that only a small number of alternatives will be considered. Which of the many conceivable ones should receive attention? Presumably those will be selected that are believed most compatible with existing values and to work most efficiently. But this presupposes that the planner knows at the beginning how the analysis will turn out; otherwise he must reject some alternatives to come up with the preferred set. At the same time there are other matters up for decision and choices must be made about whether they are to be given analytical time and attention. The planner needs rules telling him when to intervene in regard to which possible decisions and how much time to devote to each one. His estimate of the ultimate importance of the decision undoubtedly matters, but also it requires predictive ability he may not have. He is likely to resort to simple rules as the amount of money involved in the decision and an estimate of his opportunities for influencing it.

We have gone a long way from the simple advice to consider alternatives. Now we know that this command does not tell anyone which decisions should concern him, how many alternatives he should consider, how much time and attention to devote to them or whether he knows enough to make the enterprise worthwhile. To say that alternatives should be considered is to suggest that something better must exist without being able to say what it is.

Be rational! If rationality means achieving one's goals in the optimal way, it refers here to technical efficiency, the principle of least effort. As Paul Diesing argues,[13] however, one can conceive of several levels of rationality for different aspects of society. There is the rationality of legal norms and of social structures for decision, and economic rationality which is devoted to increasing national wealth.

What is good for the political system may not be good for the economy and *vice versa*. The overweening emphasis upon economic growth in

Pakistan may have contributed to the relative neglect of the question of governmental legitimacy in the eastern regions. Any analysis of public policy that does not consider incompatibilities among the different realms of rationality is bound to be partial and misleading.

Strict economic rationality means getting the most national income out of a given investment. The end is to increase real GNP, no matter who receives it, and the means is investment expenditure, no matter who pays for it. To be economically rational is to increase growth to its maximum. Speaking of economic rationality is a way of smuggling in identification with the goal of economic development without saying so.

Rationality is also used in the broader sense of reason. The rational man has goals that he tries to achieve by being systematic, efficient, consistent and so on. Since rationality in the sense of reason has no independent meaning of its own it can only have such validity as is imparted by the norms that tell us about what reasonable action is.

The injunction to plan (!!) is empty. The key terms associated with it are proverbs or platitudes. Pursue goals! Consider alternatives! Obtain knowledge! Exercise power! Obtain consent! Or be flexible but do not alter your course. Planning stands for unresolved conflicts.

Yet planning has acquired a reputation for success in some rich countries. Perhaps a certain level of affluence is required before planning becomes effective. Instead of stacking the deck against planning by asking whether it works in poor nations, let us play its best cards by looking at the record under the most propitious circumstances.

PLANNING IN RICH COUNTRIES

Although I have geared my remarks to conditions existing in poor countries, they apply to rich ones as well. Formal planning aside, they are better able than poor nations to control their future. Governments in rich nations have more resources on which to draw, more adequate machinery for mobilizing them, and more trained people to make use of them. They can afford more failures as well as capitalize on their successes. Their prosperity is not guaranteed but their chances to do well for themselves are much higher than in the poor countries. It is possible that the failure of formal economic planning in rich countries actually has been hidden by their wealth. Confrontation with experience in formal planning has been avoided by casting the debate in terms that avoid the central question.

The debate over national economic planning in the past four decades has been conducted largely in terms of dichotomies: the individual versus the state; freedom versus dictatorship; private enterprise versus state control; price systems versus hierarchical command; rational economic choice versus irrational political interference. The great questions were: could state planning be reconciled with personal liberty? Was central administrative command a better or worse way to make decisions than dependence on prices determined in economic markets? Would rational modes of economic thought, designed to increase national income in the long run, be able to overcome irrational political forces seeking to accumulate power in the short run? All these questions assume that national economic planning—as distinct from mere arbitrary political intervention—is a real possibility. But—if it doesn't work—if the goals of the plan do not move from the paper on which they are written to the society to which they are supposed to refer, then why worry about it; it can neither crush nor liberate making.

Is there a single example of successful national economic planning? The Soviet Union has had central planning and has experienced economic growth. But the growth has not been exceptional and has not followed the plan. Is there a single country whose economic life over a period of years has been guided by an economic plan so that the targets set out in the plan bear a modest resemblance to events as they actually occur? No doubt each reader will be tempted to furnish the one he has heard about. Yet the very fact (as anyone can verify by posing the same query) that is it hard to name an example s suggests that the record of planning has hardly been brilliant. For all we know, the few apparent successes (if there are any) are no more than random occurrences.

When really pushed to show results, somewhere, some place, sometime, planning advocates are likely to cite the a accomplishments of indicative planning on the French model as the modern success story of their trade. The French example is

indeed a good one because it puts the least possible demands on the planning enterprise. Where many national plans are comprehensive, in the sense that they try to set targets for virtually all sectors of the economy, the French dealt only with the major ones. While planners in some countries have to set the entire range of prices, the modified market economy in France makes this burden unnecessary. France has not been afflicted by the rapid turnover of key personnel that has contributed to the discontinuities in planning elsewhere. France is rich in many ways besides money—information, personnel, communication—that should make it easier for her planners to guide future events. Where some plans hope to be authoritative, in that both government and private industry are required to follow the guidelines contained in them, the French plans have been indicative, that is, essentially voluntary. While efforts are made to reward those who cooperate, there are no sanctions for failure to comply. French plans indicate the directions wise and prudent men would take, if they were wise and prudent. If planning does not work in France, where conditions are so advantageous, it would be unlikely to do better in less favorable circumstances.[14]

But like it or not, formal planning in France is a failure. Economic growth has taken place but not according to instructions in the plan. Targets have not been met in the first four plans. Neither for individual sectors nor for the economy as a whole have growth rates been approximated. Governments have consistently ignored the plan or opposed it in order to meet immediate needs. In order to justify the idea of planning, Steven Cohen, author of the best book on the subject, *Modern Capitalist Planning: The French Experience*,[15] suggests that if there were democratic majority agreed on its goals, if their purposes could be maintained over a period of years, if they had the knowledge and power necessary to make the world behave as they wish, if they could control the future, then central planning would work. If…!

What Cohen's book actually shows is that limited economic planning in a major industrial country with considerable financial resources and talent did not work. What hope would there be for poor nations whose accumulated wealth is definitely less, whose reservoir of human talent is so much smaller, whose whole life is surrounded by far greater uncertainties? How could planning help radically change Africa or Asia when it has failed to produce even limited changes in France?

Significant control of the future demands mobilizing knowledge, power, and resources throughout society. It does not good to propose measures that require nonexistent information, missing resources, and unobtainable consent. The planner cannot create, at the moment he needs them, things his society does not possess. He can, however, assume them to be true in that artificial world created in the plan. But planning is not a policy. It is presumably a way to create policies related to one another over time so as to achieve desired objectives. The immense presumption involved, the incredible demands, not merely on the financial, but on the intellectual resources of societal organization explain the most important thing about national planning—it does not work because no large and complex society can figure out what simple and unambiguous things it wants to do, or in what clear order or priority, or how to get them done.

Before admitting defeat the advocate of planning would at least gesture in the direction of Japan, whose extraordinary economic growth has taken place in a period during which "the government has established long-term economic plans as the guiding principle for economic policies."[16] Of the dozen or so economic plans formulated since the end of the Second World War, five were officially adopted by the government and four have advanced far enough to appraise the fit between intention and accomplishment. In his splendid account, Isamu Miyazaki notes that the Five year Plan for Economic Self-Support for fiscal years 1955-60 called for a five per cent rate of growth in gross national product. But "the economic growth rate turned out to be twice as large as what had been projected in the plan, and the growth in mining and manufacturing production and exports proved far greater than the envisaged in the plan. Thus the targets in the plan were achieved in almost two years." A second effort, the New Long-Range Economic Plan for fiscal years 1958-62, set the desired growth rate at 6.5 %. "However, in actual performance, the rate again exceeded the projection, reaching about 10% on the average

during the plan period."[17] The Doubling National Income Plan for fiscal years 1961-70, the third effort, postulated a real growth rate of some 7 to 8%. Miyazaki states that "In actual performance, however, the rate reached 11% on the average from fiscal 1961-63. Particularly notable was the performance of private equipment investment, which grew by almost 40% in fiscal 1960, followed by an additional 29% increase in fiscal 1961. This meant that the level which was expected to be reached in the final year of the plan was achieved in the first year."[18] The fourth and last national economic effort for which the returns are in, the Economic and Social Development Plan for fiscal years 1967-71, resulted in even larger gaps between promise and fulfillment. According to Miyazaki, it was estimated that the real growth rate would reach nearly 13% on the average for fiscal 1967-70 against 8.2% in the plan. The rate of increase of private equipment investment (nominal) was twice as large as the 10.6% of the forecast. Since the economic growth rate and private equipment investment have gone far beyond the projection, the plan cannot any more fulfill the role of a guide to private economic activities.[19]

Evidently the economy has been growing faster than anyone thought. Yet the purpose of plans and planners must surely be to guide economic growth in the expected direction, not to gasp in amazement as how wonderfully the country has grown contrary to (or regardless of) what they indicated. If plans are not guides, they have lost any meaning they might have had.

Questioning the meaningfulness of planning is likely to lead to impatience on the grounds that is represents man's best hope. What have you got to offer in its place? That is likely to be the response. Putting the question that way suggests that planning provides a solution to problems. But planning is not a solution to any problem. It is just a way of restating in other language the problems we do not know how to solve.

But where's the harm? If planning is not the epitome of reason, it appears innocuous enough. If some people feel better in the presence of formal planning why not let it go on?

FORMAL PLANNING: COSTS AND BENEFITS

Planning is like motherhood; everyone is for it because it seems so virtuous. Over-population on one side has not given birth to doubts on the other. If we leave out the old controversy over whether centrally directed economies are better or worse than reliance on the price mechanism, there has been virtually no discussion of possible adverse effects of formal planning. Although planners are often economists who profess to believe that there is a cost for everything, they have not applied this insight to their own activity. It may be instructive, therefore, to list a few of the possible costs of planning.

The plan may provide a substitute for action. Working on it may justify delay as the cry-word goes out, "Let's not act until the plan is ready." Delay may also be encouraged because the planning commission becomes another checkpoint in an already cumbersome administrative apparatus. If its consent or comments are required and its people overburdened, planners may discourage the speedy adaptation to emerging events that is so essential in the volatile environments of the poor countries.

Planning uses important human resources. In nations where talent is chronically scarce, men who might be contributing to important public and private decisions may be wading through huge bodies of date or constructing elaborate models whose applicability is doubtful at best. The planners not only take up their own time, they intrude on others. They call in people from the operating ministries who need to answer their questions and, if necessary, run around countering their advice. Time, attention and talent that might be spent improving the regular administration on which the nation depends, may have to be invested in internal hassling with the planners.

The direct financial cost of paying the planners and their consultants may be small, but the long-run financial costs to the nation may be high. Planners tend to be spenders. Their rationale is that they will help promote current investments that will lead to future increases in income. They, therefore, have a vested interest in increasing the total amount of investment. Frustrated at the efforts of the finance ministry to keep spending down, the planners have an incentive to get hold of their own sources of funds. They thereby contribute to one of the basic financial problems of poor countries—the fragmentation of national income. Then they become another independent entity able to resist whatever central authority exists.

Investments may come in large packages or small amounts, in humdrum improvement of human resources, or in spectacular projects. The tendency of planners is to seek the large and loud over the small and quiet. Their talents are better suited to the analysis of big projects that have a substantial impact on the economy and that, by their cost, justify expensive analytical attention. They have too few people to supervise the multitude of small projects whose total impact may nevertheless be more important to the nation than the few big projects. Their fame and fortune depend on identification with visible objects and these are not to be found in the rural classroom or the feeder road.

The stock in trade of the planner is the big model. Sometimes it appears the larger and more complex the model (though it may actually be nothing more than a long list of variables) the more important the planner. Only he can interpret it and he may gain a kind of status from being its guardian. Bad decisions may result because these models are taken beyond any merits they might have. A spurious specificity may ignore the fact that the data used is bad, that the relevant calculations cannot be performed or that the model does not apply to the case at hand. As bad decisions are dressed up in pseudo-analytical garb, ministerial officials may become unduly cynical about analysis. When the devil quotes scripture, holy writ becomes suspect.

The planner makes his way by talking about the need of considering the future in present decisions. Yet poor countries have great difficulty in knowing where they are (even where they have been) in terms of income, expenditure, manpower and the like. Retrodiction is as much their problem as prediction. Yet the planners may neglect efforts to bring knowledge up to date because they have little stake in the present. Indeed, they may work hard to create what turn out to be imaginary future problems, as a way of gaining additional influence over forthcoming decisions.

The optimism of the planners may be desirable in order to give the nation a sense of hope amidst crushing burdens. This optimism, however, may result in unreal expectations that cannot be met. Demands may be made in anticipation of future income that does not materialize. Subsequent disappointment may create political difficulty where none need have occurred.

Though their formal plans may be irrelevant, actions of planners as an interest group may have impact. There is no need for us to argue here that formal planners are necessarily wrong. It suffices to say that they have their own built-in-biases, and that these sometimes lead to unfortunate consequences. Why, then, is the worth of formal planning so rarely questioned?

Despite intermittent disaffection with planning—the contrast between the plan and the nation mocked the planners—it was difficult for national elites to forgo sight of the promised land. They so wanted an easy way out of their troubles. Besides, they soon discovered that the nonoperational quality of planning could be helpful. If it did no commit them to anything, it might yet be made into a useful instrument.

Formal planning may be useful as an escape from the seemingly insurmountable problems of the day. If life is gloomy in the present then a plan can help offset that by creating a rosier version of the future. If groups cannot be indulged in the present, they can b e shown the larger places they occupy in future plans. Formal planning can also be a way of buying off the apostles of rationality by involving hem in tasks that take them away from the real decisions.

The reputation of a nation's leaders may depend on their having a glowing plan. International elites may expect it as evidence of competence and dedication to determine control of the future rather than simply being overtaken by events. International prestige may rest to some degree on one of the few national products that are visible and transportable—a beautifully bound set of national plans.

A government may find uses for planners as a group apart from the regular bureaucratic apparatus. Planning machinery may be a way deliberately to introduce competitive elements into the administration, either as a means of provoking reform or of blocking departmental ambitions. Planners may be used as a source of ideas outside regular administrative channels (as a kind of general staff for the executive) bypassing the normal chain of command. All this, however, has little to do with their ostensible reason for being, namely, planning, but much to do with the fact that since planners do exist they may as well serve the purposes of others.

Trivial functions aside, planning might have withered from disappointments and disuse had not new clients insisted on it. When the United States made foreign aid fashionable, a number of poor countries ere in a position to secure sums of money that were large in comparison to their small budgets. This created a need for institutional mechanisms that could do two things: spend surpluses and obtain foreign aid. The United States would not, of course, do anything so simple as to give money just because a country said it needed it; capitalist America insisted upon a plan. Since an existing bureaucracy would have had no experience in putting together these documents, it was necessary to create a mechanism for preparing hem. It did not matter whether the plan worked; what did count was the ability to produce a document which looked like a plan, and that meant using economists and other technical personnel. If these skills were not available within the country, they had to be imported in the form of planners and foreign aid advisors. A demand existed and an entirely new industry was created to fill the need. Thus national planning may be justified on a strict cash basis: planners may bring in more money from abroad than it costs to support them at home.

These uses for formal planning suggest that I have been looking at plans, planners and planning commissions in the wrong way. I have been assessing (in the language of the sociologist) their manifest functions, the purpose they are supposed to serve. Formal planning also has latent functions; it serves other purposes as well.

PLANNING AS FAITH

While there is every evidence that national plans are unsuccessful, there is virtually no evidence that they do good, however, "good" might be described. Yet no one thinks of giving them up. When people continue to do things that do not help them the subject cries out for investigation. Neither the governments nor the people they rule are presumed to be masochists. Why, then, do they not change their behavior?

Planners are men of secular faith. The word "faith" is used advisedly because it is hardly possible to say that planning has been justified by works. Once the word is in them it leaps over the realm of experience. They are confirmed in their beliefs no matter what happens. Planning is good if it succeeds and society if bad if it fails. That is why planners so often fail to learn from experience. To learn one must make mistakes and planning cannot be one of them.

Planning concerns man's efforts to make the future in his own image. If he loses control of his own destiny, he fears being cast into the abyss. Alone and afraid, man is at the mercy of strange and unpredictable forces, so he takes whatever comfort he can by challenging the fates. He shouts his plans into the storm of life. Even if all he hears is the echo of his own voice, he is no longer alone. To abandon his faith in planning would unleash the terror locked in him. For if God is dead, only man can save himself.

The greater his need, the more man longs to believe in the reality of his vision. Since he can only create the future he desires on paper he transfers his loyalties to the plan. Since the end is never in sight he sanctifies the journey; the process of planning becomes holy. Since he is the end of his own striving, his reason becomes the object of his existence. Planning is reason and reason is embodied in the plan. Worshipping it, he glorified himself. But a secular idolatry is no easier to maintain than a religious one.

Faith in planning has an intermittent hold on political leaders. Their ascension to power is full of everlasting hope. The end of despair, they tell their people, is within sight. The leaders too, are overwhelmed by the gap between the future they promise and the present they cannot change. Progress is slow and painful. By allying them-selves with the forces of reason, by embracing the plan as a visible sign of salvation, they hope to overcome the past ad create a new life for their nation. When plans fail governmental leaders are tempted to abandon the god of reason. Once they have lost faith in planning, it becomes difficult for them to believe that there is any place for reasoned analysis. So they manipulate the plan and its planners for tactical purposes. If planning is reason, then reason flees when planning is in flight. Misplaced faith in the norms of rationality is easily transmitted into normless use of power.

The task of relating processes of decision to the social conditions in which they must operate is hampered because rational planning is supposed to stand as universal truth not subject to alteration through experience. It thus becomes difficult to evaluate experience; departure from the norms of planning are suspect as contradicting reason. Discussion of what seems to work in a particular context is inhibited because it may be inconsistent with "good planning practice." Rather than face up to actual conditions, planners are tempted to wish them away. If planning is a universal tool, planners find it reasonable to ask why their countries cannot live up to the requirements of rational decisionmaking. If planning is valid, they feel, nations should adjust to its demands rather than the other way around.

To save planning, planners may actually accept the blame. For if better behavior on their part would make planning work, the solution is not to abandon plans but to hire more talented planners. Martyrdom may be appropriate to their profession, but I would argue against allowing them to make the ultimate sacrifice.

Planning requires the resources, knowledge, and power of an entire people. If commodity prices suddenly fall, leading to a precipitous drop in national income, the ensuing difficulties may be attributed to faulty predictions by planners, but the relationship of the nation to international markets would seem to be the proper realm in which to seek scapegoats. Should it urn out that political leadership is divided, that may be because the planners could not convince them all, but is more likely the result of causes deeply rooted in the nation's political history. It seems odd to blame the planners because the political leaders who agreed on a particular set of priorities are suddenly replaced by another group of men with quite different preferences. If private citizens send their capital abroad rather than investing it at home, it is the values of economic elites rather than the investment plan that deserves priority investigation. When taxes are not collected because social mores prohibit direct personal confrontations, national culture, not the national plan, is the place to look. When planning is viewed as a function of the society's ability to control its future, we seem better able to explain difficulties than if we look at the alleged shortcomings of planners.

If formal planning fails not merely in one nation at one time but in virtually all nations most of the time, the defects are unlikely to be found in maladroit or untalented planners. Nor can a failure be argued successfully by saying that the countries in question are not prepared to behave rationally or to accept the advice of rational men called planners. That is only a way of saying that formal planning, after innumerable iterations, is still badly adapted to its surroundings. It cannot be rational to fail. To err is human; to sanctify the perpetuation of mistakes is something else. If governments perseverate in national planning, it must be because their will to believe triumphs over their experience. Planning is not so much a subject for the social scientist as for the theologian.

NOTES

1. *A Constant Quantity of Tears: Planning and Budgeting in Poor Countries* (The Twentieth Century Fund). This essay is a revised and expanded version of material appearing in Naomi Caiden and Aaron Wildavsky.

2. See Jeffrey L. Pressman and Aaron Wildavsky, *Implementation* (University of California Press, 1973).

3. See Andrew McFarland, *Power and Leadership in Pluralist Systems* (Stanford, California: Stanford University Press, 1969); Herbert Simon, *Models of Man* (New York: Wiley, 1957); John Harsanyi, "Measurement of Social Power, Opportunity Costs, and the Theory of Two-Person Bargaining Games," *Behavioral Science*, Vol. VII (Jan. 1962), pp. 67-80; Robert Dahl, *"Power,"* International Encyclopedia of the Social Sciences* (New York: Macmillan and Free Press, 1968), Vol. XII, pp. 405-415; James March, "The Power of Power," in David

Easton, ed., *Varieties of Political Theory* (Englewood Cliffs, N.J.: Prentice-Hall, 1966), pp. 39-70.

4. Harsanyi, *op. cit.*

5. *The New York Times,* January 25, 1971, p. 55.

6. Joseph Berliner, *Factory and Manager in the U.S.S.R.* (Cambridge: Harvard University Press, 1957); David Granick, *The Red Executive* (Garden City, N.Y.: Doubleday, 1961).

7. West Churchman, *The Systems Approach* (New York: Delacorte Press, 1968), p. 150.

8. Richard Rose, "The Variability of Party Government: *A Theoretical and Empirical Critique,"* Political Studies (Dec. 969) vol. XVII, no. 4, p. 415.

9. See David J. Berlinski, "Systems Analysis", *Urban Affairs Quarterly*, September 1970, 7, no. 1, pp. 104-126.

10. Martin Landau, "Redundancy, Rationality, and the Problem of Duplication and Overlap", *Public Administration Review* (July 1969) vol. XXIX, pp. 346-358.

11. Herbert Simon, "The Proverbs of Administration," *Public Administration Review* (Winter 1946) vol. VI, pp. 53-67.

12. It is, by the way, often difficult to know when inconsistent actions are taking place. Leaving aside obtaining accurate information, there are serious conceptual problems. Policies are often stated in general terms that leave ample scope for varying interpretations of their intent. Ambiguity sometimes performs a political function by enabling people (who might otherwise disagree if everything was made clear) to get together. There cannot then be a firm criterion against which to judge consistency. There is also the question of conflicting perspectives among actors and observers. The observer may note an apparent commitment to a certain level and type of investment and see it vitiated by diversion of funds to wage increases. To the observer this means inconsistency. The actor, however, may feel consistent in pursuing his goal of political support. Given any two policies that lead to conflicts among two values one can always find a third value by which they are reconciled. Investment seemed to bring support when it was announced and so does spending for other purposes when its turn comes. The actors' values may be rephrased as "the highest possible investment so long as it does not seriously affect immediate political support." In view of the pressures to meet the needs of different people variously situated in soci-

ety, most decisions are undoubtedly made on such a contingent basis. This is what it means to adapt to changing circumstance. As the goals of the actors shift with the times, consistency becomes a moving target, difficult to hit at the best of times, impossible to locate at the worst.

13. Paul Diesing, *Reason in Society* (Urbana: University of Illinois Press, 1962).

14. The following paragraphs on France are taken from Aaron Wildavsky, "Does Planning Work?" *Public Interest*, Summer 1971, no. 24, pp. 95-104.

15. Harvard University Press, Cambridge, Mass., 1970.

16. Isamu Miyazaki, "Economic Planning in Postwar Japan", *The Journal of the Institute of Developing Economies* (December 1970), vol. VIII, no. 4, p. 369.

17. *Ibid*, p. 373.

18. *Ibid*, p. 374.

19. *Ibid*, p. 378.

The Science of "Muddling Through"

Charles Lindblom

In this article, Charles Lindblom presents a compelling critique of the rational planning model. He argues that the formalized planning approach to decision making—the rational-comprehensive method—can be practiced only on very simple problems. For complex problems, it is not feasible to conduct a systematic comparison of a multitude of values. Thus, according to Lindblom, most decision makers rely on a method of "successive limited comparisons," or "muddling through," rather than on the rational-comprehensive method.

Suppose an administrator is given responsibility for formulating policy with respect to inflation. He might start by trying to list all related values in order of importance, e.g., full employment, reasonable business profit, protection of small savings, prevention of a stock market crash. Then all possible policy outcomes could be rated as more or less efficient in attaining a maximum of these values. This would of course require a prodigious inquiry into values held by members of society and an equally prodigious set of calculations on how much of each value is equal to how much of each other value. He could then proceed to outline all possible policy alternatives. In a third step, he would undertake systematic comparison of his multitude of alternatives to determine which attains the greatest amount of values.

In comparing policies, he would take advantage of any theory available that generalized about classes of policies. In considering inflation, for example, he would compare all policies in the light of the theory of prices. Since no alternatives are beyond his investigation, he would consider strict central control and the abolition of all prices and markets on the one hand and elimination of all public controls with reliance completely on the free market on the other, both in the light of whatever theoretical generalizations he could find on such hypothetical economies.

Finally, he would try to make the choice that would in fact maximize his values. An alternative line of attack would be to set up as his principal objective, either explicitly or without conscious thought, the relatively simple goal of keeping prices level. This objective might be compromised or complicated by only a few other goals, such as full employment. He would in fact disregard most other social values as beyond his present interest, and he would for the moment not even attempt to rank the few values that he regarded as immediately relevant. Were he pressed, he would quickly admit that he was ignoring many related values and many possible important consequences of his policies.

As a second step, he would outline those relatively few policy alternatives that occurred to him. He would then compare them. In comparing his limited number of alternatives, most of them familiar from past controversies, he would not ordinarily find a body of theory precise enough to carry him through a comparison of their respective consequences. Instead he would rely heavily on the record of past experience with small policy steps to predict the consequences of similar steps extended into the future.

Moreover, he would find that the policy alternatives combined objectives or values in different ways. For example, one policy might offer price level stability at the cost of some risk of unemployment; another might offer less price stability but also less risk of unemployment. Hence, the next step in his approach—the final selection—would combine into one the choice among values and the choice among instruments for reaching values. It would not, as in the first method of policy-making, approximate a more mechanical process of choosing the means that best satisfied goals that were previously clarified and ranked. Because practitioners of the second approach expect t achieve their goals only partially, they would expect to repeat endlessly the sequence just described, as conditions and aspirations changed and as accuracy of prediction improved.

BY ROOT OR BY BRANCH

For complex problems, the first of these two approaches is of course impossible. Although such an approach can be described, it cannot be practiced except for relatively simple problems and even then only in a somewhat modified form. It assumes intellectual capacities and sources of information that men simply do not possess, and it is even more absurd as an approach to policy when the time and money that can be allocated to a policy problem is limited, as is always the case. Of particular importance to public administrators is the fact that public agencies are in effect usually instructed not to practice the first method. That is to say, their prescribed functions and constraints—the politically or legally possible—restrict their attention to relatively few values and relatively few alternative policies among the countless alternatives that might be imagined. It is the second

method that is practiced.

Curiously, however, the literatures of decision-making, policy formulation, planning, and public administration formalize the first approach rather than the second, leaving public administrators who handle complex decisions in the position of practicing what few preach. For emphasis I run some risk of overstatement. True enough, the literature is well aware of limits on man's capacities and of the inevitability that policies will be approached in some such style as the second. But attempts to formalize rational policy formulation—to lay out explicitly the necessary steps in the process—usually describe the first approach and not the second.[1]

The common tendency to describe policy formulation even for complex problems as though it followed the first approach has been strengthened by the attention given to, and successes enjoyed by, operations research, statistical decision theory, and systems analysis. The hallmarks of these procedures, typical of the first approach, are clarity of objective, explicitness of evaluation, a high degree of comprehensiveness of overview, and wherever possible, quantification of values for mathematical analysis. But these advanced procedures remain largely the appropriate techniques of relatively small-scale problem-solving where the total number of variables to be considered is small and value problems restricted. Charles Hitch, head of the Economics Division of RAND Corporation, one of the leading centers for application of these techniques, has written:

I would make the empirical generalization from my experience at RAND and elsewhere that operations research is the art of sub-optimizing, i.e., of solving some lower-level problems, and the difficulties increase and our special competence diminishes by an order of magnitude with every level of decision making we attempt to ascent. The sort of simple explicit model which operations researchers are so proficient in using can certainly reflect most of the significant factors influencing traffic control on the George Washington Bridge, but the proportion of the relevant reality which we can represent by any such model or models in studying, say, a major foreign-policy decision, appears to be almost trivial.[2]

Accordingly, I propose in this paper to clarify and formalize the second method, much neglected in the literature. This might be described as the method of successive limited comparisons. I will contrast it with the first approach, which might be called the rational-comprehensive method.[3] More impressionistically and briefly—and therefore generally used in this article—they could be characterized as the branch method and root method, the former continually building out from the current situation, step-by-step and by small degrees; the latter starting from fundamentals anew each time, building on the past only as experience is embodied in a theory, and always prepared to start completely from the ground up.

Let us put the characteristics of the two methods side by side in simplest terms.

TABLE I.2

Rational-comprehensive (root)	Successive limited comparisons (branch)
1a Clarification of values or objectives distinct from and usually prerequisite to empirical analysis of alternative policies.	**1b** Selection of value goals and empirical analysis of the needed action are not distinct from one another but are closely intertwined.
2a Policy-formulation is therefore approached through means-end analysis: First the ends are isolated, then the means to achieve them are sought.	**2b** Since means and ends are not distinct, means-end analysis is often inappropriate or limited.
3a The test of a "good" policy is that it can be shown to be the most appropriate means to desired ends.	**3b** The test of a "good" policy is typically that various analysts find themselves directly agreeing on a policy (without their agreeing that is the most appropriate means to an agreed objective).
4a Analysis is comprehensive; every important relevant factor is taken into account.	**4b** Analysis is drastically limited:
5a Theory is often heavily relied upon.	(i) Important possible outcomes are neglected
	(ii) Important alternative potential policies are neglected.
	(iii) Important affected values are neglected.
	5b A succession of comparisons greatly reduced or eliminates reliance on theory.

Assuming that the root method is familiar and understandable, we proceed directly to clarification of its alternative by contrast. In explaining the second, we shall be describing how most administrators do in fact approach complex question, for the root method, the "best" way as a blueprint or model, is in fact not workable for complex policy questions, and administrators are forced to use the method of successive limited comparison.

Intertwining Evaluation and Empirical Analysis (1b)

The quickest way to understand how values are handled in the method of successive limited comparisons is to see how the root method often breaks down in its handling of values or objectives. The idea that values should be clarified, and in advance of the examination of alternative policies, is appealing. But what happens when we attempt it for complex social problems? The first difficulty is that on many critical values or objectives, citizens disagree, congressmen disagree, and public administrators disagree. Even where a fairly specific objective is prescribed for the administrator, there remains considerable room for disagreement on sub-objectives. Consider, for example, the conflict with respect to locating public housing, described in Meyerson and Banfield's study of the Chicago Housing Authority[4]—disagreement that occurred despite the clear objective of providing a certain number of public housing units in the city. Similarly conflicting are objectives in highway location, traffic control, minimum wage administration, development of tourist facilities in national parks, or insect control.

Administrators cannot escape these conflicts by ascertaining the majority's preference, for preferences have not been registered on most issues;

indeed, there often *are* not preferences in the absence of public discussion sufficient to bring an issue to the attention of the electorate. Furthermore, there is a question of whether intensity of feeling should be considered as well as the number of persons preferring each alternative. By the impossibility of doing otherwise, administrators often are reduced to deciding policy without clarifying objectives first.

Even when an administrator resolves to follow his own values a criterion for decisions, he often will not know how to rank them when they conflict with one another, as they usually do. Suppose, for example, that an administrator must relocate tenants living in tenements scheduled for destruction. One objective is to empty the buildings fairly promptly, another is to find suitable accommodation for persons displaced, another is to avoid friction with residents in other areas in which a large influx would be unwelcome, another is to deal with all concerned through persuasion if possible, and so on.

How does one state even to himself the relative importance of these partially conflicting values? A simple ranking of them is not enough; one needs ideally to know how much of one value is worth sacrificing for some of another value. The answer is that typically the administrator chooses—and must choose—directly among policies in which these values are combined in different ways. He cannot first clarify his values and then choose among policies.

A more subtle third point underlies both the first two. Social objectives do not always have the same relative values. One objective may be highly prized in one circumstance, another in another circumstance. If, for example, an administrator values highly both the dispatch with which his agency can carry through its projects *and* good public relations, it matters little which of the two possibly conflicting values he favors in some abstract or general sense. Policy questions arise in forms which put to administrators such a question as: Given the degree to which we are or are not already achieving the values of dispatch and the values of good public relations, is it worth sacrificing a little speed for a happier clientele, or is it better to risk offending the clientele so that we can get on with our work? The answer to such a question varies with circumstances.

The value problem is, as the example shows, always a problem of adjustments at a margin. But there is no practicable way to state marginal objectives or values except in terms of particular policies. That one value is preferred to another in one decision situation does not mean that it will be preferred in another decision situation in which it can be had only at great sacrifice of another value. Attempts to rank or order values in general and abstract terms so that they do not shift from decision to decision end up by ignoring the relevant marginal preferences. The significance of this third point thus goes very far. Even if all administrators had at hand an agreed set of values, objectives, and constraints, and an agreed ranking of these values, objectives, and constraints, their marginal values in actual choice situations would be impossible to formulate.

Unable consequently to formulate the relevant values first and then choose among policies to achieve them, administrators must choose directly amount alternative policies that offer different marginal combinations of values. Somewhat paradoxically, the only practicable way to disclose one's relevant marginal values even to oneself is to describe the policy one chooses to achieve them. Except roughly and vaguely, I know of no way to describe—or even to understand—what my relative evaluations are for, say, freedom and security, speed and accuracy in governmental decisions, or low taxes and better schools than to describe my preferences among specific policy choices that might be made between the alternatives in each of the pairs.

In summary, two aspects of the process by which values are actually handled can be distinguished. The first is clear: evaluation and empirical analysis are intertwined; that is, one chooses among values and among policies at one and the same time. Put a little more elaborately, one simultaneously chooses a policy to attain certain objectives and chooses the objectives themselves. The second aspect is related but distinct: the administrator focuses his attention on marginal or incremental values. Whether he is aware of it or not, he does not find general formulations of objectives very helpful and in fact makes specific marginal or incremental comparisons. Two policies, **X** and **Y**, confront him. Both promise the same degree of attainment of objectives *a, b, c, d,* and *e*. But **X** promises him somewhat more of *f* than does **Y**, while **Y** promises him somewhat more of *g* than does **X**. In choosing between them, he is in fact offered the alternative of a marginal or incremental amount of *f* at the expense of a marginal or incremental amount of *g*. The only values that are relevant to his choice are these increments by which the two policies differ; and, when he finally chooses between the two marginal values, he does so by making a choice between policies.[5]

As to whether to attempt to clarify objectives in advance of policy selection is more or less rational than the close intertwining of marginal evaluation and empirical analysis, the principal difference established is that for complex problems the first is impossible and irrelevant, and the second is both possible and relevant. The second is possible because the administrator need not try to analyze any values except the values by which alternative policies differ and need to be concerned with them except as they differ marginally. His need for information on values or objectives is drastically reduced as compared with the root method; and his capacity for grasping, comprehending, and relating values to one another is not strained beyond the breaking point.

Relations Between Means and Ends (2b)

Decision-making is ordinarily formalized as a means-end relationship: means are conceived to be evaluated and chosen in the light of ends finally selected independently of and prior to the choice of means. This is the means-ends relationship of the root method. But it follows from all that has just been said that such a means-end relationship is possible only to the extent that values are agreed upon, are reconcilable, and are stable at the margin. Typically, therefore, such a means-ends relationship is absent from the branch method, where means and ends are simultaneously chosen.

Yet any departure from the means-ends relationship of the root method will strike some readers as inconceivable. For it will appear to them that only in such a relationship is it possible to determine whether one policy choice is better or worse than another. How can an administrator know whether he has made a wise or foolish decision if he is without prior values or objectives by which to judge his decisions? The answer to this question calls up the third distinctive difference between root and branch methods: how to describe the best policy.

The Test of "Good" Policy (3b)

In the root method, a decision is "correct," "good," or "rational" if it can be shown to attain some specified objective, where the objective can be specified without simply describing the decision itself. Where objectives are defined only through the marginal or incremental approach to values described above, it is still sometimes possible to test whether a policy does in fact attain the desired objectives; but a precise statement of the objectives takes the form of a description of the policy chosen or some alternative to it. To show that a policy is mistaken one cannot offer an abstract argument that important objectives are not achieved; one must instead argue that another policy is more to be preferred.

So far, the departure from customary ways of looking at problem-solving is not troublesome, for many administrators will be quick to agree that the most effective discussion of the correctness of policy does take the form of comparison with other policies that might have been chosen. But what of the situation in which administrators cannot agree on values or objectives, either abstractly or in marginal terms? What then is the test of "good" policy? For the root method, there is no test. Agreement on objectives failing, there is no standard or "correctness." For the method of successive limited comparisons, the test is agreement on policy itself, which remains possible even when agreement on values is not.

It has been suggested that continuing agreement in Congress on the desirability of extending old age insurance stems from liberal desires to strengthen the welfare programs of the federal government and from conservative desires to reduce union demands for private pension plans. If so, this is an excellent demonstration of the ease with which individuals or different ideologies often can agree on concrete policy. Labor mediators report a similar phenomenon: the contestants cannot agree on criteria for settling their disputes but can agree on specific proposals. Similarly, when one administrator's objective turns out to be another's mean, they often can agree on policy.

Agreement on policy thus becomes the only practicable test of the policy's correctness. And for one administrator to seek to win the other over to agreement on ends as well would accomplish nothing and create quite unnecessary controversy.

If agreement directly on policy as a test for "best" policy seems a poor substitute for testing the policy against its objectives, it ought to be remembered that objectives themselves have no ultimate validity other than they are agreed upon. Hence agreement is the test of "best" policy in both methods. But where the root method requires agreement on what elements in the decision constitute objectives and on which of these objectives should be sought, the branch method falls back on agreement wherever it can be found.

In an important sense, therefore, it is not irrational for an administrator to defend a policy as good without being able to specify what it is good for.

Non-Comprehensive Analysis (4b)

Ideally, rational-comprehensive analysis leaves out nothing important. But it is impossible to take everything important into consideration unless "important" is so narrowly defined that analysis is in fact quite limited. Limits on human intellectual capacities and on available information set definite limits to man's capacity to be comprehensive. In actual fact, therefore, no on can practice the rational-comprehensive method for really complex problems, and every administrator faced with a sufficiently complex problem must find ways drastically to simplify.

An administrator assisting in the formulation of agricultural economic policy cannot in the first place be competent on all possible policies. He cannot even comprehend one policy entirely. In planning a soil bank program, he cannot successfully anticipate the impact of higher or lower farm income on, say, urbanization—the possible consequent loosening of family ties, possible consequent eventual need for revisions in social security and further implications for tax problems arising out of new federal responsibilities for social security and municipal responsibilities for urban services. Nor, to follow another line of repercussions, can he work through the soil bank program's effects on prices for agricultural products in foreign markets and consequent implications for foreign relations, including those arising out of economic rivalry between the United States and the U.S.S.R.

In the method of successive limited comparisons, simplification is systematically achieved in two principal ways. First, it is achieved through limitation of policy comparisons to those policies that differ in relatively small degree from policies presently in effect. Such a limitation immediately reduces the number of alternatives to be investigated and also drastically simplified the character of the investigation of each. For it is necessary to undertake fundamental inquiry into an alternative and its consequences; it is necessary only to study those respects in which the proposed alternative and its consequences differ from the status quo. The empirical comparison of marginal differences among alternative policies that differ only marginally is, of course, a counterpart to the incremental or marginal comparison of values discussed above.[6]

Relevance as Well as Realism. It is a matter of common observation that in Western democracies public administrators and policy analysts in general do largely limit their analyses to incremental or marginal differences in policies that are chose to differ only incrementally. They do not do so, however, solely because they desperately need some way to simplify their problems; they also do so in order to be relevant. Democracies change their policies almost entirely through incremental adjustments. Policy does not move in leaps and bounds.

The incremental character of political change in the United States has often been remarked. The two major political parties agree on fundamentals; they offer alternative policies to the voters only on relatively small points of difference. Both parties favor full employment, but they define it somewhat differently; both favor the development of water power resources, but in slightly different ways; and both favor unemployment compensation, but not the same level of benefits. Similarly, shifts of policy within a party take place largely through a series of relatively small changes, as can be seen in their only gradual acceptance of the idea of governmental responsibility for support of the unemployed, a change in party positions beginning in the early 30's and culminating in a sense in the Employment Act of 1946.

Party behavior is in turn rooted in public attitudes, and political theorists cannot conceive of democracy's surviving in the United States in the absence of fundamental agreement on potentially disruptive issues, with consequent limitation of policy debates to relatively small differences in policy.

Since the policies ignored by the administrator are politically impossible and so irrelevant, the simplification of analysis achieved by concentrating on policies that differ only incrementally is not a capricious kind of simplification. In addition, it can be argued that, given the limits on knowledge within which policy-makers are confined, simplifying by limiting the focus to small variations from present policy makes the most of available knowledge. Because policies being considered are like present and past policies, the administrator can obtain information and claim some insight. Non-incremental policy proposals are therefore typically not only politically irrelevant but also unpredictable in their consequences.

The second method of simplification of analysis is the practice or ignoring important possible consequences of possible policies, as well as the values attached to the neglected consequences. If this appears to disclose a shocking shortcoming of successive limited comparisons, it can be replied that, even if the exclusions are random, policies may nevertheless be more intelligently formulated than through futile attempts to achieve comprehensiveness beyond human capacity. Actually, however, the exclusions, seeming arbitrary or random from one point of view, need be neither.

Achieving a Degree of Comprehensiveness. Suppose that each value neglected by one policy-making agency were a major concern of at least one other agency. In that case, a helpful division of labor would be achieved, and no agency need find its task beyond its capacities. The shortcomings of such a system would be that one agency might destroy a value either before another agency could be activated to safeguard it or in spite of another agency's efforts. But the possibility that important values may be lost is present in any form of organization, even where agencies attempt to comprehend in planning more than is humanly possible.

The virtue of such a hypothetical division of labor is that every important interest or value has its watchdog. And these watchdogs can protect the interests in their jurisdiction in two quite different ways: first, by redressing damages done by other agencies; and, second, by anticipating and heading off injury before it occurs.

In a society like that of the United States in which individuals are free to combine to pursue almost any possible common interest they might have and in which government agencies are sensitive to the pressures of these groups, the system described is approximated. Almost every interest has its watchdog. Without claiming that every interest has a sufficiently powerful watchdog, it can be argued that our system often can assure a more comprehensive regard for the values of the whole society than any attempt at intellectual comprehensiveness.

In the United States, for example, no part of government attempts a comprehensive overview of policy on income distribution. A policy nevertheless evolves, and one responding to a wide variety of interests. A process of mutual adjustment among farm groups, labor unions, municipalities and school boards, tax authorities, and government agencies with responsibilities in the fields of housing, health, highways, national parks, fire, and police accomplishes a distribution of income in which particular income problems neglected at one point in the decision processes become central at another point.

Mutual adjustment is more pervasive than the explicit forms it takes in negotiation between groups; it persists through the mutual impacts of groups upon each other even where they are not in communication. For all the imperfections and latent dangers in this ubiquitous process of mutual adjustment, it will often accomplish an adaptation of policies to a wider range of interests than could be done by one group centrally.

Note, too, how the incremental pattern of policy-making fits with the multiple pressure pattern. For when decisions are only incremental—closely related to known policies, it is easier for one group to anticipate the kind of moves another might make and easier too for it to make correction for injury already accomplished.[7]

Even partisanship and narrowness, to use pejorative terms, will sometimes be assets to rational decision-making, for they can doubly insure that what one agency neglects, another will not; they specialize personnel to distinct points of view. The claim is valid that effective rational coordination of the federal administration, if possible to achieve at all, would require an agreed set of values[8]—if "rational" is defined as the practice of the root method of decision-making. But a high degree of administrative coordination occurs as each agency adjusts its policies to the concerns of the other agencies in the process of fragmented decision-making I have just described.

For all the apparent shortcomings of the incremental approach to policy alternatives with its arbitrary exclusion coupled with fragmentation, when compared to the root method, the branch method often looks far superior. In the root method, the inevitable exclusion of factors is accidental, unsystematic and not defensible by any argument so far developed, while in the branch method the exclusions are deliberate, systematic, and defensible. Ideally, of course, the root method does not exclude; in practice it must.

Nor does the branch method necessarily neglect long-run considerations and objectives. It is clear that important values must be omitted in considering policy, and sometimes the only way long-run objectives can be given adequate attention is through the neglect of short-run considerations. But the values omitted can be either long-run or short-run.

Succession of Comparison (5b)

The final distinctive element in the branch method is that the comparisons, together with the policy choice, proceed in a chronological series. Policy is not made once and for all; it is made and re-made endlessly. Policy-making is a process of successive approximation to some desired objectives in which what is desired itself continues to change under reconsideration.

Making policy is at best a very rough process. Neither social scientists, nor politicians, nor public administrators yet know enough about the social world to avoid repeated error in predicting the consequences of policy moves. A wise policy-maker consequently expects that his policies will achieve only part of what he hopes and at the same time will produce unanticipated consequences he would have preferred to avoid. If he proceeds through a *succession* of incremental changes, he avoids serious lasting mistakes in several ways.

In the first place, past sequences of policy steps have given him knowledge about the probable consequences of further similar steps. Second, he need not attempt big jumps toward his goals that would require predictions beyond his or anyone else's knowledge, because he never expects his policy to be a final resolution of a problem. His decision is only one step, one that if successful can quickly be followed by another. Third, he is effect able to test his previous predictions as he moves on to each further step. Lastly, he often can remedy a past error fairly quickly—more quickly than if policy proceeded through more distinct steps widely spaced in time.

Compare this comparative analysis of incremental changes with the aspiration to employ theory in the root method. Man cannot think without classifying, without subsuming one experience under a more general category of experiences. The attempt to push categorization as far as possible and to find general propositions which can be applied to specific situations is what I refer to with the word "theory." Where root analysis often leans heavily on theory in this sense, the branch method does not.

The assumption of root analysts is that theory is the most systematic and economical way to bring relevant knowledge to bear on a specific problem. Granting the assumption, an unhappy fact is that we do not have adequate theory to apply to problems in any policy area, although theory is more adequate in some areas—monetary policy, for example—than in some others. Comparative analysis, as in the branch method, is sometimes a systematic alternative to theory.

Suppose an administrator must choose among a small group of policies that differ only incrementally from each other and from present policy. He might aspire to "understand" each of the alternatives—for example, to know all the consequences of each aspect of each policy. If so, he would indeed require theory. In face, however, he would usually decide that, *for policy-making purposes*, he need know, as explained above, only the consequences of each of those aspects of the policies in which they differed from one another. For this much more modest aspiration, he requires no theory (although it might be helpful, if available), for he can proceed to isolate probable differences by examining the differences in consequences associated with past differences in policies, a feasible program b because he can take his observations from a long sequence of incremental changes.

For example, without a more comprehensive s social theory about juvenile delinquency than scholars have yet produced, one cannot possibly understand the ways in which a variety of public policies—say on education, housing, recreation, employment, race relations, and policing—might encourage or discourage delinquency. And one needs such an understanding if he undertakes the comprehensive overview of the problem prescribed in the models of the root method. If, however, one merely wants to mobilize knowledge sufficient to assist in a choice among a small group of similar policies—alternative policies on juvenile court procedures, for example—he can do so by comparative analysis of the results of similar past policy moves.

THEORISTS AND PRACTIONERS

This difference explains—in some cases at least—why the administrator often feels that the outside expert or academic problem-solver is sometimes not helpful and why they in turn often urge more theory on him. And it explains why an administrator often feels more confident when "flying by the seat of his pants" than when following the advice of theorists. Theorists often ask the administrator to go the long way round to the solution of his problems, in effect ask him to follow the best canons of the scientific method, when the administrator knows that the best available theory will work less well than more modest incremental comparisons. Theorists do not realize that the administrator is often in fact practicing a systematic method. It would be foolish to push this explanation too far, for sometimes practical decision-makers are pursuing neither a theoretical approach nor successive comparisons, nor any other systematic method.

It may be work emphasizing that theory is sometimes of extremely limited helpfulness in policy-making for at least two rather different reasons. It is greedy for facts; it can be constructed only through a great collection of observations. And it is typically insufficiently precise for application to a policy process that moves through small changes. In contrast, the comparative method both economizes on the need for facts and directs the analyst's attention to just those facts that are relevant to the fine choices faced by the decision-maker.

With respect to precision of theory, economic theory serves as an example. It predicts that an economy without money or prices would in certain specified ways misallocate resources, but this finding pertains to an alternative far removed from the kind of policies on which administrators need help. On the other hand, it is not precise enough to predict the consequences of policies restricting business mergers, and this is the kind of issue on which the administrators need help. Only in relatively restricted areas does economic theory achieve sufficient precision to go far in resolving policy questions; its helpfulness in policy-making is always so limited that it requires supplementation through comparative analysis.

SUCCESSIVE COMPARISON AS A SYSTEM

Successive limited comparisons is, then, indeed a method or system; it is not a failure of method for which administrators ought to apologize. None the less, its imperfections, which have not been explored in this paper, are many. For example the method is without a built-in safeguard for all relevant values, and it also may lead the decision-maker to overlook excellent policies for no other reason that that they are not suggested by the chain of successive policy steps leading up to the present. Hence, it ought to be said that under t his method, as well as under some of the most sophisticated variants of the root method—operations research, for example—policies will continue to be as foolish as they are wise.

Why then bother to describe the method in all the above detail? Because it is in fact a common method of policy formulation, and is, for complex problems, the principal reliance of administrators as well as of other policy analysts.[9] And because it will be superior to any other decision-making method available for complex problems in many circumstances, certainly superior to a futile attempt at superhuman comprehensiveness. The reaction of the public administrator to the exposition of method doubtless will be less a discovery of a new method than a better acquaintance with an old. But by becoming more conscious of their practice of this method, administrators might practice it with more skill and know when to extend or constrict its use. (That they sometimes practice it effectively and sometimes may not explain the extremes of opinion on "muddling through," which is both praises as a highly sophisticated for of problem-solving and denounced as no method at all. For I suspect that in so far as there is a system in what is known as "muddling through," this method is it.)

One of the noteworthy incidental consequences of clarification of the method is the light it throws on the suspicion an administrator sometimes entertains that a consultant or adviser is not speaking relevantly and responsibly when in fact by all ordinary objective evidence he is. The trouble lies in the fact that most of us approach policy problems within a framework given by our view of a chain of successive policy choices made up to the present. One's thinking about appropriate policies with respect, say, to urban traffic control is greatly influenced by one's knowledge of the incremental steps taken up to the present. An administrator enjoys an intimate knowledge of his past sequences that "outsiders" do no share, and his thinking and that of the "outsider" will consequently be different in ways that may puzzle both. Both may appear to be talking intelligently, yet each may find the other unsatisfactory. The relevance of the policy chain of succession is even more clear when an American tries to discuss, say, antitrust policy with a Swiss, for the chains of policy in the two countries are strikingly different and the two individuals consequently have organized their knowledge in quite different ways.

If this phenomenon is a barrier to communication, an understanding of it promises an enrichment of intellectual interaction in policy formulation. Once the source of difference is understood, it will sometimes be stimulating for an administrator to seek out a policy analyst whose recent experience is with a policy chain different from his own.

This raises again a question only briefly discussed above on the merits of like-mindedness among government administrators. While much of organization theory argues the virtues of common values and agreed organizational objectives, for complex problems in which the root method is inapplicable, agencies will want among their own personnel two types of diversification: administrators whose thinking is organized by reference to policy chains other than those familiar to most members of the organization and, even more commonly, administrators whose professional or personal values or interests create diversity of view (perhaps coming from different specialties, social classes, geographical areas) so that, even within a single agency, decision-making can be fragmented and parts of the agency can serve as watchdogs for other parts.

NOTES

1. James G. March and Herbert A. Simon similarly characterize the literature. They also take some important steps, as have Simon's recent articles, to describe a less heroic model of policy-making. See *Organizations* (John Wiley and Sons, 1958), p. 137.

2. "Operations Research and National Planning—A Dissent," 5 *Operations Research* 718 (October, 1957). Hitch's dissent is from particular points made in the article to which his paper is a reply; his claim that operations research is for low-level problems is widely accepted. For examples of the kind of problems to which operations research is applied, see C. W. Churchman, R. L. Ackoff and E. L. Arnoff, *Introduction to Operations Research* (John Wiley and Sons, 1957); and J. F. McCloskey and J. M. Coppinger (eds.), *Operations Research for Management*, Vol. II, (The Johns Hopkins Press, 1956).

3. I am assuming that administrators often make policy and advise in the making of policy and am treating decision-making and policy-making as synonymous for purposes of this paper.

4. Martin Meyerson and Edward D. Banfield, *Politics, Planning and the Public Interest* (The Free Press, 1955).

5. The line of argument is, of course, an extension of the theory of market choice, especially the theory of consumer choice, to public policy choices.

6. A more precise definition of incremental policies and a discussion of whether a change that

appears "small" to one observer might be seen differently by another is to be found in my "Policy Analysis," 48 *American Economic Review* 298 (June, 1958).

7. The link between the practice of the method of successive limited comparisons and mutual adjustment of interests in a highly fragmented decision-making process adds a new facet to pluralist theories of government and administration.

8. Herbert Simon, Donald W. Smithburg, and Victor A. Thompson, *Public Administration* (Alfred A. Knopf, 1950), p. 434.

9. Elsewhere I have explored this same method of policy formulation as a practiced by academic analysts of policy (Policy Analysis," *American Economic Review* 298 (June, 1958]). Although it has been here presented as a method for public administrators, it is no less necessary to

analysts more removed from immediate policy questions, despite their tendencies to describe their own analytical efforts as though they were the rational-comprehensive method with an especially heavy use of theory. Similarly, this same method is inevitably resorted to in personal problem-solving, where means and ends are sometimes impossible to separate, where aspirations or objectives undergo constant development, and where drastic simplification of the complexity of the real world is urgent if problems are to be solved in the time that can be given to the. To an economist accustomed to dealing with the marginal or incremental concept in market processes, the central idea in the method is that both evaluation and empirical analysis are incremental. Accordingly I have referred to the method elsewhere as "the incremental method."

Advocacy and Pluralism in Planning

Paul Davidoff

Paul Davidoff challenges the planning profession with a call for a new type of planner: the comprehensive city planner, who will be an advocate for the poor, broadly educated, and concerned as much with social and economic issues as with physical planning. Davidoff argues the importance of planners who are advocates rather than dispassionate professionals, and deeply involved in the politics of planning. According to Davidoff, for an effective urban democracy, planners should encourage pluralism by giving voice, power, and representation to the concerns of many interest groups, especially the poor.

The present can become an epoch in which the dreams of the past for an enlightened and just democracy are turned into a reality. The massing of voices protesting racial discrimination have roused this nation to the need to rectify racial and other social injustices. The adoption by Congress of a host of welfare measures and the Supreme Court's specification of the meaning of equal protection by law both reveal the response to protest and open the way for the vast changes still required.

The just demand for political and social equality on the part of the Negro and the impoverished requires the public to establish the bases for a society affording equal opportunity to all citizens. The compelling need for intelligent planning, for specification of new social goals and the means for achieving them, is manifest. The society of the future will be an urban one, and city planners will help to give it shape and content.

The prospect for future planning is that of a practice which openly invites political and social values to be examined and debated. Acceptance of this position means rejection of prescriptions for planning which would have the planner act solely as a technician. It has been argued that technical studies to enlarge the information available to decision makers must take precedence over statements of goals and ideals:

> We have suggested that, at least in part, the city planner is better advised to start from research into the functional aspects of cities than from his own estimation of the values which he is attempting to maximize. This suggestion springs from a conviction that at this juncture the implications of many planning decisions are poorly understood, and that no certain means are at hand by which values can be measured, ranked, and translated into the design of a metropolitan system.[1]

While acknowledging the need for humility and openness in the adoption of social goals, this statement amounts to an attempt to eliminate, or sharply reduce, the unique contribution planning can make: understanding the functional aspects of the city and recommending appropriate future action to improve the urban condition.

Another argument that attempts to reduce the importance of attitudes and values in planning and other policy sciences is that the major public questions are themselves matters of choice between technical methods of solution. Dahl and Lindblom put forth this position at the beginning of their important textbook, *Politics, Economics, and Welfare.*[2]

> In economic organization and reform, the "great issues" are no longer the great issues, if they ever were. It has become increasingly difficult for thoughtful men to find meaningful alternatives posed in the traditional choices between socialism and capitalism, planning and the free market, regulation and laissez faire, for they find their actual choices neither so simple nor so grand. Not so simple, because economic organization poses knotty problems that can only be solved by painstaking attention to technical details—how else, for example, can inflation be controlled? Nor so grand, because, at least in the Western world, most people neither can nor wish to experiment with the whole pattern of socioeconomic organization to attain goals more easily won. If for example, taxation will serve

the purpose, why "abolish the wages system" to ameliorate income inequality?

These words were written in the early 1950's and express the spirit of that decade more than that of the 1960's. They suggest that the major battles have been fought. But the "great issues" in economic organization, those revolving around the central issue of the nature of distributive justice, have yet to be settled. The world is still in turmoil over the way in which the resources of nations are to be distributed. The justice of the present social allocation of wealth, knowledge, skill, and other social goods is clearly in debate. Solutions to questions about the share of wealth and other social commodities that should go to different classes cannot be technically derived; they must arise from social attitudes.

Appropriate planning action cannot be prescribed from a position of value neutrality, for prescriptions are based on desired objectives. One conclusion drawn from this assertion is that "values are inescapable elements of any rational decision-making process"[3] and that values held by the planner should be made clear. The implications of that conclusion for planning have been described elsewhere and will not be considered in this article.[4] Here I will say that the planner should do more than explicate the values underlying his prescriptions for courses of action; he should affirm them; he should be an advocate for what he deems proper.

Determinations of what serves the public interest, in a society containing many diverse interest groups, are almost always of a highly contentious nature. In performing its role of prescribing courses of action leading to future desired states, the planning profession must engage itself thoroughly and openly in the contention surrounding political determination. Moreover, planners should be able to engage in the political process as advocates of the interests both of government and of such other groups, organizations, or individuals who are concerned with proposing policies for the future development of the community.

The recommendation that city planners represent and plead the plans of many interest groups is founded upon the need to establish an effective urban democracy, one in which citizens may be able to play an active role in the process of deciding public policy. Appropriate policy in a democracy is determined through a process of political debate. The right course of action is always a matter of choice, never the fact. In a bureaucratic age great care must be taken that choices remain in the area of public view and participation.

Urban politics, in an era of increasing government activity in planning and welfare, must balance the demands for ever-increasing central bureaucratic control against the demands for increased concern for the unique requirements of local, specialized interests. The welfare of all and the welfare of minorities are both deserving of support; planning must be so structured and so practiced as to account for this unavoidable bifurcation of the public interest.

The idealized political process in a democracy serves the search for truth in much the same manner as due process in law. Fair notice and hearings, production of supporting evidence, cross examination, reasoned decision are all means employed to arrive at relative truth: a just decision. Due process and two- (or more) party political contention both rely heavily upon strong advocacy by a professional. The advocate represents an individual, group, or organization. He affirms their position in language understandable to his client and to the decision makers he seeks to convince.

If the planning process is to encourage democratic urban government then it must operate so as to include rather than exclude citizens from participating in the process. "Inclusion" means not only permitting the citizen to be heard. It also means that he be able to become well informed about the underlying reasons for planning proposals, and be able to respond to them in the technical language of professional planners.

A practice that has discouraged full participation by citizens in plan making in the past has been based on what might be called the *"unitary plan."* This is the idea that only one agency in a community should prepare a comprehensive plan; that agency is the city planning commission or department. Why is it that no other organization within a community prepares a plan? Why is only one agency concerned with establishing both general and specific goals for community development, and with proposing the strategies and costs

required to effect the goals? Why are there not plural plans?

If the social, economic, and political ramifications of a plan are politically contentious, then why is it that those in opposition to the agency plan do not prepare one of their own? It is interesting to observe that "rational" theories of planning have called for consideration of alternative courses of action by planning agencies. As a matter or rationality it has been argued that all of the alternative choices open as means to the ends ought to be examined.[5] But those, including myself, who have recommended agency consideration of alternatives have placed upon the agency planner the burden of inventing "a few representative alternatives."[6] The agency planner has been given the duty of constructing a model of the political spectrum, and charged with sorting out what he conceives to be worthy alternatives. This duty has placed too great a burden on the agency planner, and has failed to provide for the formulation of alternatives by the interest groups who will eventually be affected by the completed plans.

Whereas in a large part of our national and local political practice contention is viewed as healthy, in city planning where a large proportion of the professions are public employees contentious criticism has not always been viewed as legitimate. Further, where only government prepares plans, and no minority plans are developed, pressure is often applied to bring all professionals to work for the ends espoused by public agency. For example, last year a Federal official complained to a meeting of planning professors that the academic planners were not giving enough support to Federal programs. He assumed that every planner should be on the side of the Federal renewal program. Of course government administrators will seek to gain the support of professionals outside of government, but such support should not be expected as a matter of loyalty. In a democratic system opposition to a public agency should be just as normal and appropriate as support. The agency, despite the fact that is concerned with planning, may be serving undesired ends.

In presenting a plea for plural planning I do not mean to minimize the importance of the obligation of the public planning agency. It must decide upon appropriate future courses of action for the community, public agencies as well as the public itself may have suffered from incomplete and shallow analysis of potential directions. Lively political dispute aided by plural plans could do much to improve the level of rationality in the process of preparing the public plan.

The advocacy of alternative plans by interest groups outside of government would stimulate city planning in a number of ways. First, it would serve as a means of better informing the public of the alternative choices open, *alternatives strongly supported by their proponents*. In current practice those few agencies which have portrayed alternatives have not been equally enthusiastic about each.[7] A standard reaction to rationalists' prescription for consideration of alternative courses of action has been "it can't be done; how can you expect planners to present alternatives which they don't approve?" The appropriate answer to that question has been that planners like lawyers may have a professional obligation to defend positions they oppose. However, in a system of plural planning, the public agency would be relieved of at least some of the burden of presenting alternatives. In plural planning the alternatives would be presented by interest groups differing with the public agency's plan. Such alternatives would represent the deep-seated convictions of t heir opponents and not just the mental exercises of rational planners seeking to portray the range of choice.

A second way in which advocacy and plural planning would improve planning practice would be in forcing the public agency to compete with other planning groups to win political support. In the absence of opposition or alternative plans presented by interest groups the public agencies have had little incentive to improve the quality of their work or the rate of production of plans. The political consumer has been offered a yes—no ballot in regard to the comprehensive plan; either the public agency's plan was to be adopted or no plan would be adopted.

A third improvement in planning practice which might follow from plural planning would be to force those who have been critical or "establishment" plans to produce superior plans, rather than only to carry out the very essential obligation of criticizing plans deemed improper.

THE PLANNER AS ADVOCATE

Where plural planning is practiced, advocacy becomes the means of professional support for competing claims about how the community should develop. Pluralism in support of political contention describes the process; advocacy describes the role performed by the professional in the process. Where unitary planning prevails, advocacy is not of paramount importance, for there is little or no competition for the plan prepared by the public agency. The concept of advocacy as taken from legal practice implies the opposition of at least two contending viewpoints in an adversary proceeding.

The legal advocate must plead for his own and his client's sense of legal propriety or justice. The planner as advocate would plead for his own and his client's view of the good society. The advocate planner would be more than a provider of information, an analyst of current trends, a simulator of future conditions, and a detailer of means. In addition to carrying out these necessary parts of planning, he would be a *proponent* of specific substantive solutions.

The advocate planner would be responsible to his client and would seek to express his client's views. This does not mean that the planner could not seek to persuade his client. In some situations persuasion might not be necessary, for the planner would have sought out an employer with whom he shared common views about desired social conditions and the means toward them. In fact one of the benefits of advocate planning is the possibility it creates for a planner to find employment with agencies holding values close to his own. Today the agency planner may be dismayed by the positions affirmed by his agency, but there may be no alternative employer.

The advocate planner would be above all a planner. He would be responsible to his client for preparing plans and for all of the other elements comprising the planning process. Whether working for the public agency or for some private organization, the planner would have to prepare plans that take account of the arguments made in other plans. Thus the advocate's plan might have some of the characteristics of a legal brief. It would be a document presenting the facts and reasons for supporting one set of proposals, and facts and reasons indicating the inferiority of counter-propos-als. The adversary nature of plural planning might, then, have the beneficial effect of upsetting the tradition of writing plan proposals in terminol-ogy which makes them appear self-evident.

A troublesome issue in contemporary planning is that of finding techniques for evaluating alterna-tive plans. Technical devices such as cost-benefit analysis by themselves are of little assistance with-out the use of means for appraising the values underlying plans. Advocate planning, by making more apparent the values underlying plans, and by making definitions of social costs and benefits more explicit, should greatly assist the process of plan evaluation. Further, it would become clear (as it is not at present) that there are no neutral grounds for evaluating a plan; there are as many evaluative systems as there are value systems.

The adversary nature of plural planning might also have a good effect on the uses of infor-mation and research in planning. One of the tasks of the advocate planner in discussing the plans prepared in opposition to his would be to point out the nature of the bias underlying information presented in other plans. In this way, as critic of opposition plans, he would be performing a task similar to the legal technique of cross-examina-tion. While painful to the planner whose bias is exposed (and no planner can be entirely free of bias) the net effect of confrontation between advo-cates of alternative plans would be more careful and precise research.

Not all the work of an advocate planner would be of an adversary nature. Much of it would be educational. The advocate would have the job of informing other groups, including pub-lic agencies, of the conditions, problems, and out-look of the group he represented. Another major educational job would be that of informing his clients of their rights under planning and renewal laws, about the general operations of city govern-ment, and of particular programs likely to affect them.

The advocate planner would devote much attention to assisting the client organization to clarify its ideas and to give expression to them. In order to make his client more powerful politically the advocate might also become engaged in expanding the size and scope of his client organi-zation. But the advocate's most important func-tion would be to carry out the planning process for the organization and to argue persuasively in favor of its planning proposals.

Advocacy in planning has already begun to emerge as planning and renewal affect the lives of more and more people. The critics of urban renewal[8] have forced response from the renewal agencies, and the ongoing debate[9] has stimulated needed self-evaluation by public agencies. Much work along the lines of advocate planning has already taken place, but little of it by professional planners. More often the work has been conduct-ed by trained community organizers or by student groups. In at least one instance, however, a plan-ner's professional aid led to the development of an alternative renewal approach, one which will result in the dislocation of far fewer families than originally comtemplated.[10]

Pluralism and advocacy are means for stimu-lating consideration of future conditions by all groups in society. But there is one social group which at present is particularly in need of the assistance of planners. This group includes organ-izations representing low-income families. At a time when concern for the condition of the poor finds institutionalization in community action programs, it would be appropriate for planners concerned with such groups to find means to plan with them. The plans prepared for these groups would seek to combat poverty and would propose programs affording new and better opportunities to the members of the organization and to families similarly situated.[11]

The difficulty in providing adequate planning assistance to organizations representing low-income families may in part be overcome by funds allocated to local anti-poverty councils. But these councils are not the only representatives of the poor; other organizations exist and seek help. How can this type of assistance be financed? This question will be examined below, when attention is turned to the means for institutionalizing plural planning.

THE STRUCTURE OF PLANNING

Planning by Special Interest Groups

The local planning process typically includes one or more "citizens" organizations concerned with the nature of planning in the community. The

Workable Program requirement for "citizen partic-ipation"[12] has enforced this tradition and brought it to most large communities. The difficulty with current citizen participation programs is that citizens are more often *reacting* to agency programs than *proposing* their concepts of appropriate goals and future action.

The fact that citizen's organizations have not played a positive role in formulating plans is to some extent a result of both the enlarged role in society played by government bureaucracies and the historic weakness of municipal party politics. There is something very shameful to our society in the necessity to have organized "citizen participation." Such participation should be the norm in an enlightened democracy. The formalization of citizen participation as a required practice in localities is similar in many respects to totalitarian shows of loyalty to the state by citizen parades.

Will a private group interested in preparing a recommendation for community development be required to carry out its own survey and analysis of the community? The answer would depend upon the quality of the work prepared by the public agency, work which should be public information. In some instances the public agency may not have surveyed or analyzed aspects the private group thinks important; or the public agency's work may reveal strong biases unacceptable to the private group. In an event, the production of a useful plan proposal will require much information concerning the present and predicted conditions in the community. There will be some costs associates with gathering that information, even if it is taken from the public agency. The major cost involved in the preparation of a plan by a private agency would probably be the employment of one or more professional planners.

What organizations might be expected to engage in the plural planning process? The first type that comes to mind are the political parties; but this is clearly as aspirational thought. There is very little evidence that local political organizations have the interest, ability, or concern to establish well developed programs for their communities. Not all the fault, though, should be placed upon the professional politicians, for the registered members of political parties have no demanded very much, if anything, from them as agents.

Despite the unreality of the wish, the desirability for active participation in the process of planning by the political parties is strong. In an ideal situation local parties would establish political platforms which would contain master plans for community growth and both the majority and minority parties in the legislative branch of government would use such plans as one basis for appraising individual legislative proposals. Further, the local administration would use its planning agency to carry out the plans it proposed to the electorate. This dream will not turn to reality for a long time. In the interim other interest groups must be sought to fill the gap caused by the present inability of political organizations.

The second set of organizations which might be interested in preparing plans for community development are those that represent special interest groups having established views in regard to proper public policy. Such organizations as chambers of commerce, real estate boards, labor organizations, pro- and anti-civil rights groups, and anti-poverty councils come to mind. Groups of this nature have often played parts in the development of community plans, but only in a very few instances have they proposed their own plans.

It must be recognized that there is strong reason operating against commitment to a plan by these organizations. In fact it is the same reason that in part limits the interests of politicians and which limits the potential for planning in our society. The expressed commitment to a particular plan may make it difficult for groups to find means for accommodating t heir various interests. In other terms, it may be simpler for professionals, politicians, or lobbyists to make deals if they have not laid their cards on the table.

There is a third set of organizations that might be looked to as proponents of plans and to whom the foregoing comments might not apply. These are the ad hoc protest associations which may form in opposition to some proposed policy. An example of such a group is a neighborhood association formed to combat a renewal plan, a zoning change, or the proposed location of a public facility. Such organizations may seek to develop alternative plans, plans which would, if effected, better serve their interests.

From the point of view of effective and rational planning it might be desirable to commence plural planning at the level of city-wide organizations, but a more realistic view is that it will start at the neighborhood level. Certain advantages of this outcome should be noted. Mention was made earlier of tension in government between centralizing and decentralizing forces. The contention aroused by conflict between the central planning agency and the neighborhood organization may indeed by healthy, leading to clearer definition of welfare policies and their relation to the rights of individuals or minority groups.

Who will pay for plural planning? Some organizations have the resources to sponsor the development of a plan. Many groups lack the means. The plight of the relatively indigent association seeking to propose a plan might be a analogous to that of the indigent client in search of legal aid. If the idea of plural planning makes sense, then support may be found from foundations or from government. In the beginning it is more likely that some foundation might be willing to experiment with plural planning as a means of making city planning more effective and more democratic. Or the Federal Government might see plural planning, if carried out by local anti-poverty councils, as a strong means of generating local interest in community affairs.

Federal sponsorship if plural planning might be seen as a more effective tool for stimulating involvement of the citizen in the future of his community than are the present types of citizen participation programs. Federal support could only be expected if plural planning were seen, not as a means of combating renewal plans, but as an incentive to local renewal agencies to prepare better plans.

The Public Planning Agency

A major drawback to effective democratic planning practice is the continuation of that non-responsible vestigial institution, the planning commission. If it is agreed that the establishment of both general policies and implementation policies are questions affecting the public interest and that public interest questions should be decided in accord with established democratic practices for decision making, then it is indeed difficult to find convincing reasons for continuing to permit independent commissions to make planning decisions.

At an earlier stage in planning the strong arguments of John T. Howard[13] and others in support of commissions may have been persuasive. But it is now more than a decade since Howard made his defense against Robert Walker's position favoring planning as a staff function under the mayor. With the increasing effect planning decisions have upon the lives of citizens the Walker proposal assumes great urgency.[14]

Aside from important questions regarding the propriety of independent agencies which are far removed from public control determining public policy, the failure to place planning decision choices in the hands of elected officials has weakened the ability of professional planners to have their proposals effected. Separating planning from local politics has made it difficult for independent commissions to garner influential political support. The commissions are not responsible directly to the electorate and in turn the electorate is, at best, often indifferent to the planning commission.

During the last decade in many cities power to alter community development has slipped out of the hands of city planning commissions, assuming they ever held it, and has been transferred to development coordinators. This has weakened the professional planner. Perhaps planners unknowingly contributed to this by their refusal to take concerted action in opposition to the perpetuation of commissions.

Planning commissions are products of the conservative reform movement of the early part of this century. The movement was essentially anti-populist and pro-aristocracy. Politics was viewed as dirty business. The commissions a re relics of a not-too-distant past when it was believed that if men of good will discussed a problem thoroughly, certainly the right solution would be forthcoming. We know today, and perhaps it was always knows, that there are no right solutions. Proper policy is that which the decision-making unit declares to be proper.

Planning commissions are responsible to no constituency. The members of the commissions, except for their chairman, are seldom knows to the public. In general the individual members fail to expose their personal views about policy and prefer to immerse them in group decision. If the members wrote concurring and dissenting opinions, then at least the commissions might stimulate thought about planning issues. It is difficult to comprehend why this aristocratic and undemocratic form of decision making should be continued. The public planning function should be carried out in the executive or legislative office and perhaps in both. There has been some question about which of these branches of government would provide the best home, but there is much reason to believe that both branches would be made more cognizant of planning issues if they were each informed by their own planning staffs. To carry this division further, it would probably be advisable to establish minority and majority planning staffs in the legislative branch.

At the root of my last suggestion is the belief that there is or should be a Republican and Democratic way of viewing city development; that there should be conservative and liberal plans, plans to support the private market and plans to support greater government control. There are many possible roads for a community to travel and many plans should show them. Explication is required of many alternative futures presented by those sympathetic to the construction of each such future. As indicated earlier, such alternatives are not presented to the public now. Those few reports which do include alternative futures do not speak in terms of interest to the average citizen. They are filled with professional jargon and present sham alternatives. These plans have expressed technical land use alternatives rather than social, economic, or political value alternatives. Both the traditional unitary plans and the new ones that present technical alternatives have limited the public's exposure to the future states that might be achieved. Instead of arousing health political contention as diverse comprehensive plans might, these plans have deflated interest.

The independent planning commission and unitary plan practice certainly should not co-exist. Separately they dull the possibility for enlightened political debate; in combination they have made it yet more difficult. But when still another hoary concept of city planning is added to them, such debate becomes practically impossible. This third of a trinity of worn-out notions is that city planning should focus only upon the physical aspects of city development.

AN INCLUSIVE DEFINITION OF THE SCOPE OF PLANNING

The view that equates physical planning with city planning is myopic. It may have had some historic justification, but is clearly out of place at a time when it is necessary to integrate knowledge and techniques in order to wrestle effectively with the myriad of problems afflicting urban populations.

The city planning profession's historic concern with the physical environment has warped its ability to see physical structures and land as servants to those who use them.[15] Physical relations and conditions have no meaning or quality apart from the way they serve their users. But this is forgotten every time a physical condition is described as good or bad without relation to a specified group of users. High density, low density, green belts, mixed uses, cluster developments, centralized or decentralized business centers are per se neither good nor bad. They describe physical relations or conditions, but take on value only when seen in terms of their social, economic, psychological, physiological, or aesthetic effects upon different users.

The profession's experience with renewal over the past decade has shown the high costs of exclusive concern with physical conditions. It has been found that the allocation of funds for removal of physical blight may not necessarily improve the over-all physical condition of a community and may engender such harsh social repercussions as to severely damage both social and economic institutions. Another example of the deficiencies of the physical bias is the assumption of city planners that they could deal with the capital budget as if the physical attributes of a facility could be understood apart from the philosophy and practice of the service conducted within the physical structure. This assumption is open to question. The size, shape, and location of a facility greatly interact with the purpose of the activity the facility houses. Clear examples of this can be seen in public education and in the provision of low cost housing. The racial and other socio-economic consequences of "physical decisions" such as location of schools and housing projects have been immense, but city planners, while acknowledging the existence of such consequences, have not sought or trained themselves to understand socio-economic problems, their causes or solutions.

The city planning profession's limited scope has tended to bias strongly many of its recommendations toward perpetuation of existing social and economic practices. Here I am not opposing the outcomes, but the way in which they are developed. Relative ignorance of social and economic methods of analysis have causes planners to propose solutions in the absence of sufficient knowledge of the costs and benefits of proposals upon different sections of the population.

Large expenditures have been made on planning studies of regional transportation needs, for example, but these studies have been conducted in a manner suggesting that different social and economic classes of the population did not have different needs and different abilities to meet them. In the field of housing, to take another example, planners have been hesitant to question the consequences of locating public housing in slum areas. In the field of industrial development, planners have seldom examined the types of jobs the community needed; it has been assumed that one job was about as useful as another. But this may not be the case where a significant sector of the population finds it difficult to get employment.

"Who gets what, when, where, why, and how" are the basic political questions which need to be raised about every allocation of public resources. The questions must be answered adequately if land use criteria are the sole or major standards for judgment.

The need to see an element of city development, land use, in broad perspective applies equally well to every other element, such as health, welfare, and recreation. The governing of a city requires an adequate plan for its future. Such a plan loses guiding force and rational basis to the degree that it deals with less than the whole that is of concern to the public.

The implications of the foregoing comments for the practice of city planning are these. First, state planning enabling legislation should be amended to permit planning departments to study and to prepare plans related to any area of public concern. Second, planning education must be redirected so as to provide channels of specialization in different parts of public planning and a core focused upon the planning process. Third,

the professional planning association should enlarge its scope so as to not exclude city planners not specializing in physical planning.

A year ago at the AIP convention it was suggested that the AIP Constitution be amended to permit city planning to enlarge its scope to all matters of public concern.[16] Members of the Institute in agreement with this proposal should seek to develop support for it at both the chapter and national level. The constitution at present states that the Institute's "particular sphere of activity shall be the planning of the unified development of urban communities and their environs and of states, regions and the nations as *expressed through determination of the comprehensive arrangement of land and land occupancy and regulation thereof.*"[17]

It is time that the AIP delete the words in my italics from its Constitution. The planner limited to such concerns is not a city planner, he is a land planner or a physical planner. A city is its people, their practices, and their political, social, cultural and economic institutions as well as other things. The city planner must comprehend and deal with all these factors.

The new city planner will be concerned with physical planning, economic planning and social planning. The scope of his work will be no wider than that presently demanded of a mayor or a city councilman. Thus, we cannot argue against an enlarged planning function on grounds that it is too large to handle. The mayor needs assistance; in particular he needs the assistance of a planner, one trained to examine needs and aspirations in terms of both short and long term perspectives. In observing the early stages of development of Community Action Programs, it is apparent that our cities are in desperate need of the type of assistance trained planners could offer. Our cities require for their social and economic programs the type of long range thought and information that have been brought forward in the realm of physical planning. Potential resources must be examined and priorities set.

What I have just proposed does not imply the termination of physical planning, but it does mean that physical planning be seen as part of city planning. Uninhibited by limitations on his work, the city planner will be able to add his expertise to the task of coordinating the operating and capital budgets and to the job of relating effects of each city program upon the others and upon the social, political, and economic resources of the community.

An expanded scope reaching all matters of public concern will make planning not only a more effective administrative tool of local government but it will also bring planning practice closer to the issues of real concern to the citizens. A system of plural city planning probably has a much greater chance for operational success where the focus is on live social and economic questions instead of rather esoteric issues relating to physical norms.

THE EDUCATION OF PLANNERS

Widening the scope of planning to include all areas of concern to government would suggest that city planners must possess a broader knowledge of the structure and forces affecting urban development. In general this would be true. But at present many city planners are specialists in only one or more of the functions of city government. Broadening the scope of planning would require some additional planners who specialize in one or more of the services entailed by the new focus.

A prime purpose of city planning is the coordination of many separate functions. This coordination calls for men holding general knowledge of the many elements comprising the urban community. Educating a man for performing the coordinative role is a difficult job, one not well satisfied by the present tradition of two years of graduate study. Training of urban planners with the skills called for in this undergraduate program affording an opportunity for holistic understanding of both urban conditions and t techniques for analyzing and solving urban problems.

The practice of plural planning requires educating planners who would be able to engage as professional advocates in the contentious work of forming social policy. The person able to do this would be one deeply committed to both the process of planning and to particular substantive ideas. Recognizing that ideological commitments will separate planners, there is tremendous need to train professionals who are competent to express their social objectives.

The great advances in analytic skills, demonstrated in the recent May issue of this *Journal* dedicated to techniques of simulating urban growth processes, portend a time when planners and the public will be better able to predict the consequences of proposed courses of action. But these advances will be of little social advantage if the proposals themselves do not have substance. The contemporary thoughts of planners about the nature of man in society are often mundane, unexciting or gimmicky. When asked to point out to students the planners who have a developed sense of history and philosophy concerning man's situation in the urban world one is hard put to come up with a name. Sometimes Goodman or Mumford might be mentioned. But planners seldom go deeper than acknowledging the goodness of green space and the soundness of proximity of linked activities. We cope with the problems of the alienated man with a recommendation for reducing the time of the journey to work.

CONCLUSION

The urban community is a system comprised of interrelated elements, but little is known about how the elements do, will, or should interrelate. The type of knowledge required by the new comprehensive city planner demands that the planning profession be comprised of groups of men well versed in contemporary philosophy, social work, law, the social sciences, and civic design. Not every planner must be knowledgeable in all these areas, but each planner must have a deep understanding of one or more of these areas and he must be able to give persuasive expression to his understanding.

As a profession charged with making urban life more beautiful, exciting, and creative, and more just, we have had little to say. Our task is to train a future generation of planners to go well beyond us in its ability to prescribe the future urban life.

NOTES

1. Britton Harris, "Plan or Projection," *Journal of the American Institute of Planners*, XXVI (November 1960) 265-272.

2. Robert Dahl and Charles Lindblom, *Politics, Economics, and Welfare* (New York: Harper and Brothers, 1953) p. 3.

3. Paul Davidoff and Thomas Reiner, "A Choice Theory of Planning," *Journal of the American Institute of Planners*, XXVIII (May 1962) 103-115.

4. *Ibid.*

5. See, for example, Martin Meyerson and Edward Banfield, *Politics, Planning and the Public Interest* (Glencoe: The Free Press, 1955) p. 314 ff. The authors state "By a *rational* decision, we mean one made in the following manner: 1. The decision-maker considers all of the alternatives (courses of action) open to him;...2. he identifies and evaluates all of the consequences which would follow from the adoption of each alternative;...3. he selects that alternative the probable consequences of which would be preferable in terms of his most valued ends."

6. Davidoff and Reiner, *Op. cit.*

7. National Capital Planning Commission, *The Nation's Capital; a Policies Plan for the year 2000* (Washington, D.C.: The Commission, 1961).

8. The most impor*tant critical studies are: Jane Jacobs,* The Life and Death of Great American Cities (New York: Random House, 1961); Martin Anderson, *The Federal Bulldozer* (Cambridge: M.I.T. Press 1964); Herbert J. Gans, "The Human Implications of Current Redevelopment and Relocation Planning, *"Journal of the American Institute of Planners*, XXV (February 1959), 15-26.

9. A recent example of heated debate appears in the following set of articles: Herbert J. Gans, "The Failure of Urban Renewal," *Commentary* 39 (April 1965) p. 29; George Raymond "Controversy," *Commentary* 40 (July 1965) p. 72; and Herbert J. Gans, "Controversy," *Commentary* 40 (July 1965) p. 77.

10. Walter Thabit, *An Alternate Plan for Cooper Square* (New York: Walter Thabit, July 1961).

11. The first conscious effort to employ the advocacy method was carried out by a graduate student of city planning as an independent research project. The author acted as both a participant and an observer of a local housing organization. See Linda Davidoff, "The Bluffs: Advocate Planning," *Comment*, Dept. of City Planning, University of Pennsylvania, (Spring 1965) p. 59.

12. See Section 101 (c) of the United States Housing Act of 1949, as amended.

13. John T. Howard, "In Defense of Planning Commissions," *Journal of the American Institute of Planners*, XVII (Spring 1951).

14. Robert Walker, *The Planning Function in Urban Government*; Second Edition (Chicago: University of Chicago Press, 1950). Walker drew the following conclusions from his examination of planning and planning commissions. "Another conclusion to be drawn from the existing composition of city planning boards is that they are not representative of the population as a whole." p. 153. "In summary the writer is of the opinion that the claim that planning commissions are more objective than elected officials must be rejected." p. 155. "From his observations the writer feels justified in saying that very seldom does a majority of any commission have any well-rounded understanding of the purposes and ramifications of planning." p. 157. "In summary, then, it was found that the average commission member does not comprehend planning nor is he particularly interested even in the range of customary physical planning." p. 158. "Looking at the planning commission at the present time, however, one is forced to conclude that, despite some examples of successful operations, the unpaid board is not proving satisfactory as planning agency," p. 165. "...(it) is believed that the most fruitful line of development for the future would be replacement of these commissions by a department of bureau attached to the office of mayor or city manager. This department might be headed by a board or by a single director, but the members or the director would in any case hold office at the pleasure of the executive on the same basis as other department heads." p. 177.

15. An excellent and complete study of the bias resulting from reliance upon physical or land use criteria appears in David Farbman, *A Description, Analysis and Critique of the Master Plan*, an unpublished mimeographed study prepared for the Univ. of Pennsylvania's Institute for Urban Studies, 1959-1960. After studying more than 100 master plans Farbman wrote: "As a result of the predominantly physical orientation of the planning profession many planners have fallen victims to a malaise which I suggest calling the "Physical Bias." This bias is not the physical orientation of the planner itself but is the result of it. ..."The physical bias is an attitude on the part of the planner which leads him to conceive of the principles and techniques of *his profession* as the key factors in determining the particular recommendations to be embodied in his plans..." "The physically biased planner plans on the assumption (conviction) that the physical problems of a city can be solved with-

in the framework of physical desiderata; in other words, that physical criteria and expertise. The physical bias produces both an inability and an unwillingness on the part of the planner to 'get behind' the physical recommendations of the plan, to isolate, examine or discuss more basic criteria..." "...There is room, then, in plan thinking, for physical principles, i.e., theories of structural inter-relationships of the physical city; but this is only a part of the story, for the structural impacts of the plan are only a part of the total impact. This total impact must be conceived as a web of physical, economic and social causes and effects," pp. 22-26.

16. Paul Davidoff, "The Role of the City Planner in Social Planning," *Proceedings of the 1964 Annual Conference*, American Institute of Planners (Washington, D.C.: The Institute, 1964) 125-131.

17. Constitution of AIP, Article II "Purposes," in *AIP Handbook & Roster*—1965, p. 8.

Author's note: The author wishes to thank Melvin H. Webber for his insightful criticism and Linda Davidoff for her many helpful suggestions and for her analysis of advocate planning. Special acknowledgement is made of the penetrating and brilliant social insights offered by the eminent legal scholar and practitioner, Michael Brodie, of the Philadelphia Bar.

Dilemmas in a General Theory of Planning

Horst W. J. Rittel

Melvin M. Webber

In this selection the authors argue that as societal problems become more complex and as the pluralism of American society increases, planning as a profession is increasingly challenged and difficult. Rittel and Webber address the issue by exploring the problems in the social professions as associated with goal-formulation, problem definition, and equity issues. These planning challenges are "inherently wicked" and cannot be addressed in the traditional scientific fashion.

George Bernard Shaw diagnosed the case several years ago; in more recent times popular protest may have already become a social movement. Shaw averred that "every profession is a conspiracy against the laity." The contemporary publics are responding as though they have made the same discovery.

Few of the modern professionals seem to be immune from the popular attack—whether they be social workers, educators, housers, public health officials, policemen, city planners, highway engineers or physicians. Our restive clients have been telling us they don't like the educational programs that schoolmen have been offering, the redevelopment projects urban renewal agencies have been proposing, the law enforcement styles of the police, the administrative behavior of the welfare agencies, the locations of the highways, and so on. In the courts, the streets, and the political campaigns, we've been hearing ever-louder public protests against the professions' diagnoses of the clients' problems, against professionally designed governmental programs, against professionally certified standards for the public services.

It does seem odd that this attack should be coming just when professionals in the social services are beginning to acquire professional competencies. It might seem that our publics are being perverse, having condoned professionalism when it was really only dressed-up amateurism and condemning professionalism when we finally seem to be getting good at our jobs. Perverse though the laity may be, surely the professionals themselves have been behind this attack as well.

Some of the generators of the confrontation have been intellectual in origin. The anti-professional movement stems in part from a reconceptualization of the professional's task. Others are more in the character of historical imperatives, i.e. conditions have been thrown up by the course of societal events that call for different modes of intervention.

The professional's job was once seen as solving an assortment of problems that appeared to be definable, understandable and consensual. He was hired to eliminate those conditions that predominant opinion judged undesirable. His record has been quite spectacular, of course; the contemporary city and contemporary urban society stand as clean evidences of professional prowess. The streets have been paved, and roads now connect all places; houses shelter virtually everyone; the dread diseases are virtually gone; clean water is piped into nearly every building; sanitary sewers are carry wastes from them; schools and hospitals serve virtually every district; and so on. The accomplishments of the past century in these respects have been truly phenomenal, however short of some persons' aspirations they might have been.

But now that these relatively easy problems have been dealt with, we have been turning our attention to others that are much more stubborn. The tests for efficiency, that were once so useful as measures of accomplishment, are being challenged by a renewed preoccupation with consequences for equity. The seeming consensus, that might once have allowed distributional problems to be dealt with, is being eroded by the growing awareness of the nation's pluralism and of the differentiation of values that accompanies differentiation of publics. The professionalized cognitive and occupational styles that were refined in the first half of this century, based in Newtonian mechanistic physics, are not readily adapted to contemporary conceptions of interacting open systems and to contemporary concerns with equity. A growing sensitivity to the waves of repercussions that ripple through such systemic networks and to the value consequences of those repercussions has generated the recent reexamination of received values and the recent search for national goals. There seems to be growing realization that a weal strut in the professional's support system lies at the juncture where goal-formulation, problem-definition and equity issues

meet. We should like to address these matters in turn.

I. GOAL FORMULATION

The search for explicit goals was initiated in force with the opening of the 1960s. In a 1960 RAND publication, Charles J. Hitch urged that "We must learn to look at *our objectives* as critically and as professionally as we look at our models and our other inputs."[1] The subsequent work in systems analysis reaffirmed that injunction. Men in a wide array of fields were prompted to redefine the systems they dealt with in the syntax of verbs rather than nouns—to ask "What do the systems do?" rather than "What are they made of?"—and then to ask the most difficult question of all: "What *should* these systems do?" Also 1960 was inaugurated with the publication of *Goals for Americans*, the report of President Eisenhower's Commission on National Goals.[2] There followed then a wave of similar efforts. The Committee for Economic Development commissioned a follow-up re-examination. So did the Brookings Institution, The American Academy of Arts and Sciences, and then President Nixon through his National Goals Research Staff. But these may by only the most apparent attempts to clarify the nation's direction.[3]

Perhaps more symptomatic in the U.S. were the efforts to install PPBS, which requires explication of *desired outcomes*; and then the more recent attempts to build systems of social indicators, which are in effect surrogates for statements of desired conditions. As we all know, it has turned out to be terribly difficult, if not impossible, to make either of these systems operational. Although there are some small success stories recounted in a few civilian agencies, successes are s till rare. Goal-finding is turning out to be an extraordinarily obstinate task. Because goal-finding is one of the central functions of planning, we shall shortly want to ask why that must be so.

At the same time that these formalized attempts were being made to discover our latent aims, the nation was buffeted by the revolt of the blacks, then by the revolt of the students, then by the widespread revolt against the war, more recently with a new consumerism and conservationism. All these movements were striking out at the underlying systemic processes of contemporary

American society. In a style rather different from those of the systems analysts and the Presidential commissioners, participants in these revolts were seeking to restructure t he value and goal systems that affect the distribution of social product and shape the directions of national policy.

Systems analysis, goals commissions, PPBS, social indicators, the several revolts, the poverty program, model cities, the current concerns with environmental quality and with the qualities of urban life, the search for new religions among contemporary youth, and the increasing attractiveness of the planning idea—all seem to be driven by a common quest. Each in its peculiar way is asking for a clarification of purposes, for a redefinition of problems, for a re-ordering of priorities to match stated purposes, for the design of new kinds of goal-directed actions, for a reorientation of the professions to the outputs of professional activities rather than to the inputs into them, and then for a redistribution of the outputs of governmental programs among the competing publics.

A deep-running current of optimism in American thought seems to have been propelling these diverse searches for direction-finding instruments. But at the same time, the Americans' traditional faith in a guaranteed Progress is being eroded by the same waves that are wearing down old beliefs in the social order's inherent goodness and in history's intrinsic benevolence. Candide is dead. His place is being occupied by a new conception of future history that, rejecting historicism, is searching for ways of exploiting the intellectual and inventive capabilities of men.

This belief comes in two quite contradictory forms. On the one hand, there is the belief in the "makeability," or unrestricted malleability, of future history by means of the planning intellect— by reasoning, rational discourse, and civilized negotiation. At the same time, there are vocal proponents of the "feeling approach," of compassionate engagement and dramatic action, even of a revival of mysticism, aiming at overcoming The System which is seen as the evil source of misery and suffering.

The Enlightenment may be coming to full maturity in the late 20th century, or it may be on its deathbed. Many Americans seem to believe both that we can perfect future history—that we can deliberately shape future outcomes to accord with

our wishes—and that there will be future history. Some have arrived at deep pessimism and some at resignation. To them, planning for large social systems has proved to be impossible without loss of liberty and equity. Hence, for them the ultimate goal of planning should be anarchy, because it should aim at the elimination of government over others. Still another group has arrived at the conclusion that liberty and equity are luxuries which cannot be afforded by a modern society, and that they should be substituted by "cybernetically feasible" values.

Professionalism has been understood to be one of the major instruments for perfectability, an agent sustaining the traditional American optimism. Based in modern science, each of the professions has been conceived as the medium through which the knowledge of science is applied. In effect, each profession has been seen as a subset of engineering. Planning and the emerging policy sciences are among the more optimistic of those professions. Their representatives refuse to believe that planning for betterment is impossible, however grave their misgivings about the appropriateness of past and present modes of planning. They have not abandoned the hope that the instruments of perfectability can be perfected. It is that view that we want to examine, in an effort to ask whether the social professions are equipped to do what they are expected to do.

II. PROBLEM DEFINITION

During the industrial age, the idea of planning, in common with the idea of professionalism, was dominated by the pervasive idea of *efficiency*. Drawn from 18th century physics, classic economics and the principle of least-means, efficiency was seen as a condition in which a specified task could be performed with low inputs of resources. That has been a powerful idea. It has long been the guiding concept of civil engineering, the scientific management movement, much of contemporary operations research; and it still pervades modern government and industry. When attached to the idea of planning, it became dominating there too. Planning was then seen as a process of designing problem-solutions that might be installed and operated cheaply. Because it was fairly easy to get consensus on the nature of problems during the early industrial period, the task could be assigned to the technically skilled, who in turn could be trusted to accomplish the simplified end-in-view. Or, in the more work-a-say setting, we could rely upon the efficiency expert to diagnose a problem and then solve it, while simultaneously reducing the resource inputs into whatever it was we were doing.

We have come to think about the planning task in very different ways in recent years. We have been learning to ask whether what we are doing is the *right* thing to do. That is to say, we have been learning to ask questions about the *outputs* of actions and to pose problem statements in valuative frameworks. We have been learning to see social processes as the links tying open systems into large and interconnected networks of systems, such that outputs from one become inputs to others. In that structural framework it has become less apparent where problem centers lie, and less apparent *where* and *how* we should intervene even if we do happen to know what aims we seek. We are now sensitized to the waves of repercussions generated by a problem-solving action directed to any one node in the network, and we are no longer surprised to find it inducing problems of greater severity at some other node. And so we have been forced to expand the boundaries of the systems we deal with, trying to internalize those externalities.

This was the professional style of the systems analysts, who were commonly seen as forbearers of the universal problem-solvers. With arrogant confidence, the early systems analysts pronounced themselves ready to take on anyone's perceived problem, diagnostically to discover its hidden character, and then, having exposed its true nature, skillfully to excise its root causes. Two decades of experience have worn the self-assurances thin. These analysts are coming to realize how valid their model really is, for they themselves have been caught by the very same diagnostic difficulties that troubled their clients.

By now we are all beginning to realize that one of the most intractable problems is that of defining problems (of knowing that distinguishes an observed condition from a desired condition) and of locating problems (finding where in the complex causal networks the trouble really lies). In turn, and equally intractable, is the problem of

identifying the actions that might effectively narrow the gap between what-is and what-ought-to-be. As we seek to improve the effectiveness of actions in pursuit of valued outcomes, as system boundaries get stretched, and as we become more sophisticated about the complex workings of open societal systems, it becomes ever more difficult to make the planning idea operational.

Many now have an image of *how* an *idealized* planning system would function. It is being seen as an on-going, cybernetic process of governance, incorporating systematic procedures for continuously searching out goals; identifying problems; forecasting uncontrollable contextual changes; inventing alternative strategies, tactics, and time-sequenced actions; stimulating alternative and plausible action sets and their consequences; evaluating alternatively forecasted outcomes; statistically monitoring those conditions of the publics and of systems that are judged to be germane; feeding back information to the simulation and decision channels so that errors can be corrected—all in a simultaneously functioning governing process. That set of steps is familiar to all of us, for it comprises what is by now the modern-classical model of planning. And yet we all know that such a planning system is unattainable, even as we seek more closely to approximate it. It is even questionable whether such a planning system is desirable.

III. PLANNING PROBLEMS ARE WICKED PROBLEMS

A great many barriers keep us from perfecting such a planning/governing system: theory is inadequate for decent forecasting; our intelligence is insufficient to our tasks; plurality of objectives held by pluralities of politics makes it impossible to pursue unitary aims; and so on. The difficulties attached to rationality are tenacious and we have so far been unable to get untangled from their web. This is partly because the classical paradigm of science and engineering—the paradigm that has underlain modern professionalism—is not applicable to the problems of open societal systems. One reason the publics have been attacking the social professions, we believe, is that the cognitive and occupational styles of the professions—mimicking the cognitive style of science and the occupational style of engineering—have just not worked on a wide array of social problems. The lay customers are complaining because planners and other professionals have not succeeded in solving the problems they claimed they could solve. We shall want to suggest that t he social professions were misled somewhere along the line into assuming they could be applied scientists— that they could solve problems in the ways scientists can solve their sorts of problems. The error has been a serious one.

The kinds of problems that planners deal with—societal problems—are inherently different from the problems that scientists and perhaps some classes of engineers deal with. Planning problems are inherently wicked.

As distinguished from problems in the natural sciences, which are definable and separable and may have solutions that are findable, the problems of governmental planning—and especially those of social or policy planning—are ill-defined; and they rely upon elusive political judgment for resolution. (Not "solution." Social problems are never solved. At best they are only re-solved—over and over again.) Permit us to draw a cartoon that will help clarify the distinction we intend.

The problems that scientists and engineers have usually focused upon are mostly "tame" or "benign" ones. As an example, consider a problem of mathematics, such as solving an equation; or the task of an organic chemist in analyzing the structure of some unknown compound; or that of the chess player attempting to accomplish checkmate in five moves. For each the mission is clear. It is clear, in turn, whether or not the problems have been solved.

Wicked problems, in contrast, have neither of these clarifying traits; and they include nearly all public policy issues—whether the question concerns the location of a freeway, the adjustment of a tax rate, the modification of school curricula, or the confrontation of crime.

There are at least en distinguishing properties of planning-type problems, i.e. wicked ones, that planners had better be alert to and which we shall comment upon in turn. As you will see, we are calling them "wicked" not because these properties are themselves ethically deplorable. We use the term "wicked" in a meaning akin to that of "malignant" (in contrast to "benign") or "vicious"

(like a circle) or "tricky" (like a leprechaun) or "aggressive" (like a lion, in contrast to the docility of a lamb). We do not mean to personify these properties of social systems by implying malicious intent. But then, you may agree that it becomes morally objectionable for the planner to treat a wicked problem as though it were a tame one, or to tame a wicked problem prematurely, or to refuse to recognize the inherent wickedness of social problems.

1. There is no definitive formulation of a wicked problem

For any given tame problem, an exhaustive formulation can be stated containing all the information the problem-solver needs for understanding and solving the problem—provided he knows his "art," of course.

This is not possible with wicked-problems. The information needed to *understand* the problem depends upon one's idea for *solving* it. That is to say: in order to *describe* a wicked-problem in sufficient detail, one has to develop and exhaustive inventory of all conceivable *solutions* ahead of time. The reason is that every question asking for additional information depends upon the understanding of the problem—and its resolution—at that time. Problem understanding and problem resolution are concomitant to each other. Therefore, in order to anticipate all questions (in order to anticipate all information required for resolution ahead of time), knowledge of all conceivable solutions is required.

Consider, for example, what would be necessary in identifying the nature of the poverty problem. Does poverty mean low income? Yes, in part. But what are the determinants of low income? Is it deficiency of the national and regional economies, or is it deficiencies of cognitive and occupational skills within the labor force? If the latter, the problem statement and the problem "solution" must encompass the educational processes. But, then, where within the educational system does the real problem lie? What then might it mean to "improve the educational system"? Or does the poverty problem reside in deficient physical and mental health? If so, we must add those etiologies to our information package, and search inside the health services for a plausible cause. Does it include cultural deprivation? spatial dislocation? problems of ego identity? deficient political and social skills?—and so on. If we can formulate the problem by tracing it to some sorts of sources—such that we can say, "aha! That's the locus of the difficulty," i.e. those are the root causes of the differences between the "is" and the "ought to be" conditions—then we have there-by also formulated a solution. To find the problem is thus the same thing as finding the solution; the problem can't be defined until the solution has been found.

The formulation of a wicked problem *is* the problem! The process of formulating the problem and of conceiving a solution (or re-solution) are identical, since every specification of the problem is a specification of the direction in which a treat-ment is considered. Thus, if we recognize defi-cient mental health services as part of the problem, then—trivially enough—"improvement of mental health services" is a specification of solution. If, as the next step, we declare the lack of community centers one deficiency of the mental health servic-es system, then "procurement of community cen-ters" is the next specification of solution. If it is inadequate treatment within community centers, then improved therapy training of staff may be the locus of solution, and so on.

This property sheds some light on the useful-ness of the famed "systems-approach" for treating wicked problems. The classical systems-approach of the military and the space programs is based on the assumption that a planning project can be organized into distinct phases. Every textbook of systems engineering starts with an enumeration of these phases "understand the problems or the mission," "gather information," "analyze infor-mation," "synthesize information and wait for the creative leap," "work out solution," or the like. For wicked problems, however, this type of scheme does not work. One cannot understand the problem without knowing about its context; one cannot meaningfully search for information without the orientation of a solution concept; one cannot first understand, then solve. The systems-approach "of the first generation" is inadequate for dealing with wicked-problems. Approaches of the "second generation" should be based on a model of planning as an argumentative process in the course of which an image of the problem and

of the solution emerges gradually among the par-ticipants, as a product on incessant judgment, sub-jected to critical argument. The methods of Operations Research play a prominent role in the systems-approach of the first generation; they become operational, however, only *after* the most important decisions have already been made, i.e. after the problem has already been tamed.

Take an optimization model. Here the inputs needed include the definition of the solution space, the system of constraints, and the perform-ance measure as a function of the planning and contextual variables. But setting up and con-straining the solution space and constructing the measure of performance is the wicked part of the problem. Very unlikely it is more essential than the remaining steps of searching for a solution which is optimal relative to the measure of per-formance and the constraint system.

2. Wicked problems have no stopping rule

In solving a chess problem or a mathematical equation, the problem-solver knows when he has done his job. There are criteria that tell when *the* or *a* solution has been found.

Not so with planning problems. Because (according to Proposition 1) the process of solving the problem is identical with the process of under-standing its nature, because there are no criteria for sufficient understanding and because there are no ends to the causal chains that link interacting open systems, the would-be planner can always try to do better. Some additional investment of effort might increase the chances of finding a bet-ter solution.

The planner terminates work on a wicked problem, not for reasons inherent in the "logic" of the problem. He stops for considerations that are external to the problem: he runs out of time, or money, or patience. He finally says, "That's good enough," or "This is the best I can do within the limitations of the project," or "I like this solution," etc.

3. Solutions to wicked problems are not true-or-false, but good-or-bad

There are conventialized criteria for objectively deciding whether the offered solution to an equa-tion or whether the proposed structural formula of a chemical compound is correct or false. They can be independently checked by other qualified persons who are familiar with the established criteria; and the answer will be normally unambiguous.

For wicked planning problems, there are no true or false answers. Normally, many parties are equally equipped, interested, and/or entitled to judge the solutions, although none has the power to set formal decision rules to determine correctness. Their judgments are likely to differ widely to accord with their group or personal interests, their special value-sets, and their ideological predilections. Their assessments of proposed solutions are expressed as "good" or "bad" or, more likely, as "better or worse" or "satisfying" or "good enough."

4. There is no immediate and no ultimate test of a solution to a wicked problem

For tame-problems one can determine on the spot how good a solution-attempt has been. More accurately, the test of a solution is entirely under the control of the few people who are involved and interested in the problem.

With wicked problems, on the other hand, any solutions, after being implemented, will generate waves of consequences over an extended—virtually an unbounded—period of time. Moreover, the next day's consequences of the solution may yield utterly undesirable repercussions which outweigh the intended advantages or the advantages accomplished hitherto. In such cases, one would have been better off if the plan had never been carried out.

The full consequences cannot be appraised until the waves of repercussions have completely run out, and we have no way of tracing *all* the waves through *all* the affected lives ahead of time or within a limited time span.

5. Every solution to a wicked problem is a "one-shot operation"; because there is no opportunity to learn by trial-and-error, every attempt counts significantly

In the sciences and in fields like mathematics, chess, puzzle-solving or mechanical engineering design, the problem-solver can try various runs without penalty. Whatever his outcome on these individual experimental runs, it doesn't matter

much to the subject-system or to the course of societal affairs. A lost chess game is seldom consequential for other chess games or for non-chess-players.

With wicked planning problems, however, *every* implemented solution is consequential. It leaves "traces" that cannot be undone. One cannot build a freeway to see how it works, and then easily correct it after unsatisfactory performance. Large public-works are effectively irreversible, and the consequences they generate have long half-loves. Many people's lives will have been irreversibly influenced, and large amounts of money will have been spent—another irreversible act. The same happens with most other large-scale public works and with virtually all public-service programs. The effects of an experimental curriculum will follow the pupils into their adult lives.

Whenever actions are effectively irreversible and whenever the half-lives of the consequences are long, *every trial counts*. And every attempt to reverse a decision or to correct for the undesired consequences poses another set of wicked problems, which are in turn subject to the same dilemmas.

6. Wicked problems do not have an enumerable (or an exhaustively describable) set of potential solutions, nor is there a well-described set of permissible operations that may be incorporated into the plan

There are no criteria which enable one to prove that all solutions to a wicked problem have been identified and considered.

It may happen than *no* solution is found, owing to logical inconsistencies in the "picture" of the problem. (For example, the problem-solver may arrive at a problem description requiring that both *A* and not-*A* should happen at the same time.) Or it might result from his failing to develop an idea f or solution (which does not mean that someone else might be more successful). But normally, in the pursuit of a wicked planning problem, a host of potential solutions arises; and another host is never thought up. It is then a matter of *judgment* whether one should try to enlarge the available set or not. And it is, of course, a matter of judgment which of these solutions should be pursued and implemented.

Chess has a finite set of rules, accounting for all situations that can occur. In mathematics, the tool chest of operations I also explicit; so, too, although less rigorously, in chemistry.

But not so in the world of social policy. Which strategies-or-moves are permissible in dealing with crime in the streets, for example, have been enumerated nowhere. "Anything goes," or at least, any new idea for a planning measure may become a serious candidate for a re-solution: What should we do to reduce street crime? Should we disarm the police, as they do in England, since even criminals are less likely to shoot unarmed men? Or repeal the laws that define crime, such as those that make marijuana use a criminal act or those that make car theft a criminal act? That would reduce crime by changing definitions. Try moral rearmament and substitute ethical self-control for police and court control? Shoot all criminals and thus reduce the numbers who commit crime? Give away free loot to would-be-thieves, and so reduce the incentive to crime? And so on.

In such fields of ill-defined problems and hence ill-definable solutions, the set of feasible plans of action relies on realistic judgment, the capability to appraise "exotic" ideas and on the amount of trust and credibility between planner and clientele that will lead to the conclusion, "OK let's try that."

7. Every wicked problem is essentially unique

Of course, for any two problems at least one distinguishing property can be found (just as any number of properties can be found which they share in common), and each of them is therefore unique in a trivial sense. But by *"essentially unique:* we mean that, despite long lists of similarities between a current problem and a previous one, there always might be an additional distinguishing property that is of overriding importance. Part of the art of dealing with wicked problems is the art of not knowing too early which type of solution to apply.

There are no *classes* of wicked problems in the sense that principles of solution can be developed to fit *all* members of a class. In mathematics there are rules for classifying families of problems—say, of solving a class of equations—whenever a certain, quite-well-specified set of characteristics matches the problem. There are explicit characteristics of tame problems that define similarities among them, in such fashion that the same set of techniques is likely to be effective on all of them.

Despite seeming similarities among wicked problems, one can never be *certain* that the particulars of a problem do not override its commonalities with other problems already dealt with.

The conditions in a city constructing a subway may look similar to the conditions in San Francisco, say; but planners would be ill-advised to transfer the San Francisco solutions directly. Differences in commuter habits or residential patterns may far outweigh similarities in subway layout, downtown layout and the rest. In the more complex world of social policy planning, every situation is likely to be one-of-a-kind. If we are right about that, the direct transference of the physical-science and engineering thoughtways into social policy might be dysfunctional, i.e. positively harmful. "Solutions" might be applied seemingly familiar problems which are quite incompatible with them.

8. Every wicked problem can be considered to be a symptom of another problem

Problems can be described as discrepancies between the state of affairs as it is and the state as it ought to be. The process of resolving the problem starts with the search for causal explanation of the discrepancy. Removal of that cause poses another problem of which the original problem is a "symptom." In turn, it can be considered the symptom of still another, "higher level" problem. Thus "crime in the streets" can be considered as a symptom of general moral decay, or permissiveness, or deficient opportunity, or wealth, or poverty, or whatever causal explanation you happen to like best. The level at which a problem is settled depends upon the self-confidence of the analyst and cannot be decided on logical grounds. There is nothing like a natural level of a wicked problem. Of course, the higher the level of a problem's formulation, the broader and more general it becomes: and the more difficult it becomes to do something about it. On the other hand, one should not try to cure symptoms: and therefore one should try to settle the problem on as high a level as possible.

Here lies a difficulty with incrementalism, as well. This doctrine advertises a policy of small steps, in the hope of contributing systematically to overall improvement. If, however, the problem is attached on too low a level (an increment), then success of resolution may result in making things worse, because it may become more difficult to deal with the higher problems. Marginal improvement does not guarantee overall improvement. For example, computerization of an administrative process may result in reduced cost, ease of operation, etc. But at the same time it becomes more difficult to incur structural changes in the organization, because technical perfection reinforces organizational patterns and normally increases the cost of change. The newly acquired power of the controllers of information may then deter later modifications of their roles.

Under these circumstances it is not surprising that the members of an organization tend to see the problems on a level below their own level. If you ask a police chief what the problems of the police are, he is likely to demand better hardware.

9. The existence of a discrepancy representing a wicked problem can be explained in numerous ways. The choice of explanation determines the nature of the problem's resolution

"Crime in the streets" can be explained by not enough police, by too many criminals, by inadequate laws, too many police, cultural deprivation, deficient opportunity, too many guns, phrenologic aberrations, etc. Each of these offers a direction for attacking crime in the streets. Which one is right? There is no rule or procedure to determine the "correct" explanation or combination of them. The reason is that in dealing with wicked problems there are several more ways of refuting a hypothesis than there are permissible in the sciences.

The mode of dealing with conflicting evidence that is customary in science is as follows: "Under conditions C and assuming the validity of hypothesis H, effect E must occur. Now, given C, E does not occur. Consequently H is to be refuted." In the context of wicked problems, however, further modes are admissible: one can deny that the effect E has not occurred, or one can explain the nonoc-

currence of E by intervening processes without having to abandon H. Here's an example: Assume that somebody chooses to explain crime in the streets by "not enough police." This is made the basis of a plan, and the size of the police force is increased. Assume further that in the subsequent years there is an increased number of arrests, but an increase of offenses at a rate slightly lower than the increase of GNP. Has the effect E occurred? Has crime in the streets been reduced by increasing the police force? If the answer is no, several nonscientific explanations may be tried in order to rescue the hypothesis H ("Increasing the police force reduces crime in the streets"): "If we had not increased the number of officers, the increase in crime would have been even greater;" "This case is an exception from rule H because there was an irregular influx of criminal elements;" "Time is too short to feel the effects yet;" etc. But also the answer "Yes, E has occurred" can be defended: "The number of arrests was increased," etc.

In dealing with wicked problems, the modes of reasoning used in the argument are much richer than those permissible in the scientific discourse. Because of the essential uniqueness of the problem (see Proposition 7) and lacking opportunity for rigorous experimentation (see Proposition 5), it is not possible to put H to a crucial test.

That is to say, the choice of explanation is arbitrary in the logical sense. In actuality, attitudinal criteria guide the choice. People choose those explanations which are most plausible to them. Somewhat but no much exaggerated, you might say that everybody picks that explanation of a discrepancy which fits his intentions best and which conforms to the action-prospects that are available to him. The analyst's "world view" is the strongest determining factor in explaining a discrepancy and, therefore, in resolving a wicked problem.

10. The planner has no right to be wrong

As Karl Popper argues in *The Logic of Scientific Discovery*,[4] it is a principle of science that solutions to problems are only hypotheses offered for refutation. This habit is based on the insight that there are no proofs to hypotheses, only potential refutations. The more a hypothesis withstands numerous attempts at refutation, the better its "corroboration" is considered to be. Consequently, the scientific community does not blame its members for postulating hypotheses that are later refuted—so long as the author abides by the rules of the game, of course.

In the world of planning and wicked problems no such immunity is tolerated. Here the aim is not to find the truth, but to improve some characteristics of the world where people live. Planners are liable for the consequences of the actions they generate; the effects can matter a great deal to those people that are touched by those actions.

We are thus led to conclude that t he problems that planners must deal with are wicked and incorrigible ones, for they defy efforts to delineate their boundaries and to identify their causes, and thus to expose their problematic nature. The planner who works with open systems is caught up in the ambiguity of their causal webs. Moreover, his would-be solutions are confounded by a still further set of dilemmas posed by the growing pluralism of the contemporary publics, whose valuations of his proposals are judged against an array of different and contradicting scales. Let us turn to these dilemmas next.

IV. THE SOCIAL CONTEXT

There was a time during the 'Fifties when the quasi-sociological literature was predicting a Mass Society—foreseen as a rather homogeneously shared culture in which most persons would share values and beliefs, would hold to common aims, would follow similar life-styles, and thus would behave in similar ways. (You will recall the popular literature on suburbia of ten years ago.) It is now apparent that those forecasts were wrong.

Instead, the high-scale societies of the Western world are becoming increasingly heterogeneous. They are becoming increasingly differentiated, comprising thousands of minority groups, *each* joined around common interests, common value systems, and shared stylistic preferences that differ from those of other groups. As the sheer volume of information and knowledge increases, as technological developments further expand the range of options, and as awareness of the liberty to deviate and differentiate spreads, more variations are *possible*. Rising affluence, or, even more, grow-

ing desire for at least subcultural identity induces groups to exploit those options and to invent new ones. We almost dare say that irregular cultural permutations are becoming the rule. We have come to realize that the melting pot never worked for large numbers of immigrants to America, [5] and that the unitary conception of "*The* American Way of Life" is now giving way to a recognition that there are numerous ways of life that are also American.

It was *pre*-industrial society that was culturally homogeneous. The industrial age greatly expanded cultural diversity. Post-industrial society is likely to be far more differentiated than any in all of past history.

It is still too early to know whether the current politicization of subpublics is going to be a long-run phenomenon or not. One could write scenarios that would be equally plausible either way. But one thing is clear: large population size will mean that small minorities can comprise large numbers of people; and, as we have been seeing, even small minorities can swing large political influence.

In a setting in which a plurality of publics is politically pursuing a diversity of goals, how is the larger society to deal with its wicked problems in a planful way? How are goals to be set, when the valuative bases are so diverse? Surely a unitary conception of *a* unitary "public welfare" is an anachronistic one.

We do not even have a theory that tells us how to find out what might be considered a societally best state. We have no theory that tells us what distribution of the social product is best—whether those outputs are expressed in the coinage of money income, information income, cultural opportunities, or whatever. We have come to realize that the concept of *the* social product is not very meaningful; possibly there is no aggregate measure for the welfare of a highly diversified society, if this measure is claimed to be objective and non-partisan. Social science has simply been unable to uncover a social-welfare function that would suggest which decisions would contribute to a societally best state. Instead, we have had to rely upon the axioms of individualism that underlie economic and political theory, deducing, in effect, that the *larger-public* welfare derives from summation of individualistic choices. And yet, we know that *this* is not necessarily so, as our current experience with air pollution has dramatized.

We also know that many societal processes have the character of zero-sum games. As the population becomes increasingly pluralistic, inter-group differences are likely to be reflected as inter-group rivalries of the zero-sum sorts. If they do, the prospects for inventing positive non-zero sum development strategies would become increasingly difficult.

Perhaps we can illustrate. A few years ago there was nearly universal consensus in American that full-employment, high productivity, and widespread distribution of consumer durables fitted into a development strategy in which all would be winters. That consensus is now being eroded. Now, when substitutes for wages are being disbursed to the poor, the college student, and the retired, as well as to the more traditional recipient of nonwage incomes, our conceptions of "employment" and of a full-employment economy are having to be revised. Now, when it is recognized that raw materials that enter the economy end up as residuals polluting the air mantle and the rivers, many are becoming wary of rising manufacturing production. And, when some of the new middle-class religions are exorcising worldly goods in favor of less tangible communal "goods," the consumption-oriented society is being challenged—oddly enough, to be sure, by those who were reared in its affluence.

What was once a clear-cut win-win strategy, that had the status of a near-truism, has now become a source of contentious differences among subpublics.

Or, if these illustrations seem to be posed at too high a level of generality, consider the sorts of inter-group conflicts imbedded in urban renewal, roadway construction, or curriculum design in the public schools. Our observation is not only that values are changing. That is true enough, and the probabilities of parametric changes are large enough to humble even the most perceptive observer of contemporary norms. Our point, rather, is that diverse values are held by different groups of individuals—that what satisfied one may be abhorrent to another, that what comprises problem-solution for one is problem-generation for another. Under such circumstances, and in the absence of an overriding social theory or an over-

riding social ethic, there is no gainsaying which group is right and which should have its ends served.

One traditional approach to the reconciliation of social values and individual choice is to entrust *de facto* decision-making to the wise and knowledgeable professional experts and politicians. But whether one finds that ethically tolerable or not, we hope we have made it clear that even such a tactic only begs the question, for there are no value-free, true-false answers to any of the wicked problems governments must deal with. To substitute expert professional judgment for those of contending political groups may make the rationales and the repercussions more explicit, but it would no necessarily make the outcomes better. The one-best answer is possible with tame problems, but not with wicked ones.

Another traditional approach to the reconciliation of social values and individual choice is to bias in favor of the latter. Accordingly, one would promote widened differentiation of goods, services, environments, and opportunities, such that individuals might more closely satisfy their individual preferences. Where large-system problems are generated, he would seek to ameliorate the effects that he judges most deleterious. Where latent opportunities become visible, he would seek to exploit them. Where positive non-zero-sum developmental strategies can be designed, he would of course work hard to install them.

Whichever the tactic, though, it should be clear that the expert is also the player in a political game, seeking to promote his private vision of goodness over others'. Planning is a component of politics. There is no escaping that truism.

We are also suggesting that none of these tactics will answer the difficult questions attached to the sorts of wicked problems planners must deal with. We have neither a theory that can locate societal goodness, nor one that might dispel wickedness, nor one that might resolve the problems of equity that rising pluralism is provoking. We are inclined to think that these theoretic dilemmas may be the most wicked conditions that confront us.

NOTES

1. Charles J. Hitch, "On the Choice of Objectives in Systems Studies" (Santa Monica,

California: The RAND Corporation, 1960; P-1955), p. 19.

    2. The report was published by Spectrum Books, Prentice-Hall, 1960.

    3. At the same time to be sure, counter voices—uncomfortable to many—were claiming that the "nation's direction" presents no meaningful reference system at all, owing to the worldwide character of the problems and the overspill of crises across national boundaries.

    4. Science Editions, New York, 1961.

    5. See an early sign of this growing realization in Nathan Glazer and Daniel Patrick Moynihan, *Beyond the Melting Pot* (Cambridge: Harvard and MIT Presses, 1963).

SUGGESTED READINGS FOR PART I

Bolan, Richard S. "Community Decision Behavior: The Culture of Planning," *Journal of the American Institute of Planners*, Vol. 35, No. 5, September 1969, pp. 301-310.

Bolan, Richard S. " Emerging Views of Planning," *Journal of the American Institute of Planners*, Vol. 33, No. 4, July 1967, pp. 233-245.

Boyer, Christine. 1983. *Dreaming the Rational City.* Cambridge: M.I.T.

Burchell, Robert W. and George Sternlieb. 1978. *Planning Theory in the 1980s.* New Brunswick: Center for Urban Policy Research.

Davidoff, Paul and Reiner, Thomas A. "A Choice Theory of Planning," *Journal of the American Institute of Planners*, Vol. 28, No. 2, May 1962, pp.103-115.

Dyckman, J.W. "Planning and Decision Theory," *Journal of the American Institute of Planners*, Vol. 27, No. 4, November 1961, pp. 335-345.

Dyckman, J. W. "The Practical Uses of Planning Theory," *Journal of the American Institute of Planners*, Vol. 35, No. 5, 1969, pp. 298-301.

Faludi, Andreas, ed. 1973. *A Reader in Planning Theory.* New York: Pergamon.

Galloway, Thomas D. and Riad C. Mahayni.. "Planning Theory in Retrospect: The Process of Paradigm Change," *Journal of the American Institute of Planners*, Vol. 43, No. 1, 1977, pp. 62-71.

Hall, Peter. 1975. *Urban and Regional Planning.* New York: Wiley.

Hall, Peter. 1988. *Cities of Tomorrow: An Intellectual History of City Planning in the Twentieth Century.* Oxford, UK: Blackwell.

Harris, Britton. "The Limits of Science and Humanism in Planning," *Journal of the American Institute of Planners*, Vol. 33, No. 5, September 1967, pp. 324-335.

Harris, Britton. "Plan or Projection: An Examination of the Use of Models in Planning," *Journal of the America Institute of Planners*, Vol. 26, No. 4, November 1960, pp. 365-272.

Hudson, Barclay. "Comparison of Current Planning Theories," *Journal of the American Planning Association*, Vol. 45, No. 4, 1979.

Klosterman, Richard E. "Arguments for and against Planning," *Town Planning Review*, Vol. 56, No. 1, 1985, pp. 5- 20.

Krieger, Martin H. "Some New Directions for Planning Theories," *Journal of the American Institute of Planners*, Vol. 40, No. 3, 1974, pp. 156-163.

Krueckeberg, Donald A. 1983. *Introduction to Planning History in the United States.* New Brunswick, NJ: Center for Urban Policy Research.

Krumholz, Norman. "A Retrospective View of Equity Planning: Cleveland 1969-1979," *Journal of the American Planning Association*, Vol. 48, No. 2, Spring 1982.

Lee, Douglass B., Jr. "Requiem for Large-Scale Models," *Journal of the American Institute of Planners*, Vol. 39. No. 3, May 1973, pp. 163-178.

Lucy, William H. "If Planning Includes Too Much, Maybe It Should Include More," *Journal of the American Planning Association*, Vol. 60, No. 3, Summer 1994, pp. 305-318.

Mandelbaum, Seymour J. "Historians and Planners: The Construction of Pasts and Futures," *Journal of the American Planning Association*, Vol. 51, No. 2, Spring, 1985, pp. 185-188.

Mumford, Lewis. 1938. *The Culture of Cities.* New York: Harcourt, Inc.

Mumford, Lewis. 1945. *City Development.* New York: Harcourt, Inc.

Mumford, Lewis. 1967. *The Myth of the Machine: The Penetration of Power.* New York: Harcourt, Inc.

Mumford, Lewis. 1968. *The Urban Prospect*. New York: Harcourt, Inc.

Schuyler, David. 1986. *The New Urban Landscape*. Baltimore: Johns Hopkins.

Scott, Mel. 1969. *American City Planning*. Berkeley: University of California Press.

Warner, Sam Bass. 1976. Street Car Suburbs: The Process of Growth in Boston. New York: Atheneum.

II
Comprehensive Planning, Land Use and Growth Management

The Goals of Comprehensive Planning

Alan Altschuler

Copyright: Reprinted with permission from the *Journal of the American Institute of Planners*, 31, 3, 1965 ©, pp. 186-197.

Alan Altschuler is interested in examining the political and administrative issues inherent in planning and land-use decisions in American cities. He focuses on how planners make difficult professional and value choices. Based on case studies of planning in Minneapolis and St. Paul, Minnesota, this selection is concerned with how planners define the public interest and engage in community goal conception. Altshuler argues that for planning to be successful, goal premises must be established in a politically compelling manner.

THE IDEAL OF COMPREHENSIVE PLANNING

Those who consider themselves comprehensive planners typically claim that their most important functions are (1) to create a master plan to guide the deliberations of specialist planners, (2) to evaluate the proposals of specialist planners in the light of the master plan, and (3) to coordinate the planning of specialist agencies so as to ensure that their proposals reinforce each other to further the public interest. Each of these functions requires for ideal performance that the comprehensive planners (a) understand the overall public interest, at least in connection with the subject matter of their plans, and (b) that they possess causal knowledge which enables them to gauge the approximate net effect of proposed actions on the public interest.

This chapter is concerned with some ways in which city planners have approached the former of these two requirements, which—contrary to most students of planning—consider the more interesting one. If comprehensive planners deal with a great many more areas of public policies than specialists, their factual and causal knowledge in each area is bound to appear shallow—at least by comparison with that of the specialists in it. Hence their claims to comprehensiveness, if they are to be persuasive, must refer primarily to a special knowledge of the public interest.

Every government planner of integrity, no matter how specialized, must be guided by some conception of the public interest. And since plans are proposals of concerted action to achieve goals, each must express his conception as a goal or series of goals for his community. He will probably conceive these goals, of course, as constantly shifting rather than highly stable, as always intermediate rather than final, and as more in the nature of criteria than of concrete destinations. Community goal conceptions are likely to have these characteristics because of the limitations on collective human foresight and imagination. Nonetheless it is impossible to plan without some sense of community goals, call them what you will.[1] Moreover, for the planning process in any community to be democratic—and I assume in these pages that it should be—the goals must win approval from a democratic political process; they must not be goals simply prescribed for the community by planners.

In this chapter we shall examine a few of the difficulties that face planners as they strive to determine community goals democratically. In the next two chapters we shall deal with the difficulties they face as they try to concert action.

IMPLICATIONS OF THE IDEAL

The comprehensive planner must assume that his community's various collective goals can somehow be measured at least roughly as to importance and welded into a single hierarchy of community objectives. In addition, he must argue that technicians like himself can prescribe courses of action to achieve these objectives without great distortion or harmful side-effects of a magnitude sufficient to outweigh the gains achieved through planning. We may conceive a continuum of faith in the feasibility and desirability of comprehensive planning. The "ideal type" defender of comprehensive planning would contend that a serious effort should be made to plan in detail the future evolution of all important economic and social patterns. Others would limit their support to the planning-in-general-outline of change in particular strategic variables.

Those who contend that comprehensive planning should play a large role in the future evolution of societies must argue that the common interests of society's members are their most important interests and constitute a large proportion of all their interests. They must assert that conflicts of interest in society are illusory, that they are about minor matters, or that they can be foreseen and resolved in advance by just arbiters (planners) who understand the total interests of all parties. Those who claim that comprehensive planning should play a large part in the future evolution of any particular economic or societal feature have to assume similar propositions with regard to conflicts of interest likely to arise in connection with it.

To the extent, then, that comprehensive planning is possible, the correct law for a society is something to be discovered, rather than willed, by public officials. The role of the politician who ignores consistency or obstructs grand schemes to placate interest groups is hard to defend. So is the concept of majority will, and the idea that party conflict is desirable. It is in this sense that the claims of planners often seem to be in conflict with those of politicians. Both claim a unique ability to judge the overall public interest. The politician's claim rests on his popular election, his knowledge of the community, his sensitivity to human needs, and his personal wisdom. The planner's claim is one of professionalism and research. If it seems somewhat devoid of human warmth, it also sounds more authoritative, more precise, more modern. As will be seen shortly, I have no wish to imply that city planners and politicians must (or, indeed, invariably do) defend their work on the basis of conflicting assumptions. It may well be that the capacities of planners and politicians are, for many purposes, suited to complement each other. Here we are not discussing everything that men called planners do, but rather some implications of the concept "comprehensiveness" in planning.

Few sophisticated American defenders of planning, certainly, believe that any group of planners can achieve a total comprehensiveness of perspective on any issue. Many do believe, however, that professional planners can come closer to achieving it on numerous vital issues than other participants in the urban decision process. The primary purpose of this chapter is to explore the theoretical foundations of this belief. It should be noted, however, that the explicit claims of practicing planners often seem to suggest that a fair approximation of genuine comprehensiveness is currently attainable. The case studies in this volume provide a number of illustrations.

CASE STUDY ILLUSTRATIONS

In his introduction to the *St. Paul Land Use Plan*, for example, Herbert Weiland, the St. Paul planning director, described his conception of the planning function in these words:

The total city planning process, of which land-use planning is but one part, involves a continuing program of deriving, organizing, and presenting a comprehensive plan for the development and renewal of [the city].... The plans must be economically feasible, and must promote the common good, and at the same time [must] preserve the rights and interests of the individual.

Long discussions with every planner involved in the preparation of the St. Paul plan persuaded me that these words were meant literally. City planning was comprehensive and for the common good, not for any lesser objectives.

Several members of the St. Paul planning staff were highly critical of C. David Locks, Weiland's predecessor, for having offered advice freely to operating agencies without first developing a comprehensive plan. Locks himself, however, had also conceived his responsibilities broadly, though he had not considered the time ripe for explicitly comprehensive planning during most of his tenure. He had written in the Planning Board's 1957 publication, *The Proposed Freeways for St. Paul*, for example, that while others had considered the cost of freeways and their effect on traffic, the Planning Board had "special responsibilities posed by virtue of its function and status as an advisory representative citizen's group concerned with the development of all facets of the community's life."[2]

In considering the development of Ancker Hospital, politicians turned finally to city planners to interpret the overall public interest. First the city planners in the St. Paul Housing and Redevelopment Authority, and eventually those in the City Planning Bureau as well, accepted the challenge with confidence. When interviewed, both groups of planners stated without hesitation that they were better equipped to interpret the public interest than the consultant hospital architect, whose primary concern was how best to build a hospital. They believed that because their perspective was broader, their recommendation was highly likely to be wiser, or more rational.[3]

In formulating the *Central Minneapolis Plan*, Rodney Engelen, with the full support of Planning Director Irvin, cast his arguments in the broadest possible terms. The operational goal of the Plan was clearly a limited one: economic growth. Engelen, however, felt that he had to justify the goal itself. He stressed the functions of downtown as bearer of culture, disseminator of news and ideas, haven for unique activities, supplier of taxes to support all public services, and so on. When interviewed, he emphasized that his concern way to enrich the lives of all citizens, not to line the pockets of downtown businessmen. It was merely fortuitous, he believed, that in this case the interests of property owners and those of society coincided. He realized that on many subjects this coincidence did not exist, or was not perceived, and that in such cases the political implementation of the public interest might be impossible.

Engelen admitted freely that no plan or evaluation could be entirely comprehensive, as did all the planners interviewed for this study when pressed. His (and their) disclaimer was perfunctory, however, as if only a minor detail were at stake. Engelen wrote, for example, that the *Central Minneapolis Plan* could not truly be termed comprehensive because "there are and will always be elements—new aspects—yet to be studied and yet to be decided upon." He thus rejected a conception of comprehensiveness that I have suggested is useless: i.e., that the comprehensive plan should deal with everything. In short, he admitted that the object of any decision is necessarily limited, at very least in time, but he preserved the implication that the planner's approach—i.e., his goal orientation—to the object may be comprehensive.

THE SEARCH FOR PLANNING GOALS

All Twin Cities planners agreed that community goals could in the final analysis be discovered only through public discussion. Planners might propose alternative articulations, but goal statements could have no claim to represent community thought unless the community or its legitimate representatives ratified them after serious discussion and deliberation. In theory the primary problem was to guide the discussion and to decide when it had gone on long enough. The primary problem in practice, it developed, was to get a discussion going.

St. Paul's planners hoped, for example, that vigorous discussion would follow publication of their *Land Use Plan*. No one showed any interest in discussing it, however. The reason seemed to be that the *Plan*'s stated goals were too general. No one knew how the application of these goals would affect him in practice. Those who were not completely uninterested in the *Plan* had learned long ago to be suspicious of high-sounding generalities. The planners had not succeeded in showing opinion leaders the relationship between the *Plan*'s stated general goals and its great mass of "standards," or more specific goals. As a result, nonplanners decided with uncoordinated unanimity to ignore the *Plan* until someone proposed specific applications of it. Only at this point, they felt, would there by anything comprehensible—whether or not comprehensible—to argue about.

Minneapolis planners argued that the St. Paul planners' premises were wrong, and would have been wrong even if discussion of their plan had developed. For a discussion truly to influence the planning process, they said, it had to begin before detailed planning got under way. In their view, no one could effectively interpolate changes into a plan after it was complete without upsetting its internal harmony. If one of the goals of a plan were changed, then in theory every specific recommendation should be altered to some extent. No one had the time or intellectual energy to do this when a plan had already taken definite shape, however. The crucial phase in the evolution of any plan, then, was the development of its first draft. Goals should be determined before this phase moved far along.

Minneapolis planners themselves tried to obtain approval for planning goals before developing their central area plan. They decided at the start that they needed a goal statement which would be both "operational" and acceptable to all "reasonable" citizens of the city. By "operational," they meant that progress toward the goal could be objectively measured, and that the broad costs, both tangible and spiritual, of striving toward it could be foreseen. Comprehensive goals, they judged, could not be operational. Therefore, reasonable men could not pass on them intelligently. It followed that goals could win intelligent public approval only if they were partial. The question was: *how* partial? Perhaps it was possible to articulate, and plan to achieve, highly general goals even if not truly comprehensive ones.

They endeavored to bring about a public discussion of essential goal options before preparing the detailed plan. Fortunately, planners and planning consultants throughout the nation had applied themselves to downtown problems in recent years, and had developed a more or less integrated theory explaining characteristic downtown problems. Consequently, Minneapolis planners were able to present their preferred goals with tightly reasoned arguments behind them. The parts were related and mutually reinforcing. The man of affairs with a limited amount of time could quickly grasp the objectives and the main lines of reasoning on which there commendations were based. The most general operational goal that the planners proposed was "the economic growth of downtown." They recognized that this goal was itself deceptive, however, in that although it sounded noncontroversial the steps necessary to its accomplishment could not keep from being controversial. in their publications on downtown planning goals, therefore, they chose to emphasize what they termed "design goals." These were in fact *types* of projects—rather than project proposals for specific streets and blocks in Minneapolis—that had been tried in other cities. The planners tried to explain the relationship between these *types* of proposals and the economic problems facing urban downtowns in the current period. It was possible to discuss the types of dislocation that might be expected, and so on, without bringing in specific project proposals. The discussion was really a model of comprehensible argument in favor of middle-range (i.e., operational but still general) planning goals. I strongly

doubt that existing theory was sufficiently developed to support comparable justifications of goal recommendations in any other area of city planning activity.[4]

Even in this area, however, the specific financial costs and unintended side effects that would arise on application in Minneapolis were difficult to foresee. Any intelligent discussion of planning goals had to take these (or their unpredictability) into account. For the discussion to be fully useful, the planners judged, its participants had to be willing to inform themselves about planning detail at some significant expenditure of time and effort. The discussion had to continue throughout the planning process, which itself would have peaks of activity but no final termination. Since the overall goal was partial, the discussants had to be urged to consider the full complexity of its side-effects. This they could not do if they confined themselves to examination of the central economic reasoning behind the "design goals."

The first problem was how to find discussants. The comprehensive planner's search is more complicated than that of any specialist. He cannot be satisfied to consult a narrow constituency. Presumably he should understand every important goal of each of society's members. If he must deal with groups rather than individuals he should not limit himself to constellations of interest that maintain permanent formal organizations. But the planners knew of no way to approach the city's "potential" groups. These would not become actual groups unless some immediate threats activated their potential members; some potential groupings of interests that the observer might identify would not become actual even then. Even those in the first category, however, had no leaders to speak for them. The abstract discussion of goals could seldom seem sufficiently immediate to spur them to organize and choose representatives. It seemed that in no other public endeavor than general goal determination was the disproportion greater between the number of groups that *might* reasonably become involved and the number that *would*.

The planners soon found that they could carry on a continuing discussion only with men whose jobs required them to spend time on the study and discussion of civic affairs. Only a few organizations in the city had such men on their payrolls.

All of these fit into a few categories. Most were large downtown business firms or organizations of businessmen. A few good government groups (supported mainly by the contributions of businesses or businessmen) had representatives who took an interest in city planning, but for the most part they were in the same position as planners: they could talk abstractly about the public interest but they could not claim any special qualifications to represent particular interests. The other permanent organizations in the city did not bother to have representatives spending the bulk of their time observing civic affairs. Each had a few continuing interests (racial issues, taxes, city hiring policy, etc.) and became politically active only when immediate threats to these arose.

Making the best of this situation, the planners tried to carry on a discussion of goals with the professional "civic affairs" representatives of downtown business. These professional discussants, however, lacked the power to commit their firms to anything; consequently, as the discussion became more specific they became more and more noncommittal. The businessmen who had the power to commit their firms to specific courses of action had neither the time nor interest to engage in almost endless discussion with the city planners. In a short while, even the professional discussants found that they had no time to study each tentative planning formulation with care. Thus, a major difficulty was revealed. Even had the planners been able to handle all the complexity of life, they would not have found laymen willing or able to evaluate their work.[5]

If it can be so difficult to spur well-informed discussion even of such limited goals as those of the *Central Minneapolis Plan*, the question necessarily arises: what should be considered an adequate discussion of planning goals? Was the discussion in this case adequate although its only participants were businessmen whose interest in the discussion was mild and who were concerned only with direct economic costs and consequences? One might say that it was, because other groups could have entered the discussion to raise additional points had they wished. I did not find any elected officials in Minneapolis, however, who accepted this reasoning. Most were rather inarticulate about their objections, but a few were able to state their views quite precisely.

Downtown businesses are, according to these objectors, "organizations in being." Their owners are accustomed to watching the civic scene and searching for issues likely to affect their interests. They enter the discussion of any proposal at a very early stage and understand its potential impact on their interests relatively early. Other members of the public, however, tend to became aware that something is afoot and then to conceptualize their interests more slowly. After the perception begins to dawn, most take quite some time to organize. The range in the amount of time, and in the degree of immediacy of a threat or opportunity, that it takes to move different types of people with potential interest in a proposal to the threshold of organizational expression is enormous. Government never moves slowly enough or poses issues clearly enough to give everyone his say. It is fair to assume, however, that only when government moves at a snail's pace and deals with issues of rather direct and immediate impact can a significant proportion of the great multitude of interests express themselves. Therefore comprehensive democratic planning is virtually impossible. No legislature or committee of interest group leaders can rationally evaluate a statement of comprehensive goals. Its members cannot, in the absence of specific project proposals and citizen reactions to them, predict how the countless measures needed to accomplish the goals will affect the overall quality of community life or the interests of their own constituents and organizations. Consequently, they are likely to prefer operating on levels where comprehension and prediction are most feasible, even if this means fragmenting policy choices rather than integrating them. In practice, this means that they will rarely commit themselves to let general and long-range goal statements guide their consideration of lower-level alternatives.

There are no doubt many local politicians in America who would not find the preceding argument a compelling one. In localities lacking a coherent "power elite" firmly committed to a plan, however, it has a high degree of plausibility as a prescription for political survival. Its specific dictates are bound to be, at a minimum, a "project" rather than a "general planning" orientation and a disinclination to deal with controversial issues.

SYSTEMATIC CRITICISMS OF THE COMPREHENSIVE PLANNING IDEAL

The crucial assumptions of those who claim that comprehensive democratic planning is possible and desirable have of course been challenged more systematically than this. Martin Meyerson argued in a 1954 article that the major attacks could be divided into two types.[6] The first is that planning limits the range of individual choice by imposing centrally made decisions. The second is that planning requires "vastly more knowledge… about a huge variety of factors" than can be obtained or grasped by any individual or closely integrated group: Meyerson asserted that the few who had tried to answer these criticisms had been more successful in answering the first than the second. They had answered the first by saying that freedom is opportunity, not just the absence of restraint; and that planning agencies are created because people sense a failure of the market and of politics to satisfy their desires. As for the second question: unfortunately, wrote Meyerson, "we all know" that the assertion that planning can provide a rational basis for substantive policy decisions is just a goal today. The danger, he went on, is that planners will become content for it to remain a goal. He left the problem with a call for research.

It is questionable, however, whether planners have answered even the first objection successfully. Though it is certainly true that freedom consists of opportunity as well as the absence of restraint, there is little agreement as to whether planning to date has anywhere in the world produced more opportunity in toto than restraint. Only "common-sense" estimates are possible, as any more precise balance sheet would have to be based on determinations of the significance of particular opportunities and restraints. Neither the philosophic (assuming values to be objective) nor the scientific (assuming them to be subjective) foundations for such determinations exist. Second, the fact that people sense a failure of the market and the political process to meet their needs hardly forces one to conclude that they are better satisfied with the planning process. A reading of American city planning publications, not to mention conversations with numerous practicing planners, reveals a preoccupation among city planners with the fail-

ure of their work to win popular approval. Moreover, the winning of popular approval would itself prove very little. Planners themselves do not hesitate to bemoan the unwisdom of many popular governmental programs. They emphasize that the public must be educated by its leaders to favor comprehensive planning. They admit that the unguided public is likely to prefer an alderman who does petty favors for constituents to one who studies the city's overall needs.

Those who have made this first objection to comprehensive planning have generally emphasized that ambitious plans can only be realized through the generous exercise of public power. They have contended that every grant of power to government increases the chance of its abuse, increases the pervading influence of bureaucracy and red tape in the lives of citizens, decreases the self-reliance of citizens, and, as the habit of delegating tasks to government becomes prevalent, undermines their healthy suspicion of those who wield power. They have said that those charged with taking a comprehensive view of political problems are necessarily charged with safeguarding the complex requisites of the social and political system entrusted to their care. In the case of American society, this means a system in which the rights of individuals to wide spheres of personal freedom are recognized.

If the planner is truly to think comprehensively, in this view, he must consider not only the goals of society, but also the framework within which these goals can be pursued. If all proposals to enlarge governmental power threaten the framework of individual liberty to some degree, the planner must share society's initial bias against them. Those who oppose planning have generally asserted that planners have a professional bias in favor of bigger and bigger government, less and less subject to pressures from interest groups. Planners, they say, are in the business of creating new proposals which call for governmental activity. The planner's own interest is in the success of his plans: that is, in additional governmental activity *ad infinitum*. Most grants of power to government are long-term ones, because the electoral process is ponderous and inflexible. To reverse a major decision once ratified is extremely difficult, though it happens occasionally, as with Prohibition. The general pattern is for public interest to focus on an issue for a short while, and then move on. The planner's bias in favor of ever-larger government should therefore disqualify him from evaluating either his own proposals or those of others. Demands for public action in modern society are so numerous that only by subjecting each to the most searching criticism, based on an initial negative bias, can the trend toward concentration of power (which admittedly cannot be stopped) be slowed to a moderate rate. When government must act to deal with some pressing issue, every effort should be made to define the problem narrowly and to deal with it specifically. The approach should be one dealing with bottlenecks, not planning the whole production line. In other words, it should be piecemeal, not comprehensive.

If these are some of the views intelligent people still can hold regarding the issue that Meyerson says planning defenders have dealt with rather successfully, we may expect to have considerable difficulty in dealing with the one he says planners have been unable to handle. In part the problem is, as Meyerson says, them ability of planners to know about the interrelations of a huge variety of factors. But every profession deals with matters of incredible complexity. No profession can bring order to the mass of facts until it knows what it hopes to accomplish. From its goals, the members of a profession can derive criteria for judging the importance of facts. Using these criteria, they can develop theories about which consequences of specific types of proposals are the most important to control. The next step is to develop techniques for controlling these consequences. All specialists have lists of techniques for dealing with the characteristic problems they encounter. Planners too have some when they act as specialists. The floor-area ratio, for example, is a characteristic device used to resolve an aesthetic problem: the fact that rigid height and bulk building regulations yield unvaried architectural patterns:

This need for criteria, however, returns comprehensive planners to their basic problem. To develop theories about what they should know when creating comprehensive plans or evaluating specialist plans comprehensively, they need to know society's goals. Unless society has goals that can be discovered and applied, the task of theory

building cannot begin. The difficulty of dealing with factual complexity will always seem insuperable, though the truly insuperable difficulty may be that of defining the aims of the theory-building endeavor. The market and political bargaining processes depend on the assumptions that only individuals have goals,[7] that these normally conflict, and that the mysteries of bargaining yield the best results possible for men. The planner cannot rely on a hypothetical invisible hand; he must validate his claim to arbitrate, whereas the bargainer must only validate his claim to negotiate. Planners cannot claim to arbitrate on the basis of their own views of the public interest. If there are important conflicts of interest in a society that cannot be resolved to the advantage of all parties, then planners require the guidance of a strong political arbitrator. The alternative is a conception that essential harmony underlies all apparent clashes of interest.

The view that clashes of interest are only apparent has always appealed to one element of the American intellect. It is assumed by most conservative defenders of laissez-faire no less than by progressive attackers of "politics." Marver Bernstein reminds us, for example, that almost all American movements for regulatory legislation have had to adjust their arguments to this conception. In order to have any chance of success, they have had to protest their general disapproval of public action, even while saying that in this particular case it was needed to stop flagrant abuses by a few unscrupulous individuals. The ostensible purpose, always, has had to be restoration of the natural harmony of interests.[8] We may conceive a progression of steps in "natural harmony" thinking from support of laissez-faire, to regulation of specific abuses, to comprehensive planning. Laissez-faire theorists, of course assume that the interests of mankind are best served with no conscious coordination of effort. Theorists of regulation assume that just as healthy human organisms often require treatment for specific ills, so with healthy economic and social systems. The next step is to say that social and economic systems are not very good self-regulators, but rather require constant, carefully planned direction and care if they are to perform adequately. In this view, suitable to an age which accepts positive government, nature provides the common ends but human intelligence and elaborately coordinated effort are required to choose and implement the proper means of achieving them.

Those who reject comprehensive planning meet this reasoning in a variety of ways. Let us consider two of those which seem most plausible.

First, many writers, including the authors of *The Federalist*, have contended that conflict of interest is an invariable feature of all societies, and that the worst conflicts of interest are between those who manipulate governmental power and those who do not. By this view, whenever all those who possess governmental power are able, let alone encouraged, to synthesize their interests into a comprehensive goal, the rest of society had better watch out. A corollary of this position is that the few goals shared by all the members of society are not the goals most important to individuals. Thus, the primary function of government should be to provide an ordered framework in which civilization can prosper. The framework may be indispensable, because freedom is meaningful only within civilized society, but from the individual's viewpoint it is still only a precondition, not a preeminent goal in itself. Except during moments of supreme crisis for a society, in this view, the normal thing is for its members to differ, for each to want to seek happiness in his own way with a minimum of organized societal interference. This argument leads naturally into the argument against planning outlined above on pages 88-89.

Second, there are those who say that even if human interests harmonize and "big government" must be tolerated in modern life, the goal of comprehensiveness in decision-making should be viewed with the utmost suspicion. These critics do not, any more than those whose views are outlined above, recommend the banishment of intelligence from the handling of human affairs. They say only that the ways of the world are often contrary to logic. Logically, the wisest decisions should be those made at the highest level, where the widest range of arguments can be considered. But in fact, because the human mind can grasp only a limited number of considerations at any time, decision-makers at the highest level can act only by drastically over-simplifying their choice problems. According to this view, any comprehensive scheme is a Procrustes bed. The decision-maker does better to recognize the unforeseen and the unique in every situation without rigid pre-

conceptions. He can, when "other things are equal," endeavor to harmonize each day's decisions with those taken previously, but he should recognize that other things often are *not* equal. What is lost in administrative unity when the piecemeal approach is employed is made up in superior contact with public opinion and the special needs of each situation.

The greatest virtue of the piecemeal approach, in this view, is that it poses a large number of policy questions. The comprehensive approach implies that politicians need only approve general policy statements periodically, leaving the rest to be deduced by experts. Politicians not unnaturally react to this idea with hostility. They recognize that if they are to be the actual deciders of policy, they must exercise their influence continuously, at levels of generality sufficiently low so that later decisions may affect the matters of interest to their constituents. They may forego interference with administration below certain levels of generality, but they must never let administrators persuade them to set the cutoff point too high. The question of where it should be is always debatable, of course. Highway engineers tend to think that the setting of highway routes should be a technical endeavor. Others, including city planners, often complain that highway engineers are inclined to handle the side-effects of route location—which may be as important as the intended effects—as peripheral matters. In a democracy, the administrators can advise but they cannot determine finally which side-effects are too important for them to handle themselves, or to ignore.

Pressure groups have a similar interest to politicians in the piecemeal approach. Their members typically are interested in direct and immediate consequences to themselves, not in the overall public interest. It is a value of the piecemeal approach that interest groups can deal with questions their members care about. They need not feel that by the time their members become aware of any threat or opportunity the issue will have been foreclosed by prior community approval of generalities. Interest groups depend for their survival on issues which move their members and on at least occasional partial successes.[9] A vigorous public opinion in turn cannot survive without vigorous interest groups, whose leaders articulate issues, command attention in the mass media, and assure supporters in dissent that they are not alone. In the absence of strong evidence to the contrary in any particular society, therefore, it should be assumed that whatever saps the vigor of interest groups saps the vigor of democracy. The ideal of comprehensive planning seems ultimately antagonistic to the level of group conflict which typically characterizes stable democratic societies. It casts doubt on the very value of public discussion, at least after the stage of determining general goals. If a group of planners can comprehend the overall public interest, then any challenge to their specific proposals must be attributable either to their own incompetence or lack of integrity, or to the selfishness and shortsightedness of their critics. Faced with such polar explanations, those who take the side of the planners are apt to conclude that competition among parties and interest groups is alien to the public interest. Dictators frequently employ this very logic to defend their systems.

Defenders of planning may meet these criticisms in part by saying that they do not rely on the idea of a comprehensive harmony of human interests. They may contend merely that maintenance of a framework in which civilization can flourish is an enormous task, requiring all of man's ingenuity and foresight. Pressure groups are currently so vigorous, they may continue, and comprehensive planning is so weak, that concern for maintaining the divisive forces in our society at adequate strength is misplaced. Even if ideal comprehensive planning is impossible and in theory "big government" threatens democracy, they may conclude, democratic societies must strive toward the first and tolerate large doses of the second if they are to meet the challenge of modern welfare expectations and rapid technological change. This argument is highly plausible, but here as elsewhere serious debates center around location of the cutoff points, and planners suffer from lack of a theory to justify their positions in these debates.

To critics of planning there is an essential difference between public actions to meet crisis threats to crucial societal values and actions to ameliorate the effects of every societal dislocation. The passionate proponents of economic reform in the1930's and of foreign aid in the postwar decade were able to argue that American democracy was in clear and mortal peril. Proponents of strong

public action to bring about desegregation in the 1960's can cite highly serious injustices and threats to domestic tranquility as the justifications for intervention. Few defenders of city planning cite such serious or immediate crises. They say instead that planning is desirable to help minimize the pains of adaptation to change, and to develop cities in which everyone's opportunity for fulfillment will be enhanced. They generally fail, however, to confront certain obvious questions squarely. How, for example, should one judge whether the alleviation of a specific social pain warrants the amount of growth in governmental power over the lives of individuals which it will require? Is it possible to achieve a high level of intelligent consensus about the substance of personal fulfillment, and the kinds of environment most conducive to it? The final judge of proposed answers to such questions must be the political process. And here is where planners' troubles have usually begun.

POLITICAL RESTRAINTS ON THE GOAL DEVELOPMENT PROCESS

Speaking broadly, there are two ways to win political acceptance for new ideas in a stable democratic system. The first is to challenge the theoretical foundations of popular beliefs with which they conflict. This way is slow at best. Moreover, it requires a highly persuasive theory. Such theories are never easily come by, nor, if they challenge older persuasive theories, do they win acceptance quickly. In the United States, the other theories with which a thoroughgoing defense of comprehensive planning would have to contend are not even perceived as theories, but rather as part of the American tradition. Perhaps in consequence, American planners have generally eschewed full-scale defense of social planning, preferring to conciliate the powerful reasoning of American conservatism rather than to challenge it directly. The only theoretical defense of public planning which planners have frequently asserted has been based on a conception of planning as businesslike foresight. The simple theories required to defend this idea of planning have won fairly easy political acceptance, but they have not dealt with the inevitable political and social implications of serious efforts to plan generally or comprehensively. It has remained necessary, therefore, to deal with these implications *ad hoc* when such efforts have been made.

One way, then, to win political acceptance for new ideas is to challenge the theoretical foundations of older ideas with which they conflict. The other way is to adapt one's own arguments and objectives to the beliefs, attitudes, and political customs already prevalent. The latter way is more likely to yield immediate results, and it minimizes the risk that no results at all will be produced. American planners almost invariably have chosen it, no doubt in part because they are influenced even more by American culture than by international planning theory. It has certainly contributed to the political security of planners and the planning function. It has perhaps obscured, however, the problem of maintaining a clear professional viewpoint.

There is no need to search far for an explanation. It is extremely difficult for any agency whose explicit function is to propose new ideas to avoid coming into frequent conflict with established ways of thinking and doing things. Even if general strategy is articulated in the most conventional possible terms, this tactical dilemma is bound to remain. With respect to planning, it is bound to be most apparent when the planning is general and community goals must be determined. Given the importance of such a determination—if it is in fact to provide a guide for future public action—and the infinite varieties of emphasis possible, one would expect that the officials making it would run the risk of offending everyone. Even if they are oblivious of their own safety, the problem of winning political approval for their proposed goal statements remains.

Two methods of dealing with this problem at the level of general goals may be outlined.[10] The first is to state goals on which all reasonable men can agree. Unfortunately, goals of this type tend not to provide any basis for evaluating concrete alternatives. Thus, the *St. Paul Land Use Plan* stated as its most general goal the "evolution of St. Paul as a better place to live and work," and the *Plan* constantly justified its more specific proposals in terms of increasing "liveability." The second alternative is to propose somewhat more controversial goals in the expectation that the community's elective policy-makers will consider, if necessary amend, and ultimately approve them. Conceivably, planners might offer elected officials several choices of goals in each area of concern, though to the extent that they did so they would reduce the possibility of all the goals finally chosen being consistent with each other. Inconsistency might be turned to positive advantage, however. Part of using this approach successfully would be to deal in "packages," so that those in the minority when one goal was approved might hope to be in the majority when others were. The objective, of course, would be to win all or almost all reasonable politicians to support of the package.

This method is tried frequently in the American system, but it seldom succeeds where the package is a set of general goals. Part of the reason, we have seen, is that many "reasonable" politicians in the system oppose general planning and the articulation of general goals on principle. Even more important is the fact that American politicians typically depend on public discussion to inform them of the interest and values affected by any proposal. If planners cannot spur adequate discussion of their goal statements, politicians cannot, and know they cannot, make informed choices among them. Even when discussion is achieved, the dictates of prudence and democratic ethics impel politicians to wait for consensus to form before acting. The upshot is that very few proposals emerge as law from American legislative processes until and unless the vast majority of articulate groups interested in them favors some version of them. In the case of novel proposals, virtual unanimity seems generally to be required unless the need for decision is seen by the vast majority to be inescapable.[10]

In the national sphere, these "rules" may be waived when survival seems to be the stake. In most areas of urban life, however, people with money can escape the worst consequences of any change. Thus, Scott Greer has characterized the American city as one of "limited liability" from the viewpoint of the individual.[11] To illustrate: if a middle-class neighborhood becomes a slum, the original residents can move out, and though this has a price it is generally easier and cheaper than fighting the trend. So long as the general standard of living is rising, most of the newcomers are taking a step upward; they are likely to be apathetic toward efforts to resist the transition, and positively hostile to programs which might "improve" the neighborhood's prospects sufficiently to drive rents up. The immediate threats in urban life, then, are of individual dislocation rather than of societal survival, or even decline.

Politicians in American society occasionally alert their constituents to specific ills and dangers, and champion specific programs for dealing with them. It has recently become fashionable, moreover, for some politicians to conduct well-publicized quests for consensual, nonoperational general goals. It is a rare politician indeed, however, who leads his constituents in formulating positive operational social goals. The quest itself would be likely to stir antagonism among those who did not believe societies should have positive goals, and it would almost certainly stir new demands against the politician's limited resources. Moreover, those few citizens who long for positive planning rarely approach unanimity in any meaningful detail on what its substance should be. The obstacles to positive political leadership are such that even those who emphasize the potential educative role of the American Presidency usually admit that the President can be effective only so long as he confines his efforts to a very few widely perceived social ills and foreign dangers. The President who obtains authority to set up general planning agencies in moments of national crisis is likely, once the crisis begins to abate, to see them scuttled by Congress while he himself is charged with Caesarism. Consider the fate of the National Resources Planning Board, abolished by Congress in 1943 though its functions had been advisory only and it had carefully avoided direct confrontations with other agencies.[12] The incomparably more significant Office of War Mobilization and Reconversion achieved immense powers of coordination in the course of its brief life, but only during total war and at the expense of adopting a highly judicialized bottleneck—as opposed to policy-oriented comprehensive—planning approach.[13] The Bureau of the Budget has nurtured its far more limited influence similarly. Few chief executives at the local level have formal powers comparable to those of the President in his, and of course none have comparable prestige.[14] In general, the American distrust of executive power has found more forceful legal expression at the local level than at the national, perhaps

because of the need for foreign and military policies nationally, and because opponents of executive power since the brief Federalist interregnum have found the constitution which it produced too difficult to change.

The opponents of planning have recognized the difference by focusing their attention on national rather than local planning efforts. Businessmen have been the primary patrons of the urban planning movement in America since its beginnings. As the planning movement has matured, moreover, fewer and fewer large property owners and executives have seen anything ironical about their providing the primary base of political support for local land-use planning while continuing bitterly to oppose anything remotely resembling national economic planning. The major reason for the survival of this apparent inconsistency has probably been that leaders of property-oriented groups have lacked confidence that they could control planning at the federal level under the President. If this view is correct, the critics have spared local planning from their attacks just *because* local politicians have had insufficient power to defy the veto groups of their political system.

THE IDEAL OF MIDDLE-RANGE PLANNING

The point has been made in previous sections that truly comprehensive goals tend not to provide any basis for evaluating concrete alternatives. It is thus difficult to stir political interest in them and impossible to plan rationally in their service. Recognizing this, at least implicitly, many contemporary planners claim to practice middle-range planning—which they define as planning for the achievement of goals that are general, but still operational. It is not very fruitful to strive for greater definitional precision than this, because the image is one of balance between the contradictory ideals of comprehensiveness and specialization. Experienced planners have a "feel" for the conception, however, and explain it to neophytes by citing illustrations. For our purpose, the *Central Minneapolis Plan* may be cited as clearly falling in the "middle range."

The middle-range planning ideal has much to recommend it, despite its imprecision. It permits the promise of meaningful political discussion and approval of planning goals, even if the achievement may in practice be highly elusive. In addition, criticisms of comprehensive planning rooted in liberal democratic theory are much less forceful when applied to middle-range planning. From the viewpoint of the general planner, however, the middle-range planning ideal has one crucial flaw. It provides no basis for the planner to claim to understand the overall public interest. Men who plan to achieve operational—even though relatively general—goals are specialist, not comprehensive, planners. Consequently, they have no obvious theoretical basis for claiming to know better than other specialists how far each specialist goal should be pursued, and with what priority.

SPECIALIZATION VS. COMPREHENSIVENESS: THE UNEASY BALANCE

The case for efforts at genuinely comprehensive planning has generally rested heavily on the thought that planners can resolve conflicts among goals in expert fashion. If they cannot, if they can only articulate specialist goals, then elected officials would seem required to act as the comprehensive arbiters of conflict. If it is assumed that arbiters operate most successfully when all important considerations are presented vigorously to them, one might argue reasonably that each important cluster of operational goals should be defended by a separate agency. Philip Selznick, for instance, has contended that leaders who wish to maximize their influence should structure their organizations so that the lines of jurisdiction dividing subunits are those along which important issues are likely to arise. His reasoning is that if issues arise within subunits they are likely to be decided by the subunit head, without the chief executive becoming aware of them. It is when subunits themselves come into conflict that arbiters at the next higher level are most likely to learn of issues.[15] Delegation of overall authority to arbitrate, in this view, even within the framework of highly general goal statements, is bound to transfer the substance of power from the delegator to the delegatee. If the delegator retains appellate jurisdiction he may dilute this effect. The more that he is committed to uphold the comprehensive policy vision of the delegatee, however, the less he

will be able to do so. In trying to persuade politicians to make this delegation and to commit themselves to comprehensive policy visions, defenders of comprehensive planning must contend that the politicians will further the welfare of their constituents by doing so. To the extent that planning agencies lack truly comprehensive perspectives, this contention becomes less and less plausible.

Beyond this, even in pursuit of their own specialist goals, planners operate in a world of whole objects, not of analytical aspects. They cannot conceive means that will further the operational goals of primary interest to them without affecting innumerable others in uncontrolled fashion. Sophisticated planners recognize this, and try not to serve their stated goals exclusively. The operational goal of the *Central Minneapolis Plan*, for example, was downtown economic growth. Its authors realized, however, that they could not reasonably ignore other goals. They wrote and spoke as though the cultural, political, spiritual, recreational, and other functions of downtown could never conflict with each other or with the economic function. In practice, they were saved by their common sense; they did not press their pursuit of economic goals sufficiently far to spur public awareness of potential serious conflicts. Conceivably, they might have listed all the significant operational goals they hoped to serve, but they would still have been left with the problem of balancing them. In short, every concrete object of planner attention is a miniature of the whole. The important analytical problems that arise in planning for an entire urban area arise in planning any section of it.[16] Perhaps the only escape is frankly to adopt a specialist orientation, even while remaining willing to adjust specific proposals as highly distasteful side-effects become apparent. It may still be plausible to maintain, however, that planners are custodians of values that somehow deserve to take precedence over the values propounded by other specialists. Let us consider the most persuasive lines of reasoning frequently advanced in support of this view.

One of the simplest was stated by Allison Dunham in a well-known article several years ago.[17] He claimed to have found after a survey of the planning literature that planners almost invariably believed that, at the very least, they were the officials best qualified to evaluate site proposals for every kind of facility. They based their position on the premise that planners were experts in the impacts of land uses on each other. The argument, in other words, was not that planners were "wiser" than operating agency officials but that on certain types of issues their specialty deserved first place in the pecking order of specialties.

Two queries come immediately to mind. First, are the impacts of uses on each other regularly more important in site decisions than the intended purposes of each use? Second, can locational problems be separated meaningfully from all other problems? For illustrative purposes, consider a central issue of the Ancker Hospital site controversy: how should the potential health benefits of a contiguous medical center be balanced against the traffic congestion it would produce? Was it possible to say in the abstract which variable deserved greater weight? Was traffic congestion more a locational problem than building the medical center? The proponents of the medical center, it will be recalled, said that it could come into being only if Ancker Hospital were built on the one available site adjacent to the city's two largest existing hospitals. The only way to argue that planners should normally be given the benefit of the doubt in disputes of this kind is to say, as Dunham did, that specialists think of the needs of their constituents, while planners think of the impact of specialist proposals on others. In this case, the constituents were sick people and hospital staff personnel, while the "others" included many of the same people, but in their other capacities—as drivers and investors, for instance. The key question is whether the "others" should have had any more presumptive right to prevail than the recognized constituents.[18]

Another objection to this definition of planner competence is that it provides only the haziest indication of the legitimate jurisdiction of planners and of government. Just what is a locational decision? It is hardly enough to say, as planners generally have, that locational decisions are those that have an impact on surrounding property or people. Almost anything I do to my property affects my neighbor in some way. For instance, if I rent out rooms in my one-family home, I have changed the use of my land and therefore made a locational decision, by a common planner definition.

Should government therefore control everything, as it already controls my right to rent out rooms? Planners deny that it should, but they have rarely asked where the cutoff point should be. They have typically been satisfied to say that government should intervene only in cases of "substantial" harm, and that common sense will prevail in interpreting the word "substantial." They may be right, but this formulation gives the citizen no theoretical guidance as to whose common sense should prevail in cases of disagreement between other decision-makers and planners.

A second persuasive line of reasoning to support the view that planners should generally prevail in such disputes is that they alone among city officials spend their days analyzing city problems from an overall point of view. Operating agency officials cannot rise above their day-to-day administrative chores, and in any event their perspectives are conditioned by the narrow responsibilities of their departments. Even politicians typically devote most of their time to maintaining contacts with, and to performing errand boy services for, their constituents. In dealing with legislative proposals, they generally focus on details of immediate interest to local groups rather than on the overall picture. In most cities, moreover, councilmen are elected from wards; in many they work only part time at their jobs; and in some each councilman heads a city department. Only planners can devote all their time to thought about city problems at the most general level.

The most obvious criticism of this position is that freedom from operating responsibility may not be the best condition in which to make high-level decisions. Some prominent decision-makers have argued that it is a poor one. Winston Churchill, for example, has written that Stafford Cripps became restive and hypercritical of his colleagues while serving as parliamentary whip during World War II. What he needed, according to Churchill's diagnosis, was responsibility which would absorb his energies and give him a sense of the concrete issues. Those who are free from operating responsibility, concluded Churchill, tend to develop an unhelpful watchdog mentality. It is unhelpful because they usually think too abstractly to be cogent critics of complex choices among policies.[19] Similarly, Chester Barnard has written that study and reflectiveness without operating responsibility tend to lead to the treatment of things by aspects rather than wholes, to a disregard of factors which cannot be expressed precisely, and to an underestimation of the need for artistry in making concrete decisions. Because so many crucial factors cannot find expression in words, Barnard concluded, the interdependencies of social life can only be grasped intuitively. Only men of long and responsible experience are likely to acquire very much of this intuitive grasp, and therefore only such men—who will also grasp the supreme difficulty of planning in this "world of unknowns"—are qualified to plan.[20] This is unquestionably a rather mystical position, but for all that it is no less a respectable and forceful one.

Barnard and Churchill agree, then, that freedom from responsibility for operating decisions is anything but fit training for planning.[21] Those who accept their view are likely to believe that any one of a number of city officials may qualify better than the planning director to serve as the wise chief advisor of politicians on broad policy issues. The Minneapolis and St. Paul city councils consistently acted on this belief. To the extent that the, desired coordination of public works, they normally relied on their city engineers to achieve it. When the Minneapolis City Council decided in 1953 to separate capital budgeting from ordinary budgeting, it set up a committee composed of politicians and civic leaders. The committee was given a small staff headed by a former city councilman. Planners were shut out of the capital budgeting process entirely. When the St. Paul City Council decided that it needed a special advisor on the interstate freeway program, it appointed City Engineer George Shepard, who had been about to retire. When Minneapolis City Engineer Hugo Erickson left the city government for private employ in the late 1950's, his successor proved inadequate (in the City Council's view) for the unofficial task of city public works coordinator. Within a year, the Council lured Erickson back into government, giving him the title of Development Coordinator. Minneapolis planners believed that they should have been given the job, but they could offer no strong arguments to support their view that Erickson was less able to take the overview than they. The politician most responsible for bringing Erickson back told me that the planners thought too abstractly and with insuffi-

cient regard to cost, whereas Erickson, though less articulate, understood the infinite, inexpressible complexity of governmental choice. In fairness to the planners, it should be added that Erickson had made his entire career in Minneapolis, looking to the City Council for his raises, perquisites, and promotions. He had risen primarily because of his technical competence, to be sure, but also because the councilmen felt confident that he would not embarrass them politically and that his overriding loyalty was to themselves. Planning Director Irvin, needless to say, could not claim similar qualifications.

A third defense that planners frequently make of their aspiration to be more than "mere" specialists is that governmental efficiency is served by having one agency keep track of everything that every city agency does, calling attention to conflicts and to means of coordinating effort for the benefit of all. The distinction between coordination and planning, however, is of practical importance only so long as planners have no power. Without power, they can as coordinators simply try to persuade groups of specialists that their respective interests will be served by improved coordination. As soon as planners begin to impose solutions or advise politicians to impose them, however, they have entered the substantive planning field. That is, they have set their perception of the public interest on substantive matters against those of the specialists who have rejected their advice. Similarly, when planners request authority to prepare a city's capital budget, they cannot justify the request on grounds of "simple efficiency," which would have to be established by the criteria of all the specialists' own goals. They must assert, at least implicitly, that they have some means of choosing among the values entrusted to each operating agency. In other words, they must claim to have goals. And the coordination of action in pursuit of substantive goals, is, if it is anything, substantive planning.

One might say that the planner needs coordinative power only because some specialists stupidly or obstinately refuse to cooperate with others in the interests of "simple efficiency," even though no significant values are threatened. The answer is that no one can determine that this is the case in any particular controversy without examining it in detail. Philip Selznick has illustrated this point clearly in his analysis of the history of the Communist party.[22] The party refused to cooperate with other leftist parties in the decade before the Popular Front, despite the obvious threat of fascism. Yet this period of isolation, Selznick contends, made the party a much more valuable tool to its masters during and after the Popular Front period. During the isolation period, the "character" of the party developed and became incorruptible. This extreme example illustrates a simple point: that cooperation and isolation in themselves have important effects on organizations. If an agency head claims that a measure advanced in the name of efficiency actually threatens important values—and any agency head who refuses the advice of the planning director will say this—no outsider can refute him until he examines the bases of his arguments in detail. If we assume that most agency heads are men of good conscience, we can likewise assume that they will have some reasons that seem genuinely sufficient to them, and that they will seem so as well to at least some reasonable outsiders. In the end, no act of coordination is without its effect on other values than efficiency.

Some planners reading this chapter will no doubt judge that the issues raised in it are "ivory tower stuff," and in the immediate sense perhaps they are—though tome they appeared quite close to the surface in the Twin Cities. The purpose of this chapter, however, has been to challenge the planning profession to reinforce its most fundamental arsenal. In the long run, I suspect, general planning and evaluation will have little effect on American cities unless their goal premises can be established in sufficiently compelling fashion (both politically and intellectually) to make politicians take notice.

NOTES

1. A few planners, mainly in the universities, have recently come to doubt this. They are taken with Herbert Simon's model of "satisficing" administrative man, which I believe they fail to understand thoroughly. Several have suggested to me that this model shows up all talk about the need for planning goals as irrelevant. The satisficing model is set forth in Herbert Simon and James G. March, *Organizations* (New York: John Wiley

and Sons, 1958), esp. pp. 140-141, 163, 175; Herbert Simon, *Models of Man* (New York: John Wiley and Sons, 1957), Chaps. 10, 14, 16; and Herbert Simon, "Theories of Decision-Making in Economics and Behavioral Science," *American Economic Review*, LXIX, No. 2 (June 1959), pp. 253-283.

According to Simon, most theorists until recently accepted the model of "maximizing" (economic) man. Maximizing man was assumed to have all the alternatives that he needed before him and to be able to rank them all with reference to the desirability of their consequences. His ranking ability rested on his possession of a "utility function," which amounted to his values or goals. For purposes of simplicity, I am leaving out here the issue of his ability to forecast consequences. Let us deal in this discussion only with the evaluation of foreseeable consequences.

Satisficing (administrative) man, on the other hand, is moved by stimuli ("e.g.," writes Simon, "a customer order or a fire gong") to search for alternatives. When he finds one that is "good enough," he intelligently avoids spending time, energy, and resources on further search.

Simon himself tends to be indifferent to high-level goal determining processes, so it is understandable that some planners should have concluded that satisficing man does not need goals. According to their interpretation, the determinants of satisficing man's choices are largely, perhaps mainly, subconscious. He knows that in any case most of the consequences of any choice are incomparable on any single operational scale of value. Consequently, being a practical man rather than a utopian intellectual, he reconciles himself to the fact that his choices are bound to be essentially intuitive. From the standpoint of an outsider, the evidence that an alternative is satisfactory is bound to be no more than that it has been chosen.

The above is a misinterpretation of Simon. In his sustained discussions of satisficing Simon always makes clear that one can only speak of an alternative's being satisfactory if it meets standards set prior to its selection. Standards, however, are neither more nor less than goals. If they are not ultimate goals, they must ultimately be evaluated on the basis of their relation to ultimate goals. The very notion of formulating precise standards of adequacy at the beginning of a search for alternatives is, it strikes me, a more literal application of means-ends language than is normally feasible at the higher levels of politics and administration. The processes of balancing ideals, estimates of feasibility, and probable costs of further search are generally far more subtle than this language suggests. The phrase that Chester Barnard frequently used, "successive approximations," seems more appropriate here. This does not mean, however, that general discussions of goals and priorities can be dispensed with in any meaningful planning exercise.

More generally, it may be noted that the satisficing model, even correctly understood, hardly represents a major advance in our understanding of human psychology. The maximizing model has long been recognized as an ideal type, a useful measuring rod against which to compare optimal aspirations with achievements, rather than as a descriptive model of human choice. It has been most useful in economics, where it has been feasible to hypothesize a single substantive goal for actors other than ultimate consumers. Use of the satisficing model, on the other hand, requires that we have substantive knowledge of such variables as the values of actors, the costs of search, and the obstacles to implementation of particular proposals. Unless observers have such knowledge, the satisficing model approaches the conception of it held by the planners mentioned above. It tells us nothing about why any particular actor considered any particular standard "good enough."

One other point worth stressing is that Simon's actors typically assess values, and consequently the significance of obstacles and costs, in purely subjective fashion. Consequently, Simon's theories are essentially theories of irresponsible choice. This may not seem terribly significant when decision-makers are choosing for themselves alone—as in the market—or for hierarchical organizations that have no pretensions of democracy or of responsibility to non-members. Such theories make both criticism and justification of choices on the basis of value considerations impossible, however, and this does matter in a democratic polity.

In *Organizations* Simon and March discuss the satisficing model in their chapter entitled "Cognitive Limits on Rationality." By contrast, my concern is with social and political obstacles to rationality. My purpose in these pages is political,

not psychological, analysis. The approach taken here is that of the politician or citizen confronted with conflicting expert arguments, and anxious to decide wisely. Either may decide whimsically in the end, but it seems both nihilistic and paralyzing to assume in the beginning that no more is possible. It is also untrue, except in a number of rather obvious senses. The goodness of ultimate goals may not be demonstrable, but they are generally not the controversial ones. All the others can be analyzed and compared in terms of the consequences, unintended as well as intended, likely to flow from pursuing them. Simon specifically admits this, but he relegates scholarly consideration of such analyses and comparisons to the Siberia of "philosophy." His followers, whether "practical men" or self-conscious "scientists," are thus led to ignore these matters. I consider this unfortunate. (This viewpoint is elaborated in my introduction to a forthcoming reader that I have edited, entitled *The Politics of American Public Administration* [New York: Dodd, Mead & Co., 1966].)

Moreover, most planners themselves consider it essential for them to be able to demonstrate the nonarbitrary nature of their recommendations. I believe that Paul Davidoff and Thomas Reiner, in their recent article, "A Choice Theory of Planning," have articulated a major preoccupation of the profession in writing: "We are concerned with the problem, so trenchantly posed by Haar, that a major task confronting the planner is to see that he acts in a nonarbitrary manner, administratively as well as conceptually. We develop in these pages a theory of nonarbitrary planning."(*Journal of the American Institute of Planners*, XXVIII, No. 2 [May 1962], 103-115. The quotation is at p. 103. The piece by Charles Haar referred to is: "The Master Plan: An Inquiry in Dialogue Form," *Journal of the American Institute of Planners*, XXV, No. 3 [August 1959 1, 133-142.) It is clearly impossible to plan nonarbitrarily without knowledge of the proper goals for the planning endeavor.

2. *The Proposed Freeways for St. Paul*, Community Plan Report 4, June 1957, p. 30.

3. Planners tend to use the words "rational" and "wise" interchangeably in evaluating public choices. This is in accord with the usage of natural law philosophers, but not with that of contemporary economic and social theorists. For the latter, the term "rational" refers to the efficiency of means where ends are known. "Wisdom" refers to deep understanding and the ability to make what are considered "good" judgments on complex human issues, when goals and efficient means are not generally known.

Consequently, the planners use of the word "rational" in the classic sense to defend their distinctly modern "expert" recommendations makes for some confusion of thought. This confusion has a political function, however. It conveys the impression that expert logic or technique can produce "good" decisions on complex human issues.

4. A major reason for this was probably that in no urban section but downtown did simple economic goals appear entirely plausible. Outside the United States, planners rarely considered them so even for downtown. See, for example, the British Town and Country Planning Association's analysis of central London problems: *The Paper Economy* (London: Town and Country Planning Association, 1962).

5. From their viewpoint as political administrators, on the other hand, Minneapolis planners and their consultants won a major, and far from inevitable, victory in persuading the professional discussants that the general lines of economic reasoning in the *Central Minneapolis Plan* were valid, and that a plan based on them would quite probably benefit downtown business. After all, even the contribution of a plan to economic growth—let alone to the public interest—was impossible to predict and difficult to identify after the fact. Trend changes after specific actions were taken were possible to measure, but no one could prove that the actions studied had caused the result. Only comparative analysis of many cities could begin to test the efficacy of particular methods, and reliable comparative data were rare.

Still, the arguments of city planners in their role as economic planners had a hardheaded quality seldom present in their other work. They wrote as though from having defined their goal clearly they could identify the major bars to progress toward it without much trouble. Knowing the enemy, they could conceive tightly reasoned, even if untested, lines of attack.

6. "Research and City Planning," *Journal of the American Institute of Planners*, XX, No. 4 (Autumn 1954), 201-205.

7. Readers will note that I say the political *bargaining* process depends on this assumption, not the political *discussion* process.

8. Marver Bernstein, *Regulating Business by Independent Commission* (Princeton: Princeton University Press, 1955), Chaps. 1, 2.

9. Not all interest groups need political successes, of course, because not all are primarily political in their orientation. Business firms, labor unions, and churches, for example ,can retain their memberships without engaging in politics. They tend to retreat from politics, however, and thus to disappear as *politically significant* interest groups, when their members perceive public discussion as invariably fruitless.

10. The phrases "vast majority" and "virtual unanimity" must be taken to mean proportions of those interested in each issue. Charles Merriam wrote thirty-five years ago in his classic description of Chicago politics that while virtually any group in the city could veto proposals affecting it, even the weakest group could get its proposals approved if no other group rose to object (*Chicago: A More Intimate View* [Chicago: University of Chicago Press, 1929]). Edward Banfield reports that Chicago's political system, run by the most powerful machine in the nation, operates still in roughly the same manner (*Political Influence* [New York: The Free Press of Glencoe, 1961]). According to Banfield, the "bosses have few or no policy objectives of their own, and therefore decide issues in response to the electoral interests of their organization (i.e., the "machine"). They seem to accept the view that electoral benefits are probable only when what we have termed the "vast majority" and "virtual unanimity" rules are followed, and when ample time is given potential interests to recognize their concern and express it.

No political machines operated in either of the two cities I studied, but the professional politicians who ran each acted similarly to the Chicago "bosses" in committing their prestige and influence.

Some members of the planning profession have themselves publicly approved the politicians' instinct. The President of the American Institute of Planners wrote in 1955, for example, that at a minimum policies adopted by government should be acceptable on a voluntary basis to 80 or 90 per cent of the public (John T. Howard, "The Planner in a Democratic Society—A Credo,"

Journal of the American Institute of Planners, XXI, No. 3 [Spring-Summer 1955], 62-65). If he meant, which I doubt he did, that it was all right for 10 or 20 per cent to be strongly opposed, he was a radical by the standards of most local politicians.

11. *The Emerging City* (New York: The Free Press of Glencoe, 1962).

12. See Edward H. Hobbs, *Behind the President* (Washington, D.C.: Public Affairs Press, 1954), Chap. 3; A. E. Holmans, *United States Fiscal Policy 1945-1959* (London: Oxford University Press, 1961), pp. 33-36; and Charles E. Merriam, "The National Resources Planning Board: A Chapter in American Planning Experience," *American Political Science Review*, XXVIII, No. 6 (December 1944), 1075-1088.

13. See Herman Somers, *Presidential Agency* (Cambridge: Harvard University Press, 1950), Chap. 2; and V. O. Key, Jr., "The Reconversion Phase of Demobilization," *American Political Science Review*, No. 6 (December 1944), 1137-1153.

14. Both of the Twin Cities had very "weak" mayors, even by local standards.

15. Philip Selznick, *Leadership in Administration* (Evanston: Row, Peterson, and Company, 1957).

16. The more limited objects (e.g., neighborhoods instead of whole cities) do present somewhat different, if not lesser, problems to the comprehensive planner. Cause and effect are easier to trace on the small scene, and important differences of interest are likely to be fewer. On the other hand, if planners emphasize the common interest of each homogeneous unit, they may well accentuate the differences between units.

17. "A Legal and Economic Basis for City Planning," *Columbia Law Review*, LVIII (May 1958), 650-671.

18. This distinction recalls John Dewey's definition of the public interest (in *The Public and Its Problems* [New York: Henry Holt and Co., 1927]) as the interest in a decision of all those not directly party to it. Critics have pointed out that the parties to the decision have some claim to be considered part of the public too, in most cases the most clearly affected part. Those who dispute over definitions of the public interest are not mere academic quibblers. The phrase "public interest" has inescapable normative, and therefore political, significance. Those whose interest is opposed to it by

a proposed definition therefore have ample reason to quibble.

19. *The Second World War*, Vol. IV: *The Hinge of Fate* (Boston: Houghton-Mifflin Co., 1950), p. 560.

Churchill was not arguing against the making of large decisions by generalists, of course. He himself was Prime Minister. Nor was he criticizing the British practice of concentrating authority within the civil service in the hands of generalists. Several points may be noted. The generalists in a British ministry exercise all formal power of decision not exercised by the minister himself. They bear responsibility as well for deciding which issues, and which specialist analyses of them, are important enough for the minister to consider. The elite corps of the generalists, the Administrative Class, are expected on entry only to think, write, and speak clearly, and to have done well in their subjects of undergraduate concentration. Any subject will do, although subjects fit for "gentlemen" (i.e., men devoted to culture rather than to making a living), notably the classics, have traditionally predominated. British administrators have no formal technical training for their work at all. They are platonic rather than functional leaders, but matured on responsibility rather than study. Those at the higher levels are notably unsympathetic to the ideal of general planning. They take well-known pride in deciding "each case on its merits."

Parenthetically, where city planners are employed in British ministries they are considered technicians, capable of contributing useful advice on specialized aspects of issues, but not of being entrusted with the power to make decisions.

20. Chester Barnard, *Organization and Management* (Cambridge: Harvard University Press, 1948), Chap. 4.

21. It should be clear that when I speak of "planning" in this chapter, I mean the work of determining overall policy guidelines for public activity, and means of implementing them. No single individual or agency makes such determinations alone in an American community. The recommendations of some, however, are bound to carry more weight than those of others. The crucial questions at issue here are (1) whether the views of planning agencies on controversial policy issues should normally be granted presumptive validity in the absence of strong evidence discrediting them; and (2) whether the training and career patterns of professional city planners equip them well for planning at the higher levels.

22. *The Organizational Weapon* (Glencoe: The Free Press, 1960).

Planning Absorbs Zoning

Carl Feiss

In this 1960s article, provocative for its time, Carl Feiss argued that zoning had not fulfilled its expectation as an effective planning tool. Feiss then called for an enlarging of the potential for planning inherent in redevelopment and renewal processes as a substitute for what he viewed as the negative impact and misuse of zoning as an instrument of planning.

The most widely employed land use control today is zoning; it is in fact the workhorse of the planning movement in this country.
— Charles M. Haar

It would be presumptuous for any one man, planner or not, to try to place zoning into perspective in the United States today. The angels of the city growth and development have feared to tread this path, though years of experience and ponderous though frequently valuable volumes are used to light the word-obscured way.

HAS ZONING WORKED?

Step back for a moment and look into the cities which others have built—others than those of us who deal only with regulatory measures and fitful plans. Further, scrutinize our ability to handle the entrepreneurs in land, building, money, water, and air. Are we peers in the power structure with those who negotiate or finance the means for the construction of what planners call "improvements" of these basic commodities? Still looking, then, we most ask ourselves whether zoning, since 1925, has helped to build or rebuild, control or stimulate, good well-planned man-made places for all the things man does in urbanized places? Is there a chance, an off-chance, that we have been captivated by a concept so persuasive and so self-propelling that it seems both a means and an end? Have we allowed ourselves to be lulled into a coma of mass acceptance of words and actions within both reality and mythology? Like the esoteric wiring of a computer, has an idea become so glitteringly enchantingly romanticized that it, as a gadget, has become for some of us as important or more important than the results it was designed to produce?

Perhaps it is the question of "the end" with which we now begin. The end is the American city you have just stepped back to look at. Do you like it? Does it work? Can you identify clearly the results of all the months and years of hard work in drafting ordinances, preparing maps, attending public hearings and Chamber of Commerce meetings, fighting in the courts, pursuing your administrative and legal responsibilities, and attending to limitless detail in the office and field? Have you achieved your ends, except in single-family districts, and are you pleased with results other than these in Class A-RI ? Dare you search for the place where you eliminated a nonconforming use?

Placing zoning in perspective, judging Its accomplishments and lack of accomplishment, we recognize today that the concept of a negative regulatory measure for the control of land use and intensity of development is philosophically opposite from the present-day concept of development and redevelopment with Its positive implications. As always the negative and positive are poles apart. We therefore find that where positive programs for development and redevelopment are under way, they frequently come in conflict with the older and more deeply entrenched regulatory measures. Or these older measures are found inadequate to meet the requirements of a positive program, and it becomes necessary to insert rules and regulations which support the design intent. Development and redevelopment imply a design intent which zoning has never served in adequate fashion, other than in broad-brush treatment of existing and expendable uses and attendant height and density controls. The results of what has been done within the powers of zoning and what is being and can be done within the powers of development and redevelopment are hardly comparable. One could cite, of course, successful instances of height control in the District of Columbia or of setback control in New York City as having a direct bearing on development design. However, this is design almost by default, since it averages a concept rather than particularizes it.

SINS OF OMISSION

We cannot hold the original inventors of zoning responsible for a philosophy that did not exist at the time they proposed this ingenious and intricate form of regulation. In fact, it was a fairly simple idea to begin with. Their ideals and their idealisms were irreproachable. Unfortunately, the concept was chiefly legal and administrative; except for its police power, it was not consciously or adequately directed towards the finite elements of community design for better living, working, and playing. We can now regret the apparently uncorrectable errors in the fundamental tenets of zoning, errors which appeared at once but have not yet been fully recognized either by zoning proponents or by the people who go along because they know no better way.

The first and perhaps the most incomprehensible error was that the draftsmen of zoning considered open land or open space to be expendable. This, perhaps more than any other legal concept or lack of legal concept, has abetted the unlimited sprawl which occurs in all urbanizing areas in this country. It should have been recognized at once that to build on land where little or no development existed was to alter its use. To build for residential or nonresidential uses on land which has been used for agricultural or other open land purposes is so clearly and obviously a change in use

that it is curious that this omission in the zoning concept was not corrected a long time ago. There are at least ten, maybe twelve, identifiable open-space or open-land uses both public and private. While some zoning ordinances do provide for agricultural uses, these are relatively few and quite weak. The result has been that space, which should have been reserved for both public and private use as part of a general plan and supported by zoning, has not been so preserved, and nowhere within the concept of zoning is there a basis for the protection of such areas. It should be clear by this time that the term "undeveloped land" must be dropped from our vocabulary and that we must substitute for it a category of open-land use, even when such open land is presently "vacant" or "unoccupied."

Granted this may appear an oversimplification of a very complex problem, but when we consider the accumulation since 1925 of results of this omission of a use category, we must realize that this basic deficiency in the zoning concept is both philosophically and actually indefensible. (I brought this matter before a meeting of zoning and planning experts in New York City nearly four years ago and was met by blank stares and defensive incredulity. It is extraordinary how strongly the adherents of zoning inviolability resent infringements on the rituals.)

THE AMATEUR HOUR

The second grave error in the philosophy of zoning is the proposition that it can be adequately and knowledgably administered by politically appointed citizens with neither technical know-how nor a plan to refer to—other than the zoning map. Our law books are now filled with many hundreds of cases, city by city, state by state, year by year, dealing with complex and often contradictory court decisions relating to the actions of local zoning boards of adjustment and the appeals from such actions. Professor Haar, quoted above, should have said that, "zoning is the work horse which *drags* the planning movement in this country." As case is added to case, legal confusion, state by state, compounds the difficulties of administering zoning at the local level by even the best-meaning and best-educated citizen zoning body.

In the first instance, the originators, as lawyers

of zoning, should have been realistic enough to recognize that technical problems as complex as are those embodied in the framing, modification, and administration of local zoning required more understanding that could reasonably be brought to bear by a voluntary group meeting once or twice a month and deluged with case after case of appeals for variances and amendments. Today, we are dealing with a concept that incomprehensible to the average person because of it legal and technical complexity. In the zoning of a city, why should we expect a citizen group to vote on the technical changes involved in densities and coverage, in the mathematics of setbacks and floor-area ratios, any more than we would expect a citizen group to pass judgment on the engineering design of a suspension bridge? The design and redesign of cities and their maintenance at the highest possible level of human, economic, and physical value is a task of such magnitude that the validity of uninformed or amateur approaches to it is subject to question. Such approaches are certainly subject to pressure by those special interests with the capacity to enter into, or to employ experts who can enter into, the details of technological complexities.

MYTH AND THEOLOGY

Part of the problem lies in a super-myth structure which has grown out of these legal and administrative complexities. There is also a compelling power of persuasion in enabling legislation and in attendant codes and ordinances which are given the powers of the public purpose through democratic means of adoption. But even more significant is that the regiments of casuists in the interpretation and ritualization of the theology of zoning have now developed the argument that these ceremonies and written dogmas are in the best interests of planning and, ergo, *pro bono publico*.

It is quite clear now that few local public documents rest on a more unstable base than does the local zoning ordinance. This instability is not so much within the law itself as it is a product of the inability of politically appointed and untutored, constantly shifting, boards of appeal or adjustment to hold to the purpose of the ordinance, which is all too frequently better served in the breach than the observance. To this we must add

the super-myth of the ability of zoning to remove nonconforming uses. Compounding these are those master plans that illustrate the zoning dream and hopefully contain those changes which nonconforming use would imply.

THE TOOL OF PLANNING!

Because of the mystical concept that has grown up that zoning "is a tool of planning," we have all hesitated to question those who have the responsibility for the use of this "tool." Regretfully, we are compelled to say that if zoning is considered a tool to attempt to pin down a land- and building-control program, the tool is hardly more than a thumb-tack to be pried loose with one fingernail at the first meeting of the board of adjustment. The tack comes out without skilled craftsmanship and very very little pressure.

What has happened is that zoning is not a tool of planning but that planning has become a tool of zoning. A master plan or general plan which deviates too much from existing zoned uses of land is considered as upsetting the acceptable tax base and real estate values, as well as interfering with the normal speculative process. This is why changes in zoning are so difficult to bring about and, when they are brought about, why so frequently they are only minor modifications of long-accepted ordinances. Few philosophic and administrative concepts have bedded down so securely so quickly. Few need such drastic reform.

The pursuit of the best public interest via the democratic process is never-ending. So also is the constant search for the improvement of human welfare. This means an ever-continuing evaluation of the strengths of the bridges between the people and their government and their law. The quasi-judicial citizen board which exists, in various capacities, in nearly every American city is one of these bridges. In the boards of appeal or boards of adjustment in zoning we find a structure that is inadequate to carry the weight of responsibility for decisions that have far-reaching effect on the nature of man-made environment. It is strongly recommended that research be done by experts in the construction of such bridges, by engineers in the process of good government and good law, to find the methods of either building anew or substituting another structure for the existing one.

It is hoped that the present zoning process can be considered an interim one. Out of consideration for those who are giving so much of their time and effort to administering the zoning process, this would be only fair. And the public, which has perhaps been inadvertently guided into the hope that the zoning processes has safeguarded and can safeguard the best interest of community development, must also come to realize that stronger and more clearly considered positive programs are needed if urban blight and decay are to be permanently eliminated and the deterioration process is to be forever halted.

We know now that zoning has not and cannot provide all the protection it was assumed it could, and that it cannot remove or alter what should not have been done in the first place.

HEN OR EGG?

Very early in the development of zoning history in this country, the urgency of the priority in time of planning over zoning was brought forward by both zoning and planning experts. The conclusion of conference after conference was that planning should always precede zoning. The objective was correct but its accomplishment was negligible. The strength of the zoning concept, myth if you will, has been such that over and over again general plans have grown out of the zoning map. Planning considerations for the future of communities have been limited by what would appear to be acceptable within the framework of local zoning practice. The reasons for this are logical and clear. The law gave support to zoning in 1925 but it has never really supported planning. The first break that planning got was in the U. S. Supreme Court decision, *Berman vs. Parker*, 1954. Herein it was stated: "The concept of the public welfare is broad and inclusive. The values it represents are spiritual as well as physical, aesthetic as well as monetary. It is within the powers of the Legislature to determine that the community should be beautiful as well as healthy, spacious as well as clean, well balanced as well as carefully patrolled." While this case concerned redevelopment in the District of Columbia, it clearly supported the concept of planning and area design. It gave a new lift to the whole process of urban planned development and in time will stand as an even greater milestone

than the *Euclid vs. Ambler* zoning case of 1925.

We have barely begun to understand what development programming we may now do within the liberalized interpretation of our powers to plan. We do not know that even the Berman-Parker case is adequate for our total purpose. Possibly this is because we are not sure what our total purpose should be. But even so, as planners, those of us who serve the public by working towards the future revitalization of communities and the building of sound new ones take comfort in the fact that such action, at least in part, has been validated as zoning was twenty-nine years earlier. This time lag however has been unfortunate. We cannot yet assess the degree of damage that has been done either by unplanned zoning action or by misguided zeal. We do know that the process has, through its complexity and frequently through its lack of direction, fixed many areas and many uses which by their very nature require reconsideration and redesign. We recognize the positive benefits that have been derived from zoning as a protective device for high-class single-family in residential areas. In this application of the zoning process throughout the country we can clearly see the physical results of the "highest type" of restriction. In other areas the protective device has been less successful, and in older areas of cities its application is barely discernible.

THE DEVELOPMENT PLAN

What we must consider now is how to reverse the priorities of planning and zoning in both strength and time. The best tool at our disposal, and also the newest, lies in the strength of urban redevelopment and renewal. Today we must think of urban development potential within the redevelopment or renewal concept as being the more positive and stronger weapon to be used by planners. No more urgent effort can be recommended than the application of these processes to local activity, all sources of financing to be considered but not to be controlling. In the process of planning and replanning and future planning for communities, design requirements for development using renewal powers and action will inevitably modify present zoning patterns. A mechanism has therefore been developed which supersedes the older one, and within the foreseeable future it can place planning in its proper and primary position in local government.

It is true that we are in the very beginning of our understanding of the redevelopment and renewal processes, having had no more than ten years experience with them. Also, there are states which have not yet passed enabling legislation and cities which have not yet adopted the necessary measures to carry out these development processes. And yet, when Baltimore can declare its downtown area blighted and subject to renewal within state law and use its own bond-issue funds to undertake the Charles Center and Civic Center development, beginning without federal assistance—and all within the last five years—we must recognize the great strength that already lies within this new concept. The renewal and revitalization and rebuilding of the Golden Triangle in Pittsburgh was accomplished this same way. This could not have been done through zoning or rezoning or any other existing mechanism of local government other than redevelopment powers. Instances are now multiplying rapidly, with both good and bad plans developing—which is to be expected at this stage of experience. However, we must recognize here a new and very vital element in the total planning of our cities and look at zoning again, in relation to this new element.

THE PLAN ABSORBS THE ZONE

A clear look at the development process raises the question of whether ultimately the controls of zoning should not be absorbed into planning districts, neighborhood, and citywide development plans and programs, staged, as is suggested in the federal community renewal program, in such a way that their accomplish merit can be carried out in sequence or, where feasible, simultaneously. The regulatory measures and covenants which go with the development plan or program on a planning district or area basis would be those which relate specifically to the design of the plan itself and to the uses and purposes to which land and buildings are to be put. A new and more vital role is automatically created for the design planner, whether in public or private service. A valid development plan must relate to a valid community plan within a political subdivision, or within a group of political subdivisions or a region or whatever you may wish. The ultimate scale is still to be established.

Inserted, also, will be required development plans for "undeveloped" land. Orderly development of open land can only take place when it has been planned in advance, as part of a process as valid as that of planning for the replanning and redesign of land cleared by urban redevelopment and urban renewal. There should be no distinction in the planning process between the replanning of old areas and the planning of new and still-to-be-developed lands. The process under consideration is not just that of the change of land use, as mentioned above, but also the creation of an orderly design for a change in land use. This could well mean a development process directed towards the creation of new communities, call them what you will. Such communities must be part of the development process within a political subdivision or of the development process which creates new political subdivisions of an orderly type. Otherwise chaos continues.

While zoning conceivably can be used as a mechanism for setting aside land for orderly development, only in rare instances has this produced desirable results without a development plan. If zoning is applied without such a plan it achieves only a fragment of a plan. Natural and human resources suffer. Highways, utilities, and services have no anchor. The administrative mechanism, which was not designed for this leadership purpose, has been proved incompetent in this role

Our thesis therefore appears to be developing that zoning be gradually eliminated as the specific regulatory measure. Substituted for it is the development planning process in selected areas—ultimately to be part of a total community renewal and conservation development process, with zoning, if it is to be retained, constituting a part of the rules, regulations, and covenant system which accompany the development plan and program.

THE DESIGN PLAN

What do we do with the mountains of zoning rules and regulations, legal decisions, and weighty processes, including the staffs and individuals who have been so intimately involved? In the first place, what is suggested here cannot be accomplished overnight. In spite of all its weaknesses, zoning must be maintained until a substitute has been found which can serve in every part of every community. Much can be chalked up to zoning experience. No matter what we do for a community in the development plan and program, there is invaluable background with zoning regulatory measures which can be transposed to those regulations which must be integral in the design plan for area development. It must be remembered that this design plan does not necessarily involve the clearance of buildings or drastic measures beyond those which would normally be required in the safeguarding or upgrading of an area. Much of what we do will be in the field of protection and conservation. In such areas we may modify the zoning approach by converting it into the performance type of regulation or, even better, making use of the newer concepts of planned development districts and planned development zones.

It can be feared that in the use of a planned development concept we may fall back again on inexperienced and incapable citizens, who make the final determination as to whether the design plan is acceptable. In other words, the equivalent of a board of adjustment may be established, but with many more difficult problems of evaluation before it. There is no gain saying that the responsibilities of a board of redevelopment and the responsibilities of a planning commission will become increasingly arduous and will require, more and more, a high type of citizen participation. The process of training and education for this type of service in itself becomes a major task. Also, there is in this country a serious scarcity of trained design planners and architects qualified to work out the intricate and appropriate schemes for the rebuilding of portions of older cities, the conservation of that which is worth selecting to be conserved, and the planning of new areas. We must devote much of our time and effort to improving our training program to meet these challenges.

It has been interesting to note the examples of success in the rebuilding of bombed out areas in Europe, particularly in the Netherlands and Great Britain, where design plans and citizens' action appear to have gone hand in hand successfully. It is certainly not beyond our capacity to develop our own abilities along these lines.

It is difficult to answer the question of whether appointed citizens and elected groups can review and administer design plans better than similarly elected boards of adjustment or appeals did for zoning. For the time being, the only valid suggestion seems to be that, where citizens' boards lack this capacity, the locality would be well advised to employ consulting boards of review or panels of trained professionals in these fields. There is one thing that should be remembered: A design plan is a visual interpretation of what should be built, can be built, should be preserved, should be removed. All the facets of a plan are clearly expressed and exposed in drawings, models, diagrams, charts, and specifications. It is not possible to hide a design plan behind the verbiage that so frequently conceals either the intent of zoning or its feasibility.

The public purpose will be expressed in its choice of design plans, since a locality must approve, through its governing body, the elements of these plans. Whether we are dealing with a small town or a big city, the public's choice will be as varied as the interests of the community itself. This is as it should be if we are ultimately and hopefully to achieve communities which have individuality and character of their own. Obviously, the opposite can occur. An unimaginative outlook may support an unimaginative plan. It certainly has in the limitless FHA subdivisions which presently cover vast areas of our urbanized land.

The history of public taste is a fascinating subject in itself. In these days of easy communication, it is all too easy to soft-sell to the national community products with little or no merit. Zoning can do little about this even in those areas where zoning for aesthetics has been an experiment. But today, hopefully and on the basis of many stimulating starts throughout the country, the replanning of old areas and the planning of new indicate that urban pride is returning, that it is becoming more and more the ambition of people our cities to live, work, and play in attractive and citing human surroundings, and that they are will to gamble on experiments as well as to fall back on safety and safeguards of the banal.

SUMMARY

In summary, then, what is recommended here? Primarily, it is that zoning should be superseded by development planning as part of comprehensive plan soon as feasible. That every area of a city should be protected and promoted by plans for improvement and development with attendant regulatory measures, which may include zoning, such plans to be given public acceptance in much the same way that zoning ordinances and maps have received public promotion and acceptance in the past. We must step forward with courage into the next stage of environmental design.

We can still make use of the experience we have gained in zoning—particularly in the design of new covenants and rules to support designed development, plans. Conceivably, zoning may remain as a generalized supporting legal measure, but it may well become a superfluous procedure. If so, it should be cut out, but not before the development planning design is well established. Otherwise we return to an even more primitive and unprotected situation (which Houston, Texas, likes), not to be recommended here. We are verging on programs for community objectives more readily achievable than in many years of modern planning history. In stepping towards comprehensive community goals through the mechanism of designed area development plans based on the growing planning powers of renewal, we will be retiring old systems with due honor, but making new history.

Building the Middle-Range Bridge for Comprehensive Planning

Martin Meyerson

This selection is Meyerson's keynote speech, delivered on May 8, 1956 at the annual meeting of the American Institute of Planners (now the American Planning Association). The text gives the reader a sense of the concerns and debates among professional planners of that period. In the speech, Meyerson suggests ways to expand the focus of the embryonic planning profession by focusing on certain functions traditionally viewed as the responsibility of local governments. He makes the argument that although the opportunity cost maybe spending less time on long-range planning, planners could bring greater efficiency to such functions—and that could translate into "daily changes of urban development."

When De Tocqueville visited here a hundred years ago, he commented that whenever two Americans got together, they formed an organization. In recent years, it has become fashionable for European observers to laugh about our tendency to elaborate on organization—now, these observers say, whenever two Americans doing the same sort of work get together, they form a profession.

PROFESSIONALIZATION

The social scientists have also focused on this tendency to professionalize. They have analyzed certain general procedures followed by all emerging professional groups. Their analyses amount to a recital of the natural history of professionalization. First, persons of imagination and vision, and a profound dissatisfaction with the world as they see it, outline the scope of new problems and propose new approaches to these problems. These are persons trained in other disciplines, often diverse disciplines; they are people of broad interests and an ability to dramatize problems and inspire others. Whatever literature is produced is polemic, general, devoted to portrayal of problems, and clamors for the attention of a citizenry already perplexed and vexed by other matters.

As more and more recognition is given to the importance of the newly discovered problems, limited funds are made available for exploring or solving these problems. More people are attracted as lay enthusiasts or as practitioners in the field; organizations are set up; conferences are held. Schools are established to give specialized training; the course of instruction grows longer and longer. A unique vocabulary is developed; nonprofessionals cannot talk it. A literature geared to specific problems emerges; nonprofessionals find it complex and dull. Soon people begin to think in terms of "careers" as well as in terms of solving problems. Salaries, job classifications, personnel qualifications, specialization within the field become important. Attempts are made to broaden functions and responsibilities, to grow bigger and bigger, to be imperialistic in scope and numbers. More and more efforts are made to make the activity expert, technical, scientific—and beyond the ken of nonprofessionals. This culminates in licensing or registration to keep out pretenders. By this time, the profession has "institutionalized"; its members acquire the power of reproduction—that is, it is the present professionals not the market situation who determine what standards must be met by new entrants.

Despite the gibes of some European observers and despite the implied gibes of the social scientists, I think our American tendency to professionalize on the whole is a good one. By being self-conscious about our work activities we do try to develop our methods and body of knowledge and to improve our competence. The danger lies in the stage when we become too rigid, when we are no longer capable of absorbing new ideas or going in new directions, or willing to discuss our problems with people in other fields. However, planning is too new an activity to be that institutionalized. We are in the expansionist, imperialistic stage, and who am I to go counter to the natural history of our emerging profession?

Therefore, I want to speak today as an imperialist for city planning. I want to speak today about expansion—about increasing our numbers, multiplying our budgets, strengthening our effectiveness, expanding our functions, and, of course, raising our salaries.

EXPANDING FUNCTIONS

I shall focus on expanded city planning functions and responsibilities which if not performed by planning agencies may very well be performed by other agencies of local government. However, I believe planning agencies are not only best equipped to perform these functions, but their own effectiveness will be enormously increased by doing so.

However, we might well ask if increasing our scope of operations will not be done by sacrificing preparation of long-range plans. Do not the administration of zoning and subdivision control already rob us of time and energy to devote to long-range planning? Of course they do. Yet they are also ways in which planning is translated effectively into daily changes of urban development.

For background to some of the additional functions I want to discuss, let me wear two hats. One is my hat at ACTION—the American Council to Improve Our Neighborhoods. The other is my hat as city planning professor. Wearing ACTION's hat, my responsibilities during the past year and more have required me to travel to many parts of the country, and to talk with many of the people who made the key decisions which shape our cities and towns. These are the mayors, the city managers, the heads of operating municipal departments, the homebuilders, the merchants and industrialists, the civic leaders. Their decisions are the decisions that set the stage for the decisions of the everyday citizen—his choices on where he lives, his kind of work, the activities he and his family will have an opportunity to participate in. And I was struck by the fact that the mayor and the merchant, the head of the renewal agency and the homebuilder are at a loss to find the specific framework to provide them with the kinds of guidance they need to make rational decisions.

As I talked with these people, it was very encouraging to me to find the respect in which they hold the city planner and to recognize it as a tribute to the responsible growth of our profession. However, their respect is rarely derived from an awareness of the importance of long-range comprehensive planning. Rather their respect is based on the project-planning accomplishments of the city planner and related officials. They speak their admiration for the highway extensions, the new zoning districts, the design of a group of public buildings, the development of a park preserve or a new terminal improvement. Partly, of course, it is because so much of our attention has necessarily gone to project-planning that little effort has been left for long-range comprehensive planning, and thus little opportunity for it to be understood, let alone for it to be vigorously supported.

Yet the framework required by the people who make some of the key decisions for both private and public community development is not provided by project-planning. Nor is the urgency of these decisions met by the kind of long-range comprehensive planning we usually do. I have concluded that a middle ground is needed. An intermediate set of planning functions must be performed on a sustained, on-going basis to provide the framework for the homebuilder who must decide how many units he should, as well as can, build next year; for the government official who must decide whether the signs of unemployment in the locality require special public action; for the appointed commissioner who has no sense of whether a particular policy which his agency might follow and obtain bonds to execute will fit in with other current city policies; for the industrialist who wants to know what specific land use changes will be made in an area within the next few years before he commits his corporation's resources; for the redevelopment agency which has no knowledge as to what the effects of previous slum-clearance projects have been and the lessons that can be learned from them.

Now changing my hat, as a professor of city planning, one of my major concerns is that we train students for the responsible posts they will hold not only this year but ten years from now. An apprenticeship might be a far superior way to a university curriculum if our main object were to prepare people for specific present jobs. What kind of a job will the planner be expected to do ten years from now? I have been trying to get some sense of this and thus of needed educational programs. I am of course talking primarily about city planning, although I believe what I am saying applies to resources planning and other kinds of planning as well. I also recognize that most city planners in the future may not work for what we

regard as city planning agencies. This does not mean that they should not be trained as city planners.

Now, wearing both my hats at the same time, I wonder very much whether the impressions I have got for the need and importance of a middle ground planning activity may not be a clue to some of the crucial functions of the profession in the years ahead, and thus a clue to planning education in the years ahead as well. The additional functions I propose are suggested not to detract from long-range planning but to make it more meaningful.

I propose that we consider whether the following middle-ground community planning functions are appropriate to our province:

1. *A Central Intelligence Function* to facilitate market operations for housing, commerce, industry and other community activities through the regular issuance of market analyses
2. *A Pulse-Taking Function* to alert the community through quarterly or other periodic reports to danger signs in blight formation, in economic changes, population movements and other shifts
3. *A Policy Clarification Function* to help frame and regularly revise development objectives of local government
4. *A Detailed Development Plan Function* to phase specific private and public programs as part of a comprehensive course of action covering not more than 10 years
5. *A Feed-Back Review Function* to analyze through careful research the consequences of program and project activities as a guide to future action

These are interrelated functions. The intelligence, pulse-taking and review functions roughly parallel the types of measures we are learning to utilize nationally, for example through the Council of Economic Advisers, to encourage equilibrium and new growth in employment and investment. On the community level, we would not want to restrict ourselves to just economic concerns. But nationally we have developed during the last twenty years a type of sensitivity to changes in the economy which permit adjustments when the economy gets markedly out of balance. We have developed a whole series of statistics and indices such as building starts, prices of hogs, consumer credit, a type of periodic information which we never had before. Then, if there are maladjustments in the economy revealed through periodic checks, we may adjust the mortgage rate, place governmental orders in areas where there is unemployment and try to take other measures to bring about equilibrium.

The five functions I want to discuss this evening envisage a similar role for the city planning agency—a role which brings planning and policy closer together. They are functions which city planning agencies to some extent fulfill already. However, they are not part of the routine view of appropriate city planning activity.

What do these five functions mean for municipal planning?

(1) The Central Intelligence Function: The planning agency as the local G2 to aid the operations of the market.

The market place—the mechanism which brings together producer and consumer, supply and demand—is the primary method under democratic capitalism by which land and other resources are allocated to those activities by which people live, work, play and raise their families.

Market decisions are more important than governmental ones in giving substance to the design and structure of our urban communities. In our cities, for example, we see that people who desire housing accommodations are more and more choosing to live in the suburbs. These represent individual choices to satisfy individual values and fit individual circumstances. But these individual choices add up to a major shift in urban patterns—not only in housing, but in shopping and many other facilities as well. The changes in urban patterns due to market selection are so decisive and have such widespread and interlocking consequences that they almost appear as though someone had directed them. (Perhaps this is the invisible hand of the market to which Adam Smith refers.)

However, the local businessman, the industrialist and the consumer rarely have the kind of accurate enough information to make rational decisions. Currently, builders, investors, business and industrial firms have such vast unknown factors with which to deal that the risks involved either operate as brakes on activity or inflate the costs of production or financing. The consumer

has to act on conjecture rather than real knowledge of choices open to him.

The city planning agency in most communities is the local unit of government best equipped to provide a market analysis function. Data would have to be obtained and analyzed continuously. Regular market reports would be issued by the planning agency. Depending on the urgency of the market decisions, some of the reports could be issued monthly, some quarterly, some semiannually, some annually. There could be special reports on the new home building market, on investment in plant, on consumer income and spending, on land and building costs. The planning agency is an appropriate one for this function, not only because it has a nucleus of people dealing with these community characteristics but also because this kind of regular and constant market analysis is crucial to the achievement of present functions of planning and some of the other ones I am discussing today.

Detailed market analysis for the city, for the metropolitan area and for subregions in this area would enable both the producer and the consumer to make more intelligent choices in respect to the location, investment, building and land utilization for industry, commerce, housing and other main facilities and activities. The political philosophy of the country rests on the market as the key means to allocate resources. If the city planning agency regularly checks and interprets the local market situation as I suggest here, it can lubricate the process of urban development and achieve many of the main objectives of city planning by facilitating intelligent individual actions.

(2) The Pulse-Taking Function: The planning agency as the watchdog for community danger signs.

It is true that most community development decisions are made through market mechanisms rather than through governmental planning mechanisms. However, one of the reasons why planning has become an accepted governmental activity is that the market has frequently exhibited such frictions and even malfunctioning that desired community ends have not been achieved. For example, a main impetus to planning came from the fact that the market was not allocating land uses in such a way as to preserve residential values during the useful life of the property. Planning was expected, through land use and other controls, to compensate for the problems—the failures—of the market.

However, planning has too often been in the position of correcting mistakes after they have happened rather than in the position of detecting and removing trouble spots before they lead to major mistakes. I therefore recommend that the planning agency submit a quarterly or other periodic report to the local chief executive alerting the community danger signs. Which neighborhoods are showing blight factors at an increased pace? Are certain transit routes losing most of their passengers? Are there signs that certain industries are about to either come in or leave the area? The planning agency should thus perpetually scan the community for indications of maladjustment. Failures of firms, increased congestion, incipient changes in land use, new demands for services might thus be detected before they gather a momentum almost impossible to stop.

To be effective the planning agency's pulse-taking report must not only alert the community to trouble spots, but must also point to remedial action. Inevitably this means a policy focus.

(3) The Policy Clarification Function: The planning agency as an aid in framing arid regularly revising development objectives of local government.

I have just suggested that the planning agency be alerted to detect any trends potentially harmful to the community. This implies that policies would be devised to halt undesirable changes and promote desired ones in the community, and that the planning agency would take some initiative in indicating the most suitable policy measures. Specific inducements to encourage private actions as well as direct public measures would be needed.

Much of the determination of community policy will evolve through the political process. In a pluralistic society such as ours, there are many conflicting values and there is, as a result, competition among goals. The competition will be expressed and settled largely through politics.

The planning agency, however, can analyze alter-native policies. It can help determine what benefits can be achieved as against what costs will be incurred by different specific policies.

Politicians could be given detailed information on the advantages and disadvantages of alternative courses of action to achieve desired goals. Planners should be prepared to say to politicians—if you wish to do such and such, then such and such consequences are likely to result. The planning agency would not be usurping the task of political decision-making but it would be making clear what the implications of alternative policy decisions are, so that more meaningful policy choices can be made. The planning agency, furthermore, can serve as the instrument for making known the policy choices once they are made. The planning agency, by suggesting revisions to policymakers on the basis of changed conditions can encourage periodic presentations of community development policy. Probably a coherent development policy statement should be consciously revealed each year through the mass media of communication.

(4) The Detailed Development Plan Function: The planning agency as the preparer of a short-range comprehensive plan spelling out specific actions to be taken.

The gap between the developmental policies of government discussed above and a long-range master plan for the future community can be bridged by the preparation of short-run plans, of five to 10 years in time span. The development plan would link measures to deal with current problems with long-range proposals to attain community goals.

For many politicians and businessmen the master plan is too generalized and too remote to seem real. For planners, on the other hand, ameliorative measures which attack symptoms rather than basic problems are too piecemeal, too hastily considered to seem worthwhile. I suggest the short-run development plan as that compromise between immediate problems and future expectations which will permit coherent policy effectuation. This type of plan preparation will require detailed, timed and localized programming of governmental policies for private as well as for public actions. Detailed cost estimates of private as well as public development, and specific administrative and legal measures to carry out the programs will have to be worked out.

Long-range comprehensive plans commonly reveal a desired state of affairs. They rarely specify the detailed courses of action needed to achieve that desired state. By their long-range nature they cannot do so. The development plan, in contrast, will indicate the specific changes in land use programmed for each year, the rate of new growth, the public facilities to be built, the structures to be removed, the private investment required, the extent and sources of public funds to be raised, the tax and other local incentives to encourage private behavior requisite to the plan. The development plan—which incidentally in a more limited form is required by law in England—would have to be acted upon each year and made an official act for the subsequent year, much as a capital budget is put into law. Revised yearly it would become the central guide to land use control, to public budgeting and to appropriate private actions to achieve directed community improvement.

(5) The Feed-Back Review Function: The planning agency as analyzer of the consequences of program and project activities in order to guide future action.

Currently, we in planning agencies have no systematic means of analyzing the effect of planning measures or programs of action. It is astonishing, for example, that we have never analyzed the effects of zoning. We have never studied what the effects of this interference in the land market have been on the monopoly position of different kinds of businesses, on the costs of land, on the encouragement or discouragement of certain types of development.

I suggest that we maintain a constant feedback of information on the intended and the unintended consequences of programs that are adopted locally. For example, if a new area is developed in the central business district with new office buildings, shopping facilities, and cultural activities, we ought to assess the unintended effects as well as the intended ones of just what happens to the older, existing sections of the central business district and to the surrounding area. Does the new development serve as catalyst and stimulator of further improvements or does it drain off activities from the remainder of the district? These kinds of questions must be asked and answered so that we can learn from our experiences and can adjust our future programming and planning.

The more such a review function is performed, the more readily it can be performed. As a body of review knowledge is built up on the parking effects of highways, on the use made of play-

grounds on whether public housing and redevelopment projects achieve their objectives, on the impact of off-street loading ordinances, the more simply can new measures be gauged.

IMPLICATIONS OF THESE FUNCTIONS FOR PLANNING AGENCIES

This may sound like a formidable range of new or at least much enlarged functions. Whether such proposals are practical depends on the situation in particular cities.

I have made a plea that we consider adding certain functions intermediate between ad hoc decisions on a subdivision plat, for example, and long range comprehensive planning. The capital budget and program in current city planning practice comes closest to this intermediate position. Of course I believe that the functions I have suggested are ones that would be of great benefit to local government and to community development. However, the functions I mentioned could be lodged in various existing or possible municipal agencies.

Assuming these functions have merit, I am convinced that the planning agency should be the appropriate niche for them. This is for us in the A.I.P. to decide, or it may be decided for us. We will not have a great deal of time in which to decide. Two cities, a large one and a moderate sized one, both known in recent years for their good government, are establishing posts called "development coordinator." Should this responsibility not have been delegated to or assumed by city planning? It is too early to say that this is prophetic of a trend. It is not too early, however, to say that planners have the opportunity to take on the development coordination function, to extend their range from the generalized plan on the one hand and the day-to-day demands on the other to the intermediate type of sustained on-going planning activities I have suggested.

But a planning agency capable of achieving some of the functions I have suggested today will require far greater specialization than we have ever had in municipal planning. It is true also that more planners will be required by specialized agencies in transportation, housing and other fields. They will be required especially in such agencies if the functions I suggest above develop.

However, the specialization will be required mostly by the planning agencies themselves to prepare detailed development plans, perpetual inventories of market characteristics and the other tasks demanded. It will require personnel with joint specialization, or more properly, people who are specialists in a particular field and generalists in planning. Joint designer planners, statistician-planners, highway expert planners, real property lawyer-planners, utility engineer-planners and other dually trained personnel will be necessary. Incentives will have to be provided to enable people willingly to acquire such dual background—in other words, we will have to pay them as well as offer intellectual satisfactions and the satisfactions which come from socially useful work.

But if we do extend our planning functions—and even if we merely try to fulfill our present tasks as we see them—we need a level of budget for local planning of a kind we have never seen before. The planner currently is responsible for advising on expenditures running into hundreds of millions of dollars and on programs intimately affecting the lives of thousands, or in some cases, millions, of people. Decisions of such far-reaching consequences should not be financed through sub-standard salaries, blighted budgets and penny pinched research. It is true that planning costs our local communities in the United States between 7½ and 10 million dollars annually. But this is insignificant when a single mile of an expressway in a single city may cost twice that much. It is unnecessary for me to point out that the total annual expenditure on city planning in the United States is less than the cost of a single public building or a fraction of the budget of my own and other academic institutions or that some of the efficiencies which can be derived from city planning in even a single city could pay for the entire cost of city planning in the country.

I do not know how much the additional functions I have suggested would cost. Costs would vary, of course, with the thoroughness of performing each function and with the size of the community. (I have completely side-stepped the issue of whether the planning agency should also attempt to administer or to oversee the short-range development plans, and if so, to what degree.) However, such planning will clearly be very costly.

My own basic premise is that good staff is essential to the performance of planning functions and good staff is expensive staff. I agree completely with the statement in the Schuster report of Great Britain that "more than ever before the planning authorities need to recruit people with first-class intellectual qualities and first-class educational attainments. Everything else that we have to say is secondary in importance to this."

It is to the credit of planning that we have been able to attract people so far through the challenge of the field rather than the remuneration offered them. However, we must recognize that just as our universities and colleges cannot well exist from the subsidy of low salaries, so planning and other governmental activities cannot sustain high quality work through the subsidy of under-paid labor. Beardsley Ruml recently advocated paying professors as much as $30,000 a year. We should hardly be expected to feel that the top jobs in planning should pay less than that.

I preambled my comments tonight with a thumbnail sketch of the natural history of all professions. Each attempts to get for itself a bigger share of the pie of responsibility, of status, of resources and of income. Just within this last week a colleague, a neighbor, and a third person whom I did not know, made the following claims in the press: The race relations expert said discrimination was America's Number One problem. The criminologist said the rising wave of juvenile crime was America's Number One problem. The third person—the psychiatric administrator—said mental health was America's Number One problem.

But these claims are not true. Naturally, you and I as city planners are convinced the Number One problem of America is the development of America's cities, their housing, their transportation and all the other elements that make them viable.

In conclusion, as an imperialist for the profession I have computed that about one-half of one per cent of municipal expenditures in the United States could result in an expenditure for planning of almost ten times what it is now. Such an expenditure I feel sure would clearly enable us to do our day-to day jobs, to do long-range planning, and to add major substance to our work through the on-going middle-range age of comprehensive planning I have described. Since Chicago 50 years ago, we have urged others to make no little plans. Let's make no little plans for the development of our

own profession in terms of resources, in terms of public support, in terms of education, and in terms of laying claim to emerging new functions.

Understanding American Land Use Regulation Since 1970

Frank J. Popper

Frank Popper examines the recent emergence of centralized, as opposed to local, land-use regulations at the regional, state, and federal levels in the United States. After analyzing and disputing two prevailing explanations for this centralization, Popper offers an alternate interpretation for the trend, one that involves practical adaptiveness and political staying power. He concludes that, "the right to make particular regulatory decisions shifts unpredictably over time from one level of government to another. No principle of administrative rationality, constitutional entitlement, economic efficiency, or even ideological predisposition truly determines the governmental locus of decisions." This article received the 1989 Award for the Best Article in the *Journal of the American Planning Association*.

Land use regulation has probably changed more since 1970 than in any comparable period in the nation's history. Two decades ago American land use regulation consisted almost entirely of local zoning; it no longer does. Instead, it has become increasingly centralized—that is, more likely to originate with regional, state, and federal agencies rather than with local ones (Healy and Rosenberg 1979; Popper 1981; DeGrove 1984). The changes in regulation have transformed American planning: its practice, its aims, its role in American government, even its attractiveness as a career. But planners have not grasped the extent of the regulatory changes, their political meaning, or their professional consequences.

Two competing interpretations—one liberal, the other conservative—now attempt to explain the recent history of American land use regulation. The liberal view maintains that the environmental shortcomings of local land use regulation, especially zoning, led to the creation in the early 1970s of new regional, state, and federal regulatory powers. Those policies, liberals contend, were largely unable to withstand the conservative onslaught—against centralized regulation, against bureaucracy, against environmentalism—that began in the

middle 1970s and crested with the Reagan administration. Thus the liberals maintain that the new centralized regulatory programs never got a chance to prove themselves. Like the local controls they were intended to supplement, they amounted to insufficient land use regulation.

The conservative perspective, on the other hand, argues that the new initiatives, far from being insufficient, created so many and such potent centralized regulatory mechanisms that the nation in effect had serious federal regulation of land use by the late 1970s and still has it m the late 1980s. The conservatives, however, maintain that the public reacted against what it rightly saw as bureaucratic overreaching: it brought conservatives to power to try to restrain the new programs, and the battle to neutralize them continues to this day. The conservatives argue that the programs in fact got a chance to prove themselves and did so too well. The conservatives believe at the centralized initiatives' key political difficulty was not that they constituted too little land use regulation as the liberals maintain, but that they constituted too much.

In this article I first examine the emergence of centralized land use regulation in America. Then I present the two existing interpretations of the overall experience of centralized regulation.[1] Next I suggest a way to reconcile the interpretations through an alternative explanation that fits the facts and explains events since 1970 better than the other two. I take a less ideological, more pragmatic approach: I argue that centralized regulation has unobtrusively succeeded in ways neither liberals nor conservatives appreciate. In particular, it has overcome its initial practical disadvantage of unfamiliarity, achieved wide (though often specialized) application, received substantial public acceptance, and even attained a measure of acquiescence from land use conservatives, including those in the Reagan administration. I conclude by exploring this revisionist interpretation's surprisingly optimistic implications for the future of American land use regulation. Much of the interpretation draws on but differs from my previous work (Popper 1981), which is to say that I changed my mind. I used to subscribe to the liberals' interpretation, but now I find the revisionist one more persuasive.

THE RISE OF CENTRALIZED REGULATION

There may never have been a time when it was as good to be an American city planner or land use lawyer as the late 1960s and early 1970s. Planning was coming alive; huge segments of the public were interested in it and its possible contributions, probably for the first time in American history. The post-World War II building boom, culminating in the record-high development rates of the late 1960s, had produced a professionally exhilarating set of environmental problems. Even more exciting, planners, land use lawyers, and their political allies had new and apparently practical solutions to those problems, which the public would accept.

There was no denying the magnitude of the country's land use difficulties. Development projects of all kinds—commercial, residential, industrial, and governmental—were getting bigger and polluting more. The interstate highway system, begun in 1956 and reaching completion from the middle 1960s on, had created vast new stretches of urban or potentially urban land. Too much of it seemed to be succumbing to formless sprawl and strip development, or to shoddily built leisure

home projects, ruinous strip mines, and polluting power plants. The nation's countryside was urbanizing rapidly and unattractively.

Under the pressures that such developments caused, long-standing deficiencies in local land use regulation became clear. Zoning, the action arm of local planning and the nation's most prevalent mechanism for land use control, seemed especially fallible. Most zoning agencies and ordinances had originated in the 1920s and 1930s, and were often inadequate to cope with the 1960s' development. They could not handle huge suburban residential projects that might affect dozens of rapidly growing localities beyond the boundaries of the regulating one. They could not deal with big energy facilities that might have regional, state, or even national impacts. They could not deal with large, complicated public works projects. In all such cases lone communities were dealing with land use questions of regional or state impacts but were making their decisions without consideration of surrounding communities and often causing harm.

Another reason local planning and zoning did not work well was that in most of the country, particularly in the small, rural communities now in the path of urban expansion, relevant laws had never really existed in the first place. Such communities espoused the American ideal of rugged individualism; many of their residents thought zoning verged on socialism. Some excellent examples of that viewpoint come from the Appalachian part of New York (Robbins 1974) and from the Missouri and Arkansas Ozarks (Lewis 1976).

In 1971 George Hartzog, director of the National Park Service, became concerned about the proliferation of commercial development on the edge of Mammoth Cave National Park in Kentucky. "I talked to those people down there about zoning," he told writer John McPhee. "'Zoning?' they said. 'Zoning?' I had the impression that I was in a foreign land" (McPhee 1977: 258). In 1971 only 30 percent of Kentucky's cities and 20 percent of its counties had zoning. Even in seemingly more urban New York state, only 40 percent of the cities had zoning, and the counties had no zoning powers at all (RuBino and Wagner 1972: 9, 16). In many rural places where zoning laws did exist, they were undemanding, unenforced, or ignored (Williams 1975).

To counter that ragged local performance, a loose coalition of environmentalists, city planners, land use lawyers, state and federal officials, progressive business people and developers, and citizen activists of all kinds emerged, bearing an alternative—more precisely, a supplement—to local land use regulation: centralized land use regulation. The coalition's goal was new regulation that would operate at higher levels of government and would apply mainly to projects that were large or in environmentally sensitive areas.

The Rockefeller Brothers Fund Task Force on Land Use and Urban Growth produced a report, *The Use of Land*, which became one of the best-known documents of the movement for higher-level regulation (Reilly 1973). It declared, "Important developments should be regulated by governments that represent all the people whose lives are likely to be affected by it, including those who could benefit from it as well as those who would be harmed by it. Where a regulatory decision significantly affects people in more than one locality, state, regional, or even federal action is necessary"(Reilly 1973: 27). From the late 1960s well into the 1970s, that approach received the imprimaturs of the nation's leading land use lawyer, Chicago's Richard Babcock (1966), the National Commission on Urban Problems (1968), the American Society of Planning officials (Heeter 1969), Ralph Nader's Study Group on Land Use in California (Fellmeth 1973), the American Bar Association (Fishman 1977), and the American Law Institute (1977). In yet another of the period's authoritative-influential documents, sponsored by the Council on Environmental Quality, Babcock's law partners Fred Bosselman and David Callies called the rising movement "The Quiet Revolution in Land Use Control " (Bosselman and Callies 1972).

As an exercise in intellectual advocacy, interest-group politics, and the self-advancement of the planning profession, the Quiet Revolution was remarkably effective. In 1969 only Hawaii—a state whose development patterns, land market, and local government structure differed deeply from those of the rest of the country—had a state law regulating land use, and it had been passed in 1961, another era entirely. By 1975 the Quiet Revolution had achieved at least 20 new environmentally-oriented state land use laws, mostly in

the northeast, the upper midwest, and the far west. Those laws variously regulated the siting and operation of all large development projects, particular kinds of large projects such as power plants or strip mines, or projects in environmentally sensitive places such as coasts, mountains, wetlands, and farmlands (Rosenbaum 1976; Healy and Rosenberg 1979; Popper 1981; DeGrove 1984). Thirty-seven states had new programs of statewide planning or statewide review of local regulatory decisions (Council of State Governments 1976: 23-26).

At the federal level the Quiet Revolution succeeded in obtaining programs where the federal government funded state ones. Through the 1972 Coastal Zone Management Act, the U.S. Department of Commerce gave the 30 Atlantic, Pacific, Gulf, and Great Lakes states grants totaling about $16 million a year to plan for and regulate coastal development. The 1977 Surface Mine Control and Reclamation Act gave the states $110 million annually in Interior Department grants to regulate strip mining. The 1970 Clean Air Act, the 1972 Clean Water Act, and the 1974 Safe Drinking Water Act gave the states a total of nearly $3 billion yearly in Environmental Protection Agency grants to carry out regulatory and construction programs with complex but definite land use implications, including controls on the location of new projects (Natural Resources Defense Council 1977: 40-97). The 1973 Flood Disaster Protection Act required that states and localities regulate development in flood plains before they (and their residents) could buy federal flood insurance or receive federal flood disaster aid (Natural Resources Defense Council 1977: 121-32).

It is hard now to recall the euphoric excitement of the land use community in the early 1970s, but it was wonderful while it lasted. Congress even came close to passing the ultimate Quiet Revolution legislation, the National Land Use Policy Act—which amounted to an extension of the Coastal Zone Management Act to all non-coastal areas of the country or, from another perspective, a national expansion of the state comprehensive laws regulating all large developments, such as those in Florida, Oregon, and Vermont (Plotkin 1987: 149-200).

The National Land Use Policy Act, as the epitome of the Quiet Revolution, would have given federal grants ($100 million annually in the 1975 bill, probably coming from the Interior Department) to draw up statewide land use plans, devise procedures to protect environmentally sensitive areas, and regulate big private developments and public works. The legislation was introduced under varying forms (and names) every year from 1968 to 1975 by liberal Democrats such as Arizona Representative Morris Udall and the late Washington Senator Henry Jackson. It reached its high tide in 1974, when the Senate passed it by a wide margin, as it had in 1972 and 1973. But the House rejected it by seven votes when President Nixon withdrew his support, reputedly in a bid for conservative votes to prevent impeachment (Lyday 1976: 40).

Planning, legal, and environmental organizations closely watched the act's progress. As a low-ranking staff member at the Chicago headquarters of the American Society of Planning Officials (ASPO) in the early 1970s, I knew that high-ranking ASPO staff members made nearly daily telephone calls to Washington to check on the bill. I assumed that much more was done at the American Institute of Planners (now merged with ASPO to form the American Planning Association), which was in Washington and, unlike ASPO, had a lobbying operation. An ASPO deputy executive director believed the act's passage would increase planners' average income by $2,000. Land use lawyers would get even more. Yet the planners, lawyers, and environmentalists were also animated by a truly public-spirited desire to show how well they would perform if given the opportunity. In 1974 the act's narrow defeat seemed to them an annoyance that would soon be rectified. Their chance would come again.

THE LIBERAL POINT: TOO LITTLE CENTRALIZED REGULATION

Land use liberals now interpret the 1974 defeat of the National Land Use Policy Act as a near miss, after which the cause of centralized land use regulation went into decline. The liberals argue that them never was enough centralized regulation, never had been, probably never would be. They believe the years since 1974 have not been good to the Quiet Revolution; in a noisy counterrevolution, the political climate has turned hostile. The

reasons are familiar: a more difficult and a volatile economy (for instance, in the energy and agricultural sectors), a resurgent conservatism, strained government finances, growing public distrust of such devices as regulation and federal grants in all fields of policy, a disenchantment with government itself.

The liberal perspective emphasizes that in recent years states have passed few new land use laws and most states still lack genuinely strong ones. Moreover, in the states that have them, the regulations have often been weakened in scope, budgets, staffing, and enforcement (Popper 1981: 116-53, 165-68; DeGrove 1984: 217-31, 308-31). Throughout the 1970s, for instance, the Florida comprehensive and California coastal programs had no enforcement staff whatever (Popper 1981: 119). Sometimes the state regulatory bodies deliberately effaced themselves, lowered their bureaucratic profile. Beginning in the late 1970s, for example, the Florida and Vermont land use programs shortened their applications and combined them with those of other state environmental agencies. They also began to hold joint hearings with state, local, and federal agencies.

By the early 1980s it was distinctly more possible in many places than it had been five years earlier for conservative state and local politicians to successfully take positions against centralized land use regulation. In 1972 Governor Ronald Reagan opposed a voters' initiative to create state commissions that would regulate development along the California coast. But when the initiative passed, he made predominantly environmentalist appointments to the commissions that were in regions where such sentiment was powerful—for instance, the areas centered around San Francisco and Santa Cruz. By contrast, in his 1982 gubernatorial race California Republican George Deukmejian made the coastal commissions a special target. Once in office, he substantially reduced their personnel and funding. In 1987, for instance, he cut $400,000 out of a budget of $5 million and closed the Santa Cruz and Santa Barbara offices.

At the federal level, there was a comparable deterioration of early 1970s planning hopes and of the federal support of state regulatory programs. At the urging of many developers and localities, Reagan administration in effect abandoned, for example, the Coastal Zone Management Act. The administration never asked for funding for it in any of its annual budget proposals; Congress had to supply the funding every year. The Reagan-era directors of the program were always publicly committed to terminating it. Many talented staffers left and their jobs went unfilled. Some operations, such as those that supplied special regulatory funds for states whose coasts were experiencing intense energy development, have been terminated (Mitchell 1986: 325-26). The Clean Air, Clean Water, Safe Drinking Water, Flood Disaster Protection, and Surface Mine Control and Reclamation acts have suffered similar neglect (Hays 1987: 501-4).

Some planners, lawyers, and environmentalists experienced a nostalgia for the National Land Use Policy Act (for example, Strong 1981). The feeling was irrational, but understandable. The legislation seemed the great might-have-been of American land use planning and the Quiet Revolution, the missed opportunity that would have convinced the public that centralized regulation could deliver something it wanted. In 1978, three years after the bill had lost any chance of passage, a group of land use professionals established the American Land Forum (I later joined its board), in large part to keep alive the impulses that animated the National Land Use Policy Act.

Thus in 1983 the forum (which by then had become the American Land Resource Association) held an open meeting at its Bethesda, Maryland, headquarters on the topic "Toward a Land Resource Policy Agenda." Charles Little, founder of the forum, suggested, "I'd like to reopen something that really interested me. Is there a piece of overarching legislation that isn't like the National Land Use Planning and Policy Act of 1974 but is something we can concoct here that would provide the policy context for all of these locally wonderful things to happen? ...I don't want to lose sight of our need to have a single, consensus-building kind of approach that would be something we would take to the doorstep of Congress and say, 'Look, here's exactly what you ought to do.'" Neil Sampson, head of the National Association of Conservation Districts, then observed, "There is some virtue in reconceptualizing the land use bill, in tearing it apart and seeing what it was and wasn't." It was left to me to be "bothered by the continual returning to the idea of

a National Land Use Policy Act or redoing it or in fact reconceptualizing it. That strikes me as the political equivalent of never getting over whomever it was you had a crush on when you were seventeen. There's a lack of consensus hereabout what overarching idea would replace the 1974-style approach" (American Land Forum 1983: 21-22). That was a minority opinion. The clear sense of the meeting was that the country needed more centralized land use regulation.

THE CONSERVATIVE COUNTERPOINT: TOO MUCH CENTRALIZED REGULATION

Land use conservatives—most developers, many local officials, nearly all libertarians, and certainly political figures such as Ronald Reagan and James Watt—see the matter differently. They emphasize the vast amount of centralized land use legislation that has passed since 1970, as well as the bureaucratic toils in which the laws have enmeshed unsuspecting homeowners, developers, and localities. The conservatives like to count up numbers of laws the contradictions between them, and the resulting long application-processing times that lead to regulatory horror stories. Conservatives-them tell the stories to embarrass and cow the agencies administering the laws (Porter 1986; Pacific Legal Foundation 1985).[2]

The conservatives can clearly produce strong evidence of excessive regulation, often out of the mouths of liberals. Chicago lawyer Fred Bosselman, shortly after the last defeat of the National Land Use Policy Act (which he helped draft), wrote that "Congress has already passed so many federal land use regulations that in a few years only a rare development project of any size will get by without two and probably more federal approvals"(Bosselman 1975: 136-37). His prediction came true. By 1979 Lance Marston, the Interior Department official who might well have directed the implementation of the National Land Use Policy Act had it passed, estimated that there had been "at least—*at least*—a 20 percent growth in federal land use programs in the last three years" (Meyer 1979: 58, emphasis in the original). He was referring to such legislation as the Surface Mine Control and Reclamation Act and the amendments to the Clean Air, Clean Water, and Safe Drinking Water acts—all of which, like the

National Land Use Policy Act, relied primarily on federal grants to states. In that light, the failure of the more lightly funded Land Use Act became almost immaterial to conservatives: far too much legislation like it (and worse, because better funded) sprang up in its wake.

At the state level the growth of land use legislation was equally impressive and equally objectionable to conservatives. By the early 1980s California had 41 state agencies besides the coastal commissions with overlapping regulatory responsibilities for the coastal zone—the Energy Commission, the Forestry Board, the State Lands Commission, the Public Utilities Commission, and so on. Six Minnesota agencies exercised 679 regulatory (and nonregulatory) powers (Popper 1981: 161; see also Bosselman, Fuerer, and Siemon 1976). These clear-it-with-yet-another regulator programs inevitably antagonized the regulated. The theme of runaway regulation—with its subthemes of delay, expense, paperwork, inconsistent rules, disappointment, and injustice for applicants—figured strongly in the important1987 Supreme Court case, *Nollan v. California Coastal Commission*, which at a minimum invalidated much of the commission's regulation concerning beach access for the public. The counsel for the victorious plaintiffs—a family that had sought to demolish a dilapidated beach house in Ventura but was overruled by the commission, which wanted plans for more public access to the beach portion of the property—was the Pacific Legal Foundation in Sacramento, probably the nation's leading conservative public-interest law firm. When one counts both state and federal agencies, most of the private land in America and all the biggest projects on it have been subject throughout the late 1970s and the entire 1980s to large amounts of centralized regulation—multiple, frustrating layers of it. Private land is now one of the most centrally regulated sectors of the American economy.

Just as centrally regulated, unbeknownst to most land use liberals, are America's *public* lands—the third of the nation, primarily in the deep-rural, intermountain west and Alaska, which the federal government owns. Those are the lands of the Interior Department's Bureau of Land Management (the largest federal land agency, which holds a fifth of the entire United States), the Interior Department's National Park Service and

its Fish and Wildlife Service, and the Agriculture Department's Forest Service: the country's national parks, forests wildlife refuges, public grazing areas, and the federally designated wildernesses within those lands. California, the nations most populous and in many ways most urban state, nonetheless is 45 percent public land, primarily away from the coast and especially east of the Central Valley. Arizona is 44 percent public land, Wyoming 48 percent. Alaska, Idaho, Nevada, Oregon, and Utah are over half public land; Nevada is an astonishing 86 percent public land. The federal holdings comprise much of America's fabled wide open spaces and its surviving frontier (Popper 1986). They are the source, through federal leasing to private contractors, of half the nation's timber, a third of its known coal and uranium reserves, four fifths of its oil shale, and similarly large proportions of its copper, silver, lead, natural gas, phosphate, potash, and grazing grass. The holdings amount to a second land tenure system in the United States, almost a sore-thumb outpost of federal-*rentier* socialism in the American economy. They are governed by federal land use laws entirely separate from those that apply to private land.

After 1970 that body of federal public-land law expanded rapidly, just like other forms of centralized land use regulation. The prime federal statute regulating the public lands is the 1976 Federal Land Policy and Management Act, which even sounds like the unpassed National Land Use Policy Act. Under the 1976 National Forest Management Act, the Forest Service is conducting what may be the largest, most detailed planning-and-regulation exercise in American history on the service's 298,000 square miles, an area more than a tenth larger than Texas (see Hunt 1987; Wilkinson and Anderson 1987). The 1980 Alaska National Interest Lands Conservation Act created ten new national parks, most bigger than any in the Lower 48. At least ten other major pieces of legislation to preserve the federal lands passed between 1970 and 1980 (Nelson 1982: 27).

All those federal-land laws greatly resemble the post-1970 private-land laws that the federal government passed. Not only do both sets of laws centralize and regulate, but they also deal with impacts that cross local and state boundaries, have a strong environmental-planning focus, and are aimed at managing growth (in the public-land case, for example, by establishing a moratorium on new coal leasing on the land in 1971 through 1981 and again in 1983 through 1985). In addition, both sets of laws try to blend conservation and development (on the public lands, through the doctrine of multiple use) and seek to preserve environmentally sensitive areas (on the public lands, national parks, wildernesses, wildlife refuges, and trails). As with the private lands, the liberal centralized regulatory efforts on the public lands provoked a conservative counterreaction that Ronald Reagan symbolized. Other potent symbols of revitalized conservatism on the public lands were James Watt, Reagan's first Interior Secretary, and the Sagebrush Rebellion, the grassroots western attempt to shrink the public-land holdings and loosen the laws regulating them. Reagan, Watt, and the Sagebrush Rebellion were highly successful, at least at the latter task: oil, gas, mineral, and timber leasing accelerated, and the government opened more land to those efforts (Popper 1984). The same pattern played itself out in the many states, both western and eastern, with large holdings in state parks and forests. (Eleven states, including such eastern ones as Connecticut, Florida, Louisiana, Michigan, Minnesota, New York, and Pennsylvania, are more than one-tenth state lands [Pekkanen 1983: 178].)

The conservatives maintain that the new programs, whether on public or private and, have overreached, gone too far. They also argue, more tellingly because less ideologically, that the programs have fallen short of many of their stated objectives even when sympathetic liberals rather than hostile conservatives administer them. It can be difficult, for instance, to show any direct, indisputable environmental results from the programs (Popper 1981: 193-94). Moreover, if the previous, solely local regulation was often unenforced or ignored, so is the new centralized regulation; a recent and generally positive study of seven state land use programs found that "the lack of an effective monitoring and enforcement component in the system has emerged as the Achilles heel in implementation" (DeGrove 1984: 391).

The centralized programs' attempts to compel, stimulate, or provide incentives for stronger local land use regulation have often proved ineffectual in the face of local resistance. Many rural localities still have weak zoning or lack it entirely (Rudel 1984), and are comfortable with the situation. Almost 30 percent of New York's municipalities, for instance, still lack zoning (McGuinness 1987: 1)—an improvement over the 60 percent figure of the early 1970s, but not huge progress.[3] And most localities are years behind in their attempts to comply with the local-planning requirements of the Florida comprehensive and California coastal laws.

More revealing, after nearly two decades of centralized programs, some planners and land use lawyers—the professional groups with the most to gain—are beginning to lose patience with the programs' deficiencies. Much of the criticisms reminiscent of the late 1960s liberal criticism of zoning (for instance, McGuinness 1987) or—most strikingly—it adopts the conservative position that almost any regulation at any level of government is objectionable excess, doomed to frustration, and also harmful to the public (for instance, Bikales 1987). By the middle 1980s, conservatives could find ample confirmation for their consistent1970s contention that the failings of the centralized programs would turn out to be much the same as those of the local programs they were supposed to supplement or improve on. Adding more programs at higher levels of government would merely spread and amplify the defects of too much regulation.

THE PRAGMATIC RESOLUTION: INCREASINGLY FAMILIAR CENTRALIZED REGULATION

There is a simpler explanation for the events since 1970. Centralized land use regulation did not collapse from insufficiency, as the liberals maintain. Nor did it collapse from overextension, as the conservatives argue. Instead it did not collapse at all: it continues to expand, but more slowly than liberals hope and conservatives fear. Its fortunes ebb and flow, depending mainly on the politics of the individual states, federal agencies, or land use fields that apply it; but on the whole it is quietly thriving. It is more tempered, more narrowly focused than it was in the early 1970s, less a subject of extravagant ideological claims (or even attention) from either liberals or conservatives. The basic problem of centralized regulation then was that the two groups—as well as the public at large—had little practical experience with it. Nearly two decades later, its unfamiliarity has diminished, and it is becoming utterly acceptable, even ordinary, to much of the political spectrum, including many of its former enemies. The agencies and laws embodying it are melting into almost boring respectability. But the price of achieving familiarity is that centralized regulation evolves in directions its friends and enemies alike might not expect or even recognize.

Given that perspective, a number of important features of the American land use scene of the late 1980s fall into place. There is, for example, more centralized regulation now than there ever has been, but that regulation is also less likely to be comprehensive, more likely to be specialized, oriented to particular purposes (Brower and Carol 1987). The trend already was visible in the late 1970s, when the executive director of the California League of Cities, Don Benninghoven, said, "There is no interest in statewide land use planning in California. None. Not by cities, not by counties, not by the state.... We've given up on the grand scheme of doing anything statewide. Instead, we concentrate on legislation on specific problems, such as coastal protection, prime agricultural land, and preserving Lake Tahoe" (*Planning* 1977: 7). The sentiment, provocative then, is now near-conventional wisdom, for the state level has seen many new centralized regulatory efforts of specialized kinds in the 1980s: programs for hazardous waste facilities, farmland protection, wetland and floodplain regulation, groundwater protection, industrial- and energy-facility siting, sensitive-area preservation (for example, along the Maryland shore of Chesapeake Bay [Powers 1986]), state parks and forests (Fund for Renewable Energy and the Environment 1988). Every state, for example, now has some form of protective legislation for farmland (National Association of State Departments of Agriculture Research Foundation Farmland Project 1987). State parks are a newly exciting land use field (Myers and Reid 1986).

The new acceptability of centralized regulation also means that the combination of even a few single-purpose laws can easily be as effective as a comprehensive land use law of the Florida-Oregon-Vermont sort. In the late 1980s New Jersey

has unobtrusively made itself a leader in combining single-purpose laws. It has state-required and state-reviewed local regulations; regional regulations for the rural fifth of the state in the Pinelands near Philadelphia and Atlantic City and for the urban 30-square-mile, high-growth Hackensack Meadowlands near New York City and Newark; state hazardous waste, coastal zone, wetland, and farmland protection laws that are among the strongest in the country (Duerksen 1983: 218-29); and the nationally unique *Mount Laurel* legislation governing the local placement and amount of new low income housing. Several of those programs only came into being after 1980. The state is seriously considering a demanding state land use plan, regional regulation of the land use impacts of transportation facilities, and a state shore-and-ocean agency with powers that would surpass those of any existing state coastal zone program.

Many of the state land use programs that dated back to the 1970s have made significant midcourse administrative corrections as centralized regulation has become more familiar in the 1980s. Most programs have tried to simplify and coordinate their bureaucratic procedures so as to defuse conservative resistance without actually undoing their regulation (Popper 1981: 165-68; Duerksen 1983: 150-68). Some programs have undergone formal self-evaluations that led to tighter regulation. The Vermont program, for instance, made two such studies (Vermont Environmental Board 1981; Byers and Wilson 1983), which finally resulted in a 1987 law that extended state regulation to developments with fewer than ten lots, thus closing a loophole builders had previously used to escape regulation.

In some states the 1970s' centralized programs have found especially high public acceptance and made hefty political gains in the 1980s. Florida passed a package of legislation in 1984, 1985, and 1986 that amounted to an entire second-generation effort at centralized regulation, a revamping and expansion of the state's 1972 comprehensive land use law (Rhodes 1986; deHaven-Smith and Patterson 1986). Many programs tried to consolidate their political support, often by at least partially winning over such former enemies as developers and local governments—for instance, by persuading developers that the programs could improve their product and so help them charge higher prices for it (DeGrove 1984: 383-84; Popper 1981: 205-6; Wilson 1987b: 34A). The Oregon program to take the most impressive case of political consolidation, first had to survive a series of developer-inspired voters' initiative that would have abolished it. The challenges, in 1976, 1978, and 1982, become progressively weaker; by the middle 1980s many of Oregon's builders and some of its local governments occasionally found themselves siding with and participating in the state's key land-and-environment citizens' watchdog group, 1000 Friends of Oregon. In 1986 Florida's program was buttressed by the formation of 1000 Friends of Florida, which was modeled on the Oregon group and expected to elicit similar support from the program's previous opponents. A review of the recent experience of the 1970s state programs concluded that "it is clear that the movement to strength the state's role in growth management is winning new support in the 1980s" (DeGrove and Stroud 1987: 8).

At the federal level, the Reagan administration always claimed that it opposed centralized land use regulation. But when forced or embarrassed by Congress, it still undertook such measure, albeit specialized, hedged, and relatively unpublicized ones. In 1981 it agreed to the Farmland Protection Policy Act, intended to prevent federal agencies' action from contributing to agricultural land loss; then it used the law mainly as a way to defer to state farmland protection programs (Dunford 1984). In 1982 it actively promoted the Coastal Barrier Resources Act, intended to restrain growth in selected barrier areas, such as island and exposed mainland beaches, the are vulnerable to damage from hurricanes, erosion, and other natural hazards (and which thus often necessitate large federal flood insurance payments). In 1987 the administration proposed to triple the size of the protected area—but it would even so have totaled barely 2,000 square miles (an area about the size of Delaware) and would still have been only on the Atlantic and Gulf coasts, a relatively small proportion of the area that might have been protected (Mitchell 1986: 320-22). In 1987 the administration agreed to an expansion of the 1977 Surface Mine Control and Reclamation Act to cover strip mines of less than two acres, a heretofore-serious loophole for coal operators. It put over 7,000 square miles of river banks into the federally protected wild and scenic river system. On the public lands it has added nearly 11,000 square miles of federally designated wilderness since 1981. The Reagan administration was not generally enamored of centralized land use regulation but did not prove as uniformly hostile to it as its liberal critics assumed.

Because the administration *was* perceived as hostile (and not just by liberals), an interesting spillover effect appeared: the long-ignored local level of land use regulation revived in many places in the 1980s. Most planners know from experience that zoning, especially in big cities, is now more pervasive, sophisticated, and effective than it has ever been. Chicago's Richard Babcock, still the nation's leading land use lawyer just as he was over 20 years ago when he endorsed centralized regulation as a supplement to zoning (Babcock 1966: 166-84), has more recently argued that zoning has a large continuing usefulness even in the absence of centralized regulation (Weaver and Babcock 1980; Babcock and Siemon 1985). In a 1986 interview he admitted zoning's defects, then said, "But what would you substitute for it? Do you want no control over development at all? That would be turning back the clock" (Knack 1987: 23). He never mentioned centralized regulation.

Zoning and local regulation, in fact, have shown a practical adaptiveness and political feasibility that no one anticipated in 1970. By the late 1980s local regulation's surprise liveliness is particularly evident in a series of stringent (and technical) growth-management initiatives in the Sun Belt. In 1986 Los Angeles voters approved a proposition to limit the floor area ratio of new buildings in many neighborhoods to 1.5, a ballot-box downzoning from the planning department's previous ratio of 3.0. The same year San Francisco voters approved a proposition tightly controlling the height, size, and number of downtown buildings (*Zoning News* 1986a: 2). In 1987 San Diego became the largest city in the nation to try to limit its population when it passed an ordinance capping the permitted number of new residential housing units at 8,000 a year, about half the number built in 1986. Even Houston, famous as the nation's largest city without zoning, was reconsidering its stance (*Zoning News* 1986b: 2-3). Meanwhile, local planners throughout the country were exploiting the many new real-world opportunities for linkage policies (Merriam, Brower, and Tegeler 1985), impact fees (Frank and Rhodes 1987), aesthetic regulation (Duerksen 1986), controls on office, commercial, and industrial growth (Fulton 1986), development moratoria (Wilson 1987b), agricultural zoning (Toner 1984), and innovative variants on permitting systems (Gordon 1984) and master plans (Lorenzen 1987).

Liberals looking at American land use in the late 1980s might easily take comfort in the acceptance of centralized regulation; conservatives might well be pleased with the limitations on it. But neither group actually is satisfied; liberals bemoan centralized regulation's shortfall, conservatives fear its overreach. Both groups misunderstand their situation. At the federal level populist conservatives preside over a nation that has more of the centralized regulation they loathe than it has had at any point in its history. In addition, while conservatives prefer local government to the federal government, they distrust all government and regulation intensely and so cannot be truly happy about the explosion of local regulation. (That was a theme in the 1987 Supreme Court case, *First English Evangelical Lutheran Church of Glendale v. County of Los Angeles*, where the Court ruled that a property owner can be compensated for an economic loss resulting from a land use regulatory decision such as a downzoning—a major conservative victory.) At the same time liberals keep wishing, mostly in vain, for more federal regulation. They do not realize that their political possibilities are now better at the state, regional, and local levels than they have ever been.

THE PRAGMATIC RESOLUTION'S IMPLICATIONS

The interpretation I have suggested has intriguing political and professional consequences that in large measure are encouraging for planners. There is now more land use regulation—centralized and local, for big projects and small, on private and public land—than ever before. The future probably will see even more regulation. Membership in environmental organizations keeps climbing steadily. The public's support for land use and environmental regulation has remained high and constant throughout the 1970s and 1980s, and shows no signs of wavering (Dunlap 1987). The

Reagan administration was not able to alter that consensus, and sometimes had to accommodate to it. The liberal impulses that drove the Quiet Revolution and the National Land Use Policy Act did not decline or disappear. They won out, and nobody noticed.

Yet in one respect the Reagan-conservative approach to land use regulation achieved an odd triumph: no one expects major federal initiatives anymore. No one, including state and local governments and planners and environmentalists, relies on such initiatives (or the prospect of them) as they did in 1972 or 1975. The federal government has become dissociated from the other parties, decoupled from them. Under Reagan federalism, each level of government and each individual government goes its own way, develops and manages and finances its own programs that spring from its own circumstances; free administrative enterprise prevails. Thus regulation can bubble up from local government and simultaneously trickle down from the state (or even federal) level. Alternatively, it need not appear at all, at any level. Or it may appear at one level and then be resisted at another, as when the federal government tries to cut back funding for state surface mine regulation or opposes state coastal zone regulation intended to restrain oil and gas drilling on the federal Outer Continental Shelf. In all such cases the rules are those of *laissez faire* bureaucratic democracy, and no outcome is foreordained (Peterson and Lewis 1986; Nathan, Doolittle, and Associates 1987).

The result can be remarkable variation across governments—here a sign of true, flexible responsiveness to the wishes of the relevant constituencies: the population gets the regulation it wants. Thus state land use regulation flourishes in Florida, New Jersey, and Oregon, but languishes in Colorado (DeGrove 1984: 291-333). Local regulation booms in California as it busts in Kansas (Rudel 1984: 494). State regulation thrives in Vermont while local regulation falters; just across the Connecticut River in New Hampshire, the situation is reversed (Merrill 1987). State and local regulators work together poorly in Maine, well in Florida and North Carolina (DeGrove 1984: 99-176, 335-70). Federally funded state coastal zone regulation performs nicely in Washington state, does not exist at all in Georgia or Illinois (Mitchell 1986; 327). The job market has adjusted accordingly; planners have gravitated to politically congenial settings. In early 1987 California counted for 11 percent of the nation's population, but 17 percent of the members of the American Planning Association. Florida had 5 percent of the American population, 8 percent of APA's members. By contrast, New York state had 7.3 percent of the population, but only 5 percent of the APA's membership.[4]

In the late 1980s American planners have plenty to do. The development boom that began in 1982 now dwarfs the late-1960s one that led to centralized regulation. But the new boom is more geographically uneven, leaves a big hole in the center of the country. The northeast and the far west, particularly in urban and suburban areas, experience near-boomtown capitalism while much of the Great Plains (Popper and Popper 1987), the south, the midwest, and the intermountain west, especially their rural areas, undergo near depression. Moreover, planners across the nation face a daunting menu of new land use issues: acid rain, the cutoff of low income housing construction, hazardous waste, foreign land ownership, suburban traffic gridlock, deindustrialization, high-tech growth corridors, affordable housing for the middle class, the greenhouse effect, LULU blockage, aging strip developments, the disappearance of small- and mid-scale farming and ranching, gentrification that displaces the poor, homelessness, and—most extensively—the simple ugliness, inconvenience, indistinctiveness, and sterility of much new 1980s development. Large areas of New Jersey, Los Angeles' San Fernando Valley, or urban and suburban Florida can be highly affluent, boast an impressive array of land use controls, and still look vile. Improving the regulations will provide work for planners at all levels of government, including federal. In truth, the professional opportunities for planners—and the chances for genuine power—have never been greater.

But it would help if planners grasped the real nature of the American federalist system of land use controls. It is so loose, so deliberately disjointed and open ended, that it is barely a system in the sense that European elite civil service bureaucracies understand the term. The right to make particular regulatory decisions shifts unpredictably over time from one level of government to another. No principle of administrative rationality, constitutional entitlement, economic efficiency, or even ideological predisposition truly determines the governmental locus of decisions. It is more often a matter of the inevitably uncertain catch-as-catch can pluralism of democratic power politics.

Thus in 1964 American land use regulation was totally local and appeared likely to stay that way. By 1974 it seemed likely to become more federal. In 1984 it had again confounded prophecy and become more state-level and local. By 1994 it may have shifted again, and our previous conceptions of it will once more look foolish. A future, more liberal, for instance, heavily promote federal regulation, revitalize some of the mechanisms the Reagan administration has neglected (say, the Clean Water Act), perhaps even support 1990s version of the National Land Use Policy Act. Yet over decades spanning several national political and ideological cycles, late-twentieth-century American society has consistently acquired more regulation, centralized and local, and more tolerance for it. The cycles have come and almost completely gone, often revealing themselves as ephemera, birds of political passage. Regulation has grown throughout and shown true political staying power. In much of the country and certainly in the large population centers, there seems to be more land use regulation every year, regardless of who is in power in Washington, the state capitals, or city hall. American planners should take heart from those trends. They can feel proud of their accomplishments since 1970.

NOTES

1.   A third, less widely held but more radical interpretation argues that centralized regulation sprang primarily from large development corporations more concerned with protecting their profits than promoting environmental quality. This interpretation disagrees with those of both the liberals and conservatives; it maintains that centralized regulation is objectionable not because in practice it is ineffective or excessively effective, but because it is ideologically regressive and socially inequitable. The interpretation agrees with the liberals that centralized regulation has faded since the middle 1970s. For examples of the interpretation, see Plotkin (1987) and Walker and

Heiman (1981). The interpretation, however trenchant, has come solely from a small number of academics and has had no influence beyond academe.

2. McClaughry (1975) presents an early prediction of those kinds of difficulties. He is a Republican conservative who in 1982 ran for the Senate from Vermont on a platform opposing the state's land use law.

3. For a similar example from Maine, see Wilson (1987a).

4. I received this information in a computer printout from the American Planning Association, dated April 7, 1987; at the time, I was a member of the APA board and received the printout in that capacity.

Author's note: This paper was originally presented at an international seminar on Urban Land Management Under Different Political Systems, in Warsaw and Lodz, Poland, September 22-23, 1987. The seminar was sponsored by the Regional Economy Department of the Polish Academy of Sciences, the Urban Development Economics Department of the University of Lodz, and the Polish Town Planners Society. Michael Greenberg, Michael Heiman, Harvey Jacobs, Janet Lynn, Robert Mason, James Mitchell, Deborah Epstein Popper, Jerzy Regulski, Neil Smith, William Toner, and three anonymous *JAPA* reviewers offered valuable comments on successive drafts.

REFERENCES

American Land Forum. 1983. Toward a Land Resource Policy Agenda. *American Land Forum* 4, 3: 11-30).

American Law Institute. 1977. *A Model Land Development Code: Official Draft*. Philadelphia: American Law Institute.

Babcock, R. 1966. *The Zoning Game: Municipal Practices and Policies*. Madison: University of Wisconsin Press.

Babcock, R., and C. Siemon. 1985. *The Zoning Game Revisited*. Cambridge, MA: Lincoln Institute of Land Policy.

Bikales, E. 1987. Ten Reasons to Dump Vermont's Act 250. *The Yankee Planner* Vol. 4, No. 1, pp. 6-7.

Bosselman, F. 1975. Commentary, pp. 136-37 in *Agenda for the New Urban Era*, edited by H. Perloff. Chicago: American Society of Planning Officials.

____ and D. Callies. 1972. *The Quiet Revolution in Land Use Control*. Washington: Government Printing Office.

Bosselman, F., D. Feurer, and C. Siemon. 1976. *The Permit Explosion: Coordination of the Proliferation*. Washington: Urban Land Institute.

Brower, D., and D. Carol, editors. 1987. *Managing Land-use Conflicts: Case Studies in Special Area Management*. Durham, NC: Duke University Press.

Byers, G., and L. Wilson. 1983. *Managing Rural Growth: The Vermont Development Review Process*. Montpelier: Vermont Environmental Board.

Council of State Governments. 1976. *State Growth Management*. Lexington, KY: Council of State Governments.

DeGrove, J. 1984. *Land, Growth and Politics*. Chicago: American Planning Association.

DeGrove, J., and N. Stroud. 1987. State Land Planning and Regulation: Innovative Roles in the 1980s and Beyond. *Land Use Law & Zoning Digest* 39, 3: 3-8.

deHaven-Smith, W., and R. Paterson. 1986. The 1986 Glitch Bill—Missing Links in Growth Management. *Florida Environmental and Urban Issues* 14, 1: 4-9.

Duerksen, C. 1983. *Environmental Regulation of Industrial Plant Siting: How to Make it Work Better*. Washington: Conservation Foundation.

____. 1986. *Aesthetics and Land-Use Controls: Beyond Ecology and Economics*. Chicago: American Planning Association.

Dunford, R. 1984. Feds Drag Their Feet on Three-Year-Old Farmland Conversion Law. *Planning* 50, 12: 24-25.

Dunlap, R. 1987. Polls, Pollution, and Politics Revisited: Public Opinion on the Environment in the Reagan Era. *Environment* 29, 4: 6-11, 32-37.

Fellmeth, R. 1973. *Politics of Land: Ralph Nader's Study Group Report on Land Use in California*. New York: Grossman.

Fishman, R., editor. 1977. *Housing for All Under Law: New Directions in Housing, Planning, and Land-Use Law*. Cambridge, MA: Ballinger.

Frank, J., and R. Rhodes, editors. 1987. *Development Exactions.* Chicago: American Planning Association.

Fulton, W. 1986. Office in the Dell. *Planning* 52, 7: 13-17.

Fund for Renewable Energy and the Environment. 1988. *The State of the States.* Washington: Fund for Renewable Energy and the Environment.

Gordon, D. 1984. The Power of the Point System. *Planning* 50, 12:15-17.

Hays, S. 1987. *Beauty, Health, and Permanence: Environmental Politics in the United States, 1955-1985.* New York: Cambridge University Press.

Healy, R., and J. Rosenberg. 1979. *Land Use and the States,* second edition. Baltimore: Johns Hopkins University Press.

Heeter, D., editor. 1969. *Toward a More Effective Land-Use Guidance System: A Summary and Analysis of Five Major Reports.* Chicago: American Society of Planning Officials.

Hunt, F. 1987. National Forest Planning: Charting the Future for 191 Million Acres of Trees and Grass. *American Land Forum* 7, 3: 18-23.

Knack, R. 1987. Troubador Babcock. *Planning* 53, 8: 21-27.

Lewis, S. 1976. Antiplanners Are Coming, Antiplanners Are Coming. *Planning* 42, 2:11-13.

Lorenzen, L. 1987. Old Faithful. *Planning* 53, 9: 11-14.

Lyday, N. 1976. *The Law of the Land: Debating National Land Use Legislation 1970-1975.* Washington: Urban Institute.

McClaughry, J. 1975. The New Feudalism—State Land Use Controls, pp. 37-57 in *No Land Is An Island: Individual Rights and Government Control of Land Use,* edited by Institute for Contemporary Studies. San Francisco: Institute for Contemporary Studies.

McGuinness, D. 1986. Fixing What's Broke. *NY Planner* 5, 6: 7.

_____. 1987. Planning Shortfalls in New York's Towns and Villages. *Small Town & Rural Planning* 7, 1: 1.

McPhee, J. 1977. *Pieces of the Frame.* New York: Farrar, Straus, and Giroux.

Merriam, D., D. Brower, and P. Tegeler, editors. 1985. *Inclusionary Zoning Moves Downtown.* Chicago: American Planning Association.

Merrill, L. 1987. The Road Not Taken. *Planning* 53, 11: 22-24.

Meyer, P. 1979. Land Rush. *Harper's* 265, 1: 45 60.

Mitchell, J. 1986. Coastal Management Since 1980: The U.S. Experience and Its Relevance for Other Countries, pp. 319-45 in *Ocean Yearbook 6,* edited by E. Borgese and N. Ginsburg. Chicago: University of Chicago Press.

Myers, P., and A. Reid. 1986. *State Parks in a New Era: A Survey of Issues and Innovations.* Washington: Conservation Foundation.

Nathan, R., F. Doolittle, and Associates. 1987. *Reagan and the States.* Princeton, NJ: Princeton University Press.

National Association of State Departments of Agriculture Research Foundation Farmland Project. 1987. *Farmland Notes* 6, 1: 1-4.

National Commission on Urban Problems. 1968. *Building the American City.* Washington: U.S. Government Printing Office.

Natural Resources Defense Council. 1977. *Land Use Controls in the United States: A Handbook on the Legal Rights of Citizens.* New York: Dial Press/James Wade.

Nelson, R. 1982. The Public Lands, pp. 14-73 in *Current Issues in Natural Resource Policy,* edited by P. Portney. Baltimore: Johns Hopkins University Press.

Pacific Legal Foundation. 1985. *The California Coastal Commission in the '80s: Disquieting Continuities and Suggestions for Reform.* Sacramento: Pacific Legal Foundation.

Pekkanen, J. 1983. The Land: Who Owns America? Part I. *Town & Country* 137, 5036: 175-86.

Peterson, G., and C. Lewis, editors. 1986. *Reagan and the Cities.* Washington: Urban Institute.

Planning. 1977. California Flirts with Growth Control. *Planning* 43, 8: 7-8.

Plotkin, S. 1987. *Keep Out: The Struggle for Land Use Control.* Berkeley: University of California Press.

Popper, D., and F. Popper. 1987. The Great Plains: From Dust to Dust. *Planning* 53, 12: 12-18.

Popper, F. 1981. *The Politics of Land-use Reform.* Madison: University of Wisconsin Press.

_____. 1984. The Timely End of the Sagebrush Rebellion. *The Public Interest* 76: 61-73.

_____. 1986. The Strange Case of the Contemporary American Frontier. *The Yale Review* 76, 1: 101-21.

Porter, D., editor. 1986. *Growth Management: Keeping on Target?* Washington: Urban Land Institute.

Powers, A. 1986. Protecting the Chesapeake Bay: Maryland's Critical Area Program. *Environment* 28, 4: 5, 44-45.

Reilly, W., editor. 1973. *The Use of Land: A Citizen's Policy Guide to Urban Growth.* New York: Crowell.

Rhodes, R. 1986. Growth Management in Florida: 1985 and Beyond. *Florida Environmental and Urban Issues* 13, 2: 1-3, 24-25.

Robbins, D. 1974. New York Towns Squelch Local Zoning Laws. *Planning* 40, 8: 6.

Rosenbaum, N. 1976. *Land Use and the Legislatures: The Politics of State Innovation.* Washington: Urban Institute.

RuBino, R., and Wagner, W. 1972. *Supplement to The States' Role in Land Resource Management.* Lexington, KY: Council of State Governments.

Rudel, T. 1984. The Human Ecology of Rural Land Use Planning. *Rural Sociology* 49, 4: 491-504.

Strong, A. 1981. *Land as a Public Good: An Idea Whose Time Has Come Again,* pp. 217-32 in *The Land Use Policy Debate in the United States,* edited by J. de Neufville. New York: Plenum Press.

Toner, W. 1984. Ag Zoning Gets Serious. *Planning* 50, 12: 19-24.

Vermont Environmental Board. 1981. *Act 250: A Performance Evaluation.* Montpelier: Vermont Environmental Board.

Walker, R., and M. Heiman. 1981. Quiet Revolution for Whom? *Annals of the Association of American Geographers* 71, 1: 67-83.

Weaver, C., and R. Babcock. 1980. *City Zoning: The Once and Future Frontier.* Chicago: American Planning Association.

Wilkinson, C., and H. Anderson. 1987. Land and Resource Planning in the National Forests. Covelo, CA: Island Press.

Williams, N. 1975. The Future of Land Use Controls, pp. 27-42 in *Future Land Use: Energy, Environmental, and Legal Constraints,* edited by R. Burchell and D. Listokin. New Brunswick, M: Rutgers University Center for Urban Policy Research.

Wilson, R. 1987a. Dire Straits. *Maine Times* 19, 28: 16-20. 1987b.

____. 1987b. Managing Maine's Growth. *Maine Times* 20, 10: 34A-35A.

Zoning News. 1986a. Is Growth Management Really Alphabet Soup? *Zoning News.* December: 2.

____. 1986b. Houston Plan Raises "Specter of Zoning." *Zoning News* December: 2-3.

The Quiet Revolution Revisited

David L. Callies

Copyright: Reprinted with permission from the *Journal of the American Planning Association*, 46, 2, 1980 ©, pp. 135-144.

This article examines the changes occurring since 1971 in what Callies and Bosselman termed "the quiet revolution" in the field of land-use controls. The changes have been anything but quiet; in fact, they are enormous, as Callies indicates: the resurgence of local government as a major factor in land use decisions, the "concomitant resurgence" in local government planning, the number of permits required for prior to development, the increased involvement of the federal government in land use control, the increasing amount and organization of citizen participation in land-use decisions, and the takings issue.

In the decade since Fred Bosselman and I prepared *The Quiet Revolution In Land Use Control* for the Council on Environmental Quality[1] there has been a virtual explosion of literature on the subject of land use controls.[2] Many of the assumptions upon which the study was based have changed, and many of its conclusions have been overtaken and, in some instances, altered by events. What follows are some observations on that intervening decade and the consequences for the "quiet revolution."

Indeed, what has happened of most significance is the passage of time—the fertile decade of the 1970s. As it took the better part of a year to compress over a dozen land use control systems into the three hundred pages that became *The Quiet Revolution*, the following survey can only be a quick summary.[3]

The Quiet Revolution was based in part on several assumptions now worth re-examining:

1. the trend away from local government land use controls (zoning, subdivisions, etc.) and toward state and regional systems;

2. the lack of comprehensive planning on the part of local communities, upon which local regulations were constructed;

3. the consequent "taking back" of police power by the states from units of local government.

The analysis led to a number of findings and conclusions, among the most salient of which were:[4]

1. the trend toward a new concept of land as both are source and a commodity (never, note, as a resource only);[5]

2. the criticism of another (e.g., state/regional) layer of regulation for regulation's sake—a sort of "insurance" that a further review of land development would somehow make the process produce better decisions;

3. the trend toward excluding or overriding local government decision-making in the new state and regional land regulation schemes;

4. increased emphasis on plans and planning in the new state and regional land regulatory schemes in contrast to the local regulatory process;

5. constitutional limits on land use regulation—the "taking" issue.

Some of these conclusions foreshadowed what has since occurred. Others missed the mark by a country mile. What follows is a brief look at what did occur.

HAWAII: WHERE "IT ALL BEGAN..."

In many respects, Hawaii was both inspiration and prototype for *The Quiet Revolution*. Its then decade old Land Use Act[6] was increasingly the subject of critical comment, classifying as it did all the land in the state into four districts and permitting local government to regulate the use of land in only one—the urban zone. The state retained the power (through its Land Use Commission) to control both the classification of land and the use of land in three of the four *zones*. While not always perfect in operation,[7] the Land Use Law nonetheless typified the overthrow of the "ancient regime" of local land use control, marking a power shift to state from local government over the use of land.

However, in the ten years since 1970, several trends have developed which have substantially altered the course of the revolution in Hawaii, where it all began. With one exception (a curious lack of case law interpreting the state and regional regulatory mechanisms that are the hallmark of the revolution), Hawaii once again typifies what the revolution has become.

The re-emergence of local government as a major force in the shaping of land use decisions

During the mid-1960s the city council and the city administration in Honolulu began taking an increasingly independent role in the conduct of land use affairs. More than sufficient land was designated "urban" to give the city and county—by now a home rule municipality with considerable independence from the state legislature—land use control over most of Oahu's[8] (and hence most of Hawaii's) population. Increasingly imaginative, sophisticated—and complicated—local land use controls were appended to the local zoning ordinance (The Comprehensive Zoning Code of 1969, as amended in 1977), which granted considerable discretion to both government and landowner in fashioning mechanisms for land development. Besides the ubiquitous planned unit development process, Honolulu incorporated a sophisticated "special design district" scheme, permitting nearly total restructuring of land use controls to fit an approved development package. That approval is almost entirely at the discretion of the city council.[9] The significance of the trend is reflected in part in the number of cases reaching the Supreme Court of Hawaii in the 1970s dealing with *local* land use controls. By and large, the cases do not reflect mundane subjects of Euclidean zoning, but rather grapple with such issues as vested rights under special and sophisticated local zoning schemes[10] and the place of planning in the local land use control hierarchy.[11] By contrast, most of the cases in the last twenty years dealing with the revolutionary *state* land use control law have been restricted largely to procedural issues, such as standing to contest Land Use Commission boundary changes.[12] While clearly significant, these do not cut to the heart of the Land Use Law in the same way that the local land use cases do to the City-County Code. There is little question that, in Hawaii at least, vigorous assertion of local land use regulation prerogatives has produced some of the sharpest controversies over land use control.

The resurgence of local planning

While it is true that comprehensive planning with teeth appears to be on the rise across the United States,[13] it is significant that in many places local governments are joining states and regions at the forefront. So it is in Hawaii. In a critical 1970 decision,[14] the Supreme Court of Hawaii made quite clear that under the current charter provisions, the City and County of Honolulu was required to amend its general plan by means of the strictest observance of procedures, and only after thorough studies and reports. This was especially necessary as local land use controls were required to follow the General Plan and especially its detailed land use maps. By means of recent charter revisions, the emphasis has shifted to the newly-drafted development plans for each of Honolulu's neighborhoods, with which all land use changes, future development approvals, and publicly-funded infrastructure improvements must comply.

This is not to imply the state does no planning of its own. The 1978 Legislature enacted a state plan[15] which is being implemented by the drafting of twelve subject-specific functional plans.[16] Once adopted by joint resolution of Hawaii's state legislature, the functional plans control both the decisions of those state agencies charged with administering the Land Use Law *and* the lands classified in the three state controlled districts,[17] as well as the infrastructure improvements to be constructed by state agencies.[18]

As the plans of the state and of the counties are to be interdependent, the issue of potential conflicts among their provisions is yet to be resolved. The State Planning Act states that each shall be drafted using the other as a basis.[19]

Citizen participation

With the resurgence in local planning has come an exponential increase in citizen participation in the land use control process which was already burgeoning at the time of *The Quiet Revolution*.[20] In Honolulu a plethora of locally-elected neighborhood boards, under the jurisdiction of the Neighborhood Commission[21] (a city agency), vie with elected city councilman for some say in the land use decisions affecting their neighborhoods.[22] Principally advisory in nature, the boards were created "to increase and assure effective citizen participation in the decisions of the City...,"[23] a stated goal of the 1972 Charter Revision Commission.[24] In particular, the Boards were to review and make recommendations on plans and zoning changes, prepare lists of recommended capital improvement projects, and set goals and objectives for neighborhood growth.[25]

Experience with the neighborhood boards has been mixed from the perspective both of the city and county and of the boards themselves. Largely without professional staff of their own, many boards tend to defer on many matters to elected members who are themselves professionals. And while participation in the selecting of neighborhood board members has been extremely uneven (from a few dozen voters in an area of several thousand residents to several thousand voters in an area of like size), board membership has already been used as a springboard to higher elected office. Moreover, while the city council has often expressed concern over the extent of local representation reflected by board decisions and positions on major policy issues (rapid transit, development planning), nevertheless the city has apparently served notice to the development community that neighborhood board consideration, if not approval, will be a prerequisite to speedy consideration of development proposals by those with formal responsibility for their approval. This has, of course, added yet another step to the development approval process.

The burgeoning of regulations on land development: a "permit explosion"

The tendency toward over-regulation of the development process is a well-documented fact of the 1970s.[26] Nowhere is that trend better illustrated than Hawaii. In conjunction with Hawaii's Coastal Zone Management Program, the state's Department of Planning and Economic Development recently released a report setting out in gruesome detail the plethora of permits potentially required of a land developer.[27] In addition to the usual local zoning, building, and subdivision approvals, development in Hawaii's extensive coastal zone could conceivably require:[28]

1.   A Special Management Plan Permit under the CZMA program,
2.   Hawaii State EIS,
3.   Shoreline Setback Permits,
4.   Conservation District Use Permit,
5.   Historic Site "Delay"/Permit,
6.   State Designated Groundwater Use Permit,
7.   Shorewaters of Hawaii Use Permit,
8.   National Pollution Discharge Elimination System Permit,
9.   County Well Permit,
10. County Grading Permit,
11. Federal EIS, and
12. Corps of Engineers Permit,

The expanded federal presence

As appears in part from the list above, many of the new requirements stem from vastly increased federal activity, especially in the environmental area,[29] with substantial impacts on land use.[30] The Water Pollution Control Act (as amended in 1972 and 1977 and now called the Clean Water Act)[31] has resulted not only in a national pollution discharge elimination system permit requirement, but also a construction management planning process in its well-known section 208. Only recently approved in Hawaii, this process will determine when and how big wastewater treatment facilities—so necessary for land development—will be constructed. NEPA's (the National Environment Policy Act's)[32] environmental impact statement requirements have spawned a plethora of litigation over the construction of such federally funded projects generating land development as new segments of Hawaii's interstate highway network.[33] To the same effect has been application of the National Historic Preservation Act through the potential listing of areas on the National Register of Historic Places and the concomitant extra burden on the

secretary of transportation in routing such highways.[34] The federal Coastal Zone Management Act has spawned a host of proposals for state and local regulation in Hawaii's coastal zone.[35] The above list is by no means exhaustive, but serves to illustrate the considerable direct effect of federal programs on land use management at the state and local level. The indirect effects may be extensive as well. Consider Hawaii's "little NEPA,"[36] which requires the filing of an environmental impact statement for significant state actions affecting the environment, clearly spawned by the example of NEPA for significant *federal* actions. Consider also the "strings" attached to flood insurance provided by the Federal Insurance Administration under the Federal Disaster Protection Act of 1973[37] in Hawaii's considerable flood prone areas.

Federal presence is felt in other ways besides state and local regulatory schemes which are required either outright or as conditions of Federal grants. Federal management of federally owned real property interests may have a considerable effect on nearby private land. Indeed, if it is sufficiently significant, the ownership of land or interests in land by the federal government may affect the use of land in an entire state. In Hawaii, the federal government not only holds large areas of land condemned for defense purposes (including choice coastal areas otherwise ripe for public or private recreational use) but also large tracts ceded to the federal government as a condition of territorial status and statehood. These so-called "ceded" lands revert to the state free of charge when they are declared "surplus" by the Administrator of the General Services Administration.[38] The release of such lands would have considerable impact on land use in Hawaii. An example of the assertion of federal jurisdiction—this time over private waters made navigable by the owners—has just recently been decided by the U.S. Supreme Court as the owner-developer of a native fishpond converted to a marina challenged successfully the Corps of Engineers' asserted power to compel public access.[39]

The "taking" issue and vested rights

Hawaii's courts have been silent on the taking issue—whether or at what point a land use regulation has the effect of taking private property for which compensation must be paid under the Fifth Amendment to the federal constitution with respect to the state's Land Use Law. The Hawaii Supreme Court has, however, recently joined the national fray over the vested rights aspect thereof: at what point do rights of an owner-developer vest so that such a development may continue—or compensation be paid for amounts expended—in the face of a new land use regulation which was not in effect when the development was in some fashion "commenced?" In a series of cases extending across the decade of the 1970s,[40] the Hawaii Supreme Court seems to favor a rule giving considerable latitude to the development community in asserting those rights.[41] In so doing it seems to be rejecting the rather stringent rules laid down in California, where it appears almost impossible for a landowner to proceed so far that a change in the rules vests his rights, short of actually commencing construction.[42] This does not bode particularly well for a regulation-oriented disposition of the taking issue should it arise in other contexts.

TESTING THE HYPOTHESES: SIMILAR TRENDS ELSEWHERE IN AND OUT OF QUIET REVOLUTION COUNTRY

While Hawaii may have been the inspiration and model for *The Quiet Revolution*, it was by no means its sole basis. Several of the areas studied in *The Quiet Revolution* have developed significant track records involving the same issues raised by the Hawaii experience. In most respects, these national trends confirm the lessons from Hawaii with respect to some of the new directions in which the revolution has gone.

The re-emergence of local government as a major source in the shaping of land use decisions

Honolulu is not by any means the only major metropolitan community which has sought (and in some measure succeeded) to wrest meaningful control over its land use policies from its state—though, as noted below, the federal government may be a more relevant and difficult adversary. In this context, California and New York come most readily to mind.

In New York, the Town of Ramapo passed appropriate amendments to its local land use reg-ulation requiring prospective residential developers to accumulate a threshold number of points, awarded for proximity to or construction of key community or infrastructure improvements. This growth-regulating ordinance was upheld in the now-famous *Golden v. Town of Ramapo* decision.[43] While concerned about potential exclusionary effects, the court noted the temporary nature of the regulations and, with respect to local regulations, had this to say.[44]

Undoubtedly, current zoning enabling legislation is burdened by the largely antiquated notion which deigns that the regulation of land use and development is uniquely a function of local government—that the public interest of the State is exhausted once its political subdivisions have been delegated the authority to zone (ALI, *A Model Land Development Code* [Tent. Draft No. 1], Intro. Mem., p. xxi). While such jurisdictional allocations may well have been consistent with formerly prevailing conditions and assumptions, questions of broader public interest have commonly been ignored.

In other words, regional and state-wide plans are fine, but meanwhile, ….

Taking a leaf from Ramapo, the City of Petaluma, California, adopted its own growth control strategy. Petaluma added to its infrastructure-sensitive system a limit of four hundred dwelling units per year and an indefinite period during which the regulations were to be effective. Although first struck down by a federal district court[45] upon a later-discredited interference-with-right-to-travel notion,[46] the ordinance was upheld by the reviewing federal appeals court.[47] Since these two decisions, so-called growth management ordinances have proliferated,[48] one of the most recently enacted being San Diego's tier-approach Growth Management Plan.[49]

While the trend toward controlling or "managing" growth at the local level (generally at the expense of the region—or at least ignoring the region's sometimes legitimate concerns) has been roundly criticized,[50] courts have generally been unresponsive, tending to uphold local land use regulations even in the face to constitutional challenge smacking of civil rights violations. In the past four years alone no less than the U.S. Supreme Court has upheld two local land use regulation schemes despite challenges alleging their discriminatory nature.

In *Eastlake v. Forest City Enterprises*,[51] the Court upheld a home rule charter amendment which subjected all prospective local zoning changes to a local referendum. The court relied in part upon what it regarded as the particularly democratic nature of the referendum process (likening it to the New England town meeting) in turning aside attacks on its potentially exclusionary nature, and its blatant disregard of local planning measures.

Again, in *Village of Arlington Heights v. MHDC*,[52] the Supreme Court upheld a local zone classification scheme which effectively excluded multiple-family housing from a Chicago suburb of some 70,000 people, despite a constitutional attack grounded upon its patently discriminatory effects. The scheme was upheld principally upon the ground that no intent to discriminate could be shown. The Court was apparently impressed that this intensely local-interest result derived from a local land use control scheme based upon a comprehensive plan.

Although the *planning* aspects are a trifle difficult to assess, it is clear the Court was unimpressed by the potentially adverse regional effects of these local land use schemes. The *Eastlake* decision especially can be viewed as a reaffirmation of the right of the local community to decide its own land use fate regardless of regional, let alone statewide, considerations which characterize the techniques examined in *The Quiet Revolution.*

The resurgence of (local) planning

Most of the regional and statutory schemes described in *The Quiet Revolution* were based, at least in part, upon comprehensive plans. The Metro Council has its Development Guide. The Bay Area Conservation and Development Commission, Hackensack Meadowlands Development Commission, and Adirondack Park Agency each has its individual plan. Even Vermont's Act 250 contemplated such a plan, though it made do with an interim one for some time after passage of the Act.

Perhaps as a result of these plan-based measures (and their subsequent upholding by the courts), local regulatory schemes which have been recently prominent also depend in part upon plans for their validity. The Ramapo[53] scheme is only one example. There are others:

1. *Baker v. City of Milwaukee*,[54] in Oregon requires that zoning decisions accord with the comprehensive plan:

[We] conclude that a comprehensive plan is the controlling land use planning instrument for a city. Upon passage of a comprehensive plan, a city assumes a responsibility to effectuate that plan and conform prior conflicting zoning ordinances to it. We further hold that the zoning decisions of a city must he in accord with that plan and a zoning ordinance which allows a more intrusive use than that described in the plan must fail.

2. *Smoke Rise, Inc. v. USCC* upheld a moratorium on sewer hookups (which limits growth) allegedly caused by inadequate regional wastewater treatment facilities, in the Washington, D.C., area:[55]

[I]t is...well established that development demand may properly be impeded where growth restrictions are imposed pursuant to well-reasoned, comprehensive plans follow the improvement of the physical infrastructure of the region.

3. *Udell v. Haas*[56] struck down zoning provisions in New York as contrary to a comprehensive plan:

[T]he mandate of the Village Law [that zoning conform to a comprehensive plan] is not merely a technicality which serves only as an obstacle course for public officials to overcome in carrying out their duties. Rather, the comprehensive plan is the essence of zoning. Without it, there can be no rational allocation of land use. It is the insurance that the public welfare is being served and that zoning does not become nothing more than just a Gallup poll.

4. *Fasano v. Board of County Commissioners of Washington County*,[57] determined the validity of a zone change based upon local comprehensive plan requirements:

[I]t must be proved that the [zone] change is in conformance with the comprehensive plan.

Even the U.S. Supreme Court, partly rehabilitating planning from the blow dealt in *City of Eastlake v. Forest City Enterprises*,[58] seems to have come round to recognizing the critical importance of comprehensive planning in local and land use decision-making. That it did so while severely blunting the anti-discriminatory sword of the Fourteenth Amendment to the U.S. Constitution is, of course, unfortunate. Nevertheless, the refusal of the Village of Arlington Heights to rezone a parcel of land in its jurisdiction so as to permit multi-family housing for those with low and moderate incomes was upheld in part on the basis of the village's comprehensive plan, which provided for such zoning only as a buffer between more and less intense land uses.[59]

Clearly the local comprehensive plan has been judicially rehabilitated to an extent that it is logically supportive of local land use decisions (and has in large measure either improved them or given courts a measure by which to judge the faulty ones) to a degree not anticipated in *The Quiet Revolution.*

Citizen participation

The increase in active citizen participation in an organized fashion was, as noted earlier. responsible for many of the "revolutionary" state and regional land use control measures analyzed in *The Quiet Revolution.*[60] The increase is a national[61]—indeed an international[62]—phenomenon.

The attitude of most elected of officials to the increased organized participation of citizens groups—whether or not through neighborhood boards as in Honolulu—has rarely been benign. The participants, however grouped, have generally organized to oppose something, presumably approved (or about to be) by their elected representative. It is therefore fair to predict that in most places confrontation (rather than cooperation) between those elected representatives and the newly-organized citizens is the order of the day.[63] The result seems to be in part a renewed focus upon and interest in the most common of issues to which citizens groups address themselves—the use of land as regulated through local planning and zoning. As the movement to organize spread, such participation has become increasingly institutionalized. The probable results are summed up nicely by two recent commentators on the local zoning scene.[64]

[I]n the success of [neighborhood] coalition may be the beginning of the demise of the

neighborhood revolution. They may topple the traditional political alliances and change political faces but revolutions do consume their own and today's dissidents can become tomorrow's central bureaucrats. Neighborhoods may find, to paraphrase Pogo's aphorism, that "we have met the government and it is us. On that day, neighborhood leaders will have to face the facts that there is more to the city than their neighborhood and that the status quo is often just another name for the stagnation in which diseases of every kind find it easy to breed.

The permit explosion

As discussed above, the incredible proliferation of permits required to undertake even a modest development has become a problem of considerable dimension during the second half of this past decade,[65] partially due to the added layer of regulation imposed by those statutes considered in *The Quiet Revolution.* Rather than truly take back some of their police power, as we observed in 1971, many states appear, on reflection, to have tapped the police power reservoir for *additional* powers.[66] Thus, while some state and regional programs did supersede or replace local land use controls, others added an additional layer or layers.[67]

As the literature reflects,[68] attempts at permit coordination or simplification have been relatively modest. Most such attempts have been limited to coordinating or simplifying the processes within one department[69] or across one type of development (such as industrial siting),[70] or one limited type of permit (such as those relating to environmental impact assessment laws).[71] General coordination or simplification by mandating across-the-board master permit forms, requiring all-agency joint hearings, or by elevating one agency or department to "land czar" status have rarely occurred. The reasons are many: local politics and friction not only between state and regional agencies on the one hand and local agencies on the other, but also among agencies at the same level; intergovernmental relations barriers due to the legally independent nature of certain local government bodies (i.e., home rule municipalities); the increasing federal presence discussed below, and the concomitant inability to coordinate many of the permits required.

However, it is hopeful to note that at least one such federal program is doing its level best by means of both regulations and funding to promote permit coordination. Under the federal Coastal Zone Management Act,[72] a measure of federal coordination with federally-approved state and local coastal zone management regulation is required under the so-called "consistency" provisions. These require federal programs to be "consistent" with local and state coastal zone regulations. Moreover, NOAA (the National Oceanic and Atmospheric Administration) has recently identified permit simplification as a major goal of the coastal zone management program, and is providing funds for investigation into its achievement.[73]

The federal incursion into land use controls

As noted above, it was the potential of a national land use policy act[74] upon which attention focused in the opening years of this decade that resulted in the virtual ignoring of the land use implications of federal environmental law. As it happened, the proposed national legislation based upon ALI's Model Land Development Code[75] never materialized, and by the mid-1970s the theoretical land use control potential of the Clean Air Act, the Water Pollution Control Act, the Solid Waste Disposal Act, and the Marine Protection, Research, and Sanctuaries Act (to name just a few) was belatedly recognized by a host of commentators.[76] In particular, recent amendments to the Clean Air Act, together with interpreting cases, provide a series of levers with which states (through the federally mandated State Implementation Plans) are to engage in air quality zoning and preconstruction reviews of new stationary pollution sources. These reviews will determine where much of new industry can locate.[77] While federal funding of wastewater treatment plants under the Water Pollution Control Act has for the most part preceded the Section 208 area wide plans that were to govern their location nevertheless the federal government did review in many significant instances the matter of location and size.[78] Such locating and sizing is critical to the location of development which increasingly must channel wastewater into such wastewater treatment plants as the deadlines creep closer for meeting effluent standards in order to obtain National Pollution Discharge Elimination System permits—needed for any discharge into the nation's "navigable" waters. Moreover, recent amendments to the Act provide for several billion dollars a year in grants for such systems, and presumably enough 208 plans will by then have been submitted to the EPA Administrator and approved so that their provisions will govern the location of many of the new wastewater treatment facilities which will be constructed as a result. If so, this federally-encouraged plan will do much to mold the shape and location of development within the regions governed by such 208 plans.

Indeed, even the National Environmental Policy Act[79] may be in for a new interpretation which will effectively result in the relocation or cancellation of major federal or federally-funded projects like dams, highways, and wastewater treatment facilities (all of which are demonstrated growth generators) rather than merely their delay. Of course, a virtually unbroken line of federal cases has determined that lack of compliance with NEPA's procedural and substantive requirements in deciding upon whether to issue, and then issuing, an environmental impact statement (EIS) is the sole ground for delaying a federal project under NEPA. Once appropriate remedial action is taken in the EIS process, then the federal action may continue regardless of the adverse environmental consequences, unless the EIS activity[80] triggers some added burden or restriction in another law or regulation, such as the National Historic Preservation Act.[81]

However, in its latest annual report to the President,[82] the Council on Environmental Quality (CEQ) would have an adverse EIS (whatever that is) result in abandonment or modification of the federal action to alleviate any adverse environmental consequences.[83] The council bases such a request for judicial re-examination upon a recent state court decision interpreting one of NEPA's so-called progeny,[84] a state environmental protection act from Washington. That act was largely copied from NEPA and, by its terms, says no more about *prohibiting* state projects on the basis of an adverse EIS than does NEPA. But in *Polygon Corp. v. City of Seattle*,[85] the Supreme Court of Washington held that an official was justified in refusing to approve a project on the ground that the required EIS disclosed a number of adverse environmental consequences. Such an interpretation as CEQ suggests for NEPA would have far-reaching consequences in the relocation, modification, or abandonment of many federal projects upon which further growth and development of a region may well depend.

The federal Coastal Zone Management Act[86] similarly has fostered state programs of coastal land use planning and controls in nearly every state with a coastal zone as defined by the Act, many of which have been partially approved. Under such programs (which are not federally mandated, but are required in order to receive certain federal grants) the coastal zone is to be regulated under a federally approved management plan with the primary goal of protecting the coastal zone. In states like California and Hawaii where, for geographical reasons, much if not most development takes place in such zones, the effect on state and local land use management and control mechanisms is considerable.

These are but examples of federal programs, all products of this decade, which have significant effects on the use of land, some far beyond those envisioned in *The Quiet Revolution*.[87]

The taking issue

As noted above, in preparing *The Quiet Revolution*, the authors were struck by the uniformity with which draftsmen and administrators of environmentally oriented legislation across the country found themselves bedeviled by the basic question: to what extent does the Constitution permit the protection of the environment by regulating the use of land without paying compensation to the landowner? At issue was the interpretation of the Fifth Amendment to The federal Constitution ending with the phrase, "nor shall private property be taken for public use without just compensation." The root of the problem was the language of Mr. Justice Holmes in the U.S. Supreme Court case, *Pennsylvania Coal v. Mahon*:[88] "The general rule at least is that while property may be regulated to a certain extent, if a regulation goes too far, it will be recognized as a taking."

Despite Brandeis' lone dissent (which, incidentally, correctly stated the law up to that time, virtually since the founding of the nation), courts have struggled with this "taking" issue for half a

century. It is this struggle, together with its English and Colonial antecedents on the one hand, and recent distinguishing of *Pennsylvania Coal* on the other, that provided the basis for a second publication by Fred Bosselman and the author (co-authored also by John Banta, now planning director for the Adirondack Park Agency) entitled *The Taking Issue: A Study of the Constitutional Limits of Governmental Authority to Regulate the Use of Privately-Owned Land Without Paying Compensation to the Owner.*[89] There, two principles were established:[90]

1. Constitutional principles governing the regulation/taking issue are adaptable to changing knowledge of factual conditions.
2. Those facts supporting the need for more environmental legislation really exist.

It was noted that *Pennsylvania Coal* was after all, an *interpretation* of a constitutional principle only, and one which appeared to ignore not only 150 years of U.S. jurisprudence, but an additional 500 years of English constitutional and legal history stretching back to the Magna Carta of 1215. After discussing the inadequate basis for *Pennsylvania Coal*, the book then described in detail cases from around the country [91] in which state supreme courts either ignored or distinguished *Pennsylvania Coal* in upholding a series of environmentally oriented land use control statutes, including several of the statutes which were the subject of case studies in *The Quiet Revolution*.[92]

The trend continues. In a footnote to a New Jersey case decided shortly after *The Taking Issue* was published, a distinguished justice allowed as how he might reconsider one of New Jersey's landmark cases against environmental regulations in light of the issues discussed in *The Taking Issue*.[93] Nor did the trends top there. In the area of vested rights, California has probably led the nation in requiring the strictest of scrutiny before a property owner may claim the right to proceed with a development following the promulgation or enactment of a restrictive land use regulation which would prohibit future developments of the same type.[94] In Vermont, the theory of Act 250 has been upheld in a series of cases involving the imposition of land use restrictions based upon environmental concerns.[95] Perhaps the Act's most severe test is yet to come: the Pyramid

Corporation has sued the state over the denial, based in part upon traffic and infrastructure priorities, of a permit to construct a shopping mall.[96] The authority of the Adirondack Park Agency to impose stringent development controls upon private lands in the six million acre Adirondack Park in New York has also been upheld.[97] The same is true for the Hackensack Meadowlands Development Commission[98] and the Tahoe Regional Planning Commission.[99] While the record is not perfect,[100] the trend is clear: the taking issue is being resolved in favor of environmental protection and land use control across the country.[101]

PROSPECTS AND PERSPECTIVES

With the hindsight of ten years, it is probably more accurate to characterize the "ancient regime" of local land use controls as having metamorphosed rather than having been overthrown. The trends toward home rule municipalities, local growth control, and strengthened local comprehensive planning, together with a host of new and more flexible local land use control techniques portend continuing increased local control. Indeed, it is a local, and not a state or regional, law which seems to have moved the Country along the land use control continuum to the preservation of the built as well as the natural environment as a valid goal of land use regulation, provided private property is not altogether stripped of value.[102]

This is not to imply that state and regional controls are either unnecessary or unavoidable. Indeed much of the resurgent local government concern with land use management results from a sensitizing from, and sometimes a reaction against, just such broader laws. But unquestionably the "revolution" has matured and passed to a more quiet stage. If local governments "feudal" land use control systems were unable to rise to the challenges of regional and statewide needs, neither were the new laws able to operate satisfactorily alone—at least as perceived by local interests.

There remains, moreover, the governed under all three levels of government: the people, dissatisfied with government of *all* levels. Citizen participation in government is on the distinct upswing, and with the blessing of the nation's highest courts.[103] Moreover, the participation is becoming

highly organized. Honolulu's neighborhood boards are but a local example of what some see as a national trend.[104] This formalization of citizen participation is perhaps worth examining in detail as an institutional mechanism for channeling citizen participation in the land use decision-making process.

That process—and the plethora of permit requirements alluded to above—threatens to choke off development, the good with the bad, if some measure of simplification or coordination or streamlining is not soon forthcoming. Adding regulation upon hearing upon review has made the process of development approval in many places—including Honolulu—both cumbersome and unwieldy beyond the point of mere frustration. There is a continuing need to explore methods of expediting the process without sacrificing its quality and ability to produce acceptable results.

Across these trends, however, cuts the increased federal control over *both* state and local land use activities as a result of the multitude of Federal programs into which state and local governments have been forced or inveigled. It may very well be, as former Judge Hufstedler observed recently from the bench of the Ninth Circuit, that:[105]

Despite this residual federal supervisory responsibility, the federal-state relationship established under [The Water Act] is "a system for the mandatory approval of a conforming State program and the consequent suspension of the federal program [which] creates a separate and independent State authority to administer the NPDES pollution controls."

But doesn't this exalt form over substance when, as in the case before that court, the California State Water Board was administering a federal permit program[106] under a federal law,[107] over which a federal official had the power of veto,[108] and pursuant to advice by a federal agency?[109] Perhaps the dissenting judge in that case had the better view, after all:[110]) [T]he EPA made all material decisions in setting the limitations of the state-issued permit. ...[T]his was federal agency action. It would be worth examining in detail both the precedent and the likely implications of such decisions. Much will in any event depend in the future on how and to whom the federal government gives out its programmatic aid: to state or to local government.

NOTES

1. F. Bosselman and D. Callies, *The Quiet Revolution in Land Use Control* (1971).

2. R. Healy, *Land Use and the States* (Resources for the Future, 1976); D. Mandelker, *Environmental and Land Controls Legislation* (1976): D. Hagman and D. Misczynski (ed.), *Windfalls for Wipeouts* (1978).

3. For other "revisits," see, e.g., Hess, "Institutionalizing the Revolution," 9 *The Urban Lawyer* at 183 (1977); R. Healy, *supra* note 2, and D. Mandelker, "The Quiet Revolution Reconsidered," 31 *Land Use Law and Zoning Digest* 4 (1979).

4. *The Quiet Revolution, supra* note 1, pp. 314-26.

5. See, Babcock and Feurer, "Land as a Commodity Affected With A Public Interest," 52 *Washington Law, Review*, 289 (1977).

6. *Hawaii Revised Statutes* ch. 205.

7. Mandelker, *supra* note 2, Ch. VlI; P. Myers, *Zoning Hawaii* (The Conservation Foundation, 1976); Lowry and McElroy, "State and Land Use Control: Some Lessons from Experience" 1 *State Planning Issues* 15 (Spring, 1976); D. Mandelker and A. Kolis, "Whither Hawaii?" 1 *University Hawaii Law Review* 48 (1979); Eckbo, Dean, Austin, and Williams, *State of Hawaii Land Use Districts and Regulations Review* (1969).

8. The city and county of Honolulu's local governmental jurisdiction is island-wide, as are those of each of Hawaii's other three principal units of local government: the County of Kauai, the County of Maui, and the County of Hawaii.

9. *1977 Cumulative Supplement of the Comprehensive Zoning Code 1969, City and County of Honolulu*, Article 15 "Special Design Districts."

10. *Life of the Land Inc. v. City Council*, 592 P.2d 26 (1979); *Denning v. Maui*, 485 P.2d 1048 (1971).

11. *Dalton v. City and County*, 462 P.2d 199 (1969).

12. *Town v. Land Use Commission*, 524 P.2d 84 (1974); *Life of the land v. Land Use Commission* (May, 1979).

13. California, Hawaii, Oregon, Florida.

14. *Dalton, supra* note 11.

15. Known as Act 100; *Hawaii Revised Statutes* ch. 226.

16. Conservation Lands, Water Resources Development, Transportation, Tourism, Historic Preservation, Education, Higher Education, Energy, Health, Recreation, Housing, and Agriculture.

17. Land Use Commission and Land Board of the Department of Land and Natural Resources, though some of the administrative authority previously exercised by these agencies now rests with the counties.

18. Act 100, *supra* note 15.

19. Act 100, *supra* note 15, §§ 52 and 61; *The Hawaii State Plan Administrative Guidelines*, (Draft of June, 1979) §§ II and III.

20. *The Quiet Revolution*, pp. 108 (citing concern over filling of San Francisco Bay), 137 (Minnesota citizen concern over sewage), and 187 (Maine citizen concern over a supertanker port). For full discussion of citizen participation, see. Reilly (ed.) *The Use of Land, A Citizen's Policy Guide to Urban Growth* (1973).

21. Revised Charter, City and County of Honolulu (1973) Ch.13.

22. Kupchak, "The Role of Neighborhood Boards is the Planning Process," *Hawaii Architect* (May, 1979).

23. Op. cit. note [19-b].

24. *Final Report of the Charter Revision Commission*, 1971-72, p. 41.

25. Op. cit., note [19-b].

26. Bosselman, Feurer, and Siemon, *The Permit Explosion* (Urban Land Institute, 1977) and Kolis (ed.), *Thirteen Perspectives on Regulatory Simplification* (Urban Land Institute, 1979).

27. *A Register of Government Permits Required for Development*, December 1977.

28. Id., pp. 63-100 (Appendix B).

29. Bosselman, Feurer, and Callies, *EPA Authority Affecting Land Use* (National Technical Information Service, 1974).

30. Bosselman, Feurer & Richter, *Federal Land Use Regulation* (Practicing Law Institute. 1977).

31. § 208, Clean Water Act, 33 U.S.C. 1251 *et seq.*

32. U.S.C. § 4321 *et seq.*

33. *Stop H-3 Assoc. v. Coleman*, 533 F.2d 434 (1976).

34. Id.

35. *Hawaii Revised Statutes* ch. 205A; *State of Hawaii Coastal Zone Management Program and Final Environmental Impact Statement* (Department of Planning and Economic Development/NOAA, 1978).

36. *Hawaii Revised Statutes* ch. 434.

37. Federal Disaster Protection Act of 1973, 12 and 42 U.S.C., P.L. 93-234.

38. P.L. 88-233, 77 Stat. 472.

39. *Kaiser Aetna v. U.S.,* _____U.S. _____, 48 *U.S. Law Week* 4045 (No. 78-738, decided Dec. 4, 1979), *reversing U.S. v. Kaiser Aetna et al.,* 584 F.2d 378. The Supreme Court affirmed the Corps of Engineers' *regulatory* authority over navigable waters, but rejected the notion that the former pond was now open to the public merely because it was navigable.

40. *Denning v. County of Maui,* 485 P.2d 1048 (1971); *Life of the Land, Inc. v. City Council,* 592 P.2d 26 (1979); *Life of the Land, Inc. v. City Council,* Harv. Sup. Ct. (No. 7240 January 11,1980).

41. *Life of the Land v. City Council, supra* note 40.

42. Hagman, "The Vesting Issue," 7 *Environmental Law,* 519 (1977). *HFH Ltd. v. Superior Ct. of Los Angeles County,* 542 P.2d 237 (1975); *Avco Community Development v. South Coast Regional Comm'n,* 533 P.2d 546 (1976).

43. *Golden v. Planning Board of the Town of Ramapo,* 285 N.E.2d291 (1972).

44. Id.

45. *Construction Industry Ass'n. of Sonoma County v. City of Petaluma,* 375 F. Supp. 574 (1974).

46. *Village of Belle Terre v. Boraas,* 416 U.S. 1 (1974).

47. *Construction Industry Ass'n. of Sonoma County v. City of Petaluma,* 522 F.2d 897 (1975).

48. See *Management and Control of Growth* (4 Vol., ULI, 1975); Codschalk and Brower, *Constitutional Issues Relating to Growth Management* (1977).

49. *A Residential Growth Management Program for San Diego* (1977); criticized, Winters, *An Independent Legal Analysis of "A Growth Management Program for San Diego"* (1978).

50. Bosselman, "Can the Town of Ramapo Pass a Law to Bind the Rights of Whole World? 1 *Florida State University, Law Review* 234 (1973).

51. *City of Eastlake v. Forest City Enterprises,* 426 U.S. 668 (1976).

52. *Metropolitan Housing Development Corp. v. Village of Arlington Heights,* 429 U.S. 252 (1977).

53. *Ramapo, supra* note 43.

54. *Baker v. City of Milwaukee,* P. 2d 772 (1975).

55. *Smoke Rise v. Washington Suburban Sanitary Commission,* 400 F. Supp. 1369 (1975).

56. 21 N.Y.2d 46 (1968), at 893-94.

57. 507 P.2d 23 (1973).

58. *Eastlake, supra* note 51.

59. *Arlington Heights, supra* note 52.

60. *Supra* note 20.

61. See, e.g., discussions in Reilly (ed.) *The Use of Land,* (1973), and Healy, *Land Use and the States, supra* note 2.

62. See, e.g., discussion in Bosselman, *In the Wake of the Tourist* (Conservation Foundation, 1978) and Noble, Banta and Rosenberg (ed.) *Groping Through the Maze* (Conservation Foundation, 1977).

63. For a full and timely discussion of such confrontations from around the country see, Babcock and Weaver, *City Zoning: The Once and Future Frontier* (American Planning Association, 1980) (draft of Oct., 1978 at ch. 14).

64. Id., at 292.

65. The Conservation Foundation, *Groping Through the Maze, supra* note 62 (1976); Bosselman, et al., *The Permit Explosion supra* note 26; Kolis (ed.) *Thirteen Perspectives on Regulatory Simplification supra* note 26.

66. Wisconsin, arguably California, and New Jersey.

67. Hawaii, New York (Adirondacks).

68. *Supra* note 1.

69. McKinney's Consolidated Laws/N.Y., § 70 et seq. (1978).

70. *The Permit Explosion,* op. cit.

71. E.g., Washington's Environmental Policy Act of 1971, Revised Code Washington Ch. 90.62.

72. 16 United States Code §§ 1451-64.

73. NOAA, *The First Five Years* (1979).

74. I.e., S.B. 268, 93rd Congress, 1st Session.

75. American Law Institute, *A Model Land Development Code* (1977).

76. Bosselman, Feurer, and Callies, *supra* note 29; Hagman, *Public Planning and Control of Urban and Land Development* (Supp. 1976) at 255; Hagman, *Urban Planning and Land Development Control,* at Ch. 20 (1975).

77. Clean Air Act, 42 United State Code § 1857 *et seq.*; Mandelker & Rothchild, "The Role of Land Use Controls in Combating Air Pollution Under the Clean Air Act of 1970," 3 Ecology Law Quarterly 235 (1973).

78. E.g., *Maryland v. Costle*, 452 F. Supp. 1154 (1978), in which the Administrator declined to fund a massive treatment plant (60 MGD) for Maryland on the twin grounds that the population projections for the area were optimistically large and the consideration of alternatives weak.

79. NEPA, *supra* note 32.

80. E.g., *Matsumoto v. Brinegar*, 568 F.2d 1289 (1978).

81. *Stop H-3 Assoc. v. Coleman, supra* note 33.

82. *Environmental Quality*, 1970.

83. Id., at 405.

84. Hagman, "NEPA's Progeny: Were the Genes Defective?"8 *Urban Law Annual* 47 (1974).

85. *The Polygon Corp. v. City of Seattle*, 578 P.2d 1309 (1978).

86. *Supra* note 72.

87. See, e.g., Bosselman, et al., *Federal Land Use Legislation, supra* note 30.

88. 260 U.S. 393, at 413 (1922).

89. Council on Environmental Quality, 1973.

90. Id., 236 *et seq.*

91. Id; Pts. I & III; see Hess, *supra* note 3.

92. Wisconsin; San Francisco; N.Y. (Adirondack Park); Vermont.

93. *AMG Associates v. Township of Springfield*, 319 A.2d 705 (1974) n. 4.

94. *Avco Community Developers, Inc. v. South Coastal Regional Commission*, 17 Cal. 3d 785, 553 P.2d 546, 132 Cal. Rptr. 386 (1976), *cert. denied*, 429 U.S. 1083 (1977); *HFH Ltd. v. Superior Court*, 15 Cal. 3d 508, 542 P.2d 237, 125 Cal. Rptr. 365 (1975); Hagman, "The Taking Issue: The HFH et al. Round," *28 Land Use Law & Zoning Digest* 5 (1975).

95. E.g., *In re Preseault*, 292 A.2d 832 (1972).

96. *Re: Pyramind Company of Burlington*: Findings of Fact and Conclusions of Law, Order Denying Land Use Permit, on Applic. #4C0281, Vt. Dist. Envir. Comm'n #4, Oct 12, 1978, appealed (Dkt. #S59-78) to Chittendon Co. Court, Nov., 1978.

97. E.g., *McCormick v. Lawrence*, 372 N.Y.S. 2d 156 (1975).

98. E.g., *Bergen Co. Sewer Authority v. HMDC*, 324 A.2d 108 (1974).

99. E.g., *League to Save Lake Tahoe v. TRPA*, 507 F.2d 517 (1974). Perhaps an irrelevant consideration, as TRPA is being dismantled.

100. For example, Florida recently lost the power to designate critical areas by order of the Governor and Cabinet sitting as the State Administration Commission under their ALI—tracking Environmental Land and Growth Management Act of 1973 in *Askew v. Cross Keys*,_____ So._____ (1979).

101. See, e.g., Mandelker, "The Quiet Revolution Reconsidered," *supra* note 3.

102. *Penn Central Transportation Co. v. City of New York:*, 98 S. Ct.2646 (1978).

103. *City of Eastlake v. Forest City Enterprises, supra* note 51.

104. Babcock and Weaver, *supra* note 63, Ch. 14; Reilly (ed.), *The Use of Land* (1973).

105. *Shell Oil Co. v. Train*, 585 F.2d 408 (9th Cir. 1978), at 410.

106. National Pollution Discharge Elimination System.

107. Clean Water Act, *supra* note 31.

108. EPA Administrator, under § 402 of the Clean Water Act.

109. Pursuant to a memorandum of understanding the state commission routinely sent permit and permit modification requests to the EPA's regional office for comment and advice. 585 P.2d 411 (1978).

110. *Shell Oil, supra* note 105, at 421.

Author's note: The author gratefully acknowledges the comments and criticism on an earlier draft of this article from Fred P. Bosselman, AICP, attorney-at-law, Chicago, and co-author of *The Quiet Revolution in Land Use, Control*; Professor and Director Tom Dinell and Professor G. Ken Lowry, of the University of Hawaii Urban and Regional Planning Program; Professor Daniel R. Mandelker, School of Law, Washington University, St. Louis; and Dr. Shelly Mark, past director of Planning, State of Hawaii, and University of Hawaii professor of Agricultural Economics.

Twentieth Century Land Use Planning

Edward J. Kaiser

David R. Godschalk

This selection presents the evolution of comprehensive land-use planning in the twentieth century. Using the metaphor of a tree, the authors move from the history ("roots") to the first 50 years into the mid-century period ("new growth") and finally to newer contemporary plans ("incorporating new branches") to illustrate how the twentieth century land-use plan has now become an intricate combination of design, policy, and management.

How a city's land is used defines its character, its potential for development, the role it can play within a regional economy and how it impacts the natural environment.

— *Seattle Planning Commission 1993*

During the twentieth century, community physical development plans have evolved from elite, City Beautiful designs to participatory, broad-based strategies for managing urban change. A review of land use planning's intellectual and practice history shows the continuous incorporation of new ideas and techniques. The traditional mapped land use design has been enriched with innovations from policy plans, land classification plans, and development management plans. Thanks to this flexible adaptation, local governments can use contemporary land use planning to build consensus and support decisions on controversial issues about space, development, and infrastructure. If this evolution persists, local plans should continue to be mainstays of community development policy into the twenty-first century.

Unlike the more rigid, rule-oriented modern architecture, contemporary local planning does not appear destined for deconstruction by a postmodern revolution. Though critics of comprehensive physical planning have regularly predicted its demise (Perin 1967, Perloff 1980, Jacobs 1992, Friedmann 1993),[1] the evidence demonstrates that spatial planning is alive and well in hundreds of United States communities. A 1994 tabulation found 2,742 local comprehensive plans prepared under state growth management regulations in twelve states. (See Table II.1.) This figure of course

significantly understates the overall nationwide total, which would include all those plans prepared in the other thirty-eight states and in the noncoastal areas of California and North Carolina. It is safe to assume that most, if not all, of these plans contain a mapped land use element.[2] Not only do such plans help decision makers to manage urban growth and change, they also provide a platform for the formation of community consensus about land use issues, now among the most controversial items on local government agendas.

This article looks back at the history of land use planning and forward to its future. It shows how planning ideas, growing from turn-of the-century roots, culminated in a midcentury consensus on a general concept—the traditional land use design plan. That consensus was stretched as planning branched out to deal with public participation, environmental protection, growth management, fiscal responsibility, and effective implementation under turbulent conditions. To meet these new challenges, new types of plans arose: verbal policy plans, land classification plans, and growth management plans. These in turn became integrated into today's hybrid comprehensive plans, broadening and strengthening the traditional approach.

Future land use planning will continue to evolve in certain foreseeable directions, as well as in ways unforeseen. Among the foreseeable developments are even more active participation by interest groups, calling for planners' skills at consensus building and managing conflict; increased use of computers and electronic media, calling for planners' skills in information management and communication; and continuing concerns over issues of diversity, sustainability, and quality of life, calling for planners' ability to analyze and seek creative solutions to complex and interdependent problems.

THE LAND USE PLANNING FAMILY TREE

We liken the evolution of the physical development plan to a family tree. The early genealogy is represented as the roots of the tree (Figure II.1). The general plan, constituting consensus practice at midcentury, is represented by the main trunk.

Since the 1970s this traditional "land use design plan" has been joined by several branches—the verbal policy plan, the land classification plan, and the development management plan. These branches connect to the trunk although springing from different planning disciplines, in a way reminiscent of the complex structure of a Ficus tree. The branches combine into the contemporary, hybrid comprehensive plan integrating design, policy, classification, and management, represented by the foliage at the top of the tree.

As we discuss each of these parts of the family tree, we show how plans respond both to social climate changes and to "idea genes" from the literature. We also draw conclusions about the survival of the tree and the prospects for new branches in the future. The focus of the article is the plan prepared by a local government—a county,

TABLE II.1. Local comprehensive plans in growth-managing states and coastal areas as of 1994

| State | Number of Comprehensive Plans | | | | Source |
	Cities/ Towns	Counties	Regions	Total	
California (coastal)	97	7	0	104	Coastal Commission
Florida	377	49	0	426	Department of Community Affairs
Georgia	298	94	0	392	Department of Community Affairs
Maine	270	0	0	270	Department of Economic and Community Development
Maryland	1	1	0	2	Planning Office
New Jersey	567	0	0	567	Community Affairs Department
North Carolina (coastal)	70	20	0	90	Division of Coastal Management
Oregon	241	36	1	278	Department of Local Community Development
Rhode Island	39	0	1	40	Department of Planning and Development
Vermont	235	0	10	245	Department of Housing and Community Affairs
Virginia	211	94	0	305	Department of Housing and Community Development
Washington	23	0	0	23	Office of Growth Management
TOTAL	**2429**	**301**	**12**	**2742**	

Compiled from telephone survey of state sources.

municipality, or urban region—for the long-term development and use of the land.[3]

ROOTS OF THE FAMILY TREE: THE FIRST 50 YEARS

New World city plans certainly existed before this century. They included L'Enfant's plan for Washington, William Penn's plan for Philadelphia, and General Oglethorpe's plan for Savannah. These plans, however, were blueprints for undeveloped sites, commissioned by unitary authorities with power to implement them unilaterally (Reps 1965).

In this century, perhaps the most influential early city plan was Daniel Burnham's plan for Chicago, published by the Commercial Club of Chicago (a civic, not a government entity) in 1909 (Schlereth 1981). The archetypical plan-as-inspirational-vision, it focuses only on design of public spaces as a City Beautiful effort.

The City Beautiful approach was soon broadened to a more comprehensive view. At the 1911 National Conference on City Planning, Frederick Law Olmsted, Jr., son of the famous landscape architect and in his own right one of the fathers of planning, defined a city plan as encompassing all uses of land, private property, public sites, and transportation. Alfred Bettman, speaking at the 1928 National Conference of City Planning, envisioned the plan as a master design for the physical development of the city's territory, including "the general location and extent of new public improvements…and in the case of private developments, the general distribution amongst various classes of land uses, such as residential, business, and industrial uses…designed for…the future, twenty-five to fifty years" (Black 1968, 352-3). Together, Olmsted and Bettman anticipated the development of the midcentury land use plan.

Another early influence, the federal Standard City Planning Enabling Act of 1928, shaped enabling acts passed by many states. However, the Act left many planners and public officials confused about the difference between a master plan and a zoning ordinance, so that hundreds of communities adopted "zoning plans" without having created comprehensive plans as the basis for zoning (Black 1968, 353). Because the Act also did not make clear the importance of comprehensiveness or define the essential elements of physical development, no consensus about the essential content of the plan existed.

Ten years later, Edward Bassett's book, *The Master Plan* (1938), spelled out the plan's subject matter and format—supplementing the 1928 Act, and consistent with it. He argued that the plan should have seven elements, all relating to land areas (not buildings) and for public buildings, public reservations, routes for public utilities, pierhead and bulkhead lines (all public facilities), and zoning districts for private lands. Bassett's views were incorporated in many state enabling laws (Haar 1955).

The physical plans of the first half of the century were drawn by and for independent commissions, reflecting the profession's roots in the Progressive Reform movement, with its distrust of politics. The 1928 Act reinforced that perspective by making the planning commission, not the legislative body, the principal client of the plan, and purposely isolating the commission from politics (Black 1968, 355). Bassett's book reinforced the reliance on an independent commission. He conceived of the plan as a "plastic" map, kept within the purview of the planning commission, capable of quick and easy change. The commission, not the plan, was intended to be the adviser to the local legislative body and to city departments (Bassett 1938).

By the 1940s, both the separation of the planning function from city government and the plan's focus on physical development were being challenged. Robert Walker, in *The Planning Function in Local Government*, argued that the "scope of city planning is properly as broad as the scope of city government (Walker 1941, 110). The central planning agency might not necessarily do all the planning but it would coordinate departmental planning in the light of general policy considerations—creating a comprehensive plan but one without a physical focus. That Idea was not widely accepted. Walker also argued that the independent planning commission should be replaced by a department or bureau attached to the office of mayor or city manager (Walker 1941, 177). That argument did take hold, and by the 1960s planning m most communities was the responsibility of an agency within local government, though planning boards still advised elected officials on planning matters.[4]

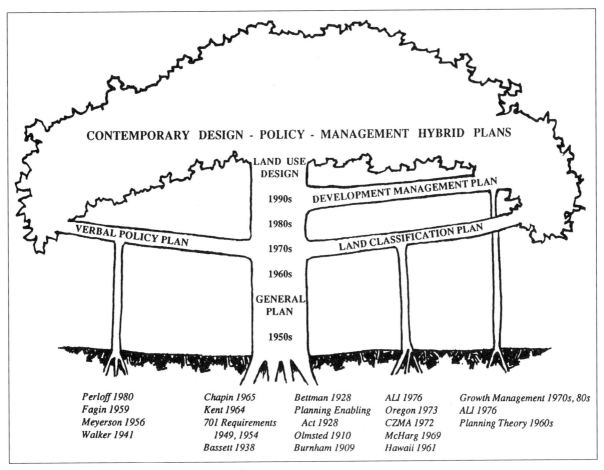

CONTEMPORARY DESIGN - POLICY - MANAGEMENT HYBRID PLANS

LAND USE
DESIGN

1990s   DEVELOPMENT MANAGEMENT PLAN

1980s

VERBAL POLICY PLAN   LAND CLASSIFICATION PLAN

1970s

1960s

GENERAL
PLAN

1950s

Perloff 1980	*Chapin 1965*	*Bettman 1928*	*ALI 1976*	*Growth Management 1970s, 80s*
Fagin 1959	*Kent 1964*	*Planning Enabling*	*Oregon 1973*	*ALI 1976*
Meyerson 1956	*701 Requirements*	*Act 1928*	*CZMA 1972*	*Planning Theory 1960s*
Walker 1941	*1949, 1954*	*Olmsted 1910*	*McHarg 1969*	
	Bassett 1938	*Burnham 1909*	*Hawaii 1961*	

Figure II.1 The family tree of land use plan

This evolution of ideas over 50 years resulted at midcentury in a consensus concept of a plan as focused on long-term physical development; this focus was a legacy of the physical design professions. Planning staff worked both for the local government executive officer and with an appointed citizen planning board, an arrangement that was a legacy of the Progressive insistence on the public interest as an anti-dote to governmental corruption. The plan addressed both public and private uses of the land, but did not deal in detail with implementation.

THE PLAN AFTER MIDCENTURY: NEW GROWTH INFLUENCES

Local development planning grew rapidly in the1950s, for several reasons. First, governments had to contend with the postwar surge of population and urban growth, as well as a need for the capital investment in infrastructure and community facilities that had been postponed during the depression and war years. Second, municipal legislators and managers became more interested in planning as it shifted from being the responsibility of an independent commission to being a function within local government. Third, and very important, Section 701 of the Housing Act of 1954 required local governments to adopt along-range general plan in order to qualify for federal grants for urban renewal, housing, and other programs, and it also made money available for such comprehensive planning.[5] The 701 program's double barreled combination of requirements and financial support led to more urban planning in the United States in the latter half of the 1950's than at any previous time in history (cited from Scott 1969, in Beal and Hollander 1979, 159).

At the same time, the plan concept was pruned and shaped by two planning educators. T.J. Kent, Jr., was a professor at the University of California at Berkeley, a planning commissioner, and a city councilman in the 1950s. His book, *The*

Urban General Plan (1964), clarified the policy role of the plan.[6] F. Stuart Chapin, Jr., was a TVA planner and planning director in Greensboro, NC in the 1940s, before joining the planning faculty at the University of North Carolina at Chapel Hill in 1949. His contribution was to codify the methodology of land use planning in the various editions of his book, *Urban Land Use Planning* (1957, 1965).[7]

What should the plan look like? What should it be about? What is its purpose (besides the cynical purpose of qualifying for federal grants)? The 701 program, Kent, and Chapin all offered answers.

The "701" Program Comprehensive Plan Guidelines

In order to qualify for federal urban renewal aid—and, later, for other grants—a local government had to prepare a general plan that consisted of plans for physical development, programs for redevelopment, and administrative and regulatory measures for controlling and guiding development. The 701 program specified what the content of a comprehensive development plan should include:

• A land use plan, indicating the locations and amounts of land to be used for residential, commercial, industrial, transportation, and public purposes
  • A plan for circulation facilities
  • A plan for public utilities
  • A plan for community facilities

T. J. Kent's Urban General Plan

Kent's view of the plan's focus was similar to that of the 701 guidelines: long-range physical development in terms of land use, circulation, and community facilities. In addition, the plan might include sections on civic design and utilities, and special areas, such as historic preservation or redevelopment areas. It covered the entire geographical jurisdiction of the community, and was in that sense comprehensive. The plan was a vision of the future, but not a blueprint; a policy statement, but not a program of action; a formulation of goals, but not schedules, priorities, or cost estimates. It was to be inspirational, uninhibited by short-term practical considerations.

Kent (1964, 65-89) believed the plan should emphasize policy, serving the following functions:
• Policy determination—to provide a process by which a community would debate and decide on its policy
• Policy communication—to inform those concerned with development (officials, developers, citizens, the courts, and others) and educate them about future possibilities
• Policy effectuation—to serve as a general reference for officials deciding on specific projects
• Conveyance of advice—to furnish legislators with the counsel of their advisors in a coherent, unified form

The format of Kent's proposed plan included a unified, comprehensive, but general physical design for the future, covering the whole community and represented by maps. (See Figure II.2.) It also contained goals and policies (generalized guides to conduct, and the most important ingredients of the plan), as well as summaries of background conditions, trends, issues, problems, and assumptions. (See Figure II.3.) So that the plan would be suitable for public debate, it was to be a complete, comprehensible document, containing factual data, assumptions, statements of issues, and goals, rather than merely conclusions and recommendations. The plan belonged to the legislative body and was intended to be consulted in decision-making during council meetings.

Kent (1964, 25-6) recommended overall goals for the plan:
• Improve the physical environment of the community to make it more functional, beautiful, decent, healthful, interesting, and efficient
• Promote the overall public interest, rather than the interests of individuals or special groups within the community
• Effect political and technical coordination in community development
• Inject long-range considerations into the determination of short-range actions
• Bring professional and technical knowledge to bear on the making of political decisions about the physical development of the community

F. Stuart Chapin, Jr.'s Urban Land Use Plan

Chapin's ideas, through focusing more narrowly on the land use plan, were consistent with Kent's in both the 1957 and 1965 editions of *Urban Land Use Planning,* a widely used text and reference work for planners. Chapin's concept of the plan was of a generalized, but scaled, design for the future use of land, covering private land uses and public facilities, including the thoroughfare network (Chapin 1957, 275-7, 378).

Chapin conceived of the land use plan as the first step in preparing a general or comprehensive plan. Upon its completion, the land use plan served as a temporary general guide for decisions, until the comprehensive plan was developed. Later, the land use plan would become a cornerstone in the comprehensive plan, which also included plans for transportation, utilities, community facilities, and renewal, only the general rudiments of which are suggested in the land use plan (Chapin 1957, 277, 388). Purposes of the plan were to guide government decisions on public facilities, zoning, subdivision control, and urban renewal, and to inform private developers about the proposed future pattern of urban development.

The format of Chapin's land use plan included a statement of objectives, a description of existing conditions and future needs for space and services, and finally the mapped proposal for the future development of the community, together with a program for implementing the plan (customarily including zoning, subdivision control, a housing code, a public works expenditure program, an urban renewal program, and other regulations and development measures) (Chapin 1957, 280-3).

The Typical General Plan of the 1950s and 1960s

Influenced by the 701 program, Kent's policy vision, and Chapin's methods, the plans of the 1950s and 1960s were based on a clear and straightforward concept: The plan's purposes were to determine, communicate, and effectuate comprehensive policy for the private and public physical development and redevelopment of the city. The subject matter was long-range physical development, including private uses of the land, circulation, and community facilities. The standard format included a summary of existing and emerging conditions and needs; general goals; and a long-range urban form in map format, accompa-

nied by consistent development policies. The coverage was comprehensive, in the sense of addressing both public and private development and covering the entire planning jurisdiction, but quite general. The tone was typically neither as "inspirational" as the Burnham plan for Chicago, nor as action-oriented as today's plans. Such was the well-defined trunk of the family tree in the 1950s and 1960s, in which today's contemporary plans have much of their origin.

CONTEMPORARY PLANS: INCORPORATING NEW BRANCHES

Planning concepts and practice have continued to evolve since midcentury, maturing in the process. By the 1970s, a number of new ideas had taken root.[8] Referring back to the family tree in Figure II.1, we can see a trunk and several distinct branches:

- *The land use design,* a detailed mapping of future land use arrangements, is the most direct descendant of the 1950s plan. It still constitutes the trunk of the tree. However, today's version is more likely to be accompanied by action strategies, also mapped, and to include extensive policies.
- *The land classification plan,* a more general map of growth policy areas rather than a detailed land use pattern, is now also common, particularly for counties, metropolitan areas, and regions that want to encourage urban growth in designated development areas and to discourage it in conservation or rural areas. The roots of the land classification plan include McHarg's *Design With Nature* (1969), the 1976 American Law Institute (ALI) Model Land Development Code, the 1972 Coastal Zone Management Act, and the 1973 Oregon Land Use Law.
- *The verbal policy plan* de-emphasizes mapped policy or end-state visions and focuses on verbal action policy statements, usually quite detailed; sometimes called a strategic plan, it is rooted in Meyerson's (1956) middle-range bridge to comprehensive planning, Fagin's (1959) policies plan, and Perloff's (1980) strategies and policies general plan.
- The development management plan lays out a specific program of actions to guide development, such as a public investment program, a development code, and a program to extend infrastructure and services; and it assumes public sec-

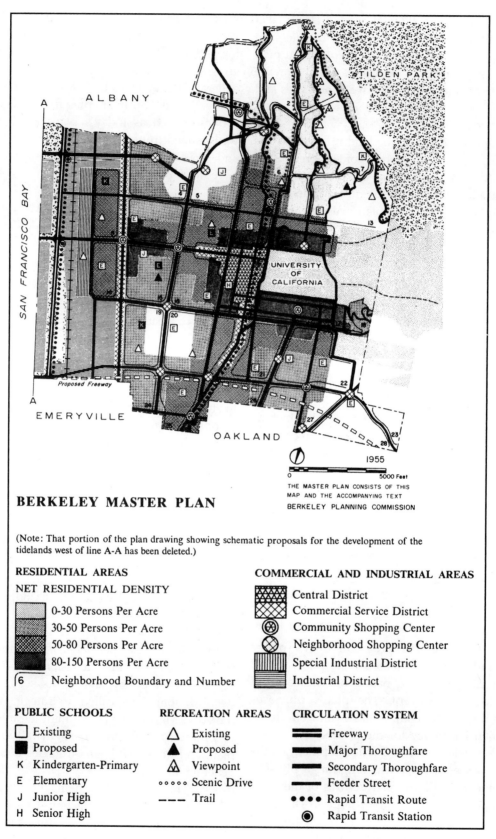

BERKELEY MASTER PLAN

1955

0   5000 Feet

THE MASTER PLAN CONSISTS OF THIS
MAP AND THE ACCOMPANYING TEXT
BERKELEY PLANNING COMMISSION

(Note: That portion of the plan drawing showing schematic proposals for the development of the tidelands west of line A-A has been deleted.)

RESIDENTIAL AREAS

NET RESIDENTIAL DENSITY

- 0-30 Persons Per Acre
- 30-50 Persons Per Acre
- 50-80 Persons Per Acre
- 80-150 Persons Per Acre
- 6 Neighborhood Boundary and Number

COMMERCIAL AND INDUSTRIAL AREAS

- Central District
- Commercial Service District
- Community Shopping Center
- Neighborhood Shopping Center
- Special Industrial District
- Industrial District

PUBLIC SCHOOLS

- ☐ Existing
- ■ Proposed
- K Kindergarten-Primary
- E Elementary
- J Junior High
- H Senior High

RECREATION AREAS

- △ Existing
- ▲ Proposed
- ⚠ Viewpoint
- ∘∘∘∘∘ Scenic Drive
- --- Trail

CIRCULATION SYSTEM

- Freeway
- Major Thoroughfare
- Secondary Thoroughfare
- Feeder Street
- •••• Rapid Transit Route
- ◉ Rapid Transit Station

Figure II.2 Example of land use design map featured in the 1950s General Plan
Source: Kent 1991, 111

THE URBAN GENERAL PLAN

Introduction: Reasons for G.P.; roles of council, CPC, citizens; historical background and context of G.P.

Summary of G.P.: Unified statement including (a) basic policies, (b) major proposals, and (c) one schematic drawing of the physical design.

Basic Policies

1. **Context of the G.P.:** Historical background; geographical and physical factors; social and economic factors; major issues, problems and opportunities.

   [facts, trends, assumptions, forecasts]

2. **Social Objectives and Urban Physical-Structure Concepts:** Value judgments concerning social objectives; professional judgments concerning major physical-structures concepts adopted as basis for G.P.

3. **Basic Policies of the G.P.:** Discussion of the basic policies that the general physical design is intended to implement.

General Physical Design

Description of plan proposals in relation to large-scale G.P. drawing and citywide drawings of:

1. Working-and-living-areas section.
2. Community-facilities section.
3. Civic-design section.
4. Circulation section.
5. Utilities section.

These drawings must remain general. They are needed because single G.P. drawing is too complex to enable each element to be clearly seen.

(Plus regional, functional, and district drawings that are needed to explain G.P.)

This diagram also suggests the contents of the official G.P. and publication as a single document.

Figure II.3 Components of the 1950s–1960s General Plan
Source: Kent 1964, 93

tor initiative for influencing the location, type, and pace of growth. The roots of the development management plan are in the environmental movement, and the movements for state growth management and community growth control (DeGrove 1984), as well as in ideas from Fagin (1959) and the ALI Code.

We looked for, but could not find, examples of land use plans that could be termed purely prototypical "strategic plans," in the sense of Bryson and Einsweiler (1988). Hence, rather than identifying strategic planning as a separate branch on the family tree of the land use plan, we see the influence of strategic planning showing up across a range of contemporary plans. We tend to agree with the planners surveyed by Kaufman and Jacobs (1988) that strategic planning differs from good comprehensive planning more in emphasis (shorter range, more realistically targeted, more market oriented) than in kind.

The Land Use Design Plan

The land use design plan is the most traditional of the four prototypes of contemporary plans and is the most direct descendent of the Kent-Chapin-701 plans of the 1950s and 1960s. It proposes a long-range future urban form as a pattern of retail, office, industrial, residential, and open spaces, and public land uses and a circulation system. Today's version, however, incorporates environmental processes, and sometimes agriculture and forestry, under the "open space" category of land use. Its land uses often include a "mixed use" category, honoring the neotraditional principle of closer mingling of residential, employment, and shopping areas. In addition, it may include a development strategy map, which is designed to bring about the future urban form and to link strategy to the community's financial capacity to provide infrastructure and services. The plans and strategies are often organized around strategic themes or around issues about growth, environment, economic development, transportation, or neighborhood/community scale change.

Like the other types of plans in vogue today, the land use design plan reflects recent societal issues, particularly the environmental crisis, the infrastructure crisis, and stresses on local government finance.[9] Contemporary planners no longer view environmental factors as development constraints, but as valuable resources and processes to be conserved. They also may question assumptions about the desirability and inevitability of urban population and economic growth, particularly as such assumptions stimulate demand for expensive new roads, sewers, and schools. While at midcentury plans unquestioningly accommodated growth, today's plans cast the amount, pace, location, and costs of growth as policy choices to be determined in the planning process.

The 1990 Howard County (Maryland) General Plan, winner of an American Planning Association (APA) award in 1991 for outstanding comprehensive planning, exemplifies contemporary land use design. (See Figure II.4.) While clearly a direct descendent of the traditional general plan, the Howard County plan adds new types of goals, policies, and planning techniques. To enhance communication and public understanding, it is organized strategically around six themes/chapters (responsible regionalism, preservation of the rural area, balanced growth, working with nature, community enhancement, and phased growth), instead of the customary plan elements. Along with the traditional land use design, the plan includes a "policy map" (strategy map) for each theme and an overall policies map for the years 2000 and 2010. A planned service area boundary is used to contain urban growth within the eastern urbanized part of the county, home to the well-known Columbia New Town.[10] The plan lays out specific next steps to be implemented over the next two years, and defines yardsticks for measuring success. An extensive public participation process for formulating the plan involved a 32-member General Plan Task Force, public opinion polling to discover citizen concerns, circulation of preplan issue papers on development impacts, and consideration of six alternative development scenarios.[11]

The Land Classification Plan

Land classification, or development priorities mapping, is a proactive effort by government to specify where and under what conditions growth will occur. Often, it also regulates the pace or timing of growth. Land classification addresses environmental protection by designating "nondevelopment" areas in especially vulnerable locations. Like the land use design, the land classification plan is spatially specific and map-oriented. However, it is less specific about the pattern of land uses within areas specified for development, which results in a kind of silhouette of urban form. On the other hand, land classification is more specific about development strategy, including timing. Counties, metropolitan areas, and regional planning agencies are more likely than cities to use a land classification plan.

The land classification plan identifies areas where development will be encouraged (called urban, transition, or development areas) and areas where development will be discouraged (open space, rural, conservation, or critical environmental areas). For each designated area, policies about the type, timing, and density of allowable development, extension of infrastructure, and development incentives or constraints apply. The planning principle is to concentrate financial resources, utilities, and services within a limited, prespecified area suitable for development, and to relieve pressure on nondevelopment areas by withholding facilities that accommodate growth.[12]

Ian McHarg's (1969) approach to land planning is an early example of the land classification concept. He divides planning regions into three categories: natural use, production, and urban. Natural use areas, those with valuable ecological functions, have the highest priority. Production areas, which include agriculture, forestry, and fishing uses, are next in priority. Urban areas have the lowest priority and are designated after allocating the land suitable to the two higher-priority uses. McHarg's approach in particular, and land classification generally, also reflect the emerging environmental consciousness of the 1960s and 1970s.

As early as 1961, Hawaii had incorporated the land classification approach into its state growth management system (DeGrove 1984). The development framework plan of the Metropolitan

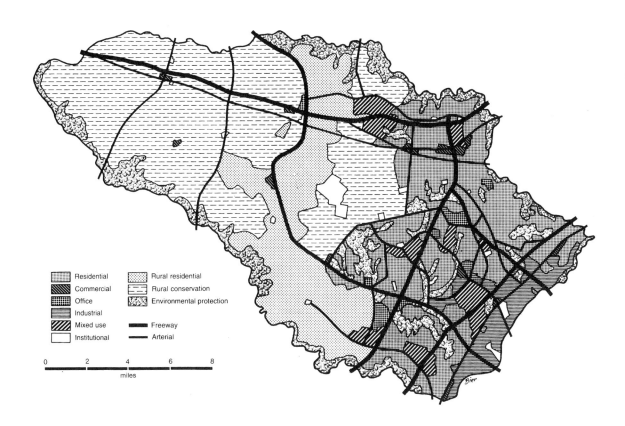

Figure II.4 Howard County, Maryland, General Plan, Land Use 2010
Source: Adapted from Howard County 1990

Council of the Twin Cities Area defined "planning tiers," each intended for a different type and intensity of development (Reichert 1976). The concepts of the "urban service area," first used in 1958 in Lexington, Kentucky, and the urban growth boundary," used throughout Oregon under its 1973 statewide planning act, classify land according to growth management policy (Abbott, Howe, and Adler 1994). Typically, the size of an urban growth area is based on the amount of land necessary to accommodate development over a period of ten or twenty years.

Vision 2005: A Comprehensive Plan for Forsyth County, North Carolina exemplifies the contemporary approach to land classification plans. The plan, which won honorable mention from APA in 1989, employs a six-category system of districts, plus a category for activity centers. It identifies both short- and long-range growth areas (4A and 4B in Figure II.5). Policies applicable to each district are detailed in the plan.

The Verbal Policy Plan Shedding the Maps

The verbal policy plan focuses on written statements of goals and policy, without mapping specific land use patterns or implementation strategy. Sometimes called a policy framework plan, a verbal policy plan is more easily prepared and flexible than other types of plans, particularly for incorporating nonphysical development policy (Perloff 1980, 233-8). Some claim that such a plan helps the planner to avoid relying too heavily on maps, which are difficult to keep up to date with the community's changes in policy (Hollander et al. 1988). The verbal policy plan also avoids falsely representing general policy as applying to specific parcels of property. The skeptics, however, claim that verbal statements in the absence of maps provide too little spatial specificity to guide implementation decisions (Reichert 1976).

The verbal policy plan may be used at any level of government, but is especially common at the state level, whose scale is unsuited to land use maps. The plan usually contains goals, facts and projections, and general policies corresponding to its purposes—to understand current and emerging conditions and issues, to identify goals to be pursued and issues to be addressed, and to formulate general principles of action. Sometimes communities do a verbal policy plan as an interim plan or a first step in the planning process. Thus, verbal policies are included in most land use design plans, land classification plans, and development management plans.

The Calvert County, MD Comprehensive Plan (Calvert County 1983), winner of a 1985 APA award, exemplifies the verbal policy plan. Its policies are concise, easy to grasp, and grouped in sections corresponding to the six divisions of county government responsible for implementation. It remains a policy plan, however, because it does not specify a program of specific actions for development management. Though the plan clearly addresses physical development and discusses specific spatial areas, it contains no land use map.

(See Figure II.6 for an illustrative page from the Calvert County plan.)

The Development Management Plan

The development management plan features a coordinated program of actions, supported by analyses and goals, for specific agencies of local government to undertake over a three-to-ten-year period. The program of actions usually specifies the content, geographic coverage, timing, assignment of responsibility, and coordination among the parts. Ideally, the plan includes most or all of the following components:[13]

•   Description of existing and emerging development conditions, with particular attention to development processes, the political-institutional context, and a critical review of the existing systems of development management

•   Statement of goals and/or legislative intent, including management-oriented goals

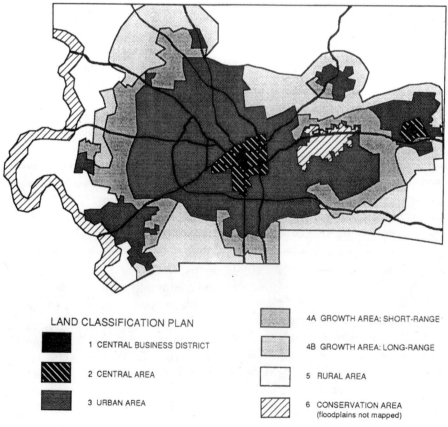

LAND CLASSIFICATION PLAN

1 CENTRAL BUSINESS DISTRICT
2 CENTRAL AREA
3 URBAN AREA
4A GROWTH AREA: SHORT-RANGE
4B GROWTH AREA: LONG-RANGE
5 RURAL AREA
6 CONSERVATION AREA (floodplains not mapped)

Figure II.5 Example of a land classification plan
Source: Adapted from Forsyth County City-County Planning Board 1988

• Program of actions—the heart of the plan—including:

1. Outline of a proposed development code, with: (a) procedures for reviewing development permits; (b) standards for the type of development, density, allowable impacts and/or performance standards; (c) site plan, site engineering, and construction practice requirements; (d) exactions and impact fee provisions and other incentives/disincentives; and (e) delineation of districts where various development standards, procedures, exactions, fees, and incentives apply
2. Program for the expansion of urban infrastructure and community facilities and their service areas
3. Capital improvement program

4. Property acquisition program
5. Other components, depending on the community situation, for example, a preferential taxation program, an urban revitalization program for specific built-up neighborhoods, or a historic preservation program

• Official maps, indicating legislative intent, which may be incorporated into ordinances, with force of law—among them, goal-form maps (e.g., land classification plan or land use design); maps of zoning districts, overlay districts, and other special areas for which development types, densities, and other requirements vary; maps of urban services areas; maps showing scheduled capital improvements; or other maps related to development management standards and procedures

Figure II.6 An excerpt from a verbal policy plan
Source: Calvert County, Maryland 1983

Industrial Districts

Industrial Districts are intended to provide areas in the county which are suitable for the needs of industry. They should be located and designed to be compatible with the surrounding land uses. either due to existing natural features or through the application of standards.

Recommendations:
1. Identify general locations for potential industrial uses.
2. Permit retail sales as an accessory use in the Industrial District.

Single-Family Residential Districts

Single-Family Residential Districts are to be developed and promoted as neighborhoods free from any land usage which might adversely affect them.

Recommendations:
1. For new development, require buffering for controlling visual, noise, and activity impacts between residential and commercial uses.
2. Encourage single-family residential development to locate in the designated towns.
3. Allow duplexes, triplexes, and fourplexes as a conditional use in the "R-1" Residential Zone so bog as the design is compatible with the single-family residential development.
4. Allow home occupations (professions and services, but not retail sales) by permitting the employment of one full-time equivalent individual not residing on the premises.

Multifamily Residential Districts

Multifamily Residential Districts provide for townhouses and multifamily apartment units. Areas designated in this category are those which are currently served or scheduled to be served by community or multi-use sewerage and water supply systems.

Recommendations:
1. Permit multifamily development in the Solomons, Prince Frederick, and Twin Beach Towns.
2. Require multifamily projects to provide adequate recreational facilities—equipment, structures, and play surfaces.
3. Evaluate the feasibility of increasing the dwelling unit density permitted in the multifamily Residential Zone (R-2).

The development management plan is a distinct type, emphasizing a specific course of action, not general policy. At its extreme the management plan actually incorporates implementation measures, so that the plan becomes part of a regulative ordinance. Although the spatial specifications for regulations and other implementation measures are included, a land use map may not be.

One point of origin for development management plans is Henry Fagin's (1959, 1965) concept of the "policies plan," whose purpose was to coordinate the actions of line departments and provide a basis for evaluating their results, as well as to formulate, communicate, and implement policy (the traditional purpose). Such a plan's subject matter was as broad as the responsibilities of the local government, including but not limited to physical development. The format included a "state of the community" message, a physical plan, a financial plan, implementation measures, and detailed sections for each department of the government.

A more recent point of origin is *A Model Land Development Code* (American Law Institute 1976), intended to replace the 1928 Model Planning Enabling Act as a model for local planning and development management. The model plan consciously retains an emphasis on physical development (unlike Fagin's broader concept), but stresses a short-term program of action, rather than a long-term, mapped goal form. The ALI model plan contains a statement of conditions and problems; objective, policies, and standards; and a short-term (from one to five years) program of specified public actions. It may also include land acquisition requirements, displacement impacts, development regulations, program costs and fund sources, and environmental, social, and economic consequences. More then other plan types, the development management plan is a "course of action" initiated by government to control the location and timing of development.[14]

The Sanibel, Florida, Comprehensive Land Use Plan (1981) exemplifies the development management plan. The plan outlines the standards and procedure of regulations (i.e., the means of implementation), as well as the analyses, goals, and statements of intent normally presented in a plan. Thus, when the local legislatures adopts the plan, it also adopts and ordinance for its implementation. Plan and implementation are merged into one instrument, as can be seen in the content of its articles:

Article 1: Preamble: including purposes and objectives, assumptions, coordination with surrounding areas, and implementation

Article 2: Elements of the Plan: Safety, Human Support Systems, Protection of Natural Environmental, Economic and Scenic Resources, Intergovernmental Coordination, and Land Use

Article 3: Development Regulations: Definitions, Maps, Requirements, Permitted Uses, Subdivisions, Mobile Home and Recreation Vehicles, Flood and Storm Proofing, Site Preparation, and Environmental Performance Standards

Article 4: Administrative Regulations (i.e., procedures): Standards, Short Form Permits, Development Permits, Completion Permits, Amendments to the Plan, and Notice, Hearing and Decision Procedures on Amendments

Figure II.7 shows the Sanibel plan's map of permitted uses, which is more like a zoning plan than a land use design plan, because it shows where regulations apply, and boundaries are exact.

THE CONTEMPORARY HYBRID PLAN: INTEGRATING DESIGN, POLICY, AND MANAGEMENT

The rationality of practice has integrated the useful parts of each of the separate prototypes reviewed here into contemporary hybrid plans that not only map and classify land use in both specific and general ways, but also propose policies and management measures. For example, Gresham, Oregon (1980) combined land use design (specifying residential, commercial, and industrial areas, and community facilities and public lands) with an overlay of land classification districts (developed, developing, rural, and conservation), and also included standards and procedures for issuing development permits (i.e., a development code). Prepared with considerable participation by citizens and interest groups, such plans usually reflect animated political debates about the costs and benefits of land use alternatives.

The states that manage growth have created new land use governance systems whose influ-

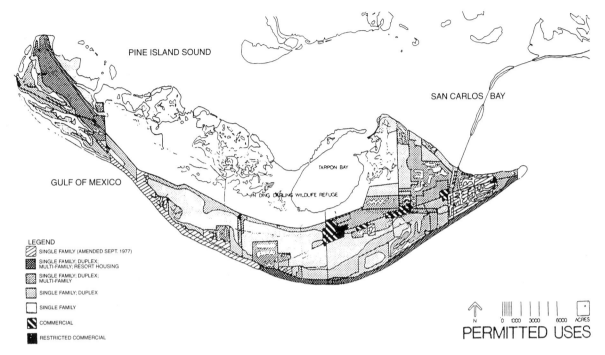

LEGEND

⬛ SINGLE FAMILY (AMENDED SEPT. 1977)

⬛ SINGLE FAMILY; DUPLEX;
MULTI-FAMILY; RESORT HOUSING

⬛ SINGLE FAMILY; DUPLEX;
MULTI-FAMILY

⬛ SINGLE FAMILY; DUPLEX

◻ SINGLE FAMILY

⬛ COMMERCIAL

⬛ RESTRICTED COMMERCIAL

PINE ISLAND SOUND

SAN CARLOS BAY

GULF OF MEXICO

TARPON BAY

J.N. DING DARLING WILDLIFE REFUGE

N 0 1000 3000 6000 ACRES

PERMITTED USES

Figure II.7. Map of permitted uses, Sanibel
Source: City of Sanibel 1981

ence has broadened the conceptual arsenals of local planners. DeGrove (1992, 161) identifies the common elements of these systems:

- consistency—intergovernmentally and internally (i.e., between plan and regulations)
- concurrency—between infrastructure and new development
- compactness—of new growth, to limit urban sprawl
- affordability—of new housing
- economic development, or "managing to grow"
- sustainability—of natural systems

DeGrove attributes the changes in planning under growth management systems to new hard-nosed concerns for measurable implementation and realistic funding mechanisms. For example, Florida local governments must adopt detailed capital improvement programs as part of their comprehensive plans, and substantial state grants may be withheld if their plans do not meet consistency and concurrency requirements.

Another important influence on contemporary plans is the renewed attention to community design. The neotraditional and transit-oriented design movements have inspired a number of pro-

posals for mixed use villages in land use plans (Calthorpe 1993; Duany and Plater-Zyberk 1991).

Toward a Sustainable Seattle: A Plan for Managing Growth (1994) exemplifies a city approach to the contemporary hybrid plan. Submitted as the Mayor's recommended comprehensive plan, it attempted to muster political support for its proposals. Three core values—social equity, environmental stewardship, and economic security and opportunity—underlie the plan's overall goal of sustainability. This goal is to be achieved by integrating plans for land use and transportation, healthy and affordable housing, and careful capital investment in a civic compact based on a shared vision. Citywide population and job growth targets, midway between growth completely by regional sprawl and growth completely by infill, are set forth within a 20-year time frame. The plan is designed to meet the requirements of the Washington State Growth Management Act.

The land use element designates urban center villages, hub urban villages, residential urban villages, neighborhood villages, and manufacturing/industrial centers, each with specific design guidelines (Figure II.8). The city's capacity for growth is identified, and then allocated according to the urban village strategy. Future development is directed to mixed-use neighborhoods, some of which are already established; existing single-family areas are protected. Growth is shaped to build community, promote pedestrian and transit use, protect natural amenities and existing residential and employment areas, and ensure diversity of people and activities. Detailed land use policies carry out the plan.

Loudoun County Choices and Changes: General Plan (1991), which won APA's 1994 award for comprehensive planning in small jurisdictions, exemplifies a county approach to the contemporary hybrid plan. Its goals are grouped into three categories:

1. Natural and cultural resources goals seek to protect fragile resources by limiting development or mitigating disturbances, while at the same time not unduly diminishing land values.

2. Growth management goals seek to accommodate and manage the county's fair share of regional growth, guiding development into the urbanized eastern part of the county or existing western towns and their urban growth areas, and conserving agriculture and open space areas in the west. (See Figure II.9.)

3. Community design goals seek to concentrate growth in compact, urban nodes to create mixed-use communities with strong visual identities, human-scale street networks, and a range of housing and employment opportunities utilizing neotraditional design concepts (illustrated in Figure II.9).

Three time horizons are addressed: the "ultimate" vision through 2040, the 20-year, long-range development pattern, and the five-year, short-range development pattern. The plan uses the concept of community character areas as an organizing framework for land use management. Policies are proposed for the overall county, as well as for the eastern urban growth areas, town urban growth areas, rural areas, and existing rural village areas. Implementation tools include capital facility and transportation proffers by developers, density transfers, community design guidelines, annexation guidelines, and an action schedule of next steps.

SUMMARY OF THE CONTEMPORARY SITUATION

Since midcentury, the nature of the plan has shifted from an elitist, inspirational, long-range vision that was based on fiscally innocent implementation advice, to a framework for community consensus on future growth that is supported by fiscally grounded actions to manage change.[15] Subject matter has expanded to include the natural as well as the built environment. Format has shifted from simple policy statements and a single large-scale map of future land use, circulation, and community facilities, to a more complex combination of text, data, maps, and time tables. In a number of states, plans are required by state law, and their content is specified by state agencies (Bollens 1993). Table 2 compares the general plan of the 1950s-1960s with the four contemporary prototype plans and the new 1990s hybrid design-policy-management plan, which combines aspects of the prototype plans.

Today's prototype land use design continues to emphasize long-range urban form for land uses, community facilities, and transportation systems as shown by a map; but the design is also expressed in general policies. Land use design is still a common form of development plan, especially in municipalities.[16]

The land classification plan also still emphasizes mapping, but of development policy rather than policy about a pattern of urban land uses. Land classification is more specific about development management and environmental protection, but less specific about transportation, community facilities, and the internal arrangement of the future urban form. County and regional governments are more likely than are municipalities to use land classification plans.

The verbal policies plan eschews the spatial specificity of land use design and land classification plans and focuses less on physical development issues. It is more suited to regions and states, or may serve as an interim plan for a city or county while another type of plan is being prepared.

The development management plan represents the greatest shift from the traditional land use plan. It embodies a short-to-intermediate-range program of governmental actions for ongoing growth management rather than for long-range comprehensive planning.

In practice, these four types of plans are not mutually exclusive. Communities often combine aspects of them into a hybrid general plan that has policy sections covering environmental/social/economic/housing/infrastructure concerns, land classification maps defining spatial growth policy, land use design maps specifying locations of particular land uses, and development management programs laying out standards and procedures for guiding and paying for growth. Regardless of the type of plan used, the most progressive planning programs today regard the plan as but one part of a coordinated growth management program, rather than, as in the 1950s, the main planning product. Such a program incorporates a capital improvement program, land use controls, small area plans, functional plans, and other devices, as well as a general plan.[17]

THE ENDURING LAND USE FAMILY TREE AND ITS FUTURE BRANCHES

For the first 50 years of this century, planning responded to concerns about progressive govern-

mental reform, the City Beautiful, and the "City Efficient." Plans were advisory, specifying a future urban form, and were developed by and for an independent commission. By midcentury this type of plan, growing out of the design tradition, had become widespread in local practice. During the 1950s and 1960s the 701 program, T.J. Kent, and F. Stuart Chapin, Jr. further articulated the plan's content and methodology. Over the last 30 years, environmental and infrastructure issues have pushed planning toward growth management. As citizen activists and interest groups have taken more of a role, land use politics have become more heated. Planning theorists, too, have questioned the midcentury approach to planning, and have proposed changes in focus, process, subject matter, and format, sometimes challenging even the core idea of rational planning. As a result, practice has changed, though not to a monolithic extent and without entirely abandoning the traditional concept of a plan. Instead, at least four distinct types of plans have evolved, all descending more or less from the mid-century model, but advocating very different concepts of what a plan should be. With a kind of

Table II.2. Comparison of plan types

| Features of Plans | 1950s General Plan | Contemporary Prototype Plans | | | | 1990s Hybrid Design-Policy-Management Plan |
		Land Use Design	Land Classification Plan	Verbal Policy Plan	Development Management Plan	
Land Use Maps	Detailed	Detailed	General	No	By growth areas	General *and* area specific
Nature of Recommendations	General community goals	Land use policies and objectives	Growth locations and incentives	Variety of community policies	Specific management actions	Policy *and* actions
Time Horizon	Long range	Long range	Long range	Intermediate range	Short range	Short *and* long range
Link to Implementation	Very weak	Weak to moderate	Moderate	Moderate	Strong	Moderate to strong
Public Participation	Pro-forma	Active	Moderate	Moderate	Active	Active
Capital Improvements	Advisory	Recommended	Recommended	Recommended	Required	Recommended to required
Land Use/ Transportation Linkage	Moderate	Strong	Weak	Varies	Strong	Strong
Environmental Protection	Weak	Moderate	Strong	Varies	Varies	Strong
Social Policy Linkage	Weak	Weak	Weak	Moderate to strong	Weak	Moderate

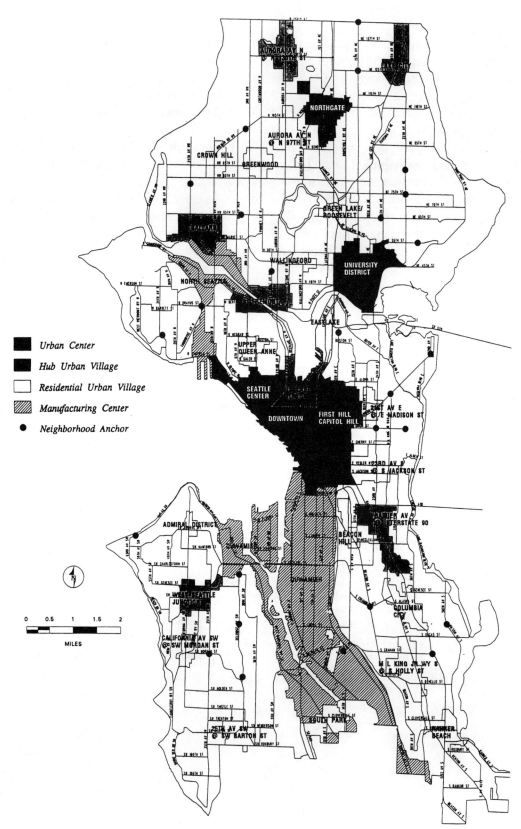

Figure II.8 Seattle urban villages strategy
Source: Seattle Planning Department 1993

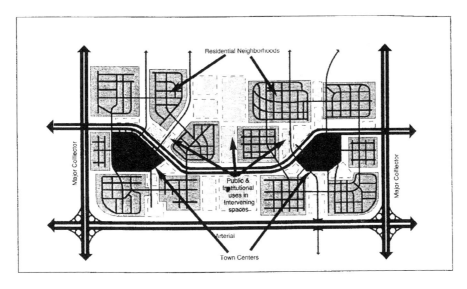

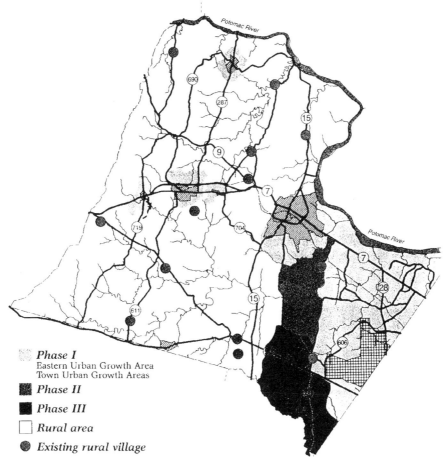

Phase I
Eastern Urban Growth Area
Town Urban Growth Areas

Phase II

Phase III

Rural area

Existing rural village

Figure II.9 Neotraditional community schematic and generalized policy planning areas, Loudoun County, Virginia General Plan
Source: Planning 60, 3: 10 (1994)

self-correcting common sense, the plans of the 1990s have subsequently incorporated the useful parts of each of these prototypes to create today's hybrid design/policy/management plans.

To return to our analogy of the plan's family tree: Roots for the physical development plan became well established during the first half of this century. By 1950, a sturdy trunk concept had developed. Since then, new roots and branches have appeared—land classification plans, verbal policy plans, and development management plans. Meanwhile development of the main trunk of the tree—the land use design—has continued. Fortunately, the basic gene pool has been able to combine with new genes in order to survive as a more complex organism—the 1990s design-policy management hybrid plan. The present family tree of planning reflects both its heredity and its environment.

The next generation of physical development plans also should mature and adapt without abandoning their heritage. We expect that by the year 2000, plans will be more participatory, more electronically based, and concerned with increasingly complex issues. An increase in participation seems certain, bolstered by interest groups' as well as governments' use of expert systems and computer databases. A much broader consideration of alternative plans and scenarios, as well as a more flexible and responsive process of plan amendment, will become possible. These changes will call upon planners to use new skills of consensus building and conflict management, as more groups articulate their positions on planning matters, and government plans and interest group plans compete, each backed by experts (Susskind and Cruikshank 1987).

With the advent of the "information highway," plans are more likely to be drafted, communicated, and debated through electronic networks and virtual reality images. The appearance of plans on CD ROM and cable networks will allow more popular access and input, and better understanding of plans' three dimensional consequences. It will be more important than ever for planners to compile information accurately and ensure it is fairly communicated. They will need to compile, analyze, and manage complex databases, as well as to translate abstract data into understandable impacts and images.

Plans will continue to be affected by dominant issues of the times: aging infrastructure and limited public capital, central city decline and suburban growth, ethnic and racial diversity, economic and environmental sustainability, global competition and interdependence, and land use/transportation/air quality spillovers. Many of these are unresolved issues from the last thirty years, now grown more complex and interrelated. Some are addressed by new programs like the Intermodal Surface Transportation Efficiency Act (ISTEA) and HUD's Empowerment Zones and Enterprise Communities. To cope with others, planners must develop new concepts and create new techniques.

One of the most troubling new issues is an attempt by conservative politicians (see the Private Property Protection Act of 1995 passed by the U.S. House of Representatives) and "wise use" (Jacobs 1995) groups to reverse the precedence of the public interest over individual private property rights. These groups challenge the use of federal, state, and local regulations to implement land use plans and protect environmental resources when the result is any reduction in the economic value of affected private property. Should their challenge succeed and become widely adopted in federal and state law, growth management plans based on regulations could become toothless. Serious thinking by land use lawyers and planners would be urgently needed to create workable new implementation techniques, setting in motion yet another planning evolution.

We are optimistic, however, about the future of land use planning. Like democracy, it is not a perfect institution but works better than its alternatives. Because land use planning has adapted effectively to this century's turbulence and become stronger in the process, we believe that the twenty-first century will see it continuing as a mainstay of strategies to manage community change.

NOTES

1. Each critic puts forth his or her own alternative to comprehensive physical planning. Some make radical recommendations, such as doing away with the mapped land-use general plan (Perloff 1980, 233-4) or even with long-range planning for Euclidean space based on straight and

parallel lines and angles of plane triangles (Friedmann 1993, 482). However, the principles embodied in their solutions tend to turn up in land use planning practice over time. Thus, we find that some comprehensive plans, such as Sanibel's, include land use regulations as recommended by Perin (1967, 337). Perloff's (1980) call for policy planning has been heeded by nearly all contemporary plans, though not to the exclusion of land use maps. Actually, no one could have foreseen in 1980 the extent to which GIS has tied policy analysis to land use mapping, suitability studies, sketch planning, and scenario development (Harris and Batty 1993). Friedmann (1993) calls for planning that is normative, innovative, political, transactive, and based on social learning. Arguably, all of these qualities may be found in leading edge examples of contemporary land use planning. Jacobs (1992) sees land use planning as a modernist conception challenged by postmodern phenomena, including a populist citizen movement, a redefinition of private property rights, and growing computer literacy. Again, these factors affect land use planning without rendering it obsolete.

2. In growth-managing states, regulations for local comprehensive plans typically specify the content of the land use elements. For example, Florida's 9J-5 rules require maps of existing and proposed land use in all local plans prepared in that state. Not only are local plans mandatory in Florida, but also they must include realistic capital improvement programs, be adopted by the governing body, and be revised every five years. There is evidence that state planning mandates improve the quality of local plans (Berke and French, 1994).

3. The land use plan typically is one element of a comprehensive or general plan, which also includes other elements, such as transportation, community facilities, and economic development. We acknowledge that these are related to land use decisions, but here we limit our attention to land use.

4. In the late 1940s more than 50 percent of all planning directors in cities with populations over 25,000 were still appointed by planning commissions. The commission was the client for the plan, and therefore the plan was not seen as something tied closely to implementation. By 1971 only 18 percent of planning directors were appointed by

such commissions, most being appointed instead by chief executives, and working directly in the executive branch (sometimes working for the planning commission as a second boss) (reported in Brooks, 1988). It was only natural that planning became more closely linked to decision making, and the role of plans was increasingly seen as more closely linked to decisions and implementation.

5. Through the end of 1964, the 701 program had allocated $79 million in grants for planning in 4,462 localities (cited in Black 1968). By its peak, 1971 through 1975, the program was allocating approximately $100 million a year. At its rescindment in 1981, the program had appropriated over $1 billion to comprehensive planning (Feiss 1985, 182).

6. Kent's book was later summarized by Alan Black, who worked originally with Kent, in a chapter on the "The Comprehensive Plan" in the 1968 edition of *Principles and Practices of Urban Planning* (the planner's "big green bible"), which summarizes the state of the art of planning practice in the 1960s (Black 1968). In testimony to the staying power of Kent's concept of the plan, the book was republished in 1991, virtually unchanged.

7. Chapin's ideas, like those of Kent, had staying power. However, to keep pace with advances in methodology, his book appeared in a third edition in 1979 and in a fourth edition in 1995 (Chapin and Kaiser 1979; Kaiser, Godschalk, and Chapin 1995).

8. A late 1970s survey, "The State of the Art in Local Planning," looked at 27 communities nominated by consulting firms and HUD staff as having "especially interesting or effective master plans" (Fishman 1978, appendix to chapter 5). Examples of our prototypes included Philadelphia (land use design), Boulder and Petaluma (growth management plan), Cleveland and Dallas (policies plan). The report looked at a number of distinguishing plan features, including whether they were top down or bottom up, the physical versus social nature of their goals, the inclusion of maps, the processes for plan preparation and revision, implementation strategies, and citizen participation approaches.

9. Social issues, such as segregation, unemployment, crime, and community disintegration,

are primarily addressed through the housing and economic development elements of comprehensive plans, although there are linkages to land use through neighborhood plans, community facility programs, and public investment strategies.

10. In this respect, the Howard County Plan also has some similarities to the prototype land classification plan.

11. For an account of the politics behind the plan (the plan was adopted but the county executive and planning director lost their positions) and an assessment of the lessons of the planning process, see Avin and Mennitto (1992).

12. Classification plans usually include more than just the two basic types of districts—development and nondevelopment. For example, the urban area might be divided into a "developed" area, consisting of the built-up central city and older suburbs, and a "transition" area, which is undeveloped or only partially developed at the time of the plan. The transition area might be divided into districts to be developed earlier (e.g., first 10 years) and districts to be developed later (e.g., years 10-20). A "rural" area might be divided into agricultural districts with a policy of long-range commitment to agricultural and forest uses, and less critical rural districts that could become urban transition in the future. "Environmentally critical" areas might be divided into areas with specific critical environmental processes, e.g., wetlands being designated as separate from water supply watersheds, width each having its own policies and development standards.

13. Adapted from plans for Breckenridge, Colorado, 1977, 1987; Gresham, Oregon, 1980; Sanibel, Florida, 1981; and Hardin County, Kentucky, 1985; see also Fagin 1959, 1965; American Law Institute 1976.

14. The idea of plan as course of action originated in the 1960s as planning theory incorporated notions from policy analysis and business administration into the rational planning model, broadening the design concept of a plan. These new concepts stressed means as much as ends, and shifted the role of government from facilitating private development to proactive guidance of growth.

15. Codification of the action requirements of land use plans can be found in the regulations implementing the Florida and Oregon growth management acts. Florida requires the provision of infrastructure "concurrently" with future development (DeGrove 1992, 16-7). Oregon requires that communities delineate and enforce urban growth boundaries (Howe 1993).

16. See, for example, the *Cleveland Civic Vision 2000 Citywide Plan* (Cleveland City Planning Commission 1991), successor to Cleveland's oft-described 1975 *Policy Planning Report*.

17. Growth management programs are related to the notion of the urban development guidance system, introduced by Chapin (1963). His concept featured the general plan as the organizing element, backed by an "urban development policies instrument," a public works program (to be followed up with a more detailed capital improvements program), an urban development code (unifying most development regulations), and a civic education/participation program.

Author's Note: We appreciate the constructive comments on earlier drafts of this article by a number of colleagues, especially Alan Black, Linda Dalton, and Kem Lowery, and by the journal's reviewers and editors. Matthew Goebel conducted the survey of comprehensive plans in growth-managing states.

REFERENCES

Abbott, Carl, Deborah Howe, and Sy Adler. 1994. *Planning the Oregon Way: A Twenty Year Evaluation.* Corvallis, OR: Oregon State University Press.

American Law Institute (ALI). 1976. *A Model Land Development Code.* Washington, DC: The American Law Institute.

Avin, Uri, and Donna Mennitto. 1992. Howard County General Plan: The Politics of Growth Management. American Institute of Certified Planners, *Planners' Casebook* (Winter): 1-8.

Bassett, Edward M. 1938. *The Master Plan.* New York: Russell Sage Foundation.

Beal, Frank, and Elizabeth Hollander. 1979. City Development Plans. *In The Practice of Local Government Planning* edited by Frank S. So, Israel Stollman, Frank Beal, and David S. Arnold. Washington, DC: International City Management Association, in cooperation with the American Planning Association.

Berke, Philip, and Steven P. French. 1994. The Influence of State Planning Mandates on Local Plan Quality. *Journal of Planning Education and Research* 13: 237-50.

Black, Alan. 1968. The Comprehensive Plan. In *Principles and Practice of Urban Planning* edited by William I. Goodman and Eric C. Freund. Washington, DC: International City Managers' Association, 349-78.

Bollens, Scott A. 1993. Restructuring Land Use Governance. *Journal of Planning Literatum* 7,3: 211-26.

Breckenridge, Town of, Comprehensive Planning Program. 1977. *Land Use Guidance System.* Breckenridge, CO: The Harris St. Group.

Breckenridge, Town of. 1987. *Land Use Guidelines.* Breckenridge, CO: Department of Community Development.

Brooks, Michael P. 1988. Four Critical Junctures in the History of the Urban Planning Profession: An Exercise in Hindsight. *Journal of the American Planning Association* 54,2: 241-8.

Bryson, John M., and Robert C. Einsweiler, eds. 1988. *Strategic Planning: Threats and Opportunities for Planners.* Chicago: Planners Press.

Calthorpe, Peter. 1993. *The Next American Metropolis.* Princeton, NJ: Princeton Architectural Press.

Calvert County, MD. 1983. *Comprehensive Plan, Calvert County, Maryland.* Prince Frederick, MD: Calvert Country.

Chapin, F. Stuart, Jr. 1957. *Urban Land Use Planning.* New York: Harper and Brothers Publishers.

Chapin, F. Stuart, Jr. 1963. Taking Stock of Techniques for Shaping Urban Growth. *Journal of the American Institute of Planners* 29,2: 76-87.

Chapin, F. Stuart, Jr. 1965. *Urban Land Use Planning.* 2d edition. Urbana, IL: The University of Illinois Press.

Chapin, F. Stuart, Jr., and Edward J. Kaiser. 1979. *Urban Land Use Planning.* 3d edition. Urbana, IL: The University of Illinois Press.

Cleveland City Planning Commission. 1975. *Policy Planning Report.* Cleveland, OH: Cleveland City Planning Commission.

Cleveland City Planning Commission. 1991. *Cleveland Civic Vision 2000 Citywide Plan.* Cleveland, OH: Cleveland City Planning Commission.

DeGrove, John M. 1984. *Land, Growth and Politics.* Washington, DC: Planners Press.

DeGrove, John M. 1992. *Planning and Growth Management in the States.* Cambridge, MA: Lincoln Institute of Land Policy.

Duany, Andres, and Elizabeth Plater-Zyberk. 1991. *Towns and Town-Making Principles.* New York: Rizzoli International Publications.

Fagin, Henry. 1959. Organizing and Carrying Out Planning Activities Within Urban Government. *Journal of the American Institute of Planners* 25,3: 109- 14.

Fagin, Henry. 1965. *The Policy Plan: Instrumentality for a Community Dialogue.* Pittsburgh, PA: Institute of Local Government, Graduate School of Public and International Affairs, University of Pittsburgh.

Feiss, Carl. 1985. The Foundations of Federal Planning Assistance. *Journal of the American Planning Association* 51,2: 175-89.

Fishman, Richard P., ed. 1978. *Housing for All Under Law: New Dimensions in Housing, Land Use and Planning Law.* Cambridge, MA: Ballinger Publishing Co.

Forsyth County City-County Planning Board. 1988. *Vision 2005: A Comprehensive Plan for Forsyth County, North Carolina.* Winston Salem, NC: Forsyth County.

Friedmann, John. 1993. Toward a Non-Euclidean Mode of Planning. *Journal of the American Planning Association* 59,4: 482-5.

Gresham Planning Division. 1980. *Gresham Community Development Plan.* Gresham, OR: Gresham Planning Division.

Gurwirt, Rob. 1994. War Over Urban Villages. *Governing* 8,2: 50-6.

Haar, Charles M. 1955. The Content of the General Plan: A Glance at History. *Journal of the American Institute of Planners* 21,2-3: 66-70.

Hardin County, Kentucky. 1985. *Development Guidance System.* Elizabethtown, KY: Hardin County Planning and Development Commission.

Harris, Britton, and Michael Batty. 1993. Locational Models, Geographic Information and Planning Support Systems. *Journal of Planning Education* and Research 12,3: 184-98.

Hollander, Elizabeth, Leslie S. Pollock, Jeffry D. Reckinger, and Frank Beal. 1988. General Development Plans. In *The Practice of Local Government Planning*, 2d edition, edited by Frank S. So and Judith Getzels. Washington, DC: ICMA Training Institute, International City Management Association.

Howard County Department of Planning and Zoning. 1990. *The 1990 General Plan... a six point plan for the future*. Ellicott City, MD: Howard County Department of Planning and Zoning.

Howe, Deborah A. 1993. Growth Management in Oregon. *In Growth Management: The Planning Challenge of the 1990's*, edited by Jay M. Stein. Newbury Park, CA: Sage Publications.

Jacobs, Harvey M. 1992. Exposing and Reframing the Unspoken Assumptions of Land Use Planning: A Postmodern View. Paper presented at the Annual Meeting of the Association of Collegiate Schools of Planning, Columbus, OH.

Jacobs, Harvey M. 1995. The Anti-Environmental 'Wise Use' Movement in America. *Land Use Law and Zoning Digest* 47, 2: 3-8.

Kaiser, Edward J., David R. Godschalk, and F. Stuart Chapin, Jr. 1995. *Urban Land Use Planning*. 4th edition. Urbana, IL: The University of Illinois Press.

Kaufman, Jerome L., and Harvey M. Jacobs. 1988. A Public Planning Perspective on Strategic Planning. In *Strategic Planning: Threats and Opportunities for Planners*, edited by John Bryson and Robert Einsweiler. Chicago: Planners Press.

Kent, T. J., Jr. 1991. *The Urban General Plan*. San Francisco, CA: Chandler Publishing Company, 1964. Reprint, Chicago: APA Planners Press.

Loudoun County General Plan. 1994. Planning 60, 3 (March): 10-11.

Loudoun County Planning Commission. 1991. *Loudoun County General Plan: Choices and Changes*. Loudoun County, VA: Loudoun County Planning Commission.

McHarg, Ian. 1969. *Design with Nature*. Garden City, NY: Natural History Press.

Meyerson, Martin. 1956. Building the Middle-Range Bridge for Comprehensive Planning. *Journal of the American Institute of Planners* 22,2: 58-64.

Perin, Constance. 1967. The Noiseless Secession from the Comprehensive Plan. *Journal of the American Institute of Planners* 33,5: 336-47.

Perloff, Harvey S. 1980. *Planning the Post-Industrial City*. Washington, DC: Planners Press.

Reichert, Peggy A. 1976. *Growth Management in the Twin Cities Metropolitan Area: The Development Framework Planning Process*. Saint Paul, MN: Metropolitan Council of the Twin Cities Area.

Reps, John. 1965. *The Making of Urban America: A History of City Planning in the United States*. Princeton, NJ: Princeton University Press.

Sanibel, City of. 1981. *Comprehensive Land Use Plan*. Sanibel, Florida: City of Sanibel.

Schlereth, Thomas J. 1981. Burnham's Plan and Moody's Manual. *Journal of the American Planning Association* 47,1: 70-82.

Scott, Mellier G. 1969. *American City Planning Since 1890* Berkeley, CA: University of California Press.

Seattle Planning Department. 1993. *A Citizen's Guide to the Draft Comprehensive Plan. Toward a Sustainable Seattle: Seattle's Plan for Managing Growth*. Seattle, WA: Seattle Planning Department.

Seattle Planning Department. 1994. *The Mayor's Recommended Comprehensive Plan. Toward a Sustainable Seattle*. Seattle, WA: Seattle Planning Department.

Susskind, Lawrence, and Jeffrey Cruikshank. 1987. *Breaking the Impasse: Consensual Approaches to Resolving Public Disputes*. New York: Basic Books.

Walker, Robert. 1941. *The Planning Function in Urban Government*. Chicago: University of Chicago Press.

Planning Through Consensus Building: A New View of the Comprehensive Planning Ideal

Judith Innes

Copyright: Reprinted with permission from the *Journal of the American Planning Association*, 62, 4, 1996 ©, pp. 460-472.

This article takes up Alan Altschuler's challenge regarding the legitimacy of comprehensive planning and argues that it is not only possible to realize, but is also intellectually defensible. Innes argues that consensus building with stakeholders offers a model for planning that responds to each of Altschuler's critiques of comprehensive planning. The article concludes with a discussion of how consensus building may be used for local comprehensive planning.

In the mid-1960s Alan Altshuler subjected the city planner's ideal of comprehensive planning to a devastating critique (1965a, 1965b). He said, in essence, that the comprehensive physical plan is neither practically feasible nor politically viable, and that the comprehensive planner has no basis for legitimacy as a professional. Meaningful public debate on comprehensive planning is virtually impossible, he claimed, because of such planning's scope and generality. He saw the role, power, and knowledge of planners as too limited, in any case, for them to prepare a comprehensive plan. Their only claim to legitimacy, he argued, is that they are experts who know and measure the public interest. Since measuring something no one can even define is clearly impossible, his implication was that no one has expertise to do comprehensive planning.[1] Altshuler ended by challenging the planning profession "to reinforce its most fundamental theoretical arsenal." Unless its premises were established in "compelling fashion," he claimed, comprehensive planning would "have little effect on American cities" (Altshuler 1965a, 194).

Altshuler's critique not only was in many ways on target, but also had a chilling effect on the development of the idea and practice of comprehensive planning. The academy turned to other ways of theorizing about planning, including systems theory, building the middle-range bridge, advocacy planning, and mixed scanning. Comprehensive planning remained in planners' lexicon and practice,

but without the benefit of the compelling arguments that Altshuler had called for.

This article takes up Altshuler's challenge. To do so is now possible, as it was not in 1965, because new practices have since developed and the literature has elaborated new knowledge and ideas about planning process. The components are now available to build theoretical and practical foundations for a meaningful and influential version of comprehensive planning.

CONSENSUS BUILDING AS A SOURCE FOR RENEWAL

The emergence of consensus building as a method of deliberation has provided the opportunity to reformulate comprehensive planning. The practice is becoming more popular as a way to address complex, controversial public issues where multiple interests are at stake.[2] Texts and how-to manuals explain how to organize groups, manage meetings, and accomplish tasks (Susskind and Cruikshank 1987; Fisher and Brown 1988; Carpenter 1989; Carpenter and Kennedy 1991; Potapchuk and Polk 1994).[3] These procedures use the tools of alternative dispute resolution, such as mediated negotiation (see, for example, Bingham 1986; Moore 1986; Buntz and Sherry 1993a, 1993b; Bacow and Wheeler 1994) and the insights of the worldwide bestseller *Getting to Yes* (Fisher and Ury 1981), which outlines how to reach mutually beneficial agreements. The methods also build on theories and practice in American pragmatism and in education, emphasizing the importance of learning communities and of empowerment (e.g., Dewey 1916; Freire 1981; and Marshall and Peters 1985).

Consensus building has emerged parallel to the idea of "communicative rationality," drawn largely from Habermas (1984), developed by Dryzek (1990,3-56) for policy making (he also calls it "discursive democracy"), and applied to planning by Forester (1989),[4] Sager (1994), and Innes (1995), among others. A decision is "communicatively rational" to the degree that it is reached consensually through deliberations involving all stakeholders,[5] where all are equally empowered and fully informed, and where the conditions of ideal speech are met (statements are comprehensible, scientifically true, and offered by those who can legitimately speak and who speak sincerely). Communicatively rational decisions, then, are those that come about because there are good reasons for them rather than because of the political or economic power of particular stakeholders. For these processes to be truly communicatively *rational*, they must also reflect "emancipatory knowledge," or knowledge of the deeper reality hidden behind popular myths, scientific theories, and the arguments and rationalizations in common use. Such knowledge can come through dialectic, self-reflection, praxis—the broad and deep experience of those who know how to do things in the world—and from discourse that challenges prevailing assumptions.[6]

Consensus building aims to resemble the theorists' account of communicative rationality. It is a method of group deliberation that brings together for face-to-face discussion a significant range of individuals chosen because they represent those with differing stakes in a problem. Facilitators, training for participants, and carefully designed procedures are intended to ensure that the mode of discourse is one where all are heard and all concerns are taken seriously.[7] Little is taken as given in the wide-ranging discussion. The process requires that participants have common information and that all become informed about each other's interests. When the group has explored interests and agreed on facts, they create options, develop criteria for choice, and make the decisions on which they can all agree. Citizens, public agencies, or even legislatures create consensus-building

groups to supplement traditional procedures for policy development and plan preparation.[8] Such groups have built consensus for planning and policy tasks on geographic scales ranging from the neighborhood to the nation. Groups have helped to plan for affordable housing (Wheeler 1993), land use at Lake Tahoe (Fulton 1989); allocating city funds in Malden, Massachusetts (Susskind and Madigan 1984); siting waste treatment facilities (Ozawa 1991); a state development and redevelopment plan in New Jersey (Innes 1992; Neuman 1993); and managing water resources and fisheries in countries around the world (Ostrom 1990).

COMPREHENSIVE PLANNING AS AN IDEAL

According to widely used texts, a comprehensive plan is a long-range physical plan for a city; it covers the city geographically; it addresses each function that makes the city work as a physical entity and that affects its physical form; it is a statement of policy rather than a program of specific actions; and it is intended to guide city officials in future actions (Black 1968; So and Getzels 1988). This view is distinct from "rational" comprehensive or "synoptic" planning, which requires clarifying objectives and developing policy by comparing all alternative means to reach objectives and then choosing the optimal method (Lindblom and Braybrooke 1963). Proponents of comprehensive city planning do not contend that every alternative must be evaluated. A comprehensive city plan is a package of policies that can respond to anticipated conditions and work together for the city as a whole. Elected officials evaluate this package as a whole, using their own methods.[9]

KENT'S VIEW OF THE COMPREHENSIVE PLAN

The most sophisticated and widely recognized version of the comprehensive city plan is in the work of T.J. Kent (1964), who laid our principles for what he preferred to call the "urban general plan."[10] Kent's book is so compelling a statement that it has been continuously in use for decades and was recently reprinted (1991). He articulated purposes for comprehensive planning that illuminate why it has been an ideal for many planners, including those in Altshuler's research.

Comprehensiveness

Kent said the plan must be comprehensive in the sense that it covers the whole city, deals with all "essential physical elements of that urban environment," and "recognizes"...its relationships with all significant factors, physical and nonphysical, local and regional, that affect the physical growth and development of the community" (98-9). It should take into account demographic and economic forecasts and anticipated technological change. It must be comprehensive in these ways in order to promote the public interest, which Kent defined as the interest of the community at large, rather than of individuals or special groups (25). Comprehensiveness facilitates consideration of the relationship between any specific question and the overall-development of the community. It facilitates the democratic determination of policies by providing a context that enables citizens and elected officials to learn, discuss, and decide in an informed way. Comprehensiveness also helps to ensure that professional and technical knowledge is brought to bear on political decisions, and it effects political and technical coordination (25-6).

Explicit Reasoning

Though the plan should be presented as a unified statement to decision-makers, Kent argued that it should explain its reasoning, identifying "the context of facts and judgments from which [it] was developed" (119-20) and making a good argument for the policies. A plan expresses value judgments, standards and principles that do not depend on scientific bases (e.g., the concept of separating industrial from residential districts). Knowledge about the interrelationship of socioeconomic issues and physical development is intuitive and speculative. Explicitness is essential so that the elected officials can make an informed final judgment (104).

Generality

Kent insisted that the plan be general, focusing on the main issues and big ideas and providing a schematic guide. It should not be a map or blueprint (102), and must be distinguishable from such implementing documents as zoning ordinances

and capital improvement programs. Although it should be inspirational, it should not be regarded as the ideal picture of the community, which is constantly evolving. Though the plan is not a prediction, its prescription should be in the possible range of outcomes. It is part intention, part feasible future. Comprehensive plans do not embody decisions, but are a tool for democratic discourse. Precise actions and implementation steps should not be decided until the future is closer and the public and policy makers have had ample communication, education, and reflection in the light of concerns embodied in the plan.

ALTSHULER'S CRITIQUE

Alan Altshuler, a political scientist, articulated the many ways that the practice of comprehensive planning fell short of these objectives in the 1960s. He based his contentions on case studies of physical planning in Minneapolis and St. Paul, in which he observed what planners did, interviewing them and others about the process (1965a). The version of comprehensive planning that he found the planners to believe in corresponds largely to Kent's. They believed the plan should guide the deliberations of specialist planners, help evaluate their proposals, and coordinate the actions of agencies (299-332).

Technical Objections

Altshuler challenged planners' expertise by saying that comprehensive plans require more knowledge than any individual can grasp. He characterized planners as researchers rather than doers, who lack the experiential knowledge to synthesize workable strategies for the plans. He argued, moreover, that planners have to measure the public interest, and that this requires them to develop a unique hierarchy of collective goals as a basis for that measurement. He made clear that in practical terms this is impossible (Altshuler 1965a, 311-4).

Political Objections

Altshuler's objections from a political perspective were equally devastating. He challenged the assumption that he contended is embedded in the idea of comprehensive planning—that the public interest is something that exists to be discovered rather than being created through political will

(1965a, 303). He pointed out that the planners' claim to know the public interest puts them at odds with politicians, who also claim to know it. He argued also that comprehensive planning cannot serve its purpose of coordination unless the planners have power to make others cooperate, which they do not (328); moreover, plans are not likely to win political acceptance if they are comprehensive, because politicians prefer having continuous influence over action, and because interest groups prefer piecemeal consideration of issues, so they can see exactly how each proposal will affect them (316-7).

Altshuler made a case that it is difficult, if not impossible, to get genuine public debate on a comprehensive plan, and yet that is essential for a plan's legitimacy. Policies and goals offered in general terms have little meaning to the public. Even if policies are posed in comparatively operational, specific terms, many of the interests are not organized to develop meaningful positions. Moreover, planning is quintessentially about new ideas, but a new idea needs plenty of discussion as well as having to win virtual unanimity to be politically acceptable (321-4).

ALTSHULER'S ASSUMPTIONS RECONSIDERED IN THE LIGHT OF CONSENSUS BUILDING

Altshuler built his arguments on assumptions that were widely shared and reasonable when he was writing. Many of these assumptions, however, are no longer so well accepted in either planning literature or practice. Consensus building, on the other hand, rests on premises that mesh more comfortably with current understandings of the link between knowledge and action.

Planner as Individual Synthesizer

Altshuler assumed that the comprehensive planner has the responsibility to absorb and evaluate all information, to develop a synthesis of relationships, and to design strategies. Comprehensive planning to him is a task processed through an individual mind. By contrast, in consensus building it is a group that, collectively, absorbs and evaluates information. While the planner[11] helps with data, ideas, and strategies, and may even write the final synthesis,

the basic elements and concept of the plan grow out of group discussion.

The Individualist Version of the Public Interest

Altshuler appears to have subscribed to a view of the public interest as an aggregation of individual interests. He assumed that the planner must either measure individuals' values on a common scale so they can be aggregated, or that the public interest must be achieved through a political process in which each group speaks independently to elected officials. By contrast, consensus building is a collective search for common ground and the opportunities for mutual benefit. It is intrinsically a method of searching for a unitary public interest that, according to Meyerson and Banfield (1955, ch. 11), may be either the set of ends shared among the individuals making up the public, or the unique interests of the body politic.[12]

Positivist, Instrumental Conception of Rationality

Altshuler applied a positivist view of knowledge and an instrumental conception of rationality as a series of calculations about the best means to the desired ends. In this view, all that counts as knowledge are measurable, observable facts and laws or principles, and therefore comprehensive planners' expertise must consist in an ability to measure the public interest. Consensus building, however, accepts as well the validity of experiential, subjective, and socially shared knowledge about many matters, including the public interest. Altshuler appears also to have been applying the synoptic view of comprehensiveness, with its assumptions about the need for means-end calculations; but in consensus building, discourse is the "calculation" method.

The Progressive Reform Model of Government

Altshuler took for granted contemporary practices of city governance that limited the potential for effective comprehensive planning. These practices, still predominant across the United States, have their roots in the Progressive era, when reformers battling corruption prepared city charters that made elected officials weak in comparison to city managers and that encouraged reliance on elite citizen commissions and freestanding public authorities to manage the city's business. This system fragmented responsibility among the players by function, divorced political decisions from much of the activity that led up to them, and encouraged the development of bureaucracy in local government, with all its standardization of tasks and agencies with narrow missions. Not only are bureaucratic agencies not designed to address the broad mission of planning, but their routinized tasks preclude the adaptability needed to coordinate with others around complex tasks. Consensus building has been instituted across the United States to compensate for the fragmentation and inflexibility of such government structures. It cuts across agencies and commissions, and brings bureaucrats, elected of officials, and citizens together for joint learning and decision making.

Few Organized Interests

At the time when Altshuler was writing, today's variety of community-based and environmental organizations was unknown. Only business, typically, was organized. Today, however, communicatively rational consensus building is a meaningful objective, because such a wide range of groups have representatives who can speak knowledgeably for their interests.

THE EVIDENCE: CASES OF CONSENSUS BUILDING

The contentions of this article are built on evidence drawn from the author's study of efforts to develop consensus over complex and controversial matters of growth and environmental policy and management within the state of California (Innes et al. 1994). Of the 14 cases, eight demonstrate fairly well the model of consensus building laid out in this article. Each of the others fall short in some significant way—for example, in one there was no group discussion, and in others meetings were not of stakeholders. It is the group of eight cases that will be described here.[13]

The purpose of the 1994 research was to advise the California legislature on the value of consensus building as a coordination technique for growth management. We chose cases where (1) the focus was growth or environmental management; (2) consensus building was central; (3) the task involved multiple issues and cut across juris-

dictional boundaries; (4) the effort had been going on long enough to assess. The cases in the group were chosen from different parts of the state.

The research team compiled detailed case histories from in-depth interviews with participants, reviews of documents, and observation of meetings. The team compared these records for similarities and differences, searching for variables and processes that were consistently associated with greater or less success in achieving agreements and in getting political support for policy or plans. Key players in each case reviewed its history for accuracy.

One case was the Growth Management Consensus Project (GMCP), a 10-month project bringing together representatives of the interests in development and growth in California to produce growth management legislation. Stakeholders came from environmental, housing, and business interests; ethnic/social equity groups; local government; and councils of government. The project was under the auspices of the state legislature and partially funded by foundations. This highly contentious group, assisted by a professional facilitator, got about 85-95 percent agreement on a series of principles for legislation before disbanding. A smaller follow-on group representing many of the stakeholders in the GMCP continued the project as the Economic and Environmental Recovery Coalition (EERC). In about two years, this second group consensually produced legislation that resolved a substantial proportion of the thorny issues originally dividing them. The legislation achieved significant support in the legislature, but failed to pass because of the state's fiscal crisis, which made some of its policies infeasible.

Two cases, the San Francisco Estuary Project (SFEP) and the Santa Monica Bay Restoration Project, were part of the U.S. Environmental Protection Agency's (EPA's) National Estuary Program, which aims to develop consensus-based management plans for large-scale water systems. Each of these two cases involved members from state and federal agencies, interest groups, and local elected bodies. Each process relied on a management committee with about 50 members, and a variety of issue-based and technical subcommittees. Each lasted five years and produced a consensus-based plan, along with findings about the status and trends of conditions in the system, and a new way of measuring water quality designed for the particular problems of each system.

A fifth case was the San Diego Regional Growth Management Strategy, created by voluntary action of the local governments of the county and staffed by planners from the regional council of government. This process produced a draft strategy for the region, as well as some intangible but significant products, such as principles about the facilities and services that should be regarded as regional, and a shared understanding that development impact fees would not suffice to fund them. The process continued with work on policies for economic development, open space acquisition, and regional infrastructure financing.

Developers in Orange County joined environmentalists, in a sixth case, to help create a Natural Communities Conservation Plan (NCCP) for endangered species. The purpose was to ensure both development and environmental protection in the coastal sage scrub habitat, which covers vast areas of prime development land and is home to several threatened species. This process has been managed by key players from the state Department of Resources and includes local governments. The results, which include guidelines for local planning based on consensually agreed upon scientific criteria, have already influenced state policy and have been adopted by two counties as official policy. A seventh case, in the Coachella Valley, was similar in purpose, producing policies and an implementation plan for development that would protect the desert habitat.

The eighth case involved environmentalists, developers, and local governments in Contra Costa County, who got together to write and pass ballot initiatives that would provide for a sales tax for highway improvements to reduce congestion, and for protection of key open space in the county.

The following sections will also draw on the author's study of the New Jersey state planning process (Innes 1992; New Jersey State Planning Commission 1992). In this process, local governments worked with state agencies in consensus building to produce a state plan. The policies of the original draft were significantly altered as a result of discussions including interest groups, state agencies, and technical experts, with the counties acting as mediators between the state and hundreds of local governments. After five years of discussion and revision, the State Planning Commission, whose members represent the full range of interests in growth, adopted the plan unanimously. Today, public agencies are quietly implementing much of it.

FINDINGS: AN OVERVIEW

The research team in the 1994 study found that in seven of the eight cases described here, groups included representatives of all active interests; and in three cases, groups sought out additional stakeholders who had not originally recognized their interest in the issue.[14] The stakeholders in all cases became better informed through the process, and valued and used their new personal and professional networks to coordinate and collaborate. In five of the cases, groups incorporated systematic technical analysis into their deliberations. The breadth of the collective knowledge and interests of group members and the lengthy periods for discussion meant that they explored a wide range of factors and their interrelationships. In all the cases, players were brought to the table and kept there, searching for agreement with their adversaries by external incentives: avoiding the costs of delay, litigation, or inaction, as well as governmental action that might impose undesirable solutions.[15]

In all the cases the groups reached agreements on significant products—legislation, indicators, scientific descriptions of the problem, lists of issues needing attention, monitoring standards, guidelines for practice, policy principles, or plans. The groups agreed on principles rather than on specific maps or detailed programs of action. With the possible exception of the Contra Costa case, all the proposals had long-term horizons and broad implications for the physical development of a geographic area. In each case, the group submitted its proposal for approval to a formal authority, such as an electorate, a legislature, or a responsible public agency, and in all cases substantial elements of the proposals were formally adopted. In short, there are many parallels between these projects and Kent's vision for the comprehensive plan.

THE PUBLIC INTEREST AND CONSENSUS BUILDING

The findings support the idea that consensus buildings results can often be regarded as approximating the public interest as conceived in the unitary version favored by planning theorists (and most common in popular usage of the term), rather than as the version which is an aggregation of individual interests.[16] As Klosterman (1980) argues, the idea of the public interest as the common good is a meaningful criterion for planning that can be assessed and agreed on with evidence and arguments within a community. His conception, which corresponds to Friedmann's (1973, 2), is consistent both with the idea of consensus building and with our findings. These practices were designed to seek what was shared or held in common. The goal of consensus building is deliberation that is informed, rakes into account the interests of all including the weakest, and uses only "good reasons" to persuade (as opposed, for example, to selfish reasons or because a player has the power to insist). The findings show that these "good reasons" came to include protecting each other's interests (because agreement depends on that) and promoting what is good for the resource or region.

Learning about the system—whether it was water, land use and transportation, or natural habitat—led to a widely shared view within all groups that "we are all in this together." Groups evaluated proposals, at least in part, by their effects on the shared systems. As Friedmann points out, "the good that is shared creates a moral community whose members agree to be jointly responsible for that which is precious to them" (1973, 2).[17] In all cases, many stakeholders came to explicitly regard their purpose in participating as at least in part a collective one, for example, to "maintain the quality of life in San Diego." Many told us they devoted hundreds of hours to the process because they "care about California" or "care about the Bay."

For a consensus group to claim to speak for a public interest, it must be widely representative of the viewpoints within that public. In almost all the cases, groups included a spokesperson for any interest group that wanted to be involved.[18] Sometimes groups actively sought out an even more diverse set of stakeholders, as did for example the SFEP, which expanded midway to include upstream water users—agriculture and the city of Sacramento. The GMCP brought representatives of the poor and of inner city ethnic groups to the table, though these had not for the most part recognized how growth management might affect them. Groups all chose to be inclusive because they wanted their proposals to have legitimacy, because they wanted to incorporate the knowledge necessary for a workable proposal, and because they wanted to put their proposals forward with broad-based political support.

REPLY TO ALTSHULER'S CRITIQUE

If we assume for the purpose of discussion that consensus building can be used for local comprehensive planning, we can respond to Altshuler's critiques.

Critique 1: Comprehensive planning assumes the public interest is out there to be discovered rather than politically willed.

In these cases, the public interest was jointly discovered and willed. Participants usually discovered goals and even strategies to which they could all agree. In the GMCP and the NCCP cases, for example, environmentalists and developers learned that they had a shared interest in certainty about what land would be protected and where development would occur. In the EERC case, group members decided they all needed to work on restructuring the state's fiscal system.

Across all cases, as participants jointly learned about the technical or political aspects of a problem, they discovered that their interests were bound together because they all depended on a common economic, fiscal, transportation, or ecological system. As a result, participants focused on how to ensure the effective working of that system.[19] For example, in the SFEP, two years of defining and debating the state of the estuary led stakeholders to agree that the water quality problem was not simply due to "end of the pipe" discharges, but that the estuary's state of health was the result of many stakeholder activities. Instead of simply monitoring and regulating dischargers, therefore, the SFEP developed a complex management plan and a new criterion for water monitoring to reflect biodiversity.

Similarly, in San Diego, local government representatives, after learning that their population growth was largely internally generated rather than due to immigration, agreed that the cost of improving infrastructure neither could nor should be met from impact fees on new developments. They agreed to develop a regional strategy to accommodate the growth of their regional economy and population. They then also agreed on which infrastructure should be regarded as regional rather than local.

Political will followed such discoveries of shared interest and agreements on strategy. In the case of the EERC, for example, participants agreed to support only growth management legislation that included *all* their agreed components. In the Contra Costa case, environmental and development interests jointly supported campaigns for a sales tax for road improvements, and for a bond issue for purchase of land for open space. With such backing, voters passed both proposals. After the SFEP process, political will helped ensure that the project's water quality measure became the centerpiece of a historic water compact in 1995, settling at least temporarily California's water wars.[20]

Critique 2: The comprehensive planner has to measure the public interest and therefore must develop a unique hierarchy of collective goals as a basis for the measurement.

If an expert is to measure the public interest, then he or she needs an objective way of aggregating multiple diverse goals. In the cases studied, no one attempted or even suggested that such a measurement be done. They neither asked experts to do it, nor tried themselves. Instead participants moved toward a strategy of action in a qualitative, discursive way. They sought shared frameworks for problems and discussed policy ideas, standards, and guidelines in the light of criteria developed within the group. Arguments had to stand the test of reasonableness, as well as to be consistent with technical information and any purposes the participants had agreed to. They combined their goals in the context of an interrelated set of strategies to which they could agree, rather than through measurement procedures. Thus, for example, in the NCCP case, participants came to understand that habitat needs could be served by protecting corridors even if development occurred along them. They then agreed to organize policies around the corridor concept, which served both environmental and development interests.

Critique 3: Comprehensive planners' legitimacy requires them to be expert in the public interest.

Though outcomes in these cases might be said to be in the public interest, determination of what these ends and actions should be was never a function of planners' expertise. It was a group choice, in which planners played a part. Nonetheless, we found planners to have substantial legitimacy among participants, who respected them for contributions they saw as essential, even when they had criticisms. Staff played many roles for which planning education and practice had prepared them, or which they were to learn after some modest training. Typically, they provided technical expertise. For example, the SANDAG[21] staff prepared population forecasts and analyses of the regional economy, which participants trusted and used. State legislative staff prepared background papers on growth management issues for the GMCP and explained political, legal, and organizational contexts. In all the cases, staff worked with group leaders to design subcommittees, tasks, agendas, and processes, and to identify additional stakeholders. Planners in New Jersey designed new processes and developed ways to help committees resolve difficult issues. In some cases, staff or consultants acted as facilitators; in many cases they introduced options; in all cases they recorded agreements, and prepared minutes and memos necessary for the processes to move forward (Innes et al. 1994, 25-7).

Staff did what Forester (1989) says planners do. They warned, framed problems, called attention, organized, negotiated, explained contexts, and tried to prevent players from manipulating or lying. They tried to create many of the conditions of ideal speech and communicative rationality. They also helped to build new practices and institutions for anticipating the future, analyzing alternatives, and deliberating. Participants recognized what planners were doing and appreciated it.

Critique 4: Planners lack the intuitive knowledge and experience to create workable comprehensive strategies.

The processes studied relied on the experiential knowledge of developers, farmers, managers of water treatment systems, citizens, and elected officials. Some stakeholders were agency staff with specialized expertise; and some were staff of private interest groups who went back to their membership to test the reactions to proposals. Someone in a group usually understood each aspect of the task in depth or had experience with it. In the NCCP, for example, developers understood how regulatory uncertainty affected their development strategy; U.S. Fish and Wildlife Service representatives understood the workings of the endangered species law and the habitat needs of the species; and local government representatives understood the preferences of their citizens and the ways localities control land use.

Planners did play key roles in developing the overall strategy and synthesis, but they did so by working interactively with the groups and usually by employing the agreements as building blocks. Planners in New Jersey began by writing a first draft of the state plan (New Jersey State Planning Commission 1988), and that became the negotiating text from which consensus groups worked. The final plan bore little resemblance to the first, with central organizing concepts changed, maps eliminated, and presentation style transformed. The result is a collective vision that was facilitated by the planners rather than synthesized by them (New Jersey State Planning Commission 1992; Innes 1992). In most of the other cases, staff suggested organizing concepts in response to group concerns, but individual group members also suggested ideas. By the time staff produced the final documents, much of the creative and synthesizing work was complete.

Critique 5: Comprehensive planning cannot serve the purpose of coordination because planners do not have the power to enforce cooperation.

Planning through consensus building did achieve coordination, but through a horizontal and selfmanaging process rather than a top-down exercise of power. People chose this method in situations where no one had the power to accomplish objectives alone. All the cases involved shared power across agencies and levels of government, and between private interests and the public sector. Coordination resulted as stakeholders learned that they could produce shared benefits through joint action. Consensus building was a coordination tool, we concluded, because it created social, intellectual, and political capital (Innes et al. 1994, 46-55; Gruber 1993). The social capital created through consensus building, that is, personal networks and trust, helped coordinate by ensuring informal communication among stakeholders. For example, in the SFEP, not only did

staff of state and regional agencies develop new working relationships, but the public sector players developed networks with the private sector representatives as well. For example, a Corps of Engineers representative began routinely calling the Sierra Club representative in the design phase of projects to identify ways to accommodate environmental concerns.

Intellectual capital included agreements on data sets, indicators, and descriptions of problematic conditions, as well as a shared understanding among the players of each other's needs and situations. When all could operate with the same information, a principal obstacle to coordination was gone. Moreover, the collective effort to understand often led to shared problem definitions and from there to coordinated action. Political capital—the players' combined capacity to influence action—also helped to coordinate, as new political alliances joined to support legislation and ensure its implementation.

Critique 6: The generality of comprehensive plans makes it impossible to get meaningful debate on them.

Although the products of first-stage consensus building typically took the form of principles, they reflected in-depth discussions that had intensively explored how general concepts would apply in specific situations. Stakeholders did not agree on a principle until they had worked out how it would affect their interests. For example, many participants in the EERC process began by wanting to require that local plans be checked for consistency with state policy. Hours of discussion convinced them that such provisions would be unenforceable (Innes et al. 1994, 87). In New Jersey, two years of discussion of a proposal to divide the state geographically into "tiers" where different development and conservation policies would apply demonstrated that the policy would create inequities and anomalies. For example, representatives of rural communities pointed out that in some areas industrial development coexisted with agriculture, so classification of an area into an agricultural zone would prevent even existing businesses from expanding, and entire communities would be cut off from development. The group then decided to use, instead, a "centers" approach that would designate a hierarchy from hamlets to large cities, to organize development and conservation policies (Innes 1992, 448-9). The specific centers are to be designated in later stages of the process.

In most of the cases, discussion was informed by technical knowledge, because experts of many kinds participated and served as staff or consultants. Stakeholders listened to experts disagree among themselves, and confronted them, challenging the data, learning about its limitations, and deciding on its implications. In the SFEP case, lay participants learned about the scientific issue through debates over characterization of the estuary and then insisted that technical information be accompanied by a set of management options. To these nontechnical participants, linking the data to such options made the information meaningful (Innes et al. 1994, 127). In several cases, stakeholders representing opposing views jointly selected a set of experts, who then pursued internal agreement on scientific questions, to be accepted by the larger group. For example, in the Natural Communities case, members of such an expert panel developed guidelines for local planning to protect the habitat, and the SFEP relied on a way of measuring water quality that was similarly developed.[22]

Critique 7: Comprehensive general plans will not gain political acceptance, because politicians prefer to maintain continuous influence, and interest groups prefer piecemeal acceptance so they can see how proposals will affect them.

For the most part, the plans and policies of these consensus processes did gain substantial political acceptance. Legislation was passed. The Coachella Valley project was implemented, and the NCCP effort continues to produce guidelines and approaches that are being used by the state and local governments. Local governments continue to support the San Diego effort. The monitoring strategies for water quality will be implemented in the San Francisco Estuary and Santa Monica Bay even though both have significant political ramifications, especially the former, which will require the state to change its historic policies for water distribution.

This is not to say that these results necessarily please the elected officials. Governor Wilson at first refused to implement the SFEP water quality monitoring plan, until federal agencies accepted it and until another consensus group of his own choosing worked out an agreement. The New Jersey State legislature at first proposed to review and possibly alter or vote down the state plan, but was dissuaded by a campaign by many lobbying groups. Our cases show that, even without support from high elected officials, broadbased consensus building can amass sufficient political capital for its results to prevail.

Consensus building can, on the other hand, help leaders develop a feasible position on a contentious issue. For example, in New Jersey, Governor Kean told the group that wanted state planning legislation that if they could design a consensus bill, he would support it. The head of the League of Municipalities helped dissuade the legislature from voting down the state plan, by arguing that the plan represented the will of the people more than it would if decided by the legislature (Innes 1992, 449). Governor Wilson authorized state agencies to take leading roles in the NCCP consensus process, which addressed politically sensitive issues of endangered species protection.

In contrast to Altshuler's expectations, the stakeholders in these eight cases wanted the formal products of consensus building to remain general, so that they pointed the direction of action, but kept options open and allowed for further learning. Participants could take this view because, unlike stakeholders in Altshuler's scenarios, they anticipated continued involvement in the next phases, policy specification and implementation. In all cases, the groups agreed to continue consensus building after the first phase.

Critique 8: Plans should be innovative, but innovations need ample discussion and near-unanimity to succeed politically. Both of these conditions are impossible with a comprehensive plan.

In several of the cases, unanticipated, innovative proposals emerged with nearly unanimous support from the consensus process. They emerged because the group's inquiry had led them to conclude that conventional solutions would not work. Innovativeness, it should be noted, can be a feature of intensive, collaborative group processes.[23] The centers policy in New Jersey, for example, was an innovation that resolved a seemingly intractable dispute. The biodiversity measure in the SFEP case was a new way to monitor water quality, requiring approaches to water management that were not part of the water agencies' organizational repertoires. The GMCP discussion transformed many participants' views so that they came to believe that social equity issues are embedded in all growth policies.

CONCLUSION

The plans, policies, and guidelines produced by the consensus processes studied here conformed in significant ways to Kent's stipulations for the urban general plan. They are comprehensive in the sense that they deal with interrelationships among physical factors—water, land use, and agriculture, for example. They are general in that they set broad principles and leave specifics for later. The discussion makes their reasoning explicit. Most of the processes were informed by technical knowledge, and all of them succeeded in coordinating across players.

One can make a good case that consensus building, properly designed, can produce decisions that approximate the public interest. In all these cases, informed and in-depth discussion occurred among a diversity of stakeholders,[24] and decisions were taken only when they were consensual. In most cases, all active interests were represented, and, in some, previously inactive interests were included. In all cases, groups found strategies that would result in shared benefit. In most cases, they made decisions they collectively regarded as beneficial to the resource or to the system as a whole. In most cases, the majority of proposals were accepted by those outside the process, and many proposals were formally adopted by voters and elected officials.

Conditions at the local level are similar to those prevailing in our cases: Multiple local agencies and interests engage in either conflict or simply uncoordinated action about the physical development and management of infrastructure, growth, and environmental resources. Individual players often have little power to achieve their missions without the cooperation of others. Yet, on the whole, municipalities seldom use consensus building for comprehensive planning. Usually, state laws already mandate procedures for public involvement, and planning commissions and public hearings are the accepted forms of public review of plans. Many stakeholders, such as residents or businesses from neighboring jurisdictions, and

state and federal regulatory agencies representing environmental or economic interests have little legitimacy as participants in local decisions about land use. Accordingly, local plans can be difficult to implement because these other stakeholders do not cooperate. With plans often lacking influence, public involvement dwindles, because the stakeholders stand aside until specific projects are on the table. That dynamic, in a vicious circle, delegitimizes the plan as a meaningful document—precisely as Altshuler contended.

The strategy and design of consensus building for local comprehensive planning is beyond the scope of this paper; as in the cases presented here, it would have to be tailor-made for each locality. Cities can start, however, by establishing stakeholder groups to work in parallel with existing city processes and advise the planning commission and city council. The group could begin conservatively, with only local stakeholders, but these might well choose to include other players whose actions would affect the city's welfare, such as absentee landlords, corporations, or environmental groups, or even state or federal agencies. Incentives are needed to bring stakeholders to the table—benefits for cooperation, and penalties or disadvantages for those stakeholders who do not participate. The cases we examined also show that players come to the table to address immediate and concrete issues. They expect short-term results, though they also need to believe there will be long-term implications. This observation suggests that such a planning process should be issue oriented and rooted in current tasks and problems, even while its goal is to develop general policies.

Setting up stakeholder groups, even with only local players, is a challenge, however, as it shifts longstanding power relationships, giving voice and legitimacy to new players and perhaps making the city the arena for conflicts that now take place at the state or regional level. Thus, local consensus building will work most effectively in the context of a nested system for planning and the management of growth, whereby the state, regions, and localities explicitly develop and coordinate their policies and priorities for allocation and regulatory decisions, with each taking into account the others'.[25]

Altshuler's critiques raise a deep contradiction in the most central of the ideas unique to city planning. To the extent that his views are widely shared, they undermine the legitimacy of both planning theory and practice. For many of the reasons Altshuler enumerates, comprehensive planning typically does not have support and understanding from the range of its constituencies. It often serves neither as a tool for discussion nor as a mechanism for coordination, and fails to get the attention it needs to provide a meaningful vision for a city.[26] Often, in the final analysis, the plan cannot even be implemented, because key players have not agreed to it. Planning ignores such issues only at its peril.

NOTES

1. Altshuler poses the issue in this way seemingly as a rhetorical device to highlight a serious conceptual problem in comprehensive planning. The public interest is at best abstract, vague and contentious as an idea. There has never been any real agreement in literature or practice about the meaning of this concept. It certainly is not in any sense measurable.

2. The terminology for these processes is still being developed, and the practices themselves are just beginning to be codified. For example, Susskind and Madigan (1984) use the term "mediated negotiation" for examples similar to our cases. This article uses the term consensus building as now having the most recognition and intuitive clarity.

3. See also the bibliography, Potapchuk and Bailey (1992), for a wide range of materials on collaborative approaches to planning and policy tasks.

4. Forester did not use the term communicative rationality, but he did introduce into planning theory the principles of civil discourse that are prerequisite to establishing communicative rationality.

5. The term stakeholder refers to groups or individuals with something significant to gain or lose as a result of the deliberations.

6. Schweiger et al. (1989) have demonstrated the truth in the idea chat when groups are designed to ensure that assumptions and proposals are challenged, by, for example, assigning devil's advocate roles to some members, they produce objectively better decisions than do groups which are merely asked to achieve consensus.

7. These procedures draw on, for example, delphi and Delbecq methods (Delbecq et al. 1975) as well as on principles developed by Fisher and Ury (1981). Typically, each person in the group expresses his or her interest without being subject to comment or criticism; brainstorming and deliberation over criteria precede choice, and the environment encourages the expression of differences without personalized conflict or premature argument over solutions. This differs from deliberation in most elected and formally appointed bodies such as planning and zoning commissions, which follow parliamentary procedure, requiring motions to be on the floor before discussion takes place (i.e., the discussion begins with solutions instead of ending with them); which employ frequent votes emphasizing differences in the group; and which do nothing to ensure that all participants express their concerns, and that all important issues and options are explored.

8. Godschalk (1992) recommends that such collaborative arrangements be institutionalized for many planning purposes.

9. This perspective begs the question of what leads up to planners selecting the elements of the package, thus leaving comprehensive planning vulnerable to critiques such as Altshuler's.

10. Indeed, those texts often cite Kent, while using the term comprehensive plan.

11. In this article I will be using the term planner for a professional who assists with consensus building. Some of the staffing our cases were trained as city planners; others had different backgrounds.

12. This notion is different enough from the former, more conventional definition of the public interest that scholars have begun to use other terms for the unitary public interest, such as common good (Bryson and Crosby 1992), or to focus on "governing the commons" (Ostrom 1990).

13. These case histories are given in full in Innes et al. (1994), Appendices 1-8, 71-231.

14. Virtually all the points made in this section apply equally well to the New Jersey case.

15. The report on this study (Innes et al. 1994) paid significant attention to the problem of the incentives and sanctions needed to get stakeholders to the table and willing to stay and seek agreements. That issue is only peripherally related to the present discussion.

16. It should be noted that no one used the term "public interest" in our interviews or in the meetings we observed. The participants were solving problems and designing policy in solely practical terms, though in the end one might agree that the results were in the public interest.

17. See also Ostrom's cases on water and fisheries management (1990). While it is unclear that one would term these *moral* communities, they certainly became communities whose members took joint responsibility for a resource.

18. Often interests were represented by public agencies whose mission coincided with those interests. For example, hunters and fishermen were represented by the state Fish and Game agency, and the interests of farmers and southern California water users were represented by the Water Resources Agency. In the EERC case, a decision was made to exclude interests who did not subscribe to some "First Principles." Over time, a widening group of interests signed on to the group, agreeing to the principles.

19. Ostrom (1990) documented a series of parallel cases where stakeholders in a common resource managed to create and administer management rules that protected the resource.

20. Although our study ended before the water compact was developed, we did some additional interviews with key players to confirm that the use of this measure was indeed an outgrowth, in part, of the SFEP.

21. San Diego Association of Governments.

22. See Ozawa (1991), and Innes (1988) for other examples of the integration of technical information into communicative planning and policy processes.

23. This has been given various labels, including "double loop learning," where the group's work leads them to question assumptions, reframe issues, and examine them from a new perspective. See Marshall and Peters (1985) and Friedmann (1987, ch. 5) for reviews of some of this extensive literature.

24. There are exceptions to these statements, of course. In the Contra Costa case, one key player concluded that he had been duped into a position harmful to his group's interest. In this case, however, the principles of communicative rationality had not been closely followed. The discussion lacked a neutral facilitator and was not pro-vided with much technical information. Moreover, it was a relatively short process of less than a year.

25. See the recommendations in Innes et al. (1994, 60-3), which describe the basic framework of such a system. Other approaches to growth management can be found in Stein (1993), particularly the chapter by Innes, "Implementing State Growth Management in the U.S." (18-43).

26. A case in point, as I write this, is a headline in the *Oakland Tribune* for Monday, March 27th, 1995: "Oakland's General Plan Update: Dull, but Important." Two hundred people out of Oakland's 300,000 came to the General Plan Fair.

Author's Note: This paper is based on the report "Coordinating Growth and Environmental Management through Consensus Building," prepared for the California Policy Seminar (Innes et al. 1994). The author thanks Yodan Rofe for his background research on comprehensive planning and his comments on the draft of this paper. The author also thanks Alan Altshuler, Karen Christensen, Judith Gruber, and an anonymous reviewer for their helpful critiques.

REFERENCES

Altshuler, Alan. 1965a. *The City Planning Process: A Political Analysis.* Ithaca, NY: Cornell University Press.

Altshuler, Alan. 1965b. The Goals of Comprehensive Planning. *Journal of the American Institute of Planners* 31,3: 186-97.

Amy, Douglas. 1987. *The Politics of Environmental Mediation.* New York: Columbia University Press.

Bacow, Lawrence, and Michael Wheeler. 1994. *Environmental Dispute Resolution.* New York: Plenum Press.

Bernstein, Richard. 1978. *The Restructuring of Social and Political Theory.* Philadelphia, PA: University of Pennsylvania Press.

Bingham, Gail. 1986. *Resolving Environmental Dispute Resolution.* Washington, DC: The Conservation Foundation.

Black, Alan. 1968. *The Comprehensive Plan. Principles and Practice of Urban Planning.* Washington, DC: International City Management Association. 349-78.

Bryson, John M., and Barbara C. Crosby. 1992. *Leadership for the Common Good. Tackling Public Problems in a Shared Power World*. San Francisco, CA: Jossey-Bass.

Buntz, Gregory C., and Susan Sherry. 1993a. A Continuum of Dispute Resolution Approaches. *Land Use Forum* 2,3: 181-4. Berkeley, CA: Continuing Education of the Bar, University of California Extension.

Buntz, Gregory C., and Susan Sherry. 1993b. Designing Dispute Resolution Systems. *Land Use Forum* 2,2: 210-3. Berkeley, CA: Continuing Education of the Bar, University of California Extension.

Carpenter, Susan. 1989. *Solving Community Problems by Consensus*. Management Information Service Report. Washington, DC: International City Management Association.

Carpenter, Susan, and W. J. P. Kennedy. 1991. *Managing Public Disputes*. San Francisco, CA: Jossey-Bass.

Delbecq, Andre L., A. H. Van de Ven, and D. Gustafson. 1975. *Group Techniques for Program Planning: A Guide to Nominal Group and Delphi Processes*. Glenview, IL: Scott Foresman.

Dewey, John. 1916. *Democracy and Education*. Toronto, Canada: MacMillan.

Dryzek, John. 1990. *Discursive Democracy: Politics, Policy and Political Science*. Cambridge, MA: Cambridge University Press.

Fisher, Roger, and Scott Brown. 1988. *Getting To Yes: Negotiating Agreement Without Giving In*. Boston, MA: Houghton Mifflin.

Fisher, Roger, and William Ury. 1981. *Getting Together: Building Relationships As We Negotiate*. New York: Penguin Group.

Forester, John. 1989. *Planning in the Face of Power*. Berkeley, CA: University of California Press.

Freire, Paulo. 1981. *Pedagogy of the Oppressed*. New York, NY: Continuum Publishing.

Friedmann, John. 1973. The Public Interest and Community Participation: Toward a Reconstruction of Public Philosophy. *Journal of the American Institute of Planners* 39,1: 4-7.

Friedmann, John. 1987. *Planning in the Public Domain: From Knowledge to Action*. Princeton: Princeton University Press.

Fulton, William. 1989. *Reaching Consensus in Land-Use Negotiations*. Planning Advisory Service Report Number 417. Chicago, IL: American Planning Association.

Godschalk, David R. 1992. Negotiating Intergovernmental Development Policy Conflicts: Practice Based Guidelines. *Journal of the American Planning Association* 58,3: 368-78.

Gruber, Judith. 1993. *Coordinating Growth Management Through Consensus Building: Incentives and the Generation of Social, Intellectual and Political Capital*. Berkeley, CA: Institute of Urban and Regional Development.

Habermas, Jurgen. 1984. *The Theory of Communicative Action*. Boston, MA: Beacon Press.

Innes, Judith E. 1988. The Power of Data Requirements. *Journal of the American Planning Association* 54,3: 275-8.

Innes, Judith E. 1992. Group Processes and the Social Construction of Growth Management: Florida, Vermont, and New Jersey. *Journal of the American Planning Association* 58,4: 440-54.

Innes, Judith E. 1995. Planning Theory's Emerging Paradigm: Communicative Action and Interactive Practice. *Journal of Planning Education and Research* 14,3: 128-35.

Innes, Judith E., Judith Gruber, Robert Thompson, and Michael Neuman. 1994. *Coordinating Growth and Environmental Management through Consensus Building*. Berkeley, CA: California Policy Seminar, University of California.

Kent, T.J. 1964. *The Urban General Plan*. San Francisco: Chandler Publishing Company. 1991. 2nd Edition. Chicago, IL: Planners Press, American Planning Association.

Klosterman, Richard E. 1980. A Public Interest Criterion. *Journal of the American Planning Association* 46 (July): 323-33.

Lindblom, Charles E. 1959. The Science of Muddling Through. *Public Administration Review* 19: 79-88.

Lindblom, Charles E., and D. Braybrooke. 1963. *A Strategy of Decision: Policy Evaluation as a Social Process*. New York: The Free Press, Macmillan.

Marshall, James, and Michael Peters. 1985. Evaluation and Education: The Ideal Community. *Policy Sciences* 18,3: 263-88.

Moore, Christopher W. 1986. *The Mediation Process: Practical Strategies for Resolving Conflict.* San Francisco, CA: Jossey Bass.

Myerson, Martin, and Edward C. Banfield. 1955. *Politics, Planning and the Public Interest.* New Jersey: The Free Press.

Neuman, Michael. 1993. Mediation in Florida and New Jersey *Land Use Forum* 2,3: 200-4. Berkeley, CA: Continuing Education of the Bar, University of California Extension.

New Jersey State Planning Commission. 1988. *Communities of Place: A Legacy for the Next Generation, the Preliminary State Development and Redevelopment Plan for the State of New Jersey.* Trenton, NJ.

New Jersey State Planning Commission. 1992. *Communities of Place: The New Jersey State Development and Redevelopment Plan.* Trenton, NJ.

Ostrom, Elinor. 1990. *Governing the Commons: The Evolution of Institutions for Collective Action.* Cambridge, U.K.: Cambridge University Press.

Ozawa, Connie P. 1991. *Recasting Science: Consensual Procedures in Public Policy Making.* Boulder, CO: Westview Press.

Potapchak, William R., and Margaret A. Bailey. 1992. *Building the Collaborative Community: A Select Bibliography for Community Leaders. Washington, DC: Program for Community Problem Solving.*

Potapchuk, William R., and Caroline G. Polk. 1994. *Building the Collaborative Community.* Washington, DC: The National Institute for Dispute Resolution (NIDR) and the Program for Community Problem Solving (PCPS).

Sager, Tore. 1994. *Communicative Planning Theory.* Aldershot, England: Avebury.

Schweiger, David M., William R. Sandberg, and Paula L. Rechner. 1989. Experiential Effects of Dialectical Inquiry, Devil's Advocacy, and Consensus Approaches to Strategic Decision Making. *Academy of Management Journal* 32,4: 745-72.

So, Frank S., and Judith Getzels. 1988. *The Practice of Local Government Planning* Washington DC: International City Management Association, Municipal Management Series.

Stein, Jay. 1993. *Growth Management: The Planning Challenge of the 1990's.* Newbury Park, CA: Sage Publications. 18-43.

Susskind, Larry, and Jeffrey Cruikshank. 1987. *Breaking the Impasse: Consensual Approaches to Resolving Public Disputes.* New York: Basic Books.

Susskind, Larry, and Denise Madigan. 1984. New Approaches to Resolving Disputes in the Public Sector. *The Justice System Journal* 9, 2: 179-203.

Wheeler, Michael. 1993. Regional Consensus on Affordable Housing: Yes in My Backyard? *Journal of Planning Education and Research* 12: 139-49.

SUGGESTED READINGS FOR PART II

Babcock, Richard and C. Siemon. *The Zoning Game Revisited.* 1985. Cambridge, MA: Lincoln Institute of Land Policy

Baer, William C. "General Plan Evaluation Criteria: An Approach to Making Better Plans," *Journal of the American Planning Association*, Vol. 63, No. 3, 1997, pp. 329-344.

Bosselman, Fred, David Callies, and John Banta. *The Taking Issue.* 1973. Washington, DC: U.S. Government Printing Office

Branch, Melville C. *Comprehensive City Planning, Introduction & Explanation.* 1985. Chicago: American Planning Association.

Bryson, John. "A Strategic Planning Process for Public and Non-Profit Organizations," *Long Range Planning*, Vol. 21, No. 1, 1988, pp. 73-81.

Chapin, F.L. Stuart, Jr. "Taking Stock of Techniques for Shaping Urban Growth," *Journal of The American Institute of Planners*, Vol. 29, No. 2, 1963, pp. 76-87.

Chapin, F.L. Stuart, and Edward J. Kaiser. *Urban Land Use Planning*, 3d ed. 1979. Urbana: The University of Illinois Press.

DeGrove, John. *Land Growth and Politics.* 1984. Chicago: American Planning Association

DeGrove, John. *Planning and Growth Management in the States: The New Frontier for Land Policy.* 1992. Cambridge, MA: Lincoln Institute of Land Policy.

Ewing, Reid. "Is Los Angeles-Style Sprawl Desirable?," *Journal of the American Planning Association*, Vol. 63, No. 1, 1997, pp. 107-126.

Fluck, Timothy Alan. *"Euclid v. Ambler*: A Retrospective," *Journal of the American Planning Association*, Vol.52, No. 3, 1986, pp. 326-337.

Godschalk, David R., David J. Brower, Larry D. McBennett, Barbara A. Vestal, and Daniel C. Herr. *Constitutional Issues of Growth Management* 1979. Chicago: American Planning Association.

Godschalk, David R. "In Defense of Growth Management," *Journal of the American Planning Association*, Vol. 58, No. 4, 1992, pp. 422-424.

Gordon, Peter and Richardson, Harry W. "Are Compact Cities a Desirable Planning Goal," *Journal of the American Planning Association*, Vol. 63, No.1, 1997, pp. 95-106.

Guttenberg, Albert Z. "A Multiple Land Use Classification System," *Journal of the American Institute of Planners*, Vol. 25, No. 3, 1959, pp. 143-150.

Haar, Charles M. "Master Planning: An Inquiry in Dialogue Form," *Journal of the American Institute of Planners*, Vol. 25, No. 3 1959, pp. 133-142.

Haar, Charles M., and Michael Allan Wolf. *Land Use Planning*. 1989. Boston: Little, Brown.

Hagman, Donald G. *Urban Planning and Land Development Control Law*. 1971. St. Paul, MN: West.

Hoch, Charles and Dalton, Linda C., ed. *The Practice of Local Government Planning*, 3d. ed. 2000. Washington, D.C.: International City Management Association.

Hoover, Robert C. "On Master Plans and Constitutions," *Journal of the American Institute of Planners*, Vol. 26, No. 1, 1960, pp. 5-24.

Howard, Ebenezer. *Garden Cities of Tomorrow*. 1946. London: Faber.

Kent, T. J. *The Urban General Plan*. 1964. San Francisco: Chandler.

Perrin, Constance. "A Noiseless Secession From the Comprehensive Plan," *Journal of the American Institute of Planners*, Vol. 33, No. 5, 1967, pp. 336-347.

Phillips, E. Barbara, and R. T. LeGates. *City Lights: An Introduction to Urban Studies*. 1981. New York: Oxford University Press.

Popper, Frank. *The Politics of Land Use Reform*. 1981. Madison: The University of Wisconsin Press.

Porter, Douglas. *Managing Growth in American Communities*. 1997. Washington, D.C.: Island Press.

Reilly, William K. *The Use of Land: A Citizen's Policy Guide to Urban Growth*. 1973. New York: Crowell.

Scott, Randall W., ed. *Management and Control of Growth*. 1971. Washington, D.C.: Urban Land Institute.

So, Frank S., and Judith Getzels, eds. *The Practice of Local Government Planning*, 2d ed. 1988. Washington, D.C.: International City Management Association.

Stein, Jay M., ed. *Growth Management: The Planning Challenge of the 1990s*. 1993. Newbury Park, CA: Sage Publications.

Strong, Ann Louise; Mandelker, Daniel R.; and Kelly, Eric Damian. "Property Rights and Takings," *Journal of the American Planning Association*, Vol. 62, No. 1, 1996, pp. 5-16.

Wilson, William. "Moles and Skylarks," Ch. 6 in *Introduction to Planning History in the United States* (Krueckeberg). 1983. New Brunswick, NJ: CUPR Press.

III
Economic, Political, Social and Strategic Issues in Planning and Development

Planning in the Face of Power

John Forester

John Forester's book is about "the vulnerabilities of democracy, about power and professional responsibility, about political action and ideology, inequality, domination, and resistance, illegitimate authority, and democratizing practices" (p. xi of the original). The author combines an analysis of social and political theory with his own empirical investigations to examine what planners do in the face of concentrated economic and political power. In this chapter, he tries to demonstrate that planners can make choices about their exercise of political power in the planning process. He argues that information is an important source of a planner's power and, if used strategically, can be a means of empowering citizens.

If planners ignore those in power, they assure their own powerlessness. Alternatively, if planners understand how relations of power shape the planning process, they can improve the quality of their analyses and empower citizen and community action. By focusing on the practical issues of information control, misinformation, and distorted communications more generally, this chapter will elaborate a pragmatic and progressive planning role for all those planning in the face of power.

Whether or not power corrupts, the lack of power surely frustrates. Planners know this only too well. They often feel overwhelmed by the exercise of private economic power, or by politics, or by both.[1] In health planning, for example, as in local land-use planning, planners must often react defensively to the initiatives of established, usually private medical care "providers" or project developers. Those providers have time, money, expertise, information, and control of- capital; the countervailing consumers, in contrast, have few such resources. Nevertheless, planners in many areas are legally mandated to make democratic citizen participation in the planning process a reality rather than a romantic promise.

Furthermore, planners often have had little influence on the implementation of their plans. Those painstaking plans have too often ended up on the shelf or have been used to further political purposes they were never intended to serve.

Given these conditions of work and the intensely political nature of planning practice, how then can planners work to fulfill their legal mandate to foster a genuinely democratic planning process? What power can planners have? In a time of retrenchment, these questions become more important than ever.

Once-and-for-all solutions in planning practice should not be expected, however, because the object of planning, future action, routinely involves the unique and novel. Even when planning serves to rationalize economic decisions, it must be attentive to the special problems presented by the case at hand. Even technical problems that can be solved with standard methods exist amid conflicting interpretations and interests, established power, and excluded segments of the population—all of which inevitably limit the efficacy of purely technical solutions. But despite the fact that planners have little influence on the structure of ownership and power in this society, they can influence the conditions that render citizens able (or unable) to participate, act, and organize effectively regarding issues that affect their lives.

This chapter seeks to demonstrate that by choosing to address or ignore the exercise of political power in the planning process, planners can make that process more democratic or less, more technocratic or less; still more dominated by the established wielders of power or less so. For instance, planners shape not only documents but also participation: who is contacted, who participates in informal design-review meetings, who persuades whom of which options for project development. Planners do so not only by shaping which facts certain citizens may have but also by shaping the trust and expectations of those citizens. Planners organize cooperation, or acquiescence, in addition to data and sketches. They are often not authoritative problem-solvers, as stereotypical engineers may be, but, instead, they are organizers (or disorganizers) of public attention: selectively shaping attention to options for action, particular costs and benefits, or particular arguments for and against proposals.[2] A key source of the planner's power to exert such influence is the control of information.[3]

This chapter therefore argues that (1) information is a complex source of power in the planning process; (2) misinformation of several distinct types—some inevitable, some avoidable, some systematic, some ad hoc—can be anticipated and counteracted by astute planners; (3) such misinformation undermines well informed planning and citizen action by manipulating citizens' beliefs, consent, trust, and sense of relevant problems, and planners can counteract these influences; (4) planners themselves sometimes participate in distorting communications and in special cases, may be justified in doing so; and (5) because planners can expect misinformation to influence processes of decision making, agenda setting, and political argument more generally, they can counteract it in several ways to foster a well-informed, democratic planning process, thereby empowering affected citizens as well.

INFORMATION AS A SOURCE OF POWER

How can information be a source of power for planners? Four ways of answering this question are rather common, but we will also consider a fifth. These reflect the perspectives of the technician, the incrementalist or pragmatist, the liberal-advocate, the structuralist, and what I will call the progressive.[4] Each perspective suggests a different basis of power that planners may cultivate in their practice. We will discuss below how the different approaches to the control and management of information can make a practical difference in planning and in broader political processes.

Although each of these perspectives will be discussed separately, in actual practice planners might combine several of them in any given case. For example, a transportation planner might strategically combine the attitudes of the technician and the progressive,[5] or a health planner might utilize approaches of both the pragmatist and the liberal-advocate.[6]

The technician. The technician supposes that power lies in technical information: knowing where the data can be found, which questions to ask, how to perform the relevant data analysis. Here, because information supplies solutions to technical problems, it is a source of power. This view reflects at once the most traditional problem-solving notion of planning and one of the profession's most criticized ideals—for it avoids, or pretends it need not concern itself directly with, politics. The technician supposes that political judgments can be avoided, that the political context at hand can be ignored. Adopting a benign view of politics, the technician believes that sound technical work will prevail on its own merits. But many planners and critics alike have been skeptical of this technocratic attitude.[7]

The incrementalist. The organizationally pragmatic incrementalist holds that information is a source of power because it responds to organizational needs. People need to know where to get information, how to get a project approved with minimum delay, and what sorts of design problems to avoid. Here, knowing the ropes is a source of power: informal networks, steady contacts, and regular communication keep planners informed. This is a social problem-solving view in which "social" is narrowly construed to mean "organizational." Planners do, of course, work in organizational networks in which different actors depend on one another for key information. Ironically, when others depend on the planners' information, that information is a source of power—despite the fact that incrementalist planners (as Lindblom suggested thirty years ago) may not know what good such power may serve beyond its impact on narrow organizational politics.[8]

The liberal-advocate. The liberal-advocate views information as a source of power because it responds to a need created by a pluralist political system; information can be used by underrepresented or relatively unorganized groups to enable them to participate more effectively in the planning process. This is the traditional advocacy planning perspective.[9] It seeks to redress inequalities of participation and distribution by bringing excluded groups into political processes with an equal chance, equal information, and equal technical resources. Traditional technical–assistance projects also fall within this view, aiming to provide technical skills and expertise so that community groups, among others, can compete on an equal footing with developers. The liberal-advocate focuses on the information needs of a particular client, i.e., the disenfranchised, the underrepresented, the poor, and the powerless.[10]

The structuralist. The structuralist paradoxically supposes that the planner's information is a source of power because it serves necessarily, first, to legitimize the maintenance of existing structures of power and ownership and, second, to perpetuate public inattention to such fundamental issues as the incompatibility of democratic political processes with a capitalist political-economy. The structuralist view, ironically, is reminiscent of the conservative functionalism of several decades ago, but now the argument takes a political-economic turn The actions of the state, and the planners who work within it, inevitably function to prop up capitalism. The structuralist perspective suggests that planners have power but, despite their best intentions, keep people in their place and protect existing power. The planners' power cannot serve freedom.[11]

The progressive. Finally, the progressive approaches information as a source of power because it can enable the participation of citizens and avoid the legitimizing functions of which the structuralist warns. The planner's information can also call attention to the structural, organizational, and political barriers that needlessly distort the information citizens rely on to act.[12] The progressive perspective thus combines the insights of the liberal and the structuralist views and goes one step further. It recognizes that political-economic power may function systematically to misinform affected publics, by misrepresenting risk or costs and benefits, for instance. The progressive view anticipates such regular, structurally rooted misinformation and organizes information to counteract this "noise" (or "ideologizing," as some would call it).[13]

Each of these planning perspectives points to a different source of the need for information, and thus defines a different basis of power: technical problems, organizational needs, political inequality, system legitimation, or citizen action.

Since the progressive view builds on the other positions, it is particularly important to consider it in more detail. Emphasizing popular participation and planners' organizing practices, the progressive view also recognizes the obstacles to such participation. We will first compare the other views; then we will examine the progressive's position.

Limitations of Common Views

The technician is not wrong so much as intentionally neglectful. Politics is thought to "get in the way" of rigorous work. The political context of planning is understood as a threat, not as an opportunity.[14] Yet it was a political process that created not only the set of problems to be addressed but the technician's job as well. Therefore one cannot choose between being technical or being political. The technician is necessarily a political actor; the crucial questions are: In what way? How covertly? Serving whom? Excluding whom?

Following the publication of Lindblom's classic article "The Science of Muddling Through," the incrementalist view first found great favor for being practical, but then inspired no end of criticism for being unprincipled, apolitical, or, in a phrase, for admonishing us to "make do."[15] In its rejection of the rational-comprehensive call to get all the facts, the incrementalist position serves as an important antidote, but it says little about the improvement of planning practice, about what planners should be doing and how they might do it.

The liberal-advocate's view gained a more explicitly ethical following, in part for addressing issues of inequality, but it has been correctly criticized for failing to address the historical and structural character of these issues.[16] The liberal-advocate has been characterized as a nurse, ministering to the sick yet unable to prevent their illnesses from occurring in the first place.

The structuralist's position is as tragic as the liberal-advocate's: pure in intention, yet frustrating in practice. Finding all planning practice to be a legitimation of the status quo, the structuralist systematically fails to address real opportunities in planning.[17] The structuralist view may fail even to identify and exploit what might be called "internal contradictions" in the structure of the political economy and the planning process in particular. The irony of the liberal-advocates' position is that their best intentions may be betrayed by their ignorance of the structural effects of political-economic organization—for example, private control of investment, or the fact that an increased number of environmental-impact reports will not prevent environmental destruction. The tragedy of the structuralist view is that its apparently comprehensive position may be wholly undialectical in that it supposes the power planners face (or serve) to be monolithic and without internal contradictions.[18]

The Progressive Analysis of Power

The progressives have problems, too. Like the more strictly technical planners, they need good information. Like liberal-advocates, they need to supply information to citizens, communities, and labor groups in order to aid their organizing and democratic efforts. Yet the progressives need to act on the basis of a political analysis that tells them how the political system in which they work will function regularly to misinform both participants in the planning process and affected citizens more generally.[19] The progressive planner needs to anticipate, for example, that developers may withhold information or misrepresent likely project consequences, such as revenues; that consultants may be used less for analysis than for legitimation; that agency meeting schedules may favor private entrepreneurs while excluding affected working people whose business is their own daily employment; that documentation provided by a project's planners for public review is not likely to discuss project flaws or alternatives as candidly as project virtues; and so on.

Unlike the incrementalist or liberal-advocate, the progressive believes that misinformation is often not an accidental problem in planning: It may well be a systemic problem to be addressed and counteracted on that basis.[20] The practical tasks facing the progressive planner, then, are like those that community organizers and political actors have traditionally performed. Health planners, for example, increasingly recognize the need for educative and organizing skills to address the problems of daily planning practice.[21] Still, developing such educative, organizing responses to expectable misinformation requires planners to address several crucial, practical questions of political and organizational analysis.

What types of misinformation can be anticipated? Are some distortions inevitable while others are avoidable? Are some distortions socially systematic while others are not? How does misinformation affect planning and citizen action? What practical responses are possible? Might planners themselves be sources of distortion? Can this be justified? How can planners expect misinformation to flow through the relations of power that structure the planning process? Finally, in the face of expectable misinformation and distortion threatening well-informed planning and citizen action, what can progressive planners do in practice? The remainder of this chapter addresses these questions and the larger question of what this analysis means for an effective, progressive planning practice.

TYPES OF MISINFORMATION

We should distinguish several types of misinformation (see Table III.1). Some misinformation will be ad hoc, random, or spontaneous. For example, in a public hearing a developer's consultant may speak too quickly or unwittingly use technical terms that the audience fails to understand. As a result, communication suffers, but hardly as the result of any systematic cause. Other instances of misinformation, though, will reflect actors' political-economic roles. Consider the remarks of James C. Miller III, executive director of a presidential task force on regulatory relief, indicating that industry representatives can be expected to exaggerate likely costs of proposed regulations, while government representatives (i.e., the regulators) can be expected to inflate the benefits of the same proposed regulations.[22] Such misrepresentations are clearly not ad hoc; they are rather structural products of political-economic relationships.

If planners can anticipate both types of misinformation (systematic and ad hoc), they can vary their practical responses accordingly. For example, impromptu and informal measures might suffice

Table III.1 Bounded rationality refined: communicative distortions as bounds to the rationality of action

Contingency of distortion	Autonomy of the source of distortion	
	Socially ad hoc	**Socially systematic structural**
	1	2
Inevitable distortions	Idiosyncratic personal traits affecting communication Random noise (cognitive limits)	Information inequalities resulting from legitimate division of labor Transmission/content losses across organizational boundaries (division of labor)
	3	4
Socially unnecessary distortions	Willful unresponsiveness Interpersonal deception Interpersonal bargaining behavior; e.g., bluffing (interpersonal manipulation)	Monopolistic distortions of exchange Monopolistic creation of needs Ideological rationalization of class or power structure (structural legitimation)

in response to nonsystematic distortions of information, because such distortions may merely be matters of blind habit. Clarifications can be requested; time for questions and cross-examination can be allotted in hearings, reviews, or commission meetings; a sensitive chairperson can intervene to suggest that a speaker speak more slowly, more directly into the microphone, less technically, and so forth.

In contrast, responses to systematic misinformation must be more strategic, based on the planner's analysis of the power structure at hand. As Steven Lukes argues, systematic misinformation is rooted in the political-economic structures that define who initiates and who reacts; who invokes authority or expertise and who is mystified or defers; who appeals to trust and who chooses to trust or be skeptical; and who defines agendas of need and who is thus defined.[23]

Some instances of misinformation might be socially necessary (that is, unavoidable), whereas still others are not. That there is some division of expertise and knowledge in society seems to be a socially, if not a biologically, necessary matter, not in the particulars of distribution (that being a political question), but in the fact of any unequal distribution at all. Some people will have developed skills for graphic arts, others for community organization, others for music composition; some might be mechanics, others painters, others farmers, and still others teachers. How the division of

labor is structured in a given society is a political question—but that there must be a division of labor in capitalist, socialist, or future societies seems to be necessary in social life. Thus, some misinformation will be unavoidable; it will flow from *some* division of labor and thus of knowledge, expertise, and access to information. Other misinformation, such as capricious propaganda, will be socially unnecessary and thus avoidable.

This analysis of misinformation and communicative distortion provides the basis for a powerful reformulation of Herbert Simon's notion of the "boundedness" of the rationality of social action.[24] The rationality of action is bounded, to be sure; but how? How inevitably? How politically? We turn to these questions below.

Some constraints on social action may be necessary, but other bounds may just be social or political artifacts—constraints that are contingent on mere relations of custom, status, or power that are hardly inevitable or immutable. Working to alter the *necessary* boundedness of rational action may be foolishness, but working to alter the *unnecessary* constraints that distort rational action may be liberating.

In addition, some constraints on social action will be the result of random disturbances, but still others will be systematic, rooted in the political-economic structures that provide the context for any action. Treating random distortions as though they were systematic is a sign of paranoia; treating systematic distortions as though they were merely ad hoc phenomena is to be ethically and politically blind, assuring only repeated surprise, disappointment, and, most likely, failure.

HOW MISINFORMATION CAN MANIPULATE ACTION

How can information and communication, always potentially distorted, shape the actions of the people with whom planners work?[25] How can a politician's promise, a developer's project proposal, or a planner's report influence the actions of city residents? Informed and unmanipulated citizen action depends on four practical criteria in social interaction.[26] In every interaction, a speaker may speak more or less (1) comprehensibly, (2) sincerely, (3) appropriately or legitimately in the context at hand, and (4) accurately. In every interaction, too, a listener's subsequent action depends in part on how these same four criteria are satisfied. Consider each briefly in turn.

First, depending on the terms in which issues are discussed, citizens may find the issues clear or barely comprehensible, relevant to their own concerns or not, framed in ordinary language or in bureaucratese. Planners may, for example, either pinpoint key issues or bury them in data, verbiage, computer printouts, or irrelevant details—and what citizens understand, their *comprehension*, will grow or suffer as a result.

Second, depending on the intentions with which issues are presented, citizens may find their trust deserved or not. Citizens may be misled by false assurances of self-protecting agency staff, by technicians who claim to be neutral, or by established interests who deceptively claim to serve the greater public good. Thus public *trust*, always precarious, may be honored or manipulated.

Third, depending on what justifications are used as issues are presented, citizens may find their consent manipulated or not. Agency staff may claim legitimacy because the proper procedures have been followed; rivals within the community may claim legitimacy because they are acting in the public interest, acting to right wrongs, or acting as representatives of populations in need. In each case, the claim to legitimacy is an attempt to shape citizens action through the mobilization of their *consent*.

Fourth, depending on the use of evidence and data, citizens may find issues either misrepresented or reported accurately. Politicians and project proponents and opponents alike may exaggerate or fabricate estimates of costs, benefits, risks, and opportunities. Whether or not the truth sets anyone free, systematic misrepresentation in the planning process is likely to breed cynicism, cripple action, and manipulate citizens' *beliefs* as well.[27]

There is no guarantee against the presence of manipulation in planning. Informed planning and citizen action are vulnerable to the mismanagement (whether ad hoc or systematic) of planners' and citizens' comprehension, trust, consent, and beliefs. Tables III.2 and III.3 show how such mismanagement can occur as the exercise of power through the processes of decision making, agenda setting, or the shaping of people's felt needs.

Responses to Misinformation

Each of the four criteria suggests how different types of misinformation can influence participation in the planning process.[28] More important, each type of misinformation calls for a different type of response from planners. The progressive planner may counter the manipulation of a neighborhood organization's trust by revealing previous instances of such misinformation presented to other neighborhoods—in the case of a developer's suspicious promise, for example. By weeding jargon out of communications and by calling attention to important planning issues that might otherwise be obscured by the sheer volume of data in consultants' reports or proposals, planners may avoid the assault on comprehension that can paralyze citizen action. A hospital administrator's inflated claim to expertise to gain the consent of consumers in a health-planning agency may be countered by marshaling dissenting expertise or by exploring the issue to clarify just what expertise is appropriate in the case at hand. Finally, planners may counteract the management of citizens' beliefs or knowledge by promoting project-review criticism and debate and by further politicizing planning processes. "Politicizing" here means more democratically structured, publicly aired political argument, not more covert wheeling and dealing.

In land-use and health-planning processes, such corrective actions are variants of organizing strategies in communities and bureaucracies. They seek to enable informed participation that recognizes the rights of others but is skeptical of the purported benevolence of established interests that stand to reap substantial private gains from proposed projects.[29] Informing the "affected but unorganized" earlier rather than later in the planning process is one simple rule of thumb that helps to counter the varieties of misinformation: commonplace acts of checking, double-checking, testing, consulting experts, seeking third-party counsel, clarifying issues, exposing assumptions, reviewing and citing the record, appealing to precedent, invoking traditional values (democratic participation, for example), spreading questions about unexplored work of Allan Jacobs in San Francisco and of Norman Krumholz in Cleveland.[30]

Yet what is crucial here is not any new progressive social technology or political gimmickry. Planners already have a vast repertoire of practical responses with which they can counteract misinformation: commonplace acts of checking, double-checking, testing, consulting experts, seeking third-party counsel, clarifying issues, exposing assumptions, reviewing and citing the record, appealing to precedent, invoking traditional values (democratic participation, for example), spreading questions about unexplored possibilities, spotlighting jargon and revealing meaning, negotiating for clearly specified outcomes and values, working through informal networks to get information, bargaining for information, holding others to public commitments, and so on.[31]

Progressive planners, therefore, must learn to anticipate misinformation before the fact, when something may still be done to counteract it. The more traditional perspectives treat information problems as either inevitable or ad hoc (see Table III.1), and as a result, planners often respond too late. The practical problem, then, is not to invent new strategies in response to misinformation—

Table III.2 Power, information, and misinformation: the management of comprehension, trust, consent, and knowledge

| Modes through which power may be exercised | Forms of misinformation | | | |
	Managing comprehension (problem framing)	Managing trust (false assurance)	Managing consent (illegitimacy)	Managing knowledge (misrepresentation)
Decision making	Resolutions passed with deliberate ambiguity; confusing rhetoric, e.g., "the truly needy"	"Symbolic" decisions (false promises)	Decisions reached without legitimate representation of public interests but appealing to public consent as if this were not the case	Decisions that misrepresent actual possibilities to the public (e.g., the effectiveness of insufficiently tested medications)
Agenda setting	Obfuscating issues through jargon or quantity of "information"	Marshaling respectable personages to gain trust (independent of substance)	Arguing, e.g., that a political issue is actually a technical issue best left to experts	Before decisions are made, misrepresenting costs, benefits, risks, true options
Shaping felt needs	Diagnosis, definition of problem or solution through ideological language	Ritualistic appeals to "openness," "public interest," and "responsiveness"; encouraging dependence on benign apolitical others	Appeals to the adequacy and efficacy of formal "participatory" processes or market mechanisms without addressing their systematic failures	Ideological or deceptive presentation of needs, requirements, or sources of satisfaction (false advertising, "analysis for hire")

such strategies abound. Instead, the planner must be able, as the progressive view suggests, to anticipate and counteract the practical misinformation likely to arise in various organizational and political processes (see Table III.2).

With such vision, progressive planners can then draw on a repertoire of responses to counteract the disabling effects of misinformation in the planning process. Only if planners anticipate these problems can they counteract misrepresentation with checking and testing of data. Only then can they defend against false appeals to trust by checking the record of past promises. Only by anticipating misinformation can planners resist obfuscation with clear and powerful writing. Only then can they address the manipulation of consent by invoking shared tradition, precedent, or established rights. The progressive approach thus draws on the vast store of strategies that planners and citizens already possess; it also suggests that planners and citizens can anticipate misinformation in time to *use* those strategies effectively, rather than looking back regretfully and saying,

"Well, what we should have done was ..."

These responses involve risks to planners that depend both on the internal support for planners in planning departments and on the external support planners receive from other agencies, community groups, or established figures.[32] How much risk is involved should be neither minimized nor exaggerated, but further assessed in theory and in practice.[33]

PLANNERS AS SOURCES OF MISINFORMATION

Planners themselves can produce misinformation. They often work within pressing time constraints, with limited data. In addition, they often face organizational and political pressures to legitimate existing processes, to mitigate or avoid conflict, and to gain consensus and consent from potentially warring factions (developers, community groups, labor representatives) whenever possible. Under such conditions, planners can sometimes exacerbate the problems caused by misinforma-

Table III.3 Power and misinformation in health planning: an illustration of the management of comprehension, trust, consent, and knowledge

| Modes through which power may be exercised | Forms of misinformation | | | |
	Managing comprehension (problem framing)	Managing trust (false assurance)	Managing consent (illegitimacy)	Managing knowledge (misrepresentation)
Decision making	Mute and suppress disagreements, differences of opinion, and conflicts within the board	Appear "democratic"; claim to be "representative," "objective"	Control committee nominations and official appointments	Focus on task only; ignore process, hide omissions
Agenda setting	Overwhelm the board with data	Ensure that sympathetic professionals chair the board and key committees	Selectively schedule and time announcements; use professional language	Avoid sensitive issues of current relevance to the agency
Shaping felt needs	Claim that the best kind of training program is one where the information flows one way, from an expert to the board members	Avoid group-process type training and training in conflict and negotiation skills	Avoid staff who are trained in community organizing	Provide information so consumers believe they need what you already think they need

Source: Adapted from Steckler and Herzog (1979).

tion: misrepresentation of facts, improper appeals to expertise or precedent, misleading statements of intentions, or the obfuscation of significant issues. Moreover, the production of misinformation by planners often does not occur just by happenstance; rather, it may be encouraged by the very structure of the bureaucracies in which the planners work.

There can be no guarantee that planners will not produce misinformation. Yet two questions are crucial for planning practice: First, when can misinformation be ethically justified or rejected?[34] Second, if misinformation cannot be prevented, what good comes from an analysis of these problems?

The ethics regarding misinformation from planners (and from professionals more generally) has been a neglected topic in the planning profession until recently. In the last several years, a number of studies have begun to address these issues, and they provide guidance for the isolated justification—but more frequently for the rejection—of planning actions that distort communications; for instance, withholding information, or exaggerating risks or uncertainties.[35] Acts depend on particular contexts for their sense and meaning; so must any ethical justification or rejection, seeking to protect human integrity, autonomy, and welfare, be interpreted and applied anew in particular historical contexts. If general ethical principles are not applied to specific cases, planners risk becoming dogmatists, blind to the requirements of specific cases, or sheer relativists, thinking that whatever seems right in the situation will suffice. Rigid adherence to formal principle, then, may callously substitute ready-made solutions for discriminating and sensitive ethical judgments. Situational relativism, in contrast, actually provides an ethics of convenience for the powerful. When the situation decides, then those with the power to define the situation really decide, and "right" is reduced to "might." Thus, at either extreme, questions of genuine justification in practice become meaningless.[36] How then are planners to apply general principles protecting integrity, autonomy, and welfare to concrete cases?

We might ordinarily wish to discourage lying, for example, because of the corrosive effect it has on social trust, but in some special circumstances we might justify it: such as deceiving a violent assailant about the whereabouts of his or her victim who has taken refuge in our house.[37] Similarly, misinforming actions by planners may at special times be justified, too, but only under particular and rare conditions, and hardly as often as might be supposed: when reasonable alternatives (as judged by a diverse, informed public) are not available; when the informed consent of others may be available (a client requests a rough summary of issues, not a more precise technical analysis); or when substantial and serious harm may be done otherwise. Each of these conditions is quite "soft" and open to a range of interpretations, but each may nevertheless be useful for the evaluation of planners' possible misinforming actions.

In the face of ever-changing historical circumstances that demand practical action, any general ethical analysis must be largely indeterminate. Yet the analysis of misinformation still can serve a politically critical function. Only after the types of misinformation that may be produced by planners are distinguished can concrete alternatives in specific circumstances be examined—and only then can we turn to the questions of justification or rejection. This chapter cannot offer ethical judgments independent of all practical cases, but it can and does serve, first, to identify the types of misinformation (whether produced or faced by planners, or both); second, to identify a repertoire of responses to misinformation; and third, to suggest how ethically to evaluate practical strategies for presenting, withholding, checking, or challenging information in the planning process. How, then, can planners work in the face of power?

THE STRUCTURAL SOURCES OF MISINFORMATION

In practice, how planners respond to misinformation will depend in part on their view of the sources of that misinformation. If they perceive misinformation to be accidental or unique to particular communities or types of projects, they are likely to work in a more ad hoc manner than if they view it as structural, to be routinely expected and countered. Questions about the sources of misinformation therefore become immediately practical. What types and mechanisms of power are faced by planners and by citizens affected by the planning process, and how influential are these modes of power? How does such power work, and how is it limited or vulnerable?

Extending Steven Lukes's cogent analysis, we can explore three answers to these questions.[38] Each answer will suggest different strategies for progressive planners to employ. One exercise of power can be understood by focusing—as the pluralists do—on decision making. Decision-makers can inform or misinform citizens effectively by virtue of their ability to prevail in formal decision-making situations.

A subtler exercise of power occurs in the setting of agendas—controlling which citizens find out what and when, about which projects, which options, and what they might be able to do as a result. Such power is immediately reminiscent of the information-brokering roles often attributed to planners: Shaping who finds out what and when often shapes action (and inaction).[39]

Yet another, still more insidious, exercise of power exists in the ability of major actors to shape the self-conceptions, the sense of legitimate expectations, and finally the needs of citizens: for example, the conceptions that citizens must acquiesce in the face of big government and big business; that socialism for poor and middle-income people is perverse, but appropriate for the wealthy who control investment; that individual market consumption will fulfill all needs; and that collective action is not a public responsibility but a nuisance.[40] Difficult to measure, this form of power nevertheless seems undeniable.

Each of these three modes of power can thwart the efforts of planners and informed citizens who seek to participate in a democratic planning process. Each of these modes—control of decision making, agenda setting, and needs shaping—can create misinformation that not only subverts informed and articulate citizen participation, but also weakens working relationships between planners and citizens. In health planning, for example, hospitals that propose expansion often utilize the pomp and circumstance of their medical staff to manipulate the trust and consent of consumer members of health-planning boards.[41] Consumer participation may then become characterized by passivity and deference, and progressive planning, staff who question the need for expansion may come to be viewed with suspicion by the consumers. In such a case, the hospital staff members exert power not through decision making, but through their ability to shape agendas of discussion and citizens' perceived needs. But how are these agendas and self-perceptions shaped? Why do the consumer board members listen?

Power as Political Communication

Hospital staff members in the above example are able to exert power because the information they present—and the way they communicate—is highly political.[42] They very selectively inform and misinform citizens. They may call attention to particular apparent needs and obscure others, whatever the resources available to meet those needs. Appealing to the public trust in their reputation and, their record of community service, hospitals may stress pressing community problems and their devotion and commitment to addressing them. They may appear to welcome legitimate, open discussion and public education while simultaneously ignoring the inability of significantly affected populations to join in those discussions. They may omit a careful analysis of public-serving alternatives to the proposed expansion and thus misrepresent the actual planning options faced by the health-planning body. In each of these cases—and they are all common enough, as any review of public participation in planning reveals—the established and often private "developer" can exert power through the control of information.

By informing or misinforming citizens, power works through the management of comprehension, or obfuscation; of trust, or false assurance; of consent, or manipulated agreement; and of knowledge, or misrepresentation.[43] Each of the three modes of power works in this way, either to thwart democratic participation and encourage passivity, or to encourage articulate political action and the realization of a democratic planning process (see Tables III.2 and III.3).[44]

Anticipating Misinformation: Progressive Planning Responses

The progressive planner seeks to anticipate and counteract misinformation that hampers publicly accessible, informed, and participatory planning. Each mode of power (decision making, agenda setting, and needs shaping) and each dimension of misinformation (obfuscation, false assurance, pretension to legitimacy, or misrepresentation of facts) may present distinct obstacles to progressive planning practice, and each obstacle calls for a distinct response.[45] As discussed here, planners can prepare participants in the planning process to face such misinformation— sometimes preparing them with facts, sometimes with questions and arguments, sometimes with expertise, and at other times just with an early warning.

Planners can respond to decision-making power by anticipating political pressures and mobilizing countervailing support.[46] Anticipating the agenda-setting attempts of established interests, planners can respond through a variety of informal, information-brokering roles, keenly attuned to the timing of the planning process, its stages and procedures, and the interests and perceptions of the participants all along the way. In addition, planners may work to include or seek ties to those traditionally excluded, encouraging attention to alternatives that dominant interests might otherwise suppress. As presented here, then, progressive planning practice represents a refinement of traditional advocacy planning, a refinement based on the practical recognition of systematic sources of misinformation. Finally, planners who anticipate the attempts of established interests to shape the perceived needs of citizens may not only work against such needs-shaping rhetoric, but they may also encourage, or ally themselves with, progressive, local organizing efforts. In the face of these modes of power, no single type of planning response will be sufficient. No doubt many strategies will be necessary if planning practitioners are to respond to, and indeed empower, citizens who hope to have an effective voice regarding the issues that affect their lives.

CONCLUSION

The power available to progressive planners encompasses the information strategies of the technician, the incrementalist, and the liberal-advocate, but it is more extensive still. Recognizing structural, routine sources of misinformation, the progressive planner seeks to anticipate and counter the efforts of interests that threaten to make a mockery of a democratic planning

process by misrepresenting cases, improperly invoking authority, making false promises, or distracting attention from key issues. In environmental planning this means beginning with the demand that impact reports be intelligible to the public and not simply commented on at public hearings once they are written. It means countering corporate misrepresentations of costs, risks, and available alternatives, too. In health planning this means attending to preventive health care as well as to curative medical care, to workplace threats as well as to medical responses. In neighborhood planning it means tempering the exaggerated claims of developers and demystifying the planning process—and the rest of local government—itself. In each area, progressive planners can encourage and inform the mobilization and action of affected citizens.

Just as each form of misinformation is a barrier to informed public participation (see Table III.2), so might an analysis of these barriers help citizens and planners alike to identify, anticipate, and overcome such obstacles to a democratic planning process. Planners can work to distinguish inevitable from avoidable distortions, ad hoc from structural distortions, and they may respond to these accordingly, so protecting reasonably informed planning and empowering citizen action as well.[47] Indeed, in a political world, any rationality in planning and administrative practice can be maintained only if analysts carefully assess the institutional contexts in which they work—as we will see in the next chapter. Anticipating and working to counteract distortions of communication that weaken democratic planning, then, progressive planning—structurally critical yet hardly fatalistic—is at once a democratizing and a practical organizing process.

NOTES

1. See Altshuler (1965), Balkas (1979), Baum (1980a, 1980b), Bradley (1979), Howe and Kaufman (1979), Page (1977), and Roche (1981).

2. Cf. Forester (1981b).

3. See, e.g., Marris and Rein (1984), Krumholz, Cogger, and Linner (1975), Benveniste (1977), Rabinowitz (1969), Kaufman (1974), and Needleman and Needleman (1974).

4. The term "progressive" is used because

"radical" has been discredited as not pragmatic, "advocate" is overly narrow, "ethical" is conventionally misunderstood to be simply idealistic, and "professional" has been reduced, colloquially, from implying a "calling" to denoting merely the possession of expertise and socioeconomic status. Our use of "progressive" appropriates those elements of the Progressive Era that called into question the structural relations of nondemocratic control of capital and investment; this use rejects, however, those elements of the same era that sought instead to rationalize, objectify, manage, and quiet the conflicts and exploitation inherent in the political- economy. In sociological terms, the problem of this chapter, and the book as a whole, is to clarify the diverse possibilities of counter-hegemonic practices.

5. E.g., Rabin (1980).

6. E.g., Bradley (1979).

7. See, e.g., Altshuler (1965), Benveniste (1977), Bradley (1979), Jacobs (1978), Krumholz, Cogger, and Linner (1975), Meltsner (1976), and Roche (1981).

8. Cf. Benveniste (1977), Kravitz (1970), Lindblom (1959), Meltsner (1976), Nilson (1979), Thompson (1967), and Wildavsky (1979).

9. The classic analysis is Davidoff (1965).

10. Cf. Davidoff (1965) and Mazziotti (1974).

11. Cf. Harvey (1978), Piven and Cloward (1971), and Saunders (1979). Like that of the other perspectives, the brief description of the structuralist perspective here is ideal-typical. Structuralist perspectives have been both forcefully presented (Poulantzas 1973) and criticized (Thompson 1980). The intention here is not to delineate substantially a structuralist position but rather to characterize it briefly, if necessarily too simply; a fuller treatment is a task for critical accounts of the way planning theory draws on the broader fields of social and political theory and political-economy. The structuralist position is sketched here to indicate that problems of local effectiveness versus system determinism (or the philosophical "problem" of voluntarism versus determinism) are always present in planning practice, as shown in the familiar question planners ask: "Am I really making a difference here, or is everything I'm doing getting washed out by the larger political and economic system?" Depending on how this question is asked, it may lead to

paralysis or, alternatively, to sharper strategic thinking. In any case, the structuralist view of information as power is presented here not to represent Marxist structuralist work in general (nor to represent all work that simply takes into account social, political, or economic structures), but instead to indicate how a view of systems-determinism might be manifest, and have extremely undialectical consequences, in practice. There are, of course, other Marxist positions, in theory and in practice, besides that of the structuralist perspective briefly presented here (Tabb and Sawers 1978).

12. Necessary and unnecessary distortions, as well as structural and nonstructural distortions, are discussed and distinguished in the next section of this chapter. These distinctions are presented schematically in Table III.1.

13. E.g., Burlage and Kennedy (1980), Burton and Murphy (1980), Bradley (1979), Forester (1981a), Freire (1970), Friedmann (1980), Gorz (1967), Hartman (1978), Kemp (1980), Kraushaar (1979), Needleman and Needleman (1974), and Schroyer (1973). Cf. Krumholz (1982).

14. Cf. Szanton (1981) and Meltsner (1976).

15. See Lindblom (1959).

16. Two fascinating discussions of the liberal attitude described so briefly here may be found in the work of John Schaar (1967) and Isaac Kramnick (1981); their essays discuss the inegalitarian ironies of traditional liberal arguments for equal opportunity. Kramnick's historical analysis suggests that the liberal doctrine of equal opportunity arose as an argument against the claims of eighteenth-century English aristocracy. Although the resulting promotion of meritocracy can be seen as an emancipatory movement in the context of aristocracy, the same doctrine of equal opportunity today, leading to the same results, meritocracy, can hardly be appreciated as emancipatory any longer.

17. See Saunders (1979).

18. It might be conjectured that planners holding such a view do not last long as planners or, alternatively, that this perspective provides an all-encompassing rationalization for planning inefficacy, if not also for finding cynical satisfaction in meeting lower expectations, Herbert Simon's "satisficing."

19. As we will see, *how* the misinformation

confronting planners comes about is a matter of the specific institutional settings in which planners work. In a capitalist political-economy in which the state functions both productively, to protect and foster capital accumulation, and reproductively, to promote and gain legitimation, the actual content of the misinformation faced by planners and citizens generally will, of course, differ in specific ways from that faced by members of bureaucratic socialist or other political-economic systems. Nevertheless, misinformation and systematic distortions of communication may be anticipated in a variety of political-economies, and our analysis here attempts only to provide a framework for research that suggests the dimensions in which hegemonic misinformation and communicative distortion can be expected to occur. It remains for analysts of planning in capitalist, bureaucratic socialist, and other political-economies to specify the contents of expectable misinformation generated in those institutional settings.

20. For the purposes of this discussion, "systemic," "systematic," and "structural" will be used virtually synonymously. Further analyses of misinformation must distinguish between distortions of communication that are rooted in (Weberian) status structures and those distortions that are rooted in (Marxist) class structures. What substantive theory of social and political-economic structure planners assume or employ will determine what sorts of structural distortions they may be able to anticipate in practice. Social and political theory, thus, informs planners' abilities to anticipate problems of practice, problems calling for preemptive response on the one hand, and threatening failure on the other (Forester 1987). See Clegg's work (1975, 1979), for example, for a critical discussion of power and structure; see also Stone (1980).

21. E.g., Bolan and Nuttal (1975), Burlage (1979), Burlage and Kennedy (1980), Checkoway (1981), Lancourt (1979), and Roche (1981).

22. See Brownstein (1981).

23. Cf. Lukes (1974), Gaventa (1980), and Forester (1982a, 1982b).

24. The next chapter develops this analysis at length. Table III.1 presents a reformulation of the meaning of the "boundedness" of rational action. These categories (necessary versus unnecessary,

ad hoc versus systematic) may provide an initial, graphic representation of the meaning of Richard Bernstein's claim that Habermas's critical communications theory of society is essentially an attempt to reformulate a comprehensive social and political theory of rationality (Bernstein 1976). See also McCarthy (1978) and note 47, below. The task of any critical social and political theory is to be able to distinguish carefully the necessary from the unnecessary, and the ad hoc from {he systematic constraints on social action (whether involving planners, citizens, decision-makers, or others) so that appropriate responses (enabling what social and political rationality there may be) will be possible. The analysis of misinformation and communicative distortion provides the basis for ethically and politically refined assessment of both (i) the problematic rationality of social and political action; and (ii) the practical responses and actions possible to counteract the threats to—and especially the systematic distortions of—socially and politically rational interaction. The paradigmatic types of systematic distortions of social action are social-psychological neurosis and political-economic ideology. In each case systematic distortions produce domination rather than emancipation (Held 1980). By providing an analysis of communicative distortions that allows actors to anticipate and then respond practically to misinforming or distorting communicative influences, a critical social theory joins an account of power relations to an account of emancipatory, politically informed and guided practice. This analysis thus suggests research to clarify, first, those bounds or constraints on rationality (types of communicative distortions) and, second, those actions and practices required to counteract or avoid those distortions mapped schematically in Table III.1.

25. Table III.2 arrays the effects of misinformation against the various levels of the exercise of power through which such misinformation may be communicated. These dimensions of Table III.2 are based on recent analyses of political power (Lukes 1974; Gaventa 1980) and of the pragmatic structure of communicative interaction (Habermas 1979; Held 1980; Shapiro 1976; McCarthy 1978; and Forester 1981c); cf. Chapter Nine. The problem of political misinformation might be approached in two ways: either by cataloguing the types of "symbolic" power that political acts may manifest (Edelman 1964, 1971, 1977) or by assessing the vulnerability of political action to distorted communications (Habermas 1970a, 1975, 1979; Bernstein 1976; Shapiro 1976). The former approach illuminates the functions of "symbolic politics," but it fails to ground those functions in an account of practical interaction, a theory of social action. Thus, the argument of this chapter complements the analysis of communicative action in planning practice (Chapters Five and Nine, for example) to consider problems of practice and relations of power directly. On parallels to Foucalt's analysis of power and discourse, see Ingram (1986).

26. Habermas (1979), Forester (1981c). See Chapter Nine for a more detailed exposition.

27. In the field of transportation planning, Yale Rabin, for example, writes: "Some believe that central city decline, minority isolation, and gasoline dependent dispersal have merely evolved from the incremental effects of millions of free choices and independent transactions in the metropolitan marketplace and that these conditions therefore simply reflect the mainstream values of a pluralistic society. The evidence, however, strongly suggests that these choices and transactions and the values which motivated them have been profoundly influenced by the systematic withholding by public officials of essential information about the fundamental nature and foreseeable impacts of highway policies and projects" (1980, 35).

28. Again, we can expect vulnerabilities of social action (to the structural management of attention, trust, consent, and knowledge) to be present whether that action (negotiating, bargaining, covering up, arguing, appealing, promising, threatening, and so on) is situated historically in capitalist or noncapitalist political-economies. But *how* actors actually face particular structural influences managing their knowledge, consent, trust, and framing of problems will vary, and must therefore be specified concretely (and strategic and practical anticipation and resistance must therefore also vary and likewise be specified) across differing political economic systems. The analysis of misinformation and response, then, may provide a framework for comparative analysis of planning practices. For work in this direction, cf. Adler (1986).

29. E.g., Checkoway (1981), Needleman and Needleman (1974), and Forester (1982b).

30. See Benveniste (1977), Jacobs (1978), Krumholz, Cogger, and Linner (1975), Lancourt (1979), Meltsner (1976), Needleman and Needleman (1974), and Roche (1981).

31. See, e.g., Goffman (1981), Lyman and Scott (1970), Needleman and Needleman (1974), Susskind and Cruickshank (1987), and Wilensky (1967).

32. See Needleman and Needleman (1974), Fainstein and Fainsten (1972), and Gondim (1986).

33. See Krumholz, Cogger, and Linner (1975); also Hoch and Cibulskis (1987).

34. Answering this question analytically will prevent unjustified acts in planning no more than distinguishing perjury from truth-telling will prevent perjury. Still, without the analytical distinctions, confusion and mystification are guaranteed, for one could never then distinguish perjury from truth-telling or outright lies from honest claims.

35. See Rohr (1978), Bok (1978), Howe and Kaufman (1979), Marcuse (1976), Euben (1981), Fleischman and Payne (1980), Forester (1980, 1981b), and Wachs (1985).

36. This analysis reflects the help of Stephen Blum. For a related analysis, see Anderson (1985).

37. See, e.g., Bok (1978).

38. See Lukes (1974), Gaventa (1980), and Roche (1981).

39. See, e.g., Meltsner (1976), Benveniste (1977), Kemp (1980), Rabinowitz (1969), Needleman and Needleman (1974), Marris and Rein (1984), and Checkoway (1986).

40. See Lukes (1974).

41. See, e.g., Clark (1977) and Checkoway (1981).

42. I.e., sociologists refer to such power as "hegemony." Cf. Thompson (1984).

43. To argue that power works as communication, in several dimensions, is not to argue that power and force are unrelated. Even dictatorial power may work far more often through the communication of the threat of force than through the application of force itself. Legitimate power, while retaining its potential use of force, appeals to and depends on consent rather than on the threat of violence. See, for example, Habermas's (1977a) discussion of Arendt's concept of power, and Pitkin's (1972) discussion of the distinction between legitimate power (authority) and illegiti-

mate power (domination); cf. Forester (1986). As applied here, and presented schematically in Chapter Nine, critical theory is an analysis of contingent, hegemonic power (cf. Giroux 1983; Marris 1982 [discussion of metaphors of power]).

44. Forester (1982b) argues that these dimensions of misinformation provide a powerful reformulation of the notions of agenda setting and mobilization of bias in discussion of political power. That essay emphasizes variations in the content of agenda setting and needs shaping; the present chapter emphasizes the types of misinformation (necessary or avoidable, ad hoc or systematic) that may be anticipated and counteracted by progressive planning practitioners. See also Chapter Five below.

45. Thus, further research should identify in detail the appropriate strategies to respond to the particular types of misinformation (see Tables III.2 and III.3).

46. See, e.g., Fisher and Foster (1978), Forester (1981b), Gaventa (1980), Hartman (1978), Kraushaar (1979), Lancourt (1979), Needleman and Needleman (1974), Roche (1981), and Scott (1985).

47. Table III.1 also allows us to locate the differences in outlook that separate several conventional planning perspectives and political sensibilities more generally. For example, incrementalists and pragmatists seem to assume a world where the significant distortions are inevitable; their typical question, then, is "What can we do, given that distortions will always haunt whatever planning we attempt?" Incrementalists, pragmatists, and technicians seem to spend little time separating socially unnecessary distortions from apparently necessary ones. While technicians hope that more powerful methods will mitigate the effects of distortion, incrementalists and pragmatists retreat to a "satisficing" position. Liberals, in contrast, find inequalities of access, knowledge, expertise, and information to be socially unnecessary and hardly inevitable, so they work to provide compensatory or remedial programs designed to overcome and eliminate those socially unnecessary distortions of human action. The liberal, though, seems generally unconcerned with distinguishing ad hoc distortions from socially systematic or structural ones. Here is the crux of the difference between the liberal and the progressive: the progressive seeks to isolate the ad hoc from the more structurally rooted distortions and then respond to each accordingly.

In terms of Table III.1, technicians may treat all information problems as if they are located in quadrant 1; incrementalists and pragmatists treat distortions as if they are located in quadrant 1 or 2. Liberals, in contrast, worry less about inevitable distortions than about politically contingent ones; thus, lacking a theory of the reproduction of social structures, they concentrate their attention in quadrant 3. Progressives, in contrast, distinguish the four quadrants and concentrate their attention on those avoidable distortions they can anticipate regularly (because these are structurally rooted) and then work to counteract, i.e., those in quadrant 4. If planners fail to distinguish the distortions in quadrant 4 from those in the other quadrants, they risk either mistaking recurring and expectable distortions for ad hoc and transient ones, or accepting avoidable distortions as if they were inevitable. In the former case, the error produces recurring surprise and avoidable distortion; in the latter case, the error produces fatalism while opportunities to improve the quality of practical work in the planning process remain unappreciated. The next chapter develops these arguments at length.

The City as a Growth Machine:
Toward a Political Economy of Place[1]

Harvey Molotch

Copyright: Molotch, Harvey; *American Journal of Sociology* ©, Vol. 82, No. 2 (Sep., 1976), pp. 309-332. Reprinted by permission of the University of Chicago Press.

In this selection Molotch outlines his theory of community growth and development, later known as Growth Machine Theory. He describes a community structure where local elites use their combined power to promote growth for personal profit. Molotch is critical of these local elites and their disregard for the common good. He concludes with a brief discussion of the "countercoalition" or in current terms, the "anti-growth movement." ·

Conventional definitions of "city," "urban place," or "metropolis" have led to conventional analyses of urban systems and urban-based social problems. Usually traceable to Wirth's classic and highly plausible formulation of "numbers, density and heterogeneity" (1938), there has been a continuing tendency, even in more recent formulations (e.g., Davis 1965), to conceive of place quite apart from a crucial dimension of social structure: power and social class hierarchy. Consequently, sociological research based on the traditional definitions of what an urban place is has had very little relevance to the actual, day-to-day activities of those at the top of local power structure whose priorities set the limits within which decisions affecting land use, the public budget, and urban social life come to be made. It has not been very apparent from the scholarship of urban social science that land, the basic stuff of place, is a market commodity providing wealth and power, and that some very important people consequently take a keen interest in it. Thus, although there are extensive literatures on community power as well as on how to define and conceptualize a city or urban place, there are few notions available to link the two issues coherently, focusing on the urban settlement as a political economy.

This paper aims toward filling this need. I speculate that the political and economic essence of virtually any given locality, in the present American context, is *growth*. I further argue that the desire for growth provides the key operative motivation toward consensus for members of politically mobilized local elites, however split they might be on other issues, and that a common interest in growth is the overriding commonality among important people in a given locale—at least insofar as they have any important local goals at all. Further, this growth imperative is the most important constraint upon available options for local initiative in social and economic reform. It is thus that I argue that the very essence of a locality is its operation as a growth machine.

The clearest indication of success at growth is a constantly rising urban-area population—a symptom of a pattern ordinarily comprising an initial expansion of basic industries followed by an expanded labor force, a rising scale of retail and wholesale commerce, more far-flung and increasingly intensive land development, higher population density, and increased levels of financial activity. Although throughout this paper I index growth by the variable population growth, it is this entire syndrome of associated events that is meant by the general term "growth."[2] I argue that the means of achieving this growth, of setting off this chain of phenomena, constitute the central issue for those serious people who care about their locality and who have the resources to make their caring felt as a political force. The city is, for those who count, a growth machine.

THE HUMAN ECOLOGY: MAPS AS INTEREST MOSAICS

I have argued elsewhere (Molotch 1967, 1973) that any given parcel of land represents an interest and that any given locality is thus an aggregate of land-based interests. That is, each landowner (or person who otherwise has some interest in the prospective use of a given piece of land) has in mind a certain future for that parcel which is linked somehow with his or her own well-being. If there is a simple ownership, the relationship is straightforward: to the degree to which the land's profit potential is enhanced, one's own wealth is increased. In other cases, the relationship may be more subtle: one has interest in an adjacent parcel, and if a noxious use should appear, one's own parcel may be harmed. More subtle still is the emergence of concern for an aggregate of parcels: one sees that one's future is bound to the future of a larger area, that the future enjoyment of financial benefit flowing from a given parcel will derive from the general future of the proximate aggregate of parcels. When this occurs, there is that "we feeling" (McKenzie 1922) which bespeaks of community. We need to see each geographical map—whether of a small group of land parcels, a whole city, a region, or a nation—not merely as a demarcation of legal, political, or topographical features, but as a mosaic of competing land interests capable of strategic coalition and action.

Each unit of a community strives, at the expense of the others, to enhance the land-use potential of the parcels with which it is associated. Thus, for example, shopkeepers at both ends of a block may compete with one another to determine in front of which building the bus stop will be placed. Or, hotel owners on the north side of a city may compete with those on the south to get a convention center built nearby (see Banfield 1961). Likewise, area units fight over highway routes, airport locations, campus developments, defense contracts, traffic lights, one-way street designations, and park developments. The intensity of group consciousness and activity waxes and wanes as opportunities for and challenges to the collective good rise and fall; but when these coalitions are of sufficiently enduring quality, they constitute identifiable, ongoing communities. Each member of a community is simultaneously the member of a number of others; hence, communities exist in a nested fashion (e.g., neighborhood within city within region), with salience of community level varying both over time and circumstance. Because of this nested nature of communities, subunits which are competitive with one another at one level (e.g., in an interblock dispute over where the bus stop should go) will be in coalition at a higher level (e.g., in an intercity rivalry over where the new port should go). Obviously, the anticipation of potential coalition acts to constrain the intensity of conflict at more local loci of growth competition.

Hence, to the degree to which otherwise competing land-interest groups collude to achieve a common land-enhancement scheme, there is community—whether at the level of a residential block club, a neighborhood association, a city or metropolitan chamber of commerce, a state development agency, or a regional association. Such aggregates, whether constituted formally or informally, whether governmental political institutions or voluntary associations, typically operate in the following way: an attempt is made to use government to gain those resources which will enhance the growth potential of the area unit in question. Often, the governmental level where action is needed is at least one level higher than the community from which the activism springs. Thus, individual landowners aggregate to extract neighborhood gains from the city government; a cluster of cities may coalesce to have an effective impact on the state government, etc. Each locality, in striving to make these gains, is in competition with other localities because the degree of growth, at least at any given moment, is finite. The scarcity of developmental resources means that government becomes the arena in which land-use interest groups compete for public money and attempt to mold those decisions which will determine the land-use outcomes. Localities thus compete with one another to gain the *preconditions* of growth. Historically, U.S. cities were created and sustained largely through this process;[3] it continues to be the significant dynamic of contemporary local political economy and is critical to the allocation of public resources and the ordering of local issue agendas.

Government decisions are not the only kinds of social activities which affect local growth chances; decisions made by private corporations also have major impact. When a national corporation decides to locate a branch plant in a given locale, it sets the conditions for the surrounding land-use pattern. But even here, government decisions are involved: plant-location decisions are made with reference to such issues as labor costs, tax rates, and the costs of obtaining raw materials and transporting goods to markets. It is government decisions (at whatever level) that help determine the cost of access to markets and raw materials. This is especially so in the present era of raw material subsidies (e.g., the mineral depletion allowance) and reliance on government approved or subsidized air transport, highways, railways, pipelines, and port developments. Government decisions influence the cost of overhead expenses (e.g., pollution abatement requirements, employee safety standards), and government decisions affect the costs of labor through indirect manipulation of unemployment rates, through the use of police to constrain or enhance union organizing, and through the legislation and administration of welfare laws (see Piven and Cloward 1972).

Localities are generally mindful of these governmental powers and, in addition to creating the sorts of physical conditions which can best serve industrial growth, also attempt to maintain the kind of "business climate" that attracts industry: for example, favorable taxation, vocational training, law enforcement, and "good" labor relations. To promote growth, taxes should be "reasonable," the police force should be oriented toward protection of property, and overt social conflict should be minimized (see Rubin 1972, p. 123; Agger, Goldrich, and Swanson 1964, p. 649).[4] Increased utility and government costs caused by new development should be borne (and they usually are—see, e.g., Ann Arbor City Planning Department [1972]) by the public at large, rather than by those responsible for the "excess" demand on the urban infrastructure. Virtually any issue of a major business magazine is replete with ads from localities of all types (including whole countries) trumpeting their virtues in just these terms to prospective industrial settlers.[5] In addition, a key role of elected and appointed officials becomes that of "ambassador" to industry, to communicate, usually with appropriate ceremony, these advantages to potential investors (see Wyner 1967).[6]

I aim to make the extreme statement that this organized effort to affect the outcome of growth distribution is the essence of local government as a dynamic political force. It is not the only function of government, but it is the key one and, ironically, the one most ignored. Growth is not, in the present analysis, merely one among a number of equally important concerns of political process (cf. Adrian and Williarns 1963). Among contemporary social scientists, perhaps only Murray Edelman (1964) has provided appropriate conceptual preparation for viewing government in such terms. Edelman contrasts two kinds of politics. First there is the "symbolic" politics which comprises the "big issues" of public morality and the symbolic reforms featured in the headlines and editorials of the daily press. The other politics is the process through which goods and services actually come to be distributed in the society. Largely unseen, and relegated to negotiations within committees (when it occurs at all within a formal government body), this is the politics which determines who, in *material terms*, gets what, where, and how (Lasswell 1936). This is the kind of politics we must talk about at the local level: it is the politics of distribution, and land is the crucial (but not the only) variable in this system.

The people who participate with their energies, and particularly their fortunes, in local affairs are the sort of persons who—at least in vast disproportion to their representation in the population—have the most to gain or lose in land-use decisions. Prominent in terms of numbers have long been the local businessmen (see Walton 1970)[7], particularly property owners and investors in locally oriented financial institutions (see, e.g., Spaulding 1951; Mumford 1961, p. 536), who need local government in their daily money-making routines. Also prominent are lawyers, syndicators, and realtors (see Bouma 1962) who need to put themselves in situations where they can be most useful to those with the land and property resources.[8] Finally, there are those who, although not directly involved in land use, have their futures tied to growth of the metropolis as a whole. At least, when the local market becomes saturated one of the few possible avenues for business expansion is sometimes the expansion of the surrounding community itself (see Adrian and Williams 1963, p. 24).[9]

This is the general outline of the coalition that actively generates the community "we feeling" (or perhaps more aptly, the "our feeling")[10] that comes to be an influence in the politics of a given locality. It becomes manifest through a wide variety of techniques. Government funds support "booster-ism" of various sorts: the Chamber of Commerce, locality-promotion ads in business journals and travel publications, city-sponsored parade floats, and stadia and other forms of support for professional sports teams carrying the locality name. The athletic teams in particular are an extraordinary mechanism for instilling a spirit of civic jingoism regarding the "progress" of the locality. A stadium filled with thousands (joined by thousands more at home before the TV) screaming for Cleveland or Baltimore (or whatever) is a scene difficult to fashion otherwise. This enthusiasm can be drawn upon, with a glossy claim of creating a "greater Cleveland," "greater Baltimore," etc., in order to gain general acceptance for local growth-oriented programs. Similarly, public school curricula, children's essay contests, soapbox derbies, spelling contests, beauty pageants, etc., help build an ideological base for local boosterism and the acceptance of growth. My conception of the territorial bond among humans differs from those cast in terms of primordial instincts: instead, I see this bond as socially organized and sustained, at least in part, by those who have a use for it (cf. Suttles 1912, pp. 111-39). I do not claim that there are no other sources of civic jingoism and growth enthusiasm in American communities, only that the growth-machine coalition mobilizes what is there, legitimizes and sustains it, and channels it as a political force into particular kinds of policy decisions.

The local institution which seems to take prime responsibility for the sustenance of these civic resources—the metropolitan newspaper—is also the most important example of a business which has its interest anchored in the aggregate growth of the locality. Increasingly, American cities are one-newspaper (metropolitan daily) towns (or one-newspaper-company towns), and the newspaper business seems to be one kind of enterprise for which expansion to other locales is especially difficult. The financial loss suffered by

the *New York Times* in its futile effort to establish a California edition is an important case in point. A paper's financial status (and that of other media to a lesser extent) tends to be wed to the size of the locality.[11] As the metropolis expands, a larger number of ad lines can be sold on the basis of the increasing circulation base. The local news paper thus tends to occupy a rather unique position: like many other local businesses, it has an interest in growth, but unlike most, its critical interest is not in the specific geographical pattern of that growth. That is, the crucial matter to a newspaper is not whether the additional population comes to reside on the north side or south side, or whether the money is made through a new convention center or a new olive factory. The newspaper has no axe to grind, except the one axe which holds the community elite together: growth. It is for this reason that the newspaper tends to achieve a statesman-like attitude in the community and is deferred to as something other than a special interest by the special interests. Competing interests often regard the publisher or editor as a general community leader, as an ombudsman and arbiter of internal bickering and, at times, as an enlightened third party who can restrain the short-term profiteers in the interest of more stable, long-term, and properly planned growth.[12] The paper becomes tbe reformist influence, the "voice of the community," restraining the competing subunits, especially the small-scale, arriviste "fast-buck artists" among them. The papers are variously successful in their continuous battle with the targeted special interests.[13] The media attempt to attain these goals not only through the kind of coverage they develop and editorials they write but also through the kinds of candidates they support for local office. The present point is not that the papers control the politics of the city, but rather that one of the sources of their special influence is their commitment to growth per se, and growth is a goal around which all important groups can rally.

Thus it is that, although newspaper editorialists have typically been in the forefront expressing sentiment in favor of "the ecology," they tend nevertheless to support growth-inducing investments for their regions. The *New York Times* likes office towers and additional industrial installations in the city even more than it loves the environment. The *Los Angeles Times* editorializes against narrow-minded profiteering at the expense of the environment but has also favored the development of the supersonic transport because of the "jobs" it would lure to Southern California. The papers do tend to support "good planning principles" in some form because such good planning is a long-term force that makes for even more potential future growth. If the roads are not planned wide enough, their narrowness will eventually strangle the increasingly intense uses to which the land will be put. It just makes good sense to plan, and good planning for "sound growth" thus is the key "environmental policy" of the nation's local media and their statesmen allies. Such policies of "good planning" should not be confused with limited growth or conservation: they more typically represent the opposite sort of goal.

Often leaders of public or quasi-public agencies (e.g., universities, utilities) achieve a role similar to that of the newspaper publisher: they become growth "statesmen" rather than advocates for a certain type or intralocal distribution of growth. A university may require an increase in the local urban population pool to sustain its own expansion plans and, in addition, it may be induced to defer to others in the growth machine (bankers, newspapers) upon whom it depends for the favorable financial and public-opinion environment necessary for institutional enhancement.

There are certain persons, ordinarily conceived of as members of the elite, who have much less, if any, interest in local growth. Thus, for example, there are branch executives of corporations headquartered elsewhere who, although perhaps emotionally sympathetic with progrowth outlooks, work for corporations which have no vested interest in the growth of the locality in question. Their indirect interest is perhaps in the existence of the growth ideology rather than growth itself. It is that ideology which in fact helps make them revered people in the area (social worth is often defined in terms of number of people one employs) and which provides the rationale for the kind of local governmental policies most consistent with low business operating costs. Nonetheless, this interest is not nearly as strong as the direct growth interests of developers, mortgage bankers, etc., and thus we find, as Schulze (1961) has observed, that there is a tendency for such executives to play a lesser local role than the

parochial, homegrown businessmen whom they often replace.

Thus, because the city is a growth machine, it draws a special sort of person into its politics. These people—whether acting on their own or on behalf of the constituency which financed their rise to power—tend to be businessmen and, among businessmen, the more parochial sort. Typically, they come to politics not to save or destroy the environment, not to repress or liberate the blacks, not to eliminate civil liberties or enhance them. They may end up doing any or all of these things once they have achieved access to authority, perhaps as an inadvertent consequence of making decisions in other realms. But these types of symbolic positions are derived from the fact of having power—they are typically not the dynamics which bring people to power in the first place. Thus, people often become "involved" in government, especially in the local party structure and fund raising, for reasons of land business and related processes of resource distribution. Some are "statesmen" who think in terms of the growth of the whole community rather than that of a more narrow geographical delimitation. But they are there to wheel and deal to affect resource distribution through local government. As a result of their position, and in part to develop the symbolic issues which will enable them (in lieu of one of their opponents or colleagues) to maintain that position of power, they get interested in such things as welfare cheating, busing, street crime, and the price of meat. This interest in the symbolic issues (see Edelman 1964) is thus substantially an aftereffect of a need for power for other purposes. This is not to say that such people don't "feel strongly" about these matters—they do sometimes. It is also the case that certain moral zealots and "concerned citizens" go into politics to right symbolic wrongs; but the money and other supports which make them viable as politicians is usually nonsymbolic money.

Those who come to the forefront of local government (and those to whom they are directly responsive), therefore, are not statistically representative of the local population as a whole, nor even representative of the social classes which produce them. The issues they introduce into public discourse are not representative either. As noted by Edelman, the distributive issues, the matters which bring people to power, are more or less deliberately dropped from public discourse (see Schattschneider 1960). The issues which are allowed to be discussed and the positions which the politicians take on them derive from the world views of those who come from certain sectors of the business and professional class and the need which they have to whip up public sentiment without allowing distributive issues to become part of public discussion. It follows that any political change which succeeded in replacing the land business as the key determinant of the local political dynamic would simultaneously weaken the power of one of the more reactionary political forces in the society, thereby affecting outcomes with respect to those other symbolic issues which manage to gain so much attention. Thus, should such a change occur, there would likely be more progressive positions taken on civil liberties, and less harassment of welfare recipients, social "deviants," and other defenseless victims.

LIABILITIES OF THE GROWTH MACHINE

Emerging trends are tending to enervate the locality growth machines. First is the increasing suspicion that in many areas, at many historical moments, growth benefits only a small proportion of local residents. Growth almost always brings with it the obvious problems of increased air and water pollution, traffic congestion, and overtaxing of natural amenities. These dysfunctions become increasingly important and visible as increased consumer income fulfills peoples other needs and as the natural cleansing capacities of the environment are progressively overcome with deleterious material. While it is by no means certain that growth and increased density inevitably bring about social pathologies (see Fischer, Baldassare, and Ofshe 1974), growth does make such pathologies more difficult to deal with. For example, the larger the jurisdiction, the more difficult it becomes to achieve the goal of school integration without massive busing schemes. As increasing experience with busing makes clear, small towns can more easily have interracial schools, whether fortuitously through spatial proximity or through managed programs.

In addition, the weight of research evidence is that growth often costs existing residents more

money. Evidently, at various population levels, points of diminishing returns are crossed such that additional increments lead to net revenue losses. A 1970 study for the city of Palo Alto, California, indicated that it was substantially cheaper for that city to acquire at full market value its foothill open space than to allow it to become an "addition" to the tax base (Livingston and Blayney 1971). A study of Santa Barbara, California, demonstrated that additional population growth would require higher property taxes, as well as higher utility costs (Appelbaum et al. 1974). Similar results on the costs of growth have been obtained in studies of Boulder, Colorado (cited in Finkler 1972), and Ann Arbor, Michigan (Ann Arbor City Planning Department 1972).[14] Systematic analyses of government costs as a function of city size and growth have been carried out under a number of methodologies, but the use of the units of analysis most appropriate for comparison (urban areas) yields the finding that the cost is directly related both to size of place and rate of growth, at least for middle-size cities (see Follett 1976; Appelbaum 1976). Especially significant are per capita police costs, which virtually all studies show to be positively related to both city size and rate of growth (see Appelbaum et al. 1974; Appelbaum 1976).

Although damage to the physical environment and costs of utilities and governmental services may rise with size of settlement, "optimal" size is obviously determined by the sorts of values which are to be maximized (see Duncan 1957). It may indeed be necessary to sacrifice clean air to accumulate a population base large enough to support a major opera company. But the essential point remains that growth is certainly less of a financial advantage to the taxpayer than is conventionally depicted, and that most people's values are, according to the survey evidence (Hoch 1972, p. 280; Finkler 1972, pp. 2, 23; Parke and Westoff 1972; Mazie and Rowlings 1973; Appelbaum et al. 1974, pp. 4.2-4.6) more consistent with small places than large. Indeed, it is rather clear that some substantial portion of the migrations to the great metropolitan areas of the last decade has been more in spite of people's values than because of them. In the recent words of Sundquist: "The notion commonly expressed that Americans have 'voted with their feet' in favor of the great cities is, on the basis of every available sampling, so much nonsense.... What is called 'freedom of choice' is, in sum, freedom of employer choice or, more precisely, freedom of choice for that segment of the corporate world that operates mobile enterprises. The real question, then, is whether freedom of corporate choice should be automatically honored by government policy at the expense of freedom of individual choice where those conflict" (1975, p. 258).

Taking all the evidence together, it is certainly a rather conservative statement to make that under many circumstances growth is a liability financially and in quality of life for the majority of local residents. Under such circumstances, local growth is a transfer of quality of life and wealth from the local general public to a certain segment of the local elite. To raise the question of wisdom of growth in regard to any specific locality is hence potentially to threaten such a wealth transfer and the interests of those who profit by it.

THE PROBLEMS OF JOBS

Perhaps the key ideological prop for the growth machine, especially in terms of sustaining support from the working-class majority (Levison 1974), is the claim that growth "makes jobs." This claim is aggressively promulgated by developers, builders, and chambers of commerce; it becomes a part of the statesman talk of editorialists and political officials. Such people do not speak of growth as useful to profits—rather, they speak of it as necessary for making jobs. But local growth does not, of course, make jobs: it distributes jobs. The United States will see next year the construction of a certain number of new factories, office units, and highways—regardless of where they are put. Similarly, a given number of automobiles, missiles, and lampshades will be made, regardless of where they are manufactured. Thus, the number of jobs in this society, whether in the building trades or any other economic sector, will be determined by rates of investment return, federal decisions affecting the money supply, and other factors having very little to do with local decision making. All that a locality can do is to attempt to guarantee that a certain proportion of newly created jobs will be in the locality in question. Aggregate employment is thus unaffected by the outcome of this competition among localities to "make" jobs.

The labor force is essentially a single national pool; workers are mobile and generally capable of taking advantage of employment opportunities emerging at geographically distant points.[15] As jobs develop in a fast-growing area, the unemployed will be attracted from other areas in sufficient numbers not only to fill those developing vacancies but also to form a work-force sector that is continuously unemployed. Thus, just as local growth does not affect aggregate employment, it likely has very little long-term impact upon the local rate of unemployment. Again, the systematic evidence fails to show any advantage to growth: there is no tendency for either larger places or more rapidly growing ones to have lower unemployment rates than other kinds of urban areas. In fact, the tendency is for rapid growth to be associated with higher rates of unemployment (for general documentation, see Follett 1976; Appelbaum 1976; Hadden and Borgatta 1965, p. 108; Samuelson 1942; Sierra Club of San Diego 1973).[16]

This pattern of findings is vividly illustrated through inspection of relevant data on the most extreme cases of urban growth: those SMSAs which experienced the most rapid rates of population increase over the last two intercensus decades. Tables III.4 and III.5 show a comparison of population growth and unemployment rates in the 25 areas which grew fastest during the 1950-60 and 1960-70 periods. In the case of both decade comparisons, half of the urban areas had unemployment rates above the national figure for all SMSAs.

Even the 25 slowest-growing (1960–70) SMSAs failed to experience particularly high rates of unemployment. Table III.6 reveals that although all were places of net migration loss less than half of the SMSAs of this group had unemployment rates above the national mean at the decade's end.

Just as striking is the comparison of growth and unemployment rates for all SMSAs in California during the 1960-66 period—a time of general boom in the state. Table III.7 reveals that among all California metropolitan areas there is no significant relationship (r = –17, z = .569) between 1960-66 growth rates and the 1966 unemployment rate. Table III.7 is also instructive (and consistent with other tables) in revealing that while there is a wide divergence in growth rates across metropolitan

Table III.4 Growth and unemployment rates for 25 fastest-growing SMSAs, 1950-60

(%)

Metropolitan Area	Rate of Growth	Unemployment Rate, 1960
1. Ft. Lauderdale-Hollywood, Florida......................	297.9	4.7
2. Anaheim-Santa Ana-Garden Grove, California....	225.6	4.6
3. Las Vegas, Nevada	163.0	6.7*
4. Midland, Texas..	162.6	4.9
5. Orlando, Florida	124.6	5.1
6. San Jose, California	121.1	7.0*
7. Odessa, Texas..	116.1	5.6*
8. Phoenix, Arizona	100.0	4.7
9. W. Palm Beach, Florida..	98.9	4.8
10. Colorado Springs, Colorado	92.9	6.1*
11. Miami, Florida	88.9	7.3*
12. Tampa-St. Petersburg, Florida	88.8	5.1
13. Tucson, Arizona	88.1	5.9*
14. Albuquerque, New Mexico....................................	80.0	4.5
15. San Bernadino-Riverside-Ontario, California	79.3	6.7*
16. Sacramento, California	74.0	6.1*
17. Albany, Georgia	73.5	4.4
18. Santa Barbara, California	72.0	3.6
19. Amarillo, Texas	71.6	3.3
20. Reno, Nevada..	68.8	6.1*
21. Lawton, Oklahoma..	64 6	5.5*
22. Lake Charles, Louisiana	62.3	7.8*
23. El Paso, Texas..	61.1	6.4*
24. Pensacola, Florida..	54.9	5.3*
25. Lubbock, Texas..	54.7	3.9
Total U.S.	18.5	5.2

Source: U.S. Bureau of the Census 1962, tables 33, 154.

*Unemployment rate above SMSA national mean.

areas, there is no comparable variation in the unemployment rates, all of which cluster within the relatively narrow range of 4.3%–6.57%. Consistent with my previous argument, I take this as evidence that the mobility of labor tends to flatten out cross-SMSA unemployment rates, regardless of widely diverging rates of locality growth. Taken together, the data indicate that local population growth is no solution to the problem of local unemployment.

It remains possible that for some reason certain specific rates of growth may be peculiarly related to lower rates of unemployment and that the measures used in this and cited studies are insensitive to these patterns.

Similarly, growth in certain types of industries may be more likely than growth in others to stimulate employment without attracting migrants. It may also be possible that certain population groups, by reason of cultural milieu, are less responsive to mobility options than others and thus provide bases for exceptions to the general argument I am advancing. The present analysis does not preclude such future findings but does assert, minimally, that the argument that growth makes jobs is contradicted by the weight of evidence that is available.[17]

I conclude that for the average worker in a fast-growing region job security has much the same sta-

Table III.5 Growth and unemployment rates of the 25 fastest-growing SMSAs, 1960-70

(%)

Metropolitan Area	Rate of Growth	Unemployment Rate, 1960
1. Las Vegas, Nevada	115.2	5.2*
2. Anaheim-Santa Ana-Garden Grove, California	101.8	5.4*
3. Oxuard-Ventura, California	89.0	5.9*
4. Ft. Lauderdale-Hollywood, Florida	85.7	3.4
5. San Jose, California	65.8	5.8*
6. Colorado Springs, Colorado	64.2	5.5*
7. Santa Barbara, California	56.4	6.4*
8. W. Palm Beach, Florida	52.9	3.0
9. Nashua, New Hampshire	47.8	2.8
10. Huntsville, Alabama	46.6	4.4
11. Columbia, Missouri	45.8	2.4
12. Phoenix, Arizona	45.8	3.9
13. Danbury, Connecticut	44.3	4.2
14. Fayetteville, Arkansas	42.9	5.2*
15. Reno, Nevada	42.9	6.2*
16. San Bernadino-Riverside-Ontario, California	41.2	5.9*
17. Houston, Texas	40.0	3.0
18. Austin, Texas	39.3	3.1
19. Dallas, Texas	39.0	3.0
20. Santa Rosa, California	39.0	7.3*
21. Tallahassee, Florida	38.8	3.0
22. Washington, D.C.	37.8	2.7
23. Atlanta, Georgia	36.7	3.0
24. Ann Arbor, Michigan	35.8	5.0*
25. Miami, Florida	35.6	3.7
Total U.S.	16.6	4.3

Source: U.S. Bureau of the Census 1972, table 3, SMSAs.

*Unemployment rate above the SMSA national mean.

tus as for a worker in a slower-growing region: there is a surplus of workers over jobs, generating continuous anxiety over unemployment[18] and the effective depressant on wages which any lumpen-proletariat of unemployed and marginally employed tends to exact (see, e.g., Bonacich 1975). Indigenous workers likely receive little benefit from the growth machine in terms of jobs; their "native" status gives them little edge over the "foreign" migrants seeking the additional jobs which may develop. Instead, they are interchangeable parts of the labor pool, and the degree of their job insecurity is expressed in the local unemployment rate, just as is the case for the nonnative worker.

Ironically, it is probably this very anxiety which often leads workers, or at least their union spokespeople, to support enthusiastically employers' preferred policies of growth. It is the case that an actual decline in local job opportunities, or economic growth not in proportion to natural increase, might induce the hardship of migration. But this price is not the same as, and is less severe than, the price of simple unemployment. It could also rather easily be compensated through a relocation subsidy for mobile workers, as is now commonly provided for high-salaried executives by private corporations and in a limited way generally by the federal tax deduction for job-related moving expenses.

Table III.6 Growth, unemployment, and net migration rates for 25 slowest-growing SMSAs, 1960-70

		(%)		
	SMSA	Rate of Growth	Net Migration	Unemployment, 1970
1.	Abilene, Texas	−5.3	−19.7	3.6
2.	Altoona, Pennsylvania	1.4	−6.6	3.5
3.	Amarillo, Texas	−3.4	−19.5	3.4
4.	Brownsville-Harlingen-San Benito, Texas	−7.1	−32.1	6.6*
5.	Charleston, West Virginia	−9.3	−19.0	4.1
6.	Duluth-Superior, Minnesota-Wisconsin	−4.1	−10.9	7.3*
7.	Gadsden, Alabama	−2.9	−12.4	7.3*
8.	Huntington-Ashland, West Virginia-Kentucky-Ohio	−0.4	−9.7	5.1*
9.	Jersey City, New Jersey	−0.5	−7.5	4.7*
10.	Johnstown, Pennsylvania	−6.4	−11.8	4.9*
11.	McAllen-Pharr-Edinburgh, Texas	−0.3	−25.4	5.9*
12.	Midland, Texas	3.4	−19.1	3.5
13.	Montgomery, Alabama	0.9	−11.1	3.8
14.	Odessa, Texas	0.9	−16.7	4.3
15.	Pittsburgh, Pennsylvania	−0.2	−7.0	4.3
16.	Pueblo, Colorado	−0.4	−12.3	5.9*
17.	St. Joseph, Missouri	−4.0	−9.2	3.9
18.	Savannah, Georgia	−0.3	−13.3	4.3
19.	Scranton, Pennsylvania	0.2	1.8	5.2*
20.	Sioux City, Iowa	3.2	13.5	4.4*
21.	Steubenville-Weirton, Ohio-West Virginia	1.3	8.9	3.7
22.	Utica-Rome, New York	-1.7	−11.2	5.7*
23.	Wheeling, West Virginia-Ohio	-4.0	−8.3	4.2
24.	Wichita Falls, Texas	−2.6	−15.1	4.0
25.	Wilkes-Barre-Hazleton, Pennsylvania	−1.3	−3.5	4.0
	Total U.S.	16.6	...	4.3

Source: U.S. Bureau of the Census 1972, table 3, SMSAs.

*Unemployment rate above SMSA national mean.

Workers' anxiety and its ideological consequences emerge from the larger fact that the United States is a society of constant substantial joblessness, with unemployment rates conservatively estimated by the Department of Commerce at 4%–8% of that portion of the work force defined as ordinarily active. There is thus a game of musical chairs being played at all times, with workers circulating around the country, hoping to land in an empty chair at the moment the music stops. Increasing the stock of jobs in any one place neither causes the music to stop more frequently nor increases the number of chairs relative to the number of players. The only way effectively to ameliorate this circumstance is to create a full-employment economy, a comprehensive system of drastically increased unemployment insurance, or some other device which breaks the connection between a person's having a livelihood and the remote decisions of corporate executives. Without such a development, the fear of unemployment acts to make workers politically passive (if not downright supportive) with respect to land-use policies, taxation programs, antipollution nonenforcement schemes which, in effect, represent income transfers from the general public to vari-

Table III.7 Growth and unemployment rates for all California SMSAs, 1960-66

SMSA	(%) Rate of Growth, 1960-66	Average Annual Change	Unemployment Rate, 1966
Anaheim-Santa Ana-Garden Grove	65.0	8.3	4.3
Bakersfield	11.1	1.7	5.2
Fresno	12.3	1.9	6.5
Los Angeles-Long Beach	11.9	1.9	4.5
Modesto	...	...	...
Oxnard-Ventura	68.8	8.7	6.0
Sacramento	20.0	3.0	5.2
Salinas-Monterey	15.9	2.4	6.1
San Bernadino-Riverside	27.9	4.0	6.2
San Diego	14.0	2.1	5.1
San Francisco-Oakland	11.1	1.7	4.4
San Jose	44.8	6.1	4.8
Santa Barbara	48.7	6.6	4.5
Santa Rosa	...	...	...
Stockton	12.5	1.9	6.3
Vallejo-Napa	20.6	3.0	4.4
California mean	27.47	3.80	5.25

Sources: For average annual change and rate of growth, U.S. Bureau of the Census 1969, table 2; for unemployment rate, 1966, State of California 1970, table C-10.

ous sectors of the elite (see Whitt 1975). Thus, for many reasons, workers and their leaders should organize their political might more consistently not as part of the growth coalitions of the localities in which they are situated, but rather as part of national movements which aim to provide full employment, income security, and programs for taxation, land use, and the environment which benefit the vast majority of the population. They tend not to be doing this at present.

THE PROBLEM OF NATURAL INCREASE

Localities grow in population not simply as a function of migration but also because of the fecundity of the existing population. Some means are obviously needed to provide jobs and housing to accommodate such growth—either in the immediate area or at some distant location. There are ways of handling this without compounding the environmental and budgetary problems of existing settlements. First, there are some localities which are, by many criteria, not overpopulated. Their atmos-

pheres are clean, water supplies plentiful, and traffic congestion nonexistent. In fact, in certain places increased increments of population may spread the costs of existing road and sewer systems over a larger number of citizens or bring an increase in quality of public education by making rudimentary specialization possible. In the state of California, for example, the great bulk of the population lives on a narrow coastal belt in the southern two-thirds of the state. Thus the northern third of the state consists of a large unpopulated region rich in natural resources, including electric power and potable water. The option chosen in California, as evidenced by the state aqueduct, was to move the water from the uncrowded north to the dense, semiarid south, thus lowering the environmental qualities of both regions, and at a substantial long-term cost to the public budget. The opposite course of action was clearly an option.

The point is that there are relatively underpopulated areas in this country which do not have "natural" problems of inaccessibility, ugliness, or lack of population-support resources. Indeed, the nation's most severely depopulated areas, the towns of Appalachia, are in locales of sufficient resources and are widely regarded as aesthetically appealing; population out-migration likely decreased the aesthetic resources of both the migrants to and residents of Chicago and Detroit, while resulting in the desertion of a housing stock and utility infrastructure designed to serve a larger population. Following from my more general perspective, I see lack of population in a given area as resulting from the political economic decisions made to populate other areas instead. If the process were rendered more rational, the same investments in roads, airports, defense plants, etc., could be made to effect a very different land-use outcome. Indeed, utilization of such deliberate planning strategies is the practice in some other societies and shows some evidence of success (see Sundquist 1975); perhaps it could be made to work in the United States as well.

As a long-term problem, natural increase may well be phased out. American birth rates have been steadily decreasing for the last several years, and we are on the verge of a rate providing for zero population growth. If a stable population actually is achieved, a continuation of the present interlocal competitive system will result in the proliferation of ghost towns and unused capital stocks as the price paid for the growth of the successful competing units. This will be an even more clearly preposterous situation than the current one, which is given to produce ghost towns only on occasion.

THE EMERGING COUNTERCOALITION

Although growth has been the dominant ideology in most localities in the United States, there has always been a subversive thread of resistance. Treated as romantic, or as somehow irrational (see White and White 1962), this minority long was ignored, even in the face of accumulating journalistic portrayals of the evils of bigness. But certainly it was an easy observation to make that increased size was related to high levels of pollution, traffic congestion, and other disadvantages. Similarly, it was easy enough to observe that tax rates in large places were not generally less than those in small places; although it received little attention, evidence that per capita government

costs rise with population size was provided a generation ago (see Hawley 1951). But few took note, though the very rich, somehow sensing these facts to be the case, managed to reserve for themselves small, exclusive meccas of low density by tightly imposing population ceilings (e.g., Beverly Hills, Sands Point, West Palm Beach, Lake Forest).

In recent years, however, the base of the antigrowth movement has become much broader and in some localities has reached sufficient strength to achieve at least toeholds of political power. The most prominent cases seem to be certain university cities (Palo Alto, Santa Barbara, Boulder, Ann Arbor), all of which have sponsored impact studies documenting the costs of additional growth. Other localities which have imposed growth controls tend also to be places of high amenity value (e.g., Ramapo, N.Y.; Petaluma, Calif.; Boca Raton, Fla.). The antigrowth sentiment has become an important part of the politics of a few large cities (e.g., San Diego) and has been the basis of important political careers at the state level (including the governorship) in Oregon, Colorado, and Vermont. Given the objective importance of the issue and the evidence on the general costs of growth, there is nothing to prevent antigrowth coalitions from similarly gaining power elsewhere—including those areas of the country which are generally considered to possess lower levels of amenity. Nor is there any reason, based on the facts of the matter, for these coalitions not to further broaden their base to include the great majority of the working class in the localities in which they appear.

But, like all political movements which attempt to rely upon volunteer labor to supplant political powers institutionalized through a system of vested economic interest, antigrowth movements are probably more likely to succeed in those places where volunteer reform movements have a realistic constituency—a leisured and sophisticated middle class with a tradition of broad-based activism, free from an entrenched machine. At least, this appears to be an accurate profile of those places in which the antigrowth coalitions have already matured.

Systematic studies of the social make up of the antigrowth activists are only now in progress (e.g., Fitts 1976), but it seems that the emerging counter-coalition is rooted in the recent environmental movements and relies on a mixture of young activists (some are veterans of the peace and civil rights movements), middle-class professionals, and workers, all of whom see their own tax rates as well as life-styles in conflict with growth. Important in leadership roles are government employees and those who work for organizations not dependent on local expansion for profit, either directly or indirectly. In the Santa Barbara antigrowth movements, for example, much support is provided by professionals from research and electronics firms, as well as branch managers of small "high-technology" corporations. Cosmopolitan in outlook and pecuniary interest, they use the local community only as a setting for life and work, rather than as an exploitable resource. Related to this constituency are certain very wealthy people (particularly those whose wealth derives from the exploitation of nonlocal environments) who continue a tradition (with some modifications) of aristocratic conservation.[19]

Should it occur, the changes which the death of the growth machine will bring seem clear enough with respect to land-use policy. Local governments will establish holding capacities for their regions and then legislate, directly or indirectly, to limit population to those levels. The direction of any future development will tend to be planned to minimize negative environmental impacts. The so-called natural process (see Burgess 1925; Hoyt 1939) of land development which has given American cities their present shape will end as the political and economic foundations of such processes are undermined. Perhaps most important, industrial and business land users and their representatives will lose, at least to some extent, the effectiveness of their threat to locate elsewhere should public policies endanger the profitability they desire. As the growth machine is destroyed in many places, increasingly it will be the business interests who will be forced to make do with local policies, rather than the local populations having to bow to business wishes. New options for taxation, creative landuse programs, and new forms of urban services may thus emerge as city government comes to resemble an agency which asks what it can do for its people rather than what it can do to attract more people. More specifically, a given industrial project will perhaps be evaluated in terms of its social utility—the usefulness of the product manufactured—either to the locality or to the society at large. Production, merely for the sake of local expansion, will be less likely to occur. Hence, there will be some pressure to increase the use value of the country's production apparatus and for external costs of production to be borne internally.

When growth ceases to be an issue, some of the investments made in the political system to influence and enhance growth will no longer make sense, thus changing the basis upon which people get involved in government. We can expect that the local business elites—led by land developers and other growth-coalition forces—will tend to withdraw from local politics. This vacuum may then be filled by a more representative and, likely, less reactionary activist constituency. It is noteworthy that where antigrowth forces have established beachheads of power, their programs and policies have tended to be more progressive than their predecessors'—on all issues, not just on growth. In Colorado, for example, the environmentalist who led the successful fight against the Winter Olympics also successfully sponsored abortion reform and other important progressive causes. The environmentally based Santa Barbara "Citizens Coalition" (with city government majority control) represents a fusion of the city's traditional left and counterculture with other environmental activists. The result of the no-growth influence in localities may thus be a tendency for an increasing progressiveness in local politics. To whatever degree local politics is the bedrock upon which the national political structure rests (and there is much debate here), there may follow reforms at the national level as well. Perhaps it will then become possible to utilize national institutions to effect other policies which both solidify the death of the growth machine at the local level and create national priorities consistent with the new opportunities for urban civic life. These are speculations based upon the questionable thesis that a reform-oriented, issue-based citizens' politics can be sustained over a long period. The historical record is not consistent with this thesis; it is only emerging political trends in the most affected localities and the general irrationality of the present urban system that suggest the alternative possibility is an authentic future.

NOTES

1. I have had the benefit of critical comments and assistance from Richard Appelbaum, Richard Baisden, Norman Bowers, Norton Long, Howard Newby, Anthony Shih, Tony Pepitone, Gerald Suttles, Gaye Tuchman, and Al Wyner.

2. This association of related phenomena is the common conceptualization which students of the economic development of cities ordinarily utilize in their analyses (see e.g., Alonso 1964, pp. 79-81; Leven 1964, pp. 140-44; Brown 1974, pp. 48-51; and Durr 1971, pp. 174-80). As Sunquist remarks in the context of his study of population policies in Western Europe, "The key to population distribution is, of course, job availability. A few persons—retired, notably, and some independent professionals such as artists, writers and inventors—may be free to live in any locality they choose but, for the rest, people are compelled to distribute themselves in whatever pattern is dictated by the distribution of employment opportunities. Some investors may locate their investment in areas of surplus labour voluntarily, and so check the migration flow, and others may be induced by government assistance to do so. But if neither of these happen—if the jobs do not go where the workers are—the workers must go to the jobs, if they are not to accept welfare as a way of life. When population distribution is an end, then, job distribution is inevitably the means" (1975, p. 13).

3. For accounts of how "boosterism" worked in this manner, see Wade (1969) and Harris (1976).

4. Agger et al. remark, on the basis of their comparative study of four U.S. cities: "[Members of the local elites] value highly harmony and unity—'pulling together.' They regard local community affairs as essentially nonpolitical, and tend to associate controversy with 'politics.' An additional factor reinforcing the value of harmony in many communities...is the nationwide competition among communities for new industries. Conflict is thought to create a highly unfavourable image to outsiders, an image that might well repel any prospective industry" (1964, p. 649).

5. See, e.g., the May 19, 1974, issue of *Forbes*, which had the following ad placed by the State of Pennsylvania: "Q: [banner headline] What state could possibly cut taxes at a time like this? A: Pennsylvania [same large type]. Pennsylvania

intends to keep showing businessmen that it means business. Pennsylvania. Where business has a lot growing for it. ..." The state of Maryland ran this ad in the same issue: "Maryland Finances the Training.... In short, we can finance practically everything you need to establish a manufacturing plant. ..."

6. The city of Los Angeles maintains an office, headed by a former key business executive, with this "liaison" as its specific task (see "L.A.'s Business Envoy Speaks Softly and Sits at a Big Desk," *Los Angeles Times* [August 26, 1974]).

7. The literature on community power is vast and controversial but has been summarized by Walton: he indicates, on the basis of 39 studies of 61 communities, that "the proportion of businessmen found in the leadership group is high irrespective of the type of power structure found" (1970, p. 446). It is my argument, of course, that this high level of participation does indeed indicate the exercise of power on behalf of at least a portion of the elite. My analysis does not assume that this portion of the elite is necessarily always united with others of high status on the concrete issues of local land use and the uses of local government.

8. Descriptions of some tactics typically employed in land-use politics are contained in McConnell (1966), Tolchin and Tolchin (1971), and Makielski (1966), but a sophisticated relevant body of literature does not yet exist.

9. Thus the stance taken by civic business groups toward growth and land-use matters affecting growth is consistently positive, although the intensity of commitment to that goal varies. In his study of New York City zoning, Makielski indicates that "the general business groups...approached zoning from an economic viewpoint , although this often led them to share the Reformer's ideology. Their economic interest in the city gave them a stake in a 'healthy,' 'growing community' where tax rates were not prohibitive, where city government was 'efficient,' and where some of the problems of the urban environment—a constricting labour force, congestion, and lack of space—were being attacked" (1966, p. 141). A similar dynamic has been observed in a medium-size Mexican city: "Despite many other differences, basic agreement on the primacy of stability and growth provides a basis for a dialogue

between government and business" (Fagen and Tuohy 1972, p. 56).

10. Bruce Pringle suggested the latter phrase to me.

11. Papers can expand into other industries, such as book publishing and wood harvesting. The point is that, compared with most other industries, they cannot easily replicate themselves across geographical boundaries through chains, branch plants, and franchises.

12. In some cities (e.g., Chicago) it is the political machine that performs this function and thus can "get things done." Political scientists (e.g., Edward Banfield) often identify success in performing this function as evidence of effective local government.

13. In his study of the history of zoning in New York City, Makielski remarks: "While the newspapers in the city are large landholders, the role of the press was not quite like that of any of the other nongovernmental actors. The press was in part one of the referees of the rules of the game, especially the informal rules—calling attention to what it considered violations" (1966, p. 189).

14. A useful bibliography of growth evaluation studies is Agelasto and Perry (undated). A study with findings contrary to those reported here (Gruen an Gruen Associates 1972) limits cost evaluation to only three municipal services and was carried out in a city which had already made major capital expenditures that provided it with huge unused capacities in water, schools, and sewage.

15. I am not arguing that the labor force is perfectly mobile, as indeed there is strong evidence that mobility is limited by imperfect information, skill limitations, and cultural and family ties. The argument is rather that the essential mobility of the labor force is sufficiently pronounced to make programs of local job creation largely irrelevant to long-term rates of unemployment.

16. This lack of relationship between local population change and unemployment has led others to conclusions similar to my own: "Economists unanimously have agreed that the only jurisdiction that should be concerned with the effects of its policies on the level of employment is the Federal government. Small jurisdictions do not have the power to effect significant changes in the level of unemployment" (Levy and Arnold 1972, p. 95).

17. It is also true that this evidence is based on federal data, accumulated through the work of socially and geographically disparate persons who had purposes at hand different from mine. This important reservation can only be dealt with by noting that the findings were consistent with the author's theoretical expectations, rather than antecedents of them. At a minimum, the results throw the burden of proof on those who would argue the opposite hypothesis.

18. For an insightful treatment of joblessness with respect to the majority of the American work force, see Levison (1974).

19. Descriptions of the social makeup of American environmentalists (who coincide as a group only roughly with the no-growth activists) and of their increasing militancy are contained in Nash (1967), Bartell (1974), Dunlap and Gale (1972), Faich and Gale (1971). For a journalistic survey of no-growth activities, see Robert Cahn, "Mr. Developer, Someone Is Watching You" (*Christian Science Monitor* [May 21, 1973], p. 9). A more comprehensive description is contained in Reilly (1973).

REFERENCES

Adrian, Charles R., and O. P. Williams. 1963. *Four Cities: A Study in Comparative Policy Making*. Philadelphia: University of Pennsylvania Press.

Agelasto, Michael A., II, and Patricia R. Perry. Undated. "The No Growth Controversy." Exchange Bibliography no. 519. Mimeographed. Box 229, Monticello, Ill.: Council of Planning Libraries.

Agger, Robert, Daniel Goldrich, and Bert E. Swanson. 1964. *The Rulers and the Ruled: Political Power and Impotence in American Communities*. New York: Wiley.

Alonso, William. 1964. "Location Theory," pp. 79-81 in *Regional Development and Planning*, edited by John Friedman and William Alonso. Cambridge, Mass.: M.I.T. Press.

Ann Arbor City Planning Department. 1972. *The Ann Arbor Growth Study*. Ann Arbor, Mich.: City Planning Department.

Appelbaum, Richard. 1976. "City Size and Urban Life: A Preliminary Inquiry into Some Consequences of Growth in American Cities."

Urban Affairs Quarterly.

Appelbaum, Richard, Jennifer Bigelow, Henry Kramer, Harvey Molotch, and Paul Relis. 1974. *Santa Barbara: The Impacts of Growth: A Report of the Santa Barbara Planning Task Force to the City of Santa Barbara.* Santa Barbara, Calif.: Office of the City Clerk. Forthcoming in abridged form as *The Effects of Urban Growth: A Population Impact Analysis*: New York: Praeger.

Banfield, Edward. 1961. *Political Influence.* New York: Macmillan.

Bartell, Ted. 1974. "Compositional Change and Attitude Change among Sierra Club Members." Mimeographed. Los Angeles: UCLA Survey Research Center.

Bonacich, Edna. 1975. "Advanced Capitalism and Black/White Race Relations in the U.S." Mimeographed. Riverside: Department of Sociology, University of California.

Bouma, Donald. 1962. "Analysis of the Social Power Position of a Real Estate Board." *Social Problems* 10 (Fall): 121-32.

Brown, Douglas. 1974. *Introduction to Urban Economics.* New York: Academic Press.

Burgess, Ernest W. 1925. *The Growth of the City: An Introduction to a Research Project.* Chicago: University of Chicago Press.

Davis, Kingsley. 1965. "The Urbanization of the Human Population." *Scientific American* 212 (September): 41-53.

Duncan, Otis Dudley. 1957. "Optimum Size of Cities," pp. 759-72 in *Cities and Societies*, edited by Paul Hatt and Albert Reiss, Jr. New York: Free Press.

Dunlap, Riley E., and Richard P. Gale. 1972. "Politics and Ecology: A Political Profile of Student Eco-Activists." *Youth and Society 3* (June): 379-97.

Durr, Fred. 1971. *The Urban Economy.* Scranton, Pa.: Intext.

Edelman, Murray. 1964. *The Symbolic Uses of Politics.* Urbana: University of Illinois Press.

Fagen, Richard R., and William S. Tuchy. 1972. *Politics and Privilege in a Mexican City.* Stanford, Calif.: Stanford University Press.

Faich, Ronald G., and Richard Gale. 1971. "Environmental Movement: From Recreation to Politics." *Pacific Sociological Review* 14 (July): 27-87.

Finkler, Earl. 1972. "No-Growth as a Planning Alternative." *Planning Advisory Report No. 283.* Chicago: American Society of Planning Officials.

Fischer, Claud, Mark Baldassare, and Richard J. Ofshe. 1974. "Crowding Studies and Urban Life: A Critical Review." Working Paper no. 242, Institute of Urban and Regional Development, University of California, Berkeley.

Fitts, Amelia. 1976. "No-Growth as a Political Issue." Ph.D. dissertation, University of California, Los Angeles.

Follett, Ross. 1976. "Social Consequences of Urban Size and Growth: An Analysis of Middle-Size U.S. Urban Areas." Ph.D. dissertation, Department of Sociology, University of California, Santa Barbara.

Gruen and Gruen Associates. 1972. *Impacts of Growth: An Analytical Framework and Fiscal Examples.* Berkeley: California Better Housing Foundation.

Hadden, Jeffrey K., and Edgar F. Borgatta. 1965. *American Cities: Their Social Characteristics.* Chicago: Rand-McNally.

Harris, Carl V. 1976. *Political Power in Birmingham, 1871-1921.* Memphis: University of Tennessee Press.

Hawley, Amos. 1951. "Metropolitan Population and Municipal Government Expenditures in Central Cities." *Journal of Social Issues 7* (January): 100–108.

Hoch, Irving. 1972. "Urban Scale and Environmental Quality," pp. 231–84 in *Population, Resources and the Environment.* U.S. Commission on Population Growth and the American Future Research Reports, edited by Ronald Ridker, vol. 3. Washington, D.C.: Government Printing Office.

Hoyt, Homer. 1939. *The Structure and Growth of Residential Neighborhoods in American Cities.* Washington, D.C.: Federal Housing Administration.

Lasswell, Harold. 1936. *Politics: Who Gets What, When, How.* New York: McGraw–Hill.

Leven, Charles. 1964. "Regional and Interregional Accounts in Perspective." *Papers, Regional Science Association* 13: 140-44.

Levison, Andrew. 1974. *The Working Class Majority.* New York: Coward, McCann & Geoghgan.

Levy, Steven, and Robert K. Arnold. 1972. "An

Evaluation of Four Growth Alternatives in the City of Milpitas, 1972-1977." Technical Memorandum Report. Palo Alto, Calif.: Institute of Regional and Urban Studies.

Livingston, Laurence, and John A. Blayney. 1971. "Foothill Environmental Design Study: Open Space vs. Development." Final Report to the City of Palo Alto. San Francisco: Livingston & Blayney.

McConnell, Grant. 1966. *Private Power and American Democracy*. New York: Knopf.

McKenzie, R. D. 1922. "The Neighborhood: A Study of Local Life in the City of Columbus, Ohio—*Conclusion*." *American Journal of Sociology* 27 (May): 780-99.

Makielski, S. J., Jr. 1966. *The Politics of Zoning: The New York Experience*. New York: Columbia University Press.

Mazie, Sara Mills, and Steve Rowlings. 1973. "Public Attitude toward Population Distribution Issues," pp. 603-15 in *Population Distribution and Policy*, edited by Sara Mazie. Washington, D.C.: Commission on Population Growth and the American Future.

Molotch, Harvey L. 1967. "Toward a More Human Ecology." *Land Economics* 43 (August): 336-41.

———. 1973. *Managed Integration: Dilemmas of Doing Good in the City*. Berkeley: University of California Press.

Mumford, Lewis. 1961. *The City in History*. New York: Harcourt Brace Jovanovich.

Nash, Roderick. 1967. *Wilderness and the American Mind*. New Haven, Conn.: Yale University Press.

Parke, Robert, Jr., and Charles Westoff, eds. 1972. "Aspects of Population Growth Policy." Report of the U.S. Commission on Population Growth and the American Future. Vol. 6. Washington, D.C.: Commission on Population Growth and the American Future.

Piven, Francis Fox, and Richard Cloward. 1972. *Regulating the Poor*. New York: Random House.

Reilly, William K., ed. 1973. *The Use of Land: A Citizens' Policy Guide to Urban Growth*. New York: Crowell.

Rubin, Lillian. 1972. *Busing and Backlash*. Berkeley: University of California Press.

Samuelson, Paul. 1942. "The Business Cycle and Urban Development," pp. 6-17 in *The Problem of the Cities and Towns*, edited by Guy Greer. Cambridge, Mass.: Harvard University Press.

Schattschneider, E. E. 1960. *The Semisovereign People*. New York: Holt, Rinehart & Winston.

Schulze, Robert O. 1961. "The Bifurcation of Power in a Satellite City," pp. 19-80 in *Community Political Systems*, edited by Morris Janowitz. New York: Macmillan.

Sierra Club of San Diego. 1973. "Economy, Ecology, and Rapid Population Growth." Mimeographed. San Diego: Sierra Club.

Spaulding, Charles. 1951. "Occupational Affiliations of Councilmen in Small Cities." *Sociology and Social Research* 35 (3): 194-200.

State of California. 1970. *California Statistical Abstract, 1970*. Sacramento: State of California.

Sundquist, James. 1975. *Dispersing Population: What America Can Learn from Europe*. Washington, D.C.: Brookings.

Suttles, Gerald. 1972. *The Social Construction of Communities*. Chicago: University of Chicago Press.

Tolchin, Martin, and Susan Tolchin. 1971. *To the Victor*. New York: Random House.

U.S. Bureau of the Census. 1962. *Census of Population*. Vol. 1, pt. 1. Washington, D.C.: Government Printing Office.

———. 1969. *Current Population Reports, Population Estimates and Projections*. Series P-25, no. 427 (July 31). Washington, D.C.: Government Printing Office.

———. 1972. *County and City Data Book*. Washington, D.C.: Government Printing Office.

Wade, Richard. 1969. *The Urban Frontier: The Rise of Western Cities*. Cambridge, Mass.: Harvard University Press.

Walton, John. 1970. "A Systematic Survey of Community Power Research," pp. 443-64 in *The Structure of Community Power*, edited by Michael Aiken and Paul Mott. New York: Random House.

White, Morton, and Lucie White. 1962. *The Intellectual versus the City*. Cambridge, Mass.: Harvard and M.I.T. Press.

Whitt, J. Allen. 1975. "Means of Movement: The Politics of Modern Transportation Systems." Ph.D. dissertation, Department of Sociology, University of California, Santa Barbara.

Wirth, Louis. 1938. "Urbanism as a Way of Life." *American Journal of Sociology* 44 (July): 1-14.

Wyner, Allen. 1967. "Governor—Salesman." *National Civic Review* 61 (February): 81-86.

Entrepreneurial Cities and Maverick Developers

Bernard J. Frieden

Lynne B. Sagalyn

Freiden and Sagalyn note that in the 1970s a city's favorite solution to solving its problems was to build a mall. Although in the complete chapter the authors focus on four case studies of varying political and social conditions, this selection contains only the most prominent example of a downtown retail success story, Boston's Faneuil Hall Marketplace. In developing the marketplace, Boston's leadership wanted to find a developer who could create a feasible retail project while preserving the architectural merit and historic character of the market buildings. James Rouse more than fit the bill, with his nerve and skill to "fit a modern retail operation inside the walls of 150-year-old warehouses on a crowded site in the heart of the city." Rouse was an optimist who believed that "the development business primarily consists of finding a way to overcome crises." This selection offers valuable insights not only into a complicated, pioneering downtown redevelopment project, but also about one of the country's most innovative and courageous developers.

While Pasadena struggled for ten years to complete its mall, more than 50 other cities decided to start their own retail ventures. Although Pasadena showed that massive subsidies would be needed to wrench these projects loose from a retail industry still attached to the suburbs, downtown coalitions ranked shopping malls high on their agenda. Every city had its own reasons, as public officials and civic leaders kept groping to figure out what made sense for downtown and what the public would accept. But no matter whether a city's immediate problem was to save a historic building, remove an eyesore, or demonstrate the mayor's competence, the favorite solution of the 1970s was to build a mall.

A LANDMARK IN BOSTON

Boston's decision to build Faneuil Hall Marketplace was exactly in tune with the mood of the times, yet it was more the result of close calls and lucky breaks than of a calculated choice in city hall. The city came close to pulling down the historic buildings in the 1950s and later nearly took the project away from the architect and developer who came up with the idea of turning them into a shopping arcade.

The once-elegant market structures began to outlive their usefulness by the early 1900s, when delivery trucks jammed the narrow, congested streets and merchants began to leave. By the 1950s, the market was dingy, deteriorating, and partly deserted. In 1956, the City Planning Board marked it for clearance to make way for office buildings.

Three years later, the Cambridge consulting firm of Adams, Howard, and Greeley drew up the first plan that advised the city to keep the three buildings as a marketplace. Kevin Lynch, an MIT professor and urban design specialist responsible for much of this plan, soon learned what some of the city's political leaders thought of historic preservation. After he finished briefing a State House committee on the new recommendations, one of the legislators took him aside to check whether he had heard his name correctly and, if so, whether he was Irish. When Lynch assured him that both points were correct, the representative whispered to him, "Tell me, why do you want to save these old Yankee buildings?"

Saving decayed buildings did not become established as city policy until the 1960s, when redevelopment director Edward Logue consulted with architectural historians and decided they were worth saving. He set the process in motion by persuading the chamber of commerce to undertake a renewal study of the waterfront area and then used the study to secure federal funds for a more detailed plan. Both the chamber's study and Logue's plan were explicit in proposing to renovate the market buildings, and city council approval of the downtown waterfront renewal plan made it official in 1964.

The renewal plan justified saving the market area as "one of the finest urban spaces in America" but was less than clear about what to do with it. Shopping was only one of several possibilities. The plan recommended keeping the few restaurants and retail food outlets that were there and improving the market by adding offices, other businesses, and apartments.

While the redevelopment authority was busy moving the food wholesalers to other quarters, Ben Thompson turned up one Sunday to photograph the interesting old buildings and began to think of how he might renovate them. Intrigued by the prospect, he pored over early photos and drawings of the Faneuil Hall markets and found in them a sense of action and excitement that he wanted to bring back to modern Boston. For ideas, he thought about Tivoli in Copenhagen, Ghirardelli Square in San Francisco, and the Farmers' Market in Los Angeles. He also started talking to Logue.

Thompson was a businessman as well as an architect. He had learned about merchandising as the founder and head of Design Research, a retail chain specializing in contemporary home furnishings. As owner of a successful restaurant in Harvard Square, he also knew the food business firsthand. Thompson saw a way to bring the traditional market back to life as part of a merchandising strategy with food as the theme.

By the time the redevelopment authority was ready to invite competitive proposals from developers, Thompson had found a Philadelphia sponsor who wanted to build the sort of retail center he had in mind. In late 1970, the firm of Van Arkel and Moss, with Thompson as architect, submitted a proposal emphasizing retailing. They planned to use the central Quincy Market building as a food arcade and to renovate the two adjoining buildings for retail stores on the ground floor with offices and either a hotel or apartments above. Two other developers who made proposals intended to have fewer stores and more offices, one even featuring a corporate headquarters in remodeled space behind the old facade.

The redevelopment authority awarded the project to Van Arkel and Moss and set up a series of tight deadlines to get the project financed, leased, and into construction. When Van Arkel and Moss was unable to meet any of these deadlines, the authority took back the project. Thompson promptly started a national search for a more capable developer but found little interest among the people he knew. The redevelopment authority, meanwhile, decided to protect the buildings by starting exterior restoration under a federal grant for historic preservation.

With more time to find a new client, Thompson wrote to James Rouse at the suggestion of a mutual friend. This time he had gone to the right address: Rouse not only wanted to do a downtown retail center but had a special interest in food markets. He had been experimenting with food courts in several of his suburban malls and was pleased with the results at Sherway Gardens near Toronto and Paramus Park in New Jersey. Rouse took one look at the Faneuil Hall site and said, "Damn, if this kind of thing can succeed in Toronto and Paramus, here right in the heart of downtown Boston it ought to be possible to produce a very special kind of place."

Rouse and Thompson agreed at once to work together and told Mayor Kevin White and redevelopment director Robert Kenney in the spring of 1972 that they wanted to develop the market complex. White and Kenney were more than encouraging. "It was like we were the knight on a white horse; we were just embraced that we were coming in to save this project," according to Rouse. While he and Thompson went about refining Thompson's earlier plans, they started negotiating the terms of an agreement with the city.

Meanwhile, one of the previous competitors for the project, Roger Webb, submitted a second proposal to Kenney. His plan was to renovate only the two warehouse buildings on either side of Quincy Market, leaving the city to improve and manage the central building. Webb and his partners were Bostonians prominent in architectural preservation, and he had recently renovated the old city hall. Their proposal was not for a retail center but for equal amounts of office space and stores in the north and south buildings.

In December, Kenney took Rouse and Thompson totally by surprise when he told them he would recommend giving the project to Roger Webb at the meeting of the redevelopment authority two days later. Rouse called his friends in Boston at once to ask them to talk to the mayor and anyone else who could help. When the authority members put off their decision, supporters of the Rouse-Thompson plan gained precious time to campaign for it. Several influential Boston bankers and property owners, convinced that Rouse and Thompson were more likely to build something of value for downtown, put pressure on Mayor White to intervene. A group of downtown executives who favored Rouse and Thompson organized themselves as Neighbors of Government Center and urged White to conduct a careful review of the two proposals.

While White pondered his decision, the redevelopment agency, Municipal Research Bureau, and Neighbors of Government Center studied the competing proposals. It was clear that selecting Rouse as developer would offer the best prospect for creating a large retail magnet in the market buildings; choosing Webb would mean saving the historic buildings without a retail focus and without the pageant of food and people that Rouse and Thompson envisioned. But the reviews focused less on what each developer would build and more on what they would do to repay the city's investment. Rouse was willing to guarantee a return of at least $600,000 a year to the city, to be paid before debt service and operating expenses, while Webb proposed to take a limited profit and turn the rest of his rental income over to the city without making any guarantees.

When the city council held hearings on the two proposals, Boston developer Norman

Leventhal, speaking for Neighbors of Government Center, told them he did not think the Webb group had the marketing expertise to handle this project. As Leventhal described the situation, Webb would have an unsupervised contract with no accountability and no obligation to provide a return for the city. The council committee on urban renewal recommended giving the project to Rouse and Thompson by a unanimous vote.

By that time, Rouse got to see the mayor. At White's suggestion, they took a walk through the run-down market buildings and stopped for a cup of coffee at a little restaurant still in business. Rouse recalls White saying, "I understand that you bulldoze your way through anything you see that you can't get done; you just bulldoze your way through." "No, we don't do that," Rouse replied, "but I'll tell you this: well fight hard for what we believe in and we will try to overcome every single roadblock there is." "How do I know you're going to do what's best for Boston?" White asked. "I don't want one of these damned buildings that really isn't right for Boston." Rouse offered to work closely with the mayor: "I'll meet with you once a week to report on everything we're doing, step by step. You can watch it all the way." As a former student of architecture at Williams College, White wanted to be involved in the design enough "to be sure they didn't muck it up with neon signs on the roof or something like that." Rouse offered him that opportunity but left town without knowing where he stood. Two days later, in late March 1973, the redevelopment authority named the Rouse Company as developer.

The Boston decision to have a downtown shopping mall was far from straightforward. It started with a decision to save the market buildings because of their architectural merit, and for most people in city government, that was always the main consideration. A fire that destroyed the historic Clinton poultry market across the street in 1971 reinforced their fears that if the Faneuil Hall markets were not soon renovated and reoccupied, they too might be lost. For the redevelopment agency, the market complex was becoming a white elephant, demanding much care and expense and providing little return. They were eager to find a developer—almost any developer—who could figure out a way to make use of it without destroying its historic character.

Nor did the redevelopment staff have any notion that retail stores in market buildings might be designed to attract large crowds of visitors to the city. "Our idea," according to research director Alex Ganz, "was to serve the growing residential market near downtown, plus office workers, and maybe increase Boston's share of retail trade just a little." But their search for a developer led to Rouse and Thompson, who did have a strategy to bring in large numbers of people for shopping and entertainment. The eventual choice of Rouse and Thompson did not mean that city officials shared their high expectations—in fact, they did not—but that key business leaders and Kevin White were impressed by Rouse's commercial success and Thompson's imaginative plans. Their proposal promised reasonable financial returns for the city while replacing the ruin outside the mayor's window.

The Boston story of chance events and happy accidents is not very different from the way other cities got started. Luck was usually as important as rational calculation. The slow pace of urban renewal in the 1950s saved Quincy Market from the bulldozer, and the readiness of the business establishment to pressure Kevin White in the 1970s gave Rouse and Thompson a chance to build their symbol of downtown revival.

JAMES ROUSE: MIXING PLEASURE WITH BUSINESS

The development team of Rouse and Thompson brought to the project special abilities that would not only help to get it built but would make it succeed even beyond the expectations of city officials. Thompson's plans were a striking achievement in themselves, fresh and ingenious in the way they adapted old buildings to new uses. Rouse added an equally essential ingredient: he knew how to turn the visions of an inspired designer into a project that could meet the commercial demands of investors, mortgage lenders, and merchants. "Profit," according to Rouse, "is the thing that hauls dreams into focus"; and he would shape these dreams into high-volume sales and high-rent space. He would go for a broader market than the restricted clientele of Thompson's avant-garde

furniture stores and upscale restaurant. Unlike the earlier urbanists, who wanted to rebuild cities for the elite, Rouse entertained middle-class shoppers and made them feel comfortable.

By the standards of the shopping center industry, whatever Rouse and Thompson did was bound to be unconventional. They were trying to fit a modern retail operation inside the walls of 150-year-old warehouses on a crowded site in the heart of the city. Only a developer with nerve and skill could do the job, and Rouse had those qualifications. A self-made man who started out as a mortgage banker, he switched to shopping center development at the age of 40 when regional malls were a new idea. He helped refine the concept by building one of the first enclosed, air-conditioned malls in the country in 1958. By the time he was 50, he embarked on another pioneering venture, building a new city of 60,000 from scratch at Columbia, Maryland. Intending Columbia as a model for future suburban growth, he took the unusual step of convening a group of social scientists and other academic advisers for ideas on planning and servicing the new community.

By the time Rouse met Thompson, he had been trying for ten years to build a shopping center downtown, first in Fort Lauderdale and then in Norfolk, Virginia, before throwing in the towel. Each abortive effort made him try harder, and when the Boston opportunity came his way in 1972, he was 58 years old and eager to try again.

Rouse's innovations usually had some underlying social concept. In his suburban malls, he tried to create community centers. At Columbia, he tried to demonstrate the advantages of a comprehensive plan for neighborhoods, parks, schools, shopping, jobs, and a town center. Further, while racial conflict was tearing other cities apart, he made a special effort to build racially integrated neighborhoods in Columbia.

He also had a special reason for wanting to build downtown shopping malls. Retailing, he believed, was one of the most important activities for regenerating cities—"a critical triggering ingredient"—because its appeal was potentially so broad. "Everything else in the center of the city serves a particular market," he said. "Offices are for office workers, the theater is for people who go to plays, the art museum is for people who go to see art. But everybody is involved in the marketplace, and as it is lively, appealing, and attractive, it draws people to the center of the city." Even Boston officials who wanted nothing more than to save the historic structures would also welcome a project that drew crowds back to the city, and Rouse was prepared to use his opportunity for that purpose.

Rouse had the resources to be an innovator at the Faneuil Hall markets. By the early 1970s, his network of successful regional malls had given him the credentials, skills, and business contacts he would need to handle a project as risky as this one. Rouse had also organized a company capable of putting visionary ideas into operation. The complexity of shopping center development demanded the talents of many experts and the leadership of more than one executive. When we speak of Rouse's work on Faneuil Hall Marketplace, we are describing the work of a managerial team headed by James Rouse as chairman and Mathias DeVito as president of the Rouse Company in the 1970s.

Rouse had an operating style well suited to working in new and unstructured situations. Unknown obstacles did not discourage him; he was an optimist who believed that close calls are normal in real estate and that "the development business primarily consists of finding a way to overcome crises." His colleagues did not always share this view, and Rouse sometimes had to calm anxious members of his own board. While he was working on Columbia, one board member called to ask whether the company was in trouble. Rouse said, "Of course we're in trouble; we're always in trouble." His director told him that Wall Street was upset because of a report that Rouse was unable to raise any more money for the sewer system in Columbia. Rouse acknowledged that the report was correct. Asked what he intended to do about it, he replied, "I haven't the foggiest notion what we're going to do about, but we'll find an answer."

With his high tolerance for risks and complexity, he was able to persuade his board to go along with projects such as Faneuil Hall, but sometimes only by the skin of his teeth. When Faneuil Hall was in its early stages and he was still juggling all the risks while trying to handle increasingly com-

plicated negotiations with the city, he made the mistake of having his project chief describe the full situation to the board. They were horrified, he recounted: "My God, there were demons at every step." The board wanted to withdraw at once, but Rouse convinced them to allocate another $500,000 to move ahead, and from then on, he was able to keep up the momentum.

Aside from a cheerful acceptance of crises, Rouse brought with him a conviction that the major obstacle to overcome was a negative frame of mind about downtown and its future. When he agreed to do the Gallery at Market East in Philadelphia at the same time as Faneuil Hall, he faced the doubts of the public, department store executives, and prospective tenants that a retail center could draw customers to that "unsafe, dirty, inconvenient" part of town. But he had resources beyond personal persuasion to win over the skeptics. His impressive track record in the suburbs helped convince investors and merchants to give his latest ideas a chance, and he had influence with businesspeople who wanted places in his suburban malls. "We had one hell of a time leasing the Gallery," he reported, but he was expanding his Cherry Hill Mall near Camden, New Jersey, and was prepared to make package deals: "We were finally very up front with the fact that any merchant who wanted to come into Cherry Hill also had to come into the Gallery."

Rouse was truly exceptional among developers in his willingness to take on the political battles that sometimes came with downtown territory. To get the Faneuil Hall project, he acknowledged "pulling every legitimate pressure we could find—which was *everything* we could find—from anybody who knew the city, knew the mayor. We did marshal a hell of a lot of support." Later, in order to build Harborplace in Baltimore, Rouse had to get voter approval in a special referendum. To win the election, he threw himself into the campaign like a professional: "Our goal was that every political club in Baltimore on election day would have to be handing out sample ballots that were for us and against the opposition, and every political club in Baltimore did. The black churches distributed 50,000 handbills in favor of Harborplace." To win support in a mostly black city, he met with 50 leading black ministers and promised minority jobs and business opportunities in the project. He was an effective campaigner, blending business purposes with his sense of social mission. "We just made our case," he explained, "and our case was honest and valid and should have been support-ed." Any developer would have been ready to state a case, but few would have been willing to mobilize political clubs and churches, and still fewer could have masterminded an election cam-paign.

Author's Notes For the profile of James Rouse, we drew on a personal interview, as well as the fol-lowing published sources: William Fulton, "The Robin Hood of Real Estate," *Planning* 51 (May 1985), 4-10; "James Wilson Rouse," *Fortune*, March 23, 1981, p. 108; Gurney Breckenfeld, "Jim Rouse Shows How to Give Downtown Retailing New Life," *Fortune*, April 10, 1978, pp. 85-91; and "Cities Are Fun," *Time*, August 24, 1981, pp. 42, 53. From Rouse's published views, we reviewed "The Regional Shopping Center: Its Role in the Community It Serves" (prepared for the Seventh Urban Design Conference, Harvard Graduate School of Design, April 26, 1963, authors' files); "Must Shopping Centers Be Inhuman," *AF* 116 June 1962), 105-108; and "You Must Take a Good Look at Your Responsibilities," *SCW* 5 (November 1976), 9-12.

For the profile of Ernest Hahn, we drew on a series of personal interviews, as well as interviews with long-time associates and staff, in particular, John Gilchrist, Jr., Ronald Hahn, Harry Newman, Jr., and Albert Sussman. We made use of "The Half Billion Dollar House That Hahn Built," *National Mall Monitor* 9 (May-June 1979), 45-52; and "Interview Ernest Hahn: "We'll Have Stable Growth …,'" *SCW* 6 (February 1977), 13-16.

The comment on developers as masters of long-drawn-out negotiations is from Leonard L. Farber, "Shopping Centers in the 1960s" (address to ICSC Conference, San Francisco, May 2, 1960).

Applying Private-Sector Strategic Planning in the Public Sector

John M. Bryson

William D. Roering

In this piece, the authors compare and contrast six approaches to private-sector strategic planning within the context of a public-sector strategic planning process. They discuss the public-sector applicability of each of the private-sec-tor approaches and explore the contingencies or conditions that govern its suc-cessful use in the public sector. Written in 1987, the article stresses the impor-tance of strategic planning and predicts it becoming a standard part of public planning in the years to follow, although the authors suggest that planners pro-ceed with much caution.

Strategic planning approaches developed in the private sector can help governments and public agen-cies become more effective—at least that is the claim of many authors, including us. Its proponents claim that strategic planning provides a set of concepts, procedures, and tools that can help public-sec-tor organizations deal with the recent dramatic changes in their environments. As two early proponents of strategic planning by governments note, "Strategic planning is a disciplined effort to produce funda-mental decisions shaping the nature and direction of governmental activities within constitutional bounds" (Olsen and Eadie 1982, 4).

What distinguishes strategic planning from more traditional planning (particularly traditional long-range comprehensive or master planning for a community) is its emphasis on (1) action, (2) consideration of a broad and diverse set of stakeholders, (3) attention to external opportunities and threats and internal strengths and weaknesses, and (4) attention to actual or potential competitors (Bloom 1986; Kaufman and Jacobs 1987).

That does not mean, however, that all approaches to what might be called corporate-style strategic planning (that is, strategic planning approaches developed in the private sector) are equally applicable to the public sector. The purposes of this article, therefore, are (1) to compare and contrast six approaches to corporate-style strategic planning, (2) to discuss their applicability to the public sector, and (3) to identify the most important contingencies that govern the successful use of these approaches in the public sector. (Actually, we present nine approaches, grouped into six categories.)

Before beginning, we should note that corporate strategic planning typically focuses on an *organization* and what it should do to improve its performance, and not on a *community*, the traditional object of attention for comprehensive planners, or on a *function*, such as transportation or health care within a community (Tomazinis 1985). We, too, focus primarily on a government corporation or agency and on how it might plan to improve its performance. But we also note where applications to communities or functions seem appropriate.

We must observe as well that careful tests of corporate-style strategic planning in the public sector are few in number. (The same, of course, can be said about approaches to comprehensive, functional, and project planning; see Bryson 1983.) Nevertheless, there is enough experience with corporate strategic planning in the private sector—and increasingly in the public sector—to reach some tentative conclusions about what seems to work under what conditions.

The rest of this article is divided into three main sections. The first presents an outline of a public-sector strategic planning process that can incorporate the six private-sector approaches to strategic planning. The second is a discussion of the six approaches: the Harvard policy model,

strategic planning systems, stakeholder management, content models (portfolio models and competitive analysis), strategic issues management, and process strategies (strategic negotiations, "logical incrementalism," and innovation). We compare and contrast those approaches along several dimensions, including their key features, assumptions, strengths, weaknesses, applicability to the public sector, and contingencies governing their use in the public sector.

The third section presents conclusions about the applicability of private-sector strategic planning to public-sector organizations and purposes. The principal conclusions are (1) that public-sector strategic planning is important and probably will become part of the standard repertoire of public planners and (2) that, nevertheless, public planners must be very careful how they engage in strategic planning, since not all approaches are equally useful and since a number of conditions govern the successful use of each approach.

A PUBLIC-SECTOR STRATEGIC PLANNING PROCESS

Author John Bryson has developed an outline of a public-sector strategic planning process that provides a framework for discussing the six corporate-style strategic planning approaches and their applicability to the public sector (see Figure III.2). The process begins with an initial agreement (or "plan for planning") among decision makers whose support is necessary for successful plan formulation and implementation. Typically they would agree on the purpose of the effort, who should be involved, what should be taken as "given," what topics should be addressed, and the form and timing of reports. Most authors agree that the support and commitment of management and the chief executive are vital if strategic planning in an organization is to succeed (Olsen and Eadie 1982). Further, the involvement of key decision makers outside the organization usually is crucial to the success of public programs if implementation will involve multiple parties and organizations (McGowan and Stevens 1983).

The second step is identification of the mandates, or "musts," confronting the government corporation or agency. Third comes clarification of the organization's mission and values, or "wants,"

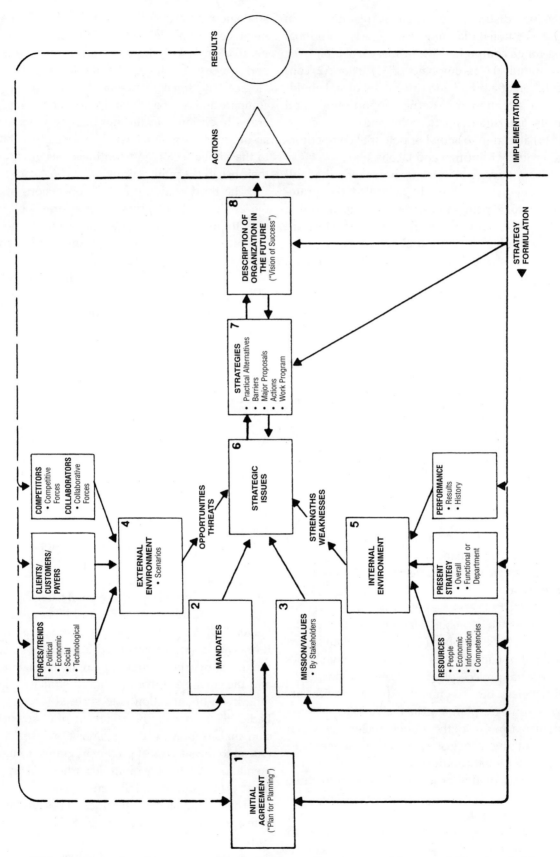

Figure III.2 Strategic planning process (Sources: Bryson, Freeman, and Roering 1986; Van de Ven, and Roering 1987)

because they have such a strong influence on the identification and resolution of strategic issues, as discussed below (Peters and Waterman 1982; Gilbert and Freeman 1985). The process draws attention in particular to similarities and differences among those who have stakes in the outcome of the process and in what the government's or agency's mission ought to be in relation to those stakeholders. "Stakeholder" is defined as any individual, group, or other organization that can place a claim on the organization's attention, resources, or output or is affected by that output. Examples of a government's stakeholders are citizens, taxpayers, service recipients, the governing body, employees, unions, interest groups, political parties, the financial community, and other governments.

Next come two parallel steps: identification of the *external* opportunities and threats the organization faces, and identification of its internal strengths and weaknesses. The distinction between what is "inside" and what is "outside" hinges on whether the organization controls the factor, which places it inside, or does not, which places it outside (Pfeffer and Salancik 1978). To identify opportunities and threats one might monitor a variety of political, economic, social, and technological forces and trends as well as various stakeholder groups, including clients, customers, payers, competitors, or collaborators. The organization might construct various scenarios to explore alternative futures in the external environment, a practice typical of private-sector strategic planning (Linneman and Klein 1983). To identify strengths and weaknesses the organization might monitor resources (inputs), present strategy (process), and performance (outputs).

Strategic planning focuses on achievement of the best "fit" between an organization and its environment. Attention to mandates and the external environment, therefore, can be thought of as planning from the "outside in." Attention to mission and values and the internal environment can be considered planning from the "inside out."

Together, the first five elements of the process lead to the sixth, identification of strategic issues (i.e., fundamental policy questions affecting the organization's mandates, mission, values, product or service level and mix, clients or users, cost, financing, or management). Usually, it is vital that strategic issues be dealt with expeditiously and

effectively if the organization is to survive and prosper. Failure to address a strategic issue typically will lead to undesirable results from a threat, failure to capitalize on an important opportunity, or both.

Strategy development, the seventh step in our outline process, begins with the identification of practical alternatives for resolving the strategic issues. Then it moves to the enumeration of barriers to the achievement of those alternatives, rather than directly to development of proposals to realize the alternatives. A focus on barriers at this point is not typical but is one way of assuring that any strategies developed deal with implementation difficulties directly rather than haphazardly.

After strategy development comes an atypical eighth step: describing the organization's potential future. This description is the organization's "vision of success" (Taylor 1984), an outline of how the organization would look if it successfully implemented its strategies and achieved its full potential. The importance of such descriptions as a guide for performance has 1ong been recognized by well-managed companies (Ouchi 1981; Peters and Waterman 1982) and organizational psychologists (Locke et al. 1981). Typically included in such descriptions are the organization's mission, its basic strategies, its performance criteria, some important decision rules, and the ethical standards expected of the organization's employees.

Those eight steps complete the strategy formulation process. Next come actions and decisions to implement the strategies and, finally, the evaluation of results.

Although our outline shows the process in a linear, sequential manner, we emphasize that the process in practice is iterative. Participants typically rethink what they have done several times before they reach final decisions. Moreover, the process doesn't always begin at the beginning. Instead, organizations typically find themselves confronted with a strategic issue that leads them to engage in strategic planning. Once engaged, the organization is then likely to go back and begin at the beginning.

The process is applicable to public organizations, functions, and communities. The only general requirement is a "dominant coalition" (Thompson 1967) willing to follow the process. For each of the approaches to corporate strategic

Table III.8 Comparison of private-sector approaches to strategic planning and their applicability to the public sector

Approach	Key features	Assumptions	Strengths	Weaknesses	Applicability to the public sector
Harvard policy model (Andrews 1980; Christensen et al. 1983)	Primarily applicable at the strategic business unit level SWOT analysis Analysis of management's values and social obligations of the firm Attempts to develop the best "fit" between a firm and its environment; i.e., best strategy for the firm	Analysis of SWOTs, management values, and social obligations of firm will facilitate identification of the best strategy Agreement is possible within the top management team responsible for strategy formulation and implementation Team has the ability to implement its decisions Implementation of the best strategy will result in improved firm performance (an assumption held in common with all strategic planning approaches)	Systematic assessment of strengths and weaknesses of firm and opportunities and threats facing firm Attention to management values and social obligations of the firm Systematic attention to the "fit" between the firm and its environment Can be used in conjunction with other approaches	Does not offer specific advice on how to develop strategies Fails to consider many existing or potential stakeholder groups	Organizations: Yes, if a strategic public planning unit can be identified and additional stakeholder interests are considered, and if a management team can agree on what should be done and haws the ability to implement its decisions Functions: SWOT analysis is applicable Communities: SWOT analysis is applicable if what is "inside" and "outside" can be specified
Strategic planning systems (Lorange 1980; Lorange et al. 1986)	Systems for formulating and implementing important decisions across levels and functions in an organization Allocation and control of resources within a strategic framework and through rational decision making Attempts to comprehensively cover all key decision areas	Strategy formulation and implementation should be rational and anticipatory An organization's strategies should form an integrated whole The organization can control centrally all or most of its internal operations Goals, objectives, and performance indicators can be specified clearly Information on performance is available at reasonable cost	Coordination of strategy formulation and implementation across levels and functions Can be used in conjunction with other approaches	Excessive comprehensiveness, prescription, and control can drive out attention to mission, strategy, and organizational structure The information requirements of planning systems can exceed the participants' ability to comprehend the information	Organizations: Less comprehensive and rigorous forms of private-sector strategic planning systems are applicable to many public-sector organizations Functions: Necessary conditions for strategic planning systems to succeed are seldom met Communities: Unlikely
Stakeholder management (Freeman 1984)	Identification of key stakeholders and the criteria they use to judge an organization's performance Development of strategists to deal with each stakeholder	An organization's survival and prosperity depend on the extent to which it satisfies its key stakeholders An organization's strategy will be successful only if it meets the needs of key stakeholders strategies to deal with each stakeholder	Recognition that many claims, both complementary and competing, are placed on an organization Stakeholder analysis (i.e., a listing of key stakeholders and of the criteria they use to judge an organization's performance) Can be used in conjunction with other approaches	Absence of criteria with which to judge different claims Need for more advice on how to develop strategies to deal with divergent stakeholder claims	Organizations: Yes, as long as agreement is possible among key decision makers over who the stakeholders are and what the organization's responses to them should be Functions: Yes, with the same caveats Communities: Yes, with the same caveats

Table III.8 Comparison of private-sector approaches to strategic planning and their applicability to the public sector *(continued)*

Approach	Key features	Assumptions	Strengths	Weaknesses	Applicability to the public sector
Content approaches					
Portfolio methods (Henderson 1979; Wind and Mahajian 1981; MacMillan 1983)	A corporation's businesses are categorized into groups based on selected dimensions for comparison and development of corporate strategy in relation to each business Attempts to balance a corporation's business portfolio to meet corporate strategic objectives	Aggregate assessment of a corporation's various businesses is important to the corporation's success Resources should be be channeled into the different businesses to meet the corporation's cash flow and investment needs A few key dimension of strategic importance can be identified against which to judge the performance of individual businesses A group exists that can make and implement decisions based on the portfolio analysis	Provides a method for evaluating a set of businesses against dimensions that are deemed to be of strategic importance to the corporation Provides a useful way of understanding some of the key economic and financial aspects of corporate strategy Can be used as part of a larger strategic planning process	Difficult to know what the relevant strategic dimensions are, what the relevant entities to be compared are, and how to classify entities against dimensions Unclear how to use the tool as part of a larger strategic planning process	Organizations: Yes, if economic, social, and political dimensions of comparison can be specified, entities to be compared can be identified, and a group exists that can make and implement decisions based on the portfolio analysis Functions: Yes, with the same caveats Communities: Yes, with the same caveats
Competitive analysis (Porter 1980; 1985; Harrigan 1981)	Analysis of key forces that shaped an industry, e.g., relative power of suppliers, threat of substitute products, threat of new entrants, amount of rivalrous activity, exit barriers to firms in the industry	Predominance of competitive behavior on the part of firms within an industry The stronger the forces that shape an industry, the lower the general level of returns in the industry The stronger the forces affecting a firm, the lower the profits for the firm Analysis of the forces will allow one to identify the best strategy whereby an industry can raise its general level of returns whereby a firm within an industry can maximize its profits	Provides a systematic method of assessing the economic aspects of an industry and the strategic options facing the industry and specific firms within it Gives relatively clear prescriptions for strategic action Can be used as a part of a larger strategic planning process	Sometimes difficult to identify what the relevant industry is Excludes consideration of potentially relevant on economic factors Tends to ignore the possibility that organizational success may turn on collaboration, not competition	Organizations: Yes, for organizations in identifiable industries (e.g., public hospitals, transit companies, recreation facilities) if a competitive analysis is coupled with a consideration of noneconomic factors and if the possibility of collaboration is also considered Functions: Yes, if the function equates to an industry Communities: No
Strategic issues management (Ansoff 1980; King 1982; Pflaum and Delmont 1987)	Attention to the recognition and resolution of strategic issues	Strategic issues are issues that can have a major influence on the organization and must be managed if the organization is to meet its objectives Strategic issues can be identified by the use of a variety of tools (e.g., SWOT analyses and environmental scanning methods) Early identification of issues will result in more favorable resolution and greater likelihood of enhanced organizational performance A group exists that is able to engage in the process and manage the issue	Ability to identify and respond quickly to issues Has a "real time" orientation and is compatible with most organizations Can be used in conjunction with other approaches	No specific advice is offered on how to frame issues other than to precede their identification with a situational analysis	Organizations: Yes, as long as there is a group able to engage in the process and manage the issue Functions: Yes, with the same caveat Communities: Yes, with the same caveat

Table III.8 Comparison of private-sector approaches to strategic planning and their applicability to the public sector *(continued)*

Approach	Key features	Assumptions	Strengths	Weaknesses	Applicability to the public sector
Process strategies					
Strategic negotiations (Pettigrew 1982; Fisher and Ury 1981; Allison 1971)	Bargaining and negotiation among two or more players over the identification and resolution of strategic issues	Organizations are "shared power" settings in which groups must cooperate, bargain, and negotiate with each other in order to achieve their ends and assure organizational survival. Strategy is created as part of a relatively constant struggle among competing groups in an organization. Strategy is the emergent product of the partial resolution of organizational issues	Recognizes that there are many actors in the strategy formulation and implementation process and that they often do not share common goals. Recognizes the desirability of bargaining and negotiation in order for groups to achieve their ends and to assure organizational survival. Can be used in conjunction with other approaches	Little advice on how to ensure technical workability and democratic responsibility—as opposed to political acceptability—of results. No assurance that overall organizational goals can or will be achieved; there may not be a whole equal to, let alone greater than, the sum of the parts	Organizatons: Yes Functions: Yes Communities: Yes
Logical incrementalism (Quinn 1980; Lindblom 1959)	Emphasizes the importance of small changes as part of developing and implementing organizational strategies. Fuses strategy formulation and implementation	Strategy is loosely linked group of decisions that are handled incrementally. Decentralized decision making is both politically expedient and necessary. Small, decentralized decisions can help identify and fulfill organizational purposes	Ability to handle complexity and changes. Attention to both formal and informal processes. Political realism. Emphasis on both minor and major decisions. Can be used in conjunction with other approaches	No guarantee that the loosely linked, incremental decisions will add up to fulfillment of overall organizational purposes	Organizations: Yes, as long as overall organizational purposes can be identified to provide a framework for incremental decisions. Functions: Yes, with the same caveat. Communities: Yes, with the same caveat
Framework for innovation (Taylor 1984; Pinchot 1985)	Emphasis on innovation as a strategy. Reliance on many elements of the other approaches and specific management practices	Change is unavoidable, and continuous innovation to deal with change is necessary if the organization is to survive and prosper. A "vision of success" is necessary to provide the organization with a common set of superordinate goals toward which to work. Innovation as a strategy will not work without an entrepreneurial company culture to support it	Allows innovation and enterpreneurship while maintaining central control on key outcomes. Fosters a commitment to innovation. Can be used in conjunction with other approaches	Costly mistakes usually are necessary as part of the process of innovation. Decentralization and local control result in some loss of accountability	Organizations: Yes, but the public is unwilling to allow public organizations to make the mistakes necessary as part of the process and development of an overall framework within which to innovate and maintain central control over key outcomes is difficult. Functions: Yes, but with the same caveats. Communities: Yes, but with the same caveats

planning we note specific contingencies that affect its application in the public sector.

APPROACHES TO CORPORATE STRATEGIC PLANNING

Although the roots of public-sector strategic planning are deep, most of the history and development of the concepts, procedures, and tools of strategic planning in this century have occurred in the private sector.[1] This history has been amply documented by others (Bracker 1980). We briefly set forth six schools of thought or models of strategic planning developed in the private sector and discuss their key features, assumptions, strengths, weaknesses, applicability to the public sector, and contingencies governing their use.

As noted above, strategic planning as a concept involves general policy and direction setting, situation assessments, strategic issue identification, strategy development, decision making, action, and evaluation. We begin with the approaches that cover more of the process and highlight policy and direction setting; then we move to approaches that focus more narrowly on elements in the later stages of the process we have outlined.

The Harvard policy model

The Harvard policy model was developed as part of, and has been included in, the business policy course taught at the Harvard Business School since the 1920s (Christensen et al. 1983 and earlier versions). The approach provides the principal inspiration behind the most widely cited recent models of public-sector strategic planning (e.g., Olsen and Eadie 1982; Sorkin, Ferris, and Hudak 1984). (See Table III.8)

The main purpose of the Harvard model is to help a firm develop the best "fit" between itself and its environment; that is, to develop the best strategy for the firm. As articulated by Andrews (1980), strategy is "a pattern of purposes and policies defining the company and its business." One discerns the best strategy by analyzing the internal strengths and weaknesses of the company and the values of senior management, then identifying the external threats and opportunities in the environment and the social obligations of the firm.

Effective use of the model presumes that agreement is possible among the members of a top management team about the firm's situation and the appropriate strategic response. Further, the model presumes the team has enough authority to enforce its decisions. A final important assumption of the model—common to all approaches to strategic planning—is that if the appropriate strategy is identified and implemented, the organization will be more effective.

The process presented in Figure 1 is strongly influenced by the Harvard model. Central to the process is attention to the internal strengths and weaknesses of the government or agency, to the values of key stakeholders (not just senior manages), and to the external threats, opportunities, and mandates (not just social obligations) affecting the government or agency.

In the business world, the Harvard model appears to be best applied at the level of the strategic business unit. A strategic business unit is a distinct business that has its own competitors and can be managed somewhat independently of other units within the organization (Rue and Holland 1986). The strategic business unit, in other words, provides an important yet bounded and manageable focus for the model. The public-sector equivalent of the strategic business unit is the strategic public planning unit, which typically would be an agency or department that addresses issues fundamentally similar in nature to one another (Montanari and Bracker 1986).

The Harvard model is also applicable at the higher and broader corporate level—in both private and public sectors—particularly if it is used with other approaches, such as the portfolio approaches to be discussed below. A portfolio approach is needed because a principal strategic concern at the corporate level is oversight of a portfolio of businesses in the private sector or a portfolio of agencies or departments in the public sector.

The systematic assessment of strengths, weaknesses, opportunuties, and threats—or SWOT analysis—is the primary strength of the Harvard model. This element of the model appears to be applicable in the public sector to organizations, functions, and communities (Sorkin, Ferris, and Hudak 1984), although in the case of communities the distinction between inside and outside may be problematic. The main weakness of the Harvard model is that it does not offer specific advice on how to develop strategies, except to note that effective strategies will build on strengths, take advantage of opportunities, and overcome or minimize weaknesses and threats.

Strategic planning systems

Strategic planning is often conceived as a system whereby manages go about making, implementing, and controlling important decisions across functions and levels in the firm. Lorange (1980), for example, has argued that any strategic planning system must address four fundamental questions: (1) Where are we going? (mission); (2) How do we get there? (strategies); (3) What is our blueprint for action? (budgets); and (4) How do we know if we are on track? (control).

Strategic planning systems vary along several dimensions: the comprehensiveness of decision areas included, the formal rationality of the decision process, and the tightness of control exercised over implementation of the decisions (Armstrong 1982). The strength of these systems is their attempt to coordinate the various elements of an organization's strategy across levels and functions. Their weakness is that excessive comprehensiveness, prescription, and control can drive out attention to mission, strategy, and organizational structure (Frederickson and Mitchell 1984; Frederickson 1984) and can exceed participants' ability to comprehend them (Bryson, Van de Ven, and Roering 1987).

Strategic planning systems are applicable to public-sector organizations, for regardless of the nature of the particular organization, it makes sense to coordinate decision making across levels and functions and to concentrate on whether the organization is implementing its strategies and accomplishing its mission. It is important to remember, however, that a strategic planning system characterized by substantial comprehensiveness, formal rationality in decision making, and tight control will work only in an organization that has a clear mission; clear goals and objectives; centralized authority; clear performance indicators; and information about actual performance available at reasonable cost (Stuart 1969; Galloway 1979). Few public-sector organizations—or functions or communities—operate under such conditions. As a result, public-sector strategic planning systems typically focus on a few areas of concern,

rely on a decision process in which politics plays a major role, and control something other than program outcomes (e.g., budget expenditures) (Wildavsky 1979).

Bryson, Van de Ven, and Roering (1987) offer an example, based on the approach used by the 3M Corporation, of how such a control system might be implemented across levels in a government corporation or agency (see Figure III.3) In the system's fist cycle, there is "bottom-up" development of strategic plans within a framework established at the top, followed by reviews and reconciliations at each succeeding level. In the second cycle, operating plans are developed to implement the strategic plans.

A similar cyclic system is used by Hennepin County, Minnesota (the county that contains Minneapolis), to address 14 areas of strategic concern (e.g., finance, employment and economic development, transportation, program fragmentation, and coordination). The system includes three cycles: strategic issue identification, strategy development, and strategy implementation (Eckhert et al. 1986).

Stakeholder management approaches

Freeman (1984) has argued that corporate strategy can be understood as a corporation's mode of relating or building bridges to its stakeholders. A stakeholder is "any group or individual who is affected by or who can affect the future of the corporation"; for example, customers, employees, suppliers, owners, governments, financial institutions, and critics. Freeman argues that a corporate strategy will be effective only if it satisfies the needs of multiple groups. Traditional private-sector models of strategy have focused only on economic actors, but Freeman argues that changes in the current business environment require that other political and social actors must be considered as well.

Because it integrates economic, political, and social concerns, the stakeholder model is one of the approaches most applicable to the public sector. Many interest groups have stakes in public organizations, functions, and communities. For example, local economic development planning typically involves government, developers, bankers, the chamber of commerce, actual or

Strategic Planning

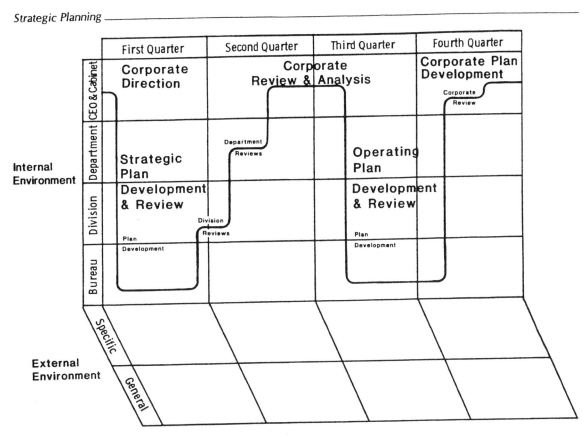

Figure III.3 Annual strategic planning process (Source: Bryson, Van de Ven, and Roering 1987)

potential employers, neighborhood groups, environmentalists, and so on. Local economic development planners would be wise to identify key stakeholders, their interests, what they will support, and strategies and tactics that might work in dealing with them (Kaufman 1979).

Bryson, Freeman, and Roering (1986) argue that an organization's mission and values ought to be formulated in stakeholder terms. That is, an organization should figure out what its mission should be in relation to each stakeholder group; otherwise, it will not be able to differentiate its responses well enough to satisfy its key stakeholders. This advice to public organizations is matched by private-sector practice in several well managed companies (O'Toole 1985). For example, the Dayton Hudson Corporation, a large retailer, identifies four key stakeholders—customers, employees, stockholders, and the communities in which they do business—and specifies what its mission is in relation to each. Dayton Hudson assumes that

if it performs well in the eyes of each of those stakeholders, its success is assured.

The strengths of the stakeholder model are its recognition of the many claims—both complementary and competing—placed on organizations by insiders and outsiders and its awareness of the need to satisfy at least the key stakeholders if the organization is to survive. The weaknesses of the model are the absence of criteria with which to judge competing claims and the need for more advice on how to develop strategies to deal with divergent stakeholder interests.

Freeman has applied the stakeholder concept primarily at the corporate and industry-wide levels in the private sector, but it seems applicable to all levels in the private and public sectors. Researchers have not yet made rigorous tests of the model's usefulness in the private or public sector, but there are several public sector case studies that indicate stakeholder analyses are quite useful as part of a strategic planning effort—for example, the city government of St. Louis Park, Minnesota (Klumpp 1986) and the Ramsey County (Minnesota) Nursing Service (Allan 1985). If the model is to be used successfully, it must be possible to achieve reasonable agreement among key decision makers about who the key stakeholders are and what the response to their claims should be.

Content approaches

The three approaches presented so far have to do more with process than with content. The process approaches do not prescribe answers, though good answers are presumed to emerge from appropriate application of them. In contrast, the tools to be discussed next—portfolio models and competitive analysis—have to do primarily with content and do yield answers. In fact, the models are antithetical to process when process concerns get in the way of developing the "right" answer.

Portfolio models. The idea of strategic planning as managing a portfolio of businesses is based on an analogy with investment practice. Just as an investor assembles a portfolio of stocks to manage risk and realize optimum returns, a corporate manager can think of the corporation as a portfolio of businesses with diverse potentials that can be balanced to manage return and cash flow. The intellectual history of portfolio theory in corporate strategy is complex (Wind and Mahajan 1981). For our purposes it is adequate to use as an example the portfolio model developed by the Boston Consulting Group: the famous "BCG Matrix" (Henderson 1979).

Bruce Henderson, founder of the Boston Consulting Group, argued that all business costs followed a well-known pattern: unit costs dropped by one-third every time volume (or turnover) doubled. Hence, he postulated a relationship, known as the *experience curve*, between unit costs and volume. This relationship leads to some generic strategic advice: gain market share, for if a firm gains market share, its unit costs will fall and profit potential will increase. Henderson argued that any business could be categorized into one of four types, depending on how its industry was growing and how large a share of the market it had: (1) high growth/ high share businesses: ("stars"), which generate substantial cash but also require large investments if their market share is

to be maintained or increased; (2) low growth/high share businesses ("cash cows"), which generate large cash flows but require low investment and therefore generate profits that can be used elsewhere; (3) low growth/low share businesses ("dogs"), which produce little cash and offer little prospect of increased share; and (4) high growth/low share businesses ("question marks"), which would require substantial investment in order to become stars or cash cows (the question is whether the investment is worth it). Generic business strategies can be adopted to meet the whole corporation's cash flow and investment needs.

Although the applications of portfolio theory to the public sector may be less obvious than those of the three approaches described above, they are nonetheless just as powerful (MacMillan 1983). Many public-sector organizations consist of "multiple businesses" that are only marginally related. Often resources from a single source are committed to these unrelated businesses. That means public-sector managers must make portfolio decisions, though usually without the help of analytical portfolio models that frame those decisions strategically. The BCG approach, like most private-sector portfolio models, uses only economic criteria, not the political or social criteria that might be necessary for public-sector applications. Private-sector portfolio approaches, therefore, must be modified substantially for public-sector use.

The Philadelphia Investment Portfolio is a public-sector example of a portfolio approach applied at the community level (Center for Philadelphia Studies 1982a; 1982b). The portfolio consists of 56 investment options (i.e., investments of public and private time and resources) arranged according to the degree to which they take advantage of ongoing trends (their "position") and the degree to which they facilitate the strategic objectives of the greater Philadelphia area (their "attractiveness"). (The judgments of position and attractiveness were formulated through the collaborative efforts of about 750 people in public, private, and nonprofit organizations who participated in the "Philadelphia: Past, Present and Future" project.) Each of the two dimensions consists of a set of economic, political, and social criteria. The creators of the portfolio view Greater Philadelphia as a community of interests and stakeholders; they strive to loosely coordinate the activities of disparate parties to achieve community goals by offering specific investment options that are attractive to specific organizations or coalitions. An organization or coalition would pursue an option because that option fit its needs or desires; but the city as a whole also would benefit from the organization's decision to invest.

The strength of portfolio approaches is that they provide a method for measuring entities of some sort (e.g., businesses, investment options, proposals, or problems) against dimensions that are deemed to be of strategic importance (e.g., share and growth or position and attractiveness) for purposes of analysis and recommendation. The weaknesses of such approaches include the difficulty of knowing what the appropriate strategic dimensions are; difficulties of classifying entities against dimensions; and the lack of clarity about how to use the tool as part of a larger strategic planning process.

If modified to include political and social factors, portfolio approaches can be used in the public sector to inform strategic decisions about organizations, functions, and communities. The approaches can be used in conjunction with process approaches, such as the one outlined in Figure 1, to provide useful information as part of an assessment of an organization, function, or community in relation to its environment. Unlike the process models, however, portfolio approaches provide an "answer" as to what that relationship should be once the dimensions of comparison and the entities to be compared are specified. The answer would be accepted only if a dominant coalition could be convinced that the answer was correct.

Competitive analysis. Another important content approach to assist with strategy selection has been developed by Michael Porter (1980, 1985) and his associates. Called competitive analysis, it assumes that by analyzing the forces that shape an industry, one can predict the general level of profits throughout the industry and the likely success of any particular strategy for a strategic business unit. Porter (1980) hypothesizes that five key forces shape an industry: relative power of customers, relative power of suppliers, threat of substitute products, threat of new entrants, and the amount of rivalrous activity among the players in the industry. Harrigan (1981) has argued that "exit

barriers"—that is, the barriers that would prevent a company from leaving an industry—are a sixth force influencing success in some industries. There are two main propositions in the competitive analysis school: (1) the stronger the forces that shape an industry, the lower the general level of returns in the industry; and (2) the stronger the forces affecting a strategic business unit, the lower the profits for that unit.

For many public-sector organizations, there are equivalents to the forces that affect private industry. Client or customer power is often exercised in the public arena, and suppliers of services (e.g., organizations providing contract services and the government's or agency's own labor supply) also can exercise power. There are fewer new entrants, but recently the private sector has begun to compete more forcefully with public organizations. And governments and agencies also often compete with one another (e.g., public hospitals for patients, or states and localities for the General Motors Saturn plant). An effective organization in the public sector, therefore, must understand the forces at work in its "industry" in order to compete effectively. On another level, planning for a specific public-sector function (e.g., health care, transportation, and recreation) can benefit from competitive analysis if the function can be considered an industry. In addition, economic development agencies must understand the forces at work in given industries and on specific firms if they are to understand whether and how to nurture those industries and firms. Finally, although communities often compete with one another, competitive analysis does not apply at that level because communities are not industries in any meaningful sense.

The strength of competitive analysis is that it provides a systematic way of assessing industries and the strategic options facing strategic business units within those industries. For public-sector applications, the weaknesses of competitive analysis are that (1) it is often difficult to know what the "industry" is and what forces affect it and (2) the key to organizational success in the public sector is often collaboration instead of competition. Competitive analyses in the public sector, therefore, must be coupled with a consideration of social and political forces and the possibilities for collaboration.

Strategic issue management

We now leave content approaches to focus again on process approaches. Strategic issue management approaches are process components or pieces of the larger strategic planning process presented in Figure III.2. Strategic issue management is primarily associated with Ansoff (1980) and focuses attention on the recognition and resolution of *strategic issues*—"forthcoming developments, either inside or outside the organization, which are likely to have an important impact on the ability of the enterprise to meet its objectives." The concept of strategic issues first emerged when practitioners of corporate strategic planning realized a step was missing between the SWOT analysis of the Harvard model and the development of strategies. That step was the identification of strategic issues. Many firms now include a strategic issue identification step as part of full-blown strategy revision exercises and also as part of less comprehensive annual strategic reviews (King 1982). Full-blown annual revision has proved impractical because strategy revision takes substantial management energy and attention, and most strategies take several years to implement anyway. Instead, most firms are undertaking comprehensive strategy revisions several years apart (typically five) and in the interim are focusing their annual strategic planning processes on the identification and resolution of a few key strategic issues that emerge from SWOT analyses, environmental scans (Hambrick 1982; Pflaum and Delmont 1987), and other analyses.

In recent years many firms have developed strategic issue management processes actually separated from their annual strategic planning processes. Many important issues emerge too quickly to be handled as part of an annual process. A separate, quick response is necessary. Typically task forces reporting directly to top management are used to develop responses to pressing issues that turn up unexpectedly.

Strategic issue management is clearly applicable to governments and agencies as well, since the agendas of these organizations consist of issues that should be managed strategically (Ring and Perry 1985). In other words, they should be managed based on a sense of mission and mandates and in the context of an environmental assessment. The strength of the approach is its ability to recognize and analyze key issues quickly. The weakness of the approach is that no specific advice is offered on exactly how to frame the issues other than to precede their identification with a situational analysis of some sort. The approach also applies to functions and places or communities, as long as some group, organization, or coalition is able to engage in the process and to manage the issue.

Process strategies

The final three process approaches to be discussed are, in effect, strategies. They are strategic negotiations, logical incrementalism, and strategic planning as a framework for innovation.

Strategic negotiations. Several writers view corporate strategy as the partial resolution of organizational issues through a highly political process (Pettigrew 1977; Mintzberg and Waters 1985). As envisioned by Pettigrew (1977), strategic negotiations are very much contextually based, as strategy is viewed as the flow of actions and values embedded in a context.

The applicability of this view of strategy to the public sector is clear when one realizes that Allison's (1971) study of the Cuban Missile Crisis provided much of the stimulus for this line of private-sector work. Negotiation has become an increasingly important focus of planning research and practice (Susskind and Ozawa 1984). An example of planning-related strategic negotiations is the Negotiated Investment Strategy project of the Charles F. Kettering Foundation (1982), in which federal, state, and local agencies in several cities worked out a coordinated investment strategy designed to meet the strategic objectives of each.

The strength of a negotiation approach is that it recognizes that power is shared in most public situations; no one person, group, or organization is "in charge," and cooperation and negotiation with others is often necessary in order for people, groups, and organizations to achieve their ends (Bryson and Einsweiler 1986). The main weakness of negotiation approaches—as expounded, for example, by Fisher and Ury (1981) in *Getting to Yes*—is that although they can show planners how to reach politically acceptable results, they are not very helpful in assuring technical workability or democratic responsibility of results.

Logical incrementalism. Incremental approaches view strategy as a loosely linked group of decisions that are handled incrementally. Decisions are handled individually below the corporate level because such decentralization is politically expedient corporate leaders should reserve their political clout for crucial decisions. Decentralization also is necessary—those closest to decisions are the only ones with enough information to make good decisions.

The incremental approach is identified principally with Quinn (1980), though the influence of Lindblom (1959) is apparent. Quinn developed the concept of *logical incrementalism*—or incrementalism in the service of overall corporate purposes—and as a result transformed incrementalism into a strategic approach. Logical incrementalism is a process approach that, in effect, fuses strategy formulation and implementation. The strengths of the approach are its ability to handle complexity and change, its emphasis on minor as well as major decisions, its attention to informal as well as formal processes, and its political realism. The major weakness of the approach is that it does not guarantee that the various loosely linked decisions will add up to fulfillment of corporate purposes. Logical incrementalism would appear to be very applicable to public-sector organizations, functions, and places or communities—the situations in which, and for which, Lindblom first developed the incremental model—as long as it is possible to establish some overarching set of strategic objectives to be served by the approach.

Strategic planning as a framework for innovation. Above we discussed strategic planning systems and noted that excessive comprehensiveness, prescription, and control could drive out attention to mission, strategy, and organizational structure. The systems, in other words, can become ends in themselves and drive out creativity, innovation, and new product and market development, without which most businesses would die (Schön 1971). Many businesses, therefore, have found it necessary to emphasize innovative strategies as a counterbalance to the excessive control orientation of many strategic planning systems. In other words, while one important reason for installing a strategic planning system is the need to exercise control across functions and levels, an equally important need for organizations is to design systems that promote creativity and entrepreneurship at the local level and prevent centralization and bureaucracy from stifling the wellsprings of business growth and change (Taylor 1984).

The framework-for-innovation approach to corporate strategic planning relies on many of the elements of the approaches discussed above, such as SWOT analyses and portfolio methods. This approach differs from earlier ones in that it emphasizes (1) innovation as a strategy, (2) specific management practices to support the strategy (e.g., project teams; venture groups; diversification, acquisition, and divestment task forces; research and development operations; new product and market groups; and a variety of organizational development techniques), (3) development of a "vision of success" that provides the decentralized and entrepreneurial parts of the organization with a common set of superordinate goals toward which to work, and (4) nurture of an entrepreneurial company culture (Pinchot 1985).

The strength of the approach is that it allows for innovation and entrepreneurship while maintaining central control. The weaknesses of the approach are that typically—and perhaps necessarily—a great many, often costly, mistakes are made as part of the innovation process and that there is a certain loss of accountability in very decentralized systems (Peters and Waterman 1982). Those weaknesses reduce the applicability of the approach to the public sector, in which mistakes are less acceptable and the pressures to be accountable for details (as opposed to results) are often greater (Ring and Perry 1985).

Nonetheless, the innovation approach would appear to be applicable to public-sector organizations when the management of innovation is needed (e.g., Zaltman, Florio, and Sikorski 1977), as in the redesign of a public service (e.g., Savas 1982). Innovation as a strategy also can and should be pursued for functions and communities. Too often a distressing equation has operated in the public sector: more money equals more service, less money equals less service. As public budgets have become increasingly strapped, there have not been enough innovation and public service redesign. The equation doesn't need to be destiny; it is possible that creative effort and innovation might actually result in *more* service for *less* money.

CONCLUSIONS

Our purpose in this paper has been to compare and contrast six approaches to corporate-style strategic planning, to discuss their applicability to the public sector, and to identify major contingencies governing their use. Several conclusions emerge from our review and analysis.

First, it should be clear that corporate strategic planning is not a single concept, procedure, or tool. In fact, it embraces a range of approaches that vary in their applicability to the public sector and in the conditions that govern their successful use. The public sector strategic planning process outlined above provides a useful framework for review and critique of the private-sector approaches to strategic planning and their applicability to the public sector. The process comprises broad policy or direction setting, internal and external assessments, attention to key stakeholders, the identification of key issues, development of strategies to deal with each issue, decision making, action, and continuous monitoring of results. The process is applicable to organizations, functions, and places or communities. The private-sector approaches to corporate strategic planning, in contrast, emphasize different parts of this whole strategic planning process, and each is focused on a given organization.

Second, although the public-sector strategic planning process is a useful framework to guide thought and action, it must be applied with care to any given situation, as is true of any planning process (Bryson and Delbecq 1979; Galloway 1979; Christensen 1985). Because every planning process should be tailored to fit specific situations, every process in practice will be a hybrid. We have outlined a number of general assumptions and conditions governing successful use of the private-sector strategic planning approaches in the public sector in order to facilitate construction of such hybrids.

Third, we think familiarity with strategic planning should be a standard part of the intellectual and skill repertoire of all public planners. Given the dramatic changes in the environments of public organizations in recent years, we expect elected public officials, public managers, and planners to pay increased attention to the formulation and implementation of effective strategies to deal with the changes. When applied appropriately to public-sector conditions, strategic planning provides a set of concepts, procedures, and tools for doing just that. We suspect the most effective public planners are now—and will be increasingly in the future—the ones who are best at *strategic* planning.

Fourth, our assertion about the increased importance of strategic planning raises the question of the appropriate role of the strategic planner. In many ways this is an old debate in the planning literature. Should the planner be a technician, politician, or hybrid, i.e., both a technician and a politician (Howe and Kaufman 1979; Howe 1980)? Or should the planner not be a planner at all, at least formally, but instead be a line manager (Bryson, Van de Ven, and Roering 1987)? We believe the strategic planner can be solely a technician only when content approaches are used. When all other approaches are used, the strategic planner should be a hybrid, so that there is some assurance that both political and technical concerns are addressed. Furthermore, since strategic planning tends to fuse planning and decision making, it is helpful to think of decision makers as strategic planners and to think of strategic planners as facilitators of strategic decision making across levels and functions in organizations and communities.

Finally, research must explore a number of theoretical and empirical issues in order to advance the knowledge ant practice of public strategic planning. In particular, contingent models for public strategic planning must be developed and tested. These models should specify key situational factors governing use; provide specific advice on how to formulate and implement strategies in different situations; be explicitly political; indicate how to deal with plural, ambiguous, or conflicting goals or objectives; link content and process; indicate how collaboration as well as competition is to be handled; and specify roles for the strategic planner. Progress has been made on all of those fronts (Checkoway 1986), but more is necessary if public-sector strategic planning is to help public organizations, functions, and communities fulfill their missions and serve their stakeholders effectively, efficiently, and responsibly.

Authors' note. The authors would like to gratefully acknowledge the helpful advice of Bob Einsweiler, Ray Burby, Ed Kaiser, and three anonymous reviewers on earlier drafts of this paper. Whatever readability the paper has we owe principally to the efforts of Barbara Crosby.

NOTE

1. The word "strategy" comes from the Greek word *stratego*, a combination of *stratos*, or army, and *ego*, or leader (O'Toole 1985). Strategic planning thus began as the art of the general and now has become the art of the general manager.

REFERENCES

Allan, J. H. 1985. A case study of the Ramsey County Nursing Service strategic planning process. Plan B paper. Minneapolis: School of Public Health, University of Minnesota.

Allison, G. T. 1971. *Essence of decision*. Boston: Little, Brown.

Andrews, K. 1980. *The concept of corporate strategy*. Rev. ed. Homewood, Ill.: R. D. Irwin.

Ansoff, I. 1980. Strategic issue rnanagement. *Strategic Management Journal* 1, 2: 131-148.

Armstrong, J. S. 1982. The value of formal planning for strategic decisions: Review of empirical research. *Strategic Management Journal* 3, 2: 197-211.

Bloom, C. 1986. Strategic planning in the public sector. *Journal of Planning Literature* 1, 2: 253-59.

Bracker, J. 1980. The historical development of the strategic management concept *Academy of Management Review* 5, 2: 219-224.

Bryson, J. M. 1983 Representing and testing procedural planning methods. In *Evaluating Urban Planning Efforts*, edited by Ian Masser. Hampshire, England: Gower.

———, and A. L. Delbecq. 1979. A contingent approach to strategy and tactics in project planning. *Journal of the American Planning Association* 45, 2: 167-179.

———, and R. C. Einsweiler, eds. 1986. *Planning and decision making in a context of shared power*. Lanham, Md.: University Press of America.

———, R E. Freeman, and W. D. Roering. 1986. Strategic planning in the public sector: Approaches and directions. In *Strategic Perspectives on Planning Practice*, edited by B. Checkoway. Lexingington, Mass.: Lexington Books.

———, A. H. Van de Ven, and W. D. Roering. 1987.

Strategic planning and the revitalization of the public service. In *Toward a New Public Service*, edited by R. Denhardt and E. Jennings. Columbia: University of Missouri Press (forthcoming).

Center for Philadelphia Studies. 1982a. *A Philadelphia prospectus*. Philadelphia: University of Pennsylvania.

———. 1982b. *Philadelphia investment portfolio*. Philadelphia: University of Pennsylvania.

Charles F. Kettering Foundation. 1982. *Negotiated investment strategy*. Dayton, Ohio: Charles F. Kettering Foundation.

Checkoway, B., ed. 1986. *Strategic perspectives on planning practice*. Lexington, Mass.: Lexington Books.

Christensen, K. S. 1985. Coping with uncertainty in planning. *Journal of the American Planning Association* 51, 1: 63-73.

Christensen, R., K. Andrews, J. Bower, R. Hammermesh, and M. Porter. 1983. *Business policy: Text and cases*. Homewood, Ill.: R. D. Irwin.

Eckhert, P., K. Korbelik, T. Delmont, and A. Pflaum. 1986. Strategic planning in Hennepin County, Minnesota: An issues management approach. Paper presented to the American Planning Association, National Planning Conference, Los Angeles. April.

Fisher, R., and W. Ury. 1981. *Getting to yes: Negotiating agreement without giving in*. New York: Penguin Books.

Fredrickson, J. W. 1984. The comprehensiveness of strategic decision processes. *Academy of Management Journal* 27, 2: 445-466.

———, and T. R. Mitchell. 1984. Strategic decision processes: Comprehensiveness and performance in an industry with an unstable environment. *Academy of Management Journal* 27, 2: 399-423.

Freeman, R. E. 1984. *Strategic management: A stakeholder approach*. Boston: Pitman.

Galloway, T. D. 1979. Comment on "Comparison of Current Planning Theories: Counterparts and Contradictions," by B. M. Hudson. *Journal of the American Planning Association* 45, 4: 399-402.

Gilbert, D. R., and R. E. Freeman. 1985. Strategic management and responsibility: A game theoretic approach. Discussion paper 22.

Minneapolis: Strategic Management Research Center, University of Minnesota.

Hambrick, D. C. 1982. Environmental scanning and organizational strategy. *Strategic Management Journal* 3, 2: 159-174.

Harrigan, K. 1981. Barriers to entry and competitive strategies. *Strategic Management Journal* 2, 4: 395-412.

Henderson, B. 1979. *Henderson on corporate strategy*. Cambridge, Mass.: Abt Books.

Howe, E. 1980. Role choices of urban planners. *Journal of the American Planning Association* 46, 4: 398-409.

——, and J. Kaufman. 1979. The ethics of contemporary American planners. *Journal of the American Planning Association* 45, 3: 243–255.

Kaufman, J. L. 1979. The planner as interventionist in public policy issues. In *Planning Theory in the 1980s*, edited by R. Burchell and G. Sternlieb. New Brunswick, N.J.: Center for Urban Policy Research, Rutgers University.

——, and H. M. Jacobs. 1987. A public planning perspective on strategic planning. *Journal of the American Planning Association* 53, 1: 21-31.

King, W. R. 1982. Using strategic issue analysis. *Long Range Planning* 15, 4: 45-49.

Klumpp, S. 1986. *Strategic planning booklet for the city of St. Louis Park*. St. Louis Park, Minn.: City of St. Louis Park.

Lindblom, C. E. 1959. The science of muddling through. *Public Administration Review* 19 (Spring): 79–88.

Linneman, R. E., and H. E. Klein.1983. The use of multiple scenarios by U.S. industrial companies: A comparison study, 1977-1981. *Long Range Planning* 16, 6: 94-101.

Locke, E. A., K. W. Shaw, L. M. Saari, and G. P. Latham. 1981. Goal setting and task performance: 1969-1980. *Psychological Bulletin* 90, 1: 125-152.

Lorange, P. 1980. *Corporate planning: An executive viewpoint*. Englewood Cliffs, N.J.: Prentice Hall.

——, M. F. S. Morton, and S. Ghoshal. 1986. *Strategic control*. St. Paul, Minn.: West.

MacMillan, I. 1983. Competitive strategies for not-for-profit agencies. *Advances in Strategic Management* 1: 61-82.

McGowan, R. P., and J. M. Stevens. 1983. Local governments initiatives in a climate of uncertainty. *Public Administration Review* 43, 2: 127-136.

Mintzberg, H., and J. A. Waters. 1985. Of strategies, deliberate and emergent. *Strategic Management Journal* 6, 3: 257-272.

Montanari, J. R., and J. S. Bracker. 1986. The strategic management process. *Strategic Management Journal* 7, 3: 251-265.

Olsen, J. B., and D. C. Eadie. 1982. *The game plan: Governance with foresight*. Washington: Council of State Planning Agencies.

O'Toole, J. 1985. *Vanguard management*. New York: Doubleday.

Ouchi, W. 1981. *Theory Z: How American business can meet the Japanese challenge*. Reading, Mass.: Addison-Wesley.

Peters, T. J., and R. H. Watennan, Jr. 1982. *In search of excellence: Lessons from America's best-run companies*. New York: Harper and Row.

Pettigrew, A. M. 1977. Strategy formulation as a political process. *International Studies in Management and Organization* 7, 2: 78-87.

Pfeffer, J., and G. R. Salanick. 1978. *The external control of organizations: A resource dependence perspective*. New York: Harper and Row.

Pflaum, A., and T. Delmont. 1987. External scanning—A tool for planners. *Journal of the American Planning Association* 53, 1: 56-67.

Pinchot G., III. 1985. *Intrapreneuring*. New York: Harper and Row.

Porter, M. 1980. *Competitive strategy*. New York: Free Press.

_____. 1985. *Competitive advantage*. New York: Free Press.

Quinn, J. B. 1980. *Strategies for change: Logical incrementalism*. Homewood, Ill.: R. D. Irwin.

Ring, P. S., and J. L. Perry. 1985. Strategic management in public and private organizations: Implications of distinctive contexts and constraints. *Academy of Management Review 10*, 2: 276-286.

Rue, L. W., and P. G. Holland. 1986. *Strategic management: Concepts and experiences*. New York: McGraw-Hill.

Savas, E. S. 1982. *Privatizing the public sector*. Chatham, N.J.: Chatham House.

Schön, D. A. 1971. *Beyond the stable state*. London: Temple Smith.

Sorkin, D. L., N. B. Ferris, and J. Hudak. 1984. *Strategies for cities and countries: A strategic planning guide*. Washington: Public Technology, Inc.

Stuart, D. G. 1969. Rational urban planning:

Problems and prospects. *Urban Affairs Quarterly* 5 (December): 151-182.

Susskind, L. E., and C. Ozawa. 1984. Mediated negotiation in the public sector: The planner as mediator. *Journal of Planning Education and Research* 4, 1: 5-15.

Taylor, B. 1984. Strategic planning—Which style do you need? *Long Range Planning* 17, 3: 51-62.

Thompson, J. D. 1967. *Organizations in action.* New York: McGraw–Hill.

Tomazinis, A. R. 1985. The logic and rationale of strategic planning. Paper presented at the 27th annual conference of the Association of Collegiate Schools of Planning, Atlanta. October.

Wildavsky, A. 1979. *Thc politics of the budgeting process.* 3d ed. Boston: Little, Brown.

Wind, Y., and V. Mahajan. 1981. Designing product and business portfolios. *Harvard Business Review* 59, 1: 155-165.

Zaltman, G., D. Florio, and L. Sikorski. 1977. *Dynamic educational change.* New York: Free Press.

SUGGESTED READINGS FOR PART III

Arnstein, Sherry R. "A Ladder of Citizen Participation," *Journal of the American Institute of Planners*, Vol. 35, No. 4, 1969, pp. 216-224.

Banfield, Edward C., and Wilson, James Q. *City Politics.* 1963. New York: Vintage Books.

Barber, Benjamin. *Strong Democracy: Participatory Politics for a New Age.* 1984. Berkeley: University of California Press.

Beauregard, Robert. *Economic Restructuring and Political Response.* 1989. Newbury Park, CA: Sage Publications.

Becker, Gary. *Human Capital*, 2d ed. New York: Columbia.

Benveniste, Guy. *Mastering the Politics of Planning.* 1989. San Francisco: Jossey-Bass Publishers.

Blakely, Edward J. *Planning Local Economic Development: Theory and Practice.* 1989. Newbury Park, CA: Sage Publications.

Bluestone, Barry, and Harrison, Bennett. *The Deindustrialization of America.* 1982. New York: Basic Books.

Blumenfeld, Hans. "The Economic Base of the Metropolis," *Journal of the American Institute of Planners*, Vol. 21, No. 4, 1955, pp. 114-132.

Braybrooke, David, and Lindblom, Charles. *A Strategy of Decision.* 1963. New York: Free Press.

Caro, Robert A. *The Power Broker.* 1974. New York: Random House/Knopf.

Catanese, Anthony James. *The Politics of Planning and Development.* 1984. Beverly Hills, CA: Sage Publications.

Checkoway, Barry. *Strategic Perspectives on Planning Practice.* 1986. Lexington, MA: Heath.

Checkoway, Barry, ed. "Paul Davidoff and Advocacy Planning in Retrospect," *Journal of the American Planning Association*, Vol. 60, No. 2, 1994, pp. 139-161.

Clavel, Pierre. *The Progressive City: Planning and Participation.* 1986. New Brunswick, NJ: Rutgers.

Davidoff, Paul and Davidoff, Linda. "Suburban Action: Advocate Planning for an Open Society," *Journal of the American Planning Association*, Vol. 36, No. 1, 1970, pp. 12-21.

Fisher, Robert, and Ury, William. *Getting to Yes.* 1983. New York: Penguin.

Gans, Herbert J. "Planning and Social Life: Friendship and Neighbor Relations in Suburban Communities," *Journal of the American Institute of Planners*, Vol. 27, No. 3, Part One, 1961, pp. 176-184.

Gans, Herbert J. *The Urban Villages: Group and Class in the Life of Italian Americans.* 1982. New York: Free Press.

Gans, Herbert J. " Deconstructing the Underclass: The Term's Danger as Planning Concept," *Journal of the American Planning Association*, Vol. 56, No. 3, 1990, pp. 271-277.

Goldsmith, William W., and Edward J. Blakely. *Separate Societies: Poverty and Inequality in U.S. Cities.* 1992. Philadelphia: Temple University Press.

Hall, Peter. *Great Planning Disasters.* 1980. London: Weidenfeld & Nicolson.

Hughes, Mark Alan. "Employment Decentralization and Accessibility: A Strategy for Stimulating Regional Mobility," *Journal of the American Planning Association*, Vol. 57, No. 3, 1991.

Jacobs, Jane. *The Economy of Cities.* 1969. New York: Random House.

Jencks, Christopher, and Peterson, Paul E. *The Urban Underclass.* 1992. Washington, D.C.: The Brookings Institution.

Krumholz, Norman. "The Cleveland Policy Planning Report," *Journal of the America Institute of Planners*, Vol. 41, No. 5, 1975, pp. 298-304.

Krumholz, Norman; Kaufman, Jerome L.; Davidoff, Paul; and Susskind, Lawrence. "A Retrospective View of Equity Planning: Cleveland 1969-79," *Journal of the American Planning Association*, Vol. 48, No. 2, 1982, pp. 163-183.

Marris, Peter, and Rein, Martin. *Dilemmas of Social Reform: Poverty and Community Action in the United States.* 1967, 1973. Chicago: Aldine.

Mills, Edward. "Economic Analysis of Urban Land Use Controls," in *Current Issues in Urban Economics* edited by Peter Mieszkowski and Mahlon Straszheim. 1979. Baltimore: Johns Hopkins.

Myrdal, Gunnar. *Rich Lands and Poor.* 1957. New York: Harper.

Orfield, Gary and Ashkinaze, Carole. *The Closing Door: Conservative Policy and Black Opportunity.* 1991. Chicago: The University of Chicago Press.

Peattie, Lisa R. "Reflections on Advocacy Planning," *Journal of the American Institute of Planners*, Vol. 34, No. 2, 1968, pp. 80-88.

Putnam, Robert D. *Bowling Alone: The Collapse and Revival of American Community.* 2001. Simon & Schuster, Inc.

Putnam, Robert D. *Better Together: Restoring the American Community.* 2003. Simon & Schuster, Inc.

Reich, Robert. *The Wealth of Nations.* 1992. New York: Vantage Books.

Rohe, W. and Gates, L. *Planning with Neighborhoods.* 1985. Chapel Hill: The University of North Carolina Press.

Rohe, W. and Mouw, Scott. "The Politics of Relocation: The Moving of the Crest Street Community," *Journal of the American Planning Association*, Vol. 57, No. 1, 1991.

Rondinelli, Dennis A. "Urban Planning as Policy Analysis: Management of Urban Change," *Journal of the American Institute of Planners*, Vol. 39, No. 1, 1973, pp. 13-22.

Rubin, Barry and Wilder, Margaret. "Urban Enterprise Zones: Employment Impacts and Fiscal Incentives," *Journal of the American Planning Association*, Vol. 55, No. 4, 1989, pp. 418-431.

Sagalyn, Lynne B. "Explaining the Improbable: Local Redevelopment in the Wake of Federal Cutbacks," *Journal of the American Planning Association*, Vol. 56, No. 4, 1990.

Schorr, Lisbeth B. *Within Our Reach.* 1988, 1989. New York: Anchor Books, Doubleday & Company, Inc.

Shalala, Donna and Vitullo-Martin, Julia. "Rethinking the Urban Crisis: Proposals for a National Urban Agenda," *Journal of the American Planning Association*, Vol. 55, No. 1, 1989, pp. 3-13.

Spain, Daphne. *Gendered Spaces.* 1992. Chapel Hill: The University of North Carolina Press.

Tabb, William K. and Sawyer, Lang. *Marxism and the Metropolis: New Perspectives in Urban Political Economy.* 1984. New York: Oxford University Press.

IV
Infrastructure: Housing and Transportation

Explaining Homelessness

Jennifer R. Wolch

Michael Dear

Andrea Akita

The problem of homelessness is as pervasive today as it was at the time of this article in the late 1980s. Solutions continue to be elusive. This article presents an explanation of the origins of some of the crises of homelessness. It examines the preconditions of homelessness as well as events that tend to perpetuate the deprivations of the homeless. The authors make the argument that planners need a comprehensive account of the problem to guide them in their choice of intervention strategies that would be considered appropriate at various stages in the cycle of homelessness.

As the number of homeless people in the United States continues to rise, various segments of government and voluntary agencies have intensified their search for ways to diminish the problem. Many policy options have come out of that search, but most have been stopgap, emergency measures to address local crises. Some cities and towns, for example, have converted old armories into temporary shelters, purchased mobile homes to shelter families, or opened urban campgrounds where the homeless can gather. In this article, we do not intend to evaluate those programmatic developments. Instead, we shall introduce into the debate a way to understand homelessness that planners and government agencies often have overlooked. Specifically, we envisage homelessness as the end state of a long and complex social and personal process. Homelessness is not a sudden event in the lives of most victims. It is more usually the culmination of a long process of economic hardship, isolation, and social dislocation—what we regard as the cycle of homelessness. It follows that planning policy aimed at addressing homelessness must also deal with the complexities involved in producing the situation. Each stage in the cycle requires different policy responses, and we must target our interventions appropriately for each stage.

In this article, we present a comprehensive "explanation" of homelessness. We begin by examining the dimensions of the problem through a simple demographic analysis that provides many clues regarding the origins and processes of the cycle. Next, we develop a three-stage model of the causes of homelessness in the United States, focusing on the structural conditions that have led to increased homelessness, and some of personal events that make people homeless. The three stages of the model provide a comprehensive account of the factors that generate homelessness.

Our analysis does not stop at that point. More and more, researchers report that life on the streets aggravates the condition of homelessness. In effect, the experience of being homeless seems to diminish people's capacities to escape from that condition. Hence, we develop the notion of "chronic homelessness" as a final stage, to convey how (for some people) the experience of homelessness becomes a downward spiral of despair and deprivation from which escape is difficult or even impossible.

Our fundamental point throughout this argument is that planners need to be aware of the complex and extended nature of the process of homelessness. Our examination makes it clear that piecemeal intervention can alleviate emergency shelter crises but such action will not resolve the long-term problem of finding permanent shelter for the homeless and returning them to the mainstream of society wherever possible, which we regard as the ultimate goal of intervention. Equally obvious is that while long-term intervention strategies are vital, they do not address the problems of survival for those presently without shelter and support. We conclude that both long- and short-term measures are necessary, but that all the solutions should be based on an integrated, comprehensive understanding of the homelessness problem. Only such a comprehensive approach will allow planners to develop workable strategies with any chance for success.

THE DIMENSIONS OF HOMELESSNESS

Robertson, Ropers, and Boyer (1984) defined "homelessness" simply as the absence of a stable residence, of a place where one can sleep and receive mail. Researchers in the field widely accept that definition and have used it in various efforts to count the homeless. It has numerous problems, however. For example, under that definition an individual living in a single-room occupancy (SRO) housing unit or with a friend or relative has a "home." In reality, however, there are degrees of homelessness, which span a continuum ranging from lack of permanent shelter to inadequate housing conditions and living arrangements (Watson and Austerberry 1986). Another definition of homelessness incorporates a dimension of disaffiliation and social isolation as well as the simple lack of shelter (Bassuk 1984). But such relative definitions, while conceptually attractive, are difficult to operationalize.

The fact that the homeless population is notoriously fugitive compounds the problems of defining homelessness. Different definitional and enumeration strategies have produced widely varied estimates of the numbers of homeless in the United States (Table IV.1). A 1984 survey that the Department of Housing and Urban Development conducted, based on shelter population and service provider information, suggested a figure between 250,000 and 350,000. On any given night, the demand for bedspaces exceeded supply by 140,000 (U.S. Department of Housing and Urban Development 1984). Human services professionals have severely criticized those figures. For instance, the National Coalition for the Homeless estimated that there were 2.5 million homeless in 1985, up

half a million since 1982 (Ito 1988). Regardless of which baseline they accept, almost all analysts agree that there has been a steady increase in the numbers of homeless since those surveys. The U.S. Conference of Mayors (1986a; 1986b) cites an average annual increase of 20 percent in the number of people seeking emergency shelter.

In addition to a rise in numbers, the composition of the homeless population is changing (Bingham, Green, and White 1987). The typical image of the homeless person as a middle-aged, male alcoholic is giving way to a much more varied picture. Now the homeless include many young people, families, children, recently unemployed, the deinstitutionalized (particularly the mentally disabled), and substance abusers (U.S. Department of Housing and Urban Development 1984; U.S. Congress 1986). The young homeless are often runaways, but the population also consists of a significant proportion of schizophrenic and other mentally disabled people who would have been institutionalized in a previous era (Bachrach 1984; Lamb 1984). Homeless families tend to be single women with their children, but two-parent families are increasingly common (Jones 1987). The unemployed span most age, gender, and racial/ethnic dimensions; many are veterans. The special problems of homeless women have attracted much recent attention (e.g., Birch 1985; Watson and Austerberry 1986).

Homelessness occurs in both urban and rural areas and in cities of all sizes. In most regions those made homeless through economic circumstances constitute fully one-half of the population in need of shelter. Another one-quarter of the population are former psychiatric patients (although that percentage may be as high as one-half in certain towns and cities). The remaining one-quarter have suffered setbacks in personal circumstances, including natural disasters and family crises (Robertson, Ropers, and Boyer 1985). There are also significant regional variations in the composition of the homeless population; for example, a significant proportion of the homeless in the southwest are native Americans.

THE PATH TO HOMELESSNESS

Figure IV.1 shows the three stages or elements we propose for the process of homelessness in the

Table IV.1 Homeless people in selected American cities

City, by region	Population[a] (1980)	Number of homeless[b] (1984)	Rate per 1,000 population[c] (Low–high)
Northeast			
Baltimore	786,775	8,000-15,000	10.17-19.07
Boston	562,994	2,000-8,000	3.55-14.21
Brockton	95,172	250	2.63
Buffalo	357,870	500	1.40
Cleveland	573,822	400-1,000	0.70-1.74
Elizabeth	106,201	300	2.82
New York	7,071,639	36,000-50,000	5.09-7.07
Philadelphia	1,688,210	8,000	4.74
Pittsburgh	423,938	1,500	3.54
Rochester	241,741	400-500	1.65-2.07
Springfield	152,319	570-780	3.74-5.12
Syracuse	170,105	450	2.65
Washington	638,333	5,000-10,000	7.83-15.67
Worcester	161,799	2,500	15.45
Southeast			
Atlanta	425,022	1,500-3,000	3.53-8.23
Birmingham	284,413	291	1.02
Jacksonville	540,920	150-300	0.28-0.55
Miami	346,865	4,000	11.53
New Orleans	557,515	700	1.26
Norfolk	266,979	100-300	0.37-1.12
Orlando	128,291	400	3.12
Richmond	219,214	2,000-4,000	9.12-18.25
Midwest			
Chicago	3,005,072	12,000-25,000	3.99-8.32
Denver	492,365	1,500-5,000	3.05-10.16
Detroit	1,203,339	2,000-8,000	1.66-6.65
Minneapolis	370,951	900	2.43
Salt Lake City	163,033	600-1,000	3.68-6.13
Tulsa	360,919	1,300	3.60
Northwest			
Portland	366,383	1,000-2,000	2.73-5.46
Seattle	493,846	500-5,000	1.01-10.12
Southwest			
Fresno	218,202	600	2.75
Los Angeles	2,966,850	22,000-30,000	7.42-10.11
Phoenix	789,850	500-6,200	0.63-7.85
San Francisco	678,974	4,500-10,000	6.63-14.73
San Jose	629,442	1,000	1.59
Tucson	330,537	3,000	9.08

a. *Source:* U.S. Department of Commerce, Bureau of the Census 1980.

b. *Source:* U.S. Department of Housing and Urban Development 1984, Table 1.

c. The choice of population base has significant impact on the calculation of the rate of homelessness. This table uses *city* population to compute the rate. However, different rates result from county or SMSA statistics. For example, for both county and SMSA in Los Angeles, the homeless rate drops to 2.94-4.01 (compared with 7.42-10.11 in the table). In New York, the SMSA-based rate of homelessness is 3.95-5.48; for the county base, 25.21-35.01. For this sample of cities, there can be no consistent rationale for city, county, or SMSA figures. That, plus the inherent unreliability in the homeless-ness figures, led us to make the arbitrary choice of city-based estimates.

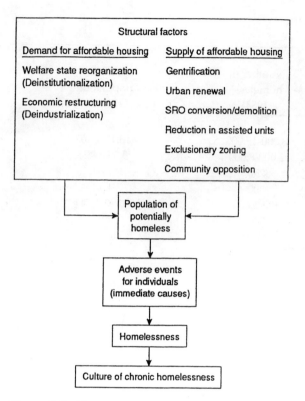

Structural factors

Demand for affordable housing	Supply of affordable housing
Welfare state reorganization (Deinstitutionalization)	Gentrification
	Urban renewal
Economic restructuring (Deindustrialization)	SRO conversion/demolition
	Reduction in assisted units
	Exclusionary zoning
	Community opposition

Population of potentially homeless

↓

Adverse events for individuals (immediate causes)

↓

Homelessness

↓

Culture of chronic homelessness

Figure IV.1 The path to homelessness.

United States. First, a set of structural (or contextual) factors operates on the national and state levels over the long term. Those factors relate especially to underlying changes in the economy and in the patterns of welfare provision. One important effect of the changes has been to increase the demand for temporary shelter. Second, our model identifies a number of components on the supply side that contribute to the increase in homelessness. Those components have combined to drastically reduce the amount of affordable accommodation available to people in marginal economic circumstances. Third, our model focuses on the individual to account for particular adverse events that Propel people into homelessness.

The structural context of homelessness

Since the 1960s, two major national trends have contributed to an increase in the population of "potentially homeless," whom we define as those living in marginal economic and housing circumstances. The trends are the reduction in public expenditures on welfare and other service-related programs and, with it, the development of the deinstitutionalization movement; and the trend

toward deindustrialization and its concomitant unemployment and poverty, which are associated with deep-seated changes in the structure of the economy.

Deinstitutionalization in the United States received a federal seal of approval in 1963 with passage of the Community Mental Health Centers Act. That legislation cleared the way for moving psychiatric patients out of mental hospitals and—according to the plan—into community-based treatment and service settings. Other deinstitutionalized groups included the mentally retarded, the physically disabled, the dependent elderly, and probationers and parolees (Dear and Wolch 1987; Lerman 1982). Unfortunately, the government subsequently allocated a woefully inadequate amount for community-based programs. As a consequence, the deinstitutionalized were no longer a priority. They tended to drift toward inner-city neighborhoods where cheap rental accommodation and most of the health and welfare services available to them existed (Wolpert, Dear, and Crawford 1975; Dear 1977; Wolch 1980). The dearth of adequate community-based shelter and service facilities even in inner–cities has caused the deinstitutionalized to become a major component of today's homeless population (Lamb 1984).

Recent reductions in social expenditures have exacerbated the plight of those vulnerable, welfare-dependent populations (Dear and Wolch 1987; Wolch and Akita 1988). Significant shifts in welfare state budgets began in the 1970s, and accelerated under the Reagan administration. Many federal programs fell to state and local governments; and the private and voluntary, and non-profit sectors had to replace other federal efforts, a trend we call "privatization." The reorganization of federal spending has pushed millions of people who depend upon social services and welfare checks to the brink of poverty or further beneath the poverty threshold, and has caused many to become homeless.

The victims of deindustrialization have joined the deinstitutionalized in the streets and on the sidewalks. "Deindustrialization" refers to the declining fortunes of the manufacturing sector in general and particularly to large-scale plant closures in the traditional centers of production in the "snowbelt" cities of the northeast (Bluestone and

Harrison 1982). The process has accelerated through the 1980s as a result of economic recession; fluctuations in the value of the dollar; and the decline of union membership and influence, which has cost jobs on the line. Those factors raised unemployment levels and created the highest rate of official poverty since the early 1960s. By 1982, 15 percent (34.4 million) of the nation's population was living below the poverty line, an increase of 40 percent since 1978 (Danziger and Feaster 1985).

The recent economic recovery has not fundamentally changed prospects for the poor. While expansion in service sector employment has somewhat offset the decline in the manufacturing sector, many of the new jobs being created are low wage, low skilled, and part time. The economic security those jobs offer is tenuous and such trends have seriously hurt many workers and their families.

The diminishing supply of affordable housing

Across America, there has been a substantial decline in the number of housing units that low income people and those in need of shelter assistance can afford (City of Chicago 1985; Baxter and Hopper 1982). Those losses have resulted primarily from downtown urban renewal, gentrification, and abandonment, and from suburban land use controls. The elimination and reduction of federal low income housing programs has also dramatically curtailed the supply of affordable shelter. Construction of low income and assisted housing has essentially stopped (*Newsweek* 1984). Currently, the net change in the publicly assisted housing stock is negative; more units are being demolished or released from subsidy requirements than are being constructed (Herbers 1987).

Competition for the remaining housing units has intensified, forcing costs up in both the owner-occupied and rental sectors of the housing market, to the point that many planners consider it a crisis situation. Brown and Apgar (1988) highlight the dimensions of that crisis. Two million households that could afford to buy a home in 1980 cannot do so today. Rents have risen at a rate 14 percent higher than prices generally. The result of rising rents and (for many) declining incomes is a dramatic increase in the amount of income people pay

for rent. It is now typical for households to spend 30 to 50 percent of income on rent; the proportion reaches almost 60 percent for single-parent households. Only 28 percent of poor renter households live in public housing or receive federal housing subsidies, leaving 5.4 million poor households competing for the stock of private sector rental housing (Brown and Apgar 1988).

The amount of housing available in the private sector rental stock is also diminishing rapidly. As more and more landlords abandon apartment buildings and houses rather than repair them, the housing supply for the poor has declined at an accelerating pace in some cities (Sternlieb et al. 1980; Dowall 1985; Wolch and Gabriel 1985; Palmer and Sawhill 1984; Wolpert and Seley 1986). The growth of service-sector employment in central business districts has attracted white-collar professionals, many of whom prefer to live in accessible central city neighborhoods (Soja, Morales, and Wolfe 1983), where they compete with poor, indigenous residents for private market housing (Lipton 1977; Noyelle 1983). The result is frequently gentrification of inner city housing which traditionally has been the major source of low income housing. At the same time, downtown service sector expansion has created jobs for many low-waged ancillary workers, increasing the demand for low cost shelter readily accessible to the downtown (Sassen-Koob 1984).

In response to the pressures of gentrification and urban renewal, developers have demolished thousands of single-room occupancy (SRO) units or converted them to condominiums. In Chicago, for example, 300 SRO units were lost to gentrification in 1981-1982, and a total of 18,000 units have been demolished or converted since 1973 (Fustero 1984; City of Chicago 1985: 23). In New York City, city-sponsored legislation encouraged the demolition of SROs and their replacement by luxury condominiums; more than 31,000 units were lost between 1975 and 1981. Chester Hartman has estimated the number of New York City SROs dropped from 170,000 in 1971 to 14,000 by the mid-1980s (quoted in Holden 1986).

The concentration of the homeless in downtown areas has been accelerated by exclusionary zoning practices and community opposition to local siting of shelters and services for the homeless (Dear and Taylor 1982; Wolch and Gabriel

1985). Many suburban jurisdictions have used zoning to limit the number and types of community-based service facilities and to restrict the development of subsidized housing projects. One of the most common zoning approaches is to require a conditional use permit for service facility siting; neighborhood opposition to the service or its clients is mobilized and results in the denial of the—use permit (Dear and Wolch 1987).

Events that precipitate homelessness

Increased demand for and diminished supply of shelter together can underlie much of the homelessness in the nation. But those problems do not explain the actual adverse events that may cause a person to become homeless. Many people experience adverse events in the housing market (eviction is one of them). For most people those occurrences represent only a temporary setback. However, for those who already live in marginal economic and housing conditions a single adverse event can be a sufficient catalyst for the fall into homelessness (McChesney 1986; Sullivan and Damrosch 1987; Farr, Koegel, and Burnam 1986; Baxter and Hopper 1982). The five most common immediate causes of homelessness that individuals report are eviction, discharge from an institution, loss of a job, personal crisis (including divorce or domestic violence), and removal of monetary or nonmonetary welfare support.

THE CULTURE OF CHRONICITY

Many homeless people are caught in a vicious cycle of deteriorating circumstances—a downward spiral that affects their mental, social, and physical well-being Unable to help themselves, refused aid, or given inappropriate assistance, their difficulties accumulate: families break up; health and appearance decline; and victimization (robbery, mugging) increases. Such circumstances threaten to create a new class, the "chronically" homeless, people for whom the experience of homelessness itself creates a new set of social and personal crises that tend to perpetuate the problem. Such individuals inhabit what we term a "culture of chronicity."

What causes a person, once homeless, to remain so? The answer to that question lies in the pathology of everyday life on the streets. Evidence

suggests that five factors determine whether or not an individual will escape homelessness (see, for example, Hope and Young 1986): experiences in temporary shelter, financial status, availability of assistance, personal status (including health), and street experience.

Living conditions in temporary and emergency shelters are often so bad that many homeless prefer to avoid them (Baxter and Hopper 1982; *New York Times* March 5, 1988). Some shelters are centers of crime, including substance abuse and personal violence. Even at best, merely having to be in one can seriously depress the morale of the newly homeless (Coleman 1986).

The management and operation of shelters can also affect the lives of the homeless. Some shelters systematically exclude certain groups through eligibility requirements (for instance, refusing admission to women or the mentally disabled). Others have obtrusive routines, including long and detailed intake procedures, or degrading and humiliating residence rules such as mandatory gynecological examinations for women (Redburn and Buss 1986).

With or without shelter, the homeless lead precarious daily lives. The financial resources most public programs offer are so low that the recipients can barely survive. For example, in 1987 general relief payments in Los Angeles County were approximately $250 per month. That allowed for three weeks' SRO accommodation, with nothing left for the fourth week's shelter or for food (Dear and Wolch 1987). The homeless typically supplement their incomes by casual day labor, begging, and prostitution (City of Chicago 1985: 33–55; Parr, Koegel, and Burnam 1986), but nonetheless do not earn enough to rent permanent shelter.

The homeless depend not only on income and financial assistance, but also on other forms of support such as food programs, job search services, and clothing provision. However, access to those services is limited and frequently involves long waiting lists and intrusive procedures. For example, Los Angeles County's "60-day rule" allows welfare officers to suspend benefits for two months for some real or perceived breach of agency rules (Dear and Wolch 1987). Those transgressions can include arriving late for an interview or failing to have a required number of job interviews in a month. Suspended claimants receive no welfare payments. For those who avoid suspension, the day is often spent standing in lines or moving between agencies in search of benefits (Rousseau 1981).

An individual's personal strength, both emotional and physical, is an important determinant of how well he or she will stand up to the rigors of life on the street. It is difficult to remain optimistic and healthy when cleanliness is an impossible goal, sleep a luxury, nutritious food scarce, and health care nonexistent. To sleep in the open in wintertime can cause death through hypothermia; in the summer, such exposure can cause sunburn or sunstroke. To stay in public shelters overnight often leaves lice infestations and empty pockets (Baxter and Hopper 1982).

Life on the street tends to exacerbate the experience of homelessness (Erickson and Wilhelm 1986; Hope and Young 1986). Although in certain respects the homeless reap some benefits from gathering in the inner city, including access to services and social support from other homeless people, they also have to contend with life in degraded physical environments.

Muggings are common, as is harassment by police and by other street people. Many homeless report that their daytime activity is "moving or walking," largely for self-protection (City of Chicago 1985).

In sum, the condition of homelessness appears to have a cumulative effect on its victims. Once on the street, physical and mental health problems rapidly surface, even among those with no previous history of such problems. As time passes, the dividing line between those with a history of mental disability and those with street-induced emotional problems becomes increasingly fuzzy (Koegel and Burnam, in press). Many people find that the descent into "chronic" homelessness can be sickeningly quick. In a bizarre concession to the speed with which lives can unravel, one shelter in Long Beach, California, refused beds to people who had been homeless for over two weeks, on the grounds that they were already beyond rehabilitation (Dear and Wolch 1987).

PUBLIC POLICY AND HOMELESSNESS

The problem of homelessness is unlikely to diminish, at least in the immediate future. The difficul-ties and adjustments of economic restructuring and of welfare state reorganization continue relatively unabated. In this section we examine some of the difficulties facing planners who wish to address the issue of homelessness.

Economic recovery and expansion may provide employment opportunities that could make it possible for some of the unemployed homeless to support themselves. However, industrial restructuring has led to the disappearance of many job categories that those people might have filled in the past (Roderick 1985). Increasingly, new jobs, primarily in the service sector, tend to be either high skill/high wage positions or low skill/low wage posts. The result seems to be a growing inequality in income distribution (Storper and Scott, in press). Many of the homeless lack skills and training for high wage jobs, and job training opportunities are scarce. A large proportion of the remaining, low wage, part time, casual jobs do not provide benefits such as health insurance or sick leave. Between 1979 and 1984, 44 percent of the net new jobs created only paid poverty level wages (Bluestone and Harrison 1987). Even full time work at the current minimum wage may not remove people from poverty status. Finally, we cannot forget that many of the homeless remain outside the labor market—either permanently (e.g., the chronic psychiatric patient) or temporarily (e.g., the single parent committed to child care).

Changes in the economic climate are likely to have only limited impact on homelessness. What future lies in the reorganized welfare state? Between 1982 and 1985, the Reagan administration cut federal programs targeted to the poor by $57 billion (adjusted for inflation; Wolch and Akita, in press). Housing in particular has fallen relative to other federal spending priorities; federal authorizations for housing were 7 percent of the total federal budget in 1978, but now they amount only to 0.7 percent (Dear 1988). Table 2 shows the extent of cuts in housing, job training, food and nutrition, social services, and income maintenance. The federal government assisted an estimated one million fewer households in 1985 than in the pre-Reagan era due to cuts in subsidized housing; 300,000 more families were living in substandard housing; hundreds of thousands have been removed from job training programs, medical insurance plans, and disability rolls; and many others have lost AFDC, foodstamps, and food nutrition benefits (Wolch and Akita, in press).

The Reagan administration has provided only extremely limited programs to the homeless. Until 1987, the administration's involvement was restricted to provision of emergency relief to meet immediate needs for food and shelter through the Federal Emergency Management Agency, the Department of Defense, the Department of Agriculture, and the Department of Housing and Urban Development; coordination of federal efforts through a federal task force on the homeless; and administrative reforms to make existing services more readily available to the homeless. Although estimates of the amount of assistance provided to the homeless through the means-tested income maintenance and service programs are difficult to obtain, in 1987 only $250 million was *specifically* targeted for the homeless (Wolch and

Akita, in press). In late 1987, Congress passed the McKinney Act, which authorized approximately $442 million in 1987 and $616 million for 1988, for a variety of homeless assistance programs; the actual appropriations, however, came to $365 million for 1987, and $356 for 1988 (*Safety Network* 1988a). Also a recently ratified housing bill authorized $15 billion to augment housing and community development programs (*Safety Network* 1988b).

Those spending commitments are important, but they will not be sufficient to bridge the growing gap between the demand for and supply of affordable housing. The National Association of Housing and Redevelopment Officials (1987) estimates that the low income population will grow by more than five million and that nearly eight million additional low cost housing units will be needed by the year 2000. In addition, the govern-

Table IV.2 Changes in federal domestic spending, 1980-1987*

	Constant 1980 dollars (in millions)			Percent change		Dollar change (in millions)	
	1980 Actual	1986 Actual	1986 Proposed	Actual	Proposed	Actual	Proposed
Subsidized housing	26.70	7.01	0.37	−74	−99	−19.69	−26.33
Public housing operating subsidies	0.75	0.86	0.78	14	47	0.11	0.03
Low rent public housing	—	0.67	1.34	—	—	0.67	1.34
Section 202	0 75	0.37	0.00	−50	−100	−0.38	0.75
Total assisted housing	28.20	8.92	2.50	−37	−65	−19.28	−25.70
CETA/JTPA (public service employment and training)	8.95	2.72	2.65	−70	−70	−6.23	−6.30
Work Incentive Program (WIN)	0.40	0.19	0.04	−53	−91	−0.21	−0.36
All employment and training[a]	10.35	3.92	3.69	−62	−64	−6.43	−6.66
Community Service Block Grants[b]	0.60	0.26	0.11	−56	−81	−0.34	−0.49
Title XX—Social Service Block Grant	2.70	1.98	2.01	−27	−25	−0.72	−0.69
Total community and social services	3.30	2.24	2.13	−41	−53	−1.06	−1.17
Food stamps	9.20	8.66	9.48	−6	3	−0.54	0.28
Child nutrition	4.00	2.84	2.57	−29	−36	−1.16	−1.43
Women, Infants and Children (WIC)	0.70	1.19	1.12	71	60	0.49	0.42
Total food/nutrition programs	13.90	12.69	13.17	18	14	−1.21	−0.73
Unemployment compensation	18.00	13.02	12.16	−28	−32	−4.98	−5.84
AFDC[c]	7.70	6.79	5.97	−12	−22	−0.91	−1.73
Supplemental Security Income	6.40	7.72	7.39	21	15	1.32	0.99
Low Income Energy Assistance	1.60	1.64	0.97	2	−39	0.04	−0.63
Medicare	32.10	52.35	50.11	63	56	20.25	18.01
Medicaid	14.05	18.66	17.69	33	26	4.61	3.64
Heath services	3.95	2.87	3.36	−27	−15	−1.08	−0.59
Total health. services	50.10	73.88	71.16	35	34	23.78	21.06

* Budget outlays are reported to reflect program levels, with the exception of housing programs, where budget authority figures are used. Percentage change totals represent averages for subcategories.
Source: Wolch and Akita, in press. Data derived from the U.S Congress, House of Representatives Committee on the Budget, 1982-1987.
   a. Includes JTPA, WIN, and other job and training programs.
   b. The Reagan Administration proposed to eliminate these programs (no budget authority requested).
   c. Figures for AFDC for 1980 were not available, therefore 1981 amounts (expressed in 1980 dollars) are used as a base.

ment will decontrol 1.9 million currently-subsidized units over the next two decades.

Other forces, beyond the purview of the federal government, influence the provision of welfare and social services to the homeless in communities. For instance, very few state or local governments have the financial resources—or political will—to address the problem comprehensively. Many urban governments have sought to shift responsibility to others, through law suits and lobbying efforts (Dear and Wolch 1987).

More and more homeless people are moving to older suburbs and outlying communities. Their visibility is mounting in tolerant liberal communities, racially-mixed suburbs, and lower income inner-ring localities, as well as in more conservative, affluent, single-family housing zones. That visibility, and the fiscal burdens associated with the homeless, have generated a backlash (Muir 1987). According to national and local advocacy groups, "1987 marked the beginning of a dangerous trend that places the aesthetic concerns of select groups of business and property owners above the life-or-death needs of the homeless" (*Safety Network* 1988c: 2). Even traditionally accepting neighborhoods are starting to squeeze out the homeless. Their efforts include "anti-bum" ordinances, increased enforcement of vagrancy laws, park-watering policies designed to make public parks soggy and uninviting, and exclusion of public and private service agencies viewed as magnets that attract more homeless persons (Winerip 1988; Ito 1988).

Another trend, potentially of vital importance, is the growth of a "new asylum movement," backed by many human services professionals who perceive the need to reestablish "comfortable, friendly asylums" for chronically ill homeless people (Bassuk 1984). Advocates of the movement come mainly from among psychiatric and penal workers. Their impetus seems to derive from a feeling of hopelessness in the face of the massive problems of the homeless population, as well as from a somewhat belated recognition that many chronically ill alcoholics, other substance abusers, and mentally disabled have already been institutionalized in prisons. For example, one-eighth of California's prison population is classified as "severely mentally ill" (Dear and Wolch 1987). If the new asylum movement continues to gain

impetus, the threat facing many of the homeless will be *reinstitutionalization* (Wolch, Nelson, and Rubalcaba, in press).

WHAT CAN PLANNERS DO?

Planners can play an important role in the search for solutions to homelessness. But first we must recognize that we are dealing with a problem that has been over two decades in the making. Hence, "quick-fix" solutions are likely to have only a superficial impact (Redburn and Buss 1986). Homelessness is an extensive, complex process. We need very different kinds of intervention to deal with the diverse aspects of the problem: economic and welfare state restructuring; the supply of affordable housing and emergency shelter; the adverse events that create homelessness; and the culture of chronic homelessness. It is beyond the scope of this article to address all aspects of public policy toward the homeless. Instead, in the final section, we emphasize those interventions that flow from our model, in which the planner's skills may have the most immediate impact. Specifically, our analysis of homelessness emphasizes the importance of local physical-spatial planning decisions to the development of adequate systems of shelter and services for the homeless and for service-dependent populations most likely to become homeless. We must design and develop such systems if homelessness is to be prevented, and if those now homeless are to regain their housing and their roles in communities and workplaces.

Emergency shelter. The most urgent problem is to provide a range of emergency shelter in all communities that have significant homelessness. Immediately available shelter is critical to prevent the descent into chronic homelessness. Planners can assist in developing estimates of the need for shelter in their communities, as well as in identifying sites suitable for new construction or conversion to shelters; they also can help providers obtain zoning approvals. In Los Angeles, city planners have become involved in such provider assistance, most recently by helping site a service facility for the homeless mentally disabled, which the Los Angeles Men's Place (LAMP) administers in an industrial-zoned area east of the central business district.

Fair-share planning. Planners need to devise "fair-share" solutions to the problem of distributing the burden of caring for the homeless. Too often shelters and services remain geographically concentrated in downtown or inner-city areas. The community backlash is partly related to the feeling that communities either are or will become "saturated" with the homeless and with service facilities designated to assist them. As we have discussed, inner-city communities have increasingly rejected services from their midst and have planned no alternative service sites as replacements; the result is a net loss of service capacity. Hence, many cities are wrestling to devise appropriate methods of planning for a more equitable distribution of shelter and services. Planners have been at the forefront in developing fair-share approaches to metropolitan housing, tax/revenue, and environment problems: we can offer valuable experience to policy makers. One example of a limited fair-share policy comes from Portland, Oregon, which has developed a fair-share plan to divert new residential service facilities from neighborhoods defined as saturated to other parts of the city. That scheme allows communities to choose between more numerous but lower impact facilities and clients or smaller numbers of higher impact installations (Dear and Wolch 1987).

Community education. Gaining community acceptance of controversial but essential facilities depends upon educating and informing neighbors of the likely impacts of such facilities. Failure to educate and involve the neighborhood in the siting process can result in refusal to allow needed facilities to be developed. Planners can help provide such information and can help devise appropriate siting strategies for targeted communities (cf., Jaffe and Smith 1986). For example, the Robert Wood Johnson Foundation program for the homeless mentally disabled has successfully incorporated community education into their siting strategy. In Ontario, Canada, planners worked with mental health providers to design and implement a community education campaign to increase acceptance of facilities for the mentally disabled. Evaluation of that program indicates that such efforts can heighten tolerance and stimulate more accepting attitudes among community residents.

Integration of physical and social planning. The problems arising from deinstitutionalization policies, so closely linked to the homeless crisis, resulted, in part, from the lack of coordination between social service policy makers and the local planners responsible for urban land use. Health service professionals commonly identify three types of shelter the homeless may need (Kaufman 1986): emergency shelter, transitional living arrangements, and permanent housing. The challenge facing planners is to assist the helping professions place their health and welfare programs in physical structures with accessible locations. Doing so involves finding sites close to established centers of need, facilitating appropriate building conversions or construction and making post-occupancy evaluations. In California initiatives are underway to begin integrating physical and social planning, the state has proposed legislation to provide local jurisdictions with community-based service facility data and encourage the use of that information in planning and zoning.

Physical-spatial design of service resources. Providing shelter alone is not typically sufficient to bring homeless people back into the mainstream of society. Since the experience of being in a shelter itself can lead to chronic homelessness if the shelter is not adequately organized, designed, and accessible to essential services, the planner's understanding of how land uses and people interact can be important in helping the community to design shelter/services systems. We use the term "service hubs" to describe collections of housing, service, and social opportunities that are close enough together that they can serve the poor and homeless in a coordinated way (Dear and Wolch 1987). The service hub is, in effect, a social support network vital to help the homeless recover. Once again, the task facing the planner is to design a built environment that promotes the development of social interaction and support. The Single Room Occupancy Housing Corporation of Los Angeles has embraced this approach. The corporation's program of SRO hotel renovation, neighborhood park improvement, and service provision is designed to make a small portion of Los Angeles' Skid Row an "island of sanity" for low income elderly and dependent SRO residents. In Ontario, Canada, the Canadian Mental Health Association has also adopted the service hub approach as part of their national policy priorities, and some Ontario cities have incorporated service hubs in their formal process of land use planning (Dear and Wolch 1987).

CONCLUSION

In this article we focused on the complexities of the homelessness problem. To break the cycle of homelessness, planners need to design interventions with an awareness of exactly where in the cycle those interventions are likely to be most effective.

Author's note: This research was supported by Grant #SES-8704256 from the National Science Foundation.

REFERENCES

Bachrach, Leona. 1984. Interpreting Research on the Homeless Mentally Ill. *Hospital and Community Psychiatry* 35: 914-16.

Bassuk, Ellen. 1984. The Homelessness Problem. *Scientific American* 251: 40-45.

Baxter, Ellen, and Kim Hopper. 1982. The New Mendicancy: Homeless in New York City. *American Journal of Orthopsychiatry* 52: 392-408.

Bingham, Richard, Roy Green, and Sammis White, eds. 1987. *The Homeless in Contemporary Society*. Newbury Park, CA: Sage.

Birch, Eugenie Ladner, ed. 1985. *The Unsheltered Woman*. New Brunswick, NJ: Center for Urban Policy Research.

Bluestone, Barry, and Bennett Harrison. 1987. The Grim Truth About the Job "Miracle." *New York Times* 1 February.

_____. 1982. *The Deindustrialization of America*. New York: Basic Books.

Brown, H. James, and William Apgar. 1988. *The State of the Nation's Housing*. Cambridge, MA: Harvard Joint Center for Housing Studies.

City of Chicago, Department of Planning. 1985. *Housing Needs of Chicago's Single, Low-Income Renters*. Chicago: City of Chicago Department of Planning.

Coleman, John. 1986. Diary of a Homeless Man, pp. 37-53 in *Housing the Homeless*, edited by Jon Erickson and Charles Wilhelm. New Brunswick, NJ: Center for Urban Policy Research.

Danzinger, Sheldon, and Daniel Feaster. 1985. Income Transfers and Poverty in the 1980s, pp. 89-117 in *American Domestic Priorities*, edited by John M. Quigley and David L. Rubinfeld. Berkeley: University of California Press.

Dear, Michael J. 1977. Psychiatric Patients in the Inner City. *Annals of the Association of American Geographers* 67: 588-94.

_____. 1988. Our "Third World" of Housing Have-nots Needs Action. *Los Angeles Times* 8 February.

Dear, Michael J., and S. Martin Taylor. 1982. *Not on Our Street*. London: Pion.

Dear, Michael J., and Jennifer R. Wolch. 1987. *Landscapes of Despair: From Deinstitutionalization to Homelessness*. Princeton, NJ: Princeton University Press.

Dowall, David. 1985. *The Suburban Squeeze*. Berkeley: University of California Press.

Erickson, Jon, and Charles Wilhelm, eds. 1986. *Housing the Homeless*. New Brunswick, NJ: Center for Urban Policy Research.

Farr, Rodger, Paul Koegel, and Audrey Burnam. 1986. A Study of Homelessness and Mental Illness in the Skid Row Area of Los Angeles. Los Angeles: County of Los Angeles Department of Mental Health.

Fustero, S. 1984. Home on the Street. *Psychology Today* 18 (February): 56-63.

Herbers, J. 1987. Outlook for Sheltering the Poor Growing Even Bleaker. *New York Times* 8 March.

Holden, C. 1986. Homelessness: Experts Differ on Root Cause. *Science* 237 (2 May): 569-70.

Hope, Marjorie, and James Young. 1986. *The Faces of Homelessness*. Lexington, MA: Lexington Books.

Ito, Sheldon. 1988. Plans to House Homeless on VA Property Dropped. *Los Angeles Times* 17 March.

Jaffe, Martin, and Thomas Smith. 1986. *Siting Group Homes for Developmentally Disabled Persons*, Planning Advisory Service Report 397. Chicago: American Planning Association.

Jones, Lanie. 1987. Youngsters Share Plight of Homeless. *Los Angeles Times* 19 May.

Kaufman, Nancy. 1986. Homeless: A Comprehensive Policy Approach, pp. 335-48 in *Housing the Homeless*, edited by Jon Wilhem and Charles Erickson. New Brunswick, NJ: Center for Urban Policy Research.

Koegel, Paul, and Audrey Burnam. In press. Problems in the Assessment of Mental Illness Among the Homeless: An Empirical Approach. In *Homelessness: The National Perspective*, edited by M. J. Robertston and M. Greenblatt. New York: Plenum Press.

Lamb, Richard. 1984. *The Homeless Mentally Ill.* Washington: American Psychiatric Association.

Lerman, Paul. 1982. *Deinstitutionalization and the Welfare State*. New Brunswick, NJ: Rutgers University Press.

Lipton, G. 1977. Evidence of Central City Revival. *Journal of the American Institute of Planners* 43: 136-47.

McChesney, Kay. 1986. New Findings on Homeless Families. Working Paper, Social Science Research Institute, University of Southern California. Los Angeles: University of Southern California.

Muir, Frederick. 1987. Homeless Plight Made Worse by Growing Backlash, Advocates Report. *Los Angeles Times* 22 December.

National Association of Housing and Redevelopment Officials. 1987. *Keeping the Commitment: An Action Plan for Better Housing and Communities for All.* Washington: National Association of Housing and Redevelopment Officials.

New York Times. 1988. Fear of Shelters Sends Many to Street. 5 March.

Newsweek. 1984. Homeless in America. *Newsweek* 103 2 January: 20-29.

Noyelle, Thierry. 1983. The Rise of Advanced Services. *Journal of the American Planning Association* 49: 280-90.

Palmer, John, and Isabel Sawhill. 1984. *The Reagan Record: An Assessment of America's Changing Domestic Priorities*. Washington: The Urban Institute.

Redburn, F. Stevens, and Terry Buss. 1986. *Responding to America's Homeless*. New York: Praeger.

Robertson, Marjorie, Richard Ropers, and R. Boyer. 1984. Emergency Shelter for the Homeless in Los Angeles County. UCLA Basic Shelter Research Project, Document #2, School of Public Health. Los Angeles: University of California, Los Angeles.

_____. 1985. The Homeless of Los Angeles County: An Empirical Evaluation. UCLA Basic Shelter Research Project, Document #4, School of Public Health. Los Angeles: University of California, Los Angeles.

Roderick, K. 1985. Homeless—Left Behind by Recovery. *Los Angeles Times* 2 February.

Rousseau, A. M. 1981. *Shopping Bag Ladies*. New York: Pilgrim Press.

Safety Network. 1988a. McKinney Funds Slashed; Homeless Lose $250 Million. January.

_____. 1988b. Housing Bill Passed, Funds Community Programs. January.

_____. 1988c. LA's Homeless Citizens, Providers Hit Hard by Backlash Activity. January.

Sassen-Koob, Saskia. 1984. The New Labor Demand in Global Cities. Pp 139-71 in *Cities in Transformation*, edited by Michael P. Smith. Beverly Hills, CA: Sage.

Soja, Edward, Rebecca Morales, and Goetz Wolff. 1983. Urban Restructuring: An Analysis of Social and Spatial Change in Los Angeles. *Economic Geography* 59: 195-230.

Sternlieb, George, James W. Hughes, Robert W. Burchell, Stephen C. Casey, Robert W. Lake, and David Listokin. 1980. *America's Housing*. New Brunswick, NJ: Center for Urban Policy Research.

Storper, Michael, and Allen J. Scott. In press. The Geographical Foundations and Social Regulation of Flexible Production Complexes. In *The Power of Geography: How Territory Shapes Social Life*, edited by Jennifer Wolch and Michael Dear. London: Allen and Unwin.

Sullivan, Patricia, and Shirley Damrosch. 1987. Homeless Women and Children, pp. 82-98 in *The Homeless in Contemporary Society*, edited by Richard Bingham, Roy Green, and Sammis White. Newbury Park, CA: Sage.

United States Conference of Mayors. 1986a. The Growth of Hunger, Homelessness and Poverty in America's Cities in 1985: A 25 City Survey. Pp 103-40 in *Hunger Among the Homeless*. Hearing before the Select Committee on Hunger, Serial No. 99-13, U.S. Congress, House. 99th Congress, 2d Session. 1986. Washington: U.S. Government Printing Office.

_____. 1986b. *The Continued Growth of Hunger, Homeless and Poverty in America's Cities: 1986.* Washington: United States Conference of Mayors.

United States Congress. House of Representatives. 1986. *Homeless Families: A Neglected Crisis.* House Report 99-982. 99th Congress, 2nd Session. Washington: U.S. Government Printing Office.

United States Department of Commerce. Bureau of the Census 1980. Census of Population. Washington: U.S. Government Printing Office.

United States Department of Housing and Urban Development. 1984. *Report to the Secretary on the Homeless and Emergency Shelters.* Joint Hearing before the Subcommittee on Housing and Community Development of the Committee on Banking, Finance, and Urban Affairs and the Subcommittee on Manpower ant Housing on the Committee on Government Operations, pp. 327-87. Banking Committee Serial No. 98091. U.S. Congress, House of Representatives, 98th Congress, 2nd Session. Washington: U.S. Government Printing Office.

Watson, Sophie, with Helen Austerberry. 1986. *Housing and Homelessness.* London: Routledge and Kegan Paul.

Winerip, Michael. 1988. Applause of Help to Homeless. *New York Times* 26 February.

Wolch, Jennifer. 1980. Residential Location of the Service-Dependent Poor. *Annals of the Association of American Geographers* 70: 330–41.

_____, and Andrea Akita. In press. The Federal Response to Homelessness and Its Implications for American Cities. *Urban Geography.*Wolch, Jennifer, and Stuart Gabriel. 1985. Dismantling the Community-Based Human Services System. *Journal of the American Planning Association* 51: 24-35.

Wolch, Jennifer, Cynthia Nelson, and Annette Rubalcaba. In press. Back to Back Wards? Prospects for the Reinstitutionalization of the Mentally Disabled. In *Location and Stigma* edited by Christopher Smith and John Giggs. London: Allen and Unwin.

Wolpert, Julian, Michael Dear, and Randi Crawford. 1975. Satellite Mental Health Facilities. *Annals of the Association of American Geographers* 65: 24-35.

Wolpert, Julian, and John Seley. 1986. Urban Neighborhoods as a National Resource: Irreversible Decisions and Their Equity Spillovers. *Geographical Analysis* 18: 81-93.

Social and Physical Planning for the Elimination of Urban Poverty

Herbert J. Gans

This paper is one of the earliest works highlighting what was then the newly forming movement for "human renewal" or what is more widely known now as community development. Gans gives a thorough overview of the history of the planning movement as a force to battle urban poverty, as well as outlining the development of social work programs that were just occurring in many American cities, such as juvenile-delinquency prevention and programs for low-income residents. He then discusses the nature of the "contemporary" urban poverty of the 1960s, an analysis of the programs he refers to as "guided mobility" planning, a discussion of the compatibility of traditional city planning with the social planning movement, and an assessment of the merit of the latter movement to both local and the federal government.

City planning has traditionally sought community betterment through so-called *physical* methods, such as the creation of efficient land-use and transportation schemes, the sorting out of diverse types of land use, and the renewal of technologically obsolescent areas and buildings to achieve functional, as well as aesthetically desirable, arrangements of structures and spaces. This paper deals with a new planning concept which places greater emphasis on economic and social methods of improving community life. In some places it is called human renewal; in others, community development; in yet others, social planning. Although none of the names is quite appropriate, the programs to which they refer are of crucial importance to the future of the city, for they seek to do away with—or at least to decimate—urban poverty and the deprivation that accompanies it. If these programs succeed, they are likely to have a lasting impact on city planning and on the other professions concerned with planning for community welfare.

The fight against poverty is not new, of course, and, in fact, the elimination of urban deprivation was one of the goals of the founders of modern city planning. The planning movement itself developed partly in reaction to the conditions under which the European immigrants who came to American cities in the mid-nineteenth century had to live. The reduction of their squalor was one of Frederick Law Olmsted's goals when he proposed the building of city parks so that the poor—as well as the rich—might have a substitute rural landscape in which to relax from urban life. It motivated the Boston civic leaders who first built playgrounds in the slums of that city and the founders of the settlement-house movement, notably Jane Addams, who argued strongly for city planning. It also sparked the efforts of those who built model tenements to improve the housing conditions of the poor. And Ebenezer Howard had this goal in mind when he proposed to depopulate the London slums through Garden Cities.

Most of these planning efforts were not aimed directly at the reduction of poverty and deprivation, but sought to use land planning, housing codes, and occasionally zoning to eliminate slums and reduce densities in the tightly packed tenement neighborhoods. The apotheosis of this approach—slum clearance—followed upon the arrival of the newest wave of poor immigrants: the southern Negroes, Puerto Ricans, and Mexicans who came to the city during World War II and in the postwar era. After a decade of noting the effects of the federal slum clearance program, however, some observers became concerned because while this method was eliminating slums, it was not contributing significantly to the improvement of the slum dwellers' living conditions.

In many cases, the reduction in the already short supply of low-cost housing brought about by slum clearance, together with faulty or nonexistent relocation planning, sent slum dwellers into adjacent slums or forced them to overcrowd declining areas elsewhere. But even where slum clearance was accompanied by adequate relocation programs, the housing of poor people in decent low-cost dwellings did not solve other—and equally pressing—problems, such as poverty, unemployment, illiteracy, alcoholism, and mental illness. Nor could rehousing alone do away with crime, delinquency, prostitution, and other deviant behavior. In short, it became clear that such physical changes as urban renewal, good housing, and modern project planning were simply not enough to improve the lives of the poverty-stricken.

As a result, planners and "housers" began to look for nonphysical planning approaches.[1] In this process, they made contact with other professions that are concerned with the low-income population; for example, social workers. Working in tandem with them and others, they have developed new programs, bearing the various names indicated above. Most often they have been referred to as social planning, a term that had been coined by social workers to describe the co-ordination of individual social-agency programs carried out by such central planning and budgeting agencies as the United Fund.[2]

Although the term has already received considerable attention in city-planning circles, I prefer to use another term. Insofar as the programs seek to aid low-income people to change their fortunes and their ways of living, they are attempts to guide them toward the social and economic mobility that more fortunate people have achieved on their own. For this reason, the programs might best be described as planning for *guided mobility*.

Such programs are now under way in many American cities. Some are designed as programs in juvenile-delinquency prevention, which have come into being under the aegis of the President's Committee on Juvenile Delinquency and work mainly with young people.[3] Others are oriented toward low-income people of all ages, and since planners have been most active in these, the rest of the article will deal primarily with such programs.[4] Although most of the programs are just getting started, some over-all similarities between them are apparent. Needless to say, any generalizations about them are preliminary, for the programs are likely to change as they progress from initial formulation to actual implementation.

The guided mobility plans and proposals which I have examined have four major programatic emphases:

1. To develop new methods of education for children from low-income and culturally deprived homes, so as to reduce functional illiteracy, school dropouts, and learning disabilities which prevent such children from competing in the modern job market in adulthood.
2. To reduce unemployment by new forms of job training among the young, by the retraining of adults, and by the creation of new jobs in the community.
3. To encourage self-help on an individual and group basis through community-organization methods that stimulate neighborhood participation.
4. To extend the amount and quality of social services to the low-income population. Among the latter are traditional case-work services, new experiments for giving professional help to the hard-to-reach, multi-problem family, and the provision of modern facilities and programs of public recreation, public health, and community-center activities.

The educational phase of guided mobility includes programs such as Higher Horizons, which attempt to draw bright children from the culturally restrictive context of low-income environments and to offer them the academic and cultural opportunities available to bright middle-class children. There are also programs to help average and backward youngsters, using remedial reading and other devices to guide them during the early school years, so that they will develop the skills and motivations to stay in school until high-school graduation. The occupational phase of the plans includes job programs which will employ young people in useful community projects and in quasi-apprentice programs in private industry, as well as various vocational-training and retraining programs for young and old alike. Meanwhile, added effort is scheduled to attract new industries and thus to bring new jobs to the community.

The extension of social services and the community-organization phase of the programs use decentralization as a means of reaching the high proportion of low-income people who usually abstain from community contact. The provision of social services to the hard-to-reach will be attempted by bringing programs to the neighborhood level, with neighborhood directors to supervise the process. In addition, the social agencies plan to co-ordinate their services, so that individual agencies working with the same individual or family know what the other is doing and duplication and contradictions can be avoided. More neighborhood facilities will also be established, including community schools, public-health clinics, and recreation centers, sometimes grouped in a "services center," so that people will be encouraged to come there when they need help.

The decentralizing of community-organization activities is intended to create a sense of neighborhood and an interest in neighborhood self-help. Community organizers will work in the neighborhood for this purpose and will try to involve "natural leaders" living in the area, who can act as a bridge between the professionals, the city, and the neighborhood population.

This is a very general description of the programs. In actuality, each community has a somewhat distinctive approach, or a different emphasis in the selection of programs, depending partly on the line-up of sponsoring agencies. But some city planners who have become interested in guided mobility programs are still preoccupied—and sometimes too much so—with traditional physical planning approaches, notably two: the realization of a neighborhood scheme—originally devised by Clarence Perry[5] and consisting of a small, clearly bounded residential area, built up at low density, with auto and pedestrian traffic carefully separated, considerable open space, and a combination elementary school and neighborhood meeting place in its center; and the provision both in such neighborhoods and in the larger community of a standard array of public facilities for recreation, health, education, culture, and other community services.

The concern with neighborhood is, of course, traditional in city planning, and even the new challenge of finding nonphysical ways of helping the low-income group has not diverted the planner from it. In some cities, guided mobility plans are thus almost appendages to physical planning programs, based on the traditional belief that the rebuilding of the city into a series of separate neighborhoods to encourage a small-townish middle-class form of family life is a proper solution even for poverty. Elsewhere, the program may be an appendage of urban-renewal activities, the main intent still being the upgrading of the physical neighborhoods. Thus, guided mobility is used partly to organize the neighborhood into undertaking—or helping the city with—this task. But in most cases, the neighborhood emphasis is based on a genuine concern that one of the causes of urban deprivation is to be found in the poor quality of neighborhood life.

The provision of public facilities is also a traditional planning emphasis, dating back to the days when the planner was an ally of the reformers who were fighting for the establishment of these facilities. Out of this has come the belief that public facilities are crucial agencies in people's lives, that up-to-date facilities and programs will encourage intensive use of them, and that this in turn will help significantly in achieving the aims of guided mobility planning.

Despite the intensity of the planner's belief in neighborhood and public facility use, there is no evidence that these two planning concepts are as important to low-income people as they are to planners. Consequently, it is fair to ask whether such concepts are as crucial to the elimination of urban poverty and deprivation as is signified by their appearance in some guided mobility plans. The answer to this question requires a brief discussion of the nature of contemporary urban poverty.

The low-income population may be divided into two major segments, which sociologists call the *working class* and the *lower class*.[6] The former consists of semiskilled and skilled blue-collar workers who hold steady jobs and are thus able to live under stable, if not affluent, conditions. Their way of life differs in many respects from that of the middle class; for example, in the greater role of relatives in sociability and mutual aid, in the lesser concern for self-improvement and education, and in their lack of interest in the good address, cultivation, and the kinds of status that are important to middle-class people. Although their ways are culturally different from the dominant middle-class norms, these are not pathological, for rates of crime, mental illness, and other social ills are not significantly higher than in the middle class. This population, therefore, has little need for guided mobility programs.

The lower class, on the other hand, consists of people who perform the unskilled labor and service functions in the society. Many of them lack stable jobs. They are often unemployed or forced to move from one temporary and underpaid job to another. Partly because of occupational instability, their lives are beset with social and emotional instability as well, and it is among them that one finds the majority of the emotional problems and social evils that are associated with the low-income population.[7]

In past generations, the American economy had considerable need for unskilled labor, and the European immigrants who performed it were able to achieve enough occupational stability to raise themselves, or their children, to working-class or even middle-class ways of living. Today, however, the need for unskilled labor is constantly decreasing and will soon be minimal. Consequently, the Negro, Puerto Rican, and Mexican newcomers who now constitute much of the American lower class find it very difficult to improve their condition.[8]

Guided mobility planning is essentially an attempt to help them solve their problems and to aid them in changing their lives. This makes it necessary to find out what causes their problems, what they themselves are striving for, and how they can be helped to achieve their objectives.

The nature of the problem is not difficult to identify. For economic reasons, and for reasons of race as well, the contemporary lower class is often barred from opportunities to hold well-paid, stable jobs, to receive a decent education, to live in good housing, or to get access to a whole series of choices and privileges that the white middle class takes for granted.

In addition, some lower-class people lack the motivations and skills that are needed not only to participate in contemporary society but, more important, to accept the opportunities if and when they become available. Moreover, the apathy, despair, and rejection which result from lack of access to crucial opportunities help bring about the aforementioned social and emotional difficulties.

There are a number of reasons for these reactions.[9] When men are long unemployed or underemployed, they feel useless and eventually become marginal members of the family. This has many consequences. They may desert their families and turn to self-destructive behavior in despair. If male instability is widespread, the woman becomes the dominant member of the family, and she may live with a number of men in the hope of finding a stable mate. The result is a family type which Walter Miller calls female-based; it is marked by free unions, illegitimate children, and what middle-class people consider to be broken homes.[10] Boys who grow up in such families may be deprived of needed male models and are likely to inherit some of the feelings of uselessness and despair they see in their fathers. In addition, the children must learn at an early age how to survive in a society in which crisis is an everyday occurrence and violence and struggle are ever-present. Thus, they may learn how to defend themselves against enemies and how to coexist with an alcoholic parent, but they do not learn how to read, how to concentrate on their studies, or how to relate to the teacher.[11] Those that do must defend their deviant behavior—and it is deviant in the lower class—against their peers, who, like peers in all other groups, demand that they conform to the dominant mode of adaptation. Also, many children grow up in households burdened with mental illness, and this scars their own emotional and social growth. Out of such conditions develops a lower-class culture with a set of behavior patterns which is useful for the struggle to survive in a lower-class milieu, but makes it almost impossible to participate in the larger society. And since the larger society rejects the lower-

class individual for such behavior, he can often develop self-respect and dignity only by rejecting the larger society. He blames it for his difficulties—and with much justification—but in this process rejects many of its values as well, becoming apathetic, cynical, and hostile even toward those that seek to help him.

This overly brief analysis is at present mostly hypothetical, for we do not yet know exactly what it is that creates the lower-class way of life. We know that the nature of family relationships, the influence of peers, the kind of home training, the adaptive characteristics of lower-class culture, the high prevalence of mental illness, and the need to cope with one crisis after another are all important factors, but we do not yet know exactly which factors are most important, how they operate to create the way of life that they do, and how they are related to the lack of opportunities that bring them about.

Similarly, we know that lower-class people are striving to change their condition, but we do not know exactly for what they are striving. It is clear that they want stable jobs and higher incomes, and there is considerable evidence of an almost magical belief in education and high occupational aspirations for the children, especially among Negroes.[12] The lack of opportunity and the constant occurrence of crises frustrate most of these aspirations before they can be implemented, but they do exist, especially among the women. On the other hand, the failure of settlement houses, social workers, and other helping agencies to reach the majority of the lower-class population suggests that these people either cannot or do not want to accept the middle-class values which these professionals preach and which are built into the welfare activities they carry out. Such programs attract the small minority desirous of or ready for middle-class life, but they repel the rest. A number of social scientists suggest that what lower-class people are striving for is the stable, family-centered life of working-class culture, and at least one delinquency-prevention program is based on such an assumption.[13]

These observations about the nature of lower-class life have many implications for guided mobility planning. As a result of the sparsity of knowledge, much research, experiment, and evaluation of experience will be necessary in order to learn what kinds of program will be successful. It is clear that the most urgent need is to open up presently restricted opportunities, especially in the occupational sphere. The guided mobility programs which stress the creation of new jobs, the attack on racial discrimination, education, and occupational training as highest-priority items are thus on the right track. Even so, new ways of bringing industry and jobs to the community must be found, for conventional programs have not been sufficiently productive. Then, ways of channeling lower-class people into new jobs, and keeping them at work even if their initial performance is not so good as that of other people or of labor-saving machines, must be invented. Racial barriers will also have to come down more quickly, especially in those spheres of life and activity most important to lower-class people, so that they can begin to feel that they have some stake in society. This too is easier said than done.

Not only is desegregation difficult to implement, but the most successful programs so far have benefited middle-class non-whites more than their less fortunate fellows. For lower-class people, access to jobs, unions, and decent low-cost housing is most important, as is the assurance of fair treatment from the police, the courts, city hall, storeowners, and helping agencies. The integration of high-priced suburban housing, expensive restaurants, or concert halls is for *them* of much less immediate significance.

Also, methods of encouraging motivations and skills and of maintaining aspirations in the face of frustration must be found. If the matriarchal lower-class family is at fault, ways of providing boys with paternal substitutes must be developed. Where the entire lower-class milieu is destructive, children may have to be removed from it, especially in their formative years. Treatments for mental illness, alcoholism, and narcotics addiction that will be effective among lower-class people have to be discovered and the causes of these ills isolated so that prevention programs may be set up. Schools must be created which can involve lower-class children. This means that they must teach the skills needed in a middle-class society, yet without the middle-class symbols and other trappings that frighten or repel the lower-class student.[14] Finally, it is necessary to develop urban renewal or other housing programs that will make livable dwellings available to the low-income population, within its price range, and located near enough to its places of employment so as not to require unreasonable amounts of travel time and expenditures.

These program requirements demand some radical changes in our ways of doing things. For example, if lower-class people are to find employment, there will need to be economic enterprises geared not solely to profit and to cost reduction but also to the social profits of integrating the unemployed. In short, eventually we shall have to give up the pretense that nineteenth-century free-enterprise ideology can cope with twentieth-century realities and learn to replan some economic institutions to help the low-income population, just as we are now redesigning public education to teach this population's children. Likewise, if lower-class people are to become part of the larger society, there must be changes in the way the police, the courts, and political structures treat them. To cite just one instance, lower-class people must be represented more adequately in local party politics, and their needs and demands must receive more adequate hearing at city hall than has heretofore been the case. Similarly, the professions that now seek to help lower-class people will have to be altered so as to be more responsive to how lower-class people define their needs, and this may mean the replacement of some professionals by skilled nonprofessionals who are more capable of achieving rapport with lower-class clients. Also, urban-renewal policy must concern itself less with "blight" removal, or with the use of new construction to solve the city's tax problems, and more with improvement of the housing conditions of the slum dwellers. Changes such as these, which require redistribution of power, income, privileges, and the alteration of established social roles, are immensely difficult to bring about. Even so, they are necessary if urban poverty and deprivation are to be eliminated.[15]

Proper guided mobility planning must be based on methods that will achieve the intended goal. If the hypotheses about the causes of urban deprivation are correct, the basic components of guided mobility planning must be able to affect the economy, the political and social structures that shore up poverty and racial—as well as class—discrimination, the focuses of lower-class culture that frustrate the response to opportunities, notably the family, the peer group, the milieu in which children grow up, and the helping agencies that now have difficulty in reaching lower-class people, especially the school. Any programs which lack these components and cannot bring about changes in the position of the lower-class population vis-a-vis the institutions named are unlikely to contribute significantly to the aim of guided mobility.

The list of basic components does not include the two that have been especially emphasized by planners: the belief in neighborhood and the importance of public facilities. This omission is not accidental, for I do not believe that these two concepts are of high priority. Indeed, it is possible that they may divert guided mobility programs from the direction they ought to take.

By focusing programs on neighborhoods as spatial units, planners are naturally drawn to what is most visible in them—the land uses, buildings, and major institutions—and their attention is diverted from what is hardest to see, the people—and social conditions—with problems. It should be clear from the foregoing analysis that the program must concentrate on the people and on the social and economic forces which foster their deprivation, rather than on neighborhood conditions which are themselves consequences of these forces.

Moreover, too much concern with neighborhoods may cause the programs to seek out the wrong people: the working-class segment of the low-income population, rather than the lower-class one. This may happen for two reasons. First, the planner often finds it difficult to distinguish between areas occupied by working-class people and those occupied by lower-class people, mainly because his concept of standard housing blinds him to differences between low-rent areas, usually occupied predominantly by the former, and slums, which house the latter. Also, working and lower-class people sometimes live together in the same planning area, especially if they are nonwhite, and a neighborhood focus makes it difficult to reach one without the other. This is undesirable because, as noted earlier, the working-class population does not need guided mobility, whereas the lower-class population needs it so badly that all resources ought to be allocated to it.

Even so, these drawbacks would not be serious if neighborhood planning could achieve the aims of guided mobility. But this is not the case, mainly because people's lives are not significantly influenced by the physical neighborhood. The important aspects of life take place within the family, the peer group, and on the job, and the neighborhood does not seem to affect these greatly. Moreover, although middle- and working-class people do sometimes participate in neighborhood activities, this is not true of lower-class people.[16] Not only do they shy away from organizational participation generally, but because of their great transience they do not spend much time in any one area. More important since life is a constant struggle for survival and an endless series o crises, lower-class people are often suspicious of their neighbors and even more so of the landlord, the storeowner, the police, and the local politician. They harbor similar feelings toward most other neighborhood institutions and local public facilities.

Thus, the lower-class population's involvement in the neighborhood is at best neutral and more often negative. Yet even if it were more positive, the components of neighborhood planning and the provision of the entire range of modern public facilities could contribute relatively little to solving the problems which concern lower-class people the most. To a poverty-stricken family, the separation of car and pedestrian traffic or the availability of park and playground within walking distance are no very crucial; their needs are much more basic.

This is not to reject the desirability of such planning concepts, but only to say that given the present condition of lower-class life, they are of fairly low priority. The location and equipment of the school are much less important than the presence of the kind of teacher who can communicate with lower-class children, and a conventional public-health facility is much less vital than an agency that can really help a mother deserted by her husband, or a person who must cope with mentally ill family members.

The standard neighborhood-and-facilities planning package canna even contribute significantly to the improvement of the lower-class milieu. The significant components of this milieu are other people, rather than environmental features, and until these other people are socially and economically secure enough to trust each other, the milieu is not likely to improve sufficiently to prevent the perpetuation of past deprivations on the young growing up within it.

In short, it seems clear that the kind of neighborhood scheme sough through traditional planning and zoning methods cannot be implemented, among lower-class people until the basic components of guided mobility programs have been effectuated. A stable, peaceful neighborhood in which there is positive feeling between neighbors assumes that people have good housing, the kind of job that frees them from worrying about where the next meal or rent money will come from, the solution of basis problems so that the landlord, the policeman, or the bill collector is n longer threatening, and the relief from recurring crises so that they ca begin to pay some attention to the world outside the household. Similarly, only when people feel themselves to be part of the larger society, an when they have learned the skills needed to survive in it will they be able to take part in school or community-center activities or to develop the ability to communicate with the staff of a health clinic.

Neighborhood planning is necessary, of course, but a social and political type which supports the community, state, and federal programs for the elimination of poverty. Thus, the methods required to help the low-income population develop the skills and attitudes prerequisite to survival in a modern society must reach into the neighborhood and the street in order to recruit people who do not, for one reason or another, come by themselves into public facilities established for such programs. Also, local political activity must be stimulated so that low-income people can use the one power they have—that of numbers and votes—to make their wishes heard at city hall and in Washington. This differs considerably from the need for "citizen participation" often called for by planners and community-organization experts; that has usually been defined as citizen consideration of—and consent to—professionally developed programs, or civic activity which is decidedly nonpolitical. The kind of local citizen participation that is needed is quite political, however, and since its aim must be to change the political status quo, it is unlikely that community organizers, who are after all employees of the existing political

institution or of establishment-dominated welfare agencies, will be able to encourage such activity even if they are personally willing to do so. Hopefully, enlightened civic leaders and politicians will eventually realize that the low-income population must be more adequately represented in the political process, but in all likelihood, they will resist any change in the existing political alignments until they have no other choice. Thus, the initiative for local political activity must come from the areas in which low-income people live. But whoever the initiating agencies may be, these are the types of neighborhood planning that are required to do something about urban poverty.

The incompatibility of traditional city-planning aims and the basic components of guided mobility programming is not to be blamed on one or another set of planners, nor indeed is it a cause for blame at all. Rather, it stems from the history and nature of modern city planning and from the basic assumptions in its approach. The description of two of these assumptions will also shed some light on the relationship between social and physical planning and their roles in the improvement of cities.

The first of these assumptions is the belief in the ability of change in the physical environment to bring about social change. Planners have traditionally acted on the assumption that the ordering of land uses, and improvements in the setting and design of buildings, highways, and other physical features of the community, would result in far-reaching improvements in the lives of those affected. The validity of this assumption has been seriously questioned in recent years, and indeed, the rise of what has been called social planning is one expression of this questioning.

But the traditional city-planning approach can also be described in another way, as being *method-oriented*. By this I mean that it has developed a repertoire of methods and techniques which have become professionally accepted and which distinguish planning from other service-giving professions. As a result, the planner concerns himself largely with improvements in these methods. In this process, however, he loses sight of the goals which his methods are intended to achieve or the problems they are to solve. Thus, he does not ask whether the methods achieve these goals or whether they achieve *any* goals.

This concern with method is not limited to the planning profession; it can be found in all professions. The attempt to maintain and improve existing methods is useful if the goals are traditional ones or if the profession deals only with routine problems. But it does not work as well when new goals are sought and when new problems arise. As I have already noted, improvements in neighborhood planning cannot contribute significantly to the new problems of the city or to the new goal of eliminating urban poverty.

What is needed instead is a *goal-oriented* or problem-oriented approach which begins, not with methods, but with the problems to be solved or the goals to be achieved. Once these are defined and agreed upon, the methods needed to achieve them can be determined through the use of professional insight, research, and experiment until the right methods—those which will solve the problem or realize the goal—are found. This approach was used in the foregoing pages, in which I questioned the usefulness of traditional planning methods and proposed instead programs to cope with the problems of the lower-class population—and their causes—as well as programs which would lead toward the goals this population was seeking for itself.

This approach is more difficult to implement than a method-oriented one, because it does not respect accepted methods—unless they work—and because it rejects the claims of professional traditions or professional] expertise that are not supported by empirical evidence. It may require new methods and new approaches and thus can wreak havoc with the established way of doing things. However much the goal-oriented approach may upset the profession in the short run, in the long run it improves its efficiency and thus its expertise and status, because its methods are likely to be much more successful, thus reducing the risk of professional failure. In an effort as pioneering and difficult as guided mobility planning, a problem- and goal-oriented approach is therefore absolutely essential.

The conception of method-oriented and goal-oriented planning can also aid our understanding of the relationship between physical and social planning. In the professional discussions of this relationship, the subject has frequently been posed as social planning versus physical planning.

Although it is not difficult to understand why the subject has been framed in this competitive way, the resulting dichotomy between social and physical planning is neither meaningful nor desirable. There are several reasons for rejecting this dichotomy.

First, social planning is said to deal with the human elements in the planning process. When planners talk of the human side of renewal or of the human factors in planning, they are suggesting by implication that physical planning is inhuman, that in its concern with land use, site design, the redevelopment of cleared land, and the city tax base it has no concern for the needs of human beings. I would not blame physical planners for objecting to this implication and am surprised that they have not done so. But even if this implication is inaccurate, the dichotomy has led to another, even more unfortunate implication, which has some truth to it. Every planning activity, like any other form of social change, creates net benefits for some people and net costs for others. These may be non-material as well as material. Whether intentionally or not, physical planning has tended to provide greater benefits to those who already have considerable economic resources or political power, be they redevelopers or tenants who profit from a luxury housing scheme, central business district retailers who gain, or expect to gain, from the ever-increasing number of plans to "revive downtown," or the large taxpayers who are helped most when planning's main aim is to increase municipal revenues. The interest in social planning is a direct result of this distribution of benefits, for it seeks to help the people who are forced to pay net costs in the physical planning process. Too often, these are poor people; for example, residents of a renewal or highway project who suffer when adequate relocation housing is lacking. Needless to say, this political bifurcation, in which physical planning benefits the well-to-do and social planning the less fortunate ones, is not a desirable state of affairs either for the community or for planning.

Finally, in actual everyday usage, the dichotomy refers to skills possessed by different types of planners. Physical planning is that set of methods which uses the traditional skills of the city planner and zoning official; social planning, that set favored by sociologically trained planners, social workers, and other professionals concerned with welfare aims. Yet if the planning activities of each are examined more closely, it becomes evident that the terms *social* and *physical* are inaccurate labels. Zoning is considered a physical planning method, but an ordinance which determines who is to live with whom and who is to work next to whom is as much social—as well as economic and political—as it is physical. So is a transportation scheme which decides who will find it easy to get in and out of the city and who will find it difficult. Conversely, social planners who urge the construction of more low-rent housing, or argue for scattered units rather than projects, are proposing physical schemes even while they are ostensibly doing social planning. Since all planning activities affect people, they are inevitably social, and the dichotomy between physical and social methods turns out to be meaningless. Moreover, in actual planning practice, no problem can be solved by any one method or any one skill. In most instances a whole variety of techniques are needed to achieve the goal.

The social-physical dichotomy is a logical consequence of viewing planning as method-oriented, because when methods are most important, there is apt to be competition between people who are skilled in the different methods. All successful professions want to apply the methods they know best, for this permits them to maintain their power and social position most easily.

If planning is conceived as goal-oriented, however, goals become most important, and methods are subordinated to the goal. In such a planning process, in which a large number of different methods are used in an integrated fashion, any single method loses its magical aura. Moreover, no goal can be defined so narrowly that it is only physical or only social. In a goal-oriented approach, then, there can be no social or physical planning. There is only *planning*: an approach which agrees upon the best goals and then finds the best methods to achieve them.

But it is not only the methods which must be reconsidered. Even the goals which are built into these methods are turning out to be less important today. The neighborhood concept has received little support from the clients of planning; the same is true of the planner's insistence on a reduction in the journey to work, which has not been accepted by the journeying populace. Also, in an age of automation and increasing unemployment, the need for economic growth, even if it is disorderly, is becoming more vital than the ordering of growth and the planner's desire for stability. It is, of course, still important to have efficient transportation schemes and to locate noxious industry away from residences; but there is less noxious industry than ever before, and for those who are affluent, the inefficiency of the automobile seems to matter little, especially if it is politically feasible to subsidize the costs of going to work by car. And even the concern with land use per use is becoming less significant. In a technology of bulldozers and rapid transportation, the qualities of the natural environment and the location of land are less important—or rather, more easily dealt with by human intervention—and increasingly, land can be used for many alternatives. The question of what is the best use, given topography and location, is thus less important than who will benefit from one use as compared to another, and who will have to pay costs, and how is the public interest affected.

One of the most important tasks in the improvement of cities is the elimination of urban poverty and of the deprivations of lower-class life. Poverty is fundamentally responsible for the slums we have been unable to eradicate by attacking the buildings and for the deprivations which ultimately bring about the familiar list of social evils. Moreover, poverty and deprivation are what makes cities so ugly and depressing, and they hasten the flight of more fortunate people into the suburbs. This in turn contributes to economic decline, the difficulties of financing municipal services, political conflict, corruption, and many of the other problems of the contemporary city.

I would not want to argue that all the city's problems can be laid at the doorstep of poverty. There are technological changes that affect its economic health and result in the obsolescence of industrial areas and street patterns. There are political rigidities that inhibit its relations with its hinterland. And the desire of most families to raise their children in low-density surroundings suggests that suburbia is not produced solely by the flight from the city and would exist without urban poverty. Even so, many of the suburbanites have come to hate the city because of the poverty they see there, and this in turn helps to create the hostility between city and suburb and the political conflict that frustrates schemes for metropolitan solutions.

If planners are genuinely concerned with the improvement of cities, the fight against poverty becomes a planning problem and one that needs to be given higher priority than it has heretofore received. A beginning is being made in the guided mobility programs that are now in operation, but a much greater effort is needed, on both the local and the federal scene, before these programs can achieve their aim. If such efforts are not made, all other schemes for improving the city will surely fail.

NOTES

1. Another impetus came from the fact that several cities scheduled urban-renewal projects in their skid-row areas, and programs to "rehabilitate" its residents were developed as part of the relocation plan.

2. The term has also been applied to plans which attempt to outline social—that is, nonphysical—goals for the entire society, a procedure that would be more aptly called *societal* planning.

3. Of these, the leading program is New York's Mobilization for Youth. This is described in Mobilization for Youth, Inc., *A Proposal for the Prevention and Control of Delinquency by Expanding Opportunities* (New York: December 1961—mimeographed).

4. Examples of the many such plans are: Action for Boston Community Development, *A Proposal for a Community Development Program in Boston* (Boston: December 1961—mimeographed); Action Housing, Inc., *...Urban Extension in the Pittsburgh Area* (Pittsburgh: September 1961—mimeographed); City of Oakland, *Proposal for a Program of Community Development* (City of Oakland, Calif.: June and December 1961—mimeographed); Community Progress, Inc., *Opening Opportunities: New Haven's Comprehensive Program for Community Progress* (New Haven, Conn.: April 1962—mimeographed); and Department of City Planning, *A Plan for the Woodlawn Community: Social Planning Factors* (Chicago: January 1962—mimeographed). My comments about the plans below are based on a number of published and unpublished documents which I have examined as well as on discussions about existing and proposed plans in which I have participated in several cities. My description of these plans is, in sociological terminology, an ideal type and does not fit exactly any one of the plans now in existence.

5. Clarence A. Perry, "The Neighborhood Unit," in *Regional Survey of New York and Its Environs* (New York: Committee on Regional Plan of New York and Its Environs, 1929), VII, 22-140.

6. Herbert J. Gans, *The Urban Villagers* (Glencoe, Ill.: Free Press, 1962), Chapter 11. See also S. M. Miller and Frank Riessman, "The Working Class Subculture: A New View," *Social Problems*, IX (1961), 86-97. The nature and extent of urban poverty are described in Michael Harrington, *The Other, America* (New York: Macmillan, 1962), Chapters 2, 4, 5, 7, 8.

7. An excellent brief description of lower-class culture may be found in Walter B. Miller, "Lower Class Culture as a Generating Milieu of Gang Delinquency," *Journal of Social Issues*, XIV (1958), 5-19. The everyday life of the lower, class is pictured in Oscar Lewis, *Five Families* (New York: Basic Books, 1959) and *The Children of Sanchez* (New York: Random House, 1961). Although Lewis' books deal with the lower class of Mexico City, his portrait applies, with some exceptions, to American cities as well.

8. For an analysis of the occupational history of the European immigrants and the more recent immigrants, see Oscar Handlin, *The Newcomers* (New York: Anchor Books, 1962).

9. For a more detailed analysis, see Gans, *op. cit.*, Chapter 12; Mobilization for Youth, Inc., *op. cit.*; and Walter B. Miller, *op. cit.*

10. Walter B. Miller, *op. cit.* This family type is particularly widespread in the Negro lower class, in which it originated during slavery.

11. The educational and other problems of the lower-class child are described in more detail in Patricia C. Sexton, *Education and Income* (New York: Viking, 1961), and Frank Riessman, *The Culturally Deprived Child* (New York: Harper, 1962).

12. For a recent example of this finding, see R. Kleiner, S. Parker, and H. Taylor, *Social Status and Aspirations in Philadelphia's Negro Population* (Philadelphia: Commission on Human Relations, June 1962—mimeographed).

13. Mobilization for Youth, Inc., *op. cit.*

14. See Sexton, op. cit., and Riessman, *op. cit.*

15. For other programatic statements, see Peter Marris, "A Report on Urban Renewal in the United States," and Leonard J. Duhl, "Planning and Poverty," in Leonard J. Duhl, ed., *The Urban Condition* (New York: Basic Books, 1963), pp. 113-134 and 295-304, respectively. See also Harrington, *op. cit.*

16. Generally speaking, middle-class people participate in formal neighborhood organizations to a much greater extent than other classes, although their social life often takes place outside the neighborhood. Working-class people are less likely to participate in formal organizations, but most of their social activities take place close to home. For a discussion of working-class attitudes toward the neighborhood, see Marc Fried and Peggy Gleicher, "Some Sources of Residential Satisfaction in an Urban 'Slum,' " *Journal of the American Institute of Planners*, XXVII (November 1961), 305-315.

Accommodating Human Unsettlement

R. Buckminster Fuller

R. Buckminster Fuller was a design philosopher who viewed the primary purpose of the design professions as a means of improving the human condition through a process of anticipating future needs. His writings tend to be speculative in nature; his discussions of architecture are secondary to his concerns with the design process and the social outcomes of built forms. In this article he reviews the proceedings of the 1976 United Nations Habitat Conference and places it in the context of his own 50-year career as an environmental designer. He argues for design responses that address the problems of housing the vast majority of humankind who must exist in unhealthy and inhuman conditions. Fuller was one of the most forceful and innovative advocates of the modern design principle of improving the environment by doing "more with less," and of the challenge of placing technology at the service of humanity.

The United Nations Conference on Human Settlements *Habitat* 1976 occurred in the penultimate year of my 1927 conceptioning of and all-out commitment to a fifty-year gestation period of economic initiatives, philosophic formulations, artifact inventions, their physical realizations, practical proving, progressive development and integration with general evolutionary events, all planned to culminate in the 1977 birth of a new World-around industry: that of an air-deliverable, air-serviceable and air-removable dwelling machine and environment controlling mass manufacturing and renting industry, which would employ humanity's maximumly informed and performing sciences and technologies and most advanced production techniques, to comprehensively and adequately accommodate all human living and development needs with the dwelling machines also serving as effective harvesters and conservers of all local income energies of the vegetation, sun and wind as well as of the energies in human and food wastes—and most importantly of all, to serve as spontaneous, comprehensively effective, self-teaching devices of both the young and the old children therein dwelling.[1]

All of the Dymaxion artifacts which I have developed have come into socio-economic use only in emergencies when all customary means of solving problems were either physically inadequate or prohibitively expensive and there were no alternatives but to use my more efficient high performance developments, reducing materials, energy, labour and overhead input costs.

When I commenced my project in 1927 at the age of 32, I was moneyless, jobless with a dependant wife and new born daughter. Despite the self-discipline of never asking anyone to listen to me, nothing could be in more marked contrast to my then unknown unlistened to sociological state than the 150 world-around audiences who have asked me to address them in each of the last five years, or the US Senate Foreign Policy Committee's invitation to me to speak to them on world political trends,[2] nor the plurality of invitations that I received to speak at the United Nations Vancouver Habitat Conference in 1976. This interest seems powerfully to suggest the relevance of my fifty-year program and the extent to which it has developed.

HABITAT AND HUMAN SETTLEMENT

I was invited to Habitat under four prime auspices; as the special guest of Habitat itself, as a member of Barbara Ward's pre-Habitat Vancouver Symposium, as President of the World Society for Ekistics and as a guest of Vancouver's Habitat Committee. I also went as leader of the combined World Game students and Earth Metabolic students *Now House* project.

On the day the Habitat conference opened, front page photographs in newspapers around the world showed the acrylic skin of my USA 275-foot diameter, geodesic dome of Montreal's Expo 67 being completely burnt out. First reports that the dome had burned to the ground were untrue; the steel structure was undamaged. Since the invisible acrylic skin had been mounted inside the spherical structure, the structural appearance had not been changed. No one was inside and no one was hurt. Within ten days even before Habitat closed, Montreal announced its intention to rehabilitate the dome.[3]

It almost seemed as though the non-structural skin of the great unharmed geodesics dome had been set afire by some mystical evolutionary wisdom to remind the world of geodesics' very high structural performance, accomplished with only three per cent of the weight of any given material necessary to produce equivalent structural and functional capabilities by any other known alter-

nate engineering systems. Apparently, the one hundred thousand geodesic domes built around the world in the last thirty years have proven their economic value, reliability and economy to such an extent that this fire brought no charges of inadequacy of geodesic dome principles. The Expo 67 dome event and the progressively increasing magnitude of human numbers interested in listening to me—as the protagonist of a design science revolution by which to accommodate physically the now evident evolutionary insistence on world-around *unsettlement of humanity*—seemed in marked contrast to related aspects of Habitat and its technological focus almost exclusively upon nationalistically emphasized, local, immobile, and "one-off" tailoring of *human settlements*.

At the opening press conference of the Barbara Ward Group at Habitat I reported that in April 1976 the Club of Rome had issued a public reversal of its 1972 L*imits to Growth*[4] concept. There had been so many contradictions of the Club's 1972 pronouncement on the limits to growth that they had reconsidered their position. I said that I felt that the Club of Rome's first statement was funded by interests that were continuing to do what money had done in the past, that is, to rationalize selfishness. Assuming the political concept of fundamental inadequacy of life support for all humans on our planet, selfishness had been able to say "I have those for whom I'm responsible and because there is not enough life support for all, I am obliged to do various things that are utterly and completely selfish." I felt that the Club of Rome's *Limits to Growth* pronouncement represented the last attempt on the part of organized capitalists' selfishness to justify to the world public why their wealth would be unable to do anything about the third world. The initial Smithsonian announcement of the *Limits to Growth* was based on work done by an MIT professor of computer sciences who was given his input data by other MIT specialists.[5] I and many others were able to make well documented and fortunately effective public announcements that the Club of Rome's *Limits to Growth* pronouncement was a sadly ignorant statement. For instance, its authors cited only the very small remaining percentages of the world's unmined metal ore reserves, and were manifestly unaware that the metals on our Earth are continually being melted out of their last use and being recirculated in amounts greatly exceeding the tonnage of metals being newly mined and added into the cumulative circulatory system approximately 3 to 1, while the interim gains in technological "know-how" take care of ever greater numbers of humans per each pound of recirculating metal or other chemical substance into which technology invests its ever improving know-how, with the result that it is now engineeringly feasible to take care of all humanity at an unprecedentedly high standard of living without mining any more metals. In my view the Club of Rome's ignorance was occasioned by the over specialization of scientists. I told the Habitat press conference that I thought the Club of Rome had manifested extraordinary courage and integrity in changing their public position, when they announced in Philadelphia that they had found on reinspection that their data was inadequate, ergo, their resulting conclusions were wrong. Later that week I received an invitation to lunch with Mr. Peccei, President of the Club of Rome, when he personally verified their new position. I applauded his integrity.

THE INFLUENCE OF FINANCE ON DEVELOPMENT

Though it produced almost no world-around newspaper reportage, the Vancover conference was an historical watershed event.[6] The old established building world was conspicuous by its absence, though there were many other powerful lobbies present such as those of the Sierra Club, Audubon Society, World Population Institute and other foundations concerned with environmental subjects. It became clear that the great banks, confronted with escalating building costs which had passed the point of no return had withdrawn all support of real estate exploiters and of obsolete building technology in general. The "big money" of the world which has gone entirely transnational had found that whereas "you can't take it with you" into the next world, you also can't take it with you around the world: ownership has now become onerous. Big money has left all the sovereignly locked-in, local-property-game-players "holding the unmovable bags" of "real estate." Machinery becomes obsolete almost overnight, is unattractive as a continuing property and must be

written off the books in five years. But machinery can be melted and reworked, to ever higher earning effectiveness only by ever improving know-how. "Know-how" has become the "apple" of transnational capitalism's eye.

As a consequence of the great 1929 crash, the monopolistic control of America's prime industrial establishments was broken. During the gradual recovery of the corporations under the aegis of the New Deal, the directors and executives of the corporations found that whether they were going to keep their jobs now, for the first time, depended entirely on the voting by stockholders to re-elect the directors and their managements, which depended entirely on whether the corporation management made profits. It was exactly at this time in history that the metals of World War I, which had been mined in such enormous profusion, began increasingly to reappear in the form of scrap. Suddenly the unforeseen recirculation of scrap began to break up the control of metal prices by the mine owners, who objected to this new development. However the new self-perpetuating managements realized that remelted metal was as pure as new metal, and more desirable because it cost less. They could make as much money by recirculation as they could by new production.

What they next found was that every time they developed a more desirable product, the sales increased. This made the wheels go round even faster so that management began to look for know-how to improve products. This brought about a completely new volition on the part of capitalism of our world. The post-1933 search for new know-how is why you see in the Sunday newspapers page after page of advertisements of great corporations looking for highly specialized, scientific and technical men with the experience generated know-how to produce new, improved and more desirable products.

All the great American corporations of yesterday have now moved out of America and their prime operations have become transnational and conglomerate and are essentially concerned with the game of selling their corporation's very complete, technical, managerial and vast credit handling and money making know-how. For this reason they are not interested in the older kind of properties. This set of unpredicted changes of volition explained the lack of concern of transnational conglomerate capitalism and their lack of opposition to the United Nations' Vancouver Conference's pre-occupation with human settlements, which they regarded as "peanuts."

The new capitalism is only mildly interested in trailers or mobile homes which are simply weather boxed platforms on which are mounted beautyrest mattresses, shower baths, washing machines, television, radio, air conditioning, lighting, cooking, refrigerating, bottled gas, tableware, toiletries, wardrobes and so forth. Mobile homes take the shape of a shoebox because they have to go through highway or railroad bridges. It is like living in the narrow shoebox shape of a railroad car.

Such mobile homes provide a place to live near jobs without having to buy a fixed home or a fixed piece of land. Because they are assemblies of mass production items their costs are low, but nowhere nearly as low as they could be if uncompromisingly designed for rental and easy maintenance rather than for sale and early replacement.

The new transitional capitalism's grand strategies are primarily formulated by international lawyers in their endeavours to vault legal barriers and avoid taxes. From 1800 to 1929, world economics were mastered by "Finance Capitalism" of the J. P. Morgan brand. From 1932 to 1952, we had "Federally Socialised Corporate Management Capitalism." Since 1952 we have had "Lawyer Desocialised and Strategied Supranational Managerial Capitalism." The grand strategy of the lawyer-managed supra-national capitalism is to keep governmental power widely deployed, ergo "conquered." Much of their media *news* has been a smoke screen diverting attention from what they were doing. For instance, while world news was spotlighted on the Korean and Vietnam wars, the great USA corporations and banks were conglomerating and moving out of America into a world theatre of operations. In 25 successive annual appropriations of Foreign Aid, totalling 100 billion dollars, "riders" required that where a USA corporation was present in the country being aided, the aid funds had to be spent through those USA corporations. In this manner, the building of the supra-national corporations' foreign manufacturing plants took all the gold out of America. When all the "gold" was gone, the USA dollar was cut loose from gold, which lowered its world purchas-

ing equity to a quarter of its pre "floated" value. This multiplied the supra-national corporations' gold backed relative monetary equity four-fold its previous value.

The world news media is controlled by transnational capitalism through advertising, its main source of income. The great corporations control that advertising. The amount of advertising placed in the media and the rates paid for it is predicated upon the size of the audience reached. Media management finds that the public appetite is for bad news. Whatever the psychological explanation may be the fact is that the media looks mainly for malignant news, rarely for benign news.

RECOMMENDATIONS FROM VANCOUVER

Though they will probably be disregarded by many nations and probably much of the world press, four noteworthy recommendations emerged from the various meetings of Barbara Ward's invited group at the Habitat Symposium, from the Non-Governmental Organizations at the Habitat Forum and from the official delegates at the UN Habitat Conference itself.[7] The four, and the conditions to which there was a response, were as follows:

First, all around the world there are large squatter settlements, as for instance in Puerto Rico, Caracas and Bombay. These squatter settlements, which may increase by as many as a million people a year, are referred to formally as "self-help" groups because they improvise something to sleep under that sheds off the rain, whether it's thee ply, corrugated paperboard or rusty corrugated iron. They are invariably on land that by law "belongs" to somebody else. The squatters are continually approached by racketeers who tell them, secretly, that the police are going to evict them, but if the squatters will pay the racketeers, arrangements can be made for them to remain. In this way the racketeers skim off all the money the squatters earn.

In order to cope with this phenomenon, the UN Vancouver Congress passed a very extraordinarily wise and humanly considerate resolution. In traveling around the world and visiting such squatter settlements, I have observed their beautiful community life. People in trouble co-operate in a thoughtful and loving way. Their way of life is so beautiful that I have always said that if I ever have to retire, it will be into one of those squatters' settlements. It was also observed by the majority of the UN delegates that the people coming to squat are very ingenious in the way they employ the limited available materials to provide shelter. Therefore, one of the first resolutions passed at the Vancouver conference and one also forged by the Barbara Ward Symposium recommended that all nations decree that all the land which these squatters occupy be made public lands, on which the people are allowed to remain. It was part of the same motion that the squatters be given much better materials with which to accomplish their environmental controlling.

The second resolution of note passed at Vancouver would remove the profit motive of real estaters who persuade farmers to give them an option on their land and then borrow government guaranteed funds to put in sewers, water and streets, thereby escalating land prices. The meeting recommended that all the nations individually arrange that whatever the increase in the value of land at the time of sale, it shall be taxed at a hundred per cent.

The third resolution that I want to draw attention to was the Barbara Ward Symposium recommendation that there should be a world moratorium on the further development of atomic energy.

The fourth resolution was one which Barbara Ward had herself conceived and introduced. It recommended that all around the world, by 1985, it be made physically and practically possible for all human beings to have fresh, safe, potable drinking, bathing and washing water. Around the world there are as yet many places where people are dying or suffering because of infected water. It is highly feasible within the present technology to make pure, safe water available to everybody anywhere.

THE WORLD GAME DOMES AND THE
NOW HOUSE

A mushroom group of foldable and moveable geodesic domes and modernized Indian tepees at Vancouver's Jericho Beach conference site demonstrated a young world's ability and inspiration to do something positive about its own future.

The World Game staff, from the Universities of Pennsylvania and Yale, called their exhibit the *Now House* because everything they had on display could be purchased now from industrial mass production sources.[8] All the labour of their production occurred under the controlled environment conditioning of factories: no rain, cold, heat, snow, ice and wind. The World Gamers exhibited four 14 foot 5/8 sphere polyester fiberglass geodesic domes with alternate translucent or opaque fiberglass hexagon or pentagon panels. These domes had no more need for old building technology than has the opening of an umbrella—a mobile, environment-controlling artifact. The World Gamers brought their exhibit from Philadelphia to Vancouver in one camper truck pulling one trailer.

The World Gamers first dug circular trenches slightly larger in diameter than the domes' circular bases. As they trenched they threw the earth into the enclosed circle and leveled it to form an elevated base for each dome. On top of the earth they laid overlapping corrugated aluminum panels which were surmounted first by aluminised foamboard to reradiate heat and next by plywood and again by indoor-outdoor carpeting. This made a very comfortable, springy and dry floor. They anchored the domes so that they could not blow away, for each one weighed only 225 pounds.

Three of the domes were positioned in a triangular pattern with ten feet between them. A high pole was mounted at the centre of the triangular area which in turn supported a watertight translucent canopy. The large triangular area between the domes and below the canopy was covered with the indoor-outdoor carpeting. The fourth dome stood mildly apart and could have been connected by a canopy but was not.

Ten of the World Gamers lived very comfortably and happily in the Now House installation. In the kitchen-bathing dome compact, economic but adequate shelving was provided on which to mount the kitchen equipment. They had a toilet which converted human waste into high-grade fertilizer. The heat necessary for this odourless process was provided alternately by electricity from the windmill hookup and by heat from the solar panel water-heating device. The toilet system produced fertilizer as a rich, dry, manured, loamlike substance which needed to be taken out of the system only once a year.

The windmill was equipped with a synchronous inverter, embodying new advanced efficiency, electronic circuitry for converting the direct current produced by the windmill into 110 volt alternating current required by most electrical equipment, making it possible to feed their alternating current directly into the public power lines. When windpower generated electricity is fed into batteries and an electric charge is later taken from the batteries for final light or power use, approximately half the energy is lost.

Feeding the unscheduled wind energy harvest directly into the power grid avoids this transfer loss. This innovation has now been accepted by the public utilities in twenty of the fifty United States. The utility companies pay the local windmill owner at wholesale rates for the energy he puts into the system and charge him at retail rates for the energy he takes out. This increases the economic advantage of both the private windmill owner and the public utilities. It is a fundamental energy "income gain" by humanity over and above dollar considerations. It is found that somewhere within a one hundred mile radius, the wind is always blowing, that is, within a two hundred mile diameter circle of 31,000 square miles. With the proliferation of such local windmills, the public utilities can progressively retire significant amounts of stand-by generating capacity, while also reducing their fossil fuel burning.

Arrayed between two of the three domes under the translucent canopy were banks of tomatoes and other food vegetation in hydroponic tanks, with noticeable growth accomplished during the short two-week period of the installation. The domes could be rotatingly rearranged with the translucent side south to impound enormous amounts of sun radiation With the translucent panels north they remained cool and let in only the north light so desirable to artists. ,

The domes that were exhibited were priced at $750 each and the cost of the total package, including $17,000 worth of equipment, amounted to $20,000. Approximately 1,000 people a day visited the *Now House* and seemed genuinely enthusiastic. Their comments and the World Gamers' experience of the operation of the complex were invaluable in consideration of future improvements.

At Habitat, as elsewhere, I pointed out that the general principle of aiming for an ever higher performance with ever less inputs of energy, time and weights of material per given level of accomplished functioning, produced sumtotally a trend toward doing so much with so little that we have now arrived at a condition where performance is approximately invisible. Form is no longer following function. Functions have become formless. World humanity's *reality* of 1900 consisted of everything people could smell, see, touch and hear. Now, three quarters of a century later, 99.9 per cent of all humanity's practical everyday, worked-with realities are only instrumentally (non-sensorially) apprehendable and employable by humans. Therefore I emphasized to the Habitat audiences that they should disregard their conditioned reflexes which spontaneously look only for immediately visible manifestations of new improved ways of living.

In 1928, at the start of my fifty-year program, the structural mast of the 1928 Dymaxion House contained all its service mechanics, as did also the first full scale prototype produced at Beech Aircraft, Wichita, Kansas, in 1944–45.[9] Following general news publication of the latter, over 37,000 orders for the house were received by mail, many with cheques, all of which had to be returned because there was then no industry to manufacture or install these air-deliverable dwelling machines. Many distributors applied for sale franchises, but the electricians and plumbers who are everywhere exclusively licensed to connect houses to the water and electricity mains said that in order to survive they would have to take apart all the Dymaxion Houses' pre-assembled plumbing and electricity manifolds and re-assemble them. This would have tripled the costs and have been as illogical as would be local electricians and plumbers taking each purchased automobile apart in the owner's frontyard and reassembling it before finally permitting its use.

To avoid this nonsensical and wasteful situation, in 1947 after twenty years of my fifty year program had passed, the grand strategy was changed to one of concentration on the improvement of the shell structures themselves. Thus was I led to design the geodesic dome. And now at the completion of my fifty year campaign the No. 2 *Now House* is becoming publicly available as the air-deliverable, only-rentable, world-around dwelling machine, right on its fiftieth birthday.

CHANGING CONCEPTIONS OF GLOBAL SCALE

World War I was so called because the stage on which it was acted was an historically unprecedented and entirely new world-around involvement. All the world's metal ore lands were involved in the production of new inanimate energy powered production machinery. When World War I was over the copper in the electric generators and motors did not rot as did the pre-World War I farm produce, nor did the copper return to the mines. The electric generators hooked up to the waterfalls kept producing electricity and the overland wires kept distributing that electricity to mass production factories and people's homes. Energy is the essence of wealth, wealth being the organized capability to support life.

When World War I was over, all the metal producing capability and energy generation persisted, with an enormous wealth gain by humanity. This high producing capability went not only into automobiles, but into farm machinery. It reduced the 90 per cent of humanity necessary on the farms to six per cent. Those not needed on the farms migrated to the cities, for food could now reach them anywhere. The new technology and its mass production under controlled environmental conditions made the old building craft technology operating under non-controlled environmental conditions, fundamentally obsolete; but society's preoccupation with accepted ways of earning its living obscured the fact. World War II took humanity's technology into the sky, deep into the ocean and eventually into outer space. These latter arts required an enormous step-up in doing more with less in order to make all logistics flyable, rocketable or electro-magnetically transmittable.

Subsequent to World War II it was found that all metals involved in the general technology of humanity were being consistently melted out of their old use forms on average every 22 years to become re-employed with an interim gained know-how to accomplish a far higher performance per pound, erg and hour technology for many times the numbers of humans served on the previous round. Japan became one of the world's greatest industrial countries employing only recirculating metal scrap.

In pre-automobile American cities and factory towns only the rich moved house, on fall and spring moving days, to bigger or smaller homes, as their changing means dictated. With the advent of the automobile, workmen could travel to better paid employment and factories could be located on new out-of-town sites. In 1950 the average American family moved out of town every six years. In 1975 the average American family was moving out of town every three years. When World War I began, the average American walked 1,100 miles a year and rode 300 miles in a vehicle of some type. In 1976, the average American still walks 1,100 miles each year but travels 20,000 miles by vehicle. And while there were no aircraft in 1900, by 1976 airport traffic was greater than that by rail when the century began. Humans with legs to move are freeing themselves from rooted dwelling patterns of earlier eras. Human settlements were inherent to agrarian and mill town ages: now human *unsettlement* is occurring.

That is why Vancouver's Habitat was an historical watershed. It marked the end of human settlement, in exclusively local geography and in major poverty. It was the beginning of the era of local geographical unsettlement and transition into the historically unprecedented and utterly unexpected condition of all humans—successfully-at-home-in-universe.

PAYING FOR THE HOMES WE NEED

At the time of the 1929 crash and following depression and the beginning of the New Deal in 1933, the United States government took over the underwriting of the obsolete building industry.[10] Cutting loose from the historical earned savings, purchasing capability and instituting purchasing capability based on future earnings of the people, the US government instituting purchasing capability based on future earnings of the people, the US government instituted 20, 30 and 40 years mortgages that need, in effect, never; be reduced so long as the periodically renegotiated interest was being paid. Had the buildings been as efficient and effective as air-space technology could render them, they would have paid for themselves in five years or better, as does all good machinery. What the government financed was the continuation and multiplication of inefficiency, manifest today in the fact that out of every 100 units of energy consumed in the US only five units of effective life supporting physical work is realized, that is, our "system" has an overall techno-economic efficiency of only five per cent. People can only have incomes through employment but 70 per cent of all the jobs in the USA are invented and produce no life support whatever. The last quarter century's vast transformation of cities all around the world to skyscraper clusters has produced space within which no life support is produced, only to accommodate job and money making. All the money making drives towards omni-automation and complete unemployment. Politics keeps inventing the jobs.

Post-1933 housing finance has shown that when the price of the median house goes above three times the median annual family income the family cannot demonstrate creditable house purchasing capability. A general condition of such inability has now been reached. Since the median family's life expectancy is 70 years and since the age of the median family's earners is 35 years, they have 35 years of life ahead but only 25 years before mandatory retirement, ergo, no more future earning years to hypothecate for home "buying" on the installment plan which (theoretically) leads towards ultimate but rarely realized "owning." To continue underwriting the inefficiencies of miniature castle building of the building and real estate enterprise system, their governments would now have to give the housing to the median class and "forget about the lower half of humanity as unhouseable." Furthermore, examination of private individual homes shows that they are only superficially individual, for the hydraulic wash away of the earth surrounding their foundations discloses the private houses to be only fancy terminal boxes mounted on the ends of pipes with the whole community functionally a unit mechanical organism.

Not only has the progressive unsettlement of humanity completely upset all historical expectancy, but as with the individual median family's inability ever again to buy its home so, too, have we exhausted the possibility of our nation's people and its businesses paying for further government underwriting of our obsolete building industry. We still have an obsolete building industry: we must try a completely new approach and our

Vancouver experience indicates one that may be appropriate.

SETTLEMENTS ON THE NORTH FACE

Those who are world travellers are familiar with the scene at the airport baggage delivery turntables: along come well-strapped bundles of tubes and blue nylon which are picked up by young people and strapped on their backs. These packs open out into very small homes, but homes they are, and very satisfactory to youth in a world where there are so many satisfactory technological complementations of such world-around living in the form of electrified and plumbinged campsites and hostels.

At our Vancouver site, in addition to the four Turtle domes there were two smaller North Face domes. The name "North Face" derives from the north face of Mount Everest, for these domes were developed by successful Everest climbers for their high altitude, advanced base, dwelling devices—designed for environmental conditions far more formidable than those with which humans anywhere had ever before swiftly and effectively coped. The North Face domes are oval in plan and are geodesic. They are made with the highest tensile strength aircraft aluminum struts and have inner and outer skins of nylon with a double skin floor. They disassemble and roll into a pack two feet long by eight inches in diameter and weigh only eight pounds. An eight-pound home compounded with a sleeping bag permits human beings to be very intimate with nature under most hostile conditions.

Despite that they were going to have to move out of town and then out of state within only five years and would have preferred to be allowed to rent acceptably built and furnished homes in acceptable localities, those humans necessitous of getting to and holding their jobs while providing their families with favourable living, learning, playing and growing conditions have been forced to buy the acceptable homes by the speculative builders, at figures that would require a minimum of 30 to 40 years to pay off. Humanity in the nonsocialist world is now being propagandised, coerced and often even forced to purchase all the immobile home properties, which gave rise to condominium or co-operative offices, apartment houses and owned single family dwellings. Yet the great industrial corporations have found such immobility to be untenable, and having now become transnational, they are concerned only with investments in service industries which rent rather than sell telephones, computers, cars, world hotelling, etc. and sell only armaments.

Eventual and perhaps even imminent, world disarmament will release the vast weapons industries for the production of air-deliverable dwelling machines. With general disarmament and the release to life promoting account of the fabulous production capacity of the world's industrial complexes will come the one day air delivery of whole cities wherein the operating energy efficiencies will be significantly multiplied and the social conditions provided by the omni-visible central community and the completely private, deployed dwelling areas; or the air delivery of single family dwelling machines to the remotest of sites; or of whole clusters of single family dwelling machines to near or far sites.

Before 1985 we will have abandoned the concept of having to earn a living. We will have given life long scholarships to everyone. We will have converted all the big city buildings to apartments and have eliminated 70 per cent of local commuting while vastly increasing long distance travel.

MORE WITH LESS: THE HOPEFUL FUTURE

In Vancouver in June 1976, the young world in its own right opened a new chapter for human society by itself becoming committed realistically to doing more with less. Before the end of the century we will find all of humanity doing so much more with so much less that it will be enjoying a higher, legitimately richer and ethically more decent standard of living than has ever been experienced by any humans before us. With economic, physical and environmental success for all will come completely new economic accounting. We now have the metals comprehensively recirculating, and the know-how to accomplish all these tasks within the limits of already mined metals.

Since all political systems are predicated upon the misconception of fundamental in adequacy of human life support on our planet, their premise will have been proven invalid. We know how to live entirely within the scope of our daily star emanating radiation and gravity, energies income, ergo within a ten year world program we can provide all humanity with an amount of energy annually equal to that enjoyed exclusively by North Americans in 1972, while concurrently phasing out all use of fossil fuels. Nor need we longer have recourse to burning up our spaceship Earth's capital inventory of atoms.

The time-energy cosmic accounting and maximum efficiency alternative technologies as exclusively employed by scenario universe and spoken of by us as "nature" will be instituted in all human affairs and will be integratively operated by world-around satellite interlinked computers. With the computers' integrative examination of the physical and metaphysical resources available to human beings, it will be discovered that we are incredibly wealthy. Wealth, as stated before, being predicated on the degree of organized competence to nurture, protect and accommodate today's and tomorrow's lives. It will be clearly manifest that we have aboard spaceship Earth four billion, billionaire, heirs-apparent who have never been notified of their magnificent inheritance which has been over long hidden within the world's obsolete laws, customs and administrations whose divorcement of money from real wealth has hidden from the whole world the late twentieth century realized existence of omnihumanity sustaining inexhaustible wealth.

NOTES

1. On the Dymaxion House see *The Harvard Crimson*, May 22, 1929, pp. 24-32.

2. *Hearings before the Committee on Foreign Relations*, US Senate, Ninety Fourth Congress, First Session, May/June 1975 (Washington, DC: US Government Printer, 1975), pp. 181-202.

3. R. Sheppard, "Buckminster Fuller Has New Dome Plan," *Montreal Star*, July 10, 1976.

4. D. H. Meadows, D. L. Meadows, J. Randers, and W. W. Behrens, *The Limits to Growth* (London: Earth Island; New York: Universe Books, 1972).

5. See J. W. Forrester, *World Dynamics* (Cambridge, MA: Wright-Allen Press, 1971).

6. For a discussion of Habitat 1976, see Humphrey Carver, "Habitat 1976: The Home of

Man," *Town Planning Review* 248, no. 3 (July 1977), pp. 281-86.

7. The resolutions and the roles of the various meetings are discussed in *Ekistics* 42, no.252 (November 1976).

8. The domes are manufactured by the Molded Fiberglass Company, Ashtabula, Ohio, and the windmill by Kedco of Inglewood, California. The synchronous inverter came from Windworks, Mukwanago, Wisconsin. In all fifty firms voluntarily equipped the *Now House*.

9. See *Fortune* magazine, April 1946, for an article "Fuller's House: It Has a Better Than Ever Chance of Upsetting the Building Industry."

10. On this and associated issues of efficiency and attitudes in the building industry, see "The - Rebirth of the American City," *Hearings before the Committee on Banking, Currency and Housing.* US House of Representatives, Ninety-Fourth Congress, Second Session, September 30, 1976 (Washington, DC: US Government Printer, 1976), pp. 1011-16.

Woman-Made America:
The Case of Early Public Housing Policy

Eugenie Ladner Birch

Copyright: Reprinted by permission from the *Journal of the American Institute of Planners*, 44, 2, 1978 ©, pp. 130-144.

This article is an excellent overview of the contribution that women made in early public housing policy and reform. Birch focuses particularly on the courageous efforts of both Edith Elmer Wood and Catherine Bauer. Women played an uncharacteristically large part in the pioneering days of the movement and became outspoken advocates for designing housing units adequate for supporting family life, rather than just providing minimal shelter. Birch outlines the beginnings of the reform, as well as the successful lobbying efforts of these women and the key pieces of legislation that resulted.

The August 19, 1937, headline announced: "Housing Bill Voted by House as Gag Blocks Opponents...Measure Is Pushed through Heated Night Session."[1] The last obstacle to the Wagner-Steagall Act fell away. As public housing became a reality, its supporters breathed with relief. For the first time, the federal government took tentative steps toward accepting permanent responsibility for the construction of decent, low-cost homes and for the elimination of hazardous, unhealthy slums. Like most social decisions in pluralistic America, neither the president nor Congress had generated this policy directly. Instead strong interest groups had captured the support of New York Senator Robert F. Wagner, and he promoted the Housing Act which responded to their ideas. In this way, housing became a legitimate national concern, to be broadened later by more ambitious legislation passed between 1949 and 1968.

The federal presence in housing matters was a major change from former practice. Until the New Deal, localities, under their police powers, were perceived as responsible for maintenance of adequate dwellings. Cities limited the scope of their work by intent and practice to regulation in the form of tenement and house codes. Traditionally, private enterprise provided all residential construction and rebuilt declining urban areas when economically feasible. However, with increasing frequency in the twentieth century, this sector had been unable or unwilling to perform these functions completely, leaving a vacuum to be filled by public endeavor.

The new federal role was the product of the efforts of the American housing movement. Consisting of an amorphous, sometimes divided, coalition of social workers, economists, labor leaders, lawyers and municipal officials, the housers waged their battle between 1914 and 1937.

Although this coalition and its approach were similar to many other alliances of the period, it differed in one significant way.[2] It was led predominantly by women. Springing from traditional female interests in social housekeeping on local levels, it grew to national importance as women united to promote their ideas. Along the way, women supplied the intellectual basis, political leadership, and executive expertise as well as the rank and file support which gave early housing policy a distinct character. This article will focus on the development of female leadership.

Two features of early housing policy can be clearly attributed to female influence. The first was the insistence that government was to build homes for the low-income slum dweller because the private sector would not do so. Earlier reformers, primarily men such as Lawrence Veiller and E. R. L. Gould, had supported publicly financed slum clearance but not governmental construction of new units. The second was the demand that the publicly constructed homes be positively supportive of family life, not merely provision of minimal shelter. Public housing architecture would reflect domestic needs as long as women anticipated in the implementation of the program.

KEY WOMEN OF THE EARLY HOUSING MOVEMENT

In the evolution of these ideas, two women played key roles. They were Edith Elmer Wood (1870–1945) and Catherine Bauer (1905-1964). Daughter of and wife of naval officers, Wood spent a good part of her life at military stations throughout the world. When she was a child, her father tutored her in languages and math. An honors graduate from Smith College at the age of eighteen, she and her mother were suffragists. An accomplished novelist, Wood became interested in housing through personal experience with unhealthy servants and the death of one of her four sons from contagion. A theorist, she approached reform by first taking a Columbia doctorate in political economy and later applying these principles to housing analysis.

Catherine Lucy Stone Bauer, a generation younger, grew up in New Jersey where her father was the state's chief highway engineer. Her mother, too, was a suffragist. A graduate of Vassar, she had

dropped out temporarily to study architecture at Cornell. A self-styled bohemian, she bounced from job to job before meeting Lewis Mumford who stimulated her interest in housing and encouraged her to write on esthetics and architecture.

Wood and Bauer had many common characteristics. Their parents encouraged self-expression and learning. They had similar educational backgrounds at women's colleges. They had literary ambitions which they turned toward achieving social good. They had pragmatic personalities which led them to temper reform theories with political reality. They differed in one major way. Wood's approach to housing reform came from the social sciences while Bauer's stemmed from architecture and planning.

Since the late nineteenth century, many other women intimately involved in housing were: Indianapolis reformer Albion Fellows Bacon; Washingtonians Mrs. Ernest P. Bicknell, Mrs. Archibald Hopkins, and the first Mrs. Woodrow Wilson; and New Yorkers Mary Kingsbury Simkhovitch, Helen Alfred, and Loula Lasker. Nonetheless, Wood and Bauer had the most significant impact on the formulation of the new policy. Wood was the pioneer who redefined the housing problem and formulated the new goals. Bauer joined her to create legislative solutions and bring political support and interest to the cause. Together, they were responsible for the passage of the Housing Act of 1937.

REDEFINING THE HOUSING PROBLEM

In the thirties, the new federal housing policy evolved from a revised perception of the problem. The laboring class became the focus. The argument held: not only had the Depression caused many workers to be unemployed, but more importantly, even in the best of times, those who did have jobs were not able to purchase or rent adequate homes at reasonable prices. As a result, the majority of low-income families were forced to live in slums or substandard units—a situation unacceptable to American society. The Wagner-Steagall Act, responding to this dilemma, would aid the worker in two ways: providing decent shelter and creating employment. Its succinct preamble stated the issue in this context. It defined the housing problem as the need:

to provide financial assistance to the States and political subdivisions thereof for the elimination of unsafe, unsanitary housing conditions, for the eradication of slums, for the provision of decent, safe and sanitary dwellings for families of low income and for the reduction of unemployment and the stimulation of business activity.... [3]

Although shelter has always been a basic need, governmental concern, stemming from the conditions caused by nineteenth century urbanization and industrialization, is relatively new. American housing reform was born in New York, scene of some of the worst examples of residential crowding, poor sanitation, and disease. Public interest was first aroused in the 1890s when *Tribune* reporter, Jacob Riis, whose vivid photographs and poignant accounts of "how the other half lived" caused progressive Governor Theodore Roosevelt to appoint a state Tenement House Commission at the turn of the century to study New York City dwellings. Headed by veteran settlement house worker, Lawrence Veiller, the commission's recommendations were embodied in the 1901 Tenement House Law, a prototype after which all of the nation's housing codes would be modeled.[4] The law established minimum standards of windows, toilets, and fire escapes in the city's multiple-unit dwellings.[5] The effect was regulatory, local and limited. It was based on Veiller's view that poor housing, caused by the unscrupulous landlord and careless tenant, was a threat to the general health, safety, and public welfare and therefore must be controlled. Writing in the early 1900s Veiller stated:

> The housing problem is the problem of enabling the great mass of people who want to live in decent surroundings and bring up their children under proper conditions to have such opportunities. It is also to a very large extent, the problem of preventing other people who do not care for decent conditions or are unable to achieve them from maintaining conditions, which are a menace to their neighbors, to the community and to civilization.[6]

For twenty years, the Veiller ideas swept the nation as reformers from Indianapolis to Philadelphia sought to introduce housing codes into their communities. Basically, these civic groups, heavily dominated by women, wished to exert social control over the slum dwellers. They never questioned the rationale nor results of their campaigns.[7] Typical of their attitudes was the declaration of a Washington, D.C. activist, Mrs. Ernest P. Bicknell, who referred to the 1914 effort to use the rules to close alley dwellings, slums peculiar to the Capital:

> Our greatest desire [is] that these people might some day be forced to live where they would be subjected to the supervision and restraint of the public street.[8]

WOOD CHALLENGES VEILLER

One volunteer worker in the Washington effort raised her voice in doubt, challenging the existing dogma. In 1913, Edith Elmer Wood undertook a survey of hundreds of alley dwellers questioning them about their conditions. She found that people lived in slums because they had no alternative. She roundly condemned "any remedial measure which simply forces them out of the alleys and makes no provision for their future as a very great hardship upon...people who in the majority of cases are deserving of every consideration."[9]

For the next five years, she broadened her studies by surveying major U.S. cities. In her first book, published in 1919, *The Housing of the Unskilled Wage Earner*, she concluded that poor housing was not the result of the malfeasance of a few landlords and tenants but of the malfunctioning of the modern industrial system and therefore must be treated differently from the traditional regulatory approach used by Veiller. In her analysis, she did not view slums as a moral problem, but as an economic issue which demanded governmental attention. To her mind, adequate shelter had to be provided through public welfare procedures. She argued,

> If our modern civilization requires workers to congregate in cities and the great value of land there puts the control of their housing outside of the hands of the workers and good housing out of their reach, then it would seem logical that housing should be accepted as a community problem—as a public service even as

water, light, transit or education—to be controlled and regulated and where necessary owned and managed by the community.[10]

In addition, Wood emphasized that the minimum standards established by Veiller were outdated and too limited for universal application. Drawing from the 1912 housing statement of the National Conference of Charities, she pointed out that the concept of adequate housing was not limited to insuring the basic health and safety of the inhabitants but also mandated decent surroundings. She established standards of density: no more than one person per room. She outlined an economic stricture: maximum rents of 20 percent of family income. She included locational demands: accessibility to places of employment.[11]

Wood desired to raise housing minimums because she realized that, although in New York City they had eliminated the worst conditions, the codes had not accomplished enough. She granted that after several years of the law's application, "There were no accumulations of filth...no dilapidation or extreme disrepair...no privy vaults... [and] there was running water in almost every apartment." Nonetheless, she charged: "only in a comparative sense can even the new law tenements be said to represent a satisfactory...standard." For there were still conditions of crowding, unpleasant and poorly designed high-density development, and relatively high rents which could be improved only by radical change.[12]

HOUSING NEEDS ANALYSIS ON A NATIONAL BASIS

Using her new standards, Wood reviewed the housing problem in a wider context, embracing the nation. At this time, Wood made the first estimates of national housing conditions. Determining the number of substandard dwellings in the country was a difficult task before the U.S. Bureau of the Census collected housing and income distribution figures. As early as 1919, Wood used primitive government statistics for average wages, number of wage earners, and costs of housing to report the dramatic finding:

> Roughly one third of the people of the United States are living under subnormal housing conditions which fall below the minimum

standard and about one tenth are living under conditions which are an acute menace to health, morals and family life.[13]

Wood continued to be the sole monitor of housing conditions during the following years. Although some writers such as Lewis Mumford and Lewis Pink covered the issue, they did not deal with the statistics. The residential market fluctuated wildly in the twenties: severe shortages and high costs in the immediate postwar period were followed by glut and inflation in the latter part of the decade.[14] Wood distinguished parameters of the problem. Writing in 1931 she observed,

> By 1926, the end of the shortage was in sight. By 1928, it had been reached. In a nationwide numerical sense, there was no longer a housing shortage. We were back where we were before the War with qualitative rather than quantitative needs. So far as net progress was concerned, ten years had been lost.[15]

Finally, when the Department of Commerce published the 1934 Real Property Inventory, Wood found figures that "block out...in vivid colors the extent of the slum clearance task that lies before us. [And it] contains facts on which to base a rational division of the field between private enterprise and public."[16] Her newsmaking analysis of the data *Slums and Blighted Areas in the United States*, published in 1935 by the Public Works Administration substantiated the earlier conclusion that one-third of the nation was ill-housed. By 1937, even Roosevelt would cite this figure in his second inaugural address. The absolute numbers in her findings of 11 million substandard units made national headlines as the *New York Times* and other newspapers gave coverage to the new conception of the housing problem.[17]

Most professionals in the field accepted Wood's analysis immediately. For example, when she published her tentative estimates in 1919, architect-houser Carol Aronovici in the *American Journal of Sociology* hailed her writing as the first "scientific discussion of the whole problem." By 1931, Executive Secretary of the Public Administration Clearing House Charles Ascher reported that public administrators regarded her work, *Recent Trends in American Housing*, as the "bible of housing." And in 1935, New Deal officials

Jacob Crane and Leon Keyserling relied upon her *Slums and Blighted Areas* as "a solid factual book."[18]

Resistance to her definition of the housing problem came from two areas: older housing reformers led by Lawrence Veiller and the real estate industry. Veiller refused to acknowledge her work because he was vehemently opposed to government construction of housing. The real estate industry shared Veiller's objections. It cried that the public sector should not compete with the private, that the state was not a good landlord, and that the workingman would become too dependent upon society if he lived in a publicly sponsored dwelling.[19]

FORMULATION OF NEW GOALS

Simultaneously with redefining the housing problem, Wood articulated new goals for social policy for its solution. Linking substandard units with their location in center city slums, she called for a program of clearance, building, loans, and code enforcement. Beginning with her 1919 book, she recommended elimination of all slums, direct public construction of new dwellings for the lowest economic third of the population, and financial assistance for the second economic third to purchase houses. These goals would be explicitly stated in the 1949 and 1968 housing acts. The Housing Act of 1949 declared that the nation was responsible for the provision of "a decent home and suitable living environment for every American family." The Housing and Urban Development Act of 1968 would reaffirm this objective and create legislation to build 26 million new residences through public and private efforts in ten years.

Wood generated these goals to be consistent with her public welfare analysis. She argued that if all citizens had a right to adequate shelter, the government must take proper action to guarantee that right. She pointed to traditional constitutional interpretations to justify this point of view. She quoted the eminent jurist Ernst Freund to demonstrate that the police power "should not only restrain and command but also render aid and service...to serve public welfare."[20] By 1949, the preamble to the housing act would clearly state this principle:

> The Congress hereby declares that the general, welfare and security of the Nation and the health and living standards of its people require housing production and...clearance of slums.[21]

PUBLIC SUPPORT AND INTEREST FOR THE CAUSE: WOMEN AND LABOR

While Wood designed her comprehensive program, she also addressed the strategic problem of how to promote its acceptance by the American public and its passage by Congress. She understood that the effort would require the demonstration of widespread political support and strong vocal alliances as well as painstaking lobbying. As early as 1914, she correctly identified two groups as having natural sympathies to her brand of housing reform. They were women and labor.

Being a suffragist, she believed women of all classes had common interests. She thought they would respond to the need to create a decent living environment for the nation's children. She, like other college educated women, was convinced that the graduates had a special responsibility to lead the movement.

> I want to see the university women of the nation become acutely—even painfully—conscious of the hardships under which more than half the mothers of our land now labor in trying to bring up children and make a real home in the cramped depressing tenements of obsolete rundown houses which are all the family income can command.... It is not impossible to bring this about but it is far from easy. It will not be done until the women of the nation organize to do it.[22]

In 1914, Wood convinced the Washington branch of the American Association of University Women (AAUW) to form a housing committee. By 1916, this local group proved to the central leadership that its work should be incorporated into its national program by arguing,

> The Association... is better fitted than any other group to determine the right direction... [for solving] the problem of securing wholesome homes for wage earners... because its members have trained minds and the habit of critical analysis, because its members are mothers who realize with especial vividness

the influence of environment on child life, because among its members are to be found architects, physicians, social workers and social economists—representatives of all the professions covering the approaches to the housing problem and finally because as an organization, it has always been distinguished for a deep sense of responsibility to the community.[23]

Wood, as head of the national housing committee during its fifteen-year existence, directed its program in two ways. The first was to develop a nationwide network of city based supporters. By 1921, there were fifty-two local groups of university women. Each one supported the reform policy and was engaged in various parochial endeavors. The Boston project participated in a housing code campaign, the New York effort lobbied on the state level for public assistance for low-cost housing construction, and the Chicago activists promoted a zoning plan which was under consideration.

Under Wood, the national committee's second function was to articulate goals and programs and use the American Association of University Women as a political base to promote them. Although the twenties were a decade in which public sympathy for housing matters was limited, the committee did have some achievements. Among its projects were lobbying for a building and housing division in the U.S. Department of Commerce established in 1922 and pressuring the Census Bureau to measure overcrowding in its 1930 tabulations.[24]

In 1929, the association's governing board, citing its interests in other areas, abolished the national housing committee. This was a great disappointment to Wood. However, this action convinced her of the need for an organization dedicated solely to housing reform. She could see from the results of the AAUW work that such a group could successfully function on grass-roots and national levels.

Wood's early efforts to generate labor support were more narrowly focused. Nonetheless, in 1914, she convinced the Central Labor Union of the District of Columbia "to instruct their delegate to the national convention of the American Federation of Labor at Philadelphia to present a resolution favoring government loans for workingmen's houses and municipal lodging."[25] Subsequently, the union adopted the motion which later became an important part of its policy.

ROLE OF THE REGIONAL PLANNING ASSOCIATION OF AMERICA

Wood's work with the American Association of University Women brought her into contact with Frederick Ackerman and Clarence Stein, members of a small circle of architects and writers centered around Charles Harris Whittaker, editor of the *Journal of the American Institute of Architects*. These men became interested in the design of low-cost dwellings during World War I when they served as advisers for U.S. government sponsored defense housing projects. Among their number were Lewis Mumford, Benton McKaye, Henry Wright, and Robert Kohn. In 1923, they formed the Regional Planning Association of America (RPAA) and invited others to join, including Edith Elmer Wood and Catherine Bauer. Through their meetings they exchanged information, encouraged each others' publications, and collaborated on experiments such as Radburn, New Jersey, a garden city. In 1933, the group divided on the issue of slum clearance. But while the RPAA lasted, it had a profound influence upon housing thought because it served as a meeting ground for leading reformers. Clarence Stein writing to Catherine Bauer recollected,

> It brought together some of those who were in search of a saner planned development on a regional basis here in the USA. Being together, talking together and working together clarified their own objectives and helped mold their own activities.[26]

ORGANIZING LOBBYING GROUPS

From the RPAA discussions Wood and Bauer gained ideas which they used in developing two major housing lobby groups. The first was the National Public Housing Conference (NPHC) founded in 1931. An outgrowth of New York socialist Norman Thomas's Committee on Civic Affairs, it quickly became independent and established, as its primary goal, the promotion of "good housing through governmental loans and public construction to those people who cannot be adequately housed at rents they can afford to pay." Women predominated in the leadership of the National Public Housing Conference. Mary Kingsbury Simkhovitch served as president. Edith Elmer Wood, Edith Abbot, Mary Harriman Rumsey, and Cornelia Bryce Pinchot were among the vice presidents. Grace Abbot, Elizabeth Coit, Loula Lasker, and Lillian Wald were some of the women who acted as the advisory committee. Helen Alfred was the executive director.[27]

The second was the Labor Housing Conference (LHC) sponsored by the Pennsylvania Federation of Labor in 1934. Its purpose was to "organize and promote a powerful and intelligent demand for workers' housing and to assist workers' groups in the formulation of their requirement." The Labor Housing Conference was the creation of architect Oscar Stonorov and union leader John Edelman of the United Hosiery Workers of Philadelphia. They were stimulated to act by the fact that in the early years of the Depression about one quarter of the union had lost homes through foreclosure. Searching for an executive secretary, they chose Catherine Bauer, author of the recently published *Modern Housing*, a book whose thesis was that America could have government sponsored housing only if workers organized to demand it.[28]

A third lobby group, the National Association of Housing Officials, (NAHO) began in 1933. Wood also was among its founding members. Its purpose was to "be a clearinghouse to collect and disseminate information and to act as a service bureau for public housing officials." Coleman Woodbury, its first permanent executive director, emphasized that its primary role was to promote better public administration.[29]

All these organizations were to be highly instrumental in the passage of New Deal housing legislation. The National Public Housing Conference initiated efforts as early as 1932. The Labor Housing Conference and the National Association of Housing Officials, founded after the first programs were in effect, became important in the fight for a permanent program.

FEDERAL HOUSING LEGISLATION

The new breed of reformers, led by Wood and Bauer, was centered primarily in the east. Consequently, New York continued to be a forerunner in housing as these activists cast about for ways to incorporate their ideas in governmental programs. In 1926, the New York State legislature passed a landmark housing law allowing tax exemptions for limited dividend companies building low-cost dwellings. Although its supporters had hoped to ease credit through a state housing bank, the legislators deferred to real estate industry complaints and deleted the provision. Wood, who viewed the program as "what is left of an effort to put my outline of a state housing policy into effect for New York," became an adviser to the state housing board, the administrator of the new law. The program would later serve as a model for the federal government.[30]

Three years after the passage of the New York law, the Depression devastated the construction industry. Urban building, which had peaked in 1925, halved by 1936. National housing starts reflected the slump—the 1925 high of almost a million fell to 93,000 by 1933. Of 13 million workers unemployed in that year, one third were in the building trades.[31]

Responding to the panic, President Herbert Hoover called a National Housing Conference in December, 1931. True to the Republican administration's leanings, the proceedings were premised on Secretary of Interior Roy L. Wilbur's warning, "Unless businessmen...accept the challenge of providing an adequate supply of housing at moderate prices, housing by public authority is inevitable."[32]

Even though the conference's climate was unsympathetic to her ideas, Wood joined more than 3,700 delegates who attended this first federally sponsored housing effort. Organized around twenty-five issues ranging from financing to minimum standards, the final recommendations were predictably conservative. The sole legislative result was the 1932 Federal Home Loan Bank Act, designed to aid beleaguered homeowners unable to meet mortgage payments. Nonetheless, in a few committees there was some debate on an expanded government role for inexpensive housing and slum clearance.

RELIEF AND CONSTRUCTION ACT: SOME PROVISION FOR HOUSING LOANS

At this time National Public Housing Conference leaders began to monitor the Washington scene carefully. They were in close communication with New York Sen. Robert F. Wagner through their president, Mary K. Simkhovitch. Simkhovitch had worked with Wagner on many local issues connected with her New York City settlement, Greenwich House. They respected each other and had a long-standing friendship. (In addition, Simkhovitch was on close terms with Eleanor Roosevelt and Secretary of Labor Frances Perkins. She used these connections to promote the cause.) Later, Wagner, with his labor sympathies, would be receptive to Bauer's overtures on behalf of the Labor Housing Conference.

As the Depression worsened, Wagner and others pressed for federal action. The National Public Housing Conference lobbyists were on the spot suggesting housing construction as an aid to recovery. The first piece of legislation they influenced was the 1932 Relief and Construction Act setting up the Reconstruction Finance Corporation to prevent industrial bankruptcies. Wagner slipped in the NPHC provision for federal loans to limited dividend companies producing low-cost homes.[33]

Although only two projects received loans, the inclusion of this provision boosted the housing movement by bringing new sources of support. Chicago observer Charles Ascher reported to Wood, There is no doubt that the ineptly worded clause in the Relief Act has given great impetus to thinking about the problem: housing has become respectable to big business. As one of the editorial writers for the *Chicago Tribune*...said to me, "We are opposed in principle to the government's going into the banking business but as long as it's there, we want to see Chicago gets its fair share." But also some of our civic leaders—big bankers and industrialists—have suddenly begun to see housing on an enormous scale as the thing to break the back of the depression: being big businessmen, they talk in terms of $100,000,000 in a fashion to take away the breath of us little folk who know that there is no plan in existence by which such work could be undertaken.[34]

NATIONAL INDUSTRIAL RECOVERY ACT AND FORMATION OF THE HOUSING DIVISION

Such talk died down with an economic rally in the summer of 1932. However, shortly after the November election of Franklin D. Roosevelt, the system faltered again and the country experienced some of the most difficult months of the Depression. The first hundred days of the presidency, featuring the creation of the early New Deal package, were to be extremely important for housing reform as activists took this opportunity to inject their ideas into federal legislation. When the National Industrial Recovery Act, a comprehensive proposal containing many items, reached Congress in May, the housers had contributed the sections creating a housing division to construct or aid in the construction of low-cost dwellings and slum clearance projects. It could make loans at 4 percent interest to limited dividend companies or grants to public authorities of up to 30 percent of costs, or directly condemn land and rebuild. Senator Wagner, with the persuasion of the National Public Housing Conference had placed these provisions in the act.[35]

Shortly before its passage, Helen Alfred, the conference's executive director, wrote jubilantly to Wood,

> What do you think of the Public Works Bill? Pretty interesting—eh? Immediately upon reading detailed news of it, we communicated with the President and a number of key people in Washington in regard to paragraph D under section 202 of Title II. We definitely requested that this paragraph read: *"Construction by public bodies* or under public regulation and control of low cost housing and slum clearance projects."[36]

Even while Congressional debate on the bill took place, housing reformers began to define the ways to implement it. In Philadelphia, the United Hosiery Workers drew up plans for what would be the first PWA housing project, the Carl Mackley homes. In New York, members of the Regional Planning Association of America outlined policy directives.

THE FIRST OBJECTIVES OF NATIONAL EMERGENCY HOUSING POLICY

The housing faction of the association—Wood, Stein, and Kohn—worked feverishly on a position paper entitled "A Housing Policy for the United States Government." They knew they were faced with a unique opportunity. Kohn wrote to Wood, "It seems likely I can make this statement the declared policy of the new Public Works Administration under the Recovery Act."[37] He was right. On June 16, Roosevelt signed the act and made Harold Ickes head of the Public Works Administration. One week later, Ickes named Kohn chief of the PWA Housing Division. When the program officially started in early July, the division had a staff of about ten and an equal number of consultants including Wood and Simkhovitch of the National Public Housing Conference.

The Regional Planning Association of America, document, which was published widely, illustrated the first principles of federal housing policy. Primarily concerned with physical and social aspects of low cost housing, it had two distinct considerations. First, the location of the projects was to be determined by regional planning and economic criteria. Second, "the complete neighborhood community [was to] be taken as the basic unit of housing." Not only should programs be dedicated to producing dwelling units, but also they should be concerned with their arrangement in large-scale developments in which provision would be made to minimize street traffic, maximize open space and parks, insure sun and air, and provide buildings for community activities.[38] Wood had emphasized these ideas in her 1923 book, *Housing Policy in Western Europe*. Bauer would repeat them in 1934 in *Modern Housing*.

The emergency housing program had a slow start. Hampered by the reticence of Congress to appropriate money, an interagency feud between controller-general John R. McCarl and administrator Ickes, and the confusion of starting a completely new agency, the housing division had processed only seven applications by the end of 1933. The program suffered further setbacks in the next years. The 1934 National Housing Act, setting up the Federal Housing Administration (FHA) to guarantee home mortgages, pitted Ickes against FHA administrator James Moffet who jockeyed for leadership in the field.[39] Later in the year, Roosevelt impounded $110 million of PWA housing funds; and in January 1935, a Kentucky court struck down federal use of eminent domain for slum clearance.[40]

THE NEED FOR A PERMANENT HOUSING POLICY

These events convinced housers that the emergency programs were impractical. Between the spring of 1935 and the summer of 1937 they hammered out the actual details of a permanent housing policy. Through Wagner and others, the Labor Housing Conference and the National Public Housing Conference brought legislation before three sessions of Congress. The 1935 versions never moved past the hearing stage. The 1936 bill passed the Senate but never got out of the house committee. With these failures, it became evident that there would be no act unless Roosevelt was behind it.

Finally, the lobbyists, through Senator Wagner, secured a campaign commitment from the president. Speaking in October, Roosevelt promised a New York City audience of 300,000,

> We have too long neglected the housing problem for our lower income groups.... We have not yet I begun adequately to spend money in order to help the families in the overcrowded sections of our cities live as American citizens have a right to live. You and I will not be content until city, state and federal government have joined with private capital in helping every American live that way.... I am confident that the next Congress will start us on our way with a sound housing policy.[41]

Following Roosevelt's election, Wagner's legislative assistant, Leon Keyserling, along with National Association of Housing Officials director Coleman Woodbury and government economist Warren J. Vinton, refashioned the previous year's bill for presentation to Roosevelt and the 1937 Congress. In the process, they frequently consulted Bauer, Wood, and Simkhovitch.

LEGISLATIVE CAMPAIGN: LHC AND NPHC LEADERS WORK NONSTOP

While this group prepared the bill, Catherine Bauer cultivated grass-roots support.[42] The National Public Housing Conference and the National Association of Housing Officials supplemented her efforts. Bauer worked from the Housing Legislation Information Office (HLIO) which she and Ernest Bohn, a Cleveland politician, long enthusiastic about federal funding for municipal problems, had started in 1936. From these headquarters, two windowless rooms located behind the stairwell of the Hays Adams Hotel, she orchestrated a masterful plan to put pressure on Roosevelt, Wagner, Rep. Henry Steagall of Alabama, head of the House Banking and Currency Committee, and other congressmen.

In the two previous years, Bauer had systematically built labor support. Personally visiting stat and local labor unions from Minneapolis to Birmingham, she convinced them to pressure the American Federation of Labor to take a strong stand on public housing. She based her strategy on the work Wood had started in 1914. By 1935 her efforts paid off. The national organization passed a resolution stating that it was in favor of "a long term permanent program to guarantee a minimum standard of decency in housing for all families." In addition, it called for the formation of local housing committees to "take the lead in developing an active demand for housing, to initiate suitable projects and to represent, protect and promote the interests of labor and consumers in the location, design, construction and management of public housing projects."[43]

This was the mandate Bauer needed. From that point on she begged, bullied, and convinced the locals to create their housing committees. She wrote innumerable pamphlets, sponsored regional labor housing meetings with leading housers as speakers, sent out periodic bulletins, gave dramatic press releases, pushed for an American Federation of Labor Housing Advisory Council of prominent leaders, and maintained constant letter and telegraph communications with key AFL supporters.

Bauer used her considerable personal talents to bring local officials into line. John Edelman, one of the Labor Housing Conference founders, never ceased to be amazed by Bauer, recording,

> The prompt and easy way in which Catherine established her relationship with the fairly hardboiled labor skates...was something no other woman...[had] accomplished.... She got herself some respectable clothes...and snuggled up to the building trades boys. And those old goats, always to a man opposed to public housing and to women's rights, to a man they fell in love with her...and introduced her around.[44]

At one critical point, she wired state federations of labor in Delaware, Maine, and Nevada saying that each state was the only one in the nation failing to give public endorsement to housing and innocently asked, "Does this mean you don't need housing or construction?" Their positive, supportive replies were prompt.[45]

Thus, she gathered labor support, instructing locals to barrage their representatives and the president with resolutions (based on a sample written by herself), letters, and telegrams of endorsement. In addition, she worked with Helen Alfred of the Public Housing Conference to round up others—civic groups, women's clubs, and government officials.

The National Public Housing Conference centered its activities in arousing grass-roots support among tenement dwellers, particularly the women who struggled to raise families in the slums. As early as the 1935 hearings on the first bill, the conference bussed a thirty-seven-member delegation of New Yorkers who presented the Senate committee with a 25,000 signature petition and heart rending testimony of their hopeless plight in the miserable homes for which they paid exorbitant rents. The mothers' descriptions of the infant mortality, debilitating disease, and criminal activities which characterized life in the slum brought increased public awareness as the *New York Times* and other newspapers gave dramatic coverage to this event. Wood's 1914 strategy: college women organizing support for housing among women and labor was coming to fruition.[46]

ROOSEVELT BACKS THE BILL

In the spring of 1937, Wagner met with Roosevelt to discuss the bill. At that time, the senator reminded the president of the reformers' work. They had endorsements from 525 local unions, 40 state federations of labor, 250 social and civic groups, 47 city councils, 34 mayors, 17 state governments, 45 religious organizations, 22 housing authorities, and 79 prominent individuals.[47]

Finally, Wagner convinced Roosevelt, who had been under considerable pressure from Secretary of Treasury Henry Morgenthau to oppose it, to make good on his campaign promise and promote the bill. The president sent word to House Banking and Currency chairman Henry Steagall to move it along. Party loyalty transformed the Alabama congressman's initial opposition to support. When Bauer, Bohn, and Keyserling went to him to talk strategy he retorted, "I'm against it, it's socialism, it's Bolshevist, it will bankrupt the country but the leader wants it…"[48] Hearing this concession, the lobbyists realized that they had conquered the worst obstacle. Although there would be more skirmishes n the congressional floor debates, the act passed the Senate, 64 to 16, and the House, 274 to 68, by the end of August.

IMPLEMENTATION OF THE WAGNER-STEAGALL ACT

The Wagner-Steagall Act called for the provision of "decent, safe and sanitary" housing. It established the United States Housing Authority to interpret this directive. Although women had played a critical role in the composition and promotion of the legislation, they did not gain leading positions in the newly formed agency. Nonetheless, they continued to have a significant impact on policy because they were important repositories of the technical knowledge which the authority's administrator, Nathan Straus, and his two deputies, Jacob Crane and Leon Keyserling, did not have. Bauer as director of information and research and Wood as a consultant on constant retainer were vitally involved in all the authority's initial activities.[49]

These women were particularly important because the new program differed considerably from the PWA one. In the new situation, local authorities would build units whose legislated cost could be no more than $4,000, not the $6,200 average of former years. New financial arrange-

ments would permit lower income tenants and the 1938 budget allocation of $500 million provided for a more massive program than the $36 million total of the PWA.

In these circumstances, the neophyte officials relied upon the wide European expertise of Wood and Bauer. Wood was particularly concerned with the issues of defining minimum standards for the units, establishing tenant selection practices, and developing financial arrangements to yield a maximum number of dwellings. Bauer helped incorporate these ideas into designs promoting community and family life.

The results reflected many of Wood's and Bauer's values. Between 1937 and 1941, the USHA sponsored 130,000 new units in 300 projects scattered throughout the nation. They were large-scale developments containing one- to three-story dwellings. They averaged 25 percent lot coverage. They featured such community facilities as meeting rooms and playgrounds. Only 4 percent of the total units were in six-story buildings and less than 1 percent in ten stories. Tenants paid no more than 20-25 percent of their incomes in rent. They lived in the city, near their work. Wood's standards of density, rent-income ratios, and physical location were met in these projects. Also, the requirement for slum clearance led to the elimination of 79,000 standard units.[50]

WAR ENDS EARLY HOUSING PROGRAM— POSTWAR PROJECTS ARE DIFFERENT

World War II brought an end to this phase of the public housing program. Under the wartime Lanham Act the government channeled funds into hastily constructed temporary dwellings for defense workers. Late in 1949 Congress passed the second major housing act providing for public construction and slum clearance. By this time the guiding lights of the earlier movement were gone Wood had died in 1945 and Bauer had retired to California to a career of teaching and consulting. Leadership of the National Public Housing Conference passed to others, and the Labor Housing Conference was inactive. A few women such as Elizabeth Wood continued to take part in the housing program but not on national policy-making levels. In addition, architectural ideas of Le Corbusier were becoming popular among designers. In this later program some of Wood's and Bauer's ideas survived but many atrophied. High density development, new tenant selection policies, and shifting American settlement patterns changed the character of public housing. Bauer, writing in 1957, bitterly criticized the new thrust of the postwar efforts. She harshly denounced them as being unfaithful to earlier plans stating,

> Life in the usual public housing project just is not the way most American families want to live. Nor does it reflect our accepted values as the way people should live.[51]

EFFECTS OF WOMEN'S PARTICIPATION

Like women's activities in the settlement house movement, consumer's leagues, and child welfare programs, female participation in housing reform had social acceptability because the reformers operated within the traditional sphere of women's interests which they merely expanded from their own homes to the city, and later, the nation. Once involved, however, women challenged contemporary definitions of the housing problem and supplied new standards and solutions. They succeeded in transferring the emphasis of housing efforts from regulation to construction. They moved motivation from social control to social justice. They allied class and sex interests to promote the cause. They influenced the shape and form of public housing architecture, making sure it safeguarded family life. Finally, they created a new profession, that of houser, as they moved from well-meaning volunteers to executive directorships of housing lobbying groups to some positions in government.

Even though women were successful in exercising this leadership in the early years of the modern housing movement, they did not sustain it. In one important sense, they failed. For when the stakes became high, in terms of large government expenditures, they lost dominance. As later housing policy demonstrates, they had not convinced their followers of the necessity of their design concepts, nor even of the efficacy of a widespread national housing program. So as they lost position, their clearly stated goals and ideas vanished also.

NOTES

1. "Housing Bill Voted by House," *New York Times*, August 19, 1937, p. 1.

2. John Buenker, *Urban Liberalism and Progressive Reform* (New York: Charles Scribner's and Sons, 1973).

3. Francesco Cordasco, ed., *Jacob Riis Revisited: Poverty and the Slum in Another Era* (Garden City: Doubleday and Co., 1968).

4. Roy Lubove, *The Progressives and the Slums: Tenement House Reform in New York City, 1890-1917* (Pittsburgh: University of Pittsburgh Press, 1962).

5. Lawrence Veiller, *A Model Tenement House Law* (New York: Russell Sage Foundation, 1910).

6. Edith Elmer Wood, *The Housing of the Unskilled Wage Earner* (New York: Macmillan, 1919), p. 18.

7. Albion Fellows Bacon, *Beauty for Ashes* (New York: Dodd, Mead & Co., 1913).

8. Mrs. Ernest P. Bicknell, "The Homemaker of the White House," *The Survey*, October 13, 1914, p. 19.

9. Edith Elmer Wood, "Four Washington Alleys," *The Survey*, December 6, 1914, pp. 251-2; statement of Mrs. Albert N. Wood, "Hearings Before the Subcommittee of the Senate Committee on the District of Columbia, Inhabited Alleys of the District of Columbia and of Unskilled Workingman," 63d Congress, 2d session, 1914, pp. 23-24.

10. Wood, *Housing the Unskilled*, p. 249.

11. Wood, *Housing*, p. 249.

12. Wood, *Housing*, p. 10.

13. Wood, *Housing*, pp. 43-46, 72, 76.

14. U.S. Bureau of the Census, *Historical Statistics of the United States* (Washington, D.C.: U.S. Government Printing Office, 1961), Series N106-115, A242-244.

15. Edith Elmer Wood, *Recent Trends in American Housing* (New York: The Macmillan Co., 1931), p. 83.

16. Edith Elmer Wood to Loula Lasker, November 24, 1934, Edith Elmer Wood Collection, Avery Library, Columbia University, Box 90-M (hereafter referred to as the EEW Collection).

17. Edith Elmer Wood, *Slums and Blighted Areas in the United States*, (Washington, D.C.: U.S. Government Printing Office, 1935); "11,000,000

Homes Put in Slum Class," *New York Times*, June 13, 1935, p. 7; "The Inaugural Address," *New York Times*, January 21, 1937, p. 1.

18. Carol Aronovici, *"Review of The Housing of the Unskilled Wage Earner,"* *American Journal of Sociology*, May, 1919, pp. 507-08; Charles Ascher Interview, New York City, October 21, 1975; Henry Churchill, "Slums and Blighted Areas," *Bulletin of Federation of Architects, Engineers, Chemists and Technicians*, December 17, 1935, p. 1.

19. Lubove, *Progressives*, p. 180.

20. Wood, *Housing*, p. 244.

21. Daniel R. Mandelker, *Housing in America* (New York: Bobbs Merrill, 1972), p. 273.

22. Edith Elmer Wood to Maxine Creviston, October 17, 1932, EEW Collection, Box 52-A.

23. Association of Collegiate Alumnae, 1919, "Report of the Committee on Housing" (The Association of Collegiate Alumnae later changed its name to the American Association of University Women).

24. In 1929 the U.S. Bureau of the Census agreed to undertake a pilot study of overcrowding in four cities but at the last moment backed out. EEW Collection, Box 25-A.

25. Edith Elmer Wood, "Reminiscences of a Housing Reformer," *Smith Quarterly*, November, 1919, p. 30.

26. Clarence Stein to Catherine Bauer, September 27, 1961, Clarence Stein Papers, Cornell University.

27. "Letterhead," National Public Housing Conference, 1931, EEW Collection, Box 39-B. Stein and Mumford later dropped out over a disagreement of emphasis. They did not favor slum clearance linked with public housing.

28. "The Reminiscences of John W. Edelman," Oral History Collection, Columbia University, 1960, pp. 91-92; Welfare Council for New York City, Housing Section, "Labor Organizes for Housing," *Housing Information Bureau Monthly Letter*, vol. 2, June 1, 1934.

29. Coleman Woodbury, Interview, Madison, Wisconsin, June 2, 1975. In 1934, NAHO held its first national conference. Bauer and Wood were among its eighty attendants. At that meeting the membership passed "A Housing Program for the United States," a memorandum criticizing current policy and suggesting new directions for the future. Although some scholars, such as Mel Scott in *American City Planning Since 1890*, view this document as the first comprehensive outline for what would become the 1937 Wagner-Steagall Act, Wood had presented the ideas much earlier in her widely read *Housing of the Unskilled Wage Earner* (1919).

30. Edith Elmer Wood to John Millar, December 16, 1932, EEW Collection, Box 32-E.

31. U.S. Department of Labor, *Building Operations in Principle Cities*, #424, 440, 500, 524, 545; Bureau of Census, *Historical Statistics*, Series N106-115, N189, D654-668; William E. Leuchtenburg, *Franklin D. Roosevelt and the New Deal* (New York: Harper and Row, 1963), pp. 13-15.

32. Mel Scott, *American City Planning Since 1890* (Berkeley: University of California Press, 1969), p. 285.

33. Joseph Huttmacher, *Senator Robert Wagner and the Rise of Urban Liberalism* (New York: Atheneum, 1958), p. 206.

34. Charles Ascher to Edith Elmer Wood, August 16, 1932, EEW Collection, Box 52-A.

35. Timothy McConnell, *The Wagner Housing Act* (Chicago: Loyola University Press, 1957), pp. 29-30.

36. Helen Alfred to Edith Elmer Wood, May 22, 1933, EEW Collection, Box 39-B.

37. Robert Kohn to Edith Elmer Wood, June 9, 1933, EEW Collection, Box 6-B.

38. Regional Planning Association of America, "A Housing Policy for the United States Government," *The Octagon*, June, 1933, pp. 28-30.

39. Harold L. Ickes, *The Secret Diary of Harold L. Ickes: The First Thousand Days, 1933-36* (New York: Simon and Schuster, 1953), pp. 230-43.

40. *United States v. Certain Lands in City of Louisville*, 9F. Supp. 137.

41. Russell B. Porter, "City Throngs Cheer Roosevelt and Landon as They Open Final Battle for the East," *New York Times*, October 29, 1936, p. 1.

42. The most thorough account of Catherine Bauer's work in these years is: M. S. Cole, "Catherine Bauer and the Public Housing Movement: 1926-1937," unpublished Ph.D dissertation, George Washington University, 1975; Ernest Bohn, Interview, June 3, 1975, Cleveland, Ohio.

43. Warren J. Vinton, "Resolution on a Public Housing Program," Warren T. Vinton papers, City Planning Collection, Cornell University.

44. John Edelman to Douglas Haskell, January 25, 1967, John Edelman papers, The Archives of Labor History and Urban Affairs, Wayne State University, Detroit.

45. Cole, "Catherine Bauer," p. 545.

46. "Slum Dwellers Plead to Senators," *New York Times*, June 5, 1935, p. 2.

47. Telegram to President Roosevelt, March 11, 1937, State Historical Society of Wisconsin, American Federation of Labor, Files of the Executive Secretary of the Labor Housing Conference.

48. Cole, "Catherine Bauer," p. 621.

49. Wood was the only houser to remain as a federal consultant from the beginning of federal involvement in 1933. Coleman Woodbury observed: "Mrs. Wood anticipated a large proportion of the issues of the thirties. When some newly born expert…would come in, he'd be busting out with [some idea]. Mrs. Wood in a quiet way, would pick it up and analyze it. She had thought about it well before and knew what ought to be done." Interview, June 2, 1975.

50. U.S. Department of the Interior, *Annual Report of the United States Housing Authority*, *1938*, (Washington, D.C.: U.S. Government Printing Office, 1939), pp. 70-96.

51. Catherine Bauer, "The Dreary Deadlock of Public Housing," *The Architectural Forum*, May 1, 1957, pp. 140 - 41.

Author's Note: A different version of this article was presented to the Columbia University Seminar on the History of the City, June, 1977. The assistance and counsel of George Collins, Deborah Gardner, Kenneth Jackson, Robert Kolody, and Chester Rapkin in encouraging the research for the preparation of this article is gratefully acknowledged.

REFERENCES

Bacon, Albion Fellows. 1913. Beauty for ashes. New York: Dodd, Mead.

Bauer, Catherine. 1957. The dreary deadlock of public housing. *Architectural Forum* 48, May: 140.

Bicknell, Mrs. Ernest P. 1914. The homemaker of the White House. *The Survey* 43, October 13: 19.

Buenker, John. 1973. Urban liberalism and progressive reform. New York: Charles Scribner's and Sons.

Cole, M. S. 1975. "Catherine Bauer and the Public Housing Movement: 1926–1937." Ph.D. dissertation, George Washington University.

Cordasco, Francesco, ed. 1968. Jacob Riis revisited: poverty and the slum in another era. Garden City: Doubleday.

Huttmacher, Joseph. 1959. Senator Robert Wagner and the rise of urban liberalism. New York: Atheneum.

Ickes, Harold L. 1953. The secret diary of Harold L. Ickes: the first thousand days, 1933–36. New York: Simon and Schuster.

Leuchtenburg, William E. 1963. Franklin D. Roosevelt and the New Deal. New York: Harper and Row.

Lubove, Roy. 1962. The progressives and the slums: tenement house reform in New York City, 1890–1917. Pittsburgh University of Pittsburgh Press.

Mandelker, Daniel R. 1972. *Housing in America*. New York: Bobbs Merrill.

McConnell, Timothy. 1957. The Wagner Housing Act. Chicago Loyola University Press.

Scott, Mel. 1969. *American city planning since 1890*. Berkeley: University of California Press.

U.S., Department of Commerce, Bureau of the Census. 1961. Historical statistics of the United States. Washington, D.C.: U.S. Government Printing Office.

U.S. Department of the Interior. 1939. Annual report of the United States Housing Authority. Washington, D.C.: U.S. Government Printing Office.

Veiller, Lawrence. 1910. A model tenement house law. New York: Russell Sage Foundation.

Wood, Edith Elmer. 1914. Four Washington alleys. *The Survey* 43, December 6: 251.

_____. 1919. The housing of the unskilled wage earner. New York: Macmillan.

_____. 1919. Reminiscences of a housing reformer. *Smith Quarterly*, November: 30.

_____. 1935. Slums and blighted areas in the United States. Washington, D.C.: U.S. Government Printing Office.

_____. 1931. *Recent trends in American housing*. New York: Macmillan.

Autos, Transit, and the Sprawl of Los Angeles: The 1920s

Martin Wachs

Copyright: Reprinted by permission of the *Journal of the American Planning Association*, 50, 3, 1984 ©, pp. 297-310.

Martin Wachs presents an historical analysis of Los Angeles to show how critical decisions made 60 and 70 years ago about land-use and transportation systems have shaped the city's current fabric. Well before the construction of its freeways, Los Angeles showed a preference for the low-density development that has become the sprawl of today. The article offers important insights into the relationship among land use, politics, cultural values, and transportation planning. It is also a lesson in how our decisions of today are shaping the landscape and development patterns for future generations.

Throughout the world, Los Angeles is known for its unique urban form and distinctive lifestyle. Some consider it glamorous and others find it sterile, but the name generally evokes images of freeways, sprawling low-density communities of single-family homes, and dependence on the automobile. Although many share these images, it proves difficult to explain how or why Los Angeles got to be the way it is. In the popular press, its decentralization is often attributed to the freeway building program and the suburban housing boom that followed the Second World War; yet historical evidence shows that the familiar Los Angeles pattern existed well before 1930 and that freeways were as much a response to decentralization as its cause.

The characteristic low density of Los Angeles was recognizable before 1900 and well established by 1930. It was the product of many interacting influences. The automobile was a critical ingredient, but so were street railways, attitudes of real estate speculators, the nature of the city's economy, and the timing of the region's most rapid growth. The decade between the end of World War I and the start of the Great Depression was probably the single most important period in the determination of Los Angeles' lifestyle and its accommodation to the automobile. Today's most complex decisions about land use, highways, and transit all have their roots in the twenties.

The automobile was being adopted widely during the 1920s, precisely when Los Angeles was experiencing its most explosive growth. At the same time, the city planning movement was attempting to establish its influence over the growth and form of the city. By studying the ideas, plans, and politics of that period, we learn that the decentralization of Los Angeles and the growth of the planning profession there had common roots.

Los Angeles in the 1920s provides another lesson to students of urban form and planning. Many portray public transit investments as ways to create urban areas of city—congested, impoverished, filthy, immoral, transient, uncertain, and heterogeneous. The late nineteenth- and early twentieth-century metropolis, as the newcomers in Los Angeles perceived it, was the receptacle for all European evils and the source of all American sins. It contradicted their long-cherished notions about the proper environment and compelled them to retreat to outskirts uncontaminated by urban vices and conducive to rural virtues. And though native [-born] Americans everywhere shared these sentiments, they formed a larger portion of the populace in Los Angeles than in other great metropolises. Here then was the basis for the extraordinary dispersal of Los Angeles.

THE ROLE OF EARLY TRANSIT SYSTEMS

Between 1870 and 1910, the technology of urban transportation was advancing substantially. Entrepreneurs were replacing horse car lines with cable, steam, and electric traction street railways in Boston, Chicago, New York, and Philadelphia.

Similar technology was introduced in Los Angeles, but there it had different effects on the city. The eastern and midwest metropolises already had become mature cities before extensive street railway networks were developed, and they were characterized by high residential densities, with living quarters in proximity to industrial and commercial districts. The street railways enabled those cities to add new residential districts beyond their older cores, through processes described by Sam Bass Warner in his classic book, *Streetcar Suburbs* (1962). Los Angeles, however, was just growing to maturity as a city when street railways were introduced, and it had never developed a significant commercial and industrial core. Its first period of rapid growth, from a population of five thousand in 1870 to nearly 320,000 in 1910, coincided with the introduction of street railways and interurban electric lines. These made residential growth possible at relatively long distances from the industrial and commercial center, even when the region's population was quite small. While new industries and businesses concentrated near the downtown railhead in the days before motor trucks and telephones, the street railways made it possible for real estate speculators to develop low-density residential estates in outlying sections catering to the obvious preferences of the newcomers. Since the denser, congested, eastern cities were regarded as sources of illness and vice, the low-density, outlying suburban growth of newer cities was regarded as an advance that contributed to substantial improvement in the quality of life. Charles Horton Cooley, who was one of the early leaders of the emerging discipline of sociology and whose doctoral dissertation was titled *A Theory of Transportation* (1894), illustrated the common view of the benefits of decentralization made by the street railways when he wrote this in 1891:

> Humanity demands that man should have sunlight, fresh air, the sight of grass and trees. It demands these things for the man himself, and it demands them still more urgently for his wife and children. No child has a fair chance in the world who is condemned to grow in the dirt and confinement, the dreariness, ugliness, and vice of the poorer quarter of a great city…. There is, then, a permanent conflict between the needs of industry and the needs of humanity. Industry says men must aggregate. Humanity says they must not, or if they must, let it be only during working hours and let the necessity not extend to their wives and children. It is the office of the city railways to reconcile these conflicting requirements. (Cooley 1891)

With preferences for single-family, low-density living so prevalent, and a population of relatively greater economic means, it was inevitable that technological advances in transit would be coupled with ventures in real estate speculation. Between 1880 and 1910, cable car and electric trolley lines were built by holders of large tracts of vacant land with the specific intention of subdividing that land and profiting from the sale of homesites made accessible to downtown by transit (Foster 1971). Often mechanically unreliable, and even more often on unsound financial footings, the street railways rarely turned profits as transportation businesses, though they often contributed to huge speculative profits in real estate. Despite many failures and bankruptcies of smaller transit companies, the period from 1901 to 1911 saw the development in Los Angeles of the largest system of interurban electric lines in the country. The Pacific Electric System, assembled and extended by Henry Huntington from seventy-two separate companies, by 1923 offered service over 1,164 miles of single track and a network that extended more than 100 miles from one end to the other. The Pacific Electric offered interurban service from Los Angeles to outlying towns and villages, while the Los Angeles Railway-operated local service on an additional 316 miles of single track within the city. Many think of the sprawling Los Angeles metropolis in terms of the automobile and freeways, but Spencer Crump (1962, 96) is more accurate when he observes that "unquestionably it was the electric interurbans which distributed the population over the countryside during the century's first decade and patterned Southern California as a horizontal city rather than one of skyscrapers and slums." By 1910, largely because of the Pacific Electric System, Los Angeles was functionally integrated with Long Beach, Santa Monica, and San Bernardino. The extent of the metropolitan region has not grown substantially since then, and most of the more recent growth has consisted instead of filling in the spaces between outlying centers associated with important stations on the Pacific Electric.

THE ARRIVAL OF THE AUTOMOBILE

During the very years of consolidation and expansion of the public transportation system, which made dispersed residential development possible in Southern California, the automobile was being introduced and perfected. At first it was available only to the wealthy. In addition, before 1920, almost all automobiles were open to the elements, and therefore extremely unattractive in the cold, rain, or snow. Early cars were difficult to operate where there were few paved roads, especially when winter weather turned dirt roads into quagmires. No wonder, then, that the auto was adopted early in Southern California. The mild and dry climate made, driving in open cars relatively comfortable and kept early roads reasonably passable. A greater proportion of Los Angeles' relatively affluent citizenry had the economic means to buy automobiles than was the case in eastern cities, and lower-density, single-family neighborhoods provided ample space to store and maintain cars, in comparison with eastern tenement communities. Thus by the end of 1919, an article in *Scientific American* describing automobile ownership patterns in the United States expressed amazement that California led the nation in per capita automobile ownership:

[I]f we had any idea that states would follow along in the approximate order of their population we would be speedily disillusioned to learn that California has 2,000 more vehicles than Pennsylvania, and leads seven other states which are credited with greater population. We find, then, that the banner is to be awarded to California, with her perpetual summer, her tourist industry, and her wonderful roads.

When that article was written, Los Angeles already had the highest ratio of automobiles per capita of any large city in the United States—about one auto per nine people. Yet Los Angeles was poised on the edge of its second and greatest boom. Between 1910 and 1920, the great aqueduct was completed from the Owens Valley, providing the city with a reliable supply of water and relief from the problem of periodic drought. Before

1910, voters in Los Angeles approved the development of a harbor at San Pedro and Wilmington, and a series of improvements to that harbor continued into the twenties, allowing Los Angeles to compete successfully to become the largest west coast port by 1930. The decade after the First World War was the city's period of most rapid growth, decentralization, and automobile acquisition, and the low-density, single-family lifestyle that has come to be identified with this city was solidified during that period of dramatic growth.

THE GREAT BOOM OF THE TWENTIES AND THE DISPERSION OF ECONOMIC ACTIVITY

Between 1920 and 1930, the population of the City of Los Angeles grew from 577,000 to 1,240,000, while the population of the county increased from 1,238,000 to 2,200,000. This phenomenal rate of increase was described by one scholar of the period as "the largest internal migration in the history of the American people" (Thornthwaite 1934, 18). By 1930, only 20 percent of the residents of Los Angeles had been born in California, while by contrast more than two-thirds of all Americans resided in the states where they were born (Findley 1958, 24). The population distribution for Los Angeles showed that it had a larger proportion of middle-aged and older residents than did the country as a whole. And median income was relatively high, at least partly because the growth rate in employed workers exceeded the growth rate in population. While manufacturing industries grew, the proportion of employed workers engaged in manufacturing declined from 28 percent in 1920 to 22 percent in 1930, and Los Angeles was increasingly described as a "white collar" town; real estate, finance, and tourism expanded most prominently (Findley 1958).

The rapid growth of Los Angeles was, of course, not accidental. Like earlier booms, it was fostered by speculators, bankers, and businessmen who derived profits from the great boom of the twenties. In 1921, the "All Weather Club" was formed to advertise the wonders of Southern California in the East and especially to promote tourism, in the belief that a substantial proportion of those who vacationed in Southern California would be "sold" on the idea of staying permanently (Foster 1971, 26).

During the first wave of Los Angeles' dispersal, between 1880 and 1910, residential subcenters grew up in outlying areas in response to accessibility provided by street railways. Most businesses, with the exception of local services, remained downtown. The boom of the twenties, however, was accompanied by decentralization of much business and commercial activity as well as the continuation of residential dispersal. By the end of the First World War, the motor truck was available to free some businesses of their dependence on proximity to rail lines, and the availability of the telephone made it possible for businesses to communicate with one another without face-to-face contact. In addition, three factors unique to Los. Angeles contributed directly to the dispersion of growth during the boom of the twenties: the central role of the petroleum industry in the local economy, the development of a port located far from the downtown area, and the adoption of a height limitation on buildings because of the danger of earthquakes.

With little coal except what was imported from great distances, local oil production fueled industrial growth and provided gasoline to operate the region's growing auto and truck fleet. As the twenties began, low petroleum prices and stable production gave way to tremendous fluctuations in prices and in the flow of capital into this industry. In 1920 there was a shortage of gasoline and a public outcry over rising gasoline pump prices. That, in turn, spurred increased investments in oil exploration, and several large, new fields were discovered in the early twenties. Later their collective production glutted the market and caused prices to plummet. Because some of the oil fields were located more than twenty miles from the central city, in places like Seal Beach, Signal Hill, and Fullerton, capital investments made in those outlying areas were another force for the spatial decentralization of Los Angeles during the twenties. Coupled with that investment was the development of refining and storage facilities near the port. The petroleum industry, one of the most important in the boom of Los Angeles in the twenties, is inherently dispersed, and that certainly contributed to the sprawl of the metropolis during the decade. To a lesser extent, the arrival of the movie industry in the twenties had a similar effect.

Seeking large lots and a variety of settings for movie production, the film industry also developed a dispersed pattern of investments as it took an important place in local economic growth.

The harbors of many eastern cities were the sources of their early commercial growth and determined the locations of their central business districts, but the Los Angeles Harbor played a small role in the early development of the town. When the seaport did begin to develop as a significant part of the local economy, between 1890 and 1920, its growth took place about twenty miles from the business center of the city. The harbor was an important element in the economic boom of the twenties, in part because of the growth in exports of the region's petroleum. The distance of the harbor from downtown meant that its growth fostered the decentralization of economic activity. In fiscal year 1920, 2,886 ships entered Los Angeles Harbor, carrying 3.5 million tons of cargo valued at $154 million. In the fiscal year ending in June 1930, the number of vessels entering the port had grown to 8,633, carrying 26 million tons of cargo valued at more than a billion dollars (Findley 1958, 110). By that time, the port of Los Angeles ranked third nationally in total commerce and second in export tonnage (Findley 1958, 111), and the associated growth in warehousing and commercial activity took place along forty miles of waterfront in the Long Beach, San Pedro, and Wilmington areas, quite distant from the traditional commercial core of the city. In response, new residential communities sprang up on previously undeveloped land between the downtown and port areas.

In 1906, after the disastrous San Francisco earthquake, the Los Angeles City Council passed an ordinance limiting the height of buildings in the city to 150 feet. The ordinance remained in effect until the mid-1950s; the only exception was the construction of the 28-story Los Angeles City Hall, completed in 1928. The limit on building height reduced the attractiveness of the central business district to office developers, thus contributing to the decentralization of economic activity. Certainly, after the elimination of the height limitation at about the same time that freeway construction was at its peak, there was a surge of high-rise development in the downtown area (Scott 1971, 189-190).

AUTOS AND TRAFFIC IN THE BOOM OF THE TWENTIES

The extensive network of interurban and local street railways at first benefited from the dispersed growth of the twenties. Because the system had been "overbuilt" in pursuit of earlier real estate profits, it had the capacity to carry more and more passengers as suburban growth accelerated after the First World War. While the Pacific Electric System had carried about 74 million passengers in 1919, in 1924 it carried its highest annual passenger total of more than 109 million, an increase of 47 percent in only six years (Crump 1962, 251). This growth, however, was much smaller than the growth in automobile ownership during the same period, and interurban patronage fell off after 1924 as reliance on the automobile increased.

The growth of Los Angeles, which peaked in the early twenties, was accompanied by the public's greater financial access to automobiles, which followed the introduction of assembly line techniques and installment buying. Expansion of the automobile industry was simultaneously the cause and the result of a decline in the price of cars. Whereas the Ford Model T sold for $950 in 1909 and a Ford runabout sold for $390 in 1916, by 1926 a Ford runabout cost $260 and a Model T carried a price tag of $290. In 1926, moreover, the price tag was attached to a car that protected its occupants better from rain, dust, and direct sun (Berger 1979, 44).

Los Angeles had an unusually high rate of automobile ownership before 1920, but during the twenties its familiar pattern of reliance on automobile travel was solidified. Between 1919 and 1929 the number of autos registered in the county increased from 141,000 to 777,000 (Foster 1971, 143). This rate of increase (about 550 percent) was many times the rate of increase in population, and the ratio of people per car dropped in ten years from nine to one to roughly three to one. Nearly fifty years passed before the city reached the present ratio of people to cars—about 1.7 to one (California Department of Transportation 1979—indicating that 1920-1930 was the watershed decade for Los Angeles' adoption of the automobile.

It is difficult and probably fruitless to determine whether the decentralization of Los Angeles caused or resulted from this explosive growth in the use of the automobile; but the combination clearly gave the city its familiar character during the twenties. Foster (1971, 144), for example, reports that despite the dispersal of economic activity,

> ...a 1933 study of traffic in ten major United States cities revealed that over twice as many vehicles invaded downtown Los Angeles in a twelve-hour period as any other city studied. Roughly 277,000 automobiles entered downtown Los Angeles' central business district. Of cities with roughly equal-sized central districts, Chicago was visited by 113,000 automobiles in the same time period, Boston by 66,000, and St. Louis by only 49,000.

A cordon count revealed that in 1924, 48 percent of all those entering the central business district of Los Angeles came by car; by 1931 another cordon count showed that the proportion had risen to 62 percent (Foster 1971, 144). Amazingly, the passage of fifty years and the construction of hundreds of miles of freeways have not really changed the basic pattern, for a 1980 cordon count showed that about two-thirds of those entering the Los Angeles CBD on a typical workday arrived in autos, vans, and trucks (Los Angeles Department of Transportation 1980).

The rapid growth in automobile ownership and use during the early twenties had two important effects on Los Angeles. First, it increased congestion on the streets at a much faster rate than street widenings, straightenings, and new street openings could cope with. Second, the growth in automobile traffic had a devastating effect on street railway operations, which already had been in financial difficulty before the widespread adoption of the automobile. The automobile first deprived the street railways of their weekend excursion traffic to beaches and mountain resorts, as people began to substitute Sunday drives for trolley car outings. For the financially strapped public transit systems, the withdrawal of that traffic was quite damaging. Their rush-hour commuting patronage remained stable at first, but profit margins disappeared because of lost revenue from recreational traffic. The loss forced a reduction in maintenance and a decrease in the frequency with which old vehicles were replaced. Some marginal routes were abandoned in the early twenties, and frequencies of service were decreased. Repeated requests for fare increases were denied by the city council, leading to further reductions in levels of service.

As transit service declined, more and more people took to automobiles for work trips, further crowding the streets that autos shared with transit cars. That, in turn, slowed transit service, increased operating costs, and caused even larger numbers of commuters to abandon the trolleys in favor of auto commuting. In spite of continued population growth, the number of revenue passengers on the Pacific Electric declined from 109 million in 1923 to 100 million in 1931 (Crump 1962, 251). The slow speeds and declining quality of transit service caused citizens to be outraged whenever proposals for fare increases were made, and the deterioration of service accelerated as traffic congestion grew. Even before 1920, the Automobile Club, the Business Men's Cooperative Association, officers of the Pacific Electric Railway, and members of the city council all had addressed the problem with a variety of proposals for potential solutions. They all widely publicized the idea that Los Angeles had a severe congestion problem primarily because it had an inadequate street system. They pointed out that Washington, D.C., at the time devoted 44 percent of its central city area to streets, and San Diego's CBD had 41 percent of its area devoted to streets, while Los Angeles' central area had narrow and discontinuous streets amounting to a mere 21.5 percent of its total downtown area. Street widenings and extensions would help automobile and transit commuters, since both modes shared the streets. In addition, proposals were made to initiate a system of traffic controls, including stop signs and traffic signals, and limitations on parking on the streets (Los Angeles Traffic Commission 1922).

From January through April 1920, the city council considered instituting a ban on curb parking in the central business district, an action that proved controversial. Some business groups supported the ban, while others opposed it vehemently, fearing that it would lead to a decline in central city sales, and an abandonment of the central district by many smaller businesses (Bottles 1983). The Board of Railway Commissioners argued that the ban was needed to reduce interference of auto traffic with the operations of the street railways and to avoid fare increases. The ban on parking was finally approved, but within days of its implementation it spurred protest meetings where hundreds of businessmen reported dramatic losses of trade. The newspapers joined in criticizing the parking ban, and the city council was finally forced to amend the ordinance, allowing 45-minute parking on the streets between the hours of 10 a.m. and 4 p.m. and keeping the no-parking rule in effect from 4 p.m. until 6:45 p.m. In the same year, the Automobile Club installed the first traffic signal as an "experiment." Despite confusion and early violations, this innovation in traffic control took hold, and in time it was widely accepted and obeyed.

THE ROLE OF CITY AND REGIONAL PLANNING

The twin explosions of population growth and automobile use occurred in the earl 1920s in Los Angeles, just as the city planning movement was gaining momentum Foster (1979) has argued that city planners were so busy establishing the legitimacy of their undertakings that they were forced to accept and adapt to the automobile rather than control it. If that occurred in eastern cities, where population growth had peaked decades earlier and urban cores of higher density were long established, it was even more obviously true in southern California, where a commitment to decentralization was stronger.

The nascent "city planning" movement of the first decade of the century had resulted in the creation of several "city beautiful" organizations, whose members feared that growth would lead to congestion and a decline in the quality of life; but the potential for profit was so great that opposition to growth was ineffectual. An accommodation was reached, over time, between boosters of growth and promoters of the "city beautiful." Both groups regarded East Coast and European cities to be models of what should be avoided in Los Angeles, and both identified high densities and congestion as the greatest dangers facing their city. Promotion of low-density and dispersed growth, they finally agreed, could serve the interests of both boosters and reformers. The city of Los

Angeles established a planning commission in 1920, and the commissioners spoke out for a dispersed city, avoiding eastern-style skyscrapers. The most tangible manifestation of their commitment to decentralization was their leadership in the creation in 1923 of the nation's first regional planning commission, joining together planning proponents from thirty-nine cities in the County of Los Angeles. In the words of Fogelson (1967, 250), "From their conception of congested eastern and midwestern metropolises, the planners assumed that the great city was no longer the most pleasant place for living or the most efficient location for working. They proposed, as an alternative, residential dispersal and business decentralization...." This view was reinforced by the appointment of real estate agents, bankers, and land developers to the two new planning commissions. While advocating orderly decentralized growth, the commissions, for all practical purposes, focused their everyday staff activities on two principal tasks: the rationalization of land subdivision activity in the county, and the provision of adequate streets and highways, primarily through negotiated agreements with the land developers.

Against the backdrop of growing traffic congestion and increasing political salience of the traffic issue, Los Angeles in the early twenties considered two different regional transportation plans that would determine the directions of transportation policy in that city for decades to come. The first dealt primarily with highways and the second primarily with transit.

THE MAJOR TRAFFIC STREET PLAN

The Automobile Club and a voluntary association of civic leaders calling itself the Los Angeles Traffic Commission both surveyed traffic conditions and called on the city council in the early twenties to develop a single comprehensive highway and street plan for Los Angeles, to include street widenings, straightenings, and extensions in accordance with a set of principles for improved traffic flow throughout the city. At the time, individual subdivisions were platted with little reference to the pattern or capacity of the overall street network, and street widenings were considered only when petitions were received from property owners along the streets. Petitions were reviewed,

on a case-by-case basis, by the city engineer. If the proposals were approved, property owners would be assessed the cost of improvements and a contractor! retained to do the work. There was no master plan for such actions, and the individual projects were uncoordinated. After several independent proposals and plans for the improvement of traffic in Los Angeles, twenty-three members of the Traffic Commission were appointed and constituted as a "Major Highways Committee," and each donated $1,000 toward financing and drafting a comprehensive traffic plan. They retained Frederick Law Olmsted, Jr., Harland Bartholomew, and Charles H. Cheney; the three considered the many independent proposals and distilled from them the influential *Major Traffic Street Plan for Los Angeles* of 1924. The plan argued for the widening, extension, and straightening of many streets and the provision of a network of major streets. It proposed the first continuous grade-separated parkway, similar to those under development at the time in the New York area. The proposed Arroyo Seco Parkway would connect Pasadena to the central business district and later would be incorporated into the freeway system as the Pasadena Freeway. Several principles were proposed that in retrospect can be seen as the rudiments of the huge regional freeway network.

A strong case was made, for example, for the separation of different classes of traffic. Through traffic should not mix with local traffic, and streetcars should be; separated, to the extent feasible, from automobiles. Underpasses and viaducts were proposed at the busiest intersections to separate traffic moving in different directions, and the concept of an elevated highway was introduced to separate automobiles from streetcars. While some of these more exotic concepts were adopted later years, the immediate effect of the plan was a general consensus for its two hundred specific proposed widenings, extensions, and straightenings of streets, and for the concept of an integrated regional road network. The plan was quickly supported by the major newspapers, business associations, the Automobile Club, and the planning commission. Foster (1971, 209) reports that even before its adoption, employees of the planning commission were referring to the plan as a comprehensive guide to the street system as they negotiated with real estate developers over individual subdivisions.

Transit executives also joined in support of the plan, believing that street improvements were an important step toward more efficient transit operations. The plan was presented to the city council in July 1924, and the Major Highways Committee of the Traffic Commission urged that a measure approving the plan be placed on the ballot at the next election to enable the citizenry to voice its support of the plan. The council voted unanimously to put the street plan on the ballot, and also to put on the ballot a $5 million bond issue to begin implementation of the plan. A combination of general revenues, bond issues, and local assessments of affected property owners was advocated as a fair and balanced way of implementing the plan over the coming years.

Support for the two ballot measures was widespread, though there was some opposition, primarily related to the high cost of the project and its financing mechanisms (Foster 1971, 158-160). Some homeowner groups thought special assessments were unfair, in that property owners abutting the improved roads would bear much of the cost, while many nonresident users would benefit. The bond issue also was opposed by some who argued that the growing population had greater need for schools and health care facilities than for roads. In fact, the proposed bond issue would raise an amount of money that could only provide a modest start toward implementing a street program expected to cost hundreds of millions. Yet a modest start was advocated precisely because the city council feared public opposition to larger spending programs. Both propositions were approved by wide margins, and the Major Traffic Street Plan had been adopted.

By the end of the twenties, only a small proportion of the projects included in the street plan had been implemented, but progress was under way. Significantly, the consensus that these projects were important remained strong throughout the Depression years, and nearly every subsequent plan for highway or freeway improvements resembled the initial one in' many ways. As new subdivisions were opened in later years, streets were extended and patterned after the 1924 plan, and its influence can be seen today throughout Los Angeles.

A COMPREHENSIVE RAPID TRANSIT PLAN

Everyone agreed the automobile was critical to the future prosperity of Los Angeles, yet few in the early twenties believed that rapid transit would not also be a critical element in the city's transportation system. Support for the highway plan and parking controls were both predicated, in part, on the improvements they would engender in transit service as well as their benefits to auto commuters. Yet the public and the press were extremely critical of the Los Angeles Railway and the Pacific Electric, complaining about the quality of service and opposing every effort to raise fares. After a series of critical articles in the local press, and outraged testimony before the city council, in 1923 the council and the Board of Public Utilities agreed to work with the railways to improve service (Bottles 1983). Although there had been many proposals for rail rapid transit projects dating back to 1906, local planners urged that transit improvements should be undertaken only in accordance with a metropolitan comprehensive plan for transit improvements. Although construction was under way on a subway project, which would permit streetcars to travel underground through one of the most congested central city areas to a downtown terminal building of the Pacific Electric, the city charter revisions of 1924 included a provision that no rapid transit construction could be undertaken until a citywide plan was completed and approved (Foster 1971,112). In 1924 the city council and the county board of supervisors agreed to share the cost of hiring a firm of transit experts to prepare a comprehensive transit plan for Los Angeles. The Chicago firm of Kelker, DeLeuw, and Company was chosen, and in 1925 they submitted the *Report and Recommendations on a Comprehensive Rapid Transit Plan for the City of Los Angeles.*

The plan called for the construction of 26.1 miles of subways and 85.3 miles of elevated railways during the next ten years and proposed many miles of feeder bus lines and bus routes in outlying areas. The report estimated the total capital cost of the transit system to be $133.4 million. The authors acknowledged that Los Angeles would continue to be a low-density metropolis of single-family homes and that rapid transit could not be financed solely from operating revenues in such an environment. It recommended that the city make special assessments in the vicinity of the stations and participate in the real estate gains that would flow from the investment by acquiring vacant property along the route; rental income in later years would go to pay off bonded indebtedness that would be used to cover construction costs. Finally, it acknowledged that an increase in transit fares would be required, probably from the 1925 level of five cents to a new level of eight cents, to make the project a reality (Kelker, DeLeuw, and Co. 1925, 163-181).

While many central city business groups supported the transit plan, and eventually some suburban chambers of commerce also endorsed it, the transit plan met from the start with much greater opposition than did the highway plan. Many questioned the wisdom of spending so much public money to benefit the privately owned Pacific Electric and Los Angeles Railway, especially considering their poor record of service. Others decried the fare increase that likely would be required. While an eight-cent fare may seem tolerable looking back on these events from the perspective of the eighties, it actually constituted a 60 percent increase in fares and was greeted by the public as would any current proposal to raise transit fares by an equivalent percentage. There was also damaging opposition to the proposal that the majority of the proposed transit routes be elevated, and many homeowner groups decried elevated transit lines as dirty, rickety, noisy, and blighting. Reports appeared in the local press of depressed property values in New York, Chicago, and Philadelphia where elevated railways already had been built. The consultants pointed out, however, that four miles of elevated line could be built for a cost equivalent to that of one mile of subway.

At the time the Kelker-DeLeuw recommendations were made, the City of Los Angeles for years had been attempting to force the major railways serving Los Angeles to abandon their separate downtown terminals and to jointly finance a "union station," located west of the plaza marking the point where the city was supposedly founded. The railroads preferred to maintain their independent terminals for a number of reasons, not the least of which was fear that they would be forced to permit intercity service by new competing carriers from the union station. At the time they could effectively exclude new rail carriers from serving

Los Angeles because the Santa Fe, Union Pacific, and Southern Pacific controlled the downtown terminals and the most economic rights-of-way providing access to downtown. The *Los Angeles Times* favored a union station at the plaza site, while several other newspapers favored the railroads' position. The railroads offered to elevate the tracks serving their existing downtown terminals, thus eliminating many grade crossings, reducing safety hazards, and easing the flow of downtown traffic. They also agreed to allow the Pacific Electric to use the proposed elevated rights-of-way, providing convenient access between the intercity railroad terminals and the public transit system. The issue became heated, and the debate lasted for years. Charges were made that crooked real estate deals were really behind the different positions, and several public commissions studied the issue without resolution. Finally, the controversy led in 1926 to two ballot propositions. The first asked voters to approve or disapprove of a union station; and the second asked them to approve or disapprove of the proposed plaza site. The battle peaked as the election neared, and the opposition to the railroads' position, articulated by the Taxpayers Anti-Elevated League, was based in large part upon the environmental damage elevated lines would have done.

Consideration of the Kelker-DeLeuw plan was deferred until the union station issue was resolved, but the implications were clear. A defeat of the railroads' proposal would severely damage prospects for implementation of the transit plan, since the acceptance of elevated railways was central to the debate over the terminal. The voters approved the concept of a union station by a margin of 61 percent to 39 percent and also chose the plaza site, though by a smaller margin. In reaching that decision, the voters had overwhelmingly rejected elevated transit. The city council could no longer consider the Kelker-DeLeuw proposal, and as the Depression arrived it had not adopted that plan or acted to implement a rapid transit system for Los Angeles.

THE LEGACY OF THE TWENTIES

City planners and businessmen agreed that dispersal of Los Angeles was desirable and recognized that pursuit of this objective required large capital investments in the capacity to move people between many activity centers. They agreed that investments in highways *and* transit would be necessary to support decentralization. Yet there were several practical reasons the highway plan was implemented while the rail transit plan was not. It appears, in retrospect, that these circumstances, rather than a clear preference for automobiles, governed decisions in the twenties.

The highway plan consisted of hundreds of individual, functional improvements that could be implemented in piecemeal fashion over many years, while the transit plan would require more "lumpy" capital investments, each quite expensive and concentrated in space and time. The tiny staff of the city planning commission, numbering about fourteen in 1925 and seventeen in 1931 (Foster 1971, 218), could address specific street dedications and widenings as it went about its primary activity of reviewing subdivision applications. The planners could use their subdivision approval authority to gain compliance from the developers, who, in the end, realized that successful marketing of their subdivisions depended on adequate street access. The financial burden of implementing the street and highway improvements was imposed on particular property owners, who recovered their costs from the sale of the subdivided lots.

The transit plan was more difficult to implement for several reasons. Because particular elements of the plan were of much larger scale and greater cost than most of the highway projects, regional tax assessments and fare increases would be required to implement them. Yet the public was already critical of the private transit companies and did not welcome the prospect of paying for improvements to services that would yield private profits. In addition (though today it seems ironic in a city internationally known for its air pollution), the elevated transit lines were viewed in the twenties as environmentally damaging. They would bring noise and shadows to a city in which sunlight and views were highly valued. The transit plan also suffered because it was closely associated with the dispute over the union station, which tended to identify the rail plan with crooked politicians, kickbacks, and land grabs. City planners were too busy implementing the highway plan and too vulnerable to political criticism to adopt a high profile in support of the rail transit plan.

As the citizens of Los Angeles debated the highway and transit plans, real estate speculators, building on widespread preferences for single-family living and the availability of autos, continued their practice of opening new subdivisions, often using fraudulent promotional tactics. By July 1925, there were nearly half a million vacant but subdivided residential lots in Los Angeles county, meaning that more than 55 percent of the subdivided lots were as yet undeveloped (Foster 1971, 183). Although the real estate speculators experienced a substantial decline in volume of transactions during the late twenties, their earlier activity ensured the continuation of the decentralized pattern that had been established in the days of the street railways.

By 1930, Los Angeles led the nation's cities in the proportion of its dwelling units that were single-family homes, at an astounding 93.7 percent. The same census showed, by comparison, that New York, Boston, and Chicago all had housing stocks of which less than 53 percent of the dwellings were single-family units (U.S. Bureau of the Census 1930, 450-51). In 1930 the Census Bureau reported that Los Angeles had a population density of only 2,812 people per square mile. That figure may be somewhat misleading, since it is based on a land area that includes the large and then-sparsely developed San Fernando Valley, annexed to the city after completion of the Owens Valley aqueduct project. Excluding that portion of the city, the density was about six thousand people per square mile, still dramatically lower than the reported figure of more than 23,000 residents per square mile in New York, nearly 18,000 per square mile in Boston, and nearly 17,000 per square mile for Chicago (U.S. Bureau of the Census 1930, 77).

By 1930 it was also clear that businesses, services, and commercial activities had dispersed to a far greater extent in the twenties than they had in the previous four decades. For example, whereas 55 percent of all the city's banks were located downtown in 1920, only ten years later that proportion had declined to 11 percent, as hundreds of branch banks opened throughout the area. The proportion of dentists' offices outside the central city increased from 16 percent in 1920 to 55 percent in 1930; and the proportion of the city's theaters that were in the central city declined from 73 percent in 1920 to just 20 percent in 1930. Whereas fewer than half of the city's delicatessens were in outlying locations in 1920, 93 percent were located outside the central city by 1930 (Reeves 1932, 19). By all accounts, then, the dispersed pattern typical of Los Angeles was clearly established during the twenties, long before the start of construction on the region's freeways.

The great boom of the twenties ended with a dramatic slowing of economic growth, bankruptcies of many real estate agents and speculators, and a slowing of the pace at which citizens of Los Angeles bought more automobiles. The pattern of the twenties persisted—the street railways slowly declined during the thirties and prospered briefly during the war years in response to gasoline rationing and military production in Los Angeles. Each year, bus routes were expanded and street railway lines abandoned. Buses could serve a large, low-density metropolitan area more economically, and that pattern had been well established before 1930. There were many proposals for transit improvements, but they all failed to capture the imagination of the public and its political leadership.

After the Second World War, when suburban growth again boomed in Los Angeles, the freeway building program began. In the early 1960s the last rail transit line was replaced by buses, and since then at least half a dozen major rapid transit plans have been considered as hundreds of miles of freeways were built. Los Angeles now has the largest all-bus transit fleet in the United States, and it appears that, after sixty. years, a start will be made soon on a rail rapid transit system. The arguments for and against the most recent subway proposals for the city have been substantially identical to those offered in the 1920s, and the major stumbling block continues to be failure to secure the necessary funding for a rail transit system in a growing and vital but decentralized metropolitan area.

Author's Note: The author gratefully acknowledges financial support from the Institute of Transportation Studies of the University of California. Deborah H. Redman conducted much of the library research necessary to identify critical sources used in this study. Scott L. Bottles provided several key interpretations of events in the 1920s. 1 also am indebted to James Clifford Findley and Mark Foster, whose doctoral dissertations were the source of a great deal of material included in this paper. Professors James J. Flink, Donald A. Krueckeberg, and John Pucher offered useful comments on the manuscript.

REFERENCES

Berger, Michael L. 1979. *The devil wagon in God's country: The automobile and social change in rural America, 1893-1929.* Hamden, Conn: Archon Books.

Bottles, Scott L. 1983. A search for rapid transit. Unpublished manuscript.

Brodsly, David. 1981. *L.A. Freeway: An appreciative essay.* Berkeley: University of California Press.

Brownell, Blaine A. 1980. Urban planning, the planning profession, and the motor vehicle in early twentieth century America. In *Shaping an Urban World*, edited by Gordon E. Cherry. London: Mansell.

California Department of Transportation and Southern California Association of Governments, 1979. *1976 urban and rural travel survey, volume IV: Summary of findings: Travel data.* Los Angeles.

Cooley, Charles Horton. 1891. The social significance of street railways. *Publications of the American Economic Association* VI: 71-73.

_____. 1894. A Theory of Transportation. *Publications of the American Economic Association* IX, 3.

Crump, Spencer, 1962. *Ride the big red cars: How trolleys helped build southern California.* Corona del Mar: Trans-Anglo Books.

Findley, James Clifford. 1958. *The economic boom of the twenties in Los Angeles.* Doctoral dissertation. Claremont: Claremont Graduate School.

Fogelson, Robert M. 1967. *The fragmented metropolis: Los Angeles, 1850–1930.* Cambridge: Harvard University Press.

Foster, Mark S. 1971. The decentralization of Los Angeles during the 1920s. Doctoral dissertation. Los Angeles: University of Southern California, Department of History.

_____. 1979. City planners and urban transportation: The American response, 1900-1940. *Journal of Urban History* 5, 3 (May): 365-396.

Kelker, DeLeuw, and Company. 1925. *Report and recommendations on a comprehensive rapid transit plan for the City and County of Los Angeles.* Chicago: Kelker, DeLeuw, and Company.

Los Angeles Department of Transportation. 1980. Central business district cordon count. Los Angeles.

Los Angeles Traffic Commission. 1922. The Los Angeles plan: A selected traffic program. December. Los Angeles.

Olmsted, Frederick Law; Harland Bartholomew; and Charles Henry Cheney. 1924. *A major traffic street plan for Los Angeles.* Prepared for the Committee on Los Angeles Plan of Major Highways of the Traffic Commission of the City and County of Los Angeles.

Reeves, Cuthbert D. 1932. *The valuation of business lots in downtown Los Angeles.* Los Angeles: Bureau of Municipal Research.

Scientific American. 1919. Automobiles and People. CXXI, 26 (December 27).

Scott, Mel. 1971. *American city planning since 1890.* Berkeley: University of California Press.

Taebel, Delbert A., and James V. Cornehls. 1977. *The political economy of urban transportation.* Port Washington, N.Y.: Kennikat Press.

Thornthwaite, C. Warren. 1934. *Internal migration in the United States.* Philadelphia: University of Pennsylvania Press.

U.S. Bureau of the Census, Department of Commerce. 1930. *Abstracts of the Census, 1930.* Washington: U.S. Government Printing Office.

Warner, Sam Bass. 1962. *Streetcar suburbs: The process of growth in Boston, 1870-1900.* Cambridge: Harvard University Press.

SUGGESTED READINGS FOR PART IV

Cervero, Robert. *Suburban Gridlock.* New Brunswick, NJ: Center for Urban Policy Research, Rutgers University. 1986.

Cervero, Robert. "Jobs-Housing Balancing and Regional Mobility," *Journal of the American Planning Association,* Vol. 55, No. 2, 1989, pp. 136-150.

Choate, Pat, and Susan Walter. *America in Ruins, Beyond the Public Works Pork Barrel.* Washington, DC: Council Of State Planning Agencies. 1981.

Dickey, J. *Metropolitan Transportation Planning.* Washington, DC: Scripta Book. 1990.

Downs, Anthony. "Growth Management: Satan or Savior? Regulatory Barriers to Affordable Housing," *Journal of the American Planning Association,* Vol. 58, No. 4, Autumn 1992, pp. 419-422.

Bratt, Rachel, ed. *Critical Perspectives on Housing.* Philadelphia: Temple University Press. 1986.

Franck, Karen, and Sherry Ahrentzen. *New Households, New Housing.* New York: Van Nostrand Reinhold. 1989.

Hanson, Susan, ed. *The Geography of Urban Transportation.* New York: Guilford Press. 1986.

Hanson, Susan, ed. *The Car and The City.* New York: Guilford Press. 1986.

Hayden, Dolores. *Redesigning the American Dream: The Future of Housing, Work, and Family Life.* New York: Norton. 1984.

Lake, Robert. *The New Suburbanites: Race and Housing in the Suburbs.* New Brunswick, NJ: Center for Urban Policy Research, Rutgers University. 1981.

Meyer, John R., and Jose A. Gomez-Ibanez. *Autos, Transit and Cities.* Cambridge, MA: Harvard. 1981.

Pickrell, Don H. "A Desire Named Streetcar: Fantasy and Fact in Rail Transit Planning," *Journal of the American Planning Association,* Vol. 58, No. 2, 1992.

Pucher, John. "Urban Travel Behavior as the Outcome of Public Policy: The Example of Modal-Split in Western Europe and North America," *Journal of the American Planning Association,* Vol. 54, No. 4, 1988.

Stein, Jay M. *Public Infrastructure Planning and Management.* Newbury Park, CA: Sage Publications. 1988.

Wachs, Martin. "Pricing Urban Transportation: A Critique of Current Policy," *Journal of the American Planning Association,* Vol. 47, No. 3, 1981.

Wachs, Martin and Margaret Crawford. *The Geography of Urban Transportation.* Ann Arbor: The University of Michigan Press. 1992.

V

Design, Place, Form and the Environment

Urban Nature and Human Design: Renewing the Great Tradition

Anne Whiston Spirn

This article calls attention to the importance of nature in city design. Anne Whiston Spirn asserts that most planners and designers have viewed natural forces as apart from, rather than as an integral part of, the city. Thus, with few exceptions, cities have failed to use the full potential of nature in creating healthy, economical, and beautiful urban environments. Spirn states that "existing knowledge about urban nature would be sufficient to produce profound changes in the form of the city, if only it were applied."

"Once we can accept that the city is as natural as the farm and as susceptible of conservation and improvement, we work free of those false dichotomies of city and country, artificial and natural, man versus other living things."

— *Kevin Lynch (1981)*

INTRODUCTION

Nature pervades the city, forging bonds between the city and the air, earth, water, and life within and around it. Urban nature consists of air, the materials suspended within it, and the light and heat transmitted through it. It is the landforms upon which the city rests and the minerals embedded in the earth beneath it; the water in rivers and reservoirs, pipes and soil; and the organisms that live within the urban habitat. But urban nature is more than a collection of individual features like wind, hills, rivers, and trees. It is the consequence of a complex interaction between the multiple purposes and activities of human beings and the natural processes that govern the movement of air, the erosion of the earth, the hydrologic cycle, and the birth and death of living organisms.

The city is part of nature. Recognition of that basic fact has powerful implications for how the city is designed, built, and maintained, and for the health, safety, and welfare of every resident. For the past century, however, consideration of nature has been viewed as pertinent mainly to the design of parks and new suburbs. But cultivation of nature is as relevant to planning transportation and sewage systems as it is to planning open space; as applicable to downtown reconstruction as to land development at the city's edge; as germane to comprehensive planning to project design. There is an historic tradition for such a field, a foundation of knowledge to support it, and projects that illustrate the beneficial application of that knowledge. This paper represents an initial effort to elucidate this tradition and is part of a larger project to trace its roots and sketch a theoretical framework.

In themselves, the forces of nature are neither benign nor hostile. Acknowledged and harnessed, they represent a powerful resource for shaping a hospitable urban habitat. Ignored or subverted, they magnify problems that have plagued cities for centuries: poisoned air and water; more frequent or more destructive natural hazards; depleted or inaccessible resources; increased energy demands and high construction and maintenance costs; and now, in many cities across the globe, a boring sameness.

Unfortunately, especially in this century, planners and designers have mostly neglected and rarely exploited natural forces within cities. The belief that the city is apart from, and even antithetical to, nature has dominated the way in which the city is perceived and continues to affect how it is built. Issues such as energy conservation, waste disposal, flood control, and water supply are treated as isolated problems, rather than as related phenomena arising from common human activities, exacerbated by a disregard for the processes of nature. Urban environmental planning has most often been a reaction to these specific problems, rather than a considered proposal for managing the relationships among them, or for seizing opportunities to solve several problems with a single solution. Solutions to narrowly defined problems are costly and inefficient and frequently precipitate other unanticipated problems. The focus on specific problems in isolation from their broader context has characterized the environmental planning literature (Galloway and Huelster 1971) and has dominated the curriculum (Deknatal 1984). This fragmented approach undermines the exploration of potential multi-purpose solutions.

More is known about urban nature today than ever before. Over the past three decades, natural scientists have amassed an impressive body of knowledge about nature in the city. Yet little of this information has been applied directly to molding the form of the city—the shape of its buildings and parks, the course of its roads, and the pattern of the whole. A small fraction of that knowledge has been employed in establishing regulations to improve environmental quality; but these have commonly been perceived as restrictive and punitive, rather than as posing opportunities for new urban forms. Regulations and their enforcement have also proven vulnerable to shifts in public policy, at the mercy of the political concerns of the moment, whereas the physical form of the city endures through generation after generation of politicians. Regulations controlling the emission of air pollutants may be altered or unenforced, for example, but urban form designed to disperse those pollutants will continue to do so regardless of changes in policy.

A few cities, however, have exploited nature ingeniously to shape an urban habitat that is safe, healthy, economical to build and maintain, beautiful, and memorable. Although such cities are not common today, they are part of an abiding tradition in city design. An overview of that tradition is outlined here, along with an assessment of existing knowledge and prospects for city design.

NATURE, HUMAN PURPOSE, AND CITY DESIGN: THE TRADITION[1]

For centuries city designers have exploited nature to promote human purposes. The roots of this tradition are as diverse as the many ways in which nature contributes to environmental quality. For example, concern for health motivated Hippocrates' observations on "airs, waters, and places" in the 5th century B.C., John Evelyn's proposals for dissipating "the Inconvenience of the Aer and Smoake of London" in the 17th century, and the sanitary reform movement in the 19th century. The desire to protect the city from hazards, both human and natural, provoked Aristotle's advice for exploiting defensible topography and securing a reliable water supply, and underlies the current interest in hazard planning. Authors through the ages have described the delights of urban groves and gardens, and contemporary social scientists have attempted to measure the pleasure that urban residents derive from plants and parks.

Nature has not meant the same thing to all people in all ages. Yet similar questions have been posed repeatedly: Does nature influence human development, or is man the sole architect of the environment in which he lives? Should man seek to coexist with nature or to dominate nature? Does man exist within nature or apart from it? Answers to these questions have profound consequences for how cities are perceived, designed, and built. To the ancient Greeks, for example, air, water, and fire were powerful elements that could determine the development and character of human cultures. The form of Greek cities was often adapted to the climate, topography, and natural hazards of their locale.

In contrast is the modern view of man as dominant and nature as fragile. This concept has spawned varied reactions; two views—the arcadian and the imperialist—represent the extremes.[2] The arcadians would protect nature, whose "harmony" they perceive as threatened by human actions.[3] The imperialists, on the other hand, would consolidate man's dominion over nature "to multiply and subdue the earth." To both arcadians and imperialists, the city has obliterated nature. Neither attitude has served the city well. Those city designers of the past century who have made important contributions to the field of urban nature and human design—Olmsted, Geddes, Mumford, McHarg, and Lynch, among them—have trod a middle ground between the arcadians and the imperialists. In so doing, they have sought to forge a consonance between natural processes and human purpose.

More than two thousand years ago, Hippocrates described the effects of "airs, waters, and places" upon human society, including the health of both individuals and the community at large. He contrasted the ill health plaguing cities that occupy damp, marshy ground or windy slopes with the benefits enjoyed by cities located to exploit sun and breezes (Hippocrates, ca. 5th century B.C.).[4] Subsequent writers suggested how cities might be sited and designed to avoid such problems. The Roman architect Vitruvius, for example, specified how the layout of streets and the orientation and arrangement of buildings should respond to seasonal patterns of sun and wind (Vitruvius, ca. 1st century B.C.).

In the 15th century, the Italian architect Alberti distilled the knowledge of ancient Greeks and Romans on the subject and added observations of his own. Alberti advocated that the siting of cities and the design of streets, squares, and buildings within them should be adapted to the character of their environment so that cities might promote health, safety, convenience, dignity, and pleasure (Alberti 1485). To Alberti, the forces of nature were powerful and deserved respect:

> We ought never to undertake any Thing that is not exactly agreeable to Nature... for Nature, if you force or wrest her out of her Way, whatever Strength you may do it with, will yet in the End overcome and break thro' all Opposition and Hindrance; and the most obstinate Violence... will at last be forced to yield to her daily and continual Perseverance assisted by Length of Time (Alberti 1485).

Alberti underscored this warning by cataloguing the disasters incurred by cities that had disre-

garded the power of nature. He also discussed landscape management techniques, including drainage, embankment, and channel improvements and forest plantation. Alberti was one of the last architects to take such a broad view. In later centuries, this tradition was continued mainly by landscape architects and engineers.[5]

When Francis Bacon stated that "nature is only to be commanded by obeying her," he represented an important change in attitude (Bacon 1624). Implicit in Bacon's statement is the conviction that nature can be understood, and through that understanding, cultivated and controlled for human benefit. John Evelyn's proposed plan to solve the air pollution of 17th century London evidenced a similar confidence. Evelyn based his plan on an understanding of the source of London's pollution and the climatic forces that acted to concentrate or disperse it. The plan is remarkable for its comprehensive scope. His recommendations, outlined in *Fumifugium: Or the Inconvenience of the Aer and Smoake of London Dissipated* (1661), included the prohibition of high-sulfur coal, the relocation of polluting land uses like tanneries from central London to outlying areas downwind of the city, and the plantation of entire blocks with trees and flowers to sweeten the air. Evelyn was also the author of *Sylva* (1664), a work on trees and their cultivation. Later, when Loudon,[6] Paxton, and Olmsted applied their experience in landscape gardening and "scientific agriculture" to the environmental problems of the 19th century city, they followed Evelyn's precedent.

By the nineteenth century, rapid urban and industrial growth produced alarming changes in both city and countryside. Many observers perceived these changes as evidence that human impact on nature was out of control, especially in large, industrial cities. George Perkins Marsh summed up that mood of disquiet in 1864:

> Man is everywhere a disturbing agent. Wherever he plants his foot, the harmonies of, nature are turned to discords... the earth is fast becoming an unfit home for its noblest inhabitant, and another era of equal human crime and human improvidence... would reduce it to such a condition of impoverished productiveness, of shattered surface, of climatic excess, as to threaten the deprivation,

barbarism, and perhaps even extinction of the species (Marsh 1864).

With the publication of *Man and Nature*, a book influential in its own time and since, Marsh became the "fountainhead of the conservation movement" (Mumford 1931). But Marsh did more than sound a warning. He proposed that man's economy be designed to work in concert with nature's: "in reclaiming and reoccupying lands laid waste by human improvidence or malice… the task… is to become a co-worker with nature in the reconstruction of the damaged fabric" (Marsh 1864).

This was an approach embraced by Marsh's contemporary, Frederick Law Olmsted. Olmsted designed parks, parkways, and residential neighborhoods as part of a broader program to promote the health and welfare of urban citizens by improving the quality of their environment. To achieve these ends, he often harnessed nature's processes in "reclaiming lands laid waste by human improvidence." For example, Olmsted's design for Boston's Back Bay transformed "the filthiest marsh and mud flats to be found anywhere in Massachusetts… a body of water so foul that even clams and eels cannot live in it"[7] into a constructed salt marsh—an attractive landscape that accepted the daily and seasonal flux of tides and floods. Olmsted argued that the employment of a "natural" water body, rather than a masonry flood storage basin, would be more effective and attractive; an amenity rather than an eyesore. His primary objective here was to improve water quality and prevent floods; enhancement of adjacent land values and provision for recreation and transportation were important, but secondary, objectives.[8] Despite the scope of Olmsted's vision, however, he still perceived the city itself as artificial, and the urban park and parkway as oases of nature in an otherwise bleak environment.

Olmsted and the sanitary engineers with whom he collaborated were part of a movement for preventative sanitation provoked by environmental health problems.[9] This sanitary reform movement had a fundamental influence on the shape of American cities, and city design was essential to their programs:

A city, most sanitarians would have agreed, should be arranged as an airy, verdant setting, free from the excessive crowding and physical congestion then common in major urban centers. Its site should be dry and readily drained of storm water. Parks and trees should be abundant enough to refresh the air. There should be ample opportunities for outdoor exercise. A pure water supply should be available as well as a water-carriage sewer system. Nuisance trades, such as slaughter-houses, should not operate within built-up districts. Sunless, ill-ventilated tenements, dark, moist, cellar dwellings, and backyard privies and cesspools should be avoided (Peterson 1979).

The introduction of public water and sewer systems and projects such as The Fens and The Riverway in Boston produced dramatic improvement in urban public health by the end of the century. During the four decades of practice, Olmsted forged new functions for urban open space that embraced concerns for health and safety, as well as beautification. Today, a century later, many prized urban amenities are the result of those efforts. Yet their broad, original purpose and the ways in which nature was exploited in their design are often forgotten. Within the field of urban nature and human design, modern practitioners have rarely advanced the impressive accomplishments of landscape architects like Olmsted and their colleagues in engineering who, together, founded the American city planning movement at the turn of the century.[10]

Soon after the turn of the century, most city designers who wished to integrate nature and city turned to new towns and suburbs; only a few remained dedicated to the reconstruction of existing city centers. Two British planners, Ebenezer Howard and Patrick Geddes, represent these divergent approaches. Ebenezer Howard rejected the old city and proposed new "garden cities," where the advantages of town and country might be combined; where industry and commerce could be integrated with homes, gardens, and farms (Howard 1902). The garden city and the new towns and "greenbelt" suburbs it inspired had as their goal the integration of nature and human settlement; but most merely incorporated the trappings of nature, like trees, lawns, and lakes, and were built with as little regard for the processes of nature as were the old cities. With few exceptions, they have utilized the same techniques of land development and building. As they have grown older and as urbanization has spread around them, they have come to exhibit many of the same environmental problems as older cities.

Patrick Geddes argued for the realization of the ideal city latent in every town. "Here or nowhere is our utopia," was his response to proponents of the new garden city movement (Geddes 1915). From his perspective as a biologist and geographer, Geddes viewed the city and its surrounding countryside as an organic whole. He advocated that city design be based upon an understanding of the natural and social history of each city and region and the needs of its current residents. To attain such an understanding, Geddes undertook "regional surveys" and displayed the results in exhibits and reports. These formed the basis for proposals that were "consistent with the unique individuality of the particular city" (Goist 1974). Geddes' regional approach has had an enduring influence upon city design through the work of Lewis Mumford.

Mumford, like his mentor Geddes, advocates that solutions to the problems facing both city and countryside depend upon perceiving both as part of a region: "Once a more organic understanding is achieved of the complex interrelations of the city and its region, the urban and the rural aspects of environment, the small-scale unit and the large–scale unit, a new sense of form will spread through both architecture and city design" (Mumford 1968). To Mumford this new urban form "must include the form-shaping contributions of nature, of river, bay, hill, forest, vegetation, climate, as well as those of human history and culture, with the complex interplay of groups, corporations, organizations, institutions, personalities" (1968). Yet Mumford's attitude to the central city is problematic. Although he speaks of integrating nature and city and the need not to "widen the retreat from the city, but to return to the original core, with a new method of containing and distributing its great numbers" (1961), nevertheless much of his work has been in support of the new town movement.

Mumford's recommendations for integrating urban nature and human purpose to produce a new city form remain very general. The importance of his contribution lies not in specific prescriptions, but in his analysis of the shortcomings of city design as it has been practiced in this century—shortcomings that include the neglect of nature. Mumford has also influenced important theorists and practitioners, among them Ian McHarg and Kevin Lynch. McHarg and Lynch share the conviction that the city must be viewed in its regional context and that urban form is an expression of the natural and cultural history of a region. To both, nature has a social value to be cultivated and incorporated into city design. From that common ground, they diverge.

An emphasis on natural processes is central to McHarg's approach: "Let us accept the proposition that nature is process, that it is interacting, that it responds to laws, representing values and opportunities for human use with certain limitations and even prohibitions" (McHarg 1968). McHarg's emphasis upon processes rather than upon features like floodplains or fault lines yields a holistic appreciation for nature and fosters designs that transcend narrow temporal and spatial limits.[11] McHarg employs a checklist of natural factors—to be addressed regardless of location, scale, or land use—which is comprehensive and ordinal: climate, geology, hydrology, soils, vegetation, and wildlife. Like Mumford, McHarg's attitude to the city is ambivalent; his greatest success has been with designs for newly urbanizing areas. His general approach, however, is equally relevant to the inner city. Balanced with other concerns, the social, economic, and aesthetic implications of nature are as important in the center of the city as they are at its edge.

Lynch's *A Theory of Good City Form* (1981) is a clearly expounded statement of what constitutes environmental quality in cities and how urban form can promote or undermine that quality. This framework incorporates all the varied ways that nature contributes to environmental quality, as well as the contribution of other social and economic factors. Good city form, as defined by Lynch, can be judged by how well it sustains life ("vitality"), by how clearly it is perceived in space and time ("sense"), how well environment and behavior "fit," and by whether these elements are provided in a manner that provides "access," "control," "efficiency," and "justice." The profound significance of urban nature for city design and the quality of human life is evident when viewed through this lens.

Lynch, in particular, stressed the importance of how people perceive the city and explored the role that nature plays in enhancing the identity, legibility, coherence, and immediacy of urban form. City form that exploits distinctive natural features enhances and intensifies a city's sense of place. City form that respects and reflects natural features and the social values they acquire has a coherent and legible structure, one that embodies shared values. City form that increases the visibility of natural processes (the passing of the seasons, the movement of water, the birth and death of living organisms), creates an environment that has both a sense of immediacy and of evolution over time. "The mental sense of connection with nature is a basic human satisfaction, the most profound aspect of sensibility.... The movements of sun and tides, the cycles of weeds and insects and men, can also be celebrated along the city pavements" (Lynch 1981).

Although Lynch's dimensions of environmental quality integrate the value of nature with other social and economic concerns, they fragment natural features and systems into categories that relate more to human needs than to the modes in which nature operates.[12] Exclusive reliance on such a framework obscures potential connections among features and activities and militates against city design that serves multiple environmental functions. The results of such an approach are already evident in the planning profession's focus on special areas like energy conservation and hazard planning to the exclusion of other related issues.[13]

If urban nature is to be wholly integrated into city design and its value fully realized, a new framework is needed: one that recognizes both the integrity and interconnectedness of the natural world and the importance of all human concerns, one that relates to all elements of urban form at all scales. Scientific knowledge exists to inform such a framework, and there are models that demonstrate the benefits such an approach would yield.

NATURE AND THE CITY: AN OVERVIEW OF THE LITERATURE

Cities do not obliterate nature, they transform it, producing a characteristically urban natural environment. All cities, by virtue of density of people and buildings and the combustion of fuel, the excavation and filling of land, the pavement of ground surface, importation of water and disposal of wastes, and the introduction of new plant and animal communities, alter the character of their original environments in similar ways. These interactions between human activities and the natural environment produce an ecosystem very different from the one that existed prior to the city. It is a system sustained by massive importation of energy and materials, a system in which human cultural processes have created a place quite different from undisturbed nature, yet united to it through the common flow of natural processes. These changes are generated not only by human activities, but also by the form of the urban fabric in which they take place. Changes in the form of the city can therefore modify many of the attributes of urban nature.

A growing literature has traced the interactions between natural processes, human purpose, and urban form. Fueled by the environmental movement and the energy crises of the 1970s, this literature on urban nature has matured in the past two decades. While the bulk of the literature deals with the description and measurement of specific natural phenomena, there is a body of work that applies that knowledge to city design. Although the literature within individual scientific disciplines is rich, cross-disciplinary studies and investigations by city designers are comparatively rare. The following paragraphs provide a brief overview of the applied literature.[14] This overview is organized by the various compartments of the physical and biological environment—air, land, water, life, and ecosystems—since this framework most closely reflects the disciplines concerned with urban nature, the natural processes involved, and the interrelationships among issues.

Urban Air

There are excellent reviews of the scientific literature on climate and air quality, including its implications for city design (Chandler 1976; Landsberg 1981), and of more specialized subjects such as air quality and urban form (Rydell and Schwartz 1968; Spirn and Batchelor 1985). These and other studies demonstrate how urban form can promote or undermine air quality, comfort, and energy conservation through its influence on air circulation and the urban heat island. Intense pedestrian-level winds, pockets of stagnant air where pollutants concentrate, and ventilating breezes, for example, can all be initiated, eliminated, or ameliorated by altering urban form. These phenomena have been observed and compared in wind tunnel tests of single buildings and building complexes, (Gandemer and Guyot 1976; Durgin and Chock 1982), of street canyons (Cermak 1975; Wedding et al. 1977), and even of entire downtown areas (Spirn 1984a; and Spirn 1984b). It is also possible to moderate or intensify the urban heat island effect at the microscale (Landsberg 1968; Hutchinson et al. 1982) and at neighborhood and city-wide scales (Landsberg 1981).

Urban Land

There are comprehensive texts on urban geology and city design (Legget 1973; Leveson 1980) and on specific problem areas like geological hazards (Bolt et al. 1975; Schuster and Krizek 1978). The U.S. government has published many case studies that demonstrate the application of geological information to city planning (Nichols and Campbell 1969; Robinson and Spieker 1978). To date, however, attention has been focused mainly on the prevention of geological hazards and the reduction of losses incurred from them. Other important issues have received less attention: how to rebuild cities following a future disaster, for example, or how to design cities that conserve and exploit mineral resources. The absence of a plan for reconstruction after a disaster has resulted, time and time again, in the repetition of past mistakes despite widespread public support for "doing it right" (Bolt et al. 1975). Existing projects demonstrate the advantages of sequential use of mineral deposits, including coordination of extraction with site preparation for anticipated future land uses (Bates 1978; Stauffer 1978).

Urban soil is an important mineral and biological resource that has received little attention. The first urban soil survey in the United States was published in 1976, and there have been few since (U.S. Soil Conservation Service 1976). A small, but growing literature documents the characteristics of urban soils and how they might be managed to support the city's landscape and help assimilate the city's wastes (Patterson 1975; Craul 1982).

Urban Water

Water is by far the city's largest import and export (Wolman 1965); in coming years the management of water resources will pose the city's greatest challenge. There are excellent sources on urban storm drainage and flood control (Dunne and Leopold 1978; Sheaffer et al. 1982; Whipple et al. 1983) and reviews of conventional and innovative sewage and water treatment methods (Barnes et al. 1981; Bastian 1981). There are projects that demonstrate the aesthetic and economic benefits of using naturally-occurring or constructed wetlands, ponds, and flood plains to prevent floods, treat waste water, protect water quality, and manage water supply resources (Poertner 1973; Wright and Taggart 1976; Notardonato and Doyle 1979; Bastian and Benforado 1983). To date, however, there is no text that incorporates storm drainage and flood control, water supply, water quality, and wastewater treatment as they relate to city design. Given the importance of water for the city and the close interrelationships among these issues, this gap in the literature is a serious one.

Urban Life

There is no single source that adequately surveys the city's many plant communities and the functions they serve. Plants, especially trees, can transform the appearance of a city, but the benefits they provide extend far beyond beautification. At the local scale, vegetation modifies microclimate (Hutchinson et al. 1982), captures particulate air pollutants (Smith and Staskawicz 1977), prevents erosion, and provides wildlife habitat (Gill and Bonnett 1973). At the city-wide scale, the cumulative effect of trees can moderate the intensity and extent of the urban heat island and can mitigate pedestrian-level wind problems (Spirn 1984b). Urban forests can be designed and managed for timber production as well as for aesthetics and recreation (Osband 1984); wetland and floodplain plant communities can be managed to improve the quality of surface waters, conserve groundwater resources, and prevent flooding (Spirn 1984a). Urban vegetation can even affect the psychological health of city residents (Lewis 1979; Francis et al. 1984) and their attitudes to the environment in which they live (Rapoport 1977).

There is a small body of literature on urban wildlife and habitats, including an overview of the field (Gill and Bonnett 1973) and reviews of specific issues, such as pest control and habitat management to attract amenity wildlife (Leedy et al. 1978). Few cities would consider the creation of wildlife habitat as a primary objective. If habitat requirements are considered when planning for other functions, however, amenity wildlife can be increased within the city and many pest problems averted. There are guidelines for such habitat design, both local and regional (Goldstein et al. 1980/81; Godron and Forman 1985).

Urban Ecosystems

Literature on urban ecosystems is scanty, but promising. The potential contribution of ecologists to urban planning and the identification of future research needs has been summarized (Holling and Orians 1971; Cooper and Vlasen 1973). Environmental models, especially in relation to air and water quality, have evolved significantly in the past two decades, and "ecological" approaches to resource and waste management have been explored (Morris 1982; Spirn 1984a). Recent developments in landscape ecology (Gordon and Forman 1985; and Forman 1981) yield new insights into spatial patterns in the urban ecosystem.

However imperfect current models are, the view of the city as an ecosystem, composed of many smaller ecosystems, is a useful strategy for city designers. Natural processes link the air, land, and water of the city and the organisms that live within it. The pathways along which energy and materials flow through the urban ecosystem are also the routes along which pollutants disseminate and where energy is stored and expended. Such an approach is as relevant to the design of a building or park as it is to the planning of a neighborhood or region. It permits a more comprehensive assessment of the costs and benefits of alternate actions than is otherwise possible.

Existing knowledge about urban nature would be sufficient to produce profound changes in the form of the city, if only it were applied. Several barriers to applying that knowledge lie within the literature itself: the fact that much material is sequestered in specialized scientific journals, conference proceedings, and technical reports; the bewildering profusion of information, often unintelligible to the lay person and sometimes contradictory; and the relative scarcity of work that assesses and synthesizes existing knowledge. Most interdisciplinary works that attempt to be comprehensive consist of books by multiple authors. While such volumes have made an important contribution, they often lack consistency, treating some subjects in great detail while others are neglected (Detwyler and Marcus 1972; Laurie 1979).[15] Rarely do they make explicit recommendations for city design; and when they do, most treat environmental planning issues at the city-wide scale only. Fortunately, there are existing projects that demonstrate the benefits of this approach.

URBAN NATURE AND CITY DESIGN: THREE CASES[16]

An emphasis upon natural processes, rather than upon the individual features that arise from them, yields a framework for city design that is dynamic rather than static, that highlights the interrelation of issues, actions, and locations, and that facilitates the integration of work at local and regional scales. Multiple benefits may be gained when storm drainage, flood control, sewage treatment, and water supply are seen as related issues that require an integrated solution, as they were in Woodlands, Texas, described below. Long-term, economical solutions are possible when depleted energy and material resources, on the one hand, and waste disposal, resulting in contamination of air, earth, and water, on the other, are perceived as a single problem with several faces. Stuttgart, in the Federal Republic of Germany, has implemented an energy conservation, air quality, and waste disposal program that recognizes these connections.

Woodlands, Texas

Woodlands, a new town now being built on 20,000 acres of pine-oak forest north of Houston will eventually be a city of 150,000 people. Water emerged as a critical factor early in the planning process. Much of Woodlands is very flat, with poorly-drained soil. The construction of a conventional storm drainage system would have entailed extensive clearance of woods and loss of much of the remainder over the long run, due to a lowered water table. It would also have increased the severity and frequency of floods downstream. In addition, since Woodlands lies atop the recharge area for an aquifer that underlies Houston, a conventional storm drainage system would have decreased the water entering the aquifer and thus contributed to ground subsidence under Houston. (Houston has already subsided ten feet in some areas due to oil and water extraction.)

The proposed solution—a "natural" drainage system—comprises ponds, wooded floodplains, and well-drained soils instead of concrete ditches. In this system, the larger floodplain network drains runoff from major storms, while well-drained soils and ponds absorb and store the rainfall from lesser storms in parks, street rights-of-way, and private yards. When compared to the cost of a more traditional system, it was estimated that the natural drainage system would save the developer over $14 million. The retention of the beautiful, wooded setting and the acquisition of a town-wide open space system are additional benefits.

The natural drainage system has structured the design of the new town. Major roads and commercial development are sited on ridgelines and higher elevations, while floodplains and recharge soils are preserved in parks and public rights-of-way. Roads, golf courses, and parks impound stormwater over sandy soils to enhance its absorption. Use of the floodplain and well-drained soils as open space works well from both ecological and social standpoints. Much of the hydrologic system is wooded; it not only soaks up and carries off rainfall, but also assimilates urban runoff and treated wastewater. Where understory is left uncleared, the woods are self-regenerating, requiring no fertilization, no new planting, no pruning, and no raking. The floodplains harbor a spectacular plant community—including large evergreen magnolias, water and willow oaks, and towering pines and a diverse, abundant native wildlife, including white-tailed deer, opossum, armadillo, and many birds—making the whole town a vast nature reserve. A continuous system of hiking, bicycle, and bridle paths runs within the drainage network, linking all parts of the town.

The quantity and quality of stormwater flowing out of the new town has been monitored since before construction began over a decade ago. Increased runoff is only one third the amount generated by a typical suburban development in Houston, and the quality of that runoff is substantially better. In April 1979, a record storm hit Houston. Nine inches of rain fell within five hours, and no house within Woodlands flooded, though adjacent subdivisions were awash (Juneja and Veltman 1979).

The plan for Woodlands thus does more than protect the health and safety of its residents. Well fitted to the hydrologic system that existed prior to its construction, it has a built-in resilience to flood or drought. The town's overall structure is coherent and meaningful; it reflects and reinforces the landforms, waterbodies, and plant communities within it and makes visible the movement of water through it. Since the drainage system must be linked, open space is accessible to every home and business. It is an efficient system, not only in its ability to drain and store stormwater, but also in its conservation of water resources, its assimilation of wastes, and its provision of low maintenance parkland that costs far less to maintain than the conventional suburban landscape of lawns and trees.

Denver

A drainage system like Woodlands' is most easily implemented in a new town, but it is practicable even in the dense cores of existing cities. For example, Denver has also implemented storm drainage and flood control plans that are based upon the hydrologic cycle. These plans tie regional flood planning to the design of specific drainage projects and reconcile the need to drain local streets and plazas with the need to protect downstream areas from increased floods. Denver's Urban Drainage and Flood Control District, formed, in 1969, coordinates the adoption and implementation of adequate and consistent floodplain regulations among local governments and undertakes master plans for individual watersheds that straddle municipal boundaries.

Rooftops, plazas, and parking lots in downtown Denver are now as much a part of these regional flood control plans as suburban creeks and the urban floodplain. The city requires new and renovated buildings in the Skyline Urban Renewal District to detain stormwater on site. The alternative, upgrading the existing storm sewer system to accommodate increased runoff, would have been an expensive burden for the city and would have increased flooding in the nearby South Platte River (Poertner 1973). The principle applied here is the same as that employed at Woodlands; developers in Denver have used rooftops, plazas, and parking lots to detain stormwater instead of ponds and soil. These fulfill their function with minimal inconvenience to pedestrians and drain gradually after a rainstorm peaks.

The riverbed, banks, and floodplain of the South Platte River have been redesigned and reshaped, not only to contain floodwaters, but also to permit their overflow into designated areas (Wright and Taggart 1976). The design of riverside amphitheatres, plazas, and sportsfields was based upon flood hydraulics, built to resist flood damage and provide flood storage. But the benefits have extended beyond public safety. The central channel of the river was dredged and refashioned not only to accommodate floodwaters, but also to create a white-water slalom run for boats. The Platte River Greenway, comprising 450 acres in eighteen parks and fifteen miles of riverside trails, is now Denver's largest park. With increased use of the river for walking, bicycling, and boating has come a heightened awareness of the river's water quality and a strong constituency for improving that quality. Many sources of water pollution have been removed from the riverbanks as a consequence; an old dump has been converted to a nature preserve; a highway maintenance yard piled with salt and sand became a park after those materials were moved to a less vulnerable spot. Citizens have brought pressure upon the city to cease dumping street sweepings and salt-laden snow in the river. Districts bordering the South Platte, among them several of Denver's lowest-income neighborhoods, have gained new parks and riverbanks free from former hazards and nuisances.

Stuttgart

Stuttgart, an industrial city of 630,000 in The Federal Republic of Germany, provides yet anoth-

er model of city design that exploits natural processes. For the past several decades Stuttgart has attempted to improve air quality and reduce the energy required to heat and cool buildings. Stuttgart lies in a valley and is plagued by persistent inversions two days out of three, a situation that resulted in frequent, unhealthy concentrations of air pollutants before the current program was implemented.

Climatologists in Stuttgart have plotted the patterns of air circulation through and around the city and continue to survey air quality to pinpoint critical areas (Franke 1976; Robel et al. 1978). These studies identified the fresh, cool air that flows through the city down canyons and along the valley bottom on calm, clear nights as a resource which ventilates and cools the city. During frequent calm periods this hill-to-valley air movement provides the only ventilation in downtown Stuttgart. Land use within these fresh air channels is therefore regulated, and many are landscaped. Together, they form a radial open space system that extends from forests at the city's outskirts to parks and pedestrian streets in the downtown. As fresh air flow's down into the valley, it is funneled into a linear park several miles long that runs through the heart of the city, bordered by institutions and businesses.

As a citywide system, these open spaces do more than promote air quality and a comfortable local climate. The forested park at the city's edge is managed for timber and for the protection of the city's water resources, including the recharge areas for its many mineral springs. The landscaped terraces and steps that tumble down the fresh air canyons create short-cuts with intermittent views of the city below. The large, downtown park is filled with sitting areas, playgrounds, flower gardens, and cafes.

Stuttgart has also decreased the emission of air pollutants through a program to reduce the energy required to heat and cool buildings. The summer heat load on downtown buildings has been reduced by converting parking lots from asphalt to turf block, and by introducing roof gardens and "wet roofs" with an inch or two of ponded water. In sections of the city where air circulation is poor, the burning of oil and coal is prohibited. Steam, produced by burning garbage in municipal incinerators, is now piped to heat individual homes and businesses in these areas; and the byproducts of cinders and ash are used in construction roadbeds.

Woodlands, Denver, and Stuttgart illustrate the benefits of applying an understanding of natural processes to city design. All three examples address the prevention of hazards, the conservation of resources, the disposal of wastes, and the protection of critical areas. But the result is more than the sum of the parts. In each case, concern for all these issues is synthesized in a single program that links citywide planning to the design of local projects. Although the impetus for each lay in concern for a single overriding problem—water in Woodlands, floods in Denver, and air pollution in Stuttgart—in each case the solution incorporated other concerns besides the primary one.

Woodlands, Denver, and Stuttgart are not isolated examples, nor do they represent revolutionary ideas. The germ of Stuttgart lay in ancient Greek city planning, and the principles upon which Woodland's and Denver's drainage systems are based were applied a century earlier by Olmsted. In these examples and the historic tradition to which they belong lies an important direction for future city design.

URBAN NATURE AND CITY DESIGN: PROSPECTS

How to integrate the diverse elements of nature with one another and with other issues facing the city? How to synthesize all this into a coherent structure that provides equitable access to the city's resources and that remains responsive to changing human needs? How to accomplish this in the dense, inner city as well as in new towns and in expanding settlements at the edge of the metropolis?

Answers will vary from city to city depending upon the overriding problems of their natural and socio-economic environments, the institutional framework within which those problems must be addressed, and the legacy of the past, as embodied in the urban fabric and in cultural traditions. Each city should first focus on those problems that are of primary importance and then, in creating solutions to those problems, find ways to accommodate other concerns. Some cities, such as Denver, must contend with recurrent natural disasters;

others, such as Stuttgart, are prone to serious, prolonged air pollution episodes. Some cities occupy ground that contains valuable mineral resources; others face growing problems of waste disposal that threaten their water supplies. Many American cities, however, share two major problems: the deterioration of urban infrastructure, including water supply and sewage treatment systems, and the decline of inner city neighborhoods. A comprehensive view of urban nature could contribute to the restoration of both.[17]

The introduction of public water supplies, storm and sanitary sewers, and public park and transportation systems in the 19th century transformed the shape of the American city. When these diverse public improvements were coordinated, they formed a coherent framework within which the growing city evolved. Many of the great urban parks and parkways built during that period, for instance, served not only to beautify the city and to provide recreation space, but also to eliminate environmental hazards and nuisances and facilitate transportation within the city. In many cities that infrastructure is now a century old and must soon be renovated or reconstructed.

In the past few decades there have also been dramatic changes in the demographics of inner cities, shifts often accompanied by a proliferation of abandoned buildings and land and a decline in public services. In some cities vacant land now comprises ten percent of the total land area, and some neighborhoods are more than half vacant. Together, the need for reinvestment in urban infrastructure, and the resource of vacant lands represent an opportunity for harnessing nature to reshape the city and, in the process, to address many other urban problems as well.

Most cities, for example, face the prospect of increased water demand and floods, accompanied by depleted water supplies and continued water contamination. Vacant lands, many of which occur in low-lying parts of the urban landscape, afford an opportunity to explore alternative solutions to these problems that might not otherwise be feasible. These include the reduction of flooding and combined sewer overflows during and following rainstorms, the exploration of alternative wastewater treatment methods, the implementation of decentralized treatment systems, and the exploitation of the residual resources in waste that would otherwise pose a disposal problem.

The development of some vacant lands to accomplish such objectives could, if designed to do so, provide recreational and aesthetic amenities, promote investment in inner city neighborhoods, and yield new funding sources for maintaining public parkland. Stormwater detention areas have been landscaped and managed as parks. Woodlands, meadows, and constructed wetlands have been used for treating wastewater, with portions also used as parkland and wildlife habitats (Bastian and Benforado 1983; Spirn 1984a). Sewage sludge poses a major disposal problem for most cities; yet sludge is extremely high in nutrients and forms an ideal soil amendment. Large-scale reclamation of urban vacant lands, whether for housing, for commerce, or for open space, will require enormous quantities of soil. Sewage sludge composted with woodchips is relatively inexpensive and has been used for such purposes in Washington, D.C., and Philadelphia (Patterson 1975; Marrazzo 1981).

The opportunities afforded by vacant land are not limited to issues of water management. In Dayton, Ohio, for example, open land (currently parking lots) surrounding the central business district has been linked to wind problems at the base of tall downtown buildings. Wind tunnel studies have suggested that these wind problems could be mitigated by adding trees or buildings to open lands upwind (Spirn 1984a).

Vacant lands are extraordinarily diverse in their physical character and social context as well as in the constellations that they form collectively. Perceived as part of the city's greater land and open space resource, and viewed together with the social and economic needs of the neighborhoods in which they occur, vacant lands represent an opportunity to integrate nature and city in new ways. In the process they can transform the city and the way people live within it.

The integration of nature and city design is now possible on a scale that was previously unimaginable. Modern science has given us a view of the natural world in which the human organism has an important but not omnipotent role and ecology has yielded a systems framework that elucidates the interactions between humans and their habitats. Information technology pro-

vides a tool for storing and correlating a complex array of data in a manner that would have been impossible even a few decades ago. If we are to realize the potential of these advances for city design, however, a means must be found to bring together those from many disciplines now working on urban nature and its implications for city design, to assemble and assess the knowledge they produce, and to stimulate the construction of projects that incorporate that information.[18]

Neither the arcadian nor the imperialist view of nature will serve to advance this field, but rather the middle ground that aspires to a beneficial meshing of the cultural processes of society and the physical and biological processes of the natural world. Such an approach could yield a new form for the city, one that would "have the biological advantages of the suburb, the social advantages of the city, and new aesthetic delights that will do justice to both modes" (Mumford 1961).

NOTES

1.   This article focuses on the role of nature in city design in Europe and North America, primarily in the United States and Great Britain. There are important traditions in other parts of the world, especially in East Asia, but their inclusion here is outside the scope of this initial article. The figures discussed here are only a few of those who have applied an understanding of nature to city design; many others have also made important contributions.

2.   The terms "arcadian" and "imperialist" are used by Donald Worster in *Nature's Economy: The Roots of Ecology* (1977). Worster demonstrates that both attitudes have been influential in ecological thought since the 18th century. The management and conservation of nature for human benefit represents a middle ground between these two poles. The distinction between preservation and conservation has split American environmentalists ever since 1897, when John Muir and Gifford Pinchot clashed bitterly over the management of Yosemite Valley. This split has permitted imperialist view to prevail.

3.   Implicit in the arcadian view is a romanticization of nature and a nostalgia for a simpler, pastoral life. This nostalgia, however, may be for a

way of life that never existed, or one that has been enjoyed only by a privileged few. See Raymond Williams, *The Country and the City* (New York: Oxford University Press, 1973), and Leo Marx, *The Machine in the Garden* (New York: Oxford University Press, 1964), for a discussion of the pastoral image in literature and society.

4. The writings attributed to Hippocrates were probably not written by a single individual, but they do provide a summary of medical thought in the late 5th century, B.C. See Clarence J. Glacken, *Traces on the Rhodian Shore* (Berkeley: University of California Press, 1967).

5. Most architects since Alberti have been concerned exclusively with the aesthetic or sociological aspects of city design and have shown little interest in nature, except for its decorative qualities. There is, however, a long-standing tradition that has addressed the relationship between architecture and climate, particularly sun and wind (Unwin 1911; Atkinson 1912; Rey 1915; Aronin 1953; Olgyay 1963; Knowles 1981).

6. See J.C. Loudon (1829) "Hints for Breathing Places..." *Gardener's Magazine* V:686-90 and M. Simo (1981) "John C. Loudon's London: On Planning and Design for the Garden Metropolis." *Garden History* 9: 184-201. Loudon presented a plan for greater London, including green "belts" and "wedges" in 1829.

7. E.W. Howe. (1881). "The Back Bay Park, Boston." Speech read before the Boston Society of Civil Engineers in March 1881. Washington, D.C.: Library of Congress, Olmsted Papers.

8. This was the first time, to this author's knowledge, that anyone had deliberately created a salt marsh (as opposed to a lake or pond) for such a purpose. Olmsted discussed both his rationale and the difficulties he encountered in a speech to the Boston Society of Architects on April 2, 1886. See Olmsted Papers, Washington, D.C.: Library of Congress.

9. Olmsted had studied civil engineering himself and was a close friend of George E. Waring, Jr., a pioneering sanitary engineer. His frequent collaboration with Waring and other sanitary engineers produced innovative designs for drainage and transportation systems in parks, parkways, and entire cities. See Schultz and McShane 1978.

10. The National Conference on City Planning, inaugurated in 1909, created the American City Planning Institute in 1917 "to study the science and advance the art of city planning." All 75 members of the ACPI were originally trained in other fields; most presidents through 1942, as well as more than half the original members, were trained as landscape architects or engineers. See John L. Hancock, "Planners in the Changing American City, 1900–1940," *AIP Journal* 33:290-304.

11. See, for example, his work on Woodlands New Community (described in this article) in which the water supply, flooding, and subsidence of Houston, over twenty miles away, were seen as related to the new town project and a solution proposed that addressed both local and regional problems. The author served as project director on two phases of this project.

12. Lynch himself does not make an explicit connection between nature and his dimensions of environmental quality, except as represented by individual natural factors. McHarg, in his own professional work and that of his associates, has increasingly incorporated social and economic concerns but in a different manner than Lynch. Narendra Juneja, a partner of McHarg's, was explicit in the assignment of social values to natural processes, distinguishing between their value to society as a whole, to specific interest groups, and to individuals. See, for example, *Medford: Performance Requirements for the Maintenance of Social Values Represented by the Natural Environment of Medford Township, New Jersey* (Philadelphia: Center for Ecological Research in Planning and Design, University of Pennsylvania, 1974) and *Environmental Resources of the Toronto Central Waterfront* (Philadelphia: Wallace McHarg Roberts and Todd, 1976). Many of the social values defined by Juneja in these reports are comparable to those utilized by Lynch, and the, emphasis on performance requirements rather than environmental determinants represents a shift from McHarg's earlier writings.

13. Specialization may be desirable and even necessary, but when planning students' sole exposure to environmental factors consists of a single specialized course in water resources, energy conservation, or waste management, those students may never gain an appreciation for the urban natural environment as a whole. See Charles Y.

Deknatal, "Choices of Orientation in Teaching Environmental Planning," *Journal of Planning Education and Research* 1984 (3): 118-125, for a review of environmental planning curriculum. Such an approach may also lead to artificial distinctions between subject areas, obscuring the connections between them. The conservation of energy and mineral resources and environmental pollution, for example, are closely related problems which demand integrated solutions.

14. Space does not permit a comprehensive review of this literature and the promise it holds for city design. A more extensive review and bibliography is provided by the author in *The Granite Garden: Urban Nature and Human Design* (New York: Basic Books, 1984).

15. Recently the profession of forestry has provided a forum for researchers and practitioners with an interest in urban nature (U.S. Forest Service 1977; Hopkins 1980), and has coined the term "urban forestry" to describe the field. Although "urban forestry" aptly captures the applied nature of the field, nevertheless, it reflects neither its breadth nor its applicability to non-forest biomes.

16. The case studies of Woodlands, Denver, and Stuttgart, as well as the introduction to this article have been adapted from my book, *The Granite Garden: Urban Nature and Human Design* (Basic Books, 1984). Copyright by Anne Whiston Spirn.

17. The author has explored this subject in greater detail, using the example of Boston, in "Reclaiming Common Ground: The Future Shape of Boston," a paper sponsored by the American Institute of Architects and McGraw-Hill Publications, delivered to the Boston Society of Architects on April 30, 1985.

18. The author is currently concluding a study of the open space potential of vacant urban lands, funded by a grant from the National Endowment for the Arts. This study defines potential open space uses broadly, including not only recreation, but also functions related to agriculture, forestry, air quality and climate, the conservation of mineral and water resources, flood control, and storm drainage, among others. The objective of the study is to enable city planners and neighborhood groups alike to evaluate the open space potential of vacant land and to weigh the benefits of open space uses with other uses, such as housing.

REFERENCES

Alberti, L.B. 1485. In *Ten Books on Architecture*, ed., J. Rykwert. New York: Transatlantic Arts, 1966.

Aristotle. 1959. *Politics and Poetics*. Translated by B. Jowett and T. Twining. New York: Viking Press.

Aronin, J.E. 1953. *Climate and Architecture*. New York: Reinhold.

Atkinson, W. 1912. *The Orientation of Buildings, or Planning for Sunlight*. New York: Wiley.

Bacon, F. *New Atlantis*. 1624. In *The Complete Essays of Francis Bacon*. New York: Washington Square Press, 1963.

Barnes, D.; Bliss, P.J.; Gould, B.W.; and Vallentine, H.R. 1981. *Water and Wastewater Engineering Systems*. Bath: Pitman.

Bastian, R.K. 1981. *Natural Systems in Wastewater Treatment and Sludge Management: An Overview*. Washington, D.C.: U.S. Environmental Protection Agency.

_____ and Benforado, J. 1983. Waste Treatment: Doing What Comes Naturally. *Technology Review*. Feb./Mar., 59-69.

Bates, R.L. 1978. Mineral Resources for a New Town. In *Geology in the Urban Environment*, eds., R.O. Urgard, G.D. McKenzie, and D. Foley. Minneapolis: Burgess.

Bolt, B.A.; Horn, W.L.; MacDonald, G.A.; and Scott, R.F. 1975. *Geological Hazards*. New York: Springer-Verlag.

Cermak, J.E. 1975. Applications of Fluid Mechanics to Wind Engineering—A Freeman Scholar Lecture. *Journal of Fluids Engineering*. 97:9-38.

Chandler, T.J. 1976. *Urban Climatology and its Relevance to Urban Design*. Technical Note 149. Geneva: World Meteorological Organization.

Cooper, W.E. and Vlasen, R.D. 1973. Ecological Concepts and Applications to Planning. In *Environment: A New Focus for Land–Use Planning*, ed., D.M. McAllister. Washington, D.C.: National Science Foundation.

Craul, P.J., ed. 1982. *Urban Forest Soils: A Reference Workbook*. Syracuse, NY: U.S. Forest Service and State University of New York.

Deknatal, C.Y. 1984. Choices of Orientation in

Teaching Environmental Planning. *Journal of Planning Education and Research*. 3:118-125.

Detwyler, T.R. and Marcus, M.G. eds. 1972. *Urbanization and Environment: The Physical Geography of the City*. Belmont, CA: Duxbury Press.

Dunne, T. and Leopold, L.B. 1978. *Water and Environmental Planning*. San Francisco: W.H. Freeman.

Durgin, F.H. and Chock, A.W. 1982. Pedestrian Level Winds: A Brief Review. *Journal of the Structural Division, Proceedings of the American Society of Civil Engineers*. 108:1751-1767.

Evelyn, Sir John. 1661. *Fumifugium: Or The Inconvenience of the Aer and Smoake of London Dissipated*. Oxford: Old Ashmolean Reprint, 1930.

_____ 1664. *Sylva*. London: Martyn and Allestry.

Forman, R.T.T. 1981. Interaction Among Landscape Elements: A Core of Landscape Ecology. In *Regional Landscape Planning: Proceedings of Educational Sessions, American Society of Landscape Architects*.

Francis, M.; Cashdan, L.; and Paxton, L. 1984. *Community Open Spaces*. Washington, D.C.: Island Press.

Franke, E., ed. 1976. *Climate: Data and Aspects for City Planning*. Translated for EPA by Literature Research Company, TR-79-0795. FBW—A Publication of Research, Building, and Living, No. 108. Stuttgart, W. Germany: Karl Kramer.

Galloway, T.D. and Huelster, R.J. 1971. Planning Literature and the Environmental Crisis: A Content Analysis. *American Institute of Planners Journal*. 37:269-274.

Gandemer, J. and Guyot, A. 1976. Integration du phenomene vent dans la conception du milieu bati. Paris: Ministere de la Qualite de la Vie.

Geddes, P. 1915. *Cities in Evolution*. London: Williams and Norgate.

Gill, D. and Bonnett, P. 1973. *Nature in the Urban Landscape: A Study of Urban Ecosystems*. Baltimore: York Press.

Glacken, C.J. 1967. *Traces on the Rhodian Shore*. Berkeley, CA: University of California Press.

Godin, G.; Wright, G.; and Shepard, R.J. 1972. Urban Exposure to Carbon Monoxide. *Archives of Environmental Health*. 25:305-313.

Gordon, M. and Forman, R.T.T. 1985. *Landscape Ecology*. New York: Wiley. In Press.

Goist, P.D. 1974. Patrick Geddes and the City. *Journal of the American Institute of Planners*. 40:31-37.

Goldstein, E.L.; Gross, M.; and DeGraaf, R.M. 1980/1981. Explorations in Bird-Land Geometry. *Urban Ecology*. 5: 113-124.

Grandjean, J. and Gilgen, A. 1976. *Environmental Factors in Urban Planning*. London: Taylor & Francis.

Hancock, J.L. 1967. Planners in the Changing American City, 1900-1940. *Journal of the American Institute of Planners*. 33:290-304.

Hippocrates. Ca. 5th century B.C. Airs, Waters, Places. In *Hippocrates*, Vol. 1. The Loeb Classical Library, ed., T.E. Page. Cambridge, MA: Harvard University Press, 1962.

Holling, C.S. and Orians, G. 1971. Toward an Urban Ecology. *Ecological Society of America Bulletin*. 52:2-6.

Hopkins, G., ed. 1980. *Proceedings of the National Urban Forestry Conference, Nov. 13-16, 1978*. 2 vols. Syracuse, NY: State University of New York.

Howard, E. 1902. *Garden Cities of To-Morrow*, ed., F.J. Osborne. Cambridge, MA: MIT Press.

Howe, E.W. 1881. The Back Bay Park, Boston. Speech read before the Boston Society of Civil Engineers in March 1881. Washington, D.C.: Library of Congress, Olmsted Papers.

Hutchinson, B.A.; Taylor, F.G.; Wendt, R.L.; and the Critical Review Panel. 1982. *Use of Vegetation to Ameliorate Building Microclimate: An Assessment of Energy Conservation Potentials*. Environmental Sciences Division Publication No. 19103. Oak Ridge, TN: Oak Ridge National Laboratory.

Juneja, N. 1974. *Medford: Performance Requirements for the Maintenance of Social Values Represented in the Natural Environment of Medford Township, N. J.* Philadelphia: University of Pennsylvania.

_____ and Veltman, J. 1979. Natural Drainage in the Woodlands. *Environmental Comment*. Nov., 7-14.

Knowles, R. 1981. *Sun, Rhythm, Form*. Cambridge, MA: MIT Press.

Landsberg, H.E. 1968. Micrometeorological Temperature Differentiation Through Urbanization. In *Urban Climates*, Technical Note 108. Brussels: World Meteorological Organization.

_____ 1981. *The Urban Climate.* New York: Academic Press.

Laurie, I.C., ed. 1979. *Nature in Cities: The Natural Environment in the Design and Development of Urban Green Space.* Chicester, England: Wiley.

Leedy, D.L.; Maestro, R.M.; and Franklin, T.M. 1978. *Planning for Wildlife in Cities and Suburbs.* Washington, D.C.: U.S. Fish and Wildlife Service, Office of Biological Services.

Legget, R.F. 1973. *Cities and Geology.* New York: McGraw-Hill.

Leveson, D. 1980. *Geology and the Urban Environment.* New York: Oxford University Press.

Lewis, C.A. 1979. Healing in the Urban Environment: A Person/Plant Viewpoint. *American Planning Association Journal.* 45:330-338.

Loudon, J.C. 1829. Hints for Breathing Places.... *Gardener's Magazine.* V:686 690.

Lynch, K. 1960. *The Image of the City.* Cambridge, MA: MIT Press.

_____ 1972. *What Time is this Place?* Cambridge, MA: MIT Press.

_____ 1976. *Managing the Sense of a Region.* Cambridge, MA: MIT Press.

_____ 1981. IA Theory of Good City Form. Cambridge, MA: MIT Press.

McHarg, I. 1964. The Place of Nature in the City of Man. *Annals of the American Academy of Political and Social Science.* 352(March):1-12.

_____ 1968. Values, Process, and Form. In Smithsonian Annual II. *The Fitness of Man's Environment.* 207-227.

_____ and Wallace, D.A., eds. 1970. *Metropolitan Open Space and Natural Process.* Philadelphia: University of Pennsylvania Press.

Marrazzo, W.J. 1981. The Selling of Waste. *EPA Journal.* 7:26-27.

Marsh, G.P. *Man and Nature.* 1864. Cambridge, MA: Harvard University Press, Belknap Press, 1974.

Morris, D. 1982. *Self-Reliant Cities: Energy and the Transformation of Urban America.* San Francisco: Sierra Club Books.

Mumford, L. 1931. *The Brown Decades.* New York: Harcourt, Brace.

_____ 1961. *The City in History.* New York: Harcourt Brace Jovanovich.

_____ 1968. *The Urban Prospect.* New York: Harcourt Brace Jovanovich.

Nichols, D.R. and Campbell, C.C., eds. 1969. *Environmental Planning and Geology: Proceedings of the Symposium on Engineering Geology in the Urban Environment.* Washington, D.C.: U.S. Geological Survey and U.S. Department of Housing and Urban Development.

Notardonato, F. and Doyle, A.F. 1979. Corps Takes New Approach to Flood Control. *Civil Engineering.* June, 65-68.

Olgyay, V. 1963. *Design with Climate: Biclimatic Approach to Architectural Regionalism.* Princeton, NJ: Princeton University Press.

Olmsted, F.L. 1886. The Problem and the Solution. Speech to the Boston Society of Architects. April 2, 1886. Washington, D.C.: Library of Congress, Olmsted Papers.

Osband, G. 1984. Managing Urban Forests. Cambridge, MA: Harvard Graduate School of Design, Dept. of Landscape Architecture. Student report.

Patterson, J.C. 1975. Enrichment of Urban Soil with Composted Sludge and Leaf Mold: Constitution Gardens. *Compost Science.* 16:18-22.

Peterson, J.A. 1979. The Impact of Sanitary Reform upon American Urban Planning, 1840-1890. *Journal of Social History.* 13:83-103.

Poertner, H.G. 1973. Better Storm Drainage Facilities at Lower Cost. *Civil Engineering.* Oct., 67-70.

Rapoport, A. 1977. *Human Aspects of Urban Form.* Oxford: Pergamon Press.

Rey, A.A. 1915. The Healthy City of the Future: Scientific Principles of Orientation for Public Roads and Dwelling. *Town Planning Review.* 6:2-9.

Robel, F.; Hoffman, U.; and Riekert, A. 1978. *Daten und Aussagen zum Stadtklima von Stuttgart auf der Grundlage der Infrarot—Thermographie.* Stuttgart, W. Germany: Chemisches Untersuchungs amt der Landeshauptstadt Stuttgart.

Robinson, G.D. and Spieker, A.M. 1978. Nature to be Commanded.... Professional Paper 950. Washington, D.C.: U.S. Geological Survey.

Rydell, C.P. and Schwartz, G. 1968. Air Pollution and Urban Form: A Review of Current

Literature. *American Institute of Planners Journal.* 34:115-120.

Schultz, S.K. and McShane, C. 1978. To Engineer the Metropolis: Sewers, Sanitation, and Planning in Late Nineteenth Century America. *Journal of American History.* 65:389-411.

Schuster, R.L. and Krizek, R.J., eds. 1978. Landslides: Analysis and Control. Special Report 176. Washington, D.C.: National Academy of Sciences.

Sheaffer, J.R.; Wright, K.; Taggart, W.; and Wright, R. 1982. *Urban Storm Drainage Management.* New York: Marcel Dekker.

Simo, M. 1981. John Claudius Loudon: On Planning and Design for the Garden Metropolis. *Garden History.* 9:184-201.

Smith, W.H. and Staskawicz, B.J. 1977. Removal of Atmospheric Panicles by Leaves and Twigs of Urban Trees: Some Preliminary Observations and Assessment of Research Needs. *Environmental Management* 1:317-330.

Southworth, M. and Southworth, S. 1973. Environmental Quality Analysis and Management for Cities and Regions: A Review of Work in the United States. *Town Planning Review.* 44:231-253.

Spirn, A.W. 1984a. *The Granite Garden: Urban Nature and Human Design.* New York: Basic Books.

_____ 1984b. Designing for Pedestrian-level Winds: The Integration of Wind Engineering Technology and Urban Design. In *Proceedings of the Conference of Educators in Landscape Architecture.* Guelph, Canada: University of Guelph.

_____ 1985. Reclaiming Common Ground: The Future Shape of Boston. Paper sponsored by the American Institute of Architects and McGraw-Hill Publications as part of a national lecture series on *The Future Shape of the City.* Presented to the Boston Society of Architects, April 30, 1985.

_____ and Batchelor, W.G. 1985. Street-level Air Pollution and Urban Form: A Review of Recent Literature. Prepared for the Boston Redevelopment Authority. Cambridge, MA: Harvard Graduate School of Design.

Stauffer, T.P. 1978. Kansas City: A Center for Secondary Use of Mined Out Space. *In Geology in the Urban Environment,* eds., R.O. Utgard, G.D. McKenzie, and D. Foley. Minneapolis: Burgess.

U.S. Soil Conservation Service. 1976. *Soil Survey of District of Columbia.* Washington, D.C.: U.S. Department of Agriculture and U.S. Department of the Interior.

Unwin, R. 1911. *Town Planning in Practice.* London: T. Fisher Unwin.

Vitruvius. Ca. 1st century B.C. In *The Ten Books on Architecture.* Cambridge, MA: Harvard University Press, 1914.

Wallace McKay Roberts and Todd. 1976. *Environmental Resources of the Toronto Central Waterfront.* Philadelphia: Wallace McKay Roberts and Todd.

Wedding, J.B.; Lombardi, D.J.; and Cermak, J.E. 1977. A Wind Tunnel Study of Gaseous Pollutants in City Street Canyons. *Journal of the Air Pollution Control Association.* 27:557-566.

Whipple, W.; Tucker, S.; Grigg, N.; Grizzard, T.; Randall, C.; and Shubinski, R. 1983. *Stormwater Management in Urbanizing Areas.* Englewood Cliffs, NJ: Prentice-Hall.

Williams, R. 1973. *The Country and the City.* New York: Oxford University Press.

Wolman, A. 1965. The Metabolism of Cities. *Scientific American.* March, 178-190.

Worster, D. 1977. *Nature's Economy: The Roots of Ecology.* Garden City, NY: Anchor Books.

Wright, K. and Taggan, W.C. 1976. The Recycling of a River. *Civil Engineering.* Nov., 42-46.

The American Public Space

J.B. Jackson

J.B. Jackson wrote about the ways that everyday experiences and the totality of natural and built environments act together to create a "sense of place." In this selection he investigates the concept of public places in the American landscape and shows how shifting social and cultural norms have transformed the ways Americans view and use open space. He also discusses the notion of "public space" in the context of a culture that places emphasis on private ownership in a country that has consumed so much of the natural landscape. Jackson argues for the ways that public space should be viewed as places that create a venue for a diverse and fragmented society to seek solace and enhance the transmission of a common set of experiences. He states: "We do well to encourage the creation of all such spaces combining recreation with knowledge of nature and our past. Their popularity is their best reason for existing."

Those of us old enough to remember what America was like a half century ago have lived through a significant but largely unnoticed development in our landscape. By that I mean not the growth of our cities but a development that came about largely as a consequence of that growth: the great increase in the number and variety of public places all over the nation.

A public place is commonly defined as a place (or space) created and maintained by public authority, accessible to all citizens for their use and enjoyment. This tells us nothing about the different ways in which we use and enjoy them, nor about the different types of public involved, but we have only to look about us to see that they are often outside the center of town and even in the open country. Many have an educational purpose: historic zones, outdoor museums, botanical gardens. And more and more spaces are being designed to give us a brief experience of nature: hiking trails and wilderness areas and beaches, for example. When we include among the newer public spaces the parking lot, the trash disposal area, and the highway, it is evident that the public is being well provided for, not only as far as places for enjoyment are concerned, but for their use as well.

Implicit in the word "public" is the presence of other people. We know better than to resent that presence; they have as much right to be there as we have. Just the same, it is characteristic of many modern public spaces that contact between persons is likely to be brief and noncommittal. Indeed, when the public is too numerous we are made uncomfortable. We did not come here for what an earlier generation called "togetherness," we came for an individual, private experience—a sequence of emotions, perceptions, sensations, of value to ourselves. This is not to say that we are unfriendly, merely that we do not necessarily associate every public place with social intercourse. We assume, in fact, that there are special places appropriate for that. Yet when we look for them today we find they are few.

CIVIC SPACE

Much has changed in America since the time when every public space was intended to be the setting for some collective, civic action. I think it can be said that beginning in the eighteenth century every public space every piece of land controlled by the authorities—was meant to serve a public institution rather than to serve the public as an aggregate of individuals. In the newer planned towns of New England an area of public land was set aside for the support of the local church and its preacher, though not for public use. Section 16 in the townships created by the National Land

Survey of 1785—the only designated public space in the township—was to support a local school. Hence its name: school section, still a feature of the western landscape. Communities more urban in character recognized the need for public spaces that the public could use; but only for the benefit of the community at large. The newly created towns of the late-eighteenth and early-nineteenth century almost invariably contained well-defined public places for the market, the drill field, the wharf, the "established" church, as well as places for a college or academy, and of course for public celebrations and public assembly. A civic function characterized them all; people were present in them to perform some public service or play some public role.

Public is a word without mystery: It derives from the Latin *populus*, and means belonging to or characteristic of the people. A public space is a people's space. But "people" as a word is less obvious. With us it simply means humanity, or a random sample of humanity, but until well into the nineteenth century it meant a specific group: sometimes the population of a nation or a town, sometimes the lowest element in that population, but always an identifiable category. Thus a common phrase in England was "the nobility, the gentry, and the public." People in this sense implied an organization and a territory; and as an organization it had an organizing or form-giving authority.

Perhaps it can be said that, as a noun, "public" implied the population, or the people, while as an adjective it referred to the authorities. Thus a public building in the eighteenth century was not a place accessible to all, for their use and enjoyment, but was the working or meeting place of the authorities.

This strictly political meaning of the word helps us interpret the kind of public place or square found in most of the new towns and cities in colonial and post-colonial America. The invaluable collections of town plans in three books by John Reps show in some detail how early planners and promoters emphasized the importance of public places.[1] Each community, each town was given a grid plan or a variation on a grid, and though many of them were little more than a cluster of square blocks, invariably there was a symmetrical array of (proposed) public buildings on a piece of public land—courthouse, market, jail, etc.

It is interesting to see how faithful colonial and frontier America was to the early Renaissance practice of according more dignity to the building than to the square in front of it. Our own perception, of course, is the opposite: In our love of open spaces we see the building as "facing" the square, the square as the focal point in the urban composition. The eighteenth-century belief was that the square, however large and imposing, derived its dignity from its association with the building, and was in fact merely the place where the inhabitants gathered to pay homage to the authorities within. Many town maps indicate proposed smaller squares, inserted into what would eventually be built-up residential areas. These were undoubtedly meant to be surrounded and dignified by public buildings, as William Penn had proposed for the four minor squares in his plan for Philadelphia. It was only in the nineteenth century that these small squares were seen and treated as parks, and this change from concentrating on the public building to concentrating on the public space would eventually produce public places bearing little or no aesthetic relationship to their urban surroundings.

Few of these neo-classical towns ever grew to resemble their paper prototypes. Many grew in an entirely unpredicted way: into monolithic compositions of identical blocks, as in Chicago, which are ideally suited to the purposes of the real estate speculator. Others did not grow at all. But their plans are no less interesting for that. They are diagrams, provincial and greatly simplified, of what Americans wanted in the way of towns: a rational, egalitarian, political ordering of spaces and structures, a sharp division between public and private, so that spaces for recreation or non-political, non-civic functions were left to the private sector to provide as best it could. The only truly public, or people's, space was the large central public square where all qualified citizens came together: a vast architectural roofless room, a stage, where all acted out their familiar assigned roles. And this, I think, is what really distinguished the traditional public space from our contemporary public space. Two centuries ago, despite the Revolution, it was still widely believed that we were *already* citizens (to the extent that we could qualify) when we appeared in public. We knew our role, our rank and place, and the structured space surrounding us merely served to confirm our status. (Much as in certain denominations we are members of the community of Christians from the moment of baptism; our subsequent participation in certain rites within the church simply *confirms* our permanent religious status.) But now we believe the contrary—that we *become* citizens by certain experiences, private as well as public. Our variety of new specialized public spaces are by way of being places where we prepare ourselves—physically, socially, and even vocationally—for the role of citizen.

DECLINE OF THE SQUARE

There are still many among us who hold that our public spaces should perform the same civilizing, political role. Nevertheless, as the nineteenth century progressed it became evident that the public square was losing prestige. During the Revolution the centers of popular excitement had been Faneuil Hall, Independence Hall, and the New York Common. But when political oratory and political demonstrations went out of fashion, the public began to frequent the busier streets, the tree-lined promenades, and the waterfront. Other developments gave the centrifugal movement further impetus. Middle-class families felt the attraction of the suburbs or of the Independent homestead. Newcomers, many from overseas, had no sentiment for the established customs, and in newer parts of town evangelical churches competed with the established church in the center. The coming of the railroad and the factory and the mill shifted leisure time activities to the less built-up outskirts of town; and finally the public buildings themselves ceased to be the locus of real power, and gradually became office buildings for the bureaucracy. In almost every American town the traits Sam Bass Warner has identified with mid-nineteenth century Philadelphia became more and more prevalent:

The effect of three decades of a building boom... was a city without squares of shops and public buildings, a city without gathering places which might have assisted in focusing the daily activities of neighborhoods. Instead of subcenters the process of building had created acres and acres of amorphous tracts—the architectural hallmark of the nineteenth and twentieth century American big

city.... Whatever community life there was to flourish from now on would have to flourish despite the physical form of the city, not because of it.[2]

Though the older towns and cities of the East retained their tradition of central park spaces, towns laid out in the Midwest and throughout the Great Plains were predominately grid plans of uniform blocks. Some of them, judging from Reps's *Cities of the American West*, provided for one or two "public squares" or "public grounds," yet few of these were centrally located and it is hard to find any of them associated with a public building. In many cases the larger spaces set aside for parks were soon subdivided into building lots. No doubt the reluctance to plan for public spaces in the potentially valuable downtown can be ascribed to the proprietor's eagerness to make money in downtown real estate. But by cutting straight through the average small American town and establishing its station and freightyards near main street, the railroad transformed the traditional center in ways that the railroad in Europe was never allowed to do: There the station was exiled to the outskirts. Thus the American town very early in the game developed a substitute social center (for men only) around the station and freightyards—a combination skidrow, wholesale district, and horse transportation complex that seems to have offered a variety of illicit and lower class attractions, as well as being a center for news. But this was a poor substitute for the traditional urban space where citizens could forgather and talk, a place described by the anthropologist R. Baumann "as special, isolated from others and enjoyed for its own sake, because talking there may be enjoyed for its own sake and not as part of another activity or for some special instrumental purpose." And so strong was the urge to have such places easily accessible yet detached from the workaday world that the American urban public, or a fraction of it, soon discovered a new and agreeable space on the outskirts of town—a favorite spot for relaxation and sociability. That was the cemetery.

THE RECREATIONAL CEMETERY

The story of the development of the so-called rural cemetery in America is familiar to anyone who knows our urban history. It began in 1831 with the designing of Mt. Auburn Cemetery in Cambridge,

Massachusetts, as a picturesque landscape of wooded hills, winding roads with paths, and rustic compositions of lawn and stream with pleasant views over the Charles, all in the style of the landscaped gardens fashionable in England at that time. This new type of cemetery immediately became a popular goal of excursions from the city. To quote Norman Newton's account, Mt. Auburn "soon became very popular as a quiet place in which to escape the bustle and clangor of the city—for strolling, for solitude, and even for family picnics. Following its success other cemeteries of the same type began to spring up."[3]

These rural cemeteries, usually located within easy reach of the city, attracted thousands of pleasure-seeking visitors, both before the presence of graves and tomb-stones, and after. A. J. Downing estimated that more than 50,000 persons visited Greenwood Cemetery in Brooklyn in the course of nine months in 1848. They came on foot and in carriages. Guidebooks in hand, they admired the monuments and the artistic planting and the views. They wandered along the lanes and paths, and rested on the expanses of lawn, sketched, ate lunch, and even practiced a little shooting. They had discovered a kind of recreation that the city had never offered.

The generally-accepted explanation for the popularity of the rural or picturesque cemetery is that it satisfied the new romantic love of nature. No doubt this had something to do with the enthusiasm, but the existence of widespread nature romanticism among working class Americans—or indeed among working class Europeans—has yet to be established. What evidence we have is largely literary, and like our contemporary environmentalism, nature romanticism seems to have been essentially a middle-class movement. In the writings of A. J. Downing, one of the most influential exponents of romanticism in architecture and landscape architecture, there are frequent suggestions that a taste for the romantic was peculiar to persons of refinement and wealth. In fact we now know enough about the fashion to recognize that a carefully-designed and well-executed picturesque landscape park called for considerable skill. It was not a "natural" space, it was (in the hands of the artist-designer) a highly structured space, a "painterly" composition whose rules and techniques were inspired by

established landscape painters. It was Olmsted who best understood the canons of the picturesque and who applied them on a grandiose scale in Central Park and Prospect Park. To the average urban working-class American, relaxing in a rural cemetery, the appeal of the new landscape was quite different from that of Downing's well-to-do patrons. He was less aware of the subtleties of romantic composition, or even of the possibility of a direct contact with nature, than of the apparent *lack* of structure. The informal landscape offered the delights of spontaneous contact with other people in a setting that in no way prescribed a certain dress code or a certain code of manners. It was a public space of a novel kind: full of surprises, where emotions and pleasures were fresh and easily shared. It was not simply another artificial space; it was an *environment*, a place for new, primarily social, experiences. It represented the rejection of structure, the rejection of classical urbanism with its historical allusions, and the rejection of architectural public space.

As further evidence that nature romanticism had little or nothing to do with the acceptance of the rural cemetery, we might consider another, less familiar example of the popular American preference for unstructured public places: the camp meetings or revivals, the evangelical gatherings which were numerous in rural and frontier communities through the first half of the nineteenth century. Each of them attracted hundreds of men and women and children, black as well as white, and each lasted several nights and days. Almost always they had a forest background. Yet despite the wilderness setting and the prevailing emotionalism, it would be hard to find any trace of nature awareness in the proceedings, nor in their religious experiences. On the contrary: The forest seemed to free men and women from *any* environmental influences. Again, it was the lack of structure, the lack of behavioral design that produced the exhilaration.

OLMSTED'S ISOLATED ART-WORKS

The park movement did not evolve out of the Great Revival, but out of the rural cemetery. It was a remarkable instance of how quickly and effectively Americans can respond to a humanitarian need—in this case the need for agreeable, healthy, and beautiful places where the urban population could enjoy itself and (of course) have contact with nature. In 1851 the New York legislature authorized the city to acquire some 840 acres for a public park. Seven years later Frederick Law Olmsted had won the design competition and work had begun on Central Park.

Ten years after that, despite the intervening war, there was not a major American city without a rural park, or the prospect of one, and many of those parks had been designed by Olmsted and his associates. Though at the beginning there were expressions of disapproval—the park would be taken over by rowdies, it was too large, it lacked the more formal qualities of the European royal parks—it was not long before parks in general were accepted as invaluable from the point of view of health, of innocent recreation, and as antidotes for the crowded and filthy city slums. Innumerable rural parks were created in smaller towns, and in the new towns of the West. It would be impossible to identify the number of college campuses, courthouses and institutional landscape designs, to say nothing of the landscaped cemeteries, that helped beautify communities throughout the country. Few of these spaces were designed by professionals. Most were the work of local amateur gardeners, and the transformation of many New England commons into neat little parks was frequently done by local women's organizations. For the most part these smaller, unpublicized parks were of no great artistic worth. They had their small lakes, their bandstands, their pretzel paths, and a monotony of elms or cottonwoods, but it must be said that they kept alive the civic tradition of public spaces at a time when the great Olmsted parks were fighting it. In those provincial parks political orators addressed the voters, band concerts were given, ethnic pageants were organized, and patriotic flowerbeds were admired. In the 1890s Frank Waugh, the landscape architect, described the typical western park as containing "race tracks, baseball grounds, camp meeting stands, carp ponds, fountains or fences."

It was this indiscriminate mixture of uses that horrified the readers of *Garden and Forest*, the organ of the Olmsted school of landscape design. For by the end of the century there had developed a very self-assured set of standards for the design of rural parks, and the most fundamental rule was

that the "primary purpose of a rural park within reach of a great city is to furnish that rest and refreshment of mind and body which come from the tranquilizing influence of contact with natural scenery." This implied two restrictions: First, no building of any kind was to be erected in the park, nor (in the words of Olmsted's son John) "formal gardens, statuary, conservatories, botanical or zoological gardens, concert groves, electric fountains or the like; also popular athletic grounds, parade grounds, ball grounds for boys and facilities for boating and bathing." These installations were not themselves objectionable, and could well have been harmonized with "contact with nature." But the park was *not* nature, or a "natural environment." It was *scenery*, a whole landscape where the visitor could wander for hours over meadows and through woods and next to lakes and streams. For such was Olmsted's ideal: The park as a three-dimensional work of art. This in turn meant that the park should be visibly isolated from the surrounding city, enclosed by an impenetrable wall of greenery, so that the outside urban world would never impinge on the "rural" landscape, or on the experience of those visitors seeking rest and "refreshment of mind and body."

OXYGEN AND VIRTUE

On aesthetic as well as on demographic grounds, there were reasons for this uncompromising isolation. But remoteness also promoted what Downing, Olmsted, and others had always considered the true role of the rural park: the physical and moral regeneration of the individual visitor. From the very beginning of the park movement there had been frequent references to the elevating influence that the rural park would have. "No one who has closely observed the conduct of the people who visit the park," Olmsted wrote, "can doubt it exercises a distinctly harmonizing and refining influence upon the most unfortunate and lawless classes of the city—an influence favorable to courtesy, self-control and temperance." To supplement this influence, Olmsted created a special park police force to control misconduct, including walking on the grass. But he also relied on the force of example to give the poor "an education to refinement and taste and the mental and moral capital of gentlemen." This was to come from observing and emulating the manners and behavior of upper-class visitors to the park. As Thomas Bender notes, "Olmsted's generation saw no difficulty in recommending that Central Park, their symbol of the democratic community, be surrounded by elegant private villas that would exert an elevating influence upon the masses who visited the park."[4]

The early vision of the rural park and its function survived intact for no more than fifty years. One of its original objectives had been the improvement of the health of city dwellers. But medical science soon proved that this was not simply a matter of fresh air and contact with nature; it was a matter of training, and the park was the appropriate place for such training. "Foul air prompts vice, " said a New York physician, "and oxygen to virtue as surely as the sunlight paints the flowers of our garden…. The varied opportunities of a park would educate [the slum child] and his family in the enjoyment of open-air pleasures. Deprived of these, he and his are educated into the ways of disease and vice by the character of their surroundings."

In the 1880s the well-organized playground movement, which had started by providing small playgrounds in the slums, demanded access to the park, and at much the same time a public eager for places to play various outdoor games brought pressure on the city to provide appropriate space. "It was easier to persuade the city fathers to make use of existing parks than to purchase additional land for recreation…. In some cases the introduction of recreational facilities was achieved with intelligence and in conformity with the original park design. In other instances the results were detrimental to the former park purpose."[5]

At the time of Olmsted's death in 1903 the park had largely ceased to be an environment in which the individual could enjoy solitary contact with nature, and had become an environment dedicated to guidance in recreation, health, citizenship, and nature knowledge. It was often crowded with cultural and recreational facilities, group activities, and increasingly populated by professional recreationists, playground supervisors, and leadership counselors. Even the definition of the park underwent drastic revision: It is now described in official documents as an open space, containing public facilities and with the appearance of a natural landscape. It is merely one element in a nation-wide ecosystem.

THE LANDSCAPE OF DIVERSITY

In retrospect, how unpredictable and how extraordinary was the change over a period of less than a century in the American concept of public spaces! The neo-classical square, in part surrounded by public buildings, and located in the heart of the city, had been the symbol of political status, recognized by all. In the 1860s, however, the rural park began to replace it in the public perception, and the rural park not only rejected any contact with architecture and formal urbanism, but was located as far as possible from workaday activities, as if to say: Here is the true center, the place where nature establishes the laws.

But perhaps the most dramatic contrast between the two public spaces was in their respective definitions of community. The neo-classical square implied a body of people, politically and socially homogeneous, inhabiting a well-defined political territory with clear-cut class divisions. The visitors to the rural park came singly, each in pursuit of an individual contact with nature, a private experience. The ideal romantic community was the garden suburb, where reverence for the environment was the only common bond, and anything like an urban or political center was discouraged. Where can such a center be seen in Olmsted's design for Riverside, the Chicago suburb? It is a pleasant tangle of curving roads and lanes where all residences are isolated by greenery. Community did not mean homogeneity or uniformity, it meant diversity, and nothing was more gratifying to Olmsted than to see a diverse public in Central Park. Again and again he described "the persons brought closely together, poor and rich, young and old, Jew and Gentile." But this was a diversity of *individuals*. When the various recreational activities invaded the park in the 1880s, what ensued was a diversity of *groups*: age groups, ethnic groups, sports groups, neighborhood groups. That was quite another kind of diversity, and the spaces occupied by these groups, if only temporarily, constituted so many public places in the strictest sense: places where like-minded people came together to share an identity.

The emergence of these hitherto non-existent

groups was probably the greatest contribution of the rural park. Long after the old-fashioned solitary pursuit of the contact with nature had vanished from the scene, these miniature societies with special identities continued to flourish and to acquire increasing public recognition over the years. Eventually they expanded beyond the park, and I think it was the automobile that encouraged this dispersal.

Though it is common practice to blame the automobile for having destroyed many territorial communities—particularly rural ones—the car has made it possible for us to come together over great distances and in a shorter length of time than ever before and this in turn has made possible the creation of many new and different public spaces throughout the landscape. Without the automobile countless recreational areas, monuments, national parks, to say nothing of remoter sections of our cities, would never have become part of those experiences which Americans always pursue. Quite aside from what they teach us, they serve as way-stations, as it were, in our American, essentially Protestant, pilgrimage of self-perfection through endless education.

We do well to encourage the creation of all such spaces combining recreation with knowledge of nature and of our past. Their popularity is their best reason for existing. Yet many of us are aware that another, no less important public space, the one where we seek out and enjoy the company and stimulation of others, has been much neglected. We have outgrown the classical monumental square with its political overtones. We now seldom congregate as citizens, and when we do, it is more to protest than to celebrate our collective identity. We have learned from experience that such oversize public spaces—and I would certainly include the Olmsted style park with its oversize natural landscapes—eventually can be subverted by the authorities and used to indoctrinate us with some establishment philosophy: the Wonders of Nature, the Wonders of Art, the Wonders of Physical Fitness, or the supreme Wonders of the Commissars looking down at us from their podium. Small, more intimate, less structured spaces are what we now prefer. "This loss of the natural impulse to monumentality," John Summerson observed, "should not be a matter of regret. It is a perfectly natural reflection of the change which is

taking place in the whole character of western culture. All those things which suggested and supported monumentality are in dissolution. The corporate or social importance of religion was one of them. The sense of the dominance of a class—of the exclusive possession of certain privileges by certain groups—was another."[6]

To these things supporting monumentality in the past must be added the concept of a monolithic Public, the concept of a homogeneous People. For the public now is a composition of constantly shifting, overlapping groups—ethnic groups, social groups, age groups, special interest groups—and each of them, at one time or another, needs its own space, distinct from the surrounding urban fabric, where its own special social forms, its own special language and set of relations, can flourish, a space which confers a brief visibility on the group. We have too few of these spaces today, too few resembling the Prado in the North End of Boston, or the ad hoc open air social spaces which often evolve in urban ethnic or racial neighborhoods and do so much to maintain a sense of local identity and custom. With great taste and infinite goodwill, landscape architects have designed many mini-parks to relieve the monotony of our towns and cities. But the Olmsted tradition persists, and what we all too often have are overelaborate spaces with the inevitable display of vegetation, the inevitable ingenious fountain, and the inevitable emphasis on individual isolation. Yet contact with other people, not contact with nature, is what most of us are really after.

A RETURN TO THE STREET

Despite our current admiration for the formal square as a feature of the urban scene, despite our attempts to introduce it in our residential areas and shopping centers and in urban renewal projects, the time is approaching, I suspect, when we will turn our attention elsewhere. There are in fact many signs that the street, or a given fragment of the street, will be the true public space of the future.

If in fact this is the case, we will be reverting, unconsciously of course, to a medieval urban concept which long preceded the Renaissance concept of the public square. In the Middle Ages it was the street—tortuous, dirty, crowded—and not the public space identified with the church or castle or market, that was the center of economic and social life. The street was the place of work, the place of buying and selling, the place of meeting and negotiating, and the scene of the important religious and civic ceremonies and processions.

But its most significant trait was its blending of domestic and public life, its interplay of two distinct kinds of space. The narrow, overcrowded buildings bordering it spilled over into the street and transformed it into a place of workshops, kitchens, and merchandising, into a place of leisure and sociability, and confrontation of every kind. It was this confusion of functions, the confusion of two different realms of law and custom, that made the medieval street a kind of city within a city, and the scene of innovations in policing, maintenance, and social reform. Until the eighteenth century the street was actually something far more extensive than the traveled space between the houses. It was the matrix of a community, always alive to threats of intrusion, jealous of privileges and customs, and conscious of its own unique character.

For many economic, social, and aesthetic reasons, we are now beginning to think of the street and its relation to its inhabitants in a way that recalls the medieval concept. Robert Gutman wrote:

The revival of interest in the urban street has been accompanied by a wholly new emphasis in the view of the street's primary social function. Put simply, what sets the contemporary idea apart from previous definitions is the conviction that the street should be designed and managed for the benefit of its residents…. These impulses to make the street work, to make it into a community, some of which are specific to the situation of the city today, have gained strength because… the residents of urban streets until recently regarded themselves as a relatively homogeneous population. This important point is often overlooked. We are concerned about the street community in large part because for the very first time in the history of cities the simple virtues and joys of urban life have been diminished for all social groups; and we connect this reduction in our level of satisfaction and safety with the breakdown of the community.[7]

Not every street can be defined as an essential spatial element in a community. The majority will continue to be public utilities. But insofar as certain streets will be seen as public places, as being closely related to their immediate built environment, they will be playing the social role we have long associated with the traditional public square: the place where we exhibit our permanent identity as members of the community. The learning experience, the experience of contact with new sensations, new people, new ideas belongs elsewhere. The street as the public space of a community, modest in size, simple in structure, will serve a strictly traditional purpose. It will be where, in the words of Paul Weiss, we recognize and abide by "a mosaic of accepted customs, conventions, habitual ways of evaluating, responding, and acting… men must, to be perfected, become social beings. They must act to make the structure of the group an integral part of themselves a desirable link with others."

NOTES

1. John Reps, *The Making of Urban America* (Princeton: Princeton University Press, 1965); *Tidewater Towns* (Williamsburg, VA: The Colonial Williamsburg Foundation, 1972); *Cities of the American West* (Princeton: Princeton University Press, 1979).

2. Sam Bass Warner Jr., *Private City* (Philadelphia University of Pennsylvania Press, 1968), p. 55.

3. Norman Newton, *Design on the Land* (Cambridge, MA: Harvard University Press, 1971), p. 268.

4. Thomas Bender, *Toward an Urban Vision* (Lexington, KY: University Press of Kentucky, 1975), p. 179.

5. George Butler, "Change in the City Parks," *Landscape* 8 (Winter 1958-59).

6. John N. Summerson, *Heavenly Mansions* (New York: Norton Library, 1963).

7. Robert Gutman, "The Street Generation," in *On Streets*, ed. Atanford Anderson (Cambridge, MA: MIT Press, 1978).

Green Cities, Growing Cities, Just Cities? Urban Planning and the Contradictions of Sustainable Development

Scott Campbell

Copyright: Reprinted by permission from the *Journal of the American Planning Association*, 62, 3, 1996 ©, pp. 296-312.

In this article Campbell examines the compatibility of sustainable development with traditional planning values. In his "the planner's triangle" model he explores the tensions and contradictions between the goals of economic vitality and environmental protection. This clash makes it difficult to actually apply the "vague idealism" of sustainable development to real-world planning issues. Campbell explores the applicability of the concept as it exists, and looks into the possibilities of redefining sustainability. He then discusses future procedural and substantive planning challenges for planners in resolving the economic-environmental conflicts and in navigating the planner's triangle.

In the coming years planners face tough decisions about where they stand on protecting the green city, promoting the economically growing city, and advocating social justice. Conflicts among these goals are not superficial ones arising simply from personal preferences. Nor are they merely conceptual, among the abstract notions of ecological, economic, and political logic, nor a temporary problem caused by the untimely confluence of environmental awareness and economic recession. Rather, these conflicts go to the historic core of planning, and are a leitmotif in the contemporary battles in both our cities and rural areas, whether over solid waste incinerators or growth controls, the spotted owls or nuclear power. And though sustainable development aspires to offer an alluring, holistic way of evading these conflicts, they cannot be shaken off so easily.

This paper uses a simple triangular model to understand the divergent priorities of planning. My argument is that although the differences are partly due to misunderstandings arising from the disparate languages of environmental, economic, and political thought, translating across disciplines alone is not enough to eliminate these genuine clashes of interest. The socially constructed view of nature put forward here challenges the view of these conflicts as a classic battle of "man versus nature" or its current variation, "jobs versus the environment." The triangular model is then used to question whether sustainable development, the current object of plannings fascination, is a useful model to guide planning practice. I argue that the current concept of sustainability, though a laudable holistic vision, is vulnerable to the same criticism of vague idealism made thirty years ago against comprehensive planning. In this case, the idealistic fascination often builds upon a romanticized view of pre-industrial, indigenous, sustainable cultures—inspiring visions, but also of limited modern applicability. Nevertheless, sustainability, if redefined and incorporated into a broader understanding of political conflicts in industrial society, can become a powerful and useful organizing principle for planning. In fact, the idea will be particularly effective if, instead of merely evoking a misty-eyed vision of a peaceful ecotopia, it acts as a lightening rod to focus conflicting economic, environmental, and social interests. The more it stirs up conflict and sharpens the debate, the more effective the idea of sustainability will be in the long run.

The paper concludes by considering the implications of this viewpoint for planning. The triangle shows not only the conflicts, but also the potential complementarity of interests. The former are unavoidable and require planners to act as mediators, but the latter area is where planners can be especially creative in building coalitions between once-separated interest groups, such as labor and environmentalists, or community groups and business. To this end, planners need to combine both their procedural and their substantive skills and thus become central players in the battle over growth, the environment, and social justice.

THE PLANNER'S TRIANGLE: THREE PRIORITIES, THREE CONFLICTS

The current environmental enthusiasm among planners and planning schools might suggest their innate predisposition to protect the natural environment. Unfortunately, the opposite is more likely to be true: our historic tendency has been to promote the development of cities at the cost of natural destruction: to build cities we have cleared forests, fouled rivers and the air, leveled mountains. That is not the complete picture, since planners also have often come to the defense of nature, through the work of conservationists, park planners, open space preservationists, the Regional Planning Association of America, greenbelt planners, and modern environmental planners. Yet along the economic-ecological spectrum, with Robert Moses, and Dave Foreman (of *Earth First!*) standing at either pole, the planner has no natural home, but can slide from one end of the spectrum to the other; moreover, the midpoint has no special claims to legitimacy or fairness.

Similarly, though planners often see themselves as the defenders of the poor and of socioeconomic equality, their actions over the profession's history have often belied that self-image (Harvey 1985). Planners' efforts with downtown redevelopment, freeway planning, public-private partnerships, enterprise zones, smokestack-chasing and other economic development strategies don't easily add up to equity planning. At best, the planner has taken an ambivalent stance between the goals of economic growth and economic justice.

In short, the planner must reconcile not two, but at least three conflicting interests: to "grow" the economy, distribute this growth fairly, and in the process not degrade the ecosystem. To classify contemporary battles over environmental racism, pollution producing jobs, growth control, etc., as simply clashes between economic growth and environmental protection misses the third issue, of

social justice. The "jobs versus environment" dichotomy (e.g., the spotted owl versus Pacific Northwest timber jobs) crudely collapses under the "economy" banner the often differing interests of workers, corporations, community members, and the national public. The intent of this paper's title is to focus planning not only for "green cities and growing cities," but also for "just cities."

In an ideal world, planners would strive to achieve a balance of all three goals. In practice, however, professional and fiscal constraints drastically limit the leeway of most planners. Serving the broader public interest by holistically harmonizing growth, preservation, and equality remains the ideal; the reality of practice restricts planners to serving the narrower interests of their clients, that is, authorities and bureaucracies (Marcuse 1976), despite efforts to work outside those limitations (Hoffman 1989). In the end, planners usually represent one particular goal—planning perhaps for increased property tax revenues, or more open space preservation, or better housing for the poor—while neglecting the other two. Where each planner stands in the triangle depicted in figure 1 defines such professional bias. One may see illustrated in the figure the gap between the call for integrative, sustainable development planning (the center of the triangle) and the current fragmentation of professional practice (the edges). This point is developed later.

The Points (Corners) of the Triangle: the Economy, the Environment, and Equity

The three types of priorities lead to three perspectives on the city: The economic development planner sees the city as a location where production, consumption, distribution, and innovation take place. The city is in competition with other cities for markets and for new industries. Space is the economic space of highways, market areas, and commuter zones.

The environmental planner sees the city as a consumer of resources and a producer of wastes. The city is in competition with nature for scarce resources and land, and always poses a threat to nature. Space is the ecological space of greenways, river basins, and ecological niches.

The equity planner sees the city as a location of conflict over the distribution of resources, of

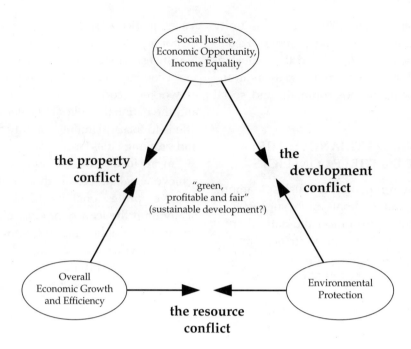

Figure V.2 The triangle of conflicting goals for planning, and the three associated conflicts. Planners define themselves, implicitly, by where they stand on the triangle. The elusive ideal of sustainable development leads to the center.

services, and of opportunities. The competition is within the city itself, among different social groups. Space is the social space of communities, neighborhood organizations, labor unions: the space of access and segregation.

Certainly there are other important views of the city, including the architectural, the psychological, and the circulatory (transportation); and one could conceivably construct a planner's rectangle, pentagon, or more complex polygon. The triangular shape itself is not propounded here as the underlying geometric structure of the planner's world. Rather, it is useful for its conceptual simplicity. More importantly, it emphasizes the point that a one-dimensional "man versus environment" spectrum misses the social conflicts in contemporary environmental disputes, such as loggers versus the Sierra Club, farmers versus suburban developers, or fishermen versus barge operators (Reisner 1987; Jacobs 1989; McPhee 1989; Tucson 1993).[1]

Triangle Axis 1: The Property Conflict

The three points on the triangle represent divergent interests, and therefore lead to three fundamental conflicts. The first conflict—between eco-

nomic growth and equity—arises from competing claims on and uses of property, such as between management and labor, landlords and tenants, or gentrifying professionals and long-time residents. This growth-equity conflict is further complicated because each side not only resists the other, but also needs the other for its own survival. The contradictory tendency for a capitalist, democratic society to define property (such as housing or land) as a private commodity, but at the same time to rely on government intervention (e.g., zoning, or public housing for the working class) to ensure the beneficial social aspects of the same property, is what Richard Foglesong (1986) calls the "property contradiction." This tension is generated as the private sector simultaneously resists and needs social intervention, given the intrinsically contradictory nature of property. Indeed, the essence of property in our society is the tense pulling between these two forces. The conflict defines the boundary between private interest and the public good.

Triangle Axis 2: The Resource Conflict

Just as the private sector both resists regulation of property, yet needs it to keep the economy flowing, so too is society in conflict about its priorities for natural resources. Business resists the regulation of its exploitation of nature, but at the same time needs regulation to conserve those resources for present and future demands. This can be called the "resource conflict." The conceptual essence of natural resources is therefore the tension between their economic utility in industrial society and their ecological utility in the natural environment. This conflict defines the boundary between the developed city and the undeveloped wilderness, which is symbolized by the "city limits." The boundary is not fixed; it is a dynamic and contested boundary between mutually dependent forces.

Is there a single, universal economic-ecological conflict underlying all such disputes faced by planners? I searched for this essential, Platonic notion, but the diversity of examples—water politics in California, timber versus the spotted owl in the Pacific Northwest, tropical deforestation in Brazil, park planning in the Adirondacks, greenbelt planning in Britain, to name a few—suggests otherwise. Perhaps there is an *Ur-Konflikt*, rooted in the fundamental struggle between human civilization and the threatening wilderness around us, and expressed variously over the centuries. However, the decision must be left to anthropologists as to whether the essence of the spotted owl controversy can be traced back to Neolithic times. A meta-theory tying all these multifarious conflicts to an essential battle of "human versus nature" (and, once tools and weapons were developed and nature was controlled, "human versus human")—that invites skepticism. In this discussion, the triangle is used simply as a template to recognize and organize the common themes; to examine actual conflicts, individual case studies are used.[2]

The economic-ecological conflict has several instructive parallels with the growth-equity conflict. In the property conflict, industrialists must curb their profit-increasing tendency to reduce wages, in order to provide labor with enough wages to feed, house, and otherwise "reproduce" itself—that is, the subsistence wage. In the resource conflict, the industrialists must curb their profit-increasing tendency to increase timber yields, so as to ensure that enough of the forest remains to "reproduce" itself (Clawson 1975; Beltzer and Kroll 1986; Lee, Field, and Burch 1990).

This practice is called "sustained yield," though timber companies and environmentalists disagree about how far the forest can be exploited and still be "sustainable." (Of course, other factors also affect wages, such as supply and demand, skill level, and discrimination, just as lumber demand, labor prices, transportation costs, tariffs, and other factors affect how much timber is harvested.) In both cases, industry must leave enough of the exploited resource, be it human labor or nature, so that the resource will continue to deliver in the future. In both cases, how much is "enough" is also contested.

Triangle Axis 3: The Development Conflict

The third axis on the triangle is the most elusive: the "development conflict," lying between the poles of social equity and environmental preservation. If the property conflict is characterized by the economy's ambivalent interest in providing at least a subsistence existence for working people, and the resource conflict by the economy's ambivalent interest in providing sustainable conditions for the natural environment, the development conflict stems from the difficulty of doing both at once. Environment-equity disputes are coming to the fore to join the older dispute about economic growth versus equity (Paehlke 1994, 349-50). This may be the most challenging conundrum of sustainable development: how to increase social equity and protect the environment simultaneously, whether in a steady-state economy (Daly 1991) or not. How could those at the bottom of society find greater economic opportunity if environmental protection mandates diminished economic growth? On a global scale, efforts to protect the environment might lead to slowed economic growth in many countries, exacerbating the inequalities between rich and poor nations. In effect, the developed nations would be asking the poorer nations to forgo rapid development to save the world from the greenhouse effect and other global emergencies.

This development conflict also happens at the local level, as in resource-dependent communities, which commonly find themselves at the bottom of the economy's hierarchy of labor. Miners, lumberjacks, and mill workers see a grim link between environmental preservation and poverty, and commonly mistrust environmentalists as elitists. Poor urban communities are often forced to make the no-win choice between economic survival and environmental quality, as when the only economic opportunities are offered by incinerators, toxic waste sites, landfills, and other noxious land uses that most neighborhoods can afford to oppose and do without (Bryant and Mohai 1992; Bullard 1990, 1993). If, as some argue, environmental protection is a luxury of the wealthy, then environmental racism lies at the heart of the development conflict. Economic segregation leads to environmental segregation: the former occurs in the transformation of natural resources into consumer products; the latter occurs as the spoils of production are returned to nature. Inequitable development takes place at all stages of the materials cycle.

Consider this conflict from the vantage of equity planning. Norman Krumholz, as the planning director in Cleveland, faced the choice of either building regional rail lines or improving local bus lines (Krumholz et al. 1982). Regional rail lines would encourage the suburban middle class to switch from cars to mass transit; better local bus service would help the inner-city poor by reducing their travel and waiting time. One implication of this choice was the tension between reducing pollution and making transportation access more equitable, an example of how bias toward social inequity may be embedded in seemingly objective transit proposals.

IMPLICATIONS OF THE PLANNER'S TRIANGLE MODEL

Conflict and Complementarity in the Triangle

Though I use the image of the triangle to emphasize the strong conflicts among economic growth, environmental protection, and social justice, no point can exist alone. The nature of the three axial conflicts is mutual dependence based not only on opposition, but also on collaboration.

Consider the argument that the best way to distribute wealth more fairly (i.e., to resolve the property conflict) is to increase the size of the economy, so that society will have more to redistribute. Similarly, we can argue that the best way to improve environmental quality (i.e., to resolve the resource conflict) is to expand the economy, thereby having more money with which to buy

environmental protection. The former is trickle-down economics; can we call the latter "trickle-down environmentalism"? One sees this logic in the conclusion of the Brundtland Report: "If large parts of the developing world are to avert economic, social, and environmental catastrophes, it is essential that global economic growth be revitalized" (World Commission on Environment and Development 1987). However, only if such economic growth is more fairly distributed will the poor be able to restore and protect their environment, whose devastation so immediately degrades their quality of life. In other words, the development conflict can be resolved only if the property conflict is resolved as well. Therefore, the challenge for planners is to deal with the conflicts between competing interests by discovering and implementing complementary uses.

The Triangle's Origins in a Social View of Nature

One of the more fruitful aspects of recent interdisciplinary thought may be its linking the traditionally separate intellectual traditions of critical social theory and environmental science/policy (e.g., Smith 1990; Wilson 1992; Ross 1994). This is also the purpose of the triangle figure presented here: to integrate the environmentalist's and social theorists world views. On one side, an essentialist view of environmental conflicts ("man versus nature") emphasizes the resource conflict. On another side, a historical materialist view of social conflicts (e.g., capital versus labor) emphasizes the property conflict. By simultaneously considering both perspectives, one can see more clearly the social dimension of environmental conflicts, that is, the development conflict. Such a synthesis is not easy: it requires accepting the social construction of nature but avoiding the materialistic pitfall of arrogantly denying any aspects of nature beyond the labor theory of value.

Environmental conflict should not, therefore, be seen as simply one group representing the interests of nature and another group attacking nature (though it often appears that way).[3] Who is to say that the lumberjack, who spends all his or her days among trees (and whose livelihood depends on those trees), is any less close to nature than the environmentalist taking a weekend walk through the woods? Is the lumberjack able to cut down trees only because s/he is "alienated" from the "true" spirit of nature—the spirit that the hiker enjoys? In the absence of a forest mythology, neither the tree cutter nor the tree hugger—nor the third party, the owner/lessee of the forest—can claim an innate kinship to a tree. This is not to be an apologist for clear-cutting, but rather to say that the merits of cutting versus preserving trees cannot be decided according to which persons or groups have the "truest" relationship to nature.

The crucial point is that all three groups have an interactive relationship with nature: the differences lie in their conflicting *conceptions* of nature, their conflicting *uses* of nature, and how they incorporate nature into their systems of values (be they community, economic, or spiritual values). This clash of human values reveals how much the ostensibly separate domains of community development and environmental protection overlap, and suggests that planners should do better in combining social and environmental models. One sees this clash of values in many environmental battles: between the interests of urban residents and those of subsidized irrigation farmers in California water politics; between beach homeowners and coastal managers trying to control erosion; between rich and poor neighborhoods, in the siting of incinerators; between farmers and environmentalists, in restrictions by open space zoning. Even then-President George Bush weighed into such disputes during his 1992 campaign when he commented to a group of loggers that finally people should be valued more than spotted owls (his own take on the interspecies equity issue). Inequity and the imbalance of political power are often issues at the heart of economic environmental conflicts.

Recognition that the terrain of nature is contested need not, however, cast us adrift on a sea of socially constructed relativism where "nature" appears as an arbitrary idea of no substance (Bird 1987; Soja 1989). Rather, we are made to rethink the idea and to see the appreciation of nature as an historically evolved sensibility. I suspect that radical environmentalists would criticize this perspective as anthropocentric environmentalism, and argue instead for an ecocentric world view that puts the Earth first (Sessions 1992; Parton 1993). It is true that an anthropocentric view, if distorted, can lead

to an arrogant optimism about civilization's ability to reprogram nature through technologies ranging from huge hydroelectric and nuclear plants down to genetic engineering. A rigid belief in the anthropocentric labor theory of value, Marxist or otherwise, can produce a modern-day Narcissus as a social-constructionist who sees nature as merely reflecting the beauty of the human aesthetic and the value of human labor. In this light, a tree is devoid of value until it either becomes part of a scenic area or is transformed into lumber. On the other hand, even as radical, ecocentric environmentalists claim to see "true nature" beyond the city limits, they are blind to how their own world view and their definition of nature itself are shaped by their socialization. The choice between an anthropocentric or an ecocentric world view is a false one. We are all unavoidably anthropocentric; the question is which anthropomorphic values and priorities we will apply to the natural and the social world around us.

SUSTAINABLE DEVELOPMENT: REACHING THE ELUSIVE CENTER OF THE TRIANGLE

If the three corners of the triangle represent key goals in planning, and the three axes represent the three resulting conflicts, then I will define the center of the triangle as representing sustainable development: the balance of these three goals. Getting to the center, however, will not be so easy. It is one thing to locate sustainability in the abstract, but quite another to reorganize society to get there.

At first glance, the widespread advocacy of sustainable development is astonishing, given its revolutionary implications for daily life (World Commission 1987; Daly and Cobb 1989; Rees 1989; World Bank 1989; Goodland 1990; Barrett and Bohlen 1991; Korten 1991; Van der Ryn and Calthorpe 1991). It is getting hard to refrain from sustainable development; arguments against it are inevitably attached to the strawman image of a greedy, myopic industrialist. Who would now dare to speak up in opposition? Two interpretations of the bandwagon for sustainable development suggest themselves. The pessimistic thought is that sustainable development has been stripped of its transformative power and reduced to its lowest common denominator. After all, if both the

World Bank and radical ecologists now believe in sustainability, the concept can have no teeth: it is so malleable as to mean many things to many people without requiring commitment to any specific policies. Actions speak louder than words, and though all endorse sustainability, few will actually practice it. Furthermore, any concept fully endorsed by all parties must surely be bypassing the heart of the conflict. Set a goal far enough into the future, and even conflicting interests will seem to converge along parallel lines. The concept certainly appears to violate the Karl Popper's requirement that propositions be falsifiable, for to reject sustainability is to embrace nonsustainability—and who dares to sketch that future? (Ironically, the nonsustainable scenario is the easiest to define: merely the extrapolation of our current way of life.)

Yet there is also an optimistic interpretation of the broad embrace given sustainability: the idea has become hegemonic, an accepted meta-narrative, a given. It has shifted from being a variable to being the parameter of the debate, almost certain to be integrated into any future scenario of development. We should therefore neither be surprised that no definition has been agreed upon, nor fear that this reveals a fundamental flaw in the concept. In the battle of big public ideas, sustainability has won: the task of the coming years is simply to work out the details, and to narrow the gap between its theory and practice.

Is Sustainable Development a Useful Concept?

Some environmentalists argue that if sustainable development is necessary, it therefore must be possible. Perhaps so, but if you are stranded at the bottom of a deep well, a ladder may be impossible even though necessary. The answer espoused may be as much an ideological as a scientific choice, depending on whether one's loyalty is to Malthus or Daly. The more practical question is whether sustainability is a useful concept for planners. The answer here is mixed. The goal may be too far away and holistic to be operational: that is, it may not easily break down into concrete, short-term steps. We also might be able to *define* sustainability yet be unable ever to actually measure it or even know, one day in the future, that we had achieved it. An old eastern proverb identifies the western

confusion of believing that to name something is to know it. That may be the danger in automatically embracing sustainable development: a facile confidence that by adding the term "sustainable" to all our existing planning documents and tools (sustainable zoning, sustainable economic development, sustainable transportation planning), we are *doing* sustainable planning. Conversely, one can do much beneficial environmental work without ever devoting explicit attention to the concept of sustainability.

Yet sustainability can be a helpful concept in that it posits the long-term planning goal of a social environmental system in balance. It is a unifying concept, enormously appealing to the imagination, that brings together many different environmental concerns under one overarching value. It defines a set of social priorities and articulates how society values the economy, the environment, and equity (Paehlke 1994, 360). In theory, it allows us not only to calculate whether we have attained sustainability, but also to determine how far away we are. (Actual measurement, though, is another, harder task.) Clearly, it can be argued that, though initially flawed and vague, the concept can be transformed and refined to be of use to planners.

History, Equity, and Sustainable Development

One obstacle to an accurate, working definition of sustainability may well be the historical perspective that sees the practice as pre-existing, either in our past or as a Platonic concept. I believe instead that our sustainable future does not yet exist, either in reality or even in strategy. We do not yet know what it will look like; it is being socially constructed through a sustained period of conflict negotiation and resolution. This is a process of innovation, not of discovery and converting the nonbelievers.

This point brings us to the practice of looking for sustainable development in pre-industrial and nonwestern cultures (a common though not universal practice). Searching for our future in our indigenous past is instructive at both the philosophical and the practical level (Turner 1983; Duerr 1985). Yet it is also problematical, tapping into a myth that our salvation lies in the pre-industrial sustainable culture. The international division of labor and trade, the movement of most people away from agriculture into cities, and exponential population growth lead us irrevocably down a unidirectional, not a circular path: the transformation of pre-industrial, indigenous settlements into mass urban society is irreversible. Our modern path to sustainability lies forward, not behind us.

The key difference between those indigenous, sustainable communities and ours is that they had no choice but to be sustainable. Bluntly stated, if they cut down too many trees or ruined the soil, they would die out. Modern society has the options presented by trade, long-term storage, and synthetic replacements; if we clear-cut a field, we have subsequent options that our ancestors didn't. In this situation, we must *voluntarily choose* sustainable practices, since there is no immediate survival or market imperative to do so. Although the long-term effects of a nonsustainable economy are certainly dangerous, the feedback mechanisms are too long-term to prod us in the right direction.

Why do we often romanticize the sustainable past? Some are attracted to the powerful spiritual link between humans and nature that has since been lost. Such romanticists tend, however, to overlook the more harsh and unforgiving aspects of being so dependent on the land. Two hundred years ago, Friedrich Schiller (1965, 28) noted the tendency of utopian thinkers to take their dream for the future and posit it as their past, thus giving it legitimacy as a cyclical return to the past.[4] This habit is not unique to ecotopians (Kumar 1991); some religious fundamentalists also justify their utopian urgency by drawing on the myth of a paradise lost. Though Marxists don't glorify the past in the same way, they, too, manage to anticipate a *static* system of balance and harmony, which nonetheless will require a cataclysmic, revolutionary social transformation to reach. All three ideologies posit some basic flaw in society—be it western materialism, original sin, or capitalism—whose identification and cure will free us from conflict. Each ideology sees a fundamental alienation as the danger to overcome: alienation from nature, from god, or from work. Each group is so critical of existing society that it would seem a wonder we have made it this far; but this persistence of human society despite the dire prognoses of utopians tells us something.

What is the fallout from such historical thinking? By neglecting the powerful momentum of modern industrial and postindustrial society, it both points us in the wrong direction and makes it easier to marginalize the proponents of sustainable development. It also carries an anti-urban sentiment that tends to neglect both the centrality and the plight of megacities. Modern humans are unique among species in their propensity to deal with nature's threats, not only through flight and burrowing and biological adaptation, nor simply through spiritual understanding, but also through massive population growth, complex social division of labor, and the fundamental, external transformation of their once-natural environment (the building of cities). Certainly the fixation on growth, industry, and competition has degraded the environment. Yet one cannot undo urban-industrial society. Rather, one must continue to innovate through to the other side of industrialization, to reach a more sustainable economy.

The cyclical historical view of some environmentalists also hinders a critical understanding of equity, since that view attributes to the environment a natural state of equality rudely upset by modern society. Yet nature is inherently neither equal nor unequal, and at times can be downright brutal. The human observer projects a sense of social equity onto nature, through a confusion, noted by Schiller, of the idealized future with myths about our natural past. To gain a sense of historical legitimacy, we project our socially constructed sense of equality onto the past, creating revisionist history in which nature is fair and compassionate. Society's path to equality is perceived not as an uncertain progress from barbarism to justice, but rather as a return to an original state of harmony as laid out in nature. In this thinking, belief in an ecological balance and a social balance, entwined in the pre-industrial world, conjures up an eco-Garden of Eden "lost" by modern society.[5]

It will be more useful to let go of this mythic belief in our involuntary diaspora from a pre-industrial, ecotopian Eden.[6] The conflation of ecological diasporas and utopias constrains our search for creative, urban solutions to social-environmental conflict. By relinquishing such mythic beliefs, we will understand that notions of equity were not lying patiently in wait in nature, to be first discovered by indigenous peoples, then lost by colonialists, and finally rediscovered by modern society in the late twentieth century. This is certainly not to say that nature can teach us nothing. The laws of nature are not the same thing, however, as natural law, nor does ecological equilibrium necessarily generate normative principles of equity. Though we turn to nature to understand the context, dynamics, and effects of the economic-environmental conflict, we must turn to social norms to decide what balance is fair and just.

How, then, do we define what is fair? I propose viewing social justice as the striving towards a more equal distribution of resources among social groups across the space of cities and of nations—a definition of "fair" distribution. It should be noted that societies view themselves as "fair" if the *procedures* of allocation treat people equally, even if the *substantive* outcome is unbalanced. (One would hope that equal treatment is but the first step towards narrowing material inequality.) The environmental movement expands the space for this "equity" in two ways: (1) intergenerationally (present versus future generations) and (2) across species (as in animal rights, deep ecology, and legal standing for trees). The two added dimensions of equity remain essentially abstractions, however, since no one from the future or from other species can speak up for their "fair share" of resources. Selfless advocates (or selfish ventriloquists) "speak for them."

This expansion of socio-spatial equity to include future generations and other species not only makes the concept more complex; it also creates the possibility for contradictions among the different calls for "fairness." Slowing worldwide industrial expansion may preserve more of the world's resources for the future (thereby increasing intergenerational equity), but it may also undermine the efforts of the underdeveloped world to approach the living standards of the west (thereby lowering international equity). Battles over Native American fishing practices, the spotted owl, and restrictive farmland preservation each thrust together several divergent notions of "fairness." It is through resolving the three sorts of conflicts on the planner's triangle that society iteratively forms its definition of what is fair.

The Path Towards Sustainable Development

There are two final aspects of the fuzzy definition of sustainability: its path and its outcome. The

basic premise of sustainable development is one that, like the long-term goal of a balanced U.S. budget, is hard not to like. As with eliminating the national debt, however, two troubling questions about sustainable development remain: How are you going to get there? Once you get there, what ate the negative consequences? Planners don't yet have adequate answers to these two questions; that is, as yet they have no concrete strategies to achieve sustainable development, nor do they know how to counter the political resistance to it.

On the *path* towards a sustainable future, the steps are often too vague, as with sweeping calls for a "spiritual transformation" as the prerequisite for environmental transformation. Sometimes the call for sustainable development seems to serve as a vehicle for sermonizing about the moral and spiritual corruption of the industrial world (undeniable). Who would not want to believe in a holistic blending of economic and ecological values in each of our planners, who would then go out into the world and, on each project, internally and seamlessly merge the interests of jobs and nature, as well as of social justice? That is, the call to planners would be to stand at every moment at the center of the triangle.

But this aim is too reminiscent of our naive belief during the 1950s and 1960s in comprehensive planning for a single "public interest," before the incrementalists and advocacy planners pulled the rug out from under us (Lindblom 1959; Altshuler 1965; Davidoff 1965; Fainstein and Fainstein 1971). I suspect that planners' criticisms of the sustainable development movement in the coming years will parallel the critique of comprehensive planning 30 years ago: The incrementalists will argue that one cannot achieve a sustainable society in a single grand leap, for it requires too much social and ecological information and is too risky. The advocacy planners will argue that no common social interest in sustainable development exists, and that bureaucratic planners will invariably create a sustainable development scheme that neglects the interests both of the poor and of nature. To both groups of critics, the prospect of integrating economic, environmental and equity interests will seem forced and artificial. States will require communities to prepare "Sustainable Development Master Plans," which will prove to be glib wish lists of goals and suspiciously vague implementation steps. To achieve consensus for the plan, language will be reduced to the lowest common denominator, and the pleasing plans will gather dust.

An alternative is to let holistic sustainable development be a long-range goal; it is a worthy one, for planners do need a vision of a more sustainable urban society. But during the coming years, planners will confront deep-seated conflicts among economic, social and environmental interests that cannot be wished away through admittedly appealing images of a community in harmony with nature. One is no more likely to abolish the economic-environmental conflict completely by achieving sustainable bliss than one is to eliminate completely the boundaries between the city and the wilderness, between the public and private spheres, between the haves and have-nots. Nevertheless, one can diffuse the conflict, and find ways to avert its more destructive fall-out.

My concern about the *ramifications* of a sustainable future is one that is often expressed: steady-state, no-growth economics would be likely to relegate much of the developing world—and the poor within the industrialized world—to a state of persistent poverty. The advocates of sustainable development rightly reject as flawed the premise of conventional economics that only a growth economy can achieve social redistribution. And growth economics has, indeed, also exacerbated the environment's degradation. However, it is wishful thinking to assume that a sustainable economy will automatically ensure a socially just distribution of resources.[7] The vision of no-growth (commonly though not universally assumed to characterize sustainable development) raises powerful fears, and planners should be savvy to such fears. Otherwise, they will understand neither the potential dangers of steady-state economics nor the nature of the opposition to sustainable development.

Rethinking/Redefining Sustainable Development

Despite the shortcomings in the current formulation of sustainable development, the concept retains integrity and enormous potential. It simply needs to be redefined and made more precise. First, one should avoid a dichotomous, black-and-white view of sustainability. We should think of American society not as a corrupt, wholly unsustainable one that has to be made pure and wholly sustainable, but rather as a hybrid of both sorts of practices. Our purpose, then, should be to move further towards sustainable practices in an evolutionary progression.

Second, we should broaden the idea of "sustainability." If "crisis" is defined as the inability of a system to reproduce itself, then sustainability is the opposite: the long-term ability of a system to reproduce. This criterion applies not only to natural ecosystems, but to economic and political systems as well. By this definition, western society already does much to sustain itself: economic policy and corporate strategies (e.g., investment, training, monetary policy) strive to reproduce the macro- and micro-economies. Similarly, governments, parties, labor unions, and other political agents strive to reproduce their institutions and interests. Society's shortcoming is that as it strives to sustain its political and economic systems, it often neglects to sustain the ecological system. The goal for planning is therefore a broader agenda: to sustain, simultaneously and in balance, these three sometimes competing, sometimes complementary systems.[8]

Third, it will be helpful to distinguish initially between two levels of sustainability: specific versus general (or local versus global). One might fairly easily imagine and achieve sustainability in a single sector and/or locality, for example, converting a Pacific Northwest community to sustained-yield timber practices. Recycling, solar power, cogeneration, and conservation can lower consumption of nonsustainable resources. To achieve complete sustainability across all sectors and/or all places, however, requires such complex restructuring and redistribution that the only feasible path to global sustainability is likely to be a long, incremental accumulation of local and industry-specific advances.

What this incremental, iterative approach means is that planners will find their vision of a sustainable city developed best at the conclusion of contested negotiations over land use, transportation, housing, and economic development policies, not as the premise for beginning the effort. To first spend years in the hermetic isolation of universities   and environmental groups, perfecting the theory of sustainable development, before testing it in community development is backwards. That approach sees sustainable development as an ideal society outside the conflicts of the planner's triangle, or as the tranquil "eye of the hurricane" at the triangle's center. As with the ideal comprehensive plan, it is presumed that the objective, technocratic merits of a perfected sustainable development scheme will ensure society's acceptance. But one cannot reach the sustainable center of the planner's triangle in a single, holistic leap to a pre-ordained balance.

THE TASK AHEAD FOR PLANNERS: SEEKING SUSTAINABLE DEVELOPMENT WITHIN THE TRIANGLE OF PLANNING CONFLICTS

The role of planners is therefore to engage the current challenge of sustainable development with a dual, interactive strategy: (1) to manage and resolve conflict; and (2) to promote creative technical, architectural, and institutional solutions. Planners must both negotiate the procedures of the conflict and promote a substantive vision of sustainable development.

Procedural Paths to Sustainable Development: Conflict Negotiation

In negotiation and conflict resolution (Bingham 1986; Susskind and Cruikshank 1987; Crowfoot and Wondolleck 1990), rather than pricing externalities, common ground is established at the negotiation table, where the conflicting economic, social, and environmental interests can be brought together. The potential rewards are numerous: not only an outcome that balances all parties, but avoidance of heavy legal costs and long-lasting animosity. Negotiated conflict resolution can also lead to a better understanding of one's opponent's interests and values, and even of one's own interests. The very process of lengthy negotiation can be a powerful tool to mobilize community involvement around social and environmental issues. The greatest promise, of course, is a win-win outcome: finding innovative solutions that would not have come out of traditional, adversarial confrontation. Through skillfully led, back-and-forth discussion, the parties can separate their initial, clashing substantive

demands from their underlying interests, which may be more compatible. For example, environmentalists and the timber industry could solve their initial dispute over building a logging road, through alternative road design and other mitigation measures (Crowfoot and Wondolleck 1990, 32-52).

However, conflict resolution is no panacea. Sometimes conflicting demands express fundamental conflicts of interest. The either-or nature of the technology or ecology may preclude a win-win outcome, as in an all-or-nothing dispute over a proposed hydroelectric project (Reisner 1987)—you either build it or you don't. An overwhelming imbalance of power between the opposing groups also can thwart resolution (Crowfoot and Wondolleck 1990, 4). A powerful party can simply refuse to participate. It is also hard to negotiate a comprehensive resolution for a large number of parties.

Planners are likely to have the best success in using conflict resolution when there is a specific, concise dispute (rather than an amorphous ideological clash); all interested parties agree to participate (and don't bypass the process through the courts); each party feels on equal ground; there are a variety of possible compromises and innovative solutions; both parties prefer a solution to an impasse; and a skilled third-party negotiator facilitates. The best resolution strategies seem to include two areas of compromise and balance: the procedural (each party is represented and willing to compromise); and the substantive (the solution is a compromise, such as multiple land uses or a reduced development density).

Procedural Paths to Sustainable Development: Redefining the Language of the Conflict

A second strategy is to bridge the chasms between the languages of economics, environmentalism, and social justice. Linguistic differences, which reflect separate value hierarchies, are a major obstacle to common solutions. All too often, the economists speak of incentives and marginal rates, the ecologists speak of carrying capacity and biodiversity, the advocate planners speak of housing rights, empowerment, and discrimination, and each side accuses the others of being "out of touch" (Campbell 1992).

The planner therefore needs to act as a translator, assisting each group to understand the priorities and reasoning of the others. Economic, ecological and social thought may at a certain level be incommensurable, yet a level may still be found where all three may be brought together. To offer an analogy, a Kenyan Gikuyu text cannot be fully converted into English without losing something in translation; a good translation, nevertheless, is the best possible way to bridge two systems of expression that will never be one, and it is preferable to incomprehension.

The danger of translation is that one language will dominance the debate and thus define the terms of the solution. It is essential to exert equal effort to translate in each direction, to prevent one linguistic culture from dominating the other (as English has done in neocolonial Africa). Another lesson from the neocolonial linguistic experience is that it is crucial for each social group to express itself in its own language before any translation. The challenge for planners is to write the best translations among the languages of the economic, the ecological, and the social views, and to avoid a quasi-colonial dominance by the economic *lingua franca*, by creating equal two-way translations.[9]

For example, planners need better tools to understand their cities and regions not just as economic systems, or static inventories of natural resources, but also as *environmental systems* that are part of regional and global networks trading goods, information, resources and pollution. At the conceptual level, translating the economic vocabulary of global cities, the spatial division of labor, regional restructuring, and technoburbs/ edge cities into environmental language would be a worthy start; at the same time, of course, the vocabulary of biodiversity, landscape linkages, and carrying capacity should be translated to be understandable by economic interests.

This bilingual translation should extend to the empirical level. I envision extending the concept of the "trade balance" to include an "environmental balance," which covers not just commodities, but also natural resources and pollution. Planners should improve their data collection and integration to support the environmental trade balance. They should apply economic-ecological bilingualism not only to the content of data, but also to the spatial framework of the data, by rethinking the geographic boundaries of planning and analysis. Bioregionalists advocate having the spatial scale for planning reflect the scale of *natural* phenomena (e.g., the extent of a river basin, vegetation zones, or the dispersion range of metropolitan air pollution); economic planners call for a spatial scale to match the *social* phenomena (e.g., highway networks, municipal boundaries, labor market areas, new industrial districts). The solution is to integrate these two scales and overlay the economic and ecological geographies of planning. The current merging of environmental Raster (grid-based) and infrastructural vector-based data in Geographic Information Systems (GIS) recognizes the need for multiple layers of planning boundaries (Wiggins 1993).

Translation can thus be a powerful planner's skill, and interdisciplinary planning education already provides some multilingualism. Moreover, the idea of sustainability lends itself nicely to the meeting on common ground of competitive value systems. Yet translation has its limits. Linguistic differences often represent real, intractable differences in values. An environmental dispute may arise not from a misunderstanding alone; both sides may clearly understand chat their vested interests fundamentally clash, no matter how expressed. At this point, translation must give way to other strategies. The difficulties are exacerbated when one party has greater power, and so shapes the language of the debate as well as prevailing in its outcome. In short, translation, like conflict negotiation, reveals both the promises and the limitations of communication-based conflict resolution.

Other Procedural Paths

Two other, more traditional approaches deserve mention. One is political pluralism: let the political arena decide conflicts, either directly (e.g., a referendum on an open space bond act, or a California state proposition on nuclear power), or indirectly (e.g., elections decided on the basis of candidates' environmental records and promised legislation). The key elements here, political debate and ultimately the vote, allow much wider participation in the decision than negotiation does. However, a binary vote cannot as easily handle complex issues, address specific land-use conflicts, or develop subtle, creative solutions. Choosing the general political process as a strategy for deciding conflict also takes the process largely out of the hands of planners.

The other traditional strategy is to develop market mechanisms to link economic and environmental priorities. Prices are made the commonality that bridges the gap between the otherwise non-commensurables of trees and timber, open space and real estate. The market place is chosen as the arena where society balances its competing values. This economistic approach to the environment reduces pollution to what the economist Edwin Mills (1978, 15) called "a problem in resource allocation." This approach can decide conflicts along the economic-environmental axis (the resource conflict), but often neglects equity. However, the market does seem to be dealing better with environmental externalities than it did ten or twenty years ago. Internalizing externalities, at the least, raises the issues of social justice and equity: e.g., who will pay for cleaning up abandoned industrial sites or compensate for the loss of fishing revenues due to oil spills. The recent establishment of a pollution credit market in the South Coast Air Quality Management District, for example, is a step in the right direction—despite criticism that the pollution credits were initially given away for free (Robinson 1993).

The role of the planner in all four of these approaches is to arrange the procedures for making decisions, not to set the substance of the actual outcomes. In some cases, the overall structure for decision-making already exists (the market and the political system). In other cases, however, the planner must help shape that structure (a mediation forum; a common language), which, done successfully, gives the process credibility. The actual environmental outcomes nevertheless remain unknowable: you don't know in advance if the environment will actually be improved. For example, environmentalists and developers heralded the Coachella Valley Fringe-Toed Lizard Habitat Conservation Plan as a model process to balance the interests of development and conservation; yet the actual outcome may not adequately protect the endangered lizard (Beatley 1992, 15-16). Similarly, although the New Jersey State Development Plan was praised for its innovative

cross-acceptance procedure, the plan itself arguably has not altered the state's urban sprawl.

The final issue that arises is whether the planner should play the role of neutral moderator, or of advocate representing a single party; this has been a longstanding debate in the field. Each strategy has its virtues.

Substantive Paths to Sustainable Development: Land Use and Design

Planners have substantive knowledge of how cities, economies, and ecologies interact, and they should put forth specific, farsighted designs that promote the sustainable city. The first area is traditional planning tools of land-use design and control. The potential for balance between economic and environmental interests exists in design itself, as in a greenbelt community (Elson 1986). Sometimes the land-use solution is simply to divide a contested parcel into two parcels: a developed and a preserved. This solution can take crude forms at times, such as the "no-net-loss" policy that endorses the dubious practice of creating wetlands. A different example, Howard's turn-of-the century Garden City (1965), can be seen as a territorially symbolic design for balance between the economy and the environment, though its explicit language was that of town-country balance. It is a design's articulated balance between the built development and the unbuilt wilderness that promises the economic environmental balance. Designs for clustered developments, higher densities, and live-work communities move toward such a balance (Rickaby 1987; Commission of the European Communities 1990; Hudson 1991; Van der Rys and Calthorpe 1991). Some dispute the inherent benefits of the compact city (Breheny 1992). A further complication is that not all economic environmental conflicts have their roots in spatial or architectural problems. As a result, ostensible solutions may be merely symbols of ecological economic balance, without actually solving the conflict.

Nevertheless, land-use planning arguably remains the most powerful tool available to planners, who should not worry too much if it does not manage all problems. The trick in resolving environmental conflicts through land-use planning is to reconcile the conflicting territorial logics of human and of natural habitats. Standard real estate development reduces open space to fragmented, static, green islands—exactly what the landscape ecologists deplore as unable to preserve biodiversity. Wildlife roam and migrate, and require large expanses of connected landscape (Hudson 1991). So both the ecological and the economic systems require the interconnectivity of a critical mass of land to be sustainable. Though we live in a three-dimensional world, land is a limited resource with essentially two dimensions (always excepting air and burrowing/mining spaces). The requirement of land's spatial interconnectivity is thus hard to achieve for both systems in one region: the continuity of one system invariably fragments continuity of the other.' So the guiding challenge for land-use planning is to achieve simultaneously spatial/territorial integrity for both systems. Furthermore, a sustainable development that aspires to social justice must also find ways to avoid the land-use manifestations of uneven development: housing segregation, unequal property-tax funding of public schools, jobs-housing imbalance, the spatial imbalance of economic opportunity, and unequal access to open space and recreation.

Substantive Paths to Sustainable Development: Bioregionalism

A comprehensive vision of sustainable land use is bioregionalism, both in its 1920s articulation by the Regional Planning Association of America (Sussman 1976) and its contemporary variation (Sale 1985; Andrus et al. 1990; Campbell 1992). The movement's essential belief is that rescaling communities and the economy according to the ecological boundaries of a physical region will encourage sustainability. The regional scale presumably stimulates greater environmental awareness: it is believed that residents of smallscale, self-sufficient regions will be aware of the causes and effects of their environmental actions, thereby reducing externalities. Regions will live within their means, and bypass the environmental problems caused by international trade and exporting pollution.

The bioregional vision certainly has its shortcomings, including the same fuzzy, utopian thinking found in other writing about sustainable

development. Its ecological determinism also puts too much faith in the regional "spatial fix": no geographic scale can, in itself, eliminate all conflict, for not all conflict is geographic. Finally, the call for regional self-reliance—a common feature of sustainable development concepts (Korten 1991, 184)—might relegate the regional economy to underdevelopment in an otherwise nationally and internationally interdependent world. Yet it can be effective to visualize sustainable regions within an interdependent world full of trade, migration, information flows and capital flows, and to know the difference between *healthy interdependence* and *parasitic dependence*, that is, a dependence on other regions' resources that is equivalent to depletion. Interdependence does not always imply an imbalance of power, nor does self-sufficiency guarantee equality. Finally, the bioregional perspective can provide a foundation for understanding conflicts among a region's interconnected economic, social and ecological networks.

Other Substantive Paths

One other approach is technological improvement, such as alternative fuels, conservation mechanisms, recycling, alternative materials, and new mass transit design. Stimulated by competition, regulation, or government subsidies, such advances reduce the consumption of natural resources per unit of production and thereby promise to ameliorate conflict over their competing uses, creating a win-win solution. However, this method is not guaranteed to serve those purposes, for gains in conservation are often cancelled out by rising demand for the final products. The overall increase in demand for gasoline despite improvements in automobile fuel efficiency is one example of how market forces can undermine technologically-achieved environmental improvements. Nor, importantly, do technological improvements guarantee fairer distribution.

The role of the planner in all these substantive strategies (land use, bioregionalism, technological improvement) is to design outcomes, with less emphasis on the means of achieving them. The environmental ramifications of the solutions are known or at least estimated, but the political means to achieve legitimacy are not. There also is a trade-off between comprehensiveness (bioregions) and short-term achievability (individual technological improvements).

Merging the Substantive and Procedural

The individual shortcomings of the approaches described above suggest that combining them can achieve both political and substantive progress in the environmental-economic crisis. The most successful solutions seem to undertake several different resolution strategies at once. For example, negotiation among developers, city planners, and land-use preservationists can produce an innovative, clustered design for a housing development, plus a per-unit fee for preserving open space. Substantive vision combined with negotiating skills thus allows planners to create win-win solutions, rather than either negotiating in a zero-sum game or preparing inert, ecotopian plans. This approach is not a distant ideal for planners: they already have, from their education and experience, both this substantive knowledge and this political savvy.

In the end, however, the planner must also deal with conflicts where one or more parties have no interest in resolution. One nonresolution tactic is the NIMBY, Not In My Back Yard, response: a crude marriage of local initiative and the age-old externalizing of pollution. This "take it elsewhere" strategy makes no overall claim to resolve conflict, though it can be a productive form of resistance rather than just irrational parochialism (Lake 1993). Nor does eco-terrorism consider balance. Instead, it replaces the defensive stance of NIMBY with offensive, confrontational, symbolic action. Resolution is also avoided out of cavalier confidence that one's own side can manage the opposition through victory, not compromise ("My side will win, so why compromise?"). Finally, an "I don't care" stance avoids the conflict altogether. Unfortunately, this ostensible escapism often masks a more pernicious NIMBY or "my side will win" hostility, just below the surface.

PLANNERS: LEADERS OR FOLLOWERS IN RESOLVING ECONOMIC-ENVIRONMENTAL CONFLICTS?

I turn finally to the question of whether planners are likely to be leaders or followers in resolving economic-environmental conflicts. One would

think that it would be natural for planners, being interdisciplinary and familiar with the three goals of balancing social equity, jobs, and environmental protection, to take the lead in resolving such conflicts. Of the conflict resolution scenarios mentioned above, those most open to planners' contributions involve the built environment and local resources: land use, soil conservation, design issues, recycling, solid waste, water treatment. Even solutions using the other approaches—environmental economic incentives, political compromise, and environmental technology innovations—that are normally undertaken at the state and federal levels could also involve planners if moved to the local or regional level.

But the planners' position at the forefront of change is not assured, especially if the lead is taken up by other professions or at the federal, not the local, level. The lively debate on whether gasoline consumption can best be reduced through higher-density land uses (Newman and Kenworthy 1989) or through energy taxes (Gordon and Richardson 1990) not only reflected an ideological battle over interpreting research results and the merits of planning intervention, but also demonstrated how local planning can be made either central or marginal to resolving environmental economic conflicts. To hold a central place in the debate about sustainable development, planners must exploit those areas of conflict where they have the greatest leverage and expertise.

Certainly planners already have experience with both the dispute over economic growth versus equity and that over economic growth versus environmental, protection. Yet the development conflict is where the real action for planners will be: seeking to resolve both environmental and economic equity issues at once. Here is where the profession can best make its unique contribution. An obvious start would be for community development planners and environmental planners to collaborate more (an alliance that an internal Environmental Protection Agency memo found explosive enough for the agency to consider defusing it) (Higgins 1994). One possible joint task is to expand current public-private partnership efforts to improve environmental health in the inner city. This urban-based effort would help planners bypass the danger of environmental elitism that besets many suburban, white-oriented environmental organizations.

If planners move in this direction, they will join the growing environmental justice movement, which emerged in the early 1980s and combined minority community organizing with environmental concerns (Higgins 1994). The movement tries to reduce environmental hazards that directly affect poor residents, who are the least able to fight pollution, be it the direct result of discriminatory siting decisions or the indirect result of housing and employment discrimination. The poor, being the least able to move away, are especially tied to place and therefore to the assistance or neglect of local planners. Understandably, local civil rights leaders have been preoccupied for so long with seeking economic opportunity and social justice that they have paid less attention to inequities in the local environment. The challenge for poor communities is now to expand their work on the property conflict to address the development conflict as well, that is, to challenge the false choice of jobs over the environment. An urban vision of sustainable development, infused with a belief in social and environmental justice, can guide these efforts.

Yet even with the rising acceptance of sustainable development, planners will not always be able, on their own, to represent and balance social, economic, and environmental interests simultaneously. The professional allegiances, skills, and bureaucracies of the profession are too constraining to allow that. Pretending at all times to be at the center of the planner's triangle will only make sustainability a hollow term. Instead, the trick will be for individual planners to identify their specific loyalties and roles in these conflicts accurately: that is, to orient themselves in the triangle. Planners will have to decide whether they want to remain outside the conflict and act as mediators, or jump into the fray and promote their own visions of ecological-economic development, sustainable or otherwise. Both planning behaviors are needed.

NOTES

1.   A curious comparison to this equity-environment economy triangle is the view of Arne Naess (1993), the   radical environmentalist who gave Deep Ecology its name in the 1970s, that the three crucial postwar political movements were the social justice, radical environmental, and peace movements, whose goals might overlap but could not be made identical.

2.   Perhaps one can explain the lack of a universal conflict in the following way: if our ideas of the economy, equity, and the environment are socially/culturally constructed, and if cultural society is local as well as global, then our ideas are locally distinct rather than universally uniform.

3.   For planners, if one is simply "planning for place," then the dispute about suburban housing versus wetlands does indeed reflect a conflict between an economic and an environmental use of a specific piece of land. But if one sees this conflict in light of "planning for people," then the decision lies between differing social groups (e.g., environmentalists, fishermen, developers) and between their competing attempts to incorporate the piece of land into their system and worldview. (This classic planning distinction between planning for people or for place begs the question: Is there a third option, "planning for nonpeople, i.e., nature"?)

4.   Schiller, using Kant's logic, recognized 200 years ago this human habit of positing the future on the past: "He thus artificially retraces his childhood in his maturity, forms for himself a *state of Nature* in idea, which is not indeed given him by experience but is the necessary result of his rationality, borrows in this ideal state an ultimate aim which he never knew in his actual state of Nature, and a choice of which he was capable, and proceeds now exactly as though he were starting afresh…."

5.   Some radical ecologists take this lost world a step further and see it not as a garden, but as wilderness (e.g., Parton 1993).

6.   I use the term diaspora to mean the involuntary dispersal of a people from their native home, driven out by a greater power (Hall 1992). The curious nature of the diaspora implied by the environmental worldview is that it is ambiguously voluntary: western positivistic thinking is the villain that we developed, but that eventually enslaved us. Then, too, diasporas invariably combine dislocations across both time and space, but the mythic "homeland" of this environmental diaspora is only from an historical era, but from no specific place.

7. The reverse may also not be automatic. David Johns (1992, 63), in advocating a broad interspecies equity, reminds us that not all forms of equity go hand-in-hand: "The nature of the linkages between various forms of domination is certainly not settled, but deep ecology may be distinct in believing that the resolution of equity issues among humans will not automatically result in an end to human destruction of the biosphere. One can envision a society without class distinctions, without patriarchy, and with cultural autonomy, that still attempts to manage the rest of nature in utilitarian fashion with resulting deterioration of the biosphere.... But the end of domination in human relations is not enough to protect the larger biotic community. Only behavior shaped by a biocentric view can do that."

8. The ambiguity of the term sustainable development is therefore not coincidental, given that reasonable people differ on which corner of the triangle is to be "sustained": a fixed level of natural resources? current environmental quality? current ecosystems? a hypothetical pre-industrial environmental state? the current material standards of living? long-term economic growth? political democracy?

9. These issues of language and translation were raised by Ngũgĩ wa Thiong'o and Stuart Hall in separate distinguished lectures at the Center for the Critical Analysis of Contemporary Cultures, Rutgers University (March 31 and April 15, 1993).

10. Conservationists have in fact installed underpasses and overpasses so that vulnerable migrating species can get around highways.

Author's Note. The author thanks Elizabeth Mueller, Susan Fainstein, Diane Massell, Jonathan Feldman, Karen Lowry, Jessica Sanchez, Harvey Jacobs, Michael Greenberg, Renée Sieber, Robert Higgins, the Project on Regional and Industrial Economics (PRIE) Seminar, and three anonymous reviewers for their comments.

REFERENCES

Altshuler, Alan. 1965. The Goals of Comprehensive Planning. *Journal of the American Institute of Planning* 31,3: 186-94.

Andrus, Van, et al., eds. 1990. *Home: A Bioregional Reader*. Philadelphia and Santa Cruz: New Catalyst/New Society.

Barrett, Gary W., and Patrick J. Bohlen. 1991. Landscape Ecology. In *Landscape Linkages and Biodiversity*, edited by Wendy E. Hudson. Washington, DC and Covelo, CA: Island Press.

Beatley, Timothy. 1992. Balancing Urban Development and Endangered Species: The Coachella Valley Habitat Conservation Plan. *Environmental Management* 16,1: 7-19.

Beatley, Timothy, and David J. Brower. 1993. Sustainability Comes to Main Street. *Planning* 59,5: 169.

Beltzer, Dena, and Cynthia Kroll. 1986. *New Jobs for the Timber Region: Economic Diversification for Northern California*. Berkeley: Institute of Governmental Studies, University of California.

Bingham, Gail. 1986. *Resolving Environmental Disputes: A Decade of Experience*. Washington, DC: The Conservation Foundation.

Bird, Elizabeth Ann R. 1987. The Social Construction of Nature: Theoretical Approaches to the History of Environmental Problems. *Environmental Review* 11,4: 255-64.

Bramwell, Anna. 1989. *Ecology in the Twentieth Century*, A History. New Haven: Yale University Press.

Breheny, M.J., ed. 1992. *Sustainable Development and Urban Form*. London: Pion.

Bryant, Bunyan, and Paul Mohai, eds. 1992. *Race and the Incidence of Environmental Hazards*. Boulder, CO: Westview Press.

Bullard, Robert D. 1990. *Dumping in Dixie: Race, Class, and Environmental Quality*. Boulder, CO: Westview Press.

Bullard, Robert D., ed. 1993. *Confronting Environmental Racism: Voices from the Grassroots*. Boston: South End Press.

Callenbach, Ernest. 1975. *Ecotopia: Tte Notebooks and Reports of William Weston*. Berkeley, CA: Banyan Tree Books.

Campbell, Scott. 1992. Integrating Economic and Environmental Planning: The Regional Perspective. Working Paper No. 43, Center for Urban Policy Research, Rutgers University.

Clawson, Marion. 1975. *Forests: For Whom and For What?* Washington, DC: Resources for the Future.

Commission of the European Communities. 1990. *Green Paper on the Urban Environment.* Brussels: EEC.

Crowfoot, James E., and Julia M. Wondolleck. 1990. *Environmental Disputes: Community Involvement in Conflict Resolution.* Washington, DC and Covelo, CA: Island Press.

Daly, Herman E. 1991. *Steady State Economics.* 2nd edition, with new essays. Washington, DC and Covelo, CA: Island Press.

Daly, Herman E., and John B. Cobb, Jr. 1989. *For the Common Good: Redirecting the Economy toward Community, the Environment, and a Sustainable Future.* Boston: Beacon Press.

Davidoff, Paul. 1965. Advocacy and Pluralism in Planning. *Journal of the American Institute of Planners* 31,4: 544-55.

Duerr, Hans Peter. 1985. *Dreamtime: Concerning the Boundary Between Wilderness and Civilization.* Oxford: Basil Blackwell.

Elson, Martin J. 1986. Green Belts: *Conflict Mediation in the Urban Fringe.* London: Heinemann.

Fainstein, Susan S., and Norman I. Fainstein. 1971. City Planning and Political Values. *Urban Affairs Quarterly* 6,3: 341-62.

Findhorn Community, The. 1975. *The Findhorn Garden: Pioneering a New Vision of Man and Nature in Cooperation.* New York: Harper and Row.

Foglesong, Richard E. 1986. *Planning the Capitalist City.* Princeton: Princeton University Press.

Friedmann, John, and Clyde Weaver. 1979. *Territory and Function: The Evolution of Regional Planning.* Berkeley and Los Angeles: University of California Press.

Goldstein, Eric A., and Mark A. Izeman. 1990. *The New York Environment Book.* Washington, DC and Covelo, CA: Island Press.

Goodland, Robert. 1990. Environmental Sustainability in Economic Development—with Emphasis on Amazonia. In *Race to Save the Tropics: Ecology and Economics for a Sustainable Future*, edited by Robert Goodland. Washington, DC and Covelo, CA: Island Press.

Gordon, Peter, and Harry Richardson. 1990. Gasoline Consumption and Cities—A Reply. *Journal of the American Planning Association.* 55,3: 342-5.

Hall, Stuart. 1992. Cultural Identity and Diaspora. *Framework* 36.

Harvey, David. 1985. *The Urbanization of Capital.* Baltimore: Johns Hopkins University Press.

Higgins, Robert R. 1994a. Race and Environmental Equity: An Overview of the Environmental Justice Issue in the Policy Process. *Polity*, forthcoming.

Higgins, Robert R. 1994b. Race, Pollution, and the Mastery of Nature. *Environmental Ethics*, forthcoming.

Hoffman, Lily. 1989. *The Politics of Knowledge: Activist Movements in Medicine and Planning.* Albany: SUNY Press.

Howard, Ebenezer. 1965. *Garden Cities of To-Morrow* (first published in 1898 as *To-Morrow: A Peaceful Path to Real Reform*). Cambridge, MA: MIT Press.

Hudson, Wendy E., ed. 1991. *Landscape Linkages and Biodiversity.* Washington, DC and Covelo, CA: Island Press.

Jacobs, Harvey. 1989. Social Equity in Agricultural Land Protection. *Landscape and Urban Planning* 17,1: 21-33.

Johns, David. 1992. The Practical Relevance of Deep Ecology. *Wild Earth* 2,2.

Korten, David C. 1991. Sustainable Development. *World Policy Journal* 9,1: 157-90.

Krumholz, Norman, et al. 1982. A Retrospective View of Equity Planning: Cleveland, 1969-1979, and Comments. *Journal of the American Planning Association* 48,2: 163-83.

Kumar, Krishan. 1991. *Utopia and Anti-Utopia in Modern Times.* Oxford and Cambridge, MA: Basil Blackwell.

Lake, Robert. 1993. Rethinking NIMBY. *Journal of the American Planning Association* 59,1: 87-93.

Lake, Robert, ed. 1987. *Resolving Locational Conflict.* New Brunswick, NJ: Center for Urban Policy Research.

Lee, Robert G., Donald R. Field, and William R. Burch, Jr., eds. 1990. *Community and Forestry: Continuities in the Sociology of Natural Resources.* Boulder, CO: Westview Press.

Lindblom, C. E. 1959. The Science of Muddling Through. *Public Administration Review* 19 (Spring): 79-88.

MacKaye, Benton. 1962 (first published in 1928 by Harcourt, Brace and Co.). *The New Exploration: A Philosophy of Regional Planning.* Urbana: University of Illinois Press.

Marcuse, Peter. 1976. Professional Ethics and Beyond: Values in Planning. *Journal of the American Institute of Planning* 42, 3: 264-74.

McPhee, John. 1989. *The Control of Nature.* New York: Farrar, Straus, Giroux.

Mills, Edwin S. 1978. *The Economics of Environmental Quality.* New York: Norton.

Naess, Arne. 1993. The Breadth and the Limits of the Deep Ecology Movement. *Wild Earth* 3,1: 74-5.

Newman, Peter W. G., and Jeffrey R. Kenworthy. 1989. Gasoline Consumption and Cities—A Comparison of U.S. Cities with a Global Survey. *Journal of the American Planning Association* 55, 1: 24-37.

Paehlke, Robert C. 1994. Environmental Values and Public Policy. In *Environmental Policy in the 1990s,* 2nd edition, edited by Norman J. Vig and Michael E. Kraft. Washington, DC: Congressional Quarterly Press.

Parton, Glenn. 1993. Why I am a Primitivist. *Wild Earth* 3,1: 12-4.

Rees, William. 1989. *Planning for Sustainable Development.* Vancouver, B.C.: UBC Centre for Human Settlements.

Reisner, Marc. 1987. *Cadillac Desert: The American West and its Disappearing Water.* New York: Penguin Books.

Rickaby, P A. 1987. Six Settlement Patterns Compared. *Environment and Planning B: Planning and Design* 14: 193-223.

Robinson, Kelly. 1993. The Regional Economic Impacts of Marketable Permit Programs: The Case of Los Angeles. In *Cost Effective Control of Urban Smog,* Federal Reserve Bank of Chicago (November): 166-88.

Ross, Andrew. 1994. *The Chicago Gangster Theory of Life: Ecology, Culture, and Society.* London and New York: Verso.

Sale, Kirkpatrick. 1985. *Dwellers in the Land: The Bioregional Vision.* San Francisco: Sierra Club Books.

Schiller, Friedrich. 1965. *On the Aesthetic Education of Man* [translated by Reginald Snell]. Originally published in 1795 as *Uber die Aesthetische Erriehung des Menschen in einer Reibe von Briefen.* New York: Friedrich Unger.

Sessions, George. 1992. Radical Environmentalism in the 90s. *Wild Earth* 2,3: 64-7.

Smith, Neil. 1990. *Uneven Development Nature, Capital and the Production of Space.* Oxford, U.K.: Blackwell.

Soja, Edward. 1989. *Postmodern Geographies: The Resurrection of Space in Critical Social Theory.* London and New York: Verso.

Susskind, Lawrence, and Jeffrey Cruikshank. 1987. Mediated Negotiation in the Public Sector: The Planner as Mediator. *Journal of Planning Education and Research* 4: 5-15.

Sussman, Carl, ed. 1976. *Planning the Fourth Migration: The Neglected Vision of the Regional Planning Association of America.* Cambridge, MA: MIT Press.

Tuason, Julie A. 1993. Economic/Environmental Conflicts in l9th-Century New York: Central Park, Adirondack State Park, and the Social Construction of Nature. Unpublished manuscript, Dept. of Geography, Rutgers University.

Turner, Frederick W. 1983. *Beyond Geography: The Western Spirit Against the Wilderness.* New Brunswick, NJ: Rutgers University Press.

Van der Ryn, Sim, and Peter Calthorpe. 1991. *Sustainable Communities: A New Design Synthesis for Cities, Suburbs and Towns.* San Francisco: Sierra Club Books.

Wiggins, Lyna. 1993. Geographic Information Systems. Lecture at the Center for Urban Policy Research, Rutgers University, April 5.

Wilson, Alexander. 1992. *The Culture of Nature: North American Landscape from Disney to the Exxon Valdez.* Cambridge, MA and Oxford, U.K.: Blackwell.

World Bank. 1989. *Striking a Balance: The Environmental Challenge of Development.* Washington, DC.

World Commission on Environment and Development (The Brundtland Commission). 1987. *Our Common Future.* Oxford: Oxford University Press.

A Theory of Urban Form

Kevin Lynch

Lloyd Rodwin

In this 1958 selection the authors examine possible analytical approaches to understanding the varied effects of different physical forms—and the location of human activities in relation to these physical forms. Lynch and Rodwin concentrate in particular on the need for analyzing urban form in relation to goal formulations and suggest techniques for studying the interrelationship.

The principal concern of the physical planner is to understand the physical environment and to help shape it to serve the community's purposes. An outsider from some other discipline would ordinarily assume that such a profession had developed some ideas concerning the diverse effects of different forms of the physical environment (not to mention the reverse effects of nonphysical forces on the environment itself). And he might be equally justified in expecting that intellectual leaders in the profession had been assiduously gathering evidence to check and reformulate these ideas so that they might better serve the practitioners in the field. A systematic consideration of the interrelations between urban forms and human objectives would seem to lie at the theoretical heart of city planning work.

But the expectation would bring a wry smile to the face of anyone familiar with the actual state of the theory of the physical environment. Where has there been any systematic evaluation of the possible range of urban forms in relation to the objectives men might have? Although most attempts at shaping or reshaping cities have been accompanied by protestations of the ends towards which the shapers are striving, yet in fact there is usually only the most nebulous connection between act and protestation. Not only are goals put in a confused or even conflicting form, but also the physical forms decided upon have very little to do with these goals. Choice of form is most often based on custom, or intuition, or on the superficial attraction of simplicity. Once constructed, forms are rarely later analyzed for their effec-tiveness in achieving the objectives originally set.

What does exist is some palliative knowledge and rules of thumb for designing street intersections, neighborhoods, and industrial areas, for separating different land uses, distinguishing different traffic functions, or controlling urban growth. Analysis of urban design is largely at the level of city parts, not of the whole. The prevailing views are static and fragmentary. When ideal models are considered, they take the form of utopias. These serve to free the imagination, but are not substitutes for adequate analysis.

There are some reasons for this unsatisfactory situation The profession is still quite young, and most of its energies are concentrated in professional practice. The men in the field are far too pre-occupied with practical problems to fashion new concepts. The profession itself developed from fields like architecture and civil engineering which have not been research minded. The professionals in the universities have taught practical courses and spent much of their time in outside practice. Research and theory under these circumstances were expendable. In the rough and tumble of daily operations, preliminary notions such as economic base studies, land use master plans, neighborhood design, or zoning and subdivision controls serve a reasonably useful function.

But the planner's situation is changing rapidly. Most of our population now lives in metropolitan regions, and the metropolitan trend is still continuing. There is not only increasing dissatisfaction with our cities, but also an awareness that it is possible to make them more delightful and more efficient places in which to live and work. Tremendous public support has been generated by organizations like The American Council to Improve Our Neighborhoods. Housing, road building, and urban renewal programs are also providing powerful instruments for the transformation of our metropolitan environment. These changing circumstances and values are interesting symptoms of the age of leisure.

The planner's tools and concepts are being subjected to a severe test by this growing demand for action. Something better than rule of thumb and shrewd improvisation is required if his services are to warrant public appreciation. In short, we need better ideas, better theory. Formulated operationally, such theory can be tested, revised, and ultimately verified. Even if initially inadequate, theories can help to develop and extend our ideas, to make them more precise, embracing, and effective. Unless planners can devise more powerful ideas for understanding and controlling the physical environment, they are not likely, and perhaps do not deserve, to be treated as more than lackeys for the performance of routine chores.

POSSIBLE ANALYTICAL APPROACHES

It is not easy to create theories "full blown." Effective theories, as a rule, are products of many men's efforts constantly reworked into a more general and more systematic form. It is also hard to locate the best starting place. In tackling the problems of the physical environment one can employ a number of approaches ranging from the descriptive to the genetic, from problem-solving to process and function analyses. All have certain advantages and disadvantages.

Description is the most obvious approach, and perhaps the weakest, standing alone. To describe the physical environment more accurately is an important aim; but since these descriptive possibilities are endless, it is difficult to be sure what is and what is not crucial or relevant. Description works best when there is enough familiarity with significance to permit vividness and terse accuracy. Too little is known about the form of the physical environment, or even about the appropriate analytical categories for analyzing these forms, to handle effective description. Description alone, moreover, yields little insight as to the underlying

mechanism of operation.

Studying how the physical environment is trans formed might be another approach. The nature of the changes can be recorded, the difficulties and directions in transition, the conditions associated with the changes, and the various social, economic, and political processes by which the alteration takes place. Often the historical, comparative, and genetic approaches are the best ways of following the dynamics of the physical environment. But there are limitations too; and these lie in the difficulty of disentangling the strategic variables which should be examined and of understanding the mechanism of change.

Another approach, now most current, is pragmatic. Each case can be considered more or less unique. The emphasis is on problem solving, or on shaping or reshaping the physical environment to eliminate specific difficulties or to achieve specific effects. Limited generalizations or rules can be formulated; but the tendency is to emphasize the uniqueness of each problem and the inapplicability of "stratospheric generalizations. " The advantage here is the "realism"; the weakness is the handicap implicit in the assumption that general ideas and theories are of almost no value as guides for dealing with specific cases or classes of cases.

A more abstract variant of problem solving might be a study of the goal-form relationship. This approach is concerned with how alternative physical arrangements facilitate or inhibit various individual and social objectives. It is an approach directly keyed to action; it would, if perfected, suggest optimum forms or a range of them, once aspirations had been clarified and decided upon. its weakness is its static nature; and its strength lies in the emphasis on the clear formulation of goals and on the probable effects of various forms of physical organization. The more that is learned about these effects, the more light will be shed on the process and perhaps even on the mechanism of change. Similarly, descriptive techniques and genetic and historical approaches might prove more effective if the emphasis were on objectives and if the evidence sought were related to the effectiveness of the environment in serving these ends. Problem solving, too, might be more systematic, less haphazard and subject to rules of thumb, if it were grounded on more solid knowledge of goal-form relationships.

This paper proposes to set forth an approach to such a theory. It will therefore necessarily deal first with the problem of analyzing urban form, secondly with the formulation of goals, and thirdly with the techniques of studying the interrelations between such forms and goals.

CRITERIA FOR ANALYTICAL CATEGORIES OF URBAN FORM

Since the work on urban form has been negligible, the first task is to decide what it is and to find ways of classifying and describing it that will turn out to be useful both for the analysis of the impact on objectives and for the practical manipulation of form. Without a clear analytical system for examining the physical form of a city, it is hardly possible to assess the effect of form or even to change it in any rational way. The seemingly elementary step of formulating an analytical system is the most crucial. Upon it hangs all the rest; and while other questions, such as the statement of objectives or the analysis of effects, may be partly the task of other disciplines, the question of city form cannot be passed off.

There are a number of criteria which a workable system must meet. First, it must apply to cities and metropolitan areas and be significant at that scale. This is simply an arbitrary definition of our particular sphere of interest, but it conceals an important distinction. There are many environmental effects which operate at larger scales (such as the influence of climate or the distribution of settlement on a national level), and even more which are effective at a smaller scale (such as the decoration of a room or the siting of a group of houses). Cities are too often regarded simply as collections of smaller environments. Most traditional design ideas (shopping centers, neighborhoods, traffic intersections, play spaces, etc.) reflect this tendency. It is usually assumed that well-designed neighborhoods, with good roads and sufficient shopping and industry, automatically produce an optimum settlement. As another example, many planners are likely to think that a beautiful city is simply the sum of a large series of small areas which are beautiful in themselves.

But this may be no more true than that a great building is a random collection of handsome rooms. Every physical whole is affected not only by the quality of its parts, but also by their total organization and arrangement. Therefore, the first criterion for form analysis is that it identify form qualities which are significant at the city or metropolitan scale, that is, which can be controlled at that scale and which also have different effects when arranged in different patterns that are describable at that scale. This criterion excludes, without in any way denying their importance, such features as intercity spacing (describable only beyond the city level) or the relation of the front door of a house to the street (which is hard to describe on the city scale unless uniform, difficult to control at that level, and whose city-wide pattern of distribution would seem to be of no importance).

The second criterion is that categories must deal solely with the physical form of the city or with the distribution of activities within it; and that these two aspects must be clearly and sharply separated. City and regional planners operate primarily upon the physical environment, although mindful of its complex social, economic, or psychological effects. They are not experts in all the planning for the future that a society engages in, but only in planning for the future development of the physical and spatial city: streets, buildings, utilities, activity distributions, spaces, and their interrelations. Although cries of dismay may greet such a reactionary and "narrow" view, the currently fashionable broader definitions lead in our judgment only to integrated, comprehensive incompetence.

A planner in this sense is aware that the final motive of his work is its human effect, and he should be well grounded, for example, in the interrelation between density and the development of children in our society. He must be quite clear that the physical or locational effects may often be the least important ones, or operate only in conjunction with other circumstances. Above all, he has to understand that the very process of achieving his proposed form, the way in which the group decides and organizes itself to carry it out, may turn out to be the most decisive effect of all. Nevertheless, he takes the spatial environment as the focus of his work, and does not pretend to be a sociologist, an economist, an administrator, or some megalomaniacal supercombination of these.

Physical form and the spatial distribution of activities in the city are partly contained in the traditional "land use" categories of the planning field. Unfortunately, these categories are analytically treacherous.

It is true that their very ambiguity is often useful in field operation, where they can be made to mean what the user wants them to mean. But for theoretical study these categories thoroughly confound two distinct spatial distributions: that of human activity, or "use" proper, and that of physical shape. The traditional concept of "single-family residential use," for example, unites a certain kind of activity: family residence (and its concomitant features of eating, sleeping, child-rearing, etc.) with a type of isolated physical structure, called a "house," which is traditionally allied with this activity. This works tolerably well in a homogeneous society, as long as people behave with docility and continue to reside in families in these houses. But if they should choose to sleep in buildings we call factories, then the whole system would be in danger. Even under present circumstances "mixed uses," or structures used now for storage, now for selling, now for religious meetings, cause trouble.

The pattern of activities and the physical pattern are often surprisingly independent of each other, and they must be separated analytically if we are to understand the effect of either. In practice, planners operate primarily upon the physical pattern, while often aiming to change the activity pattern via the physical change. Only in the negative prohibitions of some parts of the zoning ordinance do planners operate directly upon the activity pattern itself. By sharp distinction of the two, it is possible to explore how activity pattern and physical pattern interact, and which (if either) has significant effects in achieving any given objective.

This paper, however, will develop primarily the notion of the urban physical pattern, leaving the question of the activity pattern for another effort. This is done not to prejudge the relative importance of the two, but for clarity of analysis and because at present most planners operate primarily upon the physical rather than the activity patterns. The time may come, of course, when city planners may manipulate the distribution of activities in an equally direct manner. Even should this time not come and should our influence on activi-

ties continue to be indirect, it would be important to know the consequences of activity distribution.

Such nonspatial factors as the range of family income, political organization, or the social type of a city are excluded by this second criterion. This paper will also exclude factors such as the distribution of work place versus sleeping place or the quantity of flow on city streets. These latter are activity categories, properly considered under their own heading.

A third criterion of our analytical system, which adds to the problems of constructing it, is that it must be applicable to all types of urban settlement, used by any human culture. An American city, a Sumerian settlement, or a future Martian metropolis must all be capable of being subsumed under it. The categories must reach a level of generality that might be unnecessary in simply considering present-day cities in the United States. Not only is this necessary for complete analysis, but also by making our categories truly general we may uncover new form possibilities not now suspected. For example, dwelling-units-per-acre cannot be used as a basic descriptive measure, since some settlements may not have sleeping areas organized into dwelling units. (The fact of having such an organization, of course, may be part of a physical description.)

A fourth criterion is that the categories must eventually be such that they can be discovered or measured in the field, recorded, communicated, and tested. Lastly, the crucial test: all the factors chosen for analysis must have significant effect on whatever goals are important to the group using the facilities and must encompass all physical features significant for such goals.

Our aim is to uncover the important factors that influence the achievement of certain human objectives. Therefore the categories allowable here will depend upon the objectives chosen and on the threshold of effect considered significant. The categories used might shift with each new study. It is necessary, however, to set up one system of form categories so that comparisons may be made from one study to another. Therefore one must begin by considering the familiar human purposes and by guessing what physical features might be significant for those purposes. Subsequent analysis and testing will undoubtedly modify the categories based on this criterion.

In summary, the criteria for an analytic system of city form are that the categories of analysis must:

1.   Have significance at the city-wide scale, that is, be controllable and describable at that level.

2.   Involve either the physical shape or the activity distribution and not confuse the two.

3.   Apply to all urban settlements.

4.   Be capable of being recorded, communicated, and tested.

5.   Have significance for their effect on the achievement of human objectives and include all physical features that are significant.

PROPOSED ANALYTICAL SYSTEM

While several types of analytical systems might be considered, we have attempted to develop a set of abstract descriptions of the quality, quantity, or spatial distribution of various features, of types that are present in some form in all settlements. The abstractness of this system makes it difficult to conceptualize. It also divides up the total form of city, although not spatially, and it therefore raises the problem of keeping in mind the interrelations among categories. But for generality, clarity, and conciseness—and perhaps even for fresh insights—it seems to be the preferable method and will be followed in the rest of this paper.

A system for activity pattern would probably require a description of two basic aspects: Flows of men and goods, on the one hand, and, on the other, the spatial pattern of more localized activities such as exchange, recreation, sleeping, or production. Although this side of the analysis will be omitted in order to concentrate on physical pattern, a similar breakdown is feasible in the physical form description: (a) the flow *system*, excluding the flow itself; and (b) the distribution of adapted space, primarily sheltered space.

These are quite similar to the familiar duet of land use and circulation, with the content of activity removed. It may be remarked that an overtone of activity still remains, since the physical facilities are divided between those primarily used for flow, and those accommodating more fixed activities. This is a very convenient division, however, and seems to be a regular feature of all settlements.

There are many cases, of course, in which a given physical space is used both for flow and for other activities. Usually the other activities are alongside the flow, or sometimes intermixed with it, and here the space must be subdivided, or simply counted in both categories. Occasionally there may be a cyclical shift in use, as when a road is shut off for a street dance. Then, if this is important, a temporal shift of the facility from one category to another must be made. It is even conceivable that a city could contain mobile facilities in which both circulation and other activities are performed simultaneously, on the analogy of the ocean liner. But perhaps that can be faced when it happens on a scale that would be significant in a city.

Except for these difficulties, then, the division into flow system and adapted space is a convenient one. The former is usually easy to identify, and includes all the roads, paths, tubes, wires, canals, and rail lines, which are designed to facilitate the flow of people, goods, wastes, or information. The latter category, that of adapted spaces, although it seems tremendously broad, has sufficient basic similarity to be treated as an entity. It consists of all spaces that have been adapted in some way to be useful for some one or several significant noncirculatory activities.

In this country's climate, the key spaces of this nature are those enclosed and with a modified climate, that is, the city's "floor space." Elsewhere enclosure may be less important. Almost everywhere, however, the adaptation includes some modification of the ground plane, even to the cultivation of a field; and the key activities are often likely to take place in at least sheltered, if not enclosed, spaces. But in any case, the fundamental thing done to our physical environment, besides providing means for communication, is to provide spaces for various activities, to adapt the quality of those spaces, and to distribute them in an over-all pattern.

Since many of the primary adaptations of a space, such as enclosure or the provision of a smooth, level, hard, dry ground plane, are useful for many different activities, spaces are often used interchangeably. A "store-front" may be used as a store, an office, a church, a warehouse, or even a family residence. This interchangeability argues for the usefulness and necessity of generalizing adapted space into one category. Within it, one may dissect as much as necessary, dividing enclosed floor space from open space, picking out tall structuresfrom the floor space category, or hard-surfaced lots from total open space. Occasionally, purely for convenience, it may be necessary to use activity-oriented names, such as "office structure," or "parking lot." But, whenever this is done, reference is being made solely to a physical type and not to its use.

Each one of these two general categories, flow system and adapted space, could also be broken down in a parallel way for more exact analysis.

1. **Element Types:** The basic types of spaces and of flow facilities can be described qualitatively in their most significant aspects, including the extent to which the different types are differentiated in character, or to which they grade into each other.

2. **Quantity:** The quantities of houses or streets, in length or capacity or size, can then be enumerated, to give total capacity and scale.

3. **Density:** Next the intensity with which spaces or channels are packed into a given unit area can be stated; as a single quantity, if uniform, but more likely as ranges of intensity and as average and typical intensities. This is a familiar idea when applied to adapted space, particularly enclosed space, as is exemplified in the concept of the floor-area ratio. The same idea could be applied to the circulation system, calculating intensity as the flow capacity which passes in any direction through a small unit area and mapping the variation of this ratio (as in potential vehicles per hour-acre).

4. **Grain:** The extent to which these typical elements and densities are differentiated and separated in space can be defined as coarse or fine in terms of the quantity of a given type that is separated out in one cluster, and sharp or blurred in terms of the manner of separation at the boundary. Thus, house and factory building types might typically be separated in one city into large pure clusters, sharply differentiated at the edges; while in another town the grain might be very fine and the transitions generally blurred. Again, the outdoor spaces might be blurred and undifferentiated or, in the circulation system, footpaths and vehicular pavements might be sharply and coarsely separated. Essentially, this quality refers to the typical local interrelations between similar or dissimilar elements, but without reference as yet to total pattern.

5. **Focal Organization:** The spatial arrangement and interrelation of the key; points in the total environment can be examined. These might be the density peaks, the concentrations of certain dominant building types, the key open spaces, or the termini or basic intersections of the circulation systems. Consideration of the arrangement of such key points is often a shorthand method of expressing total pattern.

6. **Generalized Spatial Distribution:** This could be taken as a catchall which included the entire analysis. What is meant here is the gross pattern in two- (or three-) dimensional space, as might be expressed on a greatly simplified map or model. It would include such items as outline (or the shape of the city with reference to the noncity) and the broad pattern of zones occupied by the basic element and density types. One city might have a single central density peak; another a circle cut by pie-shaped zones of "factory" buildings; another a flow system on a rectangular grid; still another might have a uniform pattern of small interconnecting enclosed outdoor spaces surrounded by a deep belt of Free-flowing space punctuated by tall masses. Such a description would be needed whenever the notation of type, quantity, density, grain, and pattern of key points was insufficient to describe the significant total pattern.

Finally, of course, it would be necessary to interrelate the two basic categories, to show where the flow termini came with reference to the density peaks, for example, or to relate the pattern of the flow system to the general open space pattern.

The method given above is proposed as a basic system of analyzing a city's form in accordance with the original criteria. It does not try to cover all the physical features of a city, which are endless, but concentrates on those considered significant at that scale. Only systematic testing in real cities will indicate whether all the important features are included.

AN EXAMPLE OF THE ANALYTICAL SYSTEM

Since this system may be difficult to {follow in the abstract, it will perhaps clarify the proposal to use it in describing an imaginary settlement named Pone. Like any town, Pone is best described by the use of both words and precise drawings, but here words and a simple sketch must suffice.

a. Pone is made up of six types of adapted space: dirt-floored rooms, 20 by 20 feet, roofed with thatch and enclosed by adobe, each structure being free standing; concrete-floored shed spaces, 75 feet by up to 300 feet, in corrugated iron, sometimes single and sometimes in series horizontally; multistory concrete structures containing from fifty to two hundred 10 by 10 foot rooms; walled-in cultivated spaces of rectangular shape, varying from 1/2 to 3 acres; walled, stone-paved spaces pierced by paths; irregular bare dust-covered spaces which take up the remainder of the area. Pone has four types of flow channels: four-foot dirt paths, unenclosed; thirty-foot cobbled roads, enclosed in semicircular tubes of corrugated iron; an interconnecting waterproof system of four-inch pipes; and some telegraph wires.

b. There are ten thousand adobe rooms, totaling 4,000,000 square feet; fifty shed spaces, totaling 1,000,000 square feet; and four multistory structures, with 40,000 square feet of floor space. There are five thousand cultivated spaces occupying 5,000 acres, two walled and paved open spaces of 10 acres each; and the leftover dust covers 1,200 acres. There are three miles of cobbled road, each with a capacity of 400 mulecarts per hour in both directions; and 60 miles of dirt path, each able to carry 2,000 persons per hour in either direction. There are 20 miles of pipe and 2 miles of wire.

c. Density of adobe rooms varies continuously from a floor-area ratio of 0.003 to 0.3; that of the sheds from 0.3 to 0.9 (with a tendency to group at the two extremes), while the tall structures are uniformly at 5.0. Road-capacity density varies from a peak of 1,600 carts per hour-acre to a low of 20; path-capacity density varies from 4,000 persons per hour-acre to 50.

d. The three types of enclosed space are sharply differentiated and separated in plan. Cultivated spaces are mixed coarsely with the adobe rooms, while the irregular dusty areas are finely distributed throughout. Roads and paths are sharply separated and do not interconnect except at the shed spaces. Any intersections are at separated grades. They are also coarsely separated, since the roads are associated with the shed spaces.

Wires and pipes follow along paths. Pipes are dispersed, but wires serve only sheds and the multistory structures.

e. Focal points in this organization are the two rectangular paved open spaces. The first is central to the area of adobe rooms, and is the focus of converging paths. It corresponds to the peak of room density and to one of the peaks of path density. The other focal point is flanked by the multistory structures, occurs at another convergence and density peak of the path system, and is touched upon by the road system. Here occurs the major terminus and interchange point of that road system. The wire lines all pass through a central switchboard in one of the multistoried structures. The pipe lines have a single source just beyond the town boundary.

f. The settlement is round and compact, with no holes. The multistoried structures and second focus occur at the center, with the sheds occupying a narrow pie-shaped sector outwards from this. The focus of room density is slightly off center. The road system is a rectangular grid of irregular spacing, tying to the sheds, to the second focal point, and, by a single line, to the outside. The path system is irregular and capillary, but converges and intensifies at the two focal points, as noted above.

In theory (and particularly if we could use more drawings) we now know enough of the physical form to judge its value for various basic purposes at the city level of significance. One is tempted to object: Isn't this meaningless, if one knows nothing of the life that is going on within that form? Lifeless, yes, and saying little or nothing about the society of Pone (though one may make some guesses); but yet adequate, if you want to test its cost, or productive efficiency (given some productive system), or comfort (given some standards). Certainly it is the first step in trying to disentangle the effects of physical form per se, and the first step even if one wants to study the results of physical form in relation to activity pattern, or social organization, or politics. (To describe New York City in this way would, of course, take a few more pages.)

PROBLEMS OF GOAL FORMULATION

What will be the goals against which we will test this city? Unfortunately for a neat and workmanlike job, they might be almost anything. One group inhabiting Pone might find it highly satisfactory, another might find it useless or even dangerous, all depending on their several purposes and the variations in their cultures. Is there any method by which relevant goals might be set out and related to these environmental shapes? Unhappily for the reader, we now find that we must digress to consider the problems of setting up a goal system. Only after this is done will it be possible to return to the implications of the forms themselves.

The possible goals must first be considered. This may cause some confusion, since such a collection is not likely to be consistent or unified. It must be distinguished from a goal *system*, i.e., a set of selected objectives which are coherent, unified, and capable of guiding action. Construction of such a system is the desirable result of considering goal possibilities, but it can only be brought to completion by a particular group in a particular situation. Thus the possible range of goals might include both the preservation of individual life at all costs and also the maximization of human sacrifice. A particular system would have to choose, or, more probably, settle upon some intermediate stand; and this stand should be related to its other objectives.

Probably the most confusing aspect of this question is not the infinite number of goal possibilities, but rather their range of generality. Some objectives, such as "goodness," may seem to regulate almost every action, but to do so in such a vague and generalized way as to be of little help in choice. Others, such as the goal of having all children say "please" when asking for things at the table, are very clear in their implications for action,

but quite limited in their application and their consequences. These two goals are interconnected only by a long chain of explanations, situations, and interactions. It is difficult to be sure that one follows from the other and hard to weight their relative importance in relation to other goals.

To avoid such confusions, it is important that any one goal system should contain only objectives which are at approximately the same level of generality. We may smile when someone admonishes a child to "be good, and keep your fingernails clean!" But we are also exhorted to build city additions that will be good places to live in and will keep valuations high. In many cases, of course, there may be no real confusion, as when the second point is the true objective and the first is only a verbal blind.

Similarly, it is meaningless to consider beauty and fresh paint as alternative objectives: they do not operate at the same level. Each objective may in its turn be looked upon as a means of attaining some objective higher up the scale of generality. Shouting at recruits may be considered a means of overawing them, with the goal of developing obedience, which is itself directed to the building of a disciplined military force, having as its objective the winning of wars, which may be thought of as a way to gain security. When constructing a rational system for guidance in any particular situation, what must be built up is a connected hierarchy of goals, considering possible alternatives only at the same level of generality and checking lower levels for their relevance to upper levels of the system.

The more general objectives have the advantage of relative stability: they are applicable to more situations for larger groups over longer spans of time. They have the corresponding disadvantages of lack of precision and difficulty of application in any specific problem. Very often, in goal systems of real life, such general objectives may have very little connection with objectives farther down the list, being, rather, top-level show pieces, or covers for hidden motives. The operating goals are then the intermediate ones, those which actually regulate action. To develop a rational set of goals, however, the connection must be sought out, or the motives that are the true generalized goals must be revealed. The aim is to produce a system that is as coherent as possible, although this again is rare in reality.

Since reference back to very general goals is a painful one intellectually, most actions must be guided by intermediate, more concrete, objectives, which can be referred to more quickly. Only the most serious steps warrant reference to fundamentals, while everyday decisions depend on customs and precepts that are actually low-level goals. City building is important enough to be referred back to more than simple precepts; but even here decisions cannot always be brought up to the highest level of generality, since the analysis is so complex. Therefore reliance must be placed upon goals of an intermediate level. But these intermediate goals should be periodically checked for their relevance to more general objectives and to the changing situation, as well as for consistency among themselves.

It is a besetting sin to "freeze" upon rather specific goals and thus risk action irrelevant to a new situation. If it is observed, for example, that growing cities have been prosperous ones, attention may focus upon increase of population size as an objective. Actions will be directed toward stimulating growth, regardless of any consequences of dislocation, instability, or cost. Industries may be brought in which will depress the wage level and the general prosperity, because no one has stopped to examine the objectives that lie behind the growth objective, i.e., to ask the simple question: "Why do we want to grow?" Because of this continuous tendency to fix upon goals at too specific a level, it is a wise habit to challenge current goals by always pushing them back at least one step up the ladder of generality.

CRITERIA FOR THE CHOICE OF GOALS

What will be the criteria for the choice of goals in our case? If they are rational, they should be internally consistent. There should, moreover, be some possibility of moving toward their realization, now or in the future. Otherwise they are simply frustrating. To have operational meaning, they must be capable of being contradicted, thus permitting a real choice. And finally, the goals must be relevant to city form, since there are many human objectives which are little affected by environmental shape. Therefore, given one's basic values and the values of the culture in which one is operating, it is necessary to develop a set of useful intermediate objectives which are consistent, possible, operational, and relevant to the task in hand.

Devising such objectives is difficult; and it is not made easier by the fact that a planner is an individual responsible for actions or recommendations in an environment used by large numbers of people. He is not concerned simply with his own values, nor even with their interaction with the values of another individual with whom he can communicate, which is the situation of the architect with a single client. The planner's client is a large group, a difficult client to talk to, often incoherent, and usually in some conflict with itself.

To some extent the planner can rely on democratic processes to establish group objectives; to some extent he must use sociological techniques to uncover them. Often he is forced, or thinks he is forced, to rely upon his own intuition as to group objectives—a most hazardous method, since the planner is himself likely to be a member of a rather small class of that society. In any event, he must make every effort to understand his own values, as well as to uncover and clarify the goals of the society he is working for.

His troubles do not stop here. Even if he had perfect knowledge of group goals, and they proved to form a completely consistent system, he is still faced with the issue of relating them to his own personal values. He cannot be solely the handmaiden of the group, but has some responsibility (should he differ) to urge upon them a modification of their goal system or to acquaint them with new alternatives. He has a complicated role of leader and follower combined and must resolve this for himself. This is true of many other professional groups.

And should the public goals, as is most likely, prove to be internally inconsistent or in transition, then the planner must mediate these conflicts and changes. He must find the means of striking a balance and the way of preparing for the new value to come without destroying the old value still present.

But to all these everyday woes we can at the moment simply shrug our theoretical shoulders. Give us a consistent and operational system of objectives, a system possible and relevant and organized properly by levels, and we will show you the environmental forms to achieve these objectives. If your goals are superficial or short-sighted, so much the worse. That is your concern, not ours.

In western culture, general and accepted goals would probably cluster around the worth of the individual human being, around the idea of man as the measure, with an emphasis on future results and yet on the importance of process as well as final achievement. Basic values for the individual might include such things as:

a. Health, equilibrium, survival, continuity, adaptability.

b. Coherence, meaning, response.

c. Development, growth, stimulus, choice, freedom.

d. Participation, active use of powers, efficiency, skill, control.

e. Pleasure, comfort.

Upon the basis of such generalities, one can make for himself (or for his group) a set of broad goals. One way of conveniently organizing such goals may be the following:

a. Regarding the relation of men and objects: Those goals

   1. having to do with direct functioning: biological or technical goals, such as the achievement of an environment which sustains and prolongs life;

   2. having to do with sensuous interactions: psychological or esthetic goals, such as the creation of an environment which is meaningful to the inhabitant.

b. Regarding the relation of men and men: Those goals

   1. having to do with interpersonal relations: sociological and psychological goals, such as constructing surroundings which maximize interpersonal communications;

   2. or having to do with group functioning: social goals such as survival and continuity of the group.

It is important to see that a mere listing of objectives is insufficient even at this generalized level, if a policy of relative emphasis is not also included. Any real action may work for one goal and against the other, or be more or less helpful in relation to another action. Yet the choice must be made. Therefore a statement of objectives must be accompanied by a statement of relative importance: that, for example, group survival is valued

above individual survival, although both are valued. More precisely, it will have to be said that, in such-and-such a circumstance, group survival is more valued.

Since attainment of human objectives almost always entails the use of scarce resources, the next level of objectives are the economic. In their most general form, they can be described as the attainment of ends with the maximum economy of means, while keeping or making the resource level as high as possible. In all these general objectives, moreover, there is an intertwining of means and ends, of process and final achievement. Particularly where "final" achievement may be as long delayed or even as illusory, as it is in city development, the attainment of objectives may be affected more by the process itself than by the final form that is being sought.

But the goal system at this level, however consistent and relevant, is still too general for effective application to city-form decisions. Moving down to lower levels for specific guidance, how can one define a "meaningful environment," for example, or the limits within which interpersonal communication is to be maximized?

It would be possible to move down the ladder step by step, ending with some such rule as "all buildings should by their exterior form reveal to any adult inhabitant of average education and intelligence their principal internal use," or even " ....to accomplish this, the following building types shall have the following shapes...." The latter is undoubtedly an example of "misplaced concreteness"; but even the former poses problems in relating it back to the general descriptive categories of city form that were developed above. How does the "meaningfulness" of structure relate to density, or grain, or focal organization? In coming down the ladder of specificity we may find we have slipped away from relevance to form at the city scale, or have developed precepts which have multiple and complex effects on the various categories of city form.

Since the formulation of specific objectives is unavoidable, it would be preferable that they be reorganized by being grouped in terms of their relevance to the descriptive categories. Such organization is simply a tactical move, but a crucial one. It involves running through the list of descriptive categories of city form, and choosing (by intuition or prior experience) those general objectives that seem most relevant to that aspect of form.

For example, the following general goals are probably affected in some important way by the "grain" of adapted spaces in an urban settlement:

a. Optimum interpersonal communication.

b. Maximum choice of environment for the individual.

c. Maximum individual freedom in construction.

d. Optimum esthetic stimulus.

e. Maximum productive efficiency.

f. Maximum productive flexibility.

g. Minimum first cost.

h. Minimum operating cost.

By thus selecting and grouping our general goals, a hypothesis is being asserted, that, for example, "the grain of city facilities has significant (if unknown) effect on the first cost of constructing them." Such hypotheses may prove untrue, in which case the group of goals must be revised or, equally likely, it may indicate that some other objective not originally listed is also significantly affected and must be added to the list.

One objective may be significantly affected by more than one form quality and will thus appear in more than one group. Another objective may be little influenced by any one quality alone, but rather by the nature of the combination of two or more, such as the total effect of grain and density together. This is a separate point, to which we will later return.

The critical nature of the form categories previously selected now becomes apparent, since they impose their pattern upon the entire investigation. If they are not in themselves highly significant, or if they are inconsistent or poorly organized, the work must be redone. Nevertheless, by bringing in the relation to form thus early in our consideration of objectives, a much more economical and systematic attack is possible. The objectives not only contain hypotheses of relevancy, but are really turning into action questions, for example: "What grain of spaces gives a minimum first cost?"

It must be made clear that, if physical forms are considered in isolation, such action questions are not answerable. No relation between grain and first cost can be established until a construction process is postulated. Or, for another example, the impact of the grain of spaces on interpersonal communication depends also on the activity occupying those spaces. Nevertheless, once given a construction process or an activity distribution which is held constant during the test, then the differential impact of various grain alternatives can be analyzed. Thus, in a given activity context, the results of various physical patterns might be studied. Often, a principal result of a given physical pattern may occur via the manner in which it changes an activity distribution, given an assumption as to a fixed association between certain forms and certain activities.

The same limitations apply to the study of activity patterns in isolation, which are meaningless without reference to the facilities available for communication, insulation, and so on. Eventually, there would be a more complex level of analysis, in which both activity distribution and form might be allowed to vary simultaneously. Even here, however, a general cultural context is still required.

Once the general goals are arranged in terms of the type, quantity, density, grain, focal organization, and pattern of the adapted spaces and the flow system (and in the process just those objectives have been selected out which may be most critically affected by these qualities), and once a general context of culture and activity has been chosen, a more concrete level of analysis is possible. The level should be specific enough to say that "city A is closer to this objective than city B." The meaning of terms must be put in an operational, and often quantitative, way. For example, "what density of spaces allows a reasonable journey from home to work" might become: "what density (or densities) allows 75 per cent of the population to be within 30 minutes' time distance of their place of work, providing no more than 10 per cent are less than 5 minutes away from their work place?" Different city models could now be tested by this criterion.

Not all goals could be put in this quantitative form, of course. But they would at least have a testable wording, such as: "what is the density at which there is maximum opportunity for interpersonal communication within the local group, without destroying the ability of the individual to achieve privacy when desired?" Such formulations are likely to contain the words maximum, or minimum, or optimum.

The caution must be repeated that, while satisfyingly specific, such goals require continuous rechecking for relevance to the general goals and the changing situation. The home-to-work objective, for example, is simply a definition of the original word "reasonable." Next year, or in India, it might be different.

GOAL FORM INTERACTION

Having established an analytical system of urban form and groups of objectives cast in relevant operational terms, the next problem we have is the interaction of form with goal. One might begin either by considering the grain of adapted space and the objectives significantly related to it, or, alternatively, a fundamental objective and the form aspects related to it. If one of the goals is minimum first cost, for example, are the shed spaces of Pone cheaper to build when concentrated as they are in a coarse grain than if they were dispersed throughout the adobe spaces in a fine grain? Or, perhaps, does the grain of dispersion make no difference whatever? Undoubtedly, the effect of grain on cost may differ for different types of space. For example, while the grain of shed spaces was critical because they were built by mass site fabrication methods, the grain of adobe spaces might be indifferent, since they were put up singly by hand in any case. Or it might be found that dispersion of the multistory spaces among the shed spaces did not affect their cost, but dispersion among the adobe spaces did. Only in certain cases could generalizations as to grain, per se, be made. More often, the grain of a certain type of adapted space would have to be the subject of a conclusion.

The grain of the shed spaces may also affect productive efficiency. To test this, one may assume a type of activity, a given productive system, similar to the assumption of construction methods to test the cost implications. To do so does not mean that activity distribution slips in by the back door; we are still testing the impact of one or another physical quality upon the functioning of an activity which is held constant during the test. That is, given a factory system of production, which operates more easily in the wide-span shed spaces of Pone than anywhere else in the city, is that productive system more efficient if all the sheds are close together or if they are dispersed?

In this manner, the goal implications of grain could be analyzed, testing each for relevance and effect, and ending by a search to see if significant goals have been left out. If this system is successful, one should be able to say that, given such-and-such a culture, this particular grain gives best results if your goal system has these particular elements and emphases, and another grain would be better for another system. Alternatively, the objective of minimum first cost could be explored throughout all its ramifications, resulting in a statement that, given a certain culture, this particular total urban form can be constructed at a minimum first cost.

These are final stage results, difficult to attain. Partial, and still useful, conclusions are more likely, such as: if this is the contemporary American society, and if the *only* goal is productive efficiency then here is the grain to use for this type of adapted space (or: there are several equally good distributions or, perhaps, the grain is of no consequence). Of course, the answer is likely to be still more qualified. One may have to add that this grain is best in a city of small size, another in the larger city; or that optimum grain cannot be separated from density or pattern.

One further note must be made. The *process* of achieving goals or of reshaping form is, in cities, as important as the long-range goal or form. Building a new city of a specific shape may have vital side-effects on the administrative acts and organization required; sequence of development has as much to do with cost as final density. Moreover, one may have important goals which have to do mainly with the process itself, for example, that development decisions be arrived at democratically, or that people be allowed to participate in planning their dwellings, regardless of the final result.

The goal-form method, then, consists in ordering form analysis and definition of objectives so that their interrelation can be considered in a systematic and rational manner. It helps to pose the problem. There it blesses the investigator, and drops him in the mud. It has no further bearing on the analysis of any given interrelation. Each such analysis is likely to be unique and to demand its own method of solution. One might be amenable to mathematical methods; another, to sociological tools; a third, solvable only by subjective analysis; a fourth, by full-scale field tests. There is no guarantee, of course, that the fifth may be solvable at all. What is proposed is merely a way of attacking the central problems of cities in a methodical way.

This "merely," however, may in time open up new possibilities, simply because the problems are more precisely put. If the important physical properties of cities can be clearly defined, and if an operational standard can be set, such as one regarding commuting times, we may be able to study the implications of complex forms by means of new mathematical methods or with such aids as the high-speed computers.

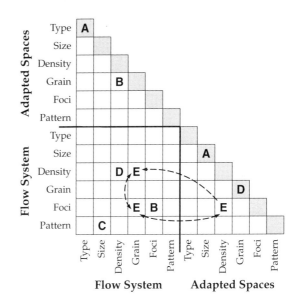

COMPLEX FORM AND GOAL RELATIONSHIPS

If form qualities and goals could be analyzed and disposed of one by one, then in time a complete structure could be built with relative ease. Unfortunately (and this is perhaps the most vulnerable point of the system) physical patterns and goals have a habit of complex interaction. There is not one goal, but many; and the presence of other goals influences the force of the original one. The city forms, which we have herded into arbitrary categories to make our analysis possible, in truth make one pattern. It is not always easy to discuss the impact of grain without specifying density or size. The consequences of the distribution of adapted spaces rests partly on the flow system allied with it.

Thus there are frequently situations where a given goal may not only be influenced by more than one form aspect, but also may at times be affected by such an intimate interaction of aspects that there is no separable cause. A convenient system of notation for such a situation might be as follows, imagining that we are concerned with five goals, A, B, C, D, and E, which have the following relationships with form:

Achievement of goal is influenced by:

    A (1) space type; (2) flow system size.

    B (1) space, density, and grain combined; (2) focal organization of space and flow system combined.

    C (1) space, size, and flow system pattern combined.

    D (1) grain of flow system; (2) density of space and flow system combined.

    E (1) grain of space, and density and focal organization of flow system all combined.

Here the appearance of a goal in the top diagonal (shaded squares) indicates that it relates to a single form quality at a time. Elsewhere its appearance shows that it is influenced by a pair of form qualities that must be considered together. One goal is shown (E) which is effected by an inseparable combination of three, and must therefore be shown as a connected triangle. If a three-dimensional notation system were used, it could occupy a single solid cube. Higher interactions would require more complicated notations.

This figure would change, of course, as the system of descriptive categories was modified. It is simply a convenient way of reminding ourselves what must be taken into account in studying goal-form interaction. It indicates, incidentally, that in this particular case two aspects of form (space pattern and flow system type) happen to be the ones that have no bearing on any goal. All the rest are involved in one way or another.

Probably these analytical methods could handle situations where pairs of qualities were involved. Triads of qualities become much more difficult, and many more are likely to make analysis impossible. Some questions may therefore be answerable, and others may resist our best efforts.

To complete the example, consider the city of Pone again. The people of Pone are simple-minded; they have few wants. They have only three goals relevant to city form:

    1. Maximum individual privacy, when not producing.

2. Maximum defensibility in war.

3. Maximum productive efficiency.

In case of conflict, goal 2 takes precedence, then goal 3. The Ponians are a simple and a rather grim people.

These goals are set in the following situation: the town produces various kinds of simple consumer goods, which it exports to the surrounding countryside in return for raw materials This production is most easily carried out in the shed spaces, directed by control functions in the multistory spaces. But the town also produces a large part of its food supply in the cultivated spaces within its limits. Other life functions, beyond production and distribution, are traditionally carried out in the adobe rooms or in the paved open spaces. Wars are fought by ground action, with simple shortrange weapons, and may occur suddenly.

The following matrix indicates the probable relevancy of various form aspects to the three goals:

That is, objective 1 is affected by the type, density, and grain of adapted spaces, all acting singly. Objective 2 is influenced by the pattern of spaces and by the density, grain and focal organization of the flow system, acting singly. It is also the prey of the combined action of the size and density of the adapted spaces. This is true because, although the larger the city the greater the defensive army that could be raised for war and the higher the density the more compact the defensive perimeter, yet in combination they may work in another way. A large, very dense city might quickly succumb to

food shortages, owing to the lack of adequate internal cultivated spaces. Therefore the optimum solution is likely to be a function of size in relation to density. Finally, objective 3 is related to the type and grain of spaces and the type and density of the flow system, acting singly, plus the combined effect of the spatial and flow-system focal organizations. The matrix indicates that the size and pattern of the flow system are meaningless to the Ponians.

The analysis on all these separate points could then be carried through and the total balance struck, comparing the actual form of Pone with any other forms within the reach of this people. One might come out with some such conclusion as: given these goals, the actual form is probably the optimum available, with the following modifications:

a. For the privacy objective, a new type of space should be substituted for the single-room adobe space.

b. For the defense objective, a better balance of size and density could be struck, particularly if the unused dust spaces were eliminated. Furthermore, if the capacity density of the flow system were stepped up and the system dispersed at finer grain throughout the settlement, then defense would be simplified.

c. For the production objective, an increase in flow capacity-density would also facilitate efficiency.

As was stated at the beginning, the high planners of Pone would also have gone on to a study of the consequences of the activity distribution in the city, and they would have ended with a higher level study of the interrelation of activity and form. But probably the reader has had enough.

EVALUATION

Application of method to a modern metropolis would obviously be far more complicated and, necessarily, more fragmentary. But the basic technique should still be applicable, though it would call for descriptions at a larger scale and goals less precisely formulated. Since the whole technique is analytical, a study of isolated parts, it will tend to give first approximations, rather coarse conclusions bristling with "ifs." It would nevertheless be the elementary knowledge upon which much more refined, and in particular much more fluid and integrated methods could be constructed.

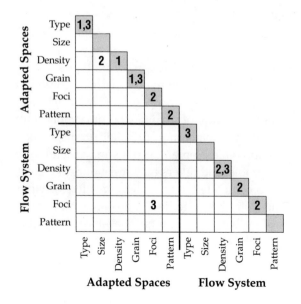

To the student of the physical environment, perhaps the most attractive features of goal-form studies are the new possibilities for research and theory. Regardless of the inadequacy of our present formulations there is a need to test and explore both the range and appropriateness of form categories. Hardly anything is known of how they interact and what the possibilities are for substitution. And instead of fragmentary notions, such as the differentiation of traffic networks, the separation or mixing of land uses, and the organization of neighborhood units, there is the prospect of a general theory of urban form for the city as a whole. If some measure of success is achieved in developing such a general theory, it should not prove too difficult to fit these miscellaneous doctrines into this broader framework, especially since these doctrines purport to modify city form in line with some more or less definite objectives.

Goal-form studies also suggest a new lead for examining city planning history. Instead of the traditional historical survey of civic design accomplishments, the adequacy of urban forms might be examined in the light of some of the major goals of different cultures. The same approach might be applied with profit to current history. Significant contemporary plans for communities might be studied to see how adequately the goals are formulated and how explicitly they are related to the physical forms proposed.

The essence of progress for most disciplines lies in finding ways of systematizing as well as extending present knowledge. Goal-form studies offer a springboard for city and regional planning to achieve this extension and synthesis.

But aside from the elegance or logic of the theoretical framework, such an analytical system may find its ultimate usefulness in providing the raw material for planning decisions. Eventually it should tell the planner: "If your only aim is productive efficiency, and if other elements are like this, and if your society does not change, then this form is the best one yet found to do the job." This is the underpinning for what in part must remain a complex art, an art yet beyond the determinability of scientific knowledge in three ways. First, in that the more complex interactions are most likely to elude rigorous theory and depend on personal judgment. Second, because the method is indifferent to the choice of values, and the choice or clarification of objectives is a fundamental part of the art of planning. And third, because the method can do no more than test form alternatives previously proposed. The creative task of imagining new form possibilities, as in all other realms of art and science, lies beyond it, although the analytical system may be suggestive in this work.

The Need for Concentration

Jane Jacobs

Jacobs's writings challenge the anti-urban, American preference for low-density development and extol the economic, social, and cultural virtues of crowded, dense, and diverse cities. In *The Death and Life of Great American Cities*, she describes her own work as no less than an "attack" on conventional planning and building practices: "My attack is not based on quibbles about rebuilding methods or hair-splitting about fashions in design. It is an attack, rather, on the principles and aims that have shaped modern, orthodox city planning and rebuilding." In this section of her chapter, "The Need for Concentration," she disputes the belief that high density correlates with "trouble" and overcrowding, and distinguishes between dense concentrations of dwellings and dwellings that are overcrowded.

CONDITION 4: *The district must have a sufficiently dense concentration of people, for whatever purpose they may be there. This includes people there because of residence.*

For centuries, probably everyone who has thought about cities at all has noticed that there seems to be some connection between the concentration of people and, the specialties they can support. Samuel Johnson, for one, remarked on this relationship back in 1785. "Men, thinly scattered," he said to Boswell, "make a shift but a bad shift, without many things… It is being concentrated which produces convenience."

Observers are forever rediscovering this relationship in new times and places. Thus in 1959, John H. Denton, a professor of business at the University of Arizona, after studying American suburbs and British "new towns" came to the conclusion that such places must rely on ready access to a city for protection of their cultural opportunities. "He based his findings," reported the *New York Times*, "on the lack of a sufficient density of population to support cultural facilities. Mr. Denton… said that decentralization produced such a thin population spread that the only effective economic demand that could exist in suburbs was that of the majority. The only goods and cultural activities available will be those that the majority requires, he observed," and so on.

Both Johnson and Professor Denton were speaking about the economic effects of large numbers of people, but not numbers loosely added up indefinitely from thinly spread populations. They were making the point that it seems to matter greatly how thinly or how thickly people are concentrated. They were comparing the effects of what we call high and low densities.

This relationship of concentration—or high density—to conveniences and to other kinds of diversity is generally well understood as it applies to downtowns. Everyone is aware that tremendous numbers of people concentrate in city downtowns and that, if they did not, there would be no downtown to amount to anything—certainly not one with much downtown diversity.

But this relationship between concentration and diversity is very little considered when it comes to city districts where residence is a chief use. Yet dwellings form a large part of most city districts. The people who live in a district also form a large share, usually, of the people who use the streets, the parks and the enterprises of the place. Without help from the concentration of the people who live there, there can be little convenience or diversity where people live, and where they require it.

To be sure, the dwellings of a district (like any other use of the land) need to be supplemented by other primary uses so people on the streets will be well spread through the hours of the day, for economic reasons. These other uses (work, entertainment, or whatever) must make intensive use of city land if they are to contribute effectively to concentration. If they simply take up physical room and involve few people, they will do little or nothing for diversity or liveliness. I think it is hardly necessary to belabor that point.

This same point is just as important, however, about dwellings. City dwellings have to be intensive in their use of the land too, for reasons that go much deeper than cost of land. On the other hand, this does not mean that everyone can or should be put into elevator apartment houses to live—or into any other one or two types of dwellings. That kind of solution kills diversity by obstructing it from another direction.

Dwelling densities are so important for most city districts, and for their future development, and are so little considered as factors in vitality, that I shall devote this chapter to that aspect of city concentration.

High dwelling densities have a bad name in orthodox planning and housing theory. They are supposed to lead to every kind of difficulty and failure.

But in our cities, at least, this supposed correlation between high densities and trouble, or high densities and slums, is simply incorrect, as anyone who troubles to look at real cities can see. Here are a few illustrations:

In San Francisco, the district of highest dwelling densities—and highest coverage of residential land with buildings too—is North Beach-Telegraph Hill. This is a popular district that has spontaneously and steadily unslummed itself in the years following the Depression and the Second World War. San Francisco's chief slum problem, on the other hand, is a district called the Western Addition, a place that has steadily declined and is now being extensively cleared. The Western Addition (which at one time, when it was new, was a good address) has a dwelling-unit density considerably lower than North Beach-Telegraph Hill's, and, for that matter, lower than the still fashionable Russian Hill's and Nob Hill's.

In Philadelphia, Rittenhouse Square is the only district that has been spontaneously upgrading and extending its edges, and is the only inner city area that has not been designated for either renewal or clearance. It has the highest dwelling density in Philadelphia. The North Philadelphia slums currently display some of the city's most severe social problems. They have dwelling densities averaging at most half those of Rittenhouse Square. Vast territories of additional decay and social disorder in Philadelphia have dwelling densities less than half those of Rittenhouse Square.

In Brooklyn, New York, the most generally admired, popular and upgrading neighborhood is Brooklyn Heights; it has much the highest density of dwellings in Brooklyn. Tremendous expanses of failed or decaying Brooklyn gray area have densities half those of Brooklyn Heights or less.

In Manhattan, the most fashionable pocket of the midtown East Side, and the most fashionable pocket of Greenwich Village have dwelling densities in the same high range as the heart of Brooklyn Heights. But an interesting difference can be observed. In Manhattan, very popular areas, characterized by high degrees of vitality and diversity, surround these most fashionable pockets. In these surrounding popular areas, dwelling densities go still higher. In Brooklyn Heights, on the other hand, the fashionable pocket is surrounded by neighborhoods where dwelling unit densities drop off; vitality and popularity drop off too.

In Boston, the North End has unslummed itself and is one of the city's healthiest areas. It has much the highest dwelling densities in Boston. The Roxbury district, which has been steadily declining for a generation, has a dwelling density about a ninth that of the North End's.[1]

The overcrowded slums of planning literature are teeming areas with a high density of dwellings. The overcrowded slums of American real life are, more and more typically, dull areas with a low density of dwellings. In Oakland, California, the worst and most extensive slum problem is an area of some two hundred blocks of detached, one- and two-family houses which can hardly be called dense enough to qualify as real city densities at all. Cleveland's worst slum prob-

lem is a square mile of much the same thing. Detroit is largely composed, today, of seemingly endless square miles of low-density failure. The East Bronx of New York, which might almost stand as a symbol of the gray belts that have become the despair of cities, has low densities for New York; in most parts of the East Bronx, densities are well below the whole city averages. (New York's average dwelling density is 55 units per net residential acre.)

However, it will not do to jump to the conclusion that all areas of high dwelling density in cities do well. They do not, and to assume that this is "the" answer would be to oversimplify outrageously. For instance, Chelsea, much of the badly failed uptown West Side, and much of Harlem, all in Manhattan, have dwelling densities in the same high ranges as those of Greenwich Village, Yorkville and the midtown East Side. Once-ultra-fashionable Riverside Drive, plagued by trouble today, has still higher dwelling densities.

We cannot understand the effects of high and low densities if we assume that the relationship between concentrations of people and production of diversity is a simple, straight mathematical affair. The results of this relationship (which Dr. Johnson and Professor Denton both spoke of in its simple, crude form), are drastically influenced by other factors too.

No concentration of residents, however high it may be, is "sufficient" if diversity is suppressed or thwarted by other insufficiencies. As an extreme example, no concentration of residence, however high, is "sufficient" to generate diversity in regimented projects, because diversity has been regimented out in any case. And much the same effects, for different reasons, can occur in unplanned city neighborhoods, where the buildings are too standardized or the blocks are too long, or there is no mixture of other primary uses besides dwellings.

However, it still remains that dense concentrations of people are *one* of the necessary conditions for flourishing city diversity. And it still follows that in districts where people live, this means there must be a dense concentration of their dwellings on the land preempted for dwellings. The other factors that influence how much diversity is generated, and where, will have nothing much to influence if enough people are not there.

One reason why low city densities conventionally have a good name, unjustified by the facts, and why high city densities have a bad name, equally unjustified, is that high densities of dwellings and overcrowding of dwellings are often confused. High densities mean large numbers of dwellings per acre of land. Overcrowding means too many people in a dwelling for the number of rooms it contains. The census definition of overcrowding is 1.5 persons per room or more. It has nothing to do with the number of dwellings on the land, just as in real life high densities have nothing to do with overcrowding.

This confusion between high densities and overcrowding, which I will go into briefly because it so much interferes with understanding the role of densities, is another of the obfuscations we have inherited from Garden City planning.

NOTE

1. Here are the density figures for these examples. They are given in numbers of dwelling units per net acre of residential land. When two figures are given, they represent a range into which the average or averages for the place concerned fall (which is the way this data is often tabulated or mapped). In San Francisco: North Beach-Telegraph Hill, 80-140, about the same as Russian Hill and Nob Hill, but the buildings cover more of the residential ground in North Beach-Telegraph Hill; the Western Addition, 55-60. In Philadelphia: Rittenhouse Square. 80-100; North Philadelphia slums, about 40; row-house neighborhoods in trouble, typically 30-45. In Brooklyn: Brooklyn Heights, 125-174 at heart and 75-124 in most of the remainder; drop-offs to 45-74 beyond; as examples of Brooklyn areas in decline or trouble, Bedford-Stuyvesant, about half at 75-124 and half at 45-74; Red Hook, mostly 45-74; some Brooklyn spots in decay as low as 15-24. In Manhattan: most fashionable pocket of midtown East Side, 125-174, rising in Yorkville to 175-254; Greenwich Village, most fashionable pocket, 124-174, rising to 175-254 for most of remainder with pocket containing stable, old, unslummed Italian community rising above 255. In Boston, North End, 275; Roxbury, 21-40.

For Boston and New York, these figures are from planning commission measurements and tabulations; for San Francisco and Philadelphia they are estimates by planning or redevelopment staff members.

Although all cities make a fetish of minute density analysis in project planning, surprisingly few have much accurate data on non-project densities. (One planning director told me he could see no reason for studying them except as light on how big the relocation problem would be if they were knocked down!) No city that I know of has studied just what localized, building-by-building variations in density go into the makeup of density averages in successful and popular neighborhoods." It's too hard to generalize about districts like that," complained a planning director when I asked him about specific density variations, at small scale, in one of his city's most successful districts. It is hard or impossible, to generalize about such districts precisely because they are, themselves, so little "generalized" or standardized in their groupings. This very capriciousness and diversity of the components is one of the most important, and most ignored, facts about density averages in successful districts.

SUGGESTED READINGS FOR PART V

Alexander, Christopher. *A New Theory of Urban Design*. New York: Oxford University Press. 1987.

Bacon, Edmund N. *Design of Cities*. New York: Penguin. 1976.

Barnett, Jonathon. *An Introduction to Urban Design*. New York: Harper & Row. 1982.

Brown, Lester, Christopher Flavin, and Sandra Postel. *Saving the Planet: How to Shape an Environmentally Sustainable Global Economy*. New York: Norton. 1991.

Cullen, Gordon. *Townscape*. New York: Reinhold. 1961.

Gratz, Roberta Brandes. The Living City: *How America's Cities Are Being Revitalized by Thinking Big in a Small Way*. New York: John Wiley & Sons, Inc. 1995.

Gratz, Roberta Brandes and Norman Mintz. *Cities Back From the Edge: New Life for Downtown.* New York: John Wiley & Sons, Inc. 2000.

Hardin, Warren. *Tragedy of the Commons.* Monticello, IL: Vance Biographies.

Hiss, Tony. *The Experience of Place.* New York: Random House, Inc. 1990.

Le Corbusier. *The City of Tomorrow and Its Planning.* New York: Dover. 1987.

Leopold, Aldo. *Sand County Almanac and Sketches.* New York: Oxford University Press. 1987.

Lynch, Kevin. *Image of the City.* Cambridge, MA: M.I.T. 1960.

Lynch, Kevin. *Site Planning*, 3d ed. Cambridge, MA: M.I.T. 1984.

Ortolano, Leonard R. 1984. *Environmental Planning and Decision Making.* New York: Wiley. 1984.

Pahlke, Robert. *Environmentalism and the Future of Progressive Politics.* New Haven: Yale. 1989.

Rybczynski, Witold. *City Life.* Touchstone Books. 1996.

Sagoff, Mark. *The Economy of the Earth.* Cambridge: Cambridge University Press. 1988.

Scully, Vincent. *American Architecture and Urbanism.* New York: Praeger. 1969.

Southworth, Michael and Eran Ben-Joseph. "Street Standards and the Shaping of Suburbia," *Journal of the American Planning Association,* Vol. 61, No. 1, 1995, pp. 65-81.

Steinberg, Saul. "Steinberg on the City," *Journal of the American Institute of Planners*, Vol. 27, No. 3, Part Two, 1961, entire issue.

Stron, Ann. *Private Property and the Public Interest.* Baltimore: Johns Hopkins. 1975.

Venturi, Robert. *Complexity and Contradiction in Architecture,* 2d ed. New York: Museum of Modern Art. 1977.

Whyte, William H. *The Last Landscape.* Garden City, NY: Doubleday. 1968.

Whyte, William H. City: *Rediscovering the Center.* New York: Doubleday. 1988.

PART
VI
International Planning

A Planned City

Lisa Peattie

In *Planning: Rethinking Ciudad Guayana*, Lisa Peattie revisits an area that she first studied over 30 years ago and described in *The View from the Barrio* (Ann Arbor: University of Michigan Press, 1968). The current book is an important, eloquently written case study both of a culture and the development planning process. Peattie is a keen observer, and her case study serves as an important source for her ideas about the practice of planning and urban design. "A Planned City," the first chapter in the book, introduces the history and context of Ciudad Guayana and then briefly addresses the question of why the planning for the city that began 20 years ago did not succeed. Peattie considers three possible explanations and then observes that the most important reason was that the planners had been unable to include local businessmen and residents in the process. Unfortunately, she finds that planning had been used to shift even more power and resources to the large corporate bodies.

While we often speak of the need for planning, we know at the same time that a number of planned cities are just awful. Indeed, there is a group of very well known planned cities that, although widely separated in space and produced by nations with sharply differing cultures and politics, share certain strikingly unappealing characteristics. Brasilia, Chandigarh, and Islamabad are particularly notable instances of the genre: cities of monumental buildings rendered sterile in effect because of the antiseptically orderly character of their setting; cities of the most rigorous separation of classes, which typically extends to excluding the poor altogether from the areas covered by planning controls; cities that seem unadapted to pedestrians, small enterprises, the modest, and the domestic.

Brazilians used to like to tell a story about a visitor to Brasilia whose belt breaks. He is depicted going desperately from place to place holding up his pants in a city that offers no convenient shopping facilities at the local or neighborhood level.

In addition to such stories, there is by now a literature of criticism on these cities, of which Epstein's *Brasilia, Plan and Reality* and Madhu Sarin's book on Chandigarh are two notable examples.[1] But so far as I know, these critiques always center around a concept of flawed planning. The planners misjudged; the planners were unsympathetic to the needs of the masses. I propose here to explore another way of thinking about the similar obnoxiousness of these planned cities: that it results from the nature and functions of central planning itself. I propose to explore this possibility via the story of another well-known planned city in Venezuela with which I myself had some years of involvement in its early days.

Ciudad Guayana, the city of this story, differs sharply from Brasilia, Chandigarh, and Islamabad in not being a government capital. It was proposed not as a seat of and monument to government, but as an industrial growth pole. In Brasilia or Chandigarh, the city's business is government; in Ciudad Guayana, government's business was industry. The announced purpose of the city was economic growth and the decentralization of development away from the capital. Nevertheless, there are certain similarities between this city and the three capitals mentioned earlier. Like them, it is characterized by strikingly large buildings in an otherwise sparsely developed area. Like them, it excludes the poor from the area of planning controls. Like them, it has an awkward, inhuman quality as a place to live.

Can it be that planning is not the way to a better environment after all?

If planning is the way to better cities, Ciudad Guayana should have turned out splendidly. It was not only located at a dramatic natural site, with a rich collection of natural resources, it was planned by an international team of experts under a powerful independent agency with extensive legal powers and ample funding.

In a national magazine article on the planning of Ciudad Guayana, one of those most involved in organizing the project wrote in 1965:

> In the lower Orinoco Valley of Venezuela, a new city is rising. Called Ciudad Guayana, this city is more than just another urban settlement; it is the focal point of an effort to establish the national economy of Venezuela on a broader and more stable basis than its present heavy dependence on petroleum. As such the city of Guayana is perhaps one of the most ambitious and significant enterprises of its kind in the world today.[2]

In 1961, when Ciudad Guayana was founded, Venezuela was completing its third decade of petroleum-driven economic growth. A nation two-thirds rural in 1936 had become two-thirds urban and was still urbanizing rapidly. Oil—still in the hands of U.S. companies—accounted for 22 percent of the Venezuelan gross national product (GNP), two-thirds of Venezuelan government revenue, and 90 percent of foreign exchange. The democratically elected Betancourt government that came to power after the years of dictatorship announced as its major strategy that of "sowing the oil"—of using the oil royalties to build a permanent economic base. The Ciudad Guayana project was part of the national planning strategy that was the outcome of the oil boom, and it was financed by the oil revenues.

The new city was to be at the junction of the Orinoco and Caroní rivers in the south of Venezuela. Eight degrees off the equator, sea level, the area was hot and dry. The existing urban settlements there lacked a phone system, a public library, a theater or a university, and even, to a great extent, piped running water! More important, in many ways, it was an airline journey or a twelve-hour drive from Caracas, the glittering city

where money and power and the contacts to get more of them were concentrated. But it had a dramatic natural site (two rivers, and a spectacular waterfall) and a rich collection of natural resources (hydroelectric power, iron, bauxite). Two U.S. companies, subsidiaries of U.S. Steel and Bethlehem Steel, were already mining iron in the area and shipping it out from company towns in the area of the proposed city. The Orinoco River provided access to cheap water transport for the heavy ore. The Venezuelan government owned and managed a dam and hydroelectric plant and was completing a steel mill. There were thus ore, energy, transportation, and the beginning of basic industry.

The program for developing these resources was backed up with both money and power. The development of the region and the planning of the new city were under the charge of a powerful development agency, the Corporacion Venezolana de Guayana (CVG), responsible only to the president of Venezuela. Its head, Colonel Alfonzo Ravard, was a military officer, an engineer with an already-established reputation as an administrator in the region. The agency's control over land—not only to regulate use but to allocate through sale or lease—superseded the powers of the local municipal government.

Furthermore, in 1961 the CVG signed an agreement with the Joint Center for Urban Studies of the Massachusetts Institute of Technology and Harvard University for research and technical assistance in regional development and in planning the city, which made available a great deal of high-powered professional expertise. The contract provided for a total of $883,700 worth of professional services over three years.[3] In July of 1964, a two-year extension was signed providing for an additional $1,081,200.[4] The CVG also funded a large staff of Venezuelan counterparts in the planning enterprise.

Twenty years later, there is a city of around 350,000 people where the planners drew plans for one—but one rather different from the planners' dream.

On the eastern side of the Caroni River there had been in 1962 the rather raggle-taggle municipal center of San Felix with its plaza and market. Now there is a vast proliferation of shantytown settlements spreading south and east of the plaza, once a comfortably shabby shaded space, now an expanse of concrete.

On the west side of the Caroni, the location of the steel mill and the modern U.S. Steel company town called Puerto Ordaz, there are commercial office blocks in several scattered groupings and the development agency's own monumental building. There are also a number of residential developments for the middle- and higher-income groups. Many of these consist of high-rise apartment buildings standing scattered about the vast sunbaked spaces. Because during the oil boom the developers overbuilt for a very small high-income market, when I visited in 1982 I was told there were eight thousand vacant apartments. A particularly luxurious development, built to house the staff of the steel mill, was too expensive even for those rather well-paid persons and was one of the empty projects.

One problem is that the major industries that were to make the city an economic growth pole are in terrible trouble: a source not of industrial dynamism and of national income but of debt and managerial concern. When oil prices suddenly soared in 1973, more than ten billion dollars of Venezuela's new OPEC riches went into Guayana,[5] largely into a fourfold expansion of the steel mill and the enlargement of productive capacity in electricity and aluminum. But the implementing agencies turned out to lack the managerial capacity to execute the ambitious projects. While the city's facilities were strained to the point of crisis, the industrial projects brought accusations of patronage and mismanagement. Meanwhile, even as oil revenues fell, the world markets for steel and aluminum dropped sharply.

But the problems of the city are not simply those of running out of money. This is not the city that the planners intended, even at reduced scale. In 1986, I am told, the vacant apartments have been filled and the city is growing. But what kind of a city is it? The planners had concerned themselves with issues of economic efficiency, amenity, social equity, and community. The city as it has evolved is conspicuously lacking on all four counts.

It lacks efficiency. Three-quarters of the population live at one end of a lineal city, and the major industries and two-thirds of the jobs are located at the other end; thus, the majority of the working population must commute daily the length of the city. They must make the commute across a classic bottleneck: a double bridge over the river that separates the two sections. This distribution of population is not at all that which was planned. Although specific predictions varied, all the planners, whether calculating by hand or by computer, proposed that "in the long run... residential growth would move westward from Puerto Ordaz in a broad band toward the steel mill, leaving only a minority of the population in San Felix."[6] The situation is at present reversed, since nearly three-quarters of the population live to the east in San Felix.

Both halves of the city lack amenity. The eastern part of the city, in which the working class lives, consists of a series of shantytown settlements. Streets are cheaply paved, if at all, and lack adequate drainage. In 1983 a study found that only a third of households in this sector were connected to the city water system.[7] Only 60 percent of the elementary school age population and 12 percent of the older youth were enrolled in school; although all schools were functioning on double shifts, the system simply lacked capacity.[8]

Puerto Ordaz, on the other side of the river where the privileged classes live, in contrast to the shantytowns of the east, is characterized by an awkward and unpleasant luxury: high-rise apartment buildings scattered widely apart, without pedestrian access, without trees and gardens, and with a deficiency of places for meeting and collective amusement.

The city lacks equity. Per capita, the development agency in 1977 had invested in the privileged Puerto Ordaz part thirty-nine times what it had invested in the working-class part[9]—and it is apparent to any casual glance.

The city lacks community. A 1983 report from the urban development agency points to the numerous factors which create a strong social segregation within the urban area: (1) natural barriers, especially the river, (2) the sharp segregation of use brought about by zoning, (3) the socioeconomic homogeneity of each residential area, and (4) the relative autonomy of the state-owned industrial enterprises. "Ciudad Guayana," the study says, "more than any other city, may be conceived of as a group of communities and a stratification of social groups."[10]

It is not only that there is no single center that serves as a point of identification for all the citizens (or more accurately in this case, the inhabitants). More striking is the fact that after twenty years, no one but the planners themselves still think of it as a single city. Ciudad Guayana as an entity exists only in the publicity flyers of the development agency. If one is to purchase a ticket at the Caracas airport, the airline will not know what you are talking about if you ask for Ciudad Guayana; you may get a ticket to Puerto Ordaz, the iron-mining company town that existed before planning began. The telephone directory has a section for Puerto Ordaz, the, west side of the river, and another, linked only by the same area code, for San Felix on the east side. Some think of three settlements, adding to San Felix and Puerto Ordaz an industrial district called Matanzas.[11]

Of those who were involved in the planning effort back in the sixties, most have left the scene; the Americans, of course, have mainly returned to the States. Many have not even been back to visit. The chief economist of the project, while based: in Boston, is an exception, for he was brought back by the development agency in the mid-seventies to work on the expansion made possible by the oil boom.

His view of the outcome of the project centers on the role of the city for national economic objectives:

> The Guayana program has achieved its basic goals. An urban-industrial hydro-power center has been established and is thriving and expanding, albeit with growing pains, rough edges and missteps. Population of Ciudad Guayana has risen from 4,000 in 1960 to 300,000 plus in the 1980s and is growing. The industrial base continues to expand; a new bauxite mine and ore processing plant are currently being brought on stream and the Guayana is again proving useful. In this time of declining oil revenues, devaluation and import restrictions, the Guayana region is serving the national economy well.[12]

The chief urban designer of the Joint Center team, Wilhelm von Moltke, visited the city for a few days in February of 1981 and even more briefly in early 1984. On both occasions he was delighted by the good results of at least one of the design team's ideas: that of laying out urbanizations in a cul-de-sac pattern with loop access roads surrounding central open spaces. Proposed by the designers as a way of creating green spaces and of building community at the neighborhood level, the scheme was subsequently abandoned in the face of criticism of its complexity and cost relative to more standard blocks. But in the experimental prototypes were the green areas and in at least one case a small community building! In other respects, however, the city was to von Moltke rather distressing. In 1981 he drafted a memorandum with his impressions for the CVG. He commended the "vitality of the city" but declared himself:

> …very disappointed in the environmental quality of the Alta Vista Center, the absence of human scale, the lack of visual structure, the lack of integration of the many large elements, the lack of concern for the pedestrian, the lack of landscaping, street furniture and other amenities.

He saw the "miscellaneous high-rise apartment buildings… in most inappropriate locations" and the "continued development of residential areas east and south-east of San Felix [which] extends the journey-to-work." He felt strongly that a height limit on buildings should have been imposed.[13]

Lloyd Rodwin revisited the city in 1977 with his wife. In the course of his trip he noted the "disastrous" decision on the part of the agency to sell off the land in the center of the city. "The values and the rents from this land," he wrote in a letter to the president of the CVG, "are essential for recapturing a reasonable share of the infrastructure investments."[14] In a more philosophical mood, a few years later, he observed:

> It turned out to be a tougher job than we thought. It was harder to find the right people. People who looked good would turn out to be disasters. There were constraints which the planning team didn't recognize.[15]

The city did not turn out as planned. One problem, of course, was the disappearance of the resource base when oil prices dropped. But this is not the whole story. There would not have been eight thousand vacant apartments in 1981 if the oil boom had continued—although it seems likely that even with the oil boom not all that building would have found a market. But the inefficiency, inequity, and lack of community characterizing the city were there before the oil boom and during the boom as they are now. Even during the boom, oil wealth did not seem to be producing a city that was agreeable to live in; on the contrary, there were protests from both the planners and the citizens as to the "crisis" produced for the city by oil-supported industrial expansion.

No, we must see the present problematic city not simply as the outcome of resource shifts; it is also the outcome of planning. The planners, their way of working, and the way that working process interacted with the other things that were going on in the city and in Venezuela constitute the roots of the present. The city was not planned as it is, but the city is the outcome of planning. The planning process helped make it what it is.

One way of explaining the undesirable outcome of the city is as planning messed up; people and institutions failed to obey the plan. The planners were unable to enforce their plans and thus to realize their dream. Rodwin's 1965 paper warned about the difficulties in implementing planning controls:

> Attracted by the prospect of jobs, poor migrants invade the area, put up makeshift shelters and exacerbate the problem of organizing land uses and public services. Most costs tend to be high, almost no amenities exist and living conditions are bleak. Understandably enough, the inhabitants become impatient with "fancy" long-range plans and delays; they grumble about the neglect of their immediate needs and care little if these needs do not fit the priorities or the plans. Up to a point their views can be slighted or ignored, but this is always dangerous. It is hardly surprising that the new city rarely measures up to the original dreams of its planners.[16]

A simpler version of this argument was provided by a Venezuelan economist with the project whom I met again, after twenty years, when I revisited the development agency's offices in

January 1982. I asked him how he thought the city had turned out. "Well," he said, "no matter how well they plan it, people keep moving in and messing it up."

This way of looking at the problem was clearly present from the beginning of the planning process. Indeed, the desire to keep people from moving in and messing up the planned city was, it will be seen, a basic reason for the separation between rich and poor, and the contrast between the settlements on the east and west of the river.

A second explanation also departs from the failure of the planners to control the actual processes of urban growth, but this time puts the blame on the planners. The planning process was too rigid. What was wanted, it is argued, was not so much a plan or final design, but a program for directing and channeling urban growth. This way of viewing the issue, like the preceding one, was also present from the beginning, put forward in a succession of consultant memoranda from the early days.

> The more fundamental problem is to view the plan not as a static design but as a path of growth.[17]

> Accept the idea that we should be making a plan for the nature, rate, quantity and quality of urban change and a plan for the development process rather than a plan for some static future state (which will never occur in just that form).[18]

> Any expectation that the ultimate appearance of the city will be like the planning team's initial blueprint will be doomed to disappointment…. One of the main factors that will control the city's future pattern will not be what is put into the blueprint as much as what will be imposed by rancho (i.e., squatter settlement) movements.[19]

The comments are surely justified; the production of a plan, in the sense of a set of visually displayed decisions as to the locations of various activities in some future state of the city, was not sufficient to direct the activities to those places. Nor could the planners stop various institutional and personal actors from doing what they wanted to do, rather than what the planners wanted them to do. Even in the early days, when the development agency had decreed a freeze on all construction until such time as the plan should have been developed, squatters continued to put up their shacks and commercial developers continued to construct buildings counter to plan; Sears was building a six-story office building while the planners debated the nature of the commercial center elsewhere in which Sears was to be the prime tenant. A focus on the plan as locational map did little to organize a process which could have negotiated such decisions.

A third view is that the planners were snobs. They were unable to plan realistically for the development of the city, since to do so would have been to recognize and provide for the needs of a mass of poor and low-status people with whom they did not wish to be identified. Snobbery identified the proper outcome of planning with the urban settings appropriate for high-income people, the "modern" with the expensive. Snobbery kept the workers at one end of the city, away from both the industrial jobs to which they would have to commute and the urbanizations of the elite.

Again, there is evidence for an endemic snobbery, both among the planners and among others of the citizenry. When I revisited the city twenty years after my first arrival and asked my cab driver what he thought of the planning, he compared San Felix, the working-class side of the river, to Puerto Ordaz, the upper-income part of the city: "San Felix is terribly planned—all shantytowns; Puerto Ordaz—that's well planned."

These three perspectives are not mutually exclusive. Indeed, I believe that they are all in various ways true. The planning process was one that focused on formal order and on the production of a somewhat statically conceived spatial plan. There was little use of the planning process as one of interacting with, and thus coming to mobilize and direct, the actions of local people. The plan was indeed altered by the initiatives of private actors, not only the squatters whom Abrams saw as shaping the urbanization pattern but also some large corporate investors who put their buildings where they chose, rather than where the plans had proposed. And indeed a strain of unrecognized, perhaps even unconscious, social snobbery in the planners responded to the demand outside the planning office for "nice" neighborhoods and a "high standard" city.

Furthermore, the three interpretations are interrelated. The social separation of the planners from the people of the site, the institutional basis of the attitudes we call snobbery, helped to drive the planning process toward formalism. The formalism, in turn, made for a process that left "implementation" for a second stage of consideration, rather than using planning to develop the social supports for a proposed development path. This process certainly left an opening for unplanned actors to develop counter to the plan.

I wish to propose, here, a fourth interpretation. This, too, does not exclude the others. It constitutes, rather, a way of thinking about the relationships between the others and between the social roots of the planning enterprise. Here, planning will be thought of as a kind of social ritual, the function of which is to legitimize government activities that, if frankly described, would arouse conflict and dissent. The so-called mistakes in planning Ciudad Guayana may be understood as the working out of certain irreducible conflicts in the real unstated goals of the project, issues that were fuzzed over by the way in which the objectives of the city were described and the way in which the planning was carried out. Planning a growth pole meant reorganizing the environment for large corporations. The planners could not have taken the local businessmen and residents into the process without diluting the overriding objective. Therefore, they left them outside. Planning was a way of shifting power and resources toward large corporate bodies. But to make this explicit would have been to threaten the political legitimacy of the government that executed the policy, and which depended on voter support. If planning had been thought of in terms of process, all this would have been quite visible. Thought of as urban design and economic targets, it became a collective product: The City Plan and The Planned City.

The planners were very idealistic people. They believed in what they were doing. One of the functions of the planning process was to construct the planning activity in a form that enabled the planners themselves to feel they were serving an essentially noble purpose. The design focus served to convert the city into a kind of monument to the idea of progress, an ideological construction within which private gain could be thought of as social progress and the general good. The attention to "good design" and values of "amenity," thought of as there for the general enjoyment, made it possible to think of an undivided community interest in the outcome of the planning process. Underlying uneasiness about class divisions and income contrasts was addressed through a focus on physical centers: neighborhood centers, the city center as "the heart of the city." Finally, the organization of an interdisciplinary team, including an anthropologist, made it possible to think of planning as addressing social issues and, indeed, as a technique of liberal reform.

NOTES

1. David G. Epstein, *Brasilia, Plan and Reality: A Study of Planned and Spontaneous Urban Development* (Berkeley: University of California Press, 1983); Madhu Sarin, *Urban Planning in the Third World: The Chandigarh Experience* (New York: Mansell Publishing, 1982).

2. Lloyd Rodwin, "Ciudad Guayana: A New City," *Scientific American*, September 1965, 122-23.

3. "Memorandum of Agreement between the Corporacion Venezolana de Fomento hereinafter Sometimes Referred to as the "Corporación and the Massachusetts Institute of Technology hereinafter Sometimes Referred to as 'M.I.T.'" (1961, Mimeographed).

4. "Memorandum of Agreement between the Corporacion Venezolana de Guayana and the Massachusetts Institute of Technology, March 1964" (Mimeographed).

5. Jackson Diehl, "Venezuela's Force-Fed Industrial Center Goes on a Crash Diet," *Washington Post*, March 4, 1983, sec. A.

6. Anthony Penfold, "Urban Transportation," in *Planning Urban Growth and Regional Development: The Experience of the Cuayana Program of Venezuela*, by Lloyd Rodwin et al. (Cambridge: MIT Press, 1969), 187-88.

7. CVG, Ministerio del Desarrollo Urbano, *Ciudad Guayana XXI: Logros, problemas y oportunidades, una sintesis del diagnostico* (Caracas: CVG, 1983), 9.

8. Ibid., 14.

9. Claude Brun M., *Ciudad Guayana mas alla de 1980* (Caracas: CVG, Division de Ingenieria y Construcci6n, Departamento de Planeamiento Urbano, 1979), 9.

10. CVG, Ministerio del Desarrollo Urbano, *Ciudad Guayana XXI*, 7.

11. Ibid., 9.

12. Alexander Ganz, letter to author, May 26, 1986.

13. "lmpressions of Ciudad Guayana from a Visit on February 25, 1981" (Typed memorandum from Willo von Moltke to General Alfonzo Ravard).

14. Lloyd Rodwin, letter to Dr. Argenis Gamboa, president of the CVG, February 2, 1977.

15. Lloyd Rodwin, interview with author, April 5, 1983.

16. Rodwin, "Ciudad Guayana," 122.

17. William Alonso, "Report Concerning Some Aspects of the Projected Guayana City" (Joint Center Guayana Project, Memorandum A-6, July 1962), 28.

18. Robert B. Mitchell, "Observations and Recommendations after Visit to Caracas, January 28-February 3, 1962" (Joint Center Guayana Project, Memorandum A-4, February 1962), 15.

19. Charles Abrams, "Report on the Development of Ciudad Guayana in Venezuela" (Joint Center Guayana Project, Memorandum A-5, January 1962), 26.

By Way of Conclusion

Hernando de Soto

This selection is the final chapter of de Soto's, *The Mystery of Capital*. It contains his concluding thoughts on the critical importance to economic development and the capitalist system of enforceable, formal property rights for the lower classes in areas such as Latin America. He looks into the early work of Marx, comments on its relevance in today's economy, and argues that there is now "enough evidence to make substantial progress in development." Finally, he concludes with a discussion of the inequitable nature of capitalism in developing nations, but notes that it is "the only game in town."

Where is the wisdom we have lost in knowledge?
Where is the knowledge we have lost in information?

—*T.S. Eliot, Choruses from "The Rock"*

THE PRIVATE CLUB OF GLOBALIZATION

Capitalism is in crisis outside the West not because international globalization is failing but because developing and former communist nations have been unable to "globalize" capital within their own countries. Most people in those nations view capitalism as a private club, a discriminatory system that benefits only the West and the elites who live inside the bell jars of poor countries.

More people throughout the world may wear Nike shoes and flash their Casio watches, but even as they consume the goods of the West, they are quite aware that they still linger at the periphery of the capitalist game. They have no stake in it. Globalization should not be just about interconnecting the bell jars of the privileged few. That kind of globalization has existed before. In the nineteenth century, Europe's ruling royals were literally one big family, related by blood and in constant contact about politics and commerce with their cousins in England, France, Holland, Spain, and Russia. Capitalism triumphed in the nineteenth century and prevailed throughout the industrialized world until the Russian Revolution and the Great Depression. But as Spain's Ortega y Gasset and the American pundit Walter Lippman pointed out, despite its dominance and sophistication, the capitalist system was always vulnerable. The American economist Lester Thurow points out that as recently as 1941,

> the United States and Great Britain were essentially the only [major] capitalist countries left on the face of the earth…. All the rest of the world were fascists, communists or Third World feudal colonies. The final crisis of the 1920s and the Great Depression of the 1930s had brought capitalism to the edge of extinction. The capitalism that now seems irresistible could, with just a few missteps, have vanished.[1]

Latin Americans do not have to be reminded. On at least four occasions since their independence from Spain in the 1820s, they have tried to become part of global capitalism and failed. They restructured their debts, stabilized their economies by controlling inflation, liberalized trade, privatized government assets (selling their railroads to the British, for example), undertook debt equity swaps, and overhauled their tax systems. At the consumer level, the Latin Americans imported all sorts of goods, from English tweed suits and Church shoes to Model T Fords; they learned English and French by listening to the radio or records; they danced the Charleston and the Lambeth Walk, and chewed Chiclets gum. But they never produced much live capital.

We may now all be benefiting from the communications revolution, and some may see progress in the fact that the Egyptian Sphinx now stares directly at the neon sign of a Kentucky Fried Chicken franchise. Nevertheless, only twenty-five of the world's two hundred countries produce capital in sufficient quantity to benefit fully from the division of labor in expanded global markets. The lifeblood of capitalism is not the Internet or fast-food franchises. It is *capital*. Only capital provides the means to support specialization and the production and exchange of assets in the expanded market. It is capital that is the source of increasing productivity and therefore the wealth of nations.

Yet only the Western nations and small enclaves of wealthy people in developing and former communist nations have the capacity to represent assets and potential and, therefore, the ability to produce and use capital efficiently. Capitalism is viewed outside the West with increasing hostility, as an apartheid regime most cannot enter. There is a growing sense, even among some elites, that if they have to depend solely and forever on the kindness of outside capital, they will never be productive players in the global capitalist game. They are increasingly frustrated at not being masters of their own fate. Since they have embarked on globalization without providing their own people with the means to produce capital, they are beginning to look less like the United States than like mercantilist Latin America with its disarray of extralegal activity.[2] Ten years ago, few would have compared the former Soviet bloc nations to Latin America. But today they look astonishingly similar strong underground economies, glaring inequality, pervasive mafias, political instability, capital flight, and flagrant disregard for law.

That is why outside the West advocates of capitalism are intellectually on the retreat. Ascendant just a decade ago, they are now increasingly viewed as apologists for the miseries and injustices that still affect the majority of people. For example, in 1999 Egypt's consultative upper house warned the government "not to be deceived any longer by calls for capitalism and globalization."[3] Having forgotten the crucial issue of property, capitalism's advocates have let themselves become identified as the defenders of the status quo, blindly trying to enforce existing written law whether it discriminates or not.

And the law in those countries does discriminate. As I illustrated in Chapter 2, at least 80 percent of the population in these countries cannot inject life into their assets and make them generate capital because the law keeps them out of the formal property system. They have trillions of dollars in dead capital, but it is as if these were isolated ponds whose waters disappear into a sterile strip of sand, instead of forming a mighty mass of water that can be captured in one unified property system and given the form required to produce capital. People hold and use their assets on the basis of myriad disconnected informal agreements where accountability is managed locally. Without the common standards that legal property brings, they lack the language necessary for their assets to talk to each other. There is no use urging them to be patient until the benefits of capitalism trickle down their way. That will never happen until the firm foundations of formal property are in place.

Meanwhile, the promoters of capitalism, still arrogant on their victory over communism, have yet to understand that their macroeconomic reforms are not enough. We must not forget that globalization is occurring because developing and former communist nations are opening up their once protected economies, stabilizing their currencies, and drafting regulatory frameworks to enhance international trade and private investment. All of this is good. What is not so good is that these reforms assume that these countries' populations are already integrated into the legal system and have the same ability to use their resources in the open market. They do not.

As I have argued in Chapter 3, most people cannot participate in an expanded market because they do not have access to a legal property rights system that represents their assets in a manner that makes them widely transferable and fungible, that allows them to be encumbered and permits their owners to be held accountable. So long as the assets of the majority are not properly documented and tracked by a property bureaucracy, they are invisible and sterile in the marketplace.

By stabilizing and adjusting by "the book," the globalizers' macroeconomic programs have dramatically rationalized the economic management of developing countries. But because their book does not address the fact that most people do not have property rights, they have done only a fraction of the work required to create a comprehensive capitalist system and market economy. Their tools are designed to work in countries where systematized law has been "globalized" internally, when inclusive property rights systems that link up to efficient monetary and investment instruments are in place—something these countries have yet to achieve.

Too many policymakers have taken an Olympian view of the globalization process. Once they stabilized and adjusted at the macro level, allowing legal business and foreign investors to prosper and orthodox economists to control the treasury, they felt they had fulfilled their duty. Because they concentrated only on policies dealing with the aggregates, they did not inquire whether people had the means to participate in an expanded market system. They forget that people are the fundamental agents of change. They forgot to focus on the poor. And they made that enormous omission because they do not operate with the concept of class in mind. In the words of one of their most outstanding pundits, they do not have "the ability to comprehend, however dimly, how other people live."[4]

Economic reformers have left the issue of property for the poor in the hands of conservative legal establishments uninterested in changing the status quo. As a result, the assets of the majority of their citizens have remained dead capital stuck in the extralegal sector. This is why the advocates of globalization and free market reforms are beginning to be perceived as the self-satisfied defenders of the interests of those who dominate the bell jar.

FACING UP TO MARX'S GHOST

Most economic reform programs in poor economies may be falling into the trap that Karl Marx foresaw: The great contradiction of the capitalist system is that it creates its own demise because it cannot avoid concentrating capital in a few hands. By not giving the majority access to expanded markets, these reforms are leaving a fertile field for class confrontation—a capitalist and free market economy for the privileged few who can concretize their property rights, and relative poverty for a large undercapitalized sector incapable of leveraging its own assets.

Class confrontations, in this day and age?

Didn't that concept come down with the Berlin Wall? Unfortunately, it did not. This may be hard for a citizen in an advanced nation to understand because in the West those discontented with the system live in "pockets of poverty." Misery in developing and former communist nations, however, is not contained in pockets; it is spread throughout society. What few pockets exist in those countries are pockets of wealth. What the West calls "the underclass" is here the majority. And in the past, when their rising expectations were not met, that mass of angry poor brought apparently solid elites to their knees (as in Iran, Venezuela, and Indonesia). In most countries outside the West, governments depend on strong intelligence services, and their elites live behind fortress-like walls for good reason.

Today, to a great extent, the difference between advanced nations and the rest of the world is that between countries where formal property is widespread and countries where classes are divided into those who can fix property rights and produce capital and those who cannot. If extralegal property rights are not accommodated, these societies May muddle along with their dual economies with the so-called law-abiding sector on one side and the impoverished extralegal sector on the other. But as information and communications continue to improve and the poor become better informed of what they do not have, the bitterness over legal apartheid is bound to grow. At some point, those outside the bell jar will be mobilized against the status quo by people with political agendas that thrive on discontent. "If we do not invent ways to make globalization more inclusive," says Klaus Schwab of the World Economic Forum, "we have to face the prospect of a resurgence of the acute social confrontations of the past, magnified at the international level."[5]

The Cold War may have ended, but the old class arguments have not disappeared. Subversive activities and an upsurge of ethnic and cultural conflicts around the world prove that when people are extremely dissatisfied they continue to constitute themselves into classes based on shared injuries. *Newsweek* notes that in the Americas since the 1980s, "each of these struggles has its own unique history, but the fighters all vilify the same enemy: the new face of Latin American Capitalism."[6] In such situations, the Marxist tool kit is better geared to explain class conflict than capitalist thinking, which has no comparable analysis or even a serious strategy for reaching the poor in the extralegal sector. Capitalists generally have no systemic explanation of how the people in the underclass got where they are and how the system could be changed to raise them up.

We must not underestimate the latent power of Marxist integrated theory at a time when masses of people with little hope are looking for a cohesive worldview to improve their desperate economic prospects. In a period of economic boom, there tends to be little time for deep thinking. Crisis, however, has a way of sharpening the mind's need for order and explanations into obsession. Marxist thinking, in whatever form it reappears—and it will—supplies a much mightier array of concepts for grappling with the political problems of capitalism outside the West than capitalist thinking does.

Marx's insights into capital, as George Soros recently observed, are often more sophisticated than those of Adam Smith.[7] Marx understood clearly that "in themselves, money and commodities are no more capital than are the means of productions and of subsistence. That they want transforming into capital."[8] He also understood that if assets could be converted into commodities and made to interact in markets, they could express values that are imperceptible to the senses but can he captured to produce rents. For Marx, property was an important issue because it was clear to him that those who appropriated the assets obtained much more than just their physical attributes. As a result, the Marxist intellectual tool kit has left anticapitalists powerful ways to explain why private property will necessarily put assets in the hands of the rich at the expense of the poor.

For those who have not noticed, the arsenal of anticapitalism and antiglobalization is building up. Today, there are serious statistics that provide the anticapitalists with just the ammunition they need to argue that capitalism is a transfer of property from poorer to richer countries and that Western private investment in developing nations is nothing short of a massive takeover of their resources by multinationals. The number of flashy cars, luxurious homes, and California-style shopping malls may have increased in most developing and former communist nations over the past

decade, but so have the poor. Nancy Birdsall and Juan Luis Londoño's research shows that poverty has grown faster and income distribution has worsened over the last decade.[9] According to a 1999 United Nations "Human Development Report," gross domestic product in the Russian Federation fell by 41 percent from 1990 to 1997, driving millions into the extralegal sector. The life expectancy of the Russian male has dropped four full years—to fifty-eight. The report blames the transition to capitalism and the effects of globalization.

These research efforts provide us with healthy warning signals, but they are also putting in place the intellectual missiles needed to discourage privatization programs and global capitalism. It is crucial, therefore, to recognize the latent Marxist paradigms and then add what we have learned in the century since Marx died. We can now demonstrate that although Marx clearly saw that parallel economic life can be generated alongside physical assets themselves—that "the predictions of the human brain appeared as independent beings endowed with life"[10]—he did not quite grasp that formal property was not simply an instrument for appropriation but also the means to motivate people to create real additional usable value. Moreover, he did not see that it is the mechanisms contained in the property system itself that give assets and the labor invested in them the form required to create capital. Although Marx's analysis of how assets become transcendent and serve greater social uses when they become exchangeable is fundamental to understanding wealth, he was not able to foresee to what degree legal property systems would become crucial vehicles for the enhancement of exchange value.

Marx understood better than anyone else in his time that in economics there is no greater blindness than seeing resources exclusively in terms of their physical properties. He was well aware that capital was "an independent substance... in which money and commodities are mere forms which it assumes and casts off in turn."[11] But he lived in a time when it was probably still too soon to see how formal property could, through representation, make those same resources serve additional functions and produce surplus value. Consequently, Marx could not see how it would be in everyone's interest to increase the range of the beneficiaries of property. Property titles were only the visible tip of a growing formal property iceberg. The rest of the iceberg is now an enormous man-made facility for drawing out the economic potential of assets. That is why Marx did not fully understand that legal property is the indispensable process that fixes and deploys capital, that without property mankind cannot convert the fruits of its labor into fungible, liquid forms that can be differentiated, combined, divided, and invested to produce surplus value. He did not realize that a good legal property system, like a Swiss army knife, has many more mechanisms than just the elementary "ownership" blade.

Much of Marx's thought is outdated because the situation today is not the same as in Marx's Europe. Potential capital is no longer the privilege of the few. After Marx's death, the West finally managed to set up a legal framework that gave most people access to property and the tools of production. Marx would probably be shocked to find how in developing countries much of the teeming mass does not consist of oppressed legal proletarians but of oppressed extralegal small entrepreneurs with a sizeable amount of assets.

Admiration for good property systems should not blind us to the fact that, as Marx noted, these systems can also be used for theft. The world will always be full of sharks expert at using property paper to skim off wealth from unsuspecting people. Yet one cannot oppose formal property systems for this reason, any more than one should abolish computers or automobiles because people use them to commit crimes. If Marx were alive today and saw the misappropriation of resources that has occurred on both sides of the former Iron Curtain, he would probably agree that looting can happen with or without property and that controlling thievery depends more on the exercise of power than on property. In addition, though Marx gave "surplus value" a very specific definition, its meaning is not chained to his pen. People have always produced surplus value pyramids, cathedrals, expensive armies, to name a few examples. Clearly much of today's surplus value in the West has originated not in scandalously expropriated labor time but in the way that property has given minds the mechanisms with which to extract additional work from commodities.

Like all of us, Marx was influenced by the social conditions and technologies of his time. The expropriation of small proprietors from their means of subsistence, the access to private property rights stemming from feudal title, the robbery of common lands, the enslavement of aboriginal populations, the looting of the conquered, and the "commercial hunting of black skins" by the colonial system may all have been essential preconditions for what Marx called the "primitive accumulation of capital." These conditions are difficult to repeat today. Attitudes have changed—to no little extent because of Marx's own writings. Looting, slavery, and colonialism now have no government's imprimatur. Most countries today are parties to treaties such as the Universal Declaration of Human Rights and have constitutions that provide equal access to property rights as one of the fundamental rights of humankind.

Moreover, as we saw in Chapter 6, authorities in developing countries have not been reticent in giving the poor access to assets. The bulk of spontaneous extralegal buildings and businesses in cities throughout the Second and Third Worlds may not have been formally titled, but governments have accepted (if only tacitly) their existence and ownership arrangements. In many developing countries during this century, large tracts of land have been given to poor farmers as part of agrarian reform programs (though without the property representations necessary to create capital). Nor have authorities in those countries been reluctant to earmark budgets for property issues. Billions of dollars have been spent on activities related to registering ownership.

PROPERTY MAKES CAPITAL "MIND FRIENDLY"

Throughout this book I have been trying to demonstrate that we now have enough evidence to make substantial progress in development. With it in hand we can move beyond the stagnant "left versus right" debate on property and avoid having to fight the same old battles all over again. Formal property is more than just ownership. As we saw in Chapter 3, it has to be viewed as the indispensable process that provides people with the tools to focus their thinking on those aspects of their resources from which they can extract capital. Formal property is more than a system for titling, recording, and mapping assets—it is an instrument of thought, representing assets in such a way that people's minds can work on them to generate surplus value. That is why formal property must be universally accessible: to bring everyone into one social contract where they can cooperate to raise society's productivity.

What distinguishes a good legal property system is that it is "mind friendly." It obtains and organizes knowledge about recorded assets in forms we can control. It collects, integrates, and coordinates not only data on assets and their potential but also our thoughts about them. In brief, capital results from the ability of the West to use property systems to represent their resources in a virtual context. Only there can minds meet to identify and realize the meaning of assets for humankind.

The revolutionary contribution of an integrated property system is that it solves a basic problem of cognition. Our five senses are not sufficient for us to process the complex reality of an expanded market, much less a globalized one. We need to have the economic facts about ourselves and our resources boiled down to essentials that our minds can easily grasp. A good property system does that—it puts assets into a form that lets us distinguish their similarities, differences, and connecting points with other assets. It fixes them in representations that the system tracks as they travel through time and space. In addition, it allows assets to become fungible by representing them to our minds so that we can easily combine, divide, and mobilize them to produce higher-valued mixtures. This capacity of property to represent aspects of assets in forms that allow us to recombine them so as to make them even more useful is the mainspring of economic growth, since growth is all about obtaining high-valued outputs from low-valued inputs.

A good legal property system is a medium that allows us to understand each other, make connections, and synthesize knowledge about our assets to enhance our productivity. It is a way to represent reality that lets us transcend the limitations of our senses. Well-crafted property representations enable us to pinpoint the economic potential of resources so as to enhance what we can do with them. They are not "mere paper": they

are mediating devices that give us useful knowledge about things that are not manifestly present.

Property records point our knowledge about things toward an end, to borrow from Thomas Aquinas, "just as the arrow is moved by the archer."[12] By representing economic aspects of the things we own and assembling them into categories that our minds can quickly grasp, property documents reduce the costs of dealing with assets and increase their value commensurately. This notion, that the value of things can be increased by reducing the costs of knowing them and transacting with them, is one of Nobel laureate Ronald Coase's major contributions. In his treatise "The Nature of the Firm," Coase established that the costs of carrying out transactions can be substantially reduced within the controlled and coordinated context of a firm.[13] In this sense, property systems are like Coase's firm—controlled environments to reduce transaction costs.

The capacity of property to reveal the capital that is latent in the assets we accumulate is born out of the best intellectual tradition of controlling our environment in order to prosper. For thousands of years our wisest men have been telling us that life has different degrees of reality, many of them invisible, and that it is only by constructing representational devices that we will be able to access them. In Plato's famous analogy, we are likened to prisoners chained in a cave with our backs to the entrance so that all we can know of the world are the shadows cast on the wall in front of us. The truth that this illustration consecrates is that many things that guide our destiny are not self-evident. That is why civilization has worked hard to fashion representational systems to access and grasp the part of our reality that is virtual and to represent it in terms we can understand.

As Margaret Boden puts it, "Some of the most important human creations have been new representational systems. These include formal notations, such as Arabic numerals (not forgetting zero), chemical formulae, or the staves, minims, and crotchets used by musicians. [Computer] programming languages are a more recent example."[14] Representational systems such as mathematics and integrated property help us manipulate and order the complexities of the world in a manner that we can all understand and that allows us to communicate regarding issues that we could not otherwise handle. They are what the philosopher Daniel Dennett has called "prosthetic extensions of the mind."[15] Through representations we bring key aspects of the world into being so as to change the way we think about it. The philosopher John Searle has noted that by human agreement we can assign "a new status to some phenomenon, where that status has an accompanying function that cannot be performed solely in virtue of the intrinsic physical features of the phenomenon in question."[16] This seems to me very close to what legal property does: It assigns to assets, by social contract, in a conceptual universe, a status that allows them to perform functions that generate capital.

This notion that we organize reality in a conceptual universe is at the center of philosophy worldwide. The French philosopher Michel Foucault labeled it the *region mediane* that provides a system of switches (*codes fondamentaux*) that constitutes the secret network where society establishes the ever-expanding range of its potential (*les conditions de possibilite*).[17] I see formal property as a kind of switchyard that allows us to extend the potential of the assets that we accumulate further and further, each time increasing capital. I have also benefited from Karl Popper's notion of *World 3*—a separate reality from *World 1* of physical objects and *World 2* of mental states—where the products of our minds take on an autonomous existence that affects the way we deal with physical reality.[18] And it is to this conceptual world that formal property takes us—a world where the West organizes knowledge about assets and extracts from them the potential to generate capital.

And so formal property is this extraordinary thing, much bigger than simple ownership. Unlike tigers and wolves, who bare their teeth to protect their territory, man, physically a much weaker animal, has used his mind to create a legal environment—property—to protect his territory. Without anyone fully realizing it, the representational system the West created to settle territorial claims took on a life of its own, providing the knowledge base and rules necessary to fix and realize capital.

THE ENEMIES OF REPRESENTATIONS

Ironically, the enemies of capitalism have always seemed more aware of the virtual origin of capital than capitalists themselves. It is this virtual aspect of capitalism that they find so insidious and dangerous. Capitalism, charges Viviane Forrester in her best-seller *L'Horreur economique*, "has invaded physical as well as virtual space.... It has confiscated and hidden wealth like never before, it has taken it out of the reach of people by hiding it in the form of symbols. Symbols have become the subjects of abstract exchanges that take place nowhere else than in their virtual world."[19] Consciously or unconsciously, Forrester is part of a long tradition of being uncomfortable with economic representations of virtual reality—those "metaphysical subtleties" that Marx thought were nevertheless necessary to understand and accumulate wealth.[20]

This fear of the virtuality of capital is understandable. Every time civilization comes up with a novel way of using representations to manage the physical world, people become suspicious. When Marco Polo returned from China, he shocked Europeans with the news that the Chinese used not metal but paper money, which people quickly denounced as alchemy. The European world resisted representative money into the nineteenth century. The latest forms of derivative money—electronic money, wire transfers, and the now omnipresent credit card—also took time to be accepted. As representations of value become less ponderous and more virtual, people are understandably skeptical. New forms of property derivatives (such as mortgage-backed securities) may help form additional capital, but they also make understanding economic life more complex. And so people are inclined to be more comfortable with the image of the noble perspiring workers of Soviet and Latin American murals, toiling in the fields or operating their machines, than with capitalists wheeling and dealing titles, shares, and bonds in the virtual reality of their computers. It is as if working with representations dirties your hands more than working with dirt and grease.

Like all representative systems—from written language to money and cyber symbols—property paper has been seen by many intellectuals as an instrument of deceit and oppression. Negative attitudes to representations have been powerful undercurrents in the formation of political ideas. The French philosopher Jacques Derrida recalls in *De la Grammatologie* how Jean Jacques Rousseau argued that writing was an important cause of human inequality. For Rousseau, those with the knowledge of writing could control written laws and official paper and, thus, the destiny of people. Claude Levi-Strauss has also argued that "the primary function of written communication is to facilitate subjugation."[21]

I am as aware as any anticapitalist of how representational systems, particularly those of capitalism, have been used to exploit and conquer, how they have left the many at the mercy of the few. I have discussed in this book how official paper has been used for outright domination. And yet the art and science of representation is one of the girders of modern society. No amount of ranting and raving against writing, electronic money, cyber symbols, and property paper will make then, disappear. Instead we must make representational systems simpler and more transparent and work hard to help people understand them. Otherwise, legal apartheid will persist, and the tools to create wealth will remain in the hands of those who live inside the bell jar.

IS SUCCEEDING AT CAPITALISM A CULTURAL THING?

Think of Bill Gates, the world's most successful and wealthiest entrepreneur. Apart from his personal genius, how much of his success is due to his cultural background and his "Protestant ethic"? And how much is due to the legal property system of the United States?

How many software innovations could he have made without patents to protect them? How many deals and long-term projects could he have carried out without enforceable contracts? How many risks could he have taken at the beginning without limited liability systems and insurance policies? How much capital could he have accumulated without property records in which to fix and store that capital? How many resources could he have pooled without fungible property representations? How many other people would he have made millionaires without being able to distribute stock options? How many economies of scale could he have benefited from if he had to operate on the basis of dispersed cottage industries that could not be combined? How would he pass on the rights to his empire to his children and colleagues without hereditary succession?

I do not think Bill Gates or any entrepreneur in the West could be successful without property rights systems based on a strong, well-integrated social contract. I humbly suggest that before any brahmin who lives in a bell jar tries to convince us that succeeding at capitalism requires certain cultural traits, we should first try to see what happens when developing and former communist countries establish property rights systems that can create capital for everyone.

Throughout history people have confused the efficiency of the representational tools they have inherited to create surplus value with the inherent values of their culture. They forget that often what gives an edge to a particular group of people is the innovative use they make of a representational system developed by another culture. For example, Northerners had to copy the legal institutions of ancient Rome to organize themselves and learn the Greek alphabet and the Arabic number symbols and systems to convey information and calculate. And so, today, few are aware of the tremendous edge that formal property systems have given Western societies. As a result, many Westerners have been led to believe that what underpins their successful capitalism is the work ethic they have inherited or the existential anguish created by their religions—in spite of the fact that people all over the world all work hard when they can and that existential angst or overbearing mothers are not Calvinist or Jewish monopolies. (I am as anxious as any Calvinist in history, especially on Sunday evenings, and in the overbearing mother sweepstakes, I would put mine in Peru up against any woman in New York.) Therefore, a great part of the research agenda needed to explain why capitalism fails outside the West remains mired in a mass of unexamined and largely untestable assumptions labeled "culture," whose main effect is to allow too many of those who live in the privileged enclaves of this world to enjoy feeling superior.

One day these cultural arguments will peel away as the hard evidence of the effects of good political institutions and property law sink in. In the meantime, as *Foreign Affairs'* Fareed Zakaria has observed,

> Culture is hot. By culture I don't mean Wagner and Abstract Expressionism—they've always

been hot—but rather culture as an explanation for social phenomena.... Cultural explanations persist because intellectuals like them. They make valuable the detailed knowledge of countries' histories, which intellectuals have in great supply. They add an air of mystery and complexity to the study of societies.... But culture itself can he shaped and changed. Behind so many cultural attitudes, tastes, and preferences lie the political and economic forces that shaped them.[22]

This is not to say that culture does not count. All people in the world have specific preferences, skills, and patterns of behavior that can be regarded as cultural. The challenge is fathoming which of these traits are really the ingrained, unchangeable identity of a people and which are determined by economic and legal constraints. Is illegal squatting on real estate in Egypt and Peru the result of ancient, ineradicable nomadic traditions among the Arabs and the Quechuas' back-and-forth custom of cultivating crops at different vertical levels of the Andes? Or does it happen because in both Egypt and Peru it takes more than fifteen years to obtain legal property rights to desert land? In my experience squatting is mainly due to the latter. When people have access to an orderly mechanism to settle land that reflects the social contract, they will take the legal route, and only a minority, like anywhere else, will insist on extralegal appropriation. Much behavior that is today attributed to cultural heritage is not the inevitable result of people's ethnic or idiosyncratic traits but of their rational evaluation of the relative costs and benefits of entering the legal property system.

Legal property empowers individuals in any culture, and I doubt that property per se directly contradicts any major culture. Vietnamese, Cuban, and Indian migrants have clearly had few problems adapting to U.S. property law. If correctly conceived, property law can reach beyond cultures to increase trust between them and, at the same time, reduce the costs of bringing things and thoughts together.[23] Legal property sets the exchange rates between different cultures and thus gives them a bedrock of economic commonalities from which to do business with each other.

THE ONLY GAME IN TOWN

I am convinced that capitalism has lost its way in developing and former communist nations. It is not equitable. It is out of touch with those who should be its largest constituency, and instead of being a cause that promises opportunity for all, capitalism appears increasingly as the leitmotif of a self-serving guild of businessmen and their technocracies. I hope this book has conveyed my belief that this state of affairs is relatively easy to correct—provided that governments are willing to accept the following:

1. The situation and potential of the poor need to be better documented.
2. All people are capable of saving.
3. What the poor are missing are the legally integrated property systems that can convert
4. Civil disobedience and the mafias of today are not marginal phenomena but the result of people marching by the billions from life organized on a small scale to life on a big scale.
5. In this context, the poor are not the problem but the solution.
6. Implementing a property system that creates capital is a political challenge because it involves getting in touch with people, grasping the social contract, and overhauling the legal system.

With its victory over communism, capitalism's old agenda for economic progress is exhausted and requires a new set of commitments. It makes no sense continuing to call for open economies without facing the fact that the economic reforms underway open the doors only for small and globalized elites and leave out most of humanity. At present, capitalist globalization is concerned with interconnecting only the elites that live inside the bell jars. To lift the bell jars and do away with property apartheid will require going beyond the existing borders of economics and law.

I am not a die-hard capitalist. I do not view capitalism as a credo. Much more important to me are freedom, compassion for the poor, respect for the social contract, and equal opportunity. But for the moment, to achieve those goals, capitalism is the only game in town. It is the only system we know that provides us with the tools required to create massive surplus value.

I love being from the Third World because it represents such a marvelous challenge—that of making a transition to a market-based capitalist system that respects people's desires and beliefs.

When capital is a success story not only in the West but everywhere, we can move beyond the limits of the physical world and use our minds to soar into the future.

Selections from *Cities in a World Economy*

Sassen Saskia

These selections are essential reading for anyone interested in understanding the new global economy and its implications for international investment. This material focuses on the implications of global change for local economic and social conditions. Sassen argues that the current transformation in the world economy—the massive changes in communication and information technologies—gives major cities a new importance as production sites. Cities are the brains of the new global economy. They are the places where financial operations tend to cluster and the places where control and coordination are located. Sassen maintains that the combination of global dispersal of economic activities and the global integration made possible by advances in telecommunication technologies have created a new strategic role for global cities. A disturbing consequence of this transformation, however, is that global cities are developing a bifurcated class structure composed of highly paid professionals at one end and low-wage, low-skilled workers at the other.

PLACE AND PRODUCTION IN THE GLOBAL ECONOMY

As the end of the twentieth century approaches, massive developments in telecommunications and the ascendance of information industries have led analysts and politicians to proclaim the end of cities. Cities, they tell us, should now be obsolete as economic entities. With large-scale relocations of offices and factories to less congested and lower cost areas than central cities, the computerized workplace can be located anywhere: in a clerical "factory" in the Bahamas or in a home in the suburbs. The growth of information industries has made it possible for outputs to be transmitted around the globe instantaneously. And the globalization of economic activity suggests that place—particularly the type of place represented by cities—no longer matters.

This is but a partial account, however. These trends are indeed all taking place, but they represent only half of what is happening. Alongside the well-documented spatial dispersal of economic activities, new forms of territorial centralization of top-level management and control operations have appeared. National and global markets, as well as globally integrated operations, require central places where the work of globalization gets done. Furthermore, information industries require a vast physical infrastructure containing strategic nodes with a hyperconcentration of facilities. Finally, even the most advanced information industries have a production process.

Once this process is brought into the analysis, funny things happen; secretaries are part of it, and so are the cleaners of the buildings where the professionals do their work. An economic configuration very different from that suggested by the concept of **information economy** emerges, whereby we recover the material conditions, production sites, and place-boundedness that are also part of globalization and the information economy. A detailed examination of the activities, firms, markets, and physical infrastructure that are involved in globalization and concentrated in cities allows us to see the actual role played by cities in a global economy. Thus when telecommunications were introduced on a large scale in all advanced industries in the 1980s, we saw the central business districts of the leading cities and international business centers of the world—New York, Los Angeles, London, Tokyo, Frankfurt, Sao Paulo, Hong Kong, and Sydney, among others—reach their highest densities ever. This explosion in the numbers of firms locating in the downtowns of major cities during that decade goes against what should have been expected according to models emphasizing territorial dispersal; this is especially true given the high cost of locating in a major downtown area.

If telecommunications has not made cities obsolete, has it at least altered the economic function of cities in a global economy? And if this is so, what does it tell us about the importance of place, of the locale, in an era dominated by the imagery and the language of economic globalization and information flows? Is there a new and strategic role for major cities, a role linked to the formation of a truly global economic system, a role not sufficiently recognized by analysts and policymakers? And could it be that the reason this new and strategic role has not been sufficiently recognized is that economic globalization—what it actually takes to implement global markets and processes—is misunderstood?

The notion of a global economy has become deeply entrenched in political and media circles all over the world. Yet its dominant images—the instantaneous transmission of money around the globe, the information economy, the neutralization of distance through **telematics**—are partial and hence profoundly inadequate representations of what globalization and the rise of information economies actually entail for cities. Missing from this abstract model are the actual material processes, activities, and infrastructures that are central to the implementation of globalization. Both overlooking the spatial dimension of economic globalization and overemphasizing the information dimensions have served to distort the role played by major cities in the current phase of economic globalization.

The last 20 years have seen pronounced changes in the geography, composition, and insti-

tutional framework of economic globalization. A world economy has been in existence for several centuries, but it has been reconstituted repeatedly over time. A key starting point for this book is the fact that, in each historical period, the world economy has consisted of a distinct combination of geographic areas, industries, and institutional arrangements. One of the important changes over the last 20 years has been the increase in the mobility of capital at both the national and especially the transnational level. The transnational mobility of capital brings about specific forms of articulation among different geographic areas and transformations in the role played by these areas in the world economy. This trend in turn produces several types of locations for international transactions, the most familiar of which are **export processing zones** and **offshore banking centers**. One question for us, then, is the extent to which major cities are yet another type of *location* for international trans actions, though clearly one at a very high level of complexity.

Increased capital mobility does not only bring about changes in the geographic organization of manufacturing production and in the network of financial markets. Increased capital mobility also generates a demand for types of production needed to ensure the management, control and servicing of this new organization of manufacturing and finance. These new types of production range from the development of telecommunications to specialized services that are key inputs for the management of a global network of factories, offices, and financial markets. The mobility of capital also includes the production of a broad array of innovations in these sectors. These types of production have their own locational patterns; they tend toward high levels of agglomeration. We will want to ask whether a focus on the *production* of these service input illuminates the question of place in processes of economic globalization particularly the kind of place represented by cities.

Specialized services for firms and financial transactions, as well as the complex markets both entail, are a layer of activity that has been central to the organization of major global processes in the 1980s. To what extent is it useful to think in terms of the broader category of cities as key locations for such activities—in addition to the more narrowly defined locations represented by headquarters of transnational corporations or offshore banking centers—to further our understanding of major aspects of the organization and management of the world economy?

Much of the scholarly literature on cities has focused on internal aspects of the urban social, economic, and political systems, and it has considered cities to be part of national urban systems. International aspects typically have been considered the preserve of nation-states, not of cities. The literature on international economic activities, moreover, has traditionally focused on the activities of multinational corporations and banks and has seen the key to globalization in the *power* of multinational firm. Again, this conceptualization has the effect of leaving no room for a possible role by cities.

Including cities in the analysis adds two important dimensions to the study of economic internationalization. First, it breaks down the national state into a variety of components that may be significant in understanding international economic activity. Second, it displaces the focus from the power of large corporations over governments and economies to the range of activities and organizational arrangements necessary for the implementation and maintenance of a global network of factories, service operations, and markets; these are all processes only partly encompassed by the activities of transnational corporations and banks. Third, it contributes to a focus on place and on the urban social and political order associated with these activities. Processes of economic globalization are thereby reconstituted as concrete production complexes situated in specific places containing a multiplicity of activities and interests, many unconnected to global processes. Focusing on cities allows us to specify a geography of strategic places on a global scale, as well as the micro-geographies and politics unfolding within these places.

A central thesis organizing this book is that the transformation during the last two decades in the composition of the world economy accompanying the shift to services and finance brings about a renewed importance of major cities as sites for certain types of activities and functions. In the current phase of the world economy, it is precisely the combination of the global dispersal of economic activities *and* global integration—under

conditions of continued concentration of economic ownership and control—that has contributed to a strategic role for certain major cities that I call **global cities** (Sassen, 1991). Some have been centers for world trade and banking for centuries, but beyond these longstanding functions, today's global cities are (1) command points in the organization of the world economy; (2) key locations and marketplaces for the leading industries of the current period, which are finance and specialized services for firms; and (3) major sites of production for these industries, including the production of innovations. Several cities also fulfill equivalent functions on the smaller geographic scales of both trans- and subnational regions.

Alongside these new global and regional hierarchies of cities is a vast territory that has become increasingly peripheral, increasingly excluded from the major economic processes that fuel economic growth in the new global economy. A multiplicity of formerly important manufacturing centers and port cities have lost functions and are in decline, not only in the less developed countries but also in the most advanced economies. This is yet another meaning of economic globalization. We can think of these developments as constituting new geographies of centrality (that cut across the old divide of poor/rich countries) and of marginality that have become increasingly evident in the less developed world and in highly developed countries as well.

The most powerful of these new geographies of centrality binds the major international financial and business centers: New York, London, Tokyo, Paris, Frankfurt, Zurich, Amsterdam, Sydney, Hong Kong, among others. But this geography now also includes cities such as Sao Paulo and Mexico City. The intensity of transactions among these cities, particularly through the financial markets, flows of services, and investment has increased sharply, and so have the orders of magnitude involved. At the same time, there has been a sharpening inequality in the concentration of strategic resources and activities between each of these cities and others in the same country. For instance, Paris now concentrates a larger share of leading economic sectors and wealth in France than it did 20 years ago, whereas Marseilles, once a major economic center, has lost its share and is suffering severe decline. Some national capitals, for example, have lost central economic functions and power to the new global cities, which have taken over some of the coordination functions, markets, and production processes once concentrated in national capitals or in major regional centers. Sao Paulo has gained immense strength as a business and financial center in Brazil over Rio de Janeiro—once the capital and most important city in the country—and over the once powerful axis represented by Rio and Brasilia, the current capital. This is one of the meanings, or consequences, of the formation of a globally integrated economic system.

What is the impact of this type of economic growth on the broader social and economic order of these cities? A vast literature on the impact of a dynamic, high-growth manufacturing sector in highly developed countries shows that it raises wages, reduces economic inequality, and contributes to the formation of a middle class. There is much less literature on the impact on the service economy, especially the rapidly growing specialized services.

Specialized services, which have become a key component of all developed economies, are not usually analyzed in terms of a production or work process. Such services are usually seen as a type of output—that is, high-level technical expertise. Thus insufficient attention has been paid to the actual array of jobs, from high paying to low paying, involved in the production of these services. A focus on production displaces the emphasis from expertise to work. Services need to be produced, and the buildings that hold the workers need to be built and cleaned. The rapid growth of the financial industry and of highly specialized services generates not only high-level technical and administrative jobs but also low-wage unskilled jobs. Together with the new interurban inequalities mentioned above, we are also seeing new economic inequalities within cities, especially within global cities and their regional counterparts.

The new urban economy is in many ways highly problematic. This is perhaps particularly evident in global cities and their regional counterparts. The new growth sectors of specialized services and finance contain capabilities for profit making that are vastly superior to those of more traditional economic sectors. The latter are essential to the operation of the urban economy and the

daily needs of residents, but their survival is threatened in a situation where finance and specialized services can earn superprofits. This sharp polarization in the profit-making capabilities of different sectors of the economy has always existed. But what we see happening today takes place on a higher order of magnitude, and it is engendering massive distortions in the operations of various markets, from housing to labor. We can see this effect, for example, in the unusually sharp increase in the beginning salaries of MBAs and lawyers and in the precipitous fall in the wages of low-skilled manual workers and clerical workers. We can see the same effect in the retreat of many real estate developers from the low- and medium-income housing market who are attracted to the rapidly expanding housing demand by the new highly paid professionals and the possibility for vast overpricing of this housing supply.

The rapid development of an international property market has made this disparity even worse. It means that real estate prices at the center of New York City are more connected to prices in London or Frankfurt than to the overall real estate market in the city. Powerful institutional investors from Japan, for instance, find it profitable to buy and sell property in Manhattan or central London. They force prices up because of the competition and raise them even further to sell at a profit. How can a small commercial operation in New York compete with such investors and the prices they can command?

The high profit-making capability of the new growth sectors rests partly on speculative activity. The extent of this dependence on speculation can be seen in the crisis of the 1990s that followed the unusually high profits in finance and real estate in the 1980s. The real estate and financial crisis, however, seems to have left the basic dynamic of the sector untouched. The crisis can thus be seen as an adjustment to more reasonable (that is, less speculative) profit levels. The overall dynamic of polarization in profit levels in the urban economy remains in place, as do the distortions in many markets.

The typical informed view of the global economy, cities, and the new growth sectors does not incorporate these multiple dimensions. Elsewhere I have argued that we could think of the dominant narrative or mainstream account of economic globalization as a narrative of eviction (Sassen, 1993). In the dominant account, the key concepts of globalization, information economy, and telematics all suggest that place no longer matters and that the only type of worker that matters is the highly educated professional. This account favors the capability for global transmission over the concentrations of established infrastructure that make transmission possible; favors information outputs over the workers producing those outputs, from specialists to secretaries; and favors the new transnational corporate culture over the multiplicity of cultural environments, including reterritorialized immigrant cultures within which many of the "other" jobs of the global information economy take place. In brief, the dominant narrative concerns itself with the upper circuits of capital, not the lower ones.

This narrow focus has the effect of excluding from the account the *place*-boundedness of significant components of the global information economy; it thereby also excludes a whole array of activities and types of workers from the story of globalization that are as vital to it as international finance and global telecommunications are. By failing to include these activities and workers, it ignores the variety of cultural contexts within which they exist, a diversity as present in processes of globalization as is the new international corporate culture. When we focus on place and production, we can see that globalization is a process involving not only the corporate economy and the new transnational corporate culture but also, for example, the immigrant economies and work cultures evident in our large cities.

The new empirical trends and the new theoretical developments have made cities prominent once again in most of the social sciences. Cities have reemerged not only as objects of study but also as strategic sites for the theorization of a broad array of social, economic, and political processes central to the current era: economic globalization and international migration; the emergence of specialized services and finance as the leading growth sector in advanced economies; and new types of inequality. In this context, it is worth noting that we are also seeing the beginning of a repositioning of cities in policy arenas. Two instances in particular stand out. One is the recent programmatic effort at the World Bank to produce analyses that show how central urban economic productivity is to macroeconomic performance. The other is the explicit competition among major cities to gain access to increasingly global markets for resources and activities ranging from foreign investment, headquarters, and international institutions to tourism and conventions.

The subject of the city in a world economy is extremely broad. The literature on cities is inevitably vast, but it focuses mostly on single cities. It is also a literature that is mostly domestic in orientation. International studies of cities tend to be comparative. What is lacking is a transnational perspective on the subject: that is to say, one that takes as its starting point a dynamic system or set of transactions that by its nature entails multiple locations involving more than one country. This contrasts with a comparative international approach, which focuses on two or more cities that may have no connections among one another.

Given the vastness of the subject and of the literature on cities and given what is lacking in much of that literature, this book focuses particularly on recent empirical and conceptual developments because they are an expression of major changes in urban and national economies and in modes of inquiry about cities. Such a choice is inevitably limited and certainly cannot account for the cases of many cities that may *not* have experienced any of these developments. Our focus on the urban impact of economic globalization, the new inequalities among and within cities, and the new urban economy is justified by the major characteristics of the current historical period and the need for social scientists to address these changes.

Chapter 2 examines key characteristics of the global economy that are important for an understanding of the impact of globalization on cities. Chapter 3 analyzes the new interurban inequalities, focusing on three key issues: (1) the impact of globalization, particularly the internationalization of production and the growth of tourism, on so-called **primate urban systems** in less developed countries; (2) the impact of economic globalization on so-called **balanced urban systems**; and (3) the possibility of the formation of a transnational urban system. A rapidly growing research literature now finds sharp increases in the linkages binding the cities that function as production sites and marketplaces for global capital. Chapter 4 focuses on the new urban economy, where finance and specialized services have emerged as driving engines for profit making. Chapter 5 examines these issues in greater detail through a series of case studies of key global cities and related issues. Chapter 6 focuses on possible new urban forms and social alignments inside these cities. Are the new social alignments inside cities merely a quantitative transformation or also a qualitative one? Chapter 7 considers this and other possibilities in summarizing the central propositions of this book.

THE URBAN IMPACT OF ECONOMIC GLOBALIZATION

Profound changes in the composition, geography, and institutional framework of the global economy have had major implications for cities. In the 1800s, when the world economy consisted largely of trade, the crucial sites were harbors, plantations, factories, and mines. Cities were already servicing centers at that time: cities typically developed alongside harbors, and trading companies were dependent on multiple industrial, banking, and other commercial services located in cities. Cities, however, were not the key production sites for the leading industries in the 1800s; the production of wealth was centered elsewhere. Today, international trade continues to be an important fact in the global economy, but it has been overshadowed both in value and in power by international financial flows, whether loans and equities or foreign currency transactions. In the 1980s, finance and specialized services have emerged as the major components of international transactions. The crucial sites for these transactions are financial markets, advanced corporate service firms, banks, and the headquarters of transnational corporations. These sites lie at the heart of the process for the creation of wealth, and they are located in cities.

Thus one of the factors influencing the role of cities in the new global economy is the change in the composition of international transactions, a factor often not recognized in standard analyses of the world economy. The current composition of international transactions shows this transformation very clearly. For instance, foreign direct investment grew three times faster in the 1980s

than the growth of the export trade. Furthermore, by the mid-1980s investment in services had become the main component in foreign direct investment flows where before it had been in manufacturing or raw materials extraction. The monetary value of international financial flows is larger than the value of international trade and of foreign direct investment. The sharp growth of international financial flows has raised the level of complexity of transactions. This new circumstance demands a highly advanced infrastructure of specialized services and top-level concentrations of telecommunications facilities. Cities are central locations for both.

A NEW GEOGRAPHY OF CENTERS AND MARGINS: SUMMARY AND IMPLICATIONS

Three important developments over the last 20 years laid the foundation for the analysis of cities in the world economy presented in this book. They are captured in the three broad propositions organizing the preceding chapters.

1. *The territorial dispersal of economic activities, of which globalization is one form, contributes to the growth of centralized functions and operations.* We find here a new logic for agglomeration and key conditions for the renewed centrality of cities in advanced economies. Information technologies, often thought of as neutralizing geography, actually contribute to spatial concentration. They make possible the geographic dispersal and simultaneous integration of many activities. But the particular conditions under which such facilities are available have promoted centralization of the most advanced users in the most advanced telecommunications centers. We see parallel developments in cities that function as regional nodes—that is, at smaller geographic scales and lower levels of complexity than global cities.

2. *Centralized control and management over a geographically dispersed array of economic operations does not come about inevitably as part of a "world system."* It requires the production of a vast range of highly specialized services, telecommunications infrastructure, and industrial services. Major cities are centers for the servicing and financing of international trade, investment, and headquarters operations. And in this sense they are strategic production sites for today's leading economic sectors. This function is reflected in the ascendance of these activities in their economies. Again, cities that serve as regional centers exhibit similar developments. This is the way in which the spatial effects of the growing service intensity in the organization of all industries materialize in cities.

3. *Economic globalization has contributed to a new geography of centrality and marginality.* This new geography assumes many forms and operates in many terrains, from the distribution of telecommunications facilities to the structure of the economy and of employment. Global cities become the sites of immense concentrations of economic power, while cities that were once major manufacturing centers suffer inordinate declines; highly educated workers see their incomes rise to unusually high levels, while low- or medium-skilled workers see theirs sink. Financial services produce superprofits while industrial services barely survive.

Let us look more closely now at this last and most encompassing of the propositions.

THE LOCUS OF THE PERIPHERAL

The sharpening distance between the extremes evident in all major cities of developed countries raises questions about the notion of "rich" countries and "rich" cities. It suggests that the geography of centrality and marginality, which in the past was seen in terms of the duality of highly developed and less developed countries, is now also evident within developed countries and especially within their major cities.

One line of theorization posits that the intensified inequalities described in the preceding chapters represent a transformation in the geography of center and periphery. They signal that peripheralization processes are occurring inside areas that were once conceived of as "core" areas—whether at the global, regional, or urban level—and that alongside the sharpening of peripheralization processes, centrality has also become sharper at all three levels.

The condition of being peripheral is installed in different geographic terrains depending on the prevailing economic dynamic. We see new forms of peripheralization at the center of major cities in developed countries not far from some of the most expensive commercial land in the world: "inner cities" are evident not only in the United States and large European cities, but also now in Tokyo (Nakabayashi, 1987; Komori, 1983; KUPI, 1981; Sassen, 1991, Chap. 9). Furthermore, we can see peripheralization operating at the center in organizational terms as well (Sassen-Koob, 1980; Wilson, 1987). We have long known about segmented labor markets, but the manufacturing decline and the kind of devaluing of nonprofessional workers in leading industries that we see today in these cities go beyond segmentation and in fact represent an instance of peripheralization.

Furthermore, the new forms of growth evident at the urban perimeter also mean crisis: violence in the immigrant ghetto of the *banlieus* (the French term for *suburbs*), exurbanites clamoring for control over growth to protect their environment, new forms of urban governance (Body-Gendrot, 1993; Pickvance & Preteceille, 1991). The regional mode of regulation in many of these cities is based on the old center/suburb model and may hence become increasingly inadequate to deal with intraperipheral conflicts—conflicts among different types of constituencies at the urban perimeter or urban region. Frankfurt, for example, is a city that cannot function without its region's towns; yet this particular *urban region* would not have emerged without the specific forms of growth in Frankfurt's center. Keil and Ronneberger (1993) note the ideological motivation in the call by politicians to officially *recognize* the region so as to strengthen Frankfurt's position in the global interurban competition. This call also provides a rationale for coherence and the idea of common interests among the many objectively disparate interests in the region: it displaces the conflicts among unequally advantaged sectors onto a project of regional competition with other regions. Regionalism then emerges as the concept for bridging the global orientation of leading sectors with the various local agendas of various constituencies in the region.

In contrast, the city discourse rather than the ideology of regionalism dominates in cities such as New York or Sao Paulo (see Toulouse, 1992). The challenge is how to bridge the inner city, or the squatters at the urban perimeter, with the center. In multiracial cities, multiculturalism has emerged as one form of this bridging. A "regional" discourse is perhaps beginning to emerge, but it has until now been totally submerged under the suburbanization banner, a concept that suggests both escape from and dependence on the city. The notion of conflict within the urban periphery among diverse interests and constituencies has not really been much of a factor in the United States. The delicate point at the level of the region has rather been the articulation between the residential suburbs and the city.

CONTESTED SPACE

Large cities have emerged as strategic territories for these developments. *First, cities are the sites for concrete operations of the economy.* For our purposes we can distinguish two forms of such concrete operations: (1) In terms of economic globalization and place, cities are strategic places that concentrate command functions, global markets, and, as demonstrated in Chapter 4, production sites for the advanced corporate service industries. (2) In terms of day-to-day work in the leading industrial complex, finance, and specialized services, we saw in Chapter 6 that a large share of the jobs involved are low paid and manual, and many are held by women and immigrants. Although these types of workers and jobs are never represented as part of the global economy, they are in fact as much a part of globalization as international finance is. We see at work here a dynamic of valorization that has sharply increased the distance between the devalorized and the valorized—indeed overvalorized—sectors of the economy. These joint presences have made cities a contested terrain.

The structure of economic activity has brought about changes in the organization of work that are reflected in a pronounced shift in the job supply, with strong polarization occurring in the income distribution and occupational distribution of workers. Major growth industries show a greater incidence of jobs at the high- and low-paying ends of the scale than do the older industries now in decline. Almost half the jobs in the producer services are lower-income jobs, and the other half are in the two highest earnings classes. On the other hand, a large share of manufacturing workers were in middle-earning jobs during the postwar period of high growth in these industries in the United States and the United Kingdom.

One particular concern here was to understand how new forms of inequality actually are constituted into new social forms, such as gentrified neighborhoods, informal economies, or downgraded manufacturing sectors. To what extent these developments are connected to the consolidation of an economic complex oriented to the global market is difficult to say. Precise empirical documentation of the linkages or impacts is impossible; the effort here is focused, then, on a more general attempt to understand the consequences of both the ascendance of such an international economic complex and the general move to a service economy.

Second, the city concentrates diversity. Its spaces are inscribed with the dominant corporate culture but also with a multiplicity of other cultures and identities, notably through immigration. The slippage is evident: the dominant culture can encompass only part of the city. And while corporate power inscribes noncorporate cultures and identities with "otherness," thereby devaluing them, they are present everywhere. The immigrant communities and informal economy described in Chapter 6 are only two instances. Diverse cultures and ethnicities are especially strong in major cities in the United States and Western Europe; these also have the largest concentrations of corporate power.

We see here an interesting correspondence between great concentrations of corporate power and large concentrations of "others." It invites us to see that globalization is not only constituted in terms of capital and the new international corporate culture (international finance, telecommunications, information flows) but also in terms of people and noncorporate cultures. There is a whole infrastructure of low-wage, nonprofessional jobs and activities that constitutes a crucial part of the so-called corporate economy.

A focus on the *work* behind command functions, on *production* in the finance and services complex, and on market*places* has the effect of incorporating the material facilities underlying globalization and the whole infrastructure of jobs and workers typically not seen as belonging to the corporate sector of the economy: secretaries and cleaners, the truckers who deliver the software, the variety of technicians and repair workers, and all the jobs having to do with the maintenance, painting, and renovation of the buildings where it is all housed.

This expanded focus can lead to the recognition that a multiplicity of economies is involved in constituting the so-called global information economy. It recognizes types of activities, workers, and firms that have never been installed in the "center" of the economy or that have been evicted from that center in the restructuring of the 1980s and have therefore been devalued in a system that puts too much weight on a narrow conception of the center of the economy. Globalization can, then, be seen as a process that involves multiple economies and work cultures.

The preceding chapters have tried to demonstrate that cities are of great importance to the dominant economic sectors. Large cities in the highly developed world are the places where globalization processes assume concrete, localized forms. These localized forms are, in good part, what globalization is about. We can then think of cities also as the place where the contradictions of the internationalization of capital either come to rest or conflict. If we consider, further, that large cities also concentrate a growing share of disadvantaged populations—immigrants in both Europe and the United States; African Americans and Latinos in the United States—then we can see that cities have become a strategic terrain for a whole series of conflicts and contradictions.

On one hand, they concentrate a disproportionate share of corporate power and are one of the key sites for the overvalorization of the corporate economy; on the other, they concentrate a disproportionate share of the disadvantaged and are one of the key sites for their devalorization.

This joint presence happens in a context where (1) the internationalization of the economy has grown sharply and cities have become increasingly strategic for global capital; and (2) marginalized people have come into representation and are making claims on the city as well. This joint presence is further brought into focus by the sharpening of the distance between the two. The center now concentrates immense power, a power that rests on the capability for global control and the capability to produce superprofits. And marginality, notwithstanding weak economic and political power, has become an increasingly strong presence through the new politics of culture and identity.

If cities were irrelevant to the globalization of economic activity, the center could simply abandon them and not be bothered by all of this. Indeed, this is precisely what some politicians argue—that cities have become hopeless reservoirs for all kinds of social despair. It is interesting to note again how the dominant economic narrative argues that place no longer matters, that firms can be located anywhere thanks to telematics, that major industries now are information-based and hence not placebound. This line of argument devalues cities at a time when they are major sites for the new cultural politics. It also allows the corporate economy to extract major concessions from city governments under the notion that firms can simply leave and relocate elsewhere, which is not quite the case for a whole complex of firms, as much of this book sought to show.

In seeking to show that (1) cities are strategic to economic globalization because they are command points, global marketplaces, and production sites for the information economy; and (2) many of the devalued sectors of the urban economy actually fulfill crucial functions for the center, this book attempts to recover the importance of cities specifically in a globalized economic system and the importance of those overlooked sectors that rest largely on the labor of women, immigrants, and, in the case of large U.S. cities, African Americans and Latinos. In fact it is the intermediary sectors of the economy (such as routine office work, headquarters that are not geared to the world markets, the variety of services demanded by the largely suburbanized middle class) and of the urban population (the middle class) that can and have left cities. The two sectors that have stayed, the center and the "other," find in the city the strategic terrain for their operations.

SUGGESTED READINGS FOR PART VI

Babcock, Blair. *Unfairly Structured Cities.* Oxford: Blackwell. 1984.

Gomez-Ibanez, Jose A., and John R. Meyer. "Privatizing and Deregulating Local Public Services: Lessons from Britain's Buses."*Journal of the American Planning Association*, Vol. 56, No. 1, 1990.

Kent, T.J., Jr. "Report on Berlin 1945" (Part One), *Journal of the American Institute of Planners*, Vol. 12, No. 1, 1946, pp. 5-17. "Report on Berlin 1945" (Part Two), *JAIP*, Vol. 12, No. 2, 1946, pp. 18-27.

Myrdal, Gunnar. *Rich Lands and Poor*. New York: Harper. 1957.

Peattie, Lisa. *The View from the Barrio*. Ann Arbor: The University of Michigan Press. 1987.

Sanyal, Bishwapriya, ed. *Breaking the Boundaries*. New York: Plenum. 1990.

Sowell, Thomas. *A Conflict of Visions*. New York: Morrow. 1987.

Todoro, Michael. *Economic Development in the Third World*. New York: Longman. 1989.

Waterson, Albert. *Development Planning: Lesson of Experience*. Baltimore: Johns Hopkins. 1969.

VII
The Profession and Practice of Planning

The Crisis of Confidence in Professional Knowledge

Donald A. Schön

In this selection Schön challenges the role of professionalism society. He examines how people have become increasingly less confident in their abilities to handle situations in practice and more dependent on professionals. Schön asks the hard questions that all professionals, including planners, must be "reflective" about —the merits of being a professional, the purpose a professional serves, and whether professional knowledge can ever be sufficient to meet the increasing demands of professional practice.

The professions have become essential to the very functioning of our society. We conduct society's principal business through professionals specially trained to carry out that business, whether it be making war and defending the nation, educating our children, diagnosing and curing disease, judging and punishing those who violate the law, settling disputes, managing industry and business, designing and constructing buildings, helping those who for one reason or another are unable to fend for themselves. Our principal formal institutions—schools, hospitals, government agencies, courts of law, armies—are arenas for the exercise of professional activity. We look to professionals for the definition and solution of our problems, and it is through them that we strive for social progress. In all of these functions we honor what Everett Hughes has called "the professions' claim to extraordinary knowledge in matters of great social importance";[1] and in return, we grant professionals extraordinary rights and privileges. Hence, professional careers are among the most coveted and remunerative, and there are few occupations that have failed to seek out professional status. As one author asked, are we seeing the professionalization of nearly everyone?[2]

But although we are wholly dependent on them, there are increasing signs of a crisis of confidence in the professions. Not only have we witnessed well-publicized scandals in which highly esteemed professionals have misused their autonomy— where doctors and lawyers, for example, have used their positions illegitimately for private

gain—but we are also encountering visible failures of professional action. Professionally designed solutions to public problems have had unanticipated consequences, sometimes worse than the problems they were designed to solve. Newly invented technologies, professionally conceived and evaluated, have turned out to produce unintended side effects unacceptable to large segments of our society. A professionally conceived and managed war has been widely perceived as a national disaster. Professionals themselves have delivered widely disparate and conflicting recommendations concerning problems of national importance, including those to which professional activities have contributed.

As a result, there has been a disposition to blame the professions for their failures and a loss of faith in professional judgment. There have been strident public calls for external regulation of professional activity, efforts to create public organizations to protest and protect against professionally recommended policies, and appeals to the courts for recourse against professional incompetence. Even in the most hallowed professional schools of medicine and law, rebellious students have written popular exposes of the amoral, irrelevant, or coercive aspects of professional education.[3]

But the questioning of professionals' rights and freedoms— their license to determine who shall be allowed to practice, their mandate for social control, their autonomy—has been rooted in a deeper questioning of the professionals' claim to extraordinary knowledge in matters of human importance. This skepticism has taken several forms. In addition to the public loss of confidence noted above, there has been a virulent ideological attack on the professions, mostly from the Left. Some critics, like Ivan Illich, have engaged in a wholesale debunking of professional claims to special expertise.[4] Others have tried to show that professionals misappropriate specialized knowledge in their own interests and the interest of a power elite intent on preserving its dominance over the rest of the society.[5] Finally, and most significantly, professionals themselves have shown signs recently of a loss of confidence in their claims to extraordinary knowledge.

As short a time ago as 1963, *Daedalus*, the highly regarded journal of the American Academy of Arts and Sciences, published a volume on the professions that began, "Everywhere in American life, the professions are triumphant." The editors of *Daedalus* found evidence of triumph in the new visibility of the professions, the growing demand for their services, and their expansion in nearly all fields of practice:

> We already devote an impressive percentage of the gross national product to the training of professionals... and the day is coming when the "knowledge industry" will occupy the same key role in the American economy that the railroad industry did a hundred years ago... At the midpoint of the fifteen year period (1955–1970) in which we are attempting to double the number of college professors—an awesome task which is made even more difficult by the simultaneous and equally grandiose expansion plans of all the other traditional professions, the spectacular proliferation of new professions and the increasing professionalization of business life—America has become more cognizant of the professions, and more dependent on their services, than at any previous time in our history. Thorsten Veblen's sixty-year-old dream of a professionally run society has never been closer to realization.[6]

The editors of *Daedalus* were by no means alone in their assessment of the situation. It was generally believed both that social needs for technical expertise were growing and that, as a cause and consequence of this growth, a professional knowledge industry had come into being. Richard Hofstadter wrote of the once self-sufficient "common man,"

> he cannot even make his breakfast without using devices, more or less mysterious to him, which expertise has put at his disposal; and when he sits down to breakfast and looks at his morning newspaper he reads about a whole range of vital and intricate issues I and acknowledges, if he is candid with himself, that he has not acquired competence to judge most of them.[7]

In his commencement address at Yale in 1962, John Kennedy had urged his young audience to "participate... in the solution of the problems that pour upon us, requiring the most sophisticated solutions to complex and obstinate issues."[8]

There were many references to a "second scientific revolution" which was producing a "knowledgeable society,"[9] an "active society," a "post-industrial society,"[10] organized around professional competence.

> The prodigious and increasing resources poured into research, the large and increasing numbers of trained people working on various natural and social "problems," and the expanding productivity resulting from this work is, at least in size, a new factor in social and... in political life. This "second scientific revolution" ...reflects both a new appreciation of the role of scientific knowledge and a new merger of western organization and scientific skills.[11]

Professionals in the labor force had risen from 4 percent in 1900, to 8 percent in 1950, to 13 percent in 1966.[12] Daniel Bell predicted that professional and technical workers would reach 15 percent of the labor force by 1975 and might well rise to 25 percent by the year 2000.[13] "The specialist in his field must be supreme," as one commentator noted, "for who, other than another similarly qualified specialist, can challenge him?"[14] Even the critics of the professions conceded that it had become impossible to conceive of a modern nation without professions.[15]

In the meantime, as the professions geared up to meet the escalating demand for their services, they suffered from overload. In the *Daedalus* volume, the essay on medicine spoke of the overtaxed physician and of the task of coordinating the proliferating specialties which had arisen out of successful medical research and practice. The essay on science complained of the dangers to scientific professionalism inherent in the bureaucracies which had grown up around scientific research. The distinguished representative of the law stressed the difficulties in maintaining the independence of the bar, the "real problem... of making legal services available on a wider basis,"[16] and the problem of managing the "burgeoning mass of data to be assimilated."[17] The teacher, the military professional, even the politician, expressed similar sentiments. As Kenneth Lynn observed,

> It is notable how many of the contributors to this symposium emphasize the multiplicity of demands that are made on the contemporary clergyman, teacher, doctor and scientists.[18]

In nearly all articles, the note most sharply sounded was the problem of a success attributed, in Bernard Barber's words, to the fact that:

> the generalized knowledge and the community orientation characteristic of professional behavior are indispensable in our society as we now know it and as we want it to be. Indeed, our kind of society can now maintain its fundamental character only by enlarging the scope for professional behavior.[19]

The success of the professionals was thought to be due, in short, to the explosion of the "knowledge industry" whose output it was the function of the professional to apply with rigor, probity, and "community orientation" to the goals and problems of American life.

The only jarring voices in this hymn of confident approbation came from the representatives of divinity and city planning. James Gustafson spoke of "the clergyman's dilemma." The clergy, he observed,

> retains a loyalty to ancient traditions in thought, in institutional life and practice. Yet it cannot simply rest its case for contemporary validity in its faithfulness to the ancient and

honorable paths of the fathers. The overused phrase "the problem of relevance" points to the reality of its dilemma ... [20]

And William Alonso spoke of his profession's "lagging understanding":

> In the past half-century our cities have outgrown our concepts and our tools, and I have tried to show how the lagging understanding of the changes in kind that go with changes in size has led us to try remedies which are unsuited to the ills of our urban areas... [21]

Yet in the period between 1963 and 1981, the expression of lagging understandings, unsuitable remedies, and professional dilemmas has become the norm, and the note of triumphant confidence in the knowledge industry is hardly to be heard at all. For in these years, both professional and layman have suffered through public events which have undermined belief in the competence of expertise and brought the legitimacy of the professions into serious question.

The nation had been enmeshed in a disastrous war which had caused it to seem at war with itself. The professional representatives of science, technology, and public policy had done very little to prevent or stop that war or to heal the rifts it produced. On the contrary, professionals seemed to have a vested interest in prolonging the conflict.

A series of announced national crises—the deteriorating cities, poverty, the pollution of the environment, the shortage of energy—seemed to have roots in the very practices of science, technology, and public policy that were being called upon to alleviate them.

Government-sponsored "wars" against such crises seemed not to produce the expected results; indeed, they often seemed to exacerbate the crises. The success of the space program seemed not to be replicable when the problems to be solved were the tangled socio-techno-politico-economic predicaments of public life. The concept of the "technological fix" came into bad odor. Indeed, some of the solutions advocated by professional experts were seen as having created problems as bad as or worse than those they had been designed to solve. Just as urban renewal had emerged in the early sixties as a destroyer of neighborhoods, its unexpected consequences attributed by critics like William Alonso to the weakness of its underlying theory, so in fields as diverse as housing, criminal justice, social services, welfare, and transportation, the most promising solutions, painstakingly worked out and advocated by the experts, came to be seen as problematic.[22] They were ineffective, they created new problems, they were derived from theories which had been shown to be fragile and incomplete. To some critics, the public predicaments of the society began to seem less like problems to be solved through expertise than like dilemmas whose resolutions could come about only through moral and political choice.[23]

Advocates for peace and for the civil rights of minorities joined forces and turned against the experts whom they saw as instruments of an all-powerful establishment. Around such issues as environmental pollution, consumer exploitation, the inequity and high cost of medical care, the perpetuation of social injustice, scientists and scientifically trained professionals found themselves in the unfamiliar role of villain.

Shortages became gluts. The 1970 census revealed that we had grossly overestimated the demand for teachers, at all levels of our education system. The shortage of scientists and engineers, so visible in the late 1950s, had evaporated by the mid–1960s. Even the much-discussed shortage of physicians began to seem, by the early 1970s, to be less a shortage than an unwillingness on the part of physicians to serve where they were most needed.

With the scandals of Medicare and Medicaid, with Watergate and its aftermath, the public image of the professions was further tarnished. Apparently professionals could not be counted on to police themselves, to live up to standards of probity which set them above the ethical level of the general public. Like everyone else, they seemed ready to put their special status to private use.

Cumulatively, these events not only undermined particular social programs, creating doubts about their underlying strategies of intervention and models of the world, but generated a pervasive sense of the complexity of the phenomena with which scientists and professionals in general were attempting to deal. The events of the mid-1960s and early 1970s eroded the confidence of the public, and of the professionals themselves, that there existed an armamentarium of theories and techniques sufficient to remove the troubles that beset society. Indeed, these troubles seemed, at least in part, attributable to the overweening pride of professional expertise.

In 1982, there is no profession which would celebrate itself in the triumphant tones of the 1963 *Daedalus* volume. In spite of the continuing eagerness of the young to embark on apparently secure and remunerative professional careers, the professions are in the midst of a crisis of confidence and legitimacy. In public outcry, in social criticism, and in the complaints of the professionals themselves, the long-standing professional claim to a monopoly of knowledge and social control is challenged—first, because professionals do not live up to the values and norms which they espouse, and second, because they are ineffective.

Professionals claim to contribute to social well-being, put their clients' needs ahead of their own, and hold themselves accountable to standards of competence and morality. But both popular and scholarly critics accuse the professions of serving themselves at the expense of their clients, ignoring their obligations to public service, and failing to police themselves effectively.[24] As one observer put it, "the more powerful the professions, the more serious the dangers of laxness in concern for public service and zealousness in promoting the practitioners' interests."[25] Surveys of client populations reveal a widespread belief that professionals overcharge for their services, discriminate against the poor and powerless in favor of the rich and powerful, and refuse to make themselves accountable to the public.[26] Among younger professionals and students, there are many who find the professions without real interest in the values they are supposed to promote: lawyers have no real interest in justice or compassion; physicians, in the equitable distribution of quality health care; scientists and engineers, in the beneficence and safety of their technologies.[27]

Evidence of professional ineffectiveness has been presented in scholarly and journalistic exposes of professionally managed disasters—the Vietnam War, the Bay of Pigs, the nuclear accident at Three Mile Island, the near-bankruptcy of New York City, to name only a few examples of this genre.[28] Critics have called attention to the technical expert's disposition to deploy his techniques, whatever the consequences. Charles Reich, for example, describes the Bureau of Reclamation as "a dam building machine which will keep building dams as long as there is running water in a stream in the United States… [without reference to] the values that dams destroy." He concludes that

> professionals… can be counted on to do their job but not necessarily to define their job.[29]

And professionals have been loudly critical of their own failure to solve social problems, to keep from creating new problems, and to meet reasonable standards of competence in their service to their clients. In this vein, Warren Burger recently lashed out at the inadequate preparation and performance of trial lawyers in America, and David Rutstein was only among the first of many physicians to reflect publicly on the failure of the health-care system to keep pace with the enormous expansion of the nation's investment in medical research and technology.[30]

Some observers have also noted a trend toward deprofessionalization. Among such diverse professional groups as engineers, teachers, musicians, scientists, physicians, and statisticians, there has been a slackening of the labor market and a decline in economic status and working conditions, a pattern of institutional change which has been variously labelled "bureaucratization," "industrialization," or even "proletarianization" of the professions.[31] Professionals are unionizing in increasing numbers, apparently in recognition of their status as workers in a bureaucracy rather than as autonomous managers of their own careers.

The crisis of confidence in the professions, and perhaps also the decline in professional self-image, seems to be rooted in a growing skepticism about professional effectiveness in the larger sense, a skeptical reassessment of the professions' actual contribution to society's well-being through the delivery of competent services based on special knowledge. Clearly, this skepticism is bound up with the questions of professional self-interest, bureaucratization, and subordination to the interests of business or government. But it also hinges centrally on the question of professional knowledge. Is professional knowledge adequate to fulfill the espoused purposes of the professions? Is it suf-

ficient to meet the societal demands which the professions have helped to create?

The crisis of confidence in the professions may not depend solely on the question of professional knowledge. On the other hand, even the muckrakers and radical critics, who emphasize professional self-interest and subordination to class-interest, envisage a purification and restructuring of the professions so that society may gain a fuller, more justly distributed access to the benefits of their special knowledge.[32] There remains, even for these critics, the question of the adequacy of professional knowledge to the needs and problems of society.

Let us consider, then, how the crisis of confidence in the professions has been interpreted by professionals who have given serious thought in their own fields to the adequacy of professional knowledge. On the whole, their assessment is that professional knowledge is mismatched to the changing character of the situations of practice—the complexity, uncertainty, instability, uniqueness, and value conflicts which are increasingly perceived as central to the world of professional practice.

In such fields as medicine, management, and engineering, for example, leading professionals speak of a new awareness of a complexity which resists the skills and techniques of traditional expertise. As physicians have turned their attention from traditional images of medical practice to the predicament of the larger health care system, they have come to see the larger system as a "tangled web" that traditional medical knowledge and skill cannot untangle. How can physicians influence a massively complex health care system which they do not understand and of which only a very small fraction is under their direct control?[33] The dean of a major school of management speaks of the inadequacy of established management theory and technique to deal with the increasingly critical task of "managing complexity."[34] The dean of a famous school of engineering observes that the nineteenth-century division of labor has become obsolete. Professionals are called upon to perform tasks for which they have not been educated, and "the niche no longer fits the education, or the education no longer fits the niche."[35]

Even if professional knowledge were to catch up with the new demands of professional practice, the improvement in professional performance. would be transitory. The situations of practice are inherently unstable. Harvey Brooks, an eminent engineer and educator, argues that professions are now confronted with an "unprecedent requirement for adaptability":

> The dilemma of the professional today lies in the fact that both ends of the gap he is expected to bridge with his profession are changing so rapidly: the body of knowledge that he must use and the expectations of the society that he must serve. Both these changes have their origin in the same common factor—technological change... The problem cannot be usefully phrased in terms of too much technology. Rather it is whether we can generate technological change fast enough to meet the expectations and demands that technology itself has generated. And the four professions—medicine, engineering, business management and education—must bear the brunt of responsibility for generating and managing this change. This places on the professional a requirement for adaptability that is unprecedented.[36]

The role of the physician will be continually reshaped, over the next decades, by the reorganization and rationalization of medical care; the proliferating roles of enterprise will call for a redefinition of the businessman's role; and architects will have to function in radically new ways as a consequence of the introduction of new building technologies, new patterns of real estate and land development, and new techniques of information processing in design. As the tasks change, so will the demands for usable knowledge, and the patterns of task and knowledge are inherently unstable.[37]

The situations of practice are not problems to be solved but problematic situations characterized by uncertainty, disorder, and indeterminacy.[38] Russell Ackoff, one of the founders of the field of operations research, has recently announced to his colleagues that "the future of operations research is past"[39] because

> managers are not confronted with problems that are independent of each other, but with dynamic situations that consist of I complex systems of changing problems that interact with each other. I call such situations messes. Problems are abstractions extracted from messes by analysis; they are to messes as atoms are to tables and charts... Managers do not solve problems they manage messes.[40]

Ackoff argues that operations research has allowed itself to become identified with techniques, mathematical models, and algorithms, rather than with "the ability to formulate management problems, solve them, and implement and maintain their solutions in turbulent environments."[41] Problems are interconnected, environments are turbulent, and the future is indeterminate just in so far as managers can shape it by their actions. What is called for, under these conditions, is not only the analytic techniques which have been traditional in operations research, but the active, synthetic skill of "designing a desirable future and inventing ways of bringing it about."[42]

The situations of practice are characterized by unique events. Erik Erikson, the psychiatrist, has described each patient as "a universe of one,"[43] and an eminent physician has claimed that "85 percent of the problems a doctor sees in his office are not in the book."[44] Engineers encounter unique problems of design and are called upon to analyze failures of structures or materials under conditions which make it impossible to apply standard tests and measurements.[45] The unique case calls for an art of practice which "might be taught, if it were constant and known, but it is not constant."[46]

Practitioners are frequently embroiled in conflicts of values, goals, purposes, and interests. Teachers are faced with pressures for increased efficiency in the context of contracting budgets, demands that they rigorously "teach the basics," exhortations to encourage creativity, build citizenship, help students to examine their values. Workers in the fields of social welfare are also torn between a professional code which advocates attention to persons and bureaucratic pressure for increased efficiency in processing cases. School superintendants, industrial managers, and public administrators are asked to respond to the conflicting demands of the many different groups which hold a stake in their enterprises. Professionals engaged in research and development are not infrequently torn between a "professional" concern for technological elegance, consumer safety, or social well-being, and an institutional demand for short-term return on investment.

In some professions, awareness of uncertainty, complexity, instability, uniqueness, and value conflict has led to the emergence of professional pluralism. Competing views of professional practice—competing images of the professional role, the central values of the profession, the relevant knowledge and skills—have come into good currency. Leston Havens has written about the "babble of voices" which confuses practitioners in the field of psychotherapy.[47] Social workers have produced multiple, shifting images of the nature of their practice, as have architects and town planners.[48] Each view of professional practice represents a way of functioning in situations of indeterminacy and value conflict, but the multiplicity of conflicting views poses a predicament for the practitioner who must choose among multiple approaches to practice or devise his own way of combining them.

In sum, when leading professionals write or speak about their own crisis of confidence, they tend to focus on the mismatch of traditional patterns of practice and knowledge to features of the practice situation—complexity, uncertainty, instability, uniqueness, and value conflict—of whose importance they are becoming increasingly aware.

Surely this is a laudable exercise in self-criticism. Nevertheless, there is something puzzling about the translation of wavering confidence in professional expertise into these particular accounts of the troubles of the professions. If it is true, for example, that social reality has shifted out from under the nineteenth-century division of labor, creating new zones of complexity and uncertainty, it is also true that practitioners in such fields as management and industrial technology do sometimes find ways to make sense of complexity and reduce uncertainty to manageable risk.

If it is true that there is an irreducible element of art in professional practice, it is also true that gifted engineers, teachers, scientists, architects, and managers sometimes display artistry in their day-to-day practice. If the art is not invariant, known, and teachable, it appears nonetheless, at least for some individuals, to be learnable.

If it is true that professional practice has at least as much to do with finding the problem as with solving the problem found, it is also true that problem setting is a recognized professional activity. Some physicians reveal skills in finding the problems of particular patients in ways that go beyond the conventional boundaries of medical diagnosis. Some engineers, policy analysts, and operations researchers have become skilled at reducing "messes" to manageable plans. For some administrators, the need to "find the right problem" has become a conscious principle of action.

And if it is true, finally, that there are conflicting views of professional practice, it is also true that some practitioners do manage to make a thoughtful choice, or even a partial synthesis, from the babble of voices in their professions.

Why, then, should leading professionals and educators find these phenomena so disturbing? Surely they are not unaware of the artful ways in which some practitioners deal competently with the indeterminacies and value conflicts of practice. It seems, rather, that they are disturbed because they have no satisfactory way of describing or accounting for the artful competence which practitioners sometimes reveal in what they do. They find it unsettling to be unable to make sense of these processes in terms of the model of professional knowledge which they have largely taken for granted. Complexity, instability, and uncertainty are not removed or resolved by applying specialized knowledge to well-defined tasks. If anything, the effective use of specialized knowledge depends on a prior restructuring of situations that are complex and uncertain. An artful practice of the unique case appears anomalous when professional competence is modelled in terms of application of established techniques to recurrent events. Problem setting has no place in a body of professional knowledge concerned exclusively with problem solving. The task of choosing among competing paradigms of practice is not amenable to professional expertise.

The events which led from the "triumphant professions" of the early 1960s to the skepticism and unease of the 1970s and early 1980s have been at least as apparent to the professionals as to the general public. But the sense of confusion and unease which is discernable among leading professionals has an additional source. Professionals have been disturbed to find that they cannot account for processes they have come to see as central to professional competence. It is difficult for them to imagine how to describe and teach what might be meant by making sense of uncertainty, performing artistically, setting problems, and choosing among competing professional paradigms, when these processes seem mysterious in the light of the prevailing model of professional knowledge.

We are bound to an epistemology of practice which leaves us at a loss to explain, or even to describe, the competences to which we now give overriding importance.

Toward a Longer View and Higher Duty for Local Planning Commissions

David J. Allor

Allor traces the history of planning commissions and the challenges they face. Planning commissioners are often poorly prepared and lack adequate training to make informed decisions about planning and development issues. Allor argues that planning commissions have the potential to be much more than simply "development processing commissions," but can be effective participants in broad community issues if they can learn from the past by "looking backward to the future."

> *Planning is the guidance of future action. In a world of intensely conflicting interests and great inequalities of status and resources, planning in the face of power is at once a daily necessity and a constant ethical challenge (John Forester 1989, 3).*

My work in training planning commissions concerns procedural aspects. In advising planning commissions with whose communities I am not familiar, I tend to avoid the underlying, but deeply felt and potentially divisive, substantive issues. I deceive neither myself nor my clients into believing that we can perceive and resolve such issues during short training sessions. This essay permits me the liberty to comment on certain values that are given form by the decisions of local planning commissions. Over the last eight years, I have been fortunate to benefit from the recurrent admonition of my frequent partner in planning commission training, C. Gregory Dale, to seek the "bigger picture." I do so here, taking the opportunity to construct a broader agenda for local planning commissions.

A HISTORY OF TURBULENCE

I have sensed in many planning commission members an emotional exhaustion and social-psychological battery as they recurrently experienced and witnessed contentious behavior in public hearings, working sessions, and deliberative meetings. Despite their conscientious efforts, many feel that the times are peculiarly difficult. Some are discouraged by the sense that they no longer are making planning decisions, but are merely refereeing continuing rounds of unresolvable disputes. Yet, as Donald A. Schön and Thomas E. Nutt point out, the entire history of planning reflects an "endemic turbulence" (1974, 181); local planning commissions have always operated within the very center of that turbulence.

Many of the early independent planning commissions were established and much of planning enabling legislation was enacted in those very turbulent years, the first three decades of the twentieth century. America then was a nation of immigrants, many from rural backgrounds, who had to adapt to the physical squalor and political corruption of the rapidly industrializing American city. The varied groups, vying for the benefits believed to await them as Americans, brought ethnic and racial prejudices to bear against each other. Economic speculation overwhelmed considerations of public health, occupational safety, and environmental responsibility. Despite all these obstacles, it was in that period that American planning commissions, those small bodies of "informed citizens," which were appointed in staggered terms of office and granted only limited control over development, first sought to give their severely divided communities a more long-range, coherent, and equitable vision of the future.

The deprivations of the Great Depression and World War II certainly aggravated poverty and internal migration. Prejudice erupted against German-Americans, Appalachian Americans, and African-Americans; most egregious of all, the internment of Japanese-Americans reflected a long-standing, deep-seated prejudice far more than an immediate, pragmatic need for national security. Local planning commissions frequently found themselves criticized simultaneously for fomenting communism in their communities and for imposing fascism on them. The planning commissions struggled with marginal resources, little professional support, and very little public support. Fortunately, however, the federal courts handed down decisions that established planning as a function of local democratic governance.

At midcentury, the work of local planning commissions helped to create wholly new communities— the suburbs, which for many embodied the vision of the future America. The new homes, new schools, new parks, and new roads all came into being through massive federal subsidies that underwrote the tradition of local comprehensive planning. Despite highly touted and hotly debated programs for urban renewal in the central cities, overt public sector disinvestment was matched by covert private sector disinvesrment, blockbusting, and redlining. The building of the new suburban society left behind the poor, the unskilled, the old, the minority, and the nonveteran. Remaining in the central city, they suffered the indignities of forced relocation, of placement in public housing, and of dependency on public assistance. As local planning commissions concen-

trated on creating new communities, American society split apart.

In the next decade, the 1960s, the longer view was nearly lost. One assassin's bullets cost the nation the vision of a "new frontier;" another assassin's bullets made evident what a long road lay ahead toward racial equality. The hope for a "great society" was lost in the carnage of international military conflict and domestic political division. Local planning commissions found themselves embattled participants in the conflicts over housing integration, school desegregation, and equal employment opportunity. Accused of complicity in institutional racism, they struggled to broaden citizen participation. The issue underlying this charge against planning commissioners was serious. Some consequences of planning, although indeed adverse, were unintended; redress was possible. If, however, adverse effects were covert and intentional, the credibility of planning was in jeopardy. Demands that the deprivations resulting from planning be compensated joined with pressures for local empowerment and gave rise to community-based advocacy planning. Despite the merits of the claims by advocacy planners, American society grew weary of social concerns and less tolerant of government programs to reduce discrimination, poverty, and unemployment.

During the last decade, as recurrent stresses arose in the American economy, the society put its faith in economic pragmatism. A shorter view dominated planning processes, replacing comprehensiveness with a focus on narrower and more immediate strategic opportunities. Local plans no longer reflected a sense of community need; instead, they were bent to serve entrepreneurial opportunity. Local communities, which had always resisted any form of regional cooperation, now competed against each other more vigorously than ever, to secure independent economic development. Planning decisions took on the character of project negotiations, with deliberations limited to the short-term balancing of vested interests. Communities that promoted "public sector-private sector partnerships" soon found themselves considered as just another corporate interest in the negotiations, and their planning staffs viewed as part of the municipal bargaining team. Local planning commissions, especially those that advertised themselves as "developer-friendly," found themselves reduced to a role appropriately described by C. Gregory Dale as a "development processing commission." When a planning staff sought to impose too stiff a set of restrictions, or alternatively, offered too weak a set of incentives, developers sought "better deals" before planning commissions and boards of zoning appeals, sometimes described as "committees of compassion." If a planning commission imposed restrictions that developers found too harsh, they shifted the negotiations to municipal councils or boards of county commissioners.

With this last decade of the century, two increasingly significant concerns have turned attention in planning back toward a view both longer and broader. The first concern recognizes the fundamental restructuring of the economy, away from the long manufacturing tradition and toward a more technologically based service economy. The effects of this restructuring will be dramatic and long lasting, touching the work and lives of future generations.

A second concern is the growing awareness that both the scale and the intensity of urban-industrial development have severely damaged the environment and irreversibly altered ecological systems. Local planning commissions must consider the very high environmental costs of transportation, sanitary sewer, solid waste, and hazardous waste disposal systems. As at the opening of the century, environmental degradation is linked directly to decline in public health; yet local planning efforts targeted toward "sustainability" and "livability" accommodate larger ecological systems only marginally. Perhaps even more embarrassing to the planning profession is the realization that local planning commissions have approved development in dangerous places. Communities are now more vulnerable to drought, earthquake, flood, hurricane, and tornado, because planning commissions have permitted and often encouraged population growth in such areas. Moreover, it is clear that localities in vulnerable areas have failed to establish and/or to enforce subdivision, land use, site design regulations, and building codes adequate to minimize recurrent "natural" disasters. Short-sighted planning has placed many in harm's way.

As the millennium approaches, I do not expect that the turbulence endemic to planning will sub-side. There is much to suggest that instead it will focus upon certain fundamental issues within American communities religion, family, and property.

RELIGIOUS PREFERENCE AND CULTURAL PLURALISM

Among the most difficult decisions made by a planning commission are those tied to issues of religion and culture. There is evidence of a present reemphasis on religious values in American society, and Concern is also rising that American communities need to be more tolerant of cultural pluralism. Planning commissions, in step with the planning profession, have long found safe ground in promoting functional values, that is, improvements of physical well-being loosely associated with the common good, general welfare, or public interest. Though no doubt sensitive to the constitutional guarantees of freedom of religion, speech, and assembly, planning commissions have maintained the separation of church and state mostly by pursuing secular, usually material, values. In doing so they have promoted cultural homogeneity, revealed in commonly shared values that would provide a foundation for planning decisions. There are now indications that this strategy is failing. Assertions of varied religious preferences and diverse claims for cultural recognition have brought new stress to planning commission decisions. In this context, two points require the patient attention of planning commissions.

First, the historical perspective shows the nation to have entrusted itself to an abstract monotheism, as demonstrated by the imprint on its legal tender and expressed in this century in the pledge of allegiance. The founders of the nation were acutely aware, however, of Europe's history of unrelenting, violent, and selective suppression of religious faiths. Religious tolerance and, in consequence, cultural tolerance were necessary for a nation begun and built by successive waves of immigrants. In actuality, though, the dominant religious note in American public life since World War II might be said to be a mild Protestantism, tempered by the gradual acceptance of Catholicism and Judaism but on less than equal terms. Neither this descriptive history, however, nor the nonspecific monotheism expressed by the founders defines the United States as an exclusively Christian nation, although adherents of some Christian groups are vocal with that claim. Their insistence that American society and polity give precedence to particular sectarian values is, I believe, an unfortunate misrepresentation of the constitutional framework that the founders hoped would keep the nation free of religious imperatives. When such claims are forwarded in local politics, planning commissions may find it difficult to maintain neutrality on sectarian issues and identify the common values that give continuity and direction to American communities.

The increasing cultural pluralism of America also complicates, in other ways, the effort to deliberate within a framework of common values. Until recently, the nation's historical record has not included recognition of either the religious preferences or the broad cultural values—or both—of, for example, Native Americans, African-Americans, Appalachian Americans, or Hispanic-Americans. These cultures, now resurgent, demand recognition, apology for historical insult, and compensation for discrimination. The adamant public expression of such claims may not always be comfortable to encounter. These current forms of turbulence may well make it more challenging for planning commissions to conduct public hearings or even their deliberative sessions, as they consider decisions with implications for deeply held religious and cultural values.

Second, a view of the future suggests that identifying the commonly held values in American communities will only become more complex. Even within the national monotheistic tradition, the increasing necessity to accommodate adherents of Islam, who themselves comprise very diverse ethnic groups, is likely to be for many Americans a disconcerting experience. New residents of American communities, the adherents to Sunnite, Shiite, or perhaps Black Moslem traditions, may be from among ethnic groups who have migrated from anywhere along the broad band stretching from the Strait of Gibraltar, across all of North Africa, the Middle East, India, and Southeast Asia, to the Philippines. Even more unfamiliar are the polytheistic, spiritualistic, ancestral, or animistic religions of Africa, India, China, Southeast Asia, Japan, northern Brazil, and the Caribbean. Yet these are possible religious

preferences for many of those who will in the future be American. Planning commissions will have to "internationalize" themselves, not only by broadening their composition but also, and more critically, by broadening their individual and collective minds.

FAMILY AND COMMUNITY

The American nuclear family, while widely recognized, was an artificial construction of post-World War II economic policy and planning process. Throughout the history of the nation, the descendants of new arrivals have sought to maintain extended family structure, multi-generational kinship, and ethnic identity. The deprivations of the Great Depression and World War II undoubtedly constrained the occupational, residential, and educational opportunities of at least one generation. That generation's pent-up demand to enjoy the bounty of peacetime (albeit cold war) America profoundly changed the countryside. Economic development policy, strongly supported by the processes of local comprehensive physical planning, led to the suburbanization of America. Scattering the population at so low a density across so vast a continent segregated American society not only by economic class and race, but also by generation. The inordinate and sustained effort to create the American nuclear family (Ozzie and Harriet and David and Rickie, living in a single-family residence in an R-1 zone) was a compounding disaster. By dividing the society intergenerationally, often abandoning grandparents in either the central city or the rural countryside, the new nuclear family pattern severed kinship ties and weakened ethnic tradition. Whereas once the old, the ill, and the dying were cared for within extended families, planners now find it a struggle to place congregate-living residences, elder apartments, nursing homes, and hospice facilities in nuclear family residential areas, as if such uses were inherent nuisances. The segregation of American society by income, by ethnicity, by race, and by generation has been horrifyingly successful in producing both social isolation and cultural banality. If contemporary planning commissions have to work so hard to reconstruct a sense of community in America, it is because antecedent planning commissions shared complicity in rendering the American community an endangered species.

Future planning commissions must not only accommodate the alternative definitions of "family" honored by the diverse cultures that make their homes in America, but also recognize the longer life expectancies of present generations. An increasing proportion of the current and future members of American communities will live two decades beyond retirement. They will become the senior members of a society stretching across four, possibly five, generations. Providing for their continued residence and, more importantly, their active participation is essential to the continuity and the vitality of American communities.

ARCHITECTURAL CONSERVATION AND COMMUNITY DESIGN

In many American communities, planning commissions have sought to strengthen the physical imagery of their communities through architectural conservation of existing structures and design regulations for new construction. Although these programs, which are often enacted as overlay zones to the zoning ordinance, may be administered by an architectural review board or design review commission, they should serve the larger purposes of community planning. In some communities there is a significant historical and architectural heritage meriting special protective regulation. In other communities, however, style-based design regulations serve simply to wrap modern construction with a cultural veneer. The current popularity of "neotraditional" planning reflects a perceived failure of modern design to express community in a meaningful way. Neotraditional planning often is no more than a random assemblage of conventional design details. Neither the local planning commission nor members of the community are able to recognize any underlying "tradition."

Planning commissions should be especially careful in adopting style-related design regulations, whether honestly seeking to conserve a design heritage or, more modestly, to borrow one. Architectural styles carry connotations of the parent cultures' attributes. While certain of those attributes may be seen as worthy of commemora-

tion and perhaps of emulation, others are problematic. Many communities in the eastern and southern United States have chosen not only to conserve but also to extend the design of their communities in colonial, federal, or ante-bellum style. Whatever the aesthetic attributes of those styles, the histories of their parent cultures include the slaughter of native populations, the enslavement of African-Americans, persecution of religious dissenters, and the denial of political and civil rights to women. Similarly, although one may recognize the positive attributes of Hispanic colonial design, one should bear in mind that the parent culture persecuted native peoples, vilified persons of mixed blood, suppressed religious dissent through the Inquisition, and subordinated women in social, political and economic affairs. In adopting style-dependent design regulations, a planning commission should examine which of the underlying cultural values it is thereby promoting.

There are two more troublesome problems with community design criteria. The first is that the choice of style expresses an underlying exclusiveness based on cultural ethnocentrism. Persons seeking to enter such a "designed" community are expected not only to live behind compatible facades, but also to subscribe to compatible values and behave in compatible manners. Those unable or unwilling to do so are dissuaded from community membership. The effect is not to build the community as a whole, but to fragment it. The second, equally dangerous possibility is that the intention of community design is disingenuous, in the sense that architectural conservation and design standards are imposed to raise economic barriers to community membership. Community design regulations can serve to implement economic discrimination.

In the future, planning commissions should rely more on design regulations that do not specifically limit style. Guidelines that offer options in siting, form, signage, construction methods, materials, and colors would be less constraining in the culturally pluralistic communities that lie ahead. Where design regulations are imposed, the economic costs associated with compliance should not be so severe as to raise the suspicion of discrimination.

PROPERTY AND COMMUNITY

Planning commissions recurrently confront a central dilemma of the American polity. Modern citizenship is predicated upon the guarantee of certain rights that attach to person. Historically, however, effective citizenship has been defined in terms of property ownership, and in some communities continues to be. For some, property ownership is the material proof that one holds an interest in the community. Conversely, persons who do not own property in the community are not accepted by some as real members. A number of prejudices about the meaning of property ownership are frequently demonstrated in the hearings and deliberations of planning commissions: renters are inferior to home owners; apartment living is morally objectionable; prefabricated housing is inferior to "real" homes; the out-of-town developer is dishonest, while the local contractor is reliable. A planning commission does have the responsibility to assess the differential impacts of development upon land; yet ownership of property, or the lack of it, does not alter the responsibility of the planning commission to treat all persons appearing before it with fairness, reasonableness, and objectivity.

In the future, full ownership of land will become less important in American society. As the economy shifts toward rapidly advancing, technologically oriented, service and information-based industries, disposable income will move away from property investment to human resource investment. The adult working population will have to commit income to recurrently upgrading skills or retraining for career changes. Similarly, for their children, far more income will have to be committed to carry them through advanced technical training or graduate professional degrees. Persons planning for retirement will choose investments other than real estate to support their continued quality of life.

Communities that have dedicated themselves narrowly to "up-scale" residential development may soon find themselves doubly restrained. The transition to the service economy will bring salary levels below those of the previously dominant manufacturing sector. The younger working population will have to postpone home ownership to secure their training and career paths. They will find it much harder to save enough for the down payment, or may not choose to commit their earnings to large and long-term mortgage debt even at low interest rates. Moreover, occupational ascent will require geographic mobility, further diminishing investment in real property. At the other end of the age scale, the elderly may seek to divest themselves of property, thereby eliminating tax and maintenance costs and reducing expenses while conserving capital assets. Where a community has not encouraged a range of residential options, retired and elderly residents may have to move, even in the absence of immediate buyers. Although providing "affordable housing" within communities is now discussed at length, local planning commissions have resisted approval of housing not only for low-income families, but also for young people and the elderly with limited incomes. In consequence, a community committed to stringent guidelines for single-family residential land use may find itself unable to provide for its mature residents and unable to attract the rising generation.

TOWARD A BROADER AGENDA

If, in the coming century, local planning commissions are to recapture the longer view, they must adopt a broader agenda. Four points are critical.

First, local planning commissions should avoid acquiring labels. A planning commission chat proclaims itself "development-friendly" may be seen as having sold off its impartiality in assessing community needs. Conversely, planning commissions that narrowly espouse "growth controls" are seen not so much as development-unfriendly, as seeking to control admission into the local democracy. A number of prejudices against renters, the elderly, and the working class are suspected to lie behind calls for controlling growth. Planning commissions must understand that neither longevity of residence nor extent of property ownership confers special privileges on citizens. The last person to have entered a democracy does not have the right to close the door to those who follow. Similarly, planning commissions that promote preservation of "community character" may be suspected of furthering economic and cultural discrimination. Large-lot subdivision regulations, low-density residential zoning, and style-based design standards may not work so much to "improve the quality of the community" as to exclude some persons from enjoying it.

The second point is that to avoid such pitfalls, planning commissions should have policies. Planning commissions should have explicit policies on economic development that relate community needs to market viability, to occupational diversity, and to employment opportunity. Residential development policies should provide a range of density, style, and tenancy options appropriate for income levels of the population. A growth control policy should incorporate not only the sentiments of the community but also the constraints of ecological systems, the funding limits for public infrastructure, and the operating costs of essential public services. Planning commissions should have policies on education, recreation and open space; on environmental conservation and historic preservation; on transportation, public services, and public infrastructure. Policies are crucial, because they both incorporate the larger values of a community and establish reasonable and equitable processes by which to realize them.

The third point is that—amazing thought!—planning commission policies should be meaningfully integrated in an officially adopted, regularly updated, long-range, comprehensive plan. The horizon of that plan should never be less than the full term of the longest general obligation, capital improvement bond issue, and it should be implemented through a capital improvements program coordinated with both subdivision and zoning regulations. It is disappointing that few communities have capital improvements programs; instead, capital improvements are funded piece-meal through compulsory dedications, exactions, and development fees. Local planning commissions that narrowly tinker with the land-use pattern through zoning regulation condemn themselves to recurrent, parsimonious land-use disputes. If the members of a planning commission are embarrassed, frustrated, and bored by such disputes, the problem is of their own making.

Fourth and finally, if a local planning commission truly pursues the longer view, it must invert the order of its business to reflect that priority. It must clearly and consistently signal to those who

come before it with specific applications that the general plan and public policies guide deliberation and decision. The New Business section of every planning commission agenda should begin with issues related to the comprehensive plan, followed by consideration of policies, followed by review of the capital improvements program, followed by amendments to the subdivision regulation and zoning ordinance—and only then consider specific applications. No doubt, planning commissions adopting such an agenda would be seen in the short run as less compassionate to the community and less friendly to developers. Nevertheless, the central responsibility of the planning commission is to provide collective good judgment and intelligent direction in service to the future of its community. The commission must learn to reserve for itself both time and priority to deliberate fundamental issues, to incorporate these into plan and into policy, to implement them through incentives and regulations, and to decide specific applications reasonably and equitably in accord with the plan.

LOOKING BACKWARD TO THE FUTURE

In closing I ask planning commissions to be aware of their place in history. Their decisions, although most frequently recommendations, if they are implemented irrevocably alter the lives of the members of the community and even of generations yet unborn. The decisions of planning commissions shape the patterns of social interaction: of residence, work, education, and play. Local planning commissions cannot escape the responsibility to maintain both the longer view and faithfulness to higher duty. They must understand that their judgments are assertions of values.

The present century, opened with the extension of voting rights to women. In the century's third quarter, civil rights, voting rights, and economic rights were assured to minorities. In its closing decade, guarantees of nondiscrimination were extended to community members with mental and physical disabilities. That history reflects the admirable struggle of American society to expand opportunities, to assure equal rights, and to promote tolerance. I ask that local planning commissions do those same things.

REFERENCES

Allor, David J. 1984. *The Planning Commissioners Guide: Processes for Reasoning Together*. Chicago: Planners Press.

Forester, John. I9S9. *Planning in the Face of Power*. Berkeley: University of California Press.

Schön, Donald A., and Thomas E. Nutt. 1974. Endemic Turbulence: The Future for Planning Education. In *Planning In America: Learning From Turbulence*, edited by David R. Godschalk. Washington. DC; American Institute of Planners, 181-205.

Author's Note. I wish to acknowledge the critical comments on the draft of this essay by C. Gregory Dale, AICP, past APA Ohio Chapter president, and by Anne F. McBride, AICP, current Ohio Planning Conference president.

Why We Need a New Vision

Anthony Downs

For more than half a century, metropolitan areas across the country have grown and developed in a pattern of low-density sprawl, contributing to many of the country's economic problems. The flaws in this country's dominant vision—single-family house, the affinity for automobiles, work in low-rise buildings, and life in small communities free from signs of poverty—undermine our society and its future well-being. Downs argues that the pattern of land consumption created by this vision has led to absorption of too much open space, a lack of affordable housing, excessive automobile travel, and other problems. He asserts that the social inconsistencies manifested by this pattern threaten to weaken the economic and social functioning of many metropolitan areas and thus the country's entire economy. Thus, Downs says, a change in our vision of how metropolitan areas ought to develop is necessary to break the cycle of social inconsistencies and environmental destruction.

For half a century, America has had one dominant vision of how its metropolitan areas ought to grow and develop. It is best described as unlimited low-density sprawl. This vision encompasses personal and social goals—a home in the suburbs, a car, good schools, responsive local government—that most Americans cherish. Most metropolitan areas have successfully realized the vision. Yet this achievement has contributed to unexpected growth-related dilemmas that threaten the long-run viability of American society—something the American public and most leaders have yet to realize. They have not, therefore, even begun to confront the need to alter the vision to resolve its problems. Yet these problems must be resolved if American society is to prosper.

As a result of increasingly intrusive difficulties during the 1980s, a remarkable transformation occurred in the attitude of hundreds of local governments. They had, for many years, considered growth a source of economic benefits and welcomed more jobs and more people. But now, many have come to regard growth as responsible for traffic congestion, air pollution, loss of open space, higher taxes to pay for additional infrastructure, and a lack of affordable housing. They have adopted policies designed to control growth in their communities. Known as growth management, the policies are explicit attempts to limit the proliferation of new housing and commercial and industrial buildings; the addition of roads, schools, and other social infrastructure; and increases in population and jobs within existing facilities.[1]

Growth management in some form is nothing new; communities have long tried to shape their development through zoning laws and other ordinances. But adopting policies specifically designed to restrict growth itself *is* relatively new. These policies have been advanced mostly in the past two decades, and they have spread rapidly. One reason is that once a few local governments in a metropolitan area have adopted growth management policies, others nearby come under pressure to do likewise to avoid being swamped by the development their neighbors have excluded. Growth management has become important mainly where there has been economic prosperity and rapid expansion of population and jobs. This applies to a minority of metropolitan areas, probably containing less than 30 percent of the nation's people. But they include California, Florida, and the Northeast, traditionally America's economically most dynamic regions.

It is not easy to manage growth effectively—if at all. Most metropolitan areas have dozens or even hundreds of local governments that exercise sovereignty over land use within their jurisdictions. But the problems growth management is supposed to solve are mainly regional.

And even policies that any one community adopts often have regional implications. For example, when Petaluma, California, limited the number of housing units that could be built there each year, neighboring Santa Rosa experienced spillover housing demand. Rents and home prices increased and vacancies fell. More important, almost all growth management efforts themselves increase housing costs, which reduces the number of houses and apartments available to low- and moderate-income people. Thus, well-meaning local efforts to manage growth could make society as a whole worse off, without doing much to solve growth-related problems.

The most dangerous result of growth management policies is that they help perpetuate the concentration of very poor households in depressed neighborhoods in big cities and older suburbs. These neighborhoods contain a small percentage of the U.S. population, but they are riddled with the most virulent forms of four problems that are undermining social cohesion and economic efficiency throughout the nation: exploding rates of crime and violence, increased numbers of children growing up in poverty, poor-quality public education, and failure to integrate workers into the mainstream workforce. These problems affect every community in the nation, but many Americans still do not recognize how serious they are. One reason is that the problems have intensified and spread gradually. Dramatic incidents such as the 1992 Los Angeles riots have been rare. They have, however, diverted attention from the reality that these problems are worsening nationwide, not just in inner cities.

In America, it normally takes a social crisis to overcome resistance to addressing conditions that are dangerous but that benefit large numbers of people. That is precisely the case with these four problems: they are aggravated by low-density growth and other practices that benefit a great many people. Thus, they do not seem threatening enough to overcome the inertia of the status quo. Yet if the problems are not attacked vigorously, they will gravely impair the political unity, productivity, and economic efficiency of American society and the personal security of everyone. Carrying out such attacks will, however, require changing our vision of how growth ought to occur.

In this confusing environment, it is hard for individual communities to decide how best to respond to rapid growth. Are the undesirable conditions really caused primarily by growth? Which policies might succeed in ameliorating them? Which might have severe side effects or make conditions worse? Is limiting local growth desirable at all for either a given locality or society as a whole? If so, what should the goals of such limitations be? To what extent do communities need to coordinate growth management policies with other communities to achieve effective results? Can multiplicity of governments in metropolitan areas manage growth effectively, or does that arrangement need to be modified? If so, how?

This book seeks to answer these questions. It considers the problems associated with rapid metropolitan growth from a perspective that encompasses inner-city problems. And it examines the effects of growth management in communities that have tried to alter the course of urban growth. The book also analyzes three other ways growth could occur, alternatives that might reduce the problems that have arisen from pursuit of unlimited low-density development. This analysis necessarily focuses on the relationships between the suburbs and central cities. Finally, the book attempts to identify the policies likely to be most effective in helping to resolve growth-related problems.

THE DOMINANT VISION

Ironically, the underlying cause of recent hostility toward growth has been the overwhelmingly successful realization of Americans' common vision of how growth ought to occur. Unlimited low-density development has dominated nearly all American policies affecting metropolitan area growth for more than four decades.

The first dement of this vision is ownership of detached single-family homes on spacious lots. A 1993 poll conducted by the Federal National Mortgage Association showed that 86 percent of American households believed owning a home was better than renting, 83 percent believed owning was a good investment, and 73 percent preferred a single-family detached home with a yard.[2] Owning such a home has become the heart of the American dream, the prevailing image of how a household succeeds. Realization of this dream implies low-density settlement.

The second element is ownership of automotive vehicles. Nearly every American wants to be able to leap into his or her car, van, or truck and zoom off on an uncongested road to wherever he or she wants to go, in total privacy and great comfort.

The third element is working in low-rise workplaces—offices or industrial buildings or shopping centers in attractively landscaped, park-like settings. Each structure is, of course, to be accompanied by its own free parking lot.

The fourth element is residence in small communities with strong local governments. Americans want these governments to control land use, public schools, and other things affecting the quality of neighborhood life. This form of governance permits residents to have an influential voice in shaping their environment.

The fifth element is an environment free from the signs of poverty. Unlike the other four, this element is not acknowledged or even consciously desired. But it inevitably results from two conditions for housing production that are explicitly desired by most Americans: no construction of "substandard" housing and few housing subsidies for low-income households.[3] Thus the dominant

approach to housing the poor in the United States is the trickle-down process. Low-income people are housed in older units formerly occupied by the nonpoor. The result is concentration of the poorest households in neighborhoods where the oldest, most deteriorated housing is located—usually central cities and older suburbs.

These five elements define much of what passes for the American dream in the minds of most suburbanites and many city dwellers. The dements add up to a relatively unconstrained individualism. In effect, each person, household, or business seeks an environment that maximizes its own well-being without very much regard to the possible effects on society as a whole. Pursuing the realization of each element reinforces achievement of one or more of the others. A community of single-family homes creates the need for private transportation. And once households own cars, they can commute to widely scattered low-density workplaces.

The value and attainability of this vision has been reinforced through constant promotion by the real estate industry and suburban communities. Homebuilders, realtors, advertisers, town governments, and local planning officials sing the praises of suburban lifestyles and uncrowded, safe communities. This vision is now so strongly entrenched that it has become almost political suicide for elected officials to challenge any of its elements.

PROBLEMS OF THE LOW-DENSITY VISION

Unfortunately, this model of development is riddled with internal inconsistencies that have created severe disparities between vision and reality. The ubiquity of the private automobile and its needs, for instance, have compromised the dream of open roads and fresh air. These inconsistencies are now becoming more apparent because the vision's dements have been achieved more completely than ever. Automobile ownership and use greatly accelerated during the 1980s.[4] More cars meant more traffic congestion and air pollution and high costs for building and widening roads. However, most Americans do not realize that success in attaining their goals is responsible for other results they abhor. Even when confronted by overwhelming evidence, they find it much easier to blame traffic congestion and other urban ills on some scapegoat than to recognize that their own habitual behavior causes them.

Most suburbanites blame congestion and delay on real estate developers and the latest residents to arrive in their communities. They often adopt strong growth management policies in response to these problems. But most policies do not attack the problems' fundamental causes, so the policies cannot remedy them effectively.

EXCESSIVE TRAVEL

A primary flaw in the dominant vision is that it generates excessive travel. A pattern of single-family housing and low-density workplaces spreads homes and jobs widely. People have to travel long distances from where they live to where they work, shop, or play. In theory, if jobs spread out as much as housing, dispersion would not increase average travel distances as long as people lived near where they worked. But jobs have not spread out as widely as housing, and cross-commuting is common because people do not choose homes near their jobs. In both 1980 and 1990, about 30 percent of all U.S. commuters traveled 30 minutes or more to their jobs, though the average time was 20 minutes.[5] From 1983 to 1990, the average household vehicle trip increased from 7.9 to 9.0 miles and the average commute from 8.6 to 10.9 miles. Average vehicle miles traveled per household rose 29 percent.[6]

These increases can be considered excessive only in relation to some standard. But more travel has generated more traffic congestion, expense, time spent driving, and air pollution than many Americans can tolerate easily.[7] Therefore, it is reasonable to conclude that people are traveling much more than they would prefer. And expanding mass transit is not likely to remedy the problem. Buses or fixed-rail transit can operate efficiently only if at least one end of most journeys is concentrated in a few points of destination. But when both homes and jobs are widely scattered, concentration no longer prevails, even if there are a few major nodes, such as a downtown. Low-density settlements cannot efficiently support mass transit.

So single-family homeownership and low-density workplaces provide strong incentives for households to use private vehicles. In 1983, 87 percent of all U.S. households owned at least one motor vehicle, and 53 percent owned two or more. Even among households with incomes less than $10,000, more than 60 percent owned at least one car or truck; among those with incomes of $40,000 or more, 99 percent owned at least one, and 87 percent owned two or more.[8] Because of automobile ownership and low-density settlements, nearly all American workers commute by private vehicles. In 1990, only 5 percent of all rush-hour commuters used public transit, 86 percent used private vehicles, and 73 percent drove to work alone.[9] The result, of course, is peak-hour traffic congestion.

Such congestion could have been mitigated if a lot more streets and roads had been built, or existing ones expanded, in the 1980s. But people wanted to avoid the expense and the disruptions of acquiring land and building more highways. Those costs were collective: bearing them required communities to raise public funds and choose rights-of-way. Suburban citizens could not, however, agree about who was to bear the costs, so no one did, and roads that might have better accommodated the explosion of the vehicle population were not built.[10]

Americans usually believe these problems are caused by high-density development. Because traffic is most congested near big-city downtowns, regional shopping centers, and large outlying office parks, they think high-density land use must cause the congestion. It is true that the most intense local congestion is often found near high-density sites because they generate many vehicle movements in a small area. In fact, some experts argue that the spreading out of jobs and housing around the edges of metropolitan areas has helped Americans adjust to massive increases in urban population, jobs, and vehicle use without creating even more local congestion.[11] But when large areas are developed with high average densities rather than low ones, total travel and general congestion are reduced.

LACK OF AFFORDABLE HOUSING

The dominant vision's second flaw is that it focuses on relatively high-cost housing. Areas of new growth developed to its specifications provide few dwellings that low- and moderate-income households can afford. Yet these households are an integral part of American life, even in the suburbs. They provide workers for low-wage jobs essential to fast-food establishments, gas stations, laundries, hospitals, shopping centers, lawn care firms, and so on. And moderate-wage workers are often the backbone of police and fire protection, teaching, and other local government services.

Among the 92 million U.S. households in 1990, one-third did not live in single-family homes and one-third were renters.[12] But the low density of metropolitan development does not include dwelling units appropriate to these people. Although suburbs do contain multifamily dwellings, such housing is not part of the dominant vision, and its construction is often opposed by local residents. Besides, most low- and moderate-income people cannot afford to live in new housing. To maintain desirable environments, American communities require that new housing meet quality requirements that are very high by world or even Western European and Japanese standards. These requirements are designed by middle-class architects, planners, and citizens in conformity with what they believe is decent housing. But their concept of decency far surpasses what is necessary for human health and safety. Consequently, all new American dwellings are too costly for low-income people to occupy without direct subsidies. But subsidies are provided for only a few of the many households with incomes low enough to be eligible for them. So poor people live in unsubsidized older dwellings.

At first glance, nothing seems wrong with this practice; it has provided adequate shelter for millions for many years. However, trickle-down only works in metropolitan areas with more housing units available than households to occupy them. Then, when a household moves into a newly built unit, it leaves a vacant unit behind that some less affluent household can occupy. That household, in turn, leaves another unit behind and so on. But when net housing construction is lower than net household formation, such chains of moves cannot occur as effectively. This happens nationally when housing starts are down and happens more often in fast-growing metropolitan areas such as many in California and Florida. By the time older units do become available they may be deteriorated and inadequate. Yet their rents may still be high in relation to the low incomes of the poor.

The trickle-down process also helps generate a socioeconomic hierarchy of neighborhoods that separates low-income households from moderate, middle-, and upper-income ones. The poor become concentrated in the most deteriorated housing at the centers of cities because it is the cheapest. In 1990, 10.4 million people lived in census tracts where 40 percent or more of the residents had money incomes below the poverty level. Some 17 percent of black and 11 percent of Hispanic Americans lived in extreme poverty areas of America's 100 largest central cities, compared with only 1 percent of whites. Three-fourths of the residents of these concentrations lived in the nation's central cities; less than 5 percent lived in suburbs.[13] High unemployment, crime, broken families, drug abuse, mental illness, disability, children born out of wedlock, gang membership, and structural deterioration are endemic there. Schools and other public services are of much lower quality than services in the rest of the metropolitan area. Young people find it difficult to escape from poverty.

These inner-city maladies have undermined the ability of central cities to perform economic and social functions crucial to the welfare of all residents, including suburban residents. This problem is the most harmful result of pursuing the dominant vision of metropolitan development, although that pursuit is not its only cause. Until America makes far more progress at coping with crime and other problems, especially in inner cities, the problems will cripple its ability to compete in a global economy and to function as a viable democracy.

In contrast to these inner-city neighborhoods, most suburbs have been built since World War II. Total suburban population rose from 41 million in 1950 to 115 million in 1990, an increase of 181 percent compared with a 65 percent increase in total population. The proportion of Americans living in suburbs rose from 27 percent to 46 percent.[14]

Historically, suburban employers of low- and moderate-income workers have relied on those living in older city neighborhoods. However, this arrangement has gradually deteriorated. Many more new jobs are being created in the suburbs than in central cities. And the sheer size of Los

Angeles, northern New Jersey, and other fast-growing areas means that most older, less costly housing is many miles from where new jobs are located. Thus, workers living in older, more central neighborhoods often have a hard time looking for jobs, or commuting when they do find them.

Finally, the economic expansion of the 1980s drove the unemployment rate below 7 percent nationally.[15] This prosperity and demographic changes in the U.S. age distribution created a nationwide shortage of entry-level workers. As a result, before the 1990 recession, far-out suburbs of many metropolitan areas were experiencing acute shortages of low-wage and even moderate-wage labor. These shortages were gone by the 1990-91 recession, but they will reappear when unemployment rates fall as the economy expands. Thus, the low-density vision's focus on relatively costly single-family housing and its reliance on trickle-down housing are inconsistent with the need for low- and moderate-wage workers in every community in every metropolitan area.[16]

FINANCING INTRASTRUCTURE FAIRLY

Another flaw in the dominant vision is its lack of consensus about how best to finance new schools, roads, and sewage and water systems. There is also no consensus on how to pay for increasing the capacity of existing facilities in established areas through which new residents will pass on their way to and from work or shopping. The lack of consensus creates political conflicts, often resulting in gross underfunding of facilities and services. Residents of fast-growing areas want most of the added infrastructure to be paid for by newcomers through impact fees, exactions, proffers, and permit fees.[17] Residents regard these tactics as merely requiring newcomers to pay their fair share because they will be the main beneficiaries. Residents, thus, typically vote against most increases in general taxes or bonding powers to pay for expanded facilities. But developers and potential newcomers believe the entire community should share in the costs. Because existing residents benefited from past general financing of infrastructure, it is unfair for them to change the rules. Also, growth creates greater economic prosperity, which aids everyone. Finally, loading the marginal costs of growth onto new developments

raises housing costs, unfairly reducing homeownership and rental opportunities of people with low and moderate incomes.

Political resolution of this controversy is inherently biased in favor of existing residents: potential newcomers cannot vote on local government policies that affect their welfare. Even so, it is difficult to force newcomers to pay all the marginal costs of growth. Some costs spring from more intensive use of existing facilities by both newcomers and previous residents.

Faced with this situation, residents often choose to hold down taxes by providing inadequate facilities for newcomers and even for themselves. New housing and commercial subdivisions may get built without adequate sewers, streets, and schools, as has been happening in Florida for some time. The dominant vision of how metropolitan areas ought to develop offers no guidance on how to resolve these problems.

SITING LOCALLY UNDESIRABLE LAND USES

The dominant vision also contains no effective means of resolving conflicts between the welfare of a metropolitan area as a whole and the welfare of its parts. Government decision making powers, especially those controlling land use, are divided among many communities, sp each local government has a parochial viewpoint. Public officials are not primarily concerned with the welfare of the area as a whole or of society as a whole. Still, every society must have some facilities—airports, expressways, jails, garbage incinerators, landfills—that benefit society as a whole but have unpopular effects on their immediate surroundings. These essential facilities, known as locally undesirable land uses, or LULUs, promote an attitude called NIMBY, or not in my back yard.

In an urban society designed in accordance with low-density growth, it is difficult to find a politically acceptable location for a needed but locally undesirable facility. Residents near every potential site pressure their local governments to oppose putting it there, and those governments have the power to reject the facility because controls over land use have been divided among myriad local entities. Officials are motivated to reject the facility because they are politically responsible only to their own residents. The resulting paralysis has virtually halted airport construction in the United States and blocked creation of thousands of other badly needed facilities. Low- and moderate-income households themselves are regarded as undesirable by many middle- and upper-income people, who fear the market values of their homes will plummet and property taxes will skyrocket. Thus, NIMBY reinforces the dominant vision's failure to provide housing that low- and moderate-income people can afford.

PAYING THE COSTS

Another flaw in the vision is its failure to compel people whose behavior generates significant social costs to pay for those costs directly. Every driver who enters a well-traveled highway during rush hour adds to congestion, slowing down all other drivers to some extent and costing them lost time. Drivers who make the same trip during nonpeak hours do not generate this cost. It would, therefore, be socially efficient if solo drivers on major roads were charged a direct fee for traveling during peak hours but not at other times. These charges would encourage more people to drive in nonpeak periods or to share rides. The money could be used to improve the nation's transportation system.[18] Politicians, however, have usually refused to adopt peak-hour road-use pricing because it would penalize low-income drivers. Also, time-differentiated road pricing runs counter to the "right" of citizens to use private vehicles to go anywhere anytime.

Another example of creating social costs without paying for them is the exclusionary zoning in many suburbs. Middle- and upper-income households often pressure local governments to adopt regulations that greatly increase the costs of homes. The residents believe such regulations help maximize home values. But exclusionary requirements force low- and moderate-income workers to live far from suburban jobs and commute long distances, which increases traffic congestion and air pollution and imposes time losses on all commuters. The people who lobby local governments to adopt exclusionary regulations do not have to pay the social costs they are generating for others.

ABSORBING TOO MUCH OPEN SPACE

The dominant vision encourages converting too much open space into urban uses. Of course, any settlement pattern accommodating additional population and economic development will convert some open space to urban uses, so conversion should not be considered excessive per se. But low-density settlement requires much larger areas to accommodate any given total population than higher-density settlement does. That, in turn, decreases the access of metropolitan area dwellers to open space. Some planners also criticize suburban sprawl because it swallows prime agricultural land and often encroaches upon environmentally sensitive areas. Because the United States produces agricultural surpluses, conversion of agricultural land probably does not diminish the nation's welfare much, but losses of accessible open space and environmentally sensitive areas clearly reduce the quality of life.

The pattern of development typical in U.S. metropolitan areas also bypasses parcels of vacant land, spreading development out farther than low net residential densities would otherwise require. This increases infrastructure costs. And many small pieces of open space that are skipped remain privately owned and are too scattered to be used as recreational areas. Local governments are not motivated to buy and set aside large parcels of land for open space accessible to people throughout the region. They may create parks for their own residents, but they do not want to spend money on people living elsewhere.

Finally, many environmentalists believe low-density growth threatens wetlands, forests, river basins, and habitats of threatened species. Developers, they contend, should be prohibited from converting such land to urban uses through regulatory procedures, rather than by having public authorities purchase it. The environmentalists oppose public purchase because they do not believe taxpayers will fund as many purchases as are socially desirable.

These social costs of the dominant vision are harder to quantify, even in theory, than its other flaws. It is impossible to establish scientifically just how much open space is necessary for a good quality of life or just how accessible it should be. But these criticisms have had a powerful political impact on growth management policies. In Oregon and Florida, a major motivation for adopting statewide land use planning and urban growth boundaries was fear that development would convert open land in the Willamette River Valley and the Everglades to scattered urban uses.

THE DOMINANT VISION AND SOCIAL INCONSISTENCIES

The flaws in the dominant vision have undermined the desirability of the environment produced by pursuing that vision: the results are inconsistent with the high quality of life it promises. These flaws threaten to weaken the economic and social functioning of many metropolitan areas and, therefore, of the entire U.S. economy and society.

This situation illustrates a fundamental problem in democracies. They have great difficulty solving the long-run problems created by policies that provide short-run benefits. Once people receive the benefits, they do not want to give them up. But they cannot agree how to distribute the long-run costs necessary to sustain the benefits. Each group of beneficiaries tries to shift as many of the costs as possible onto other groups. In some cases, the costs are not paid at all. Ultimately, such a failure undermines or offsets the short-run benefits. Increased traffic congestion and air pollution offset some of the benefits people sought when they moved to low-density suburbs. Yet these problems are partly caused by the very low density these people insisted on.

A major focus of this book is how America can reduce the harm these social inconsistencies can do to the quality of life in metropolitan areas. But before that can happen, people must realize that the problems they associate with growth are, in fact, caused primarily by their own behavior. They cannot improve conditions without altering their vision of how metropolitan areas ought to develop. Achieving such a transformation is difficult and is made even more so because each person is part of a group, and the behavior of the group must change to affect the overall result. Consequently, each person believes what he or she does will make no difference, and the motivation to change remains weak.

Most Americans do not recognize their responsibility in causing the growth-related social problems they dislike. It will take strong and persistent leadership from those who do realize it to convince them. A primary goal of this book is to help public and private parties exercise such leadership.

NOTES

1. Throughout this book, population growth will be used as a proxy for these other forms of development because it is highly correlated with them and detailed data about it are more readily available.
2. Fannie Mae, "Fannie Mae National Housing Survey 1993," Washington, D.C., 1993, pp. 6, 16, 17.
3. These two conditions may seem natural to most Americans, but they are not in the rest of the world. New substandard housing in the form of barrios or shantytowns is the main method of housing the urban poor in most less developed societies. Extensive use of public housing subsidies is a major method of providing housing for the urban poor in many Western European nations. Anthony Downs, "Housing the Urban Poor: The Economics of Various Strategies," *American Economic Review*, vol. 59 (September 1969), pp. 646-51.
4. From 1980 through 1988, the number of cars and trucks in use in the United States increased by 31.9 million, or 22.8 percent; the population increased by 18.3 million, or 8.0 percent. Surfaced road mileage increased by only 4.3 percent. Motor Vehicle Manufacturers Association, *Motor Vehicle Facts & Figures '89* (Detroit 1989), pp. 28-29,84; and Bureau of the Census, *Statistical Abstract of the United States: 1989* (Department of Commerce 1989), p. 7.
5. Data for 1980 from Alan E. Pisarski, *Commuting in America: A National Report on Commuting Patterns and Trends* (Westport, Conn.: Eno Foundation for Transportation, 1987), p. 60. Data for 1990 from Center for Urban Transportation Research, *Florida Demographics and the Journey to Work: A County Data Book* (University of South Florida 1993), p. 21.

6. Office of Highway Information Management, Federal Highway Administration, "1990 Nationwide Personal Transportation Study: Early Results," Department of Transportation, August 1991, pp. 8-9, 20.

7. For example, the Bay Area Council reported that 38 percent of the 630 respondents in a 1990 poll cited traffic congestion as the area's biggest problem, compared with only 8 percent for each of the three problems ranked next. This 38 percent was up one-third form the 1989 pool. Congestion has been the most-cited problem for eight straight years. Bay Area Council, *Bay Area Poll* (January 1991).

8. Motor Vehicle Manufacturers Association, *Motor Vehicle Facts & Figures '88* (Detroit 1988), p. 45.

9. Center for Urban Transportation Research, *Florida Demographics and the Journey to Work*, p.21.

10. Lack of roadbuilding is only one cause of growing peak-hour traffic congestion. Congestion would undoubtedly have increased significantly from 1980 to 1990 even if many roads had been built. For in-depth analysis, see Anthony Downs, *Stuck in Traffic: Coping with Peak-Hour Traffic Congestion* (Brookings 1992), chap. 1.

11. Peter Gordon and Harry W. Richardson, "Trends in Congestion in Metropolitan Areas," paper prepared for the Symposium for the Study on Urban Transportation Congestion Pricing, National Research Council, Washington, D.C., June 1993, p. 1.

12. Of all occupied units 64 percent were owner occupied. Bureau of the Census, *Statistical Abstract of the United States: 1992* (Department of Commerce 1992), p. 716. Also, 64 percent of the entire housing inventory consisted of single-family units. Bureau of the Census, "1990 Housing Highlights: United States," CH-S-1-1, Department of Commerce, July 1991.

13. Author's calculations using data from Ronald B. Mincy, "The Under Class: Changing Concept, Constant Reality," Urban Institute, Washington, D.C., May 1993; John D. Kasarda, "Inner-City Concentrated Poverty and Neighborhood Distress: 1970 to 1990" in Fannie Mae, *Housing Policies for Distressed Urban Neighborhoods* (1993), p. 20; and Bureau of the Census, "Poverty in the United States: 1990," *Current Population Reports*, series P-60, no. 175 (Department of Commerce, 1991), p. 15. I am greatly indebted to the authors for their assistance.

14. Author's calculations based on data from Bureau of the Census, *Statistical Abstract of the United States: 1992*, p. 8.

15. *Economic Report of the President, January 1993*, table B-30.

16. U.S. public policy does not rely solely on tricke-down to house the poor, the federal public housing program, the federal section 8 subsidy program, and state issuance of federal tax-exempt bonds do finance low-income housing. In 1988 there were 1.45 million low-income public housing units, while in 1989 there were 6.37 million low-income renter households and another 11.5 million with very low incomes. And most public housing units are in central cities. Data on households are from an unpublished tabulation of American Housing Survey data for 1989 done by Carla Pedone of the Congressional Budget Office. Data on public housing units are from Bureau of the Census, *Statistical Abstract of the United States: 1992*, p. 724.

17. For an analysis of the nature and effects of such fees, see Alan A. Altshuler and Jose A. Gómez-Ibáñez, *Regulation for Revenue: The Political Economy of Land Use Exactions* (Brookings, 1993).

18. For a detailed analysis of peak-hour road pricing, see Downs, *Stuck in Traffic*, chap. 4. Also see Kenneth A. Small, Clifford Winston, and Carol A. Evans, *Road Work: A New Highway Pricing and Investment Policy* (Brookings 1989).

SUGGESTED READINGS FOR PART VII

Argyris, Chris and Donald A. Schön. *Theory in Practice: Increasing Professional Effectiveness.* San Francisco: Jossey-Bass. 1974.

Beauregard, Robert A. "Occupational Transformations in Urban and Regional Planning, 1960 to 1980," *Journal of Planning Education and Research*, Vol. 5, No. 1, pp. 10-16.

Beckman, Norman. "The Planner as Bureaucrat," *Journal of the American Institute of Planners*, Vol. 30, No. 4, 1964, pp. 216-224.

Gleick, James. *Chaos: Making a New Science*. New York: Viking Penguin. 1987.

Hiltner, Seward. "Planning as a Profession," *Journal of the American Institute of Planners*, Vol. 22, No. 4, 1957, pp. 162-167.

Howard, John T. "In Defense of Planning Commissions," *Journal of the American Institute of Planners*, Vol. 17, No. 2, 1951, pp. 89-94.

Howard, John T. "The Planner in a Democratic Society - A Credo," *Journal of the American Institute of Planners*, Vol. 21, Nos. 2-3, 1955, pp. 62-65.

Howe, Beth and Jerome L. Kaufman. "The Ethics of Contemporary American Planners," *Journal of the American Planning Association*, Vol. 45, No. 3, 1979, pp. 243-255.

Isserman, Andrew. "Dare to Plan: An Essay on the Role of the Future in Planning Frontier and Edgetown," *Town Planning Review*, Vol. 65, No. 4, 1985.

Krieger, Martin H. 1975. "What Do Planners Do?" *Journal of the American Institute of Planners*, Vol. 41, No. 5, 1975.

Louv, Richard. *Children's Future: Listening to the American Family. New Hope for the Next Generation*. Boston: Houghton Mifflin. 1990.

Marcuse, Peter. "Professional Ethics and Beyond: Values in Planning," *Journal of the American Institute of Planners*, Vol. 22, No. 2, 1956, pp. 58-64.

Michael, Donald N. *On Learning to Plan—and Planning to Learn*. San Francisco: Jossey-Bass. 1973.

Nash, Peter H. and Dennis Durden. "A Task Force Approach to Replace the Planning Board," *Journal of the American Institute of Planners*, Vol. 30, No. 1, 1964, pp. 10-26.

Perloff, Harvey S. *Education for Planning: City, State and Regional*. Baltimore: Johns Hopkins. 1957.

Schön, Donald A. "Some of What a Planner Knows: A Case Study of Knowing-in-Practice," *Journal of the American Planning Association*, Vol. 48, No. 3, 1982, pp. 351-364.

Schorr, Lisbeth B. *Within Our Reach*. New York: Anchor Books, Doubleday & Co., Inc. 1988.

Sennett, Richard. *The Conscience of the Eye*. New York: Knopf. 1990.

Shalala, Donna E., and Julia Vitullo-Martin. "Rethinking the Urban Crisis: Proposals for a National Urban Agenda," *Journal of the American Planning Association*, Vol. 55, No. 1, 1989.

Teitz, Michael B. "Planning Education and the Planning Profession," *Journal of Planning Education and Research*, Vol. 3, No. 2, pp. 75-77.

Van Der Ryn, Sim, and Peter Calthorpe. *Sustainable Communities: A New Design Synthesis for Cities, Suburbs and Towns*. San Francisco: Sierra Club Books. 1986.

Vernon, Raymond, William Alonso, Anthony Downs, Peter Hall, and Lawrence Susskind. "The Coming Global Metropolis: Symposium Essays," *Journal of the American Planning Association*, Vol. 57, No. 1, 1991.

Webber, Melvin M. "Comprehensive Planning and Social Responsibility: Toward an AIP Consensus on the Profession's Role and Purposes," *Journal of the American Institute of Planners*, Vol. 29, No. 4, 1963, pp. 232-241.

Wilson, William Julius. *The Truly Disadvantaged: The Inner City, the Underclass, and Public Policy*. Chicago: The University of Chicago Press. 1987.

ABOUT THE AUTHORS

Andrea Akita has been a planner for the Single Room Occupancy Housing Corporation in Los Angeles, and coauthored with Jennier Wolch an analysis of the federal response to the homeless and its implications for cities in the United States.

David J. Allor was a professor in the School of Planning and a fellow at the Center for the Study of Dispute Resolution, University of Cincinnati. He wrote *The Planning Commissioners Guide: Processes for Reasoning Together*.

Alan A. Altshuler is Ruth and Frank Stanton Professor of Urban Policy and Planning at Harvard University and Director of the Taubman Center for State and Local Government. He has been dean of the Graduate School of Public Administration at New York University, professor of Political Science and Urban Planning at the Massachusetts Institute of Technology, and Secretary of Transportation for the Commonwealth of Massachusetts. His books include *The City Planning Process*; *Community Control*; *The Urban Transportation System*; *The Future of the Automobile*; and *Regulation for Revenue: Governance and Opportunity in Metropolitan America*.

Eugenie L. Birch is professor and chair of the Department of City and Regional Planning at the University of Pennsylvania. Her research is in two fields—the history of planning and contemporary planning and housing—and her articles have appeared in such publications as the *Journal of Urban History*, *Journal of Planning Education and Research*, *Journal of the American Planning Association*, and *Planning* magazine. She is a former president of the Association of Collegiate Schools of Planning and the Society of American City and Regional Planning History.

John M. Bryson is a professor at the Hubert H. Humphrey Institute of Public Affairs at the University of Minnesota. His areas of focus include leadership, strategic management, and the design of organizational community change processes. His publications include *Strategic Planning for Public and Nonprofit Organizations* and *Leadership for the Common Good (co-author)*.

David L. Callies is Benjamin A. Kudo Professor of Law at the University of Hawaii at Manoa. He is widely recognized for his work with local, state, and national government agencies in land-use management and control, transportation policy, and intergovernmental relations. Professor Callies's publications include *Taking Land: Compulsory Purchase and Regulation in Asia-Pacifc Countries (co-author)*, *Preserving Paradise: Why Regulation Won't Work*, and *Regulating Paradise: Land Use Controls in Hawaii*, *The Quiet Revolution in Land Use Control (co-author)*; *The Taking Issue; Cases and Materials on Land Use (3rd ed.)*, and *Property Law and the Public Interest*. He is co-editor of *Land Use and Environmental Law Review* and past managing editor of the *Michigan Journal of Law Reform*.

Scott Campbell is a faculty member in the College of Architecture and Urban Planning at the University of Michigan. His research and teaching are in the areas of planning and theory and history, economic development, sustainable development, and regional planning. His publications include *Readings in Urban Theory* and *Readings in Planning Theory* (co-editor); *The Rise of the Gunbelt* (co-editor); and the forthcoming *Cold War Metropolis: The Fall and Rebirth of Berlin as a World City*.

Paul Davidoff served as a planner for the Delaware Cornmission; the New Canaan Planning Commission; Vorhees, Walker, Smith & Smith; and the New York City Planning Commission. He was also a faculty member in the City Planning Department, University of Pennsylvania and a director of the graduate program of the Urban Planning Program at Hunter College. He was the unsuccessful Democratic candidate for the U.S. Congress from the 26th Congressional District in New York in 1968. In 1969, with Neil Gold, he formed and became executive director of the Suburban Action Institute, which became the Metropolitan Action Institute in 1980.

Michael Dear is professor of geography and director of the Southern California Studies Center at the University of Southern California. His research interests focus on comparative urbanism, and his most recent publications are *The Postmodern Urban Condition* and *Postborder City* (edited with Gustavo Leclerc).

Hernando de Soto is president of the Institute for Liberty and Democracy (ILD), headquartered in Peru and regarded by *The Economist* as the second most important think tank in the world. *Time* recently named him one of the five leading Latin

American innovators of the century. As Personal Representative and Principal Advisor to the President of Peru, he initiated that country's economic and political reforms. His book, *The Other Path*, was a bestseller throughout Latin America.

Anthony Downs is a Senior Fellow at the Brookings Institution in Washington, D.C. He previously served as a member and then chairman of Real Estate Research Corporation, a nationwide consulting firm advising private and public decision-makers on real estate investment, housing policies, and urban affairs. He has served as a consultant to many of the nation's largest corporations, to major developers, to dozens of government agencies at local, state, and national levels (including the U.S. Department of Housing and Urban Development), and to many private foundations. He is also a director or trustee of the MassMutual Life Insurance Company, General Growth Properties, Bedford Property Investors, the NAACP Legal and Educational Property Trust, Penton Media Inc., the Urban Land Institute, the Urban Institute, and the National Housing Partnership Foundation.

Carl Feiss was an architect and urban planner who helped create the Federal Historic Preservation Act of 1966, and the National Register of Historic Places. He was credited with elevating urban planning to a distinct discipline, and aided in the historic preservation of Annapolis, Maryland; Alexandria, Virginia; Charleston, South Carolina; and Savannah, Georgia. He was director of the housing and planning division of the Columbia University School of Architecture before moving on to head the Denver planning commission. In 1950, he came to Washington as chief planner for what was then called "slum clearance," and ran programs that would later become the Department of Housing and Urban Development. He later was an independent consultant, and then returned to teaching in 1973 at the University of Florida's College of Architecture (now the College of Design, Construction and Planning), where he founded the Urban and Regional Development Center, the forerunner of the Department of Urban and Regional Planning.

John Forester is a professor and past chair of the Department of City and Regional Planning at Cornell University. His work explores the micro-politics and ethics of planning practice, including the ways planners work in the face of power and conflict. His books include *Planning in the Face of Power*; *Making Equity Planning Work: Leadership in the Public Sector* (with Norman Krumholz), *The Deliberative Practitioner: Encouraging Participatory Planning Processes*, and *Israeli Planners and Designers: Profiles of Community Builders* (co-editor).

Bernard Frieden has served in various positions at the Massachusetts Institute of Technology (M.I.T.), including chairman of the M.I.T.-Harvard Joint Center for Urban Studies and as Associate Dean of the School of Architecture and Planning. His *The Environmental Protection Hustle* (1979) showed how newly enacted environmental laws were vulnerable to exploitation by groups with narrow, often non-environmental objectives. His *Downtown, Inc.* (coauthor), a study of festival marketplace development in American downtown areas during the 1970s and 1980s, is a highly regarded work on the political economy of downtown revitalization in American since World War II.

R. Buckminster Fuller was an architect, engineer, inventor, and philosopher, best known in architectural history for his use of the geodesic dome as a structural form. He was a writer and publisher, the principal of the Dymaxion and Geodesic Corporations, and Professor of Design at Southern Illinois University. His numerous writings include books, *Critical Path*; *Earth Inc.*; *Operating Manual for Spaceship Earth*; and *Synergetics: Explorations in the Geometry of Thinking*.

Herbert Gans is a sociologist and educator. A prolific author, his publications include *The Urban Villagers*, *The Levittowners*, *People and Plans*, *Popular Culture and High Culture*, *Deciding What's News*, *The War Against the Poor*, and *Making Sense of America*.

David R. Godschalk is Stephen Baxter Professor of Planning and former department chair at the University of North Carolina in Chapel Hill. He is the former editor of the *Journal of the American Institute of Planners* and has served on the editorial boards of the *Journal of the American Planning Association* and the *Journal of Planning Education and Research*. His writings include *Constitutional Issues of Growth Management* (coauthor), *Understanding Growth Management: The Planner as Dispute Resolver*, and (with Edward J. Kaiser) *Urban Land Use Planning* (fourth edition, University of Illinois Press, 1995).

J.B. Jackson was an architectural and landscape critic and writer who popularized the study of vernacular places and structures. He was a professor both at Harvard University and the University of California, Berkeley. His books include *American Space*; *Discovering the Vernacular Landscape*; *The Necessity for Ruins*; and *A Sense of Place, A Sense of Time*.

Jane Jacobs challenged conventional ideas about physical planning and argued the virtues of big, diverse, crowded, and dense cities. Her writings include *The Death and Life of Great American Cities*; *The Economy of Cities*; *Cities and the Wealth of Nations*; *A Question of Separatism: Quebec and the Struggle over Sovereigny*; *Systems of Survival*; and *The Nature of Economics*.

Edward J. Kaiser is professor emeritus and former chair of the Department of City and Regional Planning at the University of North Carolina at Chapel Hill. He is a former editor of the *Journal of the American Institute of Planners* and a member of several journal editorial boards, including the *Journal of the American Planning Association*. Kaiser is co-author with David R. Godschalk of *Urban Land Use Planning* (fourth edition, University of Illinois Press, 1995).

Charles Lindblom, Sterling Professor Emeritus of Economics and Political Science at Yale University, is a past president of the American Political Science Association and of the Association for Comparative Economic Studies. His publications include *The Policy-Making Process*; *The Intelligence of Democracy*; *Unions and Capitalism*; *Politics, Economics and Welfare* (with R.A. Dahl); *A Strategy of Decision* (with D. Braybrooke); *Politics and Markets*; *Usable Knowledge* (with D.K. Cohen); *Inquiry and Change*; and *The Market System*.

Kevin Lynch was a professor in the Urban Studies and Planning Program at the Massachusetts Institute of Technology. Lynch's numerous writings, including *Images of the City, A Theory of Good City Form, What Time Is This Place?* and *Site Planning* all emphasized the importance of people's perceptions in designing the environment. Lynch was also a partner in the environmental design firm of Carr, Lynch Associates, which was involved in many important projects, including site planning for the town of Columbia, Maryland.

Martin Meyerson is president emeritus of the University of Pennsylvania. He previously served as chair of the University of Pennsylvania Foundation and as head of the program policy group of the University's Fels Center of Government. Meyerson was the first urban specialist to become president of a research university. He has worked on problems of urban, regional, national, cultural development for governments and organizations in various countries and is principal author of the following books: *Politics, Planning and the Public Interest* (with Edward Banfield); *Housing, People and Cities*; *Face of the Metropolis*; *Boston: The Job Ahead*; and *Gladly Learn and Gladly Teach*. He holds 23 honorary degrees from universities and colleges in the United States and abroad.

Harvey Molotch is a professor of sociology at the University of California, Santa Barbara and professor of Metropolitan Studies and Sociology, New York University. He is a prolific author. His works include: *Where Stuff Comes From: Forces that Shape the Products of Everyday Life* (Routledge, forthcoming 2003). He is the co-author of *Building Rules: How Local Controls Shape Community*; *Environments and Economies*; *Urban Fortunes: The Political Economy of Place*; and *The Effects of Urban Growth: A Population Impact Analysis*.

Lisa Peattie is professor emeritus and senior lecturer in the Department of Urban Studies and Planning, at the Massachusetts Institute of Technology. She has also been a visiting professor at the University of California and a consultant to the World Bank and the United Nations. Peattie has conducted research in a wide variety of settings, including the Fox Indians of Iowa; New York City public schools; public housing in Boston; a new planned city in Venezuela; and low-income neighborhoods in Cairo, Lima, Bogota, and Mexico City. She is the author of *The View from the Barrio*, *Thinking about Development*, *Making Work* (with William Ronco), *Women's Claims* (with Martin Rein), and *Planning: Rethinking Ciudad Guayana*.

John Reps, emeritus professor of city and regional planning and one of the founders of the City and Regional Planning Department at Cornell University, was a renowned historian of urban plans. His books included *The Making Urban America*, *Bird's Eye Views*, *Historic Lithographs of North American Cities*, *Cities of the Mississippi*, and *Nineteenth-Century Images of Urban Development* (with photographer Alex MacLean).

Horst W.J. Rittel was a professor of the Sciences of Design at the University of California, Berkeley and, concurrently, professor of architecture and director of the Institute for the Foundation of Planning at the University of Stuttgart.

Lloyd Rodwin was a Ford International Professor Emeritus of Urban Studies at the Massachusetts Institute of Technology, and the co-founder of the MIT-Harvard Joint Center for Urban Studies. He was the author or editor of 11 books, including the forthcoming *The Profession of City Planning: Changes, Images and Challenges, 1950-2000* (with Bishwapriya Sanyal), *Cities of the Mind* (with Robert Hollister), and *Rethinking the Development Experience: Essays Provoked by the Work of Albert Hirschman* (edited with Don Schön).

William D. Roering has research interests in managerial cognition and decision-making, cooperative and competitive relationships, and moral reasoning and business ethics. His work has been published in the *Journal of Management Inquiry*, *Public Administration Review*, and *Business Horizons*. He has also contributed chapters to several research volumes, including *Research in the Management of Innovation, Advances in Global High Technology Management* and *Advances in Strategic Management*. He is a member of the Academy of Management and Strategic Management Society. He was also the Recipient of the Best Article of the Year Award from the *Journal of the American Planning Association*.

Lynne B. Sagalyn is an expert in real estate equity securities and public development finance. Her research and writings in real estate investment, securitization, urban development, and public policy have been published in both academic and professional journals. She has recently completed *Times Square Roulette: Remaking the City Icon* and is co-author (with Bernard Frieden) of *Downtown, Inc.: How America Rebuilds Cities*. Sagalyn sits on a number of boards, including United Dominion Realty Trust, Capital Trust, J.P. Morgan U.S. Real Estate and Growth Fund, and the Retail Initiative.

Saskia Sassen is professor of urban planning and serves on the faculty of the School of International and Public Affairs at Columbia University. Her work focuses on international, regional, and urban economic development, on

international labor migration, and, most recently, on questions of governance in the global economy. Sassen's books include *The Mobility of Labor and Capital*; *The Global City: New York, London, Tokyo*; *Cities in a World Economy*; and *Immigration Policy in a World Economy*. Sassen has been a member of several research groups, including a Japan-based project on economic restructuring in the United States and Japan sponsored by the U.N. Center on Regional Development and others. She also has been a consultant to various organizations, including several United Nations projects, the National Urban League, the New York City Office of Economic Development, the Public Broadcasting Corporation, and the Ford Foundation.

Donald A. Schön was Ford Professor Emeritus and senior lecturer in the School of Architecture and Planning at the Massachusetts Institute of Technology. He developed the concept of the reflective practitioner through his works, which included *Beyond the Stable State*, *The Reflective Practitioner*, and *Educating the Reflective Practitioner*. He served during the Kennedy administration as director of the Institute for Applied Technology in the National Bureau of Standards, Department of Commerce, where he continued through 1966. He then co-founded and directed the Organization for Social and Technological Innovation, a nonprofit social research and development firm in the Boston area, through 1973. He was the youngest invitee ever to give the prestigious Reith Lectures for the British Broadcasting Corporation.

Anne Whiston Spirn is a professor of landscape architecture at the University of Pennsylvania and is the author of *The Granite Garden: Urban Nature and Human Design*.

Martin Wachs is director of the Institute of Transportation Studies at the University of California, Berkeley, where he also holds faculty appointments as professor of City and Regional Planning and of Civil and Environmental Engineering. He served previously as professor of Urban Planning and director of the Institute of Transportation Studies at UCLA. He is the author or editor of four books and has written over 100 articles on transportation and planning policy, including the transportation needs of elderly and handicapped people, fare and subsidy policies in urban transportation, the problems of crime in public transit systems, and methods for the evaluation of alternative transportation projects. He currently serves on the executive committee of the Transportation Research Board and recently completed a term as a member of the California Commission on Transportation Investment.

Melvin M. Webber is Professor Emeritus of Planning at the University of California, Berkeley.

Mark A. Weiss is a public policy scholar at the Woodrow Wilson International Center in Washington, D.C. He was special assistant to the Secretary of the U.S. Department of Housing and Urban Development from 1993 to 1997. He is a known expert on urban and regional development, housing and community development, eonomic and business development, public policy and planning.

Aaron Wildavsky was founding dean of the Graduate School of Public Policy at the University of California, Berkeley. A former president of the American Political Science Association, he also taught at Oberlin College in Ohio. His writings include *Cultural Theory* (with Richard Ellis and Michael Thompson), *The Rise of Radical Egalitarianism*, and *Searching for Safety*.

Jennifer R. Wolch is a professor of Geography and Urban and Regional Planning, and director of the Center for Sustainable Cities at the University of Southern California. In the 1980s, her research focused on problems of service-dependent and homeless people in American cities, social policy, and human service delivery. She was director of the Los Angeles Homelessness Project, 1987-94.

ABOUT THE EDITOR

Jay M. Stein, FAICP, is professor and dean of the College of Design, Construction and Planning at the University of Florida. He previously served as chair of the Department of Urban and Regional Planning at the University of Florida, chair and acting dean at the School of Architecture and Planning, University of Buffalo, UPS Foundation visiting professor at Stanford, and as a faculty member in the Department of City and Regional Planning at the Georgia Institute of Technology. The author of numerous articles and books, he has recently edited a trilogy of classic reading texts in urban planning, real estate and development, and architecture (co-editor). He previously served as a two-term member of the editorial board of the *Journal of the American Planning Association* and currently serves on three other editorial boards of planning related journals.

Index